Brains Confounded
by the Ode of Abū Shādūf Expounded

Letter from the General Editor

The Library of Arabic Literature series offers Arabic editions and English translations of significant works of Arabic literature, with an emphasis on the seventh to nineteenth centuries. The Library of Arabic Literature thus includes texts from the pre-Islamic era to the cusp of the modern period, and encompasses a wide range of genres, including poetry, poetics, fiction, religion, philosophy, law, science, history, and historiography.

Books in the series are edited and translated by internationally recognized scholars and are published in parallel-text format with Arabic and English on facing pages, and are also made available as English-only paperbacks.

The Library encourages scholars to produce authoritative, though not necessarily critical, Arabic editions, accompanied by modern, lucid English translations. Its ultimate goal is to introduce the rich, largely untapped Arabic literary heritage to both a general audience of readers as well as to scholars and students.

The Library of Arabic Literature is supported by a grant from the New York University Abu Dhabi Institute and is published by NYU Press.

Philip F. Kennedy
General Editor, Library of Arabic Literature

هزّ القحوف
بشرح قصيد أبي شادوف

يوسف الشربينيّ

المجلّد الثاني

LIBRARY OF
المكتبة
ARABIC
العربية
LITERATURE

Brains Confounded by the Ode of Abū Shādūf Expounded

Yūsuf al-Shirbīnī

Volume Two

Edited and translated by
Humphrey Davies

Volume editors
James E. Montgomery
Geert Jan van Gelder

NEW YORK UNIVERSITY PRESS
New York

NEW YORK UNIVERSITY PRESS
New York

Library of Congress Cataloging-in-Publication Data
Names: Shirbini, Yusuf ibn Muhammad, active 1665-1687, author. | Davies, Humphrey T. (Humphrey Taman), editor translator. | Shirbini, Yusuf ibn Muhammad, active 1665-1687. Hazz al-quhuf fi sharh qasid Abi Shaduf. English. | Shirbini, Yusuf ibn Muhammad, active 1665-1687. Hazz al-quhuf fi sharh qasid Abi Shaduf.
Title: Brains confounded by the ode of Abu Shaduf expounded / Yusuf Ibn Muhammad Ibn Abd al-Jawad Ibn Khidr al-Shirbini; edited and translated by Humphrey Davies.
Description: New York : New York Univeristy Press, 2016. | In English with orginal Arabic text. | Includes bibliographical references and index.
Identifiers: LCCN 2016006848 (print) | LCCN 2016008844 (ebook) | ISBN 9781479882342 (cl : alk. paper) | ISBN 9781479838905 (cl : alk. paper) | ISBN 9781479822362 (e-book) | ISBN 9781479888252 (e-book) | ISBN 9781479809721 (e-book) | ISBN 9781479892389 (e-book)
Subjects: LCSH: Villages--Egypt--Early works to 1800. | Egypt--Rural conditions--Early works to 1800. | Social problems in literature--Early works to 1800. | Satire, Arabic--Egypt--Early works to 1800. | Arabic literature--Egypt--Early works to 1800.
Classification: LCC HN786.A8 .S5513 2016 (print) | LCC HN786.A8 (ebook) | DDC 307.760932--dc23
LC record available at http://lccn.loc.gov/2016006848

New York University Press books are printed on acid-free paper, and their binding materials are chosen for strength and durability.

Series design by Titus Nemeth.

Typeset in Tasmeem, using DecoType Naskh and Emiri.

Typesetting and digitization by Stuart Brown.

Manufactured in the United States of America
c 10 9 8 7 6 5 4 3 2 1

Table of Contents

هزّ القحوف
بشرح قصيد أبي شادوف

Brains Confounded by the Ode of Abū Shādūf Expounded

المجلّد الثاني

Part Two

بسم الله الرحمن الرحيم

(الحمد لله) ربّ العالمين * والصلاة والسلام على سيّدنا محمد أشرف النبيّين * وعلى آله وصحبه أجمعين * (وبعد) فيقول العبد الفقير إلى الله تعالى يوسف بن محمّد بن عبد الجواد بن خضر الشربينيّ كان الله له ورحم سلفه إنّه لمّا كانت الهمّة البارده * والفكرة الكاسده * تحرّكت أيّاماً قلائل * لتأليف كتاب صار في الأوراق حاصل * في أحوال أهل الريف باتّفاق * وما لهم من نظم ونثر وحبّ واشتياق * وصار جزءاً لا يُرى في الكثافة له شبيه * ولا يكترث به ذو فضل في العلوم نبيه * وكان كالمقدّمة للقصيد * وقد حوى معاني تشبه قحوف الجريد * وخُتِمَ بالأرجوزة الحاوية لما فيه من النثر والأشعار * وغايته أنّه اغتراف من بنات الأفكار * أردت اتّصاله بهذا الجزء الثاني * وحلّ معاني القصيد الّتي عليه مدار تلك المباني * فحرّكتُ فكرتي الخامله * وأطلقتُ عِنان اليراع لبيان تلك الأمور الحاصله * لحلّ معاني نظم القصيد * منسكباً عليه انسكاب الوابل على الصعيد * بألفاظ يفوح معناها كريح الفَسْوى * ومعاني تشبه في الوضع خابط عَشْوى * فساعدتني الفكرة لما إليه قصدت * وتحرّكت معي لما إليه أردت * وهذا أوان الشروع في المقصود * بعون الملك المعبود * فأقول ١٠٩

In the Name of God, the Merciful, the Compassionate

Praise be to God, Lord of the Worlds, and blessings and peace upon our master Muḥammad, noblest of prophets, and upon his family and companions, one and all! To proceed. The humble slave of the Almighty, Yūsuf ibn Muḥammad ibn ʿAbd al-Jawād ibn Khiḍr al-Shirbīnī declares (and may God be for him and have mercy on his forebears): after frigid determination and sluggish lucubration had bestirred themselves for a few days and been constrained to produce a book that's now on paper contained, on the conditions of the people of the countryside as it may be, and on their love and longing and their prose and poetry, which work became a Part in coarseness without peer, to which no man of virtue and discerning scholarship would ever give ear, which was to serve as an introduction to the coming Ode, which motifs like the prickly ends of palm fronds included and with an *urjūzah*—a summary of all that's in it of poetry and prose—concluded and which, to cut the story short, was a dollop of my inspired thought, I determined to add thereto this second part and unravel the meanings of the Ode, which are the point from which its formal constructions depart; so I set my lethargic brain to work, allowing my pen on the elucidation of the matters therein to go berserk and to unravel the motifs that the Ode contains, descending upon it like a downpour on Upper Egypt when it rains, with expressions whose sense wafts about like a fart, and motifs thrown together without method or art. And indeed, my brain assisted me in that for which I strove and bestirred itself with me to attain the goal at which I drove; and now's the moment to set out in pursuit of that thing, with the help of God, the Worshipped King. I therefore declare: 9.1

(ذكر نسب الناظم وما حواه * وذكر الموضع الذي
ضمّه وآواه * وسبب سعادته وحصولها *
وصفة لحيته هل كانت طويلة أو قلّ طولها *
وكيف مال عليه الدهر في آخر الزمان *
حتّى أنشأ هذا القصيد واشتهر عنه وبان) *

١،١٠ فنقول أمّا نسبه فعلى أقوال فمنهم من صرّح أنّه أبو شادوف بن أبو جاروف بن شقادف بن لقالق بن بحلق بن عفلق بن عفر بن دعموم بن فلحس بن خرا الحس فإذا ذقت الكلام بمعقول *عرفت انتهاء نسبه على هذا القول * وقيل أبو شادوف بن أبو جاروف بن بردع بن زوبع بن بحلق بن عفلق بن بهدل بن عوكل بن عمره بن كل خرا فانتهى نسبه على القول الأوّل لابن خرا الحس وعلى الثاني لابن كل خرا والثاني أصحّ لأنّ أكل الخرا أبلغ من لحسه

٢،١٠ (وأمّا قريته) ففيها خلاف قيل إنّه من تَلّ فندروك وقيل من كفرشمرطاطي وهو الصحيح لأنّ الناظم صرّح بذلك في بعض أشعاره فقال [وافر]

١،٢،١٠ أَنَا يَا نَاسُ فِي قَوْلِي دَلَايِل وَنَظْمِي حَقُّ مَاهُوشِي هَبَايِل
أَبُو شَادُوفْ أَنَا قَالْلِي أَبُويَهْ عَلَيْهِ وَجِدَّتِي دِيكْ أُمُّ نَايِل

An Account of the Lineage of the Poet and Its Components, and of the Place That Took Him to Its Bosom and Gave Him Shelter from His Earliest Moments, and of the Origins of His Fortune and How It Was Brought, and of the Nature of His Beard, Whether It Was Long or Short, and of How, at the End, by Fate He Was O'erthrown, as a Result of Which He Composed This Ode for Which He Became Famous and Well Known

His Lineage

We declare: opinions differ concerning his lineage. Some state that he was Abū Shādūf son of Abū Jārūf son of Shaqādif son of Laqāliq (Storks) son of Baḥlaq (Goggle-Eye) son of ʿAflaq (Big Flabby Vagina) son of ʿAfr (Dust) son of Duʿmūm son of Falḥas[1] son of Kharā Ilḥas (Lick-Shit). If you ingest these words with your rational faculty, you will realize that this is the end of his ancestry. Others, however, say he was Abū Shādūf son of Abū Jārūf son of Bardaʿ (Donkey Saddle) son of Zawbaʿ (Dust Storm) son of Baḥlaq son of ʿAflaq son of Bahdal (Disheveled) son of ʿAwkal son of ʿAmrah[2] son of Kul Kharā (Eat-Shit). Thus, according to the first version, his genealogy ends with "son of Lick-Shit" and according to the second with "son of Eat-Shit"; however, the second is more correct because to eat shit is more eloquent than to lick it. 10.1

His Village

As for his village, it is a matter of dispute. Some say that he was from Tall Fandarūk and others from Kafr Shammirṭāṭī,[3] the latter being correct, for the poet himself says so in some verses of his, to wit: 10.2

Me, good people, my words are a guide 10.2.1
    And my verses speak true, no tomfooleries hide.
Abū Shādūf am I. My dad told me the tale,
    And likewise my grandma, old Umm Nāyil,

بِأَنِّي قَدْ تَرَبَّيْتْ يَا جَمَاعَهْ   بِكَفْرٍ يَعْرِفُوهْ نَاسْ أَوَايِلْ
يُسَمَّى كَفْرْ شَمَّرْ لِي وَطَاطِي   فَكُنْ صَاحِبْ فَهَامَهْ يَا فَسَاقِلْ
وَذَا قَوْلِي وَأَبُو شَادُوفِ إِسْمِي   وَشِعْرِي حَقّْ مَنْ جَانِي يُسَايِلْ

وسمعتُ شعرًا لبعض أهل الريف يدلّ أنّه من تلّ فندروك وهو هذا [وافر] ٢،٢،١٠

سَمِعْنَا مِنْ قَدِيمٍ وَمِنْ جَدِيدِ   كَلَامًا مَاكِنَّا شِبْهَ ٱلْحَدِيدِ
أَبُو شَادُوفِ عَنْهُ خَبَّرُونَا   بِقَوْلٍ حَقّْ جَانَا بِٱلْوَكِيدِ
بِتَلّْ فَنْدَرُوكْ فِيهِ تَرَبَّى   وَعَاشْ يَا قَوْمْ وَأَنْشَا لُو قَصِيدِ
وَذَا قَوْلِي وَأَنَا غِنْدَافُ إِسْمِي   وَكَمْ مِنْ نَظْمْ أَجِيبُو مِنْ بِعِيدِ

وقد يُجمَع بين الروايتين فيقال إنه وُلِدَ في كفرشمرطاطي وتربّى في تلّ فندروك

(وأمّا صفة لحيته) فقال بعضهم كانت طويلة جدًّا وقال آخر كانت معتدلة في الطول ٣،١٠ والقصر وقد يجمع بين القولين فيقال إنّه لمّا كان في ابتداء عمره في سعادة كاملة ونعمة وافرة كما سيأتي كانت طويلة لكثرة ما كان يتعهّدها بدهن الفراخ والزيت الحارّ والتمشّط وإصلاح الشعر ونحو ذلك فلمّا كبر وتغيّر عليه الزمان واعتراه الهمّ والأحزان قلّ طُولُهَا من أكل الطبوع والصئبان ونحو ذلك أي إنّها نشأت في الأوّل طويلة ثمّ إنّها عَرُضَتْ فعرضُها ضَرَّ طُولَهَا فلا تعارض بين الروايتين كما قال الشاعر [خفيف]

Of how, good folk, I was raised
In a hamlet known since olden days
Called Kafr Shammir-lī wa-Ṭāṭī[4]—
So, Fasāqil,[5] be a wise laddie!
These are my verses, Abū Shādūf's my name,
And any who comes to inquire my verse can claim.

And I heard verses by a country person that indicate that he was from Tall Fandarūk, as follows: 10.2.2

We have heard in days old and new
Speech strong as iron and as true—
Of Abū Shādūf they did us tell,
In words very trusty and confirmed as well,
That Tall Fandarūk was his childhood abode,
And there he lived, good people, and composed an ode.
These are my verses, Ghindāf's my name,
And verse far-fetched is the name of my game!

The two versions may be reconciled by saying that he was born in Kafr Shammirṭāṭī and raised in Tall Fandarūk.

The Shape of His Beard

As for the shape of his beard, some say it was very long, while others say it 10.3
was moderate in both length and shortness. The two accounts may be reconciled by saying that, at the beginning of his life—when, as we shall see, he enjoyed perfect good fortune and abundant blessings—his beard was long because he groomed it frequently with chicken fat and linseed oil and combed it and tended its hairs and so on; however, when he grew old and his fortunes changed and care and sorrows overtook him, it became less commode-ious[6] because of his eating dirt and nits and so on. In other words, it grew long at first and then later it grew wide, with the result that its width rendered its length odious, and, as such, there is no contradiction between the two versions. As the poet says:

ذَقَنٌ طالَتْ فأَفسَدَت عِندَما ضَرَّ طولُها
قَصَّروها فأصلَحَت عِندَما قَلَّ طولُها

٤،١٠ (وقيل) من الدليل على قلّة عقل الرجل صِغَرُ رأسه وطول لحيته وإن كان اسمه يحيى فقد فقد العقل بالكليّة وفي المثل طويل ذقن قليل عقل (كما اتّفق أنّ بعضهم كان له صاحب طويل اللحية يؤدّب الأطفال) ففقده أيّاماً فسأل عنه فقيل هو منقطع في بيته حزين قال فظنّ صديقه أنّه مات له ولد أو أحد من أقاربه فذهب إليه فرآه في حالة الحزن وهو يبكي وينوح فقال له يا أخي عظّم الله أجرك وأحسن عزاك ورحم ميّتك كلّ نفس ذائقة الموت فقال له أتظنّ أنّه مات لي أحد فقال له فما الخبر فقال له الشيخ اعلم أنّي كنت جالساً ذات يوم فسمعت رجلاً ينشد ويقول [بسيط]

يا أُمَّ عمرٍو جزاكِ الله مَكرُمَةً رُدّي عَلَيَّ فؤادي أَينَما كانا
لا تأخُذينَ فؤادي تلعَبينَ بِهِ فكَيفَ يلعَبُ بالإِنسانِ إِنسانا

فقلت في نفسي لولا أنّ أمّ عمرو هذه من أحسن الناس وأجملهم ما قيل فيها هذا الشعر فشغفت بها أيّاماً وانقطعت بحبّها ثمّ إنّي جلست يوماً من الأيّام زماناً فسمعت قائلاً يقول [وافر]

إِذا ذَهَبَ الحِمارُ بِأُمِّ عَمرٍو فلا رَجَعَتْ ولا رَجَعَ الحِمارُ

فقلت لولا أنّ أمّ عمرو ماتت ما قيل فيها هذا البيت فداخلني الحزن واعتراني الأسف قال فتحقّق صاحبه قلّة عقله وتركه ومضى

٥،١٠ (وقيل مرّ بعضهم في يوم شديد البرد) فرأى رجلاً صغير الرأس طويل اللحية وعليه قميص واحد وهو يرتعد من شدّة البرد ورأى تحت إبطه حِرام أبيض من الصوف

A beard grew long and got quite nasty,
So that its length became quite odious.
They cut it short and it got much nicer,
When its length was less commode-ious.

Some say that it is sign of a lack of brains when a man's head is small and his beard long, and if his name is Yaḥyā as well, he hasn't a hope of brains at all; and the proverb says, "Long beard, little brain." Thus it came about that a man had a friend with a long beard who was a teacher of young children.[7] On one occasion, after he had failed to see him for some days, the man asked after his friend and was told, "He has shut himself up in his house to grieve." The man thought that he must have lost a child or one of his relatives, so he went to see him and found him grief-stricken and weeping and wailing. "My brother," said the first, "may God make great your recompense and make good your consolation and have mercy on the departed! Every soul must taste death!" "Think you that one of mine has died?" said the other. "What then?" said the first. "Know," said the shaykh, "that I was sitting one day when I heard a man recite the following verses: 10.4

O Umm ʿAmr, God reward you well,
Give me back my heart, wherever it may be![8]
Don't take my heart to make of it your toy—
How can a girl with a young man's heart make free?

"—so I said to myself, 'Were not this Umm ʿAmr one of the best and most beautiful of people, these verses would not have been said of her!' and I fell madly in love with her and shut myself away with her love. Then one day I sat for a while and I heard someone say:

When the donkey went off with Umm ʿAmr,
She never came back, and neither did the donkey

"—so I thought, 'If Umm ʿAmr were not dead, they would not have made up this verse about her' and I was overcome with grief and afflicted by sorrow." This made his friend realize how stupid the man was and he left him and went his way.

And the story is told that one extremely cold day a certain person was going 10.5
along when he saw a man with a small head and long beard wearing nothing

مطويّ فقال له لأيّ شيء لا تضع هذا الحرام عليك يقيك ألم البرد فقال أخشى من نزول المطر عليه فيبتلّ فيذهب حسنه وتزول بهجته قال فتحقّق الرجل قلّة عقله وتركه ومضى

٦،١٠ وأجود اللحاء ما كان معتدلة متساوية الشعر لا طويلة ولا قصيرة (فإن قيل) إنّ فرعون كانت لحيته تزيد عن طوله شِبْرًا أو شبرين على ما قيل ومع هذا كان عارفًا فطنًا (قلنا الجواب) أنّ الله تعالى كان قد أعطاه ثلاث آيات منها طول لحيته وأنّها كانت خضراء اللون ولم يكن لمثله ذلك وكان له جواد يضع قدمه عند منتهى بصره وترتفع رجلاه إذا صعد ويداه إذا هبط أو يقال إنّه وإن كان على غاية من المعرفة فهو في حكم مسلوب العقل لادّعائه الإلهيّة وارتكابه الأمور الشنيعة ونحو ذلك فالكلام على حقيقته كما تقدّم انتهى

٧،١٠ (وقيل أحذر الناس وأشطنهم الأجاردة) فينبغي لمن صاحبهم أن يكون منهم على حذر لشدّة حذقهم وقوّة معرفتهم وكثرة محاورتهم للأمور (كما اتّفق أنّ بعض الملوك قال لوزيره مَنْ أشطن الناس وأحذرهم قال الأُجْرود) قال أريد أن تطلّعني على حقيقة ذلك فقال تصنع طعاماً وتصنع له ملاعق كلّ ملعقة ثلاثة أذرع وتأمر الناس يحضروا لأكل الطعام فإذا حضروا وجلسوا تأمرهم أن لا يأكلوا إلّا بالملاعق وأنّ الرجل منهم لا يمسك الملعقة إلّا من طرفها ويأكل وتنظر ما يظهر لك قال ففعل الملك ما أمره به الوزير وحضر الناس للطعام فلمّا جلسوا أمرهم أن لا يأكلوا إلّا بالملاعق وأن لا أحد يتجاوز بالمسك طرف الملعقة كما مرّ قال فأرادوا الأكل فلم يقدروا وأرادوا القيام فمنعهم الملك وأمرهم بالجلوس فصار الرجل منهم يملأ الملعقة وأراد أن يدخل ما فيها فمه فتطول عن فمه وتفوت قفاه فتحيّروا في أمره فبينما هم على هذه الحالة إذ دخل عليهم رجل أجرود فقال لهم ما بالكم لا تأكلون من الطعام فأخبروه بالقضيّة فقال

but a shift and shivering from the cold. Noticing that the man had a white woolen mantle folded under his arm, he asked him, "Why don't you put on the mantle to protect yourself from the cold?" The man replied, "I'm afraid that the rain will get on it and make it wet, and then it won't be lovely and new-looking anymore." This made the man realize how stupid he was and he left him and went his way.

The finest beard is middling, with hairs of even length, neither long nor 10.6
short. If it be said, "Pharaoh's beard was longer than he was tall, by one or two spans, or so it is reported, and even so he was wise and full of insight," we respond, "The explanation is that the Almighty gave him three miraculous signs, one of them being the length of his beard, which was also green and the like of which was vouchsafed to no other of his sort. He also had a steed that placed its front foot at the farthest point that it could see and raised its hind legs when it ascended and its front legs when it descended. Or it may be said that, even though he possessed extraordinary knowledge, he was effectively bereft of intelligence because he claimed to be divine and perpetrated heinous acts and so on. Thus what we have said is correct as stated above. End."

It is said that the most quick-witted and devilishly clever of men are those 10.7
who have no beard at all. Anyone associating with them must be on guard, because of their great intelligence, breadth of knowledge, and finesse. Thus it happened that a certain king once asked his minister, "Who are the most devilishly clever and quick-witted of men?" and the minister answered, "Those who have no beard." "I want you," said the king, "to demonstrate the truth of that for me." Said the minister, "You must prepare some food and make spoons for the food, each spoon three cubits in length, and order people to come and eat. When the people have come and sat down, order them to eat with nothing but those spoons and tell them that no one may touch the spoon except by the handle and that he may eat in no other way. Then watch what happens." The king did as the minister instructed him, and the people came for the food. When they sat down, he ordered that they eat only with the spoons and told them that no one should touch any part of the spoon but the handle, as described. They wanted to eat but could not, and they wanted to leave, but the king stopped them and ordered them to sit. One of them would fill the spoon and try to put what was in it in his mouth, but it would miss his mouth and stick out over his shoulder, and no one knew what to do. While they were thus engaged, a man with no beard entered. "How is it that you are not eating

هذا أمر سهل أنا أدلّكم على حيلة تأكلون بها ولا تخالفوا أمر الملك كلّ رجل منكم يُطعِم الّذي قبالة وجهه وكذلك الآخر يمدّ ملعقته يطعم من أطعمه حتّى تكتفوا من الطعام والملاعق على حالها فصار هذا يُلقِم هذا بملعقته والآخر يفعل مع الآخر مثل ما فعل معه حتّى اكتفوا جميعاً قال فتعجّب الملك من حيلة هذا الأجرود وقوّة شيطنته وشدّة فراسته وأمر له بِصِلَةٍ وأخلع على الوزير

٨،١٠ (ووقف رجل أجرود بين يدي بعض الملوك) يشكو خصمه فقال له الملك إنّي متعجّب من شكواك يعني إنك أجرود لا يغلب عليك أحد فقال له العفو يا ملك إن كان في وجهي بعض شعرات فإنّ خصمي أملس لا شعر بوجهه قال فضحك الملك وأنصفه من خصمه وأمر له بصلة

٩،١٠ (وأمّا سبب سعادته في ابتداء أمره وكيف مال عليه الدهر) فعلى أقوال أحدها إنه لمّا نشأ وصار له من العمر عشر سنين كان في قوّة وشهامة ومعرفة في رعي الغنم والنطّ في الغيط والمشي في الحرّ حافي عريان وكان يشيل الجلّة الخضراء على رأسه من الغيط إلى داره في أسرع زمن حتّى أنّ الرطوبة المتحلّلة منها كانت تسيل على وجهه وربّما عطش فشرب منها وربّما عمّ ما يسيل منها بقيّة جسده كما هو عادة أولاد الأرياف وكان يمكث الشهر والشهرين لا يغسل له وجهاً إلّا أن صادفه رشاش بول عجلة أو بقرة وهو سارح إلى الغيط أو مروّح فيمعكه بيده فيكون قائماً مقام الماء لغسل وجهه وكان مع هذه النظافة الفشرويّة لا يغفل عن ضرب الأولاد ولعب الكورة حول الحارات والنطّ على المزابل والأجران ولعب الدارة * والطبلة والزُمّاره * والعياط

the food?" he asked, so they told him the problem. "That's easy," he said, "I will show you a stratagem that will allow you to eat without disobeying the king's command: each one of you will feed the man sitting opposite him, and that man likewise will feed the one who feeds him. That way you will eat your fill with the spoons as they are." So this man started feeding morsels to that one and likewise that man to this one till all had eaten their fill. The king was amazed at the beardless man's stratagem and the force of his cunning and his great insight and ordered that he be given a gift and bestowed a robe of honor on the minister.

And once a beardless man stood before a certain king and brought a complaint against an opponent. The king said to him, "I am amazed at your complaint. After all, you are beardless, and no one should be able to get the better of you." "Pardon, O king," replied the man, "but my face has the odd hair, while my opponent is completely smooth, without a single hair on his face!" The king laughed and gave the man his due against his opponent and ordered that he be given a gift. 10.8

The Origins of His Good Fortune in His Early Days and How Fate Came to Turn Against Him

As for the origins of the poet's good fortune in his early days and how fate came to turn against him, accounts differ. One says that, when he was grown and had reached ten years of age, he was strong, lusty, and well versed in pasturing flocks, gamboling in fields, and walking barefoot and naked in the heat, and that he would haul wet manure on his head from the field to his house in the shortest time imaginable, so that the liquid released would run over his face, and from this, if he ever got thirsty, he would drink; and sometimes what ran down from it would cover the rest of his body, as is typically the case among country boys. And he would go for a month or even two without giving his face a wash, unless he should happen to get doused in urine by a calf or a cow as he was on his way to or from the fields, in which case he would rub it in with his hand, using it in place of water to wash his face. Despite this fatuous cleanliness, he never passed up an opportunity to beat up the other children, play ball around the village quarters, gambol on the dung heaps and threshing floors, play at *dārah* and on the drums and *zummārah*, making a tumult and wild sounds, and beating the hounds, and other crud and crap, to the point that 10.9

والغاره * وضرب الكلاب * والسخام والهباب * حتّى أنّه من دون رفاقته صار يومه بيومين * وشهره بشهرين * كما قال فيه شاعر القريتين * شعر [وافر]

أَبُو شَادُوفِ مِنْ يَوْمُو مُجَعْمِصْ شَبِيهُ ٱلْجَرْوِ يِتْنَطَّطْ بِقُوَّهْ ١،٩،١٠
وَيَسْرَحْ غَيْطْ أَبُو مَعْرَهْ يُجَمِّعْ مِنَ ٱلْجِلَّهْ ٱلطَّرِيَّهْ فِي ٱلْقُرُوَّهْ
وَهُوْ عُرْيَانْ وَشَايِلْ فَوْقْ رَاسُو وَوَجْهُو صَارْ كَمَا وَجْهِ ٱلْبَعْوَّهْ
وَمَا قَدْ سَالْ مِنَ ٱلْجِلَّهْ ٱلطَّرِيَّهْ يَسِيلْ عَلَيْهْ وَمَا عِنْدُو مُرُوَّهْ
وَيَقْعُدْ شَهْرْ مَا يَغْسِلْ لِوَجْهُو وَلَا شَهْرَيْنْ وَجِسْمُو فِيهِ قُوَّهْ
يُسَرِّحْ لِلضُّحَى فِي ٱلْجُرْنِ يِكْنُسْ وَيَطْرُدْ شِبْهْ كَلْبَتْنَا ٱمّْ صَرْوَهْ ٢،٩،١٠
وَيَا زَيْنَكْ يَاَبُو شَادُوفِ لَمَّا يِجِي ٱلْجَامُوسْ يِقَعْ فِي وَسْطِ رَبْوَهْ
وَيِنْزِلْ يِنْغِرِزْ فِيهَا وَرَاهُمْ تَقُولْ ٱنْتَا كَمَا عِفْرِيتِ خَلْوَهْ
أَبُو شَادُوفِ مِنْ صُغْرُو مُدَلَّلْ تَرَبَّا عِنْدَنَا كَلْبَ ٱبْنِ جَرْوَهْ
أَبُو شَادُوفْ عَطَاهُ ٱللّٰهُ نِعْمَهْ لِبِسْ لِبْدَهْ وَعِنْدُو ٱلْيَوْمْ فَرْوَهْ
وَٱبُوهْ ٱلْيَوْمْ شَيْخُ ٱلْكَفْرِ قَاعِدْ حِدَا ٱلصَّرَّافْ رُكْبَهْ جَنْبْ حِدْوَهْ
يِقُولْ سِيدِي[1] يِقُولْ لُهْ يَا مُعَرَّصْ تِحُطُّ ٱلْمَالْ أَوْ أُخَلِّيكْ دَعْوَهْ ٣،٩،١٠
وَهُوْ مِنْ مِتْلْ أَبُو شَادُوفْ وَجِدُّهْ وَٱبُوهْ وَعَمَّتُو بِنْتْ ٱمّْ فَسْوَهْ
وَنِخْتِمْ قَوْلَنَا بِمْدِيحْ مُحَمَّدْ رَسُولْ ٱللّٰهِ كَمْ زَاحْ كُلّْ بَلْوَهْ
عَلَيْهْ[2] يَا رَبَّنَا صَلِّي وَسَلِّمْ وَأَصْحَابُو ٱلْكِرَامْ أَهْلُ ٱلْفُتُوَّهْ

وكان الناس يحسدوا والده عليه وعلى قوّته وشطارته وشدّة معرفته في نقر الطبلة وصوت الزُمّارة وكان أبوه قد ملك في حال حياته حماراً أعرج وعنزين وحِصّة في ١٠،١٠

١ بي: يا سيّدي. ٢ بي: عليهِ.

he was the one among his companions who knew best how to make two days of every one and of every month two. As the Bard of the Two Villages[9] put it:

Abū Shādūf from day one's been cocky— 10.9.1
Like a puppy he bounces all over
And goes to Abū Maʿrah's field and gathers
Fresh dung on a platter.
He'll be naked, with a load on his head,
And his face like the face of an ogre,
And the wet dung that's gone runny
Will have run down upon him, and there's nothing brave in his manner.
He goes for a month without washing his face,
Or for two, and his body's still got power:
After sweeping the threshing floors all morning long, 10.9.2
He'll still dash about like our bitch Umm Ṣarwah.
How fine you look, Abū Shādūf (when
He comes to the buffaloes and falls into ordure
And gets down and wallows there behind them).
You'd say you were the afreet of some cloister!
All his life Abū Shādūf's been pampered:
Like a puppy dog he grew up among us and scampered.
Abū Shādūf, God grant him ease,
Put on a cap and today has a sheepskin fur.
Today his father's shaykh of the hamlet and sits
Knee to sandal with the tax collector.
The first says, "Master!" The other, "You pimp! 10.9.3
Cough up the taxes or I'll use you others to deter."
This is from the likes of Abū Shādūf and his grandfather[10]
And his father and his father's sister, Umm Faswah's[11] daughter,
And we close our words with praise for Muḥammad—
How many a calamity he has swept away, God's Messenger!
On him, O Lord, pour blessings and peace,
As on his noble companions, of knightly order!

Indeed, people used to envy his father for having a son so strong and so smart and such an expert at banging the drum and playing the *zummārah*. 10.10

ثور الساقية ونصف بقرة وعشر فرخات وديكهم وأربع كيلات نُخال ورُبعَين شعير وملك نحو أربعمائة قرص جلّة ومطمورة يخزن فيها الزبل أيّام الشتاء وكان عنده قُلّة مكسورة وزير أقلم وجيروانة يكنس بها الجرن وكلب يحرس الدار فلمّا تمّت له هذه السعادة توفّى إلى رحمة الله تعالى كما في الغالب أنّ الفقير يوم يسعد يموت وما أحسن ما قال الشاعر [متقارب]

إذا تَمَّ شَيءٌ بَدا نقصُهُ   تَوَقَّعْ[1] زَوالاً إذا قِيلَ تَمّ

١١،١٠ فكفّنه ولده أبو شادوف في رداء من محر الكتّان ودفنه في تربة تعرف بتربة ابن خاروق بسنط كفر[2] شمرطاطي وقيل بكفر تلّ فندروك وقد يجمع بين القولين فيقال مات في كفرشمرطاطي ودفن في كفر تلّ فندروك وقبره الآن يعرف بقبر أبو جاروف تزوره الفلّاحون ويلعبون بجانبه الكورة وربّما تبول عليها البهائم في بعض الأوقات وقد رثاه بعض شعراء الأرياف بأبيات فقال [وافر]

١،١١،١٠ أَلا كُونُوا ٱسْعِفُونِي يا جَماعَهْ   وَإِبْكُوا يا مُشاهْ فِي كُلّ ساعَهْ
أَبُو جارُوفْ وَلّى ٱلْيَوْمَ عَنّا   وَخَلَّى ٱلْعَنْزَ وَٱلْبَقْرَهْ بِتاعَهْ
وَخَلّى بِنْتْ عَمُّو أُمَّ فَلْحَسْ   عَلَيهِ ٱلْيَوْمَ تَبْكِي وَسْطَ قاعَهْ
وَأَبُو شادُوفْ يُعَيِّطْ مَلُو رَاسُو   أَبُويا ماتْ وَعُدْنا فِي بَشاعَهْ
وَراحْ مَنْ كانَ شَيْخَ ٱلْكَفْرِ يُحْكَمْ   عَلَى ٱلجِدْعانْ وَدَوْلِيكَ ٱلرِّباعَهْ
٢،١١،١٠ وَلَمّا كانَ يَرْكَبْ يَوْمَ غارَهْ   عَلَى كَلْبُهْ وَيَدَّلَّعْ دِلاعَهْ
وَيَلْبِسْ لِبْدَتُو مِنْ فَوْق رَاسُو   وَدَقْنُو بارِدَهْ فِيها سَقاعَهْ
وَحَوْلُو جَرْوِ إِبْنِ خَرا ٱنْتَ فَلْحَسْ   وَمُشاةُ ٱلْكَفْرِ ما مِنْهُمْ نَجاعَهْ

١ بي: توفّي. ٢ بي: سنط بكفر.

Now, his father had acquired, in the course of his life, a lame donkey, two goats, a share in the ox that turned the waterwheel, half a cow, ten hens with their rooster, four bushels of bran, and two quarterns of barley. He also owned about four hundred dung cakes and a bin in which he stored chicken droppings during the winter, and he had a broken water jug, a striped earthenware water butt, a besom to sweep the threshing floor, and a dog to guard the house. Once he had achieved this state of luxury, he died and passed into the mercy of the Almighty, in keeping with the common rule that the day a poor man gets rich, he dies—a point well made by the poet[12] who said:

When a thing's complete, decline sets in.
Expect extinction when men say, "Done!"

So his son Abū Shādūf wrapped him in a cloak of combed linen and buried him in a grave known as "the grave of Ibn Kharūf" at the acacia trees of Kafr Shammirṭāṭī, or, as some say, at Kafr Tall Fandarūk; but the two statements may be combined, in which case one would say, "He died in Kafr Shammirṭāṭī and was buried in Kafr Tall Fandarūk." His grave is now known as "the grave of Abū Jārūf," and the peasants visit it and play ball next to it, and the animals urinate on it from time to time. A country poet elegized him in the following lines: **10.11**

Ah come, good people, to my aid, **10.11.1**
And weep, *mushāh*, time and again!
Abū Jārūf today away from us has turned,
While his goat and cow remain.
He's left his father's brother's daughter, Umm Falḥas,[13]
In an empty chamber today to weep and complain,
And Abū Shādūf bawls fit to burst,
"My father's dead and it's all gone awful again!"
Gone is the hamlet's shaykh who ruled
O'er the brave lads and all those men!
And when, to go raiding, he used to mount **10.11.2**
His dog and primp and preen,
And put his cap atop his head—
His beard sticking out and looking mean—
And about him were Jarw Ibn Kharā Inta Falḥas[14]
And the *mushāh* of the hamlet, none worth a bead,

تقُولْ رَيِّسْ عَلَى جَوْقِ ٱلْمَغَانِي   أَوِ ٱلْخَلْبُوصْ جَا يِشْفَعْ شَفَاعَهْ
وَجِيصُو رَاحْ يَا ٱللهْ ارحم عِضَامُو   وَبَشْبِشْ طُوبتُو فِي كُلِّ سَاعَهْ
وَٱبُو شَادُوفْ يَا ٱللهْ أبقِي شبابو   وَيُصْبِحْ شَيْخَنَا صَاحِبْ نَفَاعَهْ   ١٠،١١،٣
وَيِبْقَى مِثْلْ أَبُوهْ رَاكِبْ وَحَوْلُو   جَمَاعَهْ فِي جَمَاعَهْ فِي جَمَاعَهْ
وَيِتْعَنْطَزْ وَيَسْرَحْ فِي ٱلضَّهَارِي   وَيِجَعْمَصْ وَيُقْعُدْ فِي ٱلشِّرَاعَهْ
وَنِخْتِمْ قَوْلَنَا وَٱلدَّائِمْ ٱللهْ   وَدَا ٱلْكَاسْ حَقّْ مَا فِيهِ ٱنْدِفَاعَهْ
وَٱنَا شَاطِرْ وَشَاعِرْ طُولَ عُمْرِي   وَٱلْضُمْ لَضْمْ يِتْلَمَّعْ لِمَاعَهْ
جَعَلْتُو فِيهِ يِحْزَنْ مَنْ يَشُوفُو   وَوَدَّعْتُو بِقَوْلِي ٱلْيَوْمْ وَدَاعَهْ   ١٠،١١،٤
وَٱصَالْ عَالزَّيْنْ أُصَلِّي طُولَ عُمْرِي   نَبِيِّ ٱللهْ وَأَطْلُبْ لِي شَفَاعَهْ
وَمِنْ بَعْدِ ٱلصَّلَاةِ اسْمَعْ لِقَوْلِي[1]   وَضَرْبَهْ دَمّْ تِكْتِمْ دِي ٱلْجَمَاعَهْ

قال فلمّا فرغ العزا وراق الزمان * وأخذ خاطر أبو شادوف المشايخ والجدعان *   ١٠،١٢
وتصدّق على والده بالفطير * المعمول بالنخالة والشعير * وليّس قبره بالوحل والجلّه * وعمل بجانبه مدود العجله * سحب النبّوت * وتمشّى كالنُعوت * واتمشيخ على الكفر * وأطاعه زيد وعمرو * وجلس على ركبة ونصف مورّط * وعيّط واتنطّط * وغنّا وقال * وافتخر بهذا المقال * وأنشد وجعل يقول شعر [وافر]

أَبُو شَادُوفْ عُمْرِي يَا سَلَامَهْ   أَقُولُ ٱلْقَوْلْ وَٱنَا صَاحِبْ فَهَامَهْ   ١٠،١٢،١
وَلَوْلَا أَنْ أَبُويَهْ فِي تُرَابُو   أَنَا فِي ٱلْكَفْرِ شَيْخْ بِلَا مَلَامَهْ
وَأَحْكُمْ عَٱلْمُشَاهْ وَٱسْرَحْ وَٱرَوِّحْ   وَٱخُوضْ ٱلْبَحْرْ إِلَى حَدِّ ٱلْحَزَامَهْ

١ الأصل: قولي.

You'd have said he was head of a band of musicians,
Or the buffoon who'd come to plead!
Gone now is his fart, God bless his bones
And moisten his head-brick[15] time and again!
As to Abū Shādūf, God preserve his youth 10.11.3
And make him our shaykh, to rule to our gain,
Like his father mounted, and may his army
Troop after troop after troop contain,
And may he buck like a donkey and set off around noon
And lounge about pompously and sit in the *shirāʿah*.[16]
Thus we end our words, and God alone endures,
And death's a cup from which none may abstain!
And I'm a smart guy and all my life a poet,
And I string together verses that shimmer and shine.
These I've made so all who behold them may mourn, 10.11.4
And today with my words I've sent him off fine,
And for the rest of my days I'll praise the Beauteous,
God's Prophet, and pray his intercession to gain.
Now the blessing's done, so hear what I say:
I hope you're all snuffed by a clot on the brain!

And when the wake was over and the dust had settled and Abū Shādūf had received the condolences of the shaykhs and the brave lads, and he had distributed bran-and-barley pastries as alms for the repose of his father's soul and had plastered his grave with mud and dung, and built the calf's trough next to it, he put his cudgel over his shoulder and stepped out like a fine steed, and played the shaykh over the hamlet, and every Zayd and ʿAmr[17] obeyed, and he sat on his ass with one knee up and one knee on the ground, and shouted and jumped, both up and down, and sang and made up poetry, of which he was proud, declaiming and saying out loud: 10.12

Me, Abū Shādūf—O Salāmah[18]— 10.12.1
All my life I've made up verses and I'm a bright guy,
And now my father's in his grave[19]
I'm shaykh of the hamlet, which none can decry!
And I rule the foot soldiers and come and go,
And I wade in the river up to my thigh,

وَٱشِدُّ عَلَى ٱلْحُمَارْ وَٱرْكَبْ وَحَوْلِي   جَمَاعَهْ شِبْهْ شَمْعَهْ فِي ضَلاَمَهْ
أَبُو عُنْطُوزْ وَٱبُو بُزْبُوزْ وَعَفْلَقْ   وَدَمْ إِلْحَسْ قَفَاكْ وَأَبُو عِمَامَهْ
وَٱنَا مَا عَادْ كَيْفِي ٱلْيَوْمْ وَاحِدْ   وَٱضَالْ إِنِّي مُجَمْعَصْ فِي شَهَامَهْ ٢،١٢،١٠
وَأَطْحَنْ قَرْنْ مِنْ خَالَفْ كَلاَمِي   بِنَبُّوتِي وَٱكْسِرْ بُو عِضَامَهْ
أَبُويَهْ كَانْ قَبْلِي شَيْخْ عَلَيْكُمْ   فَخَلُّونِي وَرُوحُوا بِالسَّلاَمَهْ
وَنَخْتِمْ قَوْلَنَا بِمَدِيحْ مُحَمَّدْ   وَأَصْحَابُو ٱلْمِلاَحْ أَهْلِ ٱلْكَرَامَهْ

١٣،١٠ قال فعند ذلك حسدوه المشايخ والجدعان على مشيخة الكفر الّتي حصلت له بعد والده على التِركة فأغرَوا عليه الحكّام فأرسلوا إليه وعارضوه في جانب منها وقيل فيها كلّها ولم ينفعه إلّا مطمورة الزبل الّتي ادّخرها وهي الّتي كانت سبب سعادته بعد موت أبيه على ما قيل ثمّ صار يداري الناس ويتملّق لهم بالكلام إلى أن تناست القضيّة ودخل فصل الشتاء ففتح المطمورة ليلاً وباع الزبل وكثر عليه الرزق على هذا القول وقيل إنّه اقترض عشرين نصفاً وأخذ بهم بيضاً وطلع مصر فصادف عيد النصارى فباع البيض بزيادة عن ثمنه فكان هذا السبب لسعادته وقد يجمع بين القولين فيقال إنّه باع الزبل وأخذ بثمنه بيضاً فكانت سعادته من مجموع الزبل وثمن البيض فلا تعارض في ذلك وكان يعطي ويتكرّم فقصدته الشعراء والأدباء من أطراف البلاد حتّى أنّه أجاز شاعراً بخمسين بيضة وكيلة شعير وأعطى آخر مائة قرص جلّة وجاءه آخر بغرارة فملأها زبل من أوّلها إلى آخرها ودفعها له وكان قد أقبل عليه الرزق بزيادة عن والده فكان عنده وزّتين وعشرين ديك وقفص فراخ جريد ونبّوت أعوج ولِبدة وخَلَقة

And I saddle my donkey and mount, around me
A company like to a candle in the night sky,
With Abū ʿUntūz and Abū Buzbūz[20] and ʿAflaq,
While Blood-Lick-the-Back-of-Your-Neck and Abū *ʿimāmah*[21] are nigh.
These days the world doesn't hold my like, 10.12.2
And I'll boss you forever and go on being a helluva guy,
And with my cudgel I'll break the bones and smash the pate
Of any who disobey.
My father before me was shaykh over you,
So let me be, and be on your way!
And we close our words with praise of Muḥammad
And his dandy companions, the people of generosity!

At this the shaykhs and the brave lads envied him the shaykhdom of the hamlet, to which he had succeeded after his father's death, and they incited the authorities against him, and the latter sent for him and deprived him of a part or, as some say, of all of it, and he had nothing to fall back on but the binful of droppings, which he had kept out of sight and which had been the source of his prosperity after his father's death, or so they say. However, he set about sucking up to people and flattering them, until the matter was forgotten and the winter came and he opened the bin one night and sold the droppings and made a good living, according to this version of events. Others, however, say that he borrowed twenty silver pieces and bought eggs with them and went to Cairo, where he happened to arrive on the feast of the Christians,[22] so he sold the eggs for more than they were worth, and this was the source of his prosperity. The two versions may be reconciled by saying that he sold the droppings and bought eggs with the proceeds, so that his prosperity was the sum of the price of the droppings and the price of the eggs, and from this perspective there is no contradiction. And he took to handing out money and dispensing hospitality, and poets and men of letters from the farthest hamlets sought him out. One poet he rewarded with fifty eggs and a measure of barley, and to another he gave a hundred dung cakes, and yet another brought him a sack, which he filled with droppings from top to bottom and gave him in payment. He became even richer than his father, for he had two geese, twenty roosters, a chicken hutch made out of palm ribs, a crooked staff, a felt cap, 10.13

زرقاء وقُفّة ملانة نخال وعشر حِزَم عروق جزر ناشف وغير ذلك ولم يزل على هذه الحالة يبارك له المولى في رزقه فإنّما الرزق من الله تعالى

١٤،١٠ (كما اتّفق أنّ بعض الصالحين كان فقيرًا جدًّا) فبينما هو نائم إذ هتف به هاتف يقول له يا فلان امض إلى محلّ كذا خذ منه ألف دينار فقال أفيهم بركة قال لا قال اذهب عنّي فأتاه ثاني مرّة وقال له اذهب إلى المحلّ الفلانيّ خذ منه خمسمائة دينار فقال أفيهم بركة قال لا قال اذهب عنّي ولم يزل يأتيه مرّة بعد أخرى حتّى قال له اذهب إلى محلّ كذا وخذ منه دينارًا واحدًا فقال أفيه بركة قال نعم فقال إذًا آخذه فذهب وأخذ الدينار وبورك له فيه وصار في نعمة زائدة وسعادة وافرة فالشخص إذا قَنِعَ شَبِعَ وبورك له في قليله قال الوليّ العارف بالله تعالى سيّدي يحيى البهلول رضي الله عنه ونفعنا به آمين [وزن غير معروف]

واستقنع بقليلك   يأتيك الله بكثير

وقال [وزن غير معروف]

كم من عارض بعد رشاش   ينهلّ من المُزْن

١٥،١٠ وقال الشافعيّ رضي الله عنه [متقارب مع كسر]

وجدتُ القناعةَ كنزَ الغنا   فصرتُ بأذيالها ممتسكْ
فَلا ذا يَراني عَلى بابِهِ   ولا ذا يَراني لَه[1] منهمكْ
أَمُرُّ عَلى النّاس بلا درهمٍ   ولا لي مطالب كأنّي ملكْ

١٦،١٠ حتّى مال عليه الدهر والزمان * وجفَتْه الأهل والخلاّن * ونَفِدَ جميع ما كان معه من المال * وصار في أكبر الهمّ وأشدّ الأحوال * ولم يجد له خِلاًّ ولا مساعد * ولم

---

١ بي (في جميع النسخ): عليه.

a tattered blue shift, a basket full of bran, ten bunches of dry carrots, and other stuff too, and he continued thus, with the Lord blessing his prosperity—for prosperity comes from the Almighty alone.

In illustration of which, we might mention that it happened that a certain righteous man was very poor. Once, while asleep, he heard a voice say to him of a sudden, "You! Go to such-and-such a place and take from there a thousand dinars!" "Has the Lord blessed them?" he asked. "No," said the voice. "Leave me!" said the man. Then the voice came to him again and said, "Go to such-and-such a place and take from there five hundred dinars!" "Has the Lord blessed them?" he asked. "No," said the voice. "Leave me!" said the man. The voice kept coming to him again and again, until it said to him, "Go to such-and-such a place and take from there one dinar!" "Has the Lord blessed it?" he asked. "Yes," said the voice. "Then I will take it," said the man, and he went and he took the dinar and was blessed in it and obtained great ease and abundant riches, for if a man is content with what he has he will not suffer want, and the little he has will be blessed. As says the Righteous Saint and Initiate of the Almighty, My Master Yaḥyā al-Buhlūl,[23] may the Almighty be pleased with him and benefit us and all Muslims through him, amen: 10.14

Be content with the little you have
And God will give you much!

And he says:

How many a cloud after sprinkling
Lets fall a heavy shower!

And al-Shāfiʿī,[24] may God be pleased with him, has said: 10.15

I found acceptance of my lot a treasure house of riches,
And to its skirts began to cling.
Now no man finds me at his door
Or chasing him for anything.
I move among mankind without a single cent
And have no wants, just like a king.

Thus it was till fate and fortune against him turned, and he was by relatives and boon companions spurned, and all that he had owned was spent, and he found himself in the greatest woe and severest predicament, of all friends 10.16

يبق إلّا ما خلَفه له الوالد * وأخذ مشيخة الكفر من كان له خديم * ولم ير له مساعداً ولا حميم * كما هو عادة الدهر في رفع السافل * وخفض السادة الأماثل * فهو كالميزان في فعله * أو المُنخَل في حاله ونقله * كما قال الشاعر هذه الأبيات [وافر]

رَأَيتُ الدَّهرَ يَرفَعُ كُلَّ وَغدٍ   ويَخفِضُ كُلَّ ذي شِيَمٍ شريفَهْ
كَمِثلِ البَحرِ يُغرِقُ كُلَّ حيٍّ   ولا يَنفَكُّ يَطفو فيه[1] جِيفَهْ
أو الميزانِ يَخفِضُ كُلَّ وافٍ   ويَرفَعُ كُلَّ ذي زِنَةٍ خَفِيفَهْ

١٧،١٠ وقال بعضهم [سريع]

الدَّهرُ كالمُنخَلِ في فِعلِهِ   فاعْجَبْ لِما يَصنَعُهُ المُنخَلْ
يَحُطُّ لُبَّ اللُّبِّ مِن تحتِهِ   ويَرفَعُ القِشْرَةَ والفَشْوَلْ

فحوادث الدهر تأتي على غرر * وتُذهِب الشخص على خطر *

١٨،١٠ وقد قلت في مطلع قصيدة من هذا المعنى هذه الأبيات [بسيط]

حَوادِثُ الدَّهرِ قَد تَأتي عَلَى خَطَرِ   فاحذَر عَواقِبَها تَنجو مِنَ الضَّرَرِ
واعدُد لها مِن دُروعِ الصَّبرِ سابِغةً[2]   تَقيكَ شِدَّتَها[3] إذ تَرمِ بالشَّرَرِ
ودَعْ زَمانَ الصِّبا أغصانُه يَبِسَتْ   مِن بَعدِ نَضرَتِها في المَغرِسِ النَّضِرِ
كانَت لَيالي بِها اللَّذّاتُ مُثمِرَةً   قَطَفتُ مِنها ثِمارَ العِزِّ في الصِّغَرِ[4]

إلى آخر هذه الأبيات

١٩،١٠ فليس لحوادث الدهر إلّا الصبر الجميل * والتسليم إلى الربّ الجليل * وممّن دهمه حادث الزمان * وانصرفت عنه الأهل والخلّان * (ما يحكى أنّ بعض الحسدة وشّى

---

١ بي: فيه كل. ٢ بي: سابقةً. ٣ بي: شرتها. ٤ بي: الصَفَرِ.

and helpers bereft, no wealth remaining but what his father'd left, and those who were once his servants took over the shaykhdom of the hamlet, while he could find neither helper nor friend—for such is the way of Fate: it raises up the lowly, and brings down the noble and exemplary, it being like a balance in its action, or like a sieve in its working and extraction—as the poet[25] says in the following verses:

I see Fate lifts every scoundrel high
And humbles those with noble traits—
Just like the sea, which drowns all living things
While every stinking carcass to its surface levitates,
Or like the scale, which raises all that's light
But sinks with weights.

And another has said: 10.17

Fate's like a sieve in how it works,
So wonder at what the sieve achieves—
The densest grains it puts below,
And on the top the husks and chaff it leaves

—for the accidents of Fate may be cause for alarm, and drive a man into the way of harm.

In the opening lines of an ode of mine on the same theme I say: 10.18

The accidents of Fate may be to your peril—
So beware their outcome and escape any harm that might transpire.
Prepare against them an ample coat of mail from patience,
To protect you from their fierceness when showered with their fire
And leave behind the time of youth—its boughs have dried
That in the verdant nursery once were full of juice.
They were nights bowed down with pleasures
From which, when young, I gathered glory's fruits

—and so on to the end of these verses.

Nothing but "patience fair"[26] against the accidents of Fate can remedy afford—that, and submission to the Majestic Lord; and apropos of those caught unawares by fate's blows and abandoned by kin and fellows, is the story that is told of how a certain envious person slandered the vizier and 10.19

بالوزير الكاتب ابن مُقْلة) الذي انفرد في زمانه بعلوّ الخط وحسنه وادّعى أنّه دلس على الملك في بعض الأمور قال فأمر الملك بقطع يده فلمّا فعل به هذا الأمر لزم بيته وانصرفت عنه الأصدقاء والمحبّون ولم يأته أحد إلى نصف النهار فتبيّن للملك أنّ الكلام عليه باطل فأمر بقتل الرجل الّذي وشّى به وأعاد ابن مقلة إلى ما كان عليه وندم الملك على ما فعله معه من قطع يده فلمّا رأوا إخوانه عَوْد النعمة إليه عادوا له يهنّوه وأقبلوا إليه يتعذّرون له فعند ذلك أنشد يقول شعر [بسيط]

تَخالَفَ النّاسُ والزَّمانُ ... فَحَيثُ كانَ الزَّمانُ كانوا
عاداني الدَّهرُ نِصفَ يَومٍ ... فانكَشَفَ النّاسُ لي وبانوا
يا أيُّها المُعرِضون عنّي ... عودوا فَقَدْ عادَ لِيَ الزَّمانُ

وقيل مكث يكتب بيده اليسرى بقية عمره ولم يتغيّر خطّه حتّى مات

(ومن النوادر الدالّة على فصاحة ابن مقلة) ما اتّفق أنّ رجلاً كتب رقعة وألقاها ٢٠،١٠
إليه بحضرة الملك ليقرأها عليه وكلّ لفظ منها فيه حرف الراء وكان ابن مقلة لا يقدر أن ينطق بهذا الحرف وصورتها أمر أمير الأمراء أن يُحفَرَ بيرًا على قارعة الطريق يشرب منه الشارد والوارد قال فلمّا أن تأمّلها غيّر الألفاظ وأتى بالمعنى وقال حكم حاكم الحكّام أن يُجعَلَ جُبًّا على شاطئ الوادي ليستقي منه الغادي والبادي وكان هذا من قوّة بلاغته رحمه الله تعالى وقيل أربعة يُضرَب منهم المثل حسّان بن ثابت في الفصاحة ولُقمان في الحكمة وابن أدهم في الزهد وابن مقلة في حسن الكتابة والخطّ قال الشاعر يصف هذه الأربعة بهذه الأبيات [طويل]

فَصاحَةُ حَسّانٍ وَخَطُّ ابن مُقْلَةٍ ... وحِكمَةُ لُقمانٍ وزُهدُ ابنِ أَدهَمِ
إذا اجتَمَعوا في المَرءِ والمَرءُ مُفلِسٌ ... ونُودي عَلَيه لا يُباعُ بِدِرهَمِ

calligrapher Ibn Muqlah—who was unique in his age for the sublime beauty of his hand—claiming that he had cheated the king in some matter. The king, in consequence, ordered Ibn Muqlah's hand cut off. After the command had been carried out, Ibn Muqlah kept to his house, while his friends and dear ones abandoned him and up to the middle of the day no one came to see him. Then the king discovered that the accusation against him was false, ordered that the man who had slandered him be killed, and restored Ibn Muqlah to his previous position, repenting that he had had his hand cut off. When Ibn Muqlah's brethren saw that he was returned to favor, they came back to him and visited him to make their excuses, at which he recited the following verses:[27]

Man and time succeed each other in reciprocity,
So, as time is, man must too be.
Fate savaged me for half a day,
And man's nature was thus revealed and made clear to me.
O you who turned away,
Return, for time itself's turned back to me.

It is said that he continued to write with his left hand for the rest of his life, and his writing did not change to the day he died.

A curious anecdote attesting to Ibn Muqlah's mastery of the language relates **10.20**
that a man once wrote something on a scrap of paper and tossed it to him in the presence of the king for him to read to him, and every word contained the letter r, which Ibn Muqlah could not pronounce. The message read as follows: "The ruler of rulers requires a spring drilled right by the road so every transient and traveler may drink." After glancing at it, Ibn Muqlah changed the words and kept the meaning, saying: "The king of kings commands that a well be dug next to the wadi, so all who come and go may wet their whistles." This was an example of his extraordinary skill with words, may the Almighty have mercy on him. It is said there are four men whose qualities have become proverbial: Ḥassān ibn Thābit for eloquence, Luqmān for wisdom, Ibn Adham for self-denial, and Ibn Muqlah for beauty of writing and script. Said the poet, describing these four:

Ḥassān's tongue and Ibn Muqlah's hand,
The wisdom of Luqmān and the self-denial of Ibn Adham,
Were these brought together in one bankrupt,
And he were hawked for sale, he'd not bring in one dirham.

٢١،١٠ وأمّا ضدّ هذه الأربعة فلله درّ من قال فيها [طويل]

سَماجَةُ أُطروشٍ وثُقْل ابن قَينةٍ   وغَفلَةُ قَرنانٍ وعَكسُ ابنِ أَيهَمِ
إذا اجتَمعوا في المرءِ والمرءُ مُوسِرٌ   لَكانَ فَصيحَ القومِ عِندَ التَكلُّمِ

٢٢،١٠ وممّا دهمه حادث الدهر * وعلاه الهمّ والقهر * فأصبح بعد العزّ حقيرا * وبعد الغنا فقيرا * (كما اتّفق أنّ رجلاً ركبته الديون فترك عياله وخرج هائماً على وجهه) إلى أن أقبل بعد أيّام على مدينة عالية الأصوار عظيمة البنيان فدخلها في حالة الذلّ والانكسار وقد اشتدّ به الجوع وآلمه السفر فمرّ في بعض شوارعها فرأى جماعة من الأكابر متوجّهين فذهب معهم إلى أن انتهوا إلى محلّ يشبه محلّ الملوك فدخلوا ذلك المكان وهو تابعهم إلى أن انتهوا إلى رجل جالس في هيبة عظيمة وحوله الغلمان والخدم كأنّه من أبناء الوزراء فلمّا رآهم قام لهم وأكرمهم قال فأخذ الرجل المذكور الوهم واندهش ممّا رأى من البنيان والخدم والحشم فتأخّر إلى ورائه وهو في حيرة وكربة وخائف على نفسه حتّى جلس في محلّ بعيد منفرد عن الناس بحيث لا يراه أحد فبينما هو جالس إذ أقبل عليه رجل ومعه أربع كلاب من كلاب الصيد وعليهم أنواع الخزّ والديباج وفي أعناقها أطواق الذهب بسلاسل من الفضّة فربط كلّ كلب منهم في محلّ مُعَدّ له ثمّ غاب وأتى بأربع أصحن من الذهب ملآنين من الطعام المفتخر ووضع لكلّ واحد منهم صحناً على انفراده ثمّ مضى وتركهم قال فصار هذا الرجل ينظر إلى الطعام من شدّة الجوع ويريد أن يتقدّم إلى كلب منهم يأكل معه فيمنعه الخوف منهم فنظر إليه كلب منهم فعرف حاله فامتنع عن الأكل وأشار إليه فدنا منه فأشار إليه ثانياً أن كُل من هذا الصحن فتأخّر الكلب عن الصحن فأكل الرجل حتّى اكتفى وأراد أن يذهب فأشار إليه الكلب أن خُذ الصحن ببقيّة ما فيه من الطعام قال فأخذه ووضعه في كمّه ووقف ساعة فلم يأت أحد يسأل عن الصحن فمضى به إلى حال سبيله ثمّ سافر إلى مدينة أخرى فباع الصحن وأخذ بثمنه بضائع وتوجّه إلى بلده فباع ما

As for the opposites of these four,[28] how well the poet put it in the following lines: 10.21

Uṭrūsh is odious, Ibn Qaynah discourteous,
Qarnān's credulous, and Ibn Ayham's obstreperous.
Were all these faults combined in one with wealth endowed,
He'd be "the people's orator" whenever he made a sound!

Concerning another who was caught unawares by Fate's blows and overcome by oppression and woes—so that after he was exalted he became debased, and after riches saw his wealth effaced—is the story that is told of a man who was burdened with debts and left his children and wandered aimlessly until he came to a high-walled city, mightily built. He entered, abject and broken in spirit, devoured by hunger and exhausted by travel, and was walking along one of its streets when he saw a company of eminent persons proceeding together. He joined them and they came to a place like a king's palace, and they entered, the man following, and they continued until they came to a man sitting in great state, with pages and servants around him, as though he were the son of a viceroy, and this man, when he saw them, rose to greet them and paid them great honor. The subject of our tale was overcome with amazement and taken aback by the magnificence of the place and the servants and retainers, and he retired in a state of perplexity and apprehension, afraid for his safety, and sat down in a spot far removed from the people, where none could catch sight of him. While he was thus seated, a man came towards him with four hunting dogs dressed in silks and brocades and with gold collars and silver chains around their necks. The man tied each dog in its appointed place and disappeared and returned with four golden dishes filled with sumptuous food and placed before each dog its own dish. Then he went away and left them. The man was so hungry that he started to eye the food, and wanted to go up to one of the dogs and eat with it, but fear prevented him from approaching them. One of the dogs, however, looked at him, understood his plight, and, ceasing to eat, signaled to him to approach. The man drew near, and again the dog made a sign, as though to say, "Eat from this dish," and drew back from the dish, so the man ate until he was full and wanted to leave. At this, the dog made a sign to him as if to say, "Take this dish with the remaining food," so the man picked it up and put it in his sleeve and waited a while, but no one came looking for the dish, so he took it and went his way. Then he journeyed to another 10.22

معه وقضى ما عليه من الدين وكثر عليه الرزق وصار في نعمة كبيرة زائدة وبركة عميمة مدّة من الزمان ثمّ إنّه قال لنفسه لا بدّ أنّك تسافر إلى مدينة صاحب الصحن وتأخذ له هديّة سنيّة تكافئه بها وتدفع له ثمنه وإن كان أنعم به عليك كلب من كلابه ثمّ إنّه أخذ هديّة تليق بمقام الرجل وأخذ معه ثمن الصحن وسافر أيّاماً وليالي حتّى أقبل على تلك المدينة وطلع إليها يريد الاجتماع به حتّى أقبل إلى محلّه فلم ير إلّا طَلَلا باليا * وغراباً ناعيا * وديارا قد أقفرت * وأحوالاً قد تغيّرت * وحالاً للقلوب قد أَرْجَفَ * ومحلاً تركه الدهر ﴿قاعًا صفصفا﴾ * كما قال بعضهم [طويل]

سَرَى طَيْفُ سُعْدى طارِقًا يَستَفِزُّني سُحَيْـرًا وصَحبي بالدِّيارِ رُقودُ
فَلَمّـا انتَبَهـنا لِلخَيـالِ الّذي سَـرَى أَرَى الدّارَ قَفْـرًا والمَزارُ بَعيدُ

٢٣،١٠ فلمّا شاهد تلك الأطلال الباليه * ورأى ما صنع الدهر بها علانيه * اعترته الحيرة عن يقين * والتفت فرأى رجلاً مسكين * في حالة تقشعرّ منها الجلود * ورؤية يحنّ إليها الجلمود * فقال له يا هذا ما صنع الدهر والزمان * بصاحب هذا المكان * وأين بدوره السافره * ونجومه الزاهره * وما هذا الحادث الّذي حدث على بنيانه * وما هذا الأمر الّذي لم يُبقِ منه غير جدرانه * فقال له هذا المسكين * وهو يتأوّه من قلب حزين * أمّا في كلام الرسول عبرة لمن اقتدى به وسمعه * حقّ على الله أن لا يرفع شيئاً في هذه الدار إلّا وضعه * وإن كان سؤالك عن أمر وسبب * فليس مع انقلاب الدهر عجب * أنا صاحب هذا المكان ومُنْشيه * وساكنه وبانيه * وصاحب بدوره السافره * وأمواله الفاخره * وتحفه الزاهيه * وجواره الباهيه * ولكنّ الزمان قد مال * فأَذهب الخدم والمال * وصيّرني في هذه الحالة الراهنه * ودهمني بحوادث كانت عنده كامنه * وسؤالك هذا عن أمر وسبب * فأخبرني عنه واترك العجب * قال فأخبره بالقصّه * وهو في تألّم وغُصّه * وقال

city and sold the dish and bought goods with the proceeds and made his way to his own town, where he sold what he had and paid off his debts, and his business increased and he found himself in a state of the greatest ease and general good fortune. When some time had passed, he said to himself, "You must make a journey to the city of the owner of the dish and take with you a splendid gift in recompense and pay him back the price of the dish, even though one of his dogs made you a present of it." So he took a gift befitting the man's standing and took with him the price of the dish, and he journeyed by day and by night until he came to that city and went up into it, hoping to meet with the man. However, on approaching that place, he nothing saw but crumbling ruins and cawing ravens, dwellings reduced to desolation and all things in deterioration, a sight to leave the heart in a state of agitation and a place turned by Fate into «a scene of devastation».[29] As the poet[30] says:

> Suʿdā's ghost agliding came and woke me in alarm
> At break of dawn, my fellows in their homes yet still asleep,
> But when aroused by that night phantom gliding,
> I found the house bereft, the tryst too far to keep.

When the man observed that wasted debris, and beheld what fate had 10.23
wrought for all to see, perplexity assailed him for sure, and, turning, a pitiful man he saw, his state fit to make the skin creep, the sight of him enough to make a stone weep. "You there!" he said. "What have Fate and time made of the master of this facade? Where are those suns that shimmered and stars that glimmered? What blow upon his edifice could fall that would leave nothing standing but the wall?" That pitiful man responded for his part, moaning from a grieving heart, "Is there not guidance in the Messenger's words for those who follow his example and heed his admonition that 'It is God's right to raise up naught in this Abode that He does not then subject to demolition'? If your question be for good reason and cause, know that there is nothing in the vicissitudes of Fate that calls for pause. I am the master of this place and its erector, its occupant and its constructor, the owner of its shimmering suns and overwhelming sums and master of this place replete with so many a brilliant bauble and slave girl adorable—but Fate turned its back, put servants and money to the sack, and drove me to this present state, catching me unawares with concealed blows with which it lies in wait. However, your question surely is for good cause and reason raised, so inform me of what they may be and

له قد جئتك بهديّة فيها النفوس ترغب * وثمن صحنك الّذي أخذتُه من الذهب * فإنّه كان سبباً لغنائي بعد الفقر * ولزوال ما كان عندي من الهمّ والحصر * قال فهزّ الرجل رأسه وبكى * وأنّ واشتكى * وقال يا هذا أظنّك مجنون * فإن هذا أمر لا يكون * كلب من كلابنا تكرّم عليك بصحن من الذهب * أَفَأَرْجِعُ فيه ولو كنتُ في أشدّ الهمّ والوَصَب * والله لم يأتني منك شيء يساوي قُلامه * فامض من حيث جئت بالسلامه * قال فقبّل الرجل أقدامه ويديه * وانصرف راجعاً يثني بالمديح عليه * ثمّ إنّه عند فراقه ووداعه * أنشد هذا البيت الّذي يُلتَذّ بسماعه * فقال [خفيف]

ذَهَبَ النّاسُ والكِلابُ جَميعاً   فَعَلى النّاسِ والكِلابِ السَّلامُ

٢٤،١٠ (وقد ناب مؤلّف هذا الكتاب من كيد الدهر نائب) * ورمته الليالي بسهام الهموم من قِسِيّ المصائب * فأصبح بعد الجمع وحيدا * وبعد الأنس فريدا * يسامر النجوم * ويساور الهموم * يسكُب على فراق الأحِبّة الدموع * ويرجو عَوْد الدهر وهيهات الرجوع * قال الشاعر [بسيط]

فَلَيتَ شِعري والدُّنيا مَفرَّقةٌ   بَينَ الرِّفاقِ وأَيّامُ الوَرى دُوَلُ
هَل تَرجِعُ الدّارُ بَعدَ البُعدِ آنِسةً   وهَل تَعودُ لَنا أَيّامُنا الأُوَلُ

٢٥،١٠ لكن الصبر على غدوات الأيّام * من شِيَم السادة الكرام * شعر [بسيط]

اصبر فَفي الصَّبرِ فضلٌ[١] لو عَلِمتَ به   لَكُنتَ بادَرتَ شُكرًا صاحِبَ النِّعَمِ
واعلَم بأَنَّكَ إن لَم تَصطَبِرْ كَرَمًا   صَبَرتَ قَهرًا على ما خُطَّ بالقَلَمِ

١ بي: فضلا.

cease to be amazed!" The other then related to him his tale, with a lump in his throat and great travail, telling him, "I have brought you a gift such as any might desire, plus the price of your golden dish that I did acquire, for it was a cause of my becoming rich after poverty and of my relief from dire straits and misery." The man then wagged his head and wailed, and moaned and railed, and he said, "You are crazy, sir, it seems to me, for such a thing can never be. A dog of ours made you a gift of a dish of gold, and I should now go back on that? Never, though I were subject to woe and misery untold! By God, I will not take from you one fingernail sliver, so return in peace to the place whence you came hither!" The man then kissed his feet and hands, and, extolling the other's worth, set off for his native lands, and, as he left him and was bidding him good-bye, spoke this verse on which the ear must love to dwell:

> Gone are the men and the dogs together,
> So to men and dogs alike, farewell!

Likewise the author of this book from fortune's plots has suffered blows, after the nights had shot him with woe's arrows from disaster's bows, so that he found himself, after companionship, on his own, after sweet intimacy, alone, conversing with the stars, wrestling with his cares, over the departure of his dear ones pouring his lament, and hoping—faint hope!—that Fate might yet relent. As the poet says: 10.24

> Would that I knew—for the world tears friends apart
> And the stars of men both wax and wane—
> Will the house, after parting, fill once more with cheer,
> And will those first days of ours return again?

However, patience with life's perfidies is a mark of the noble man: 10.25

> Patience! You'd rush to thank the Lord of Every Boon
> If you but knew what benefits in patience lie!
> And know that should you not endure with grace
> What by the Pen is writ, you will, perforce, comply!

(وكلّ هذا توطئة لما نال الناظم من الهموم * وما اعتراه من منطوق حوادث دهره والمفهوم * وهو الّذي كان سبباً لإنشاء هذا القصيد * وشكواه هذا الأمر الوافر المديد * فقال) [طويل] ٠٫١١

ص

يَقُولُ أَبُو شَادُوفٍ مِنْ عُظْمِ مَا شَكَا   مِنَ ٱلْقِلِّ جِسْمُو مَا يَضَالْ نَحِيفْ ١٫١١

ش

هذا الكلام له بحر وقدّ * وتقاطيع ومدّ * فبحره الطويل المديد * الناقص المزيد * ومن جعله من بحر الكامل * قال فيه متهابل متهابل * ومن قاسه ببحر الوافر * قال هو البحر الزاخر * ومن نسبه لبحر البسيط * قال هو من معنى الهلط والتخبيط * ومن قارنه ببحر السلسله * قال هو من معنى هلهله هلهله * ومن قارنه ببقيّة البحور * قال في تمثيله أنت حمار أو ثور * وأمّا قدّه المعهود * فعلى وزن برّوة تخلّي الماضغين جلود * وأمّا تقاطيعه المذكوره * فهي هذه الكلمات المنشوره * ١٫١٫١١

يقول	أبوشا	دوف من	عظم ما	شكى
نبول	عليها	في الضحى	مع غرو	بها

ومجموع هذا الكلام * من هذا النظام *

The Ode of Abū Shādūf with Commentary

All of which paves the way for the woes that on our own poet were inflicted, and the accidents of fate, both overt and covert, with which he was afflicted and which were the reason for his composing this ode, and of his complaint, profuse and extended, against all that fate on him bestowed. Thus he says: 11.0

TEXT

yaqūlu abū shādūfi[31] *min ʿuẓmi mā shakā* 11.1
mina l-qilli jismū mā yaḍāl naḥīf

Says Abū Shādūf: from all he has suffered
of want, his body's ever skinny

COMMENTARY

These words are metered[32] and tuned,[33] have feet, and may be crooned.[34] The meter's the one that's both "Long" and "Extended"[35]—and impaired and distended. Those who claim its meter's "the Perfect" say it goes "without intellect, without intellect (*mutahābilun mutahābilun*),"[36] while those who compare it to that called "the Exuberant" say, "This is the meter luxuriant!" and those who assign it to "the Diffused" say, "It's flabby and confused!" while those who compare it to the Meter of the Chain[37] say it goes "featherbrain, featherbrain (*halhalah halhalah*),"[38] and those who compare it to other metrical clocks use, to represent it, "You're a *donkey* or an *ox*." Its usual tune goes to the measure "If you chew a bit of soap, it'll make you like leather."[39] Its feet, of which we've already made mention, appear as follows, when in articulation:[40] 11.1.1

yaqūlu	*abū shā*	*dūfi min*	*ʿuẓmi mā*	*shakā*
nabūlu	*ʿalayhā*	*fī l-ḍuḥā*	*maʿ ghurū*	*bihā*

and the whole of the Ode is in the same mode, namely:

(نبول عليها في الضحى مع غروبها)

فإذا عرفت البحر والقدّ * والتقاطيع والمدّ * فلنشرع لك الآن في شرح الكلام على حسب التواقيع * أو على نمط الفراقيع *

٢،١،١١ فنقول قوله (يقول) أي يريد أن ينشئ[١] قولاً في الخارج فيه شرح حاله ودليل على ما نابه من حوادث الزمان * وما أصابه من دواعي الهمّ والأحزان * والقول له مصادر واشتقاقات فمصدره قال يقول قولاً ومقالة وربّما يزاد فيه قلّة وقيلولة واشتقاقه من القَيْلولة أو من القُلَل أو من الأقوال أو من قالوا أو قلنا

٣،١،١١ وإنّما زدت هذه المصادر الفشرويّة وهذه الاشتقاقات الهباليّة إلّا لنبني عليها ما سأذكره لك (ممّا اتّفق لي مع بعض من يدّعي العلم وهو جاهل) وما ذاك إلّا أنّي لمّا توجّهت إلى الحجّ إلى بيت الله الحرام سنة أربعة وسبعين وألف وبلغت بَنْدَر القُصَيْر أنتظر خروج السفن فجلست أيّاماً بزاوية على البحر المالح أَعِظ الناس فبينما أنا ذات يوم في هذا المكان أقرأ فيه * وأبيّن للناس الكلام ومعانيه * وأنا في هيئة تشين النظر * وفي أُهْبة ذهاب وسفر * وبهللة وهبال * وهلفطة ومقال * إذ أقبل عليّ بلا محاله * رجل يشبه دائرة الهاله * طويل هبيل * فظّ ثقيل * له عمّة كالهَيُولى في العظم * وطيلسان نُسِجَ من صوف الغنم * ثمّ جلس يريد الضرر * ونظر إليّ شذر * فظهر لي منه الشرّ والجدال * ومنتظر منّي متى قلت قال * وكان الأمر كما ذكرت * وما إليه بهذا المعنى أشرت * فابتدأت في الكلام * وقلت قال النبيّ عليه الصلاة والسلام * فعند ذلك قال لي بلفظ كثيف * ما معنى قال في التصريف * فلمّا سمعت سؤاله * تحقّقت جهله وهباله * وعلمت أنّه خالي من العلوم * وجاهل بالمنطوق والمفهوم * فقلت له إنّ قال يتصرّف منه أسماء وأفعال *

---

١ بي: ينشي.

nabūlu ʿalayhā fī l-ḍuḥā maʿ ghurūbihā
We urinate upon it in the forenoon and at sunset.

Now that you know the meter and tune, the feet and the croon, let me embark on the exposition of the verse according to its rhythmic pattern, or in firecracker fashion.

Thus we declare: 11.1.2

yaqūlu ("Abū Shādūf says")—i.e., he intends to initiate speech (*qawl*) external to himself that will contain an explanation of his state and evidence of the accidents of Time with which he was inflicted, and the occasions for woe and grief with which he was inflicted. The word *qawl* has paradigms and etymologies. The paradigm is *qāla*, *yaqūlu*, *qawlan*, and *maqālatan*, to which may be added *qullatan* ("water pitcher")[41] and *qaylūlatan* ("midday snooze").[42] It is derived from *qaylūlah* or from *qulal* ("water pitchers") or from *aqwāl* ("sayings") or from *qālū* ("they said") or *qulnā* ("we said").[43]

I have added these facetious paradigms and silly etymologies simply as a point of departure for the account that I shall relate to you of an encounter I once had with one of those persons who claim learning while in fact they are ignorant, to wit that, when I went on pilgrimage to God's Holy House[44] in the year 1074[45] and had reached the port of al-Quṣayr and was waiting there for the ships to leave, I stayed for a few days at a hostel on the sea, preaching to the people. One day, as I was reciting the Qur'an there, explaining the words and their meanings to the people to make them clear, a sorry sight to see, accoutered for travel by sea, engaged in buffoonery and deliration, and cant and speechification,[46] there came towards me—let no one doubt my say-so!—a man round as a halo, tall and cretinous, gross and hebetudinous, with a turban huge as the Primordial Lump, and a woolen shawl draped over his chump. Clearly up to no good, he sat himself down and fixed me with a frown, while his determination to involve me in trouble and contention plainly could be read, since he could barely wait for me to say the word "Said . . ." And so it was as I've described, and in the manner that I've implied, for no sooner had I begun to give my lesson, and declared, "Said the Prophet, upon him peace and benison . . ." than he asked me in tones unrefined, "What's the meaning of 'said' *when it's declined*?" When I heard his query, and understood his ignorance and inanity, I realized that in learning he was so far from an adept as to be 11.1.3

وهي قال يقول قولاً ومقالة وقلّة وقَيلولة على الكمال * وإن أردت جعلت لك بيقين * تصريف هذه الستّة ستّاً وثلاثين * فقال لي وهذا التصريف في أيّ متن من المتون * فقلت له في ديوان ابن سودون * فركن إلى قولي على جهل منه وعمى * فعرفت أنه لا يدري الاسم ولا المسمّى * ثمّ انقاد إليّ بعد الدعوى والهيس * انقياد الغنم للتيس * وامتثل الأمر في رواحه ومقبله * حتّى مضى إلى حال سبيله *

(فإن قيل) لأيّ شيء خلبطتَ على هذا السائل في هذه المصادر والاشتقاقات * ووسّعت عليه في هذه الأمور الهباليّات * كنت تقتصر على ما قالوه في كتب الصرف * ولا تجرف الكلام جرف * (قلنا الجواب) نعم كان ينبغي هذا الكلام * ولكن مع من يدري العلم بالتمام * وأمّا الجاهل البليد * والفظّ العنيد * فليس له إلّا ما يناسب جهله من دشّ الكلام * والعجرفة فيما يليق بذلك المقام * فكان ما سبق من الجواب وحاله * مناسب لسؤاله وهباله * فاتّضح الإشكال * عن وجه هذا الهبال * ٤،١،١١

(مسألة هباليّة) ما الحكمة في أنّ الناظم ابتدأ كلامه بصيغة المضارع ولم يأت بصيغة الماضي كما قال صاحب ألفيّة النحو رحمه الله تعالى قال محمّد هو ابن مالك (الجواب الفشرويّ) أنّ هذا الفعل الماضي الّذي هو قال يتولّد منه المضارع وهو يقول ويقول يأتي منه قولاً كما سبق في تأصيل الأفعال والأسماء فاكتفى بالفرع عن الأصل أو أنّه أراد تعداد الأمور الّتي حصلت له من تغيّر الزمان وانقلابه ولم يكن أخبر عنها سابقاً بلفظ الماضي فأراد الإخبار عنها بلفظ المضارع الّذي هو يقول وإن كان في معنى الماضي صورةً وفي معنى المضارع حقيقةً قال الشاعر [طويل] ٥،١،١١

فقالَ هو الماضي يَقولُ مُضـارِعٌ وإنْ كان ذا الماضي له في الحقيقةِ

quite unaware of the difference between word and concept. So I said to him, "From *qāl* both nouns and verbs we may decline: *qāla, yaqūlu, qawlan,* and *maqālatan* or *qullatan* or *qaylūlatan* in fine—and if you like I'll make you up, for sure, in addition to these six, thirty more!" Said he to me, "In what standard text is this declension shown?" Said I, "In the collected works of Ibn Sūdūn!" Then he accepted my words—he was that ignorant and benighted—and I realized that he couldn't tell the name from the thing cited. Thenceforth, after all the pretension and bluster, he followed me as a sheep its master, and submitted in his comings and goings to my sway, till he departed and went his way.

If it be said, "How come you set out to confuse this inquirer with such para- 11.1.4
digms and etymologies, and you gave him such good measure of imbecilities, when you should have stuck to what they'd say in a grammar book, instead of ladling out such gobbledygook?" we reply, "All well and good, but that only goes for those who understand scholarship as one should. As for the dumb ignoramus, who's gross and pertinacious, his ignorance calls for nothing better than whatever nonsense one may churn out, and the haughtiness befitting the condition of such a lout. Thus the reply that I have given above—taken as it came—was quite appropriate to a question so inane. The problem's now revealed, the silliness no longer concealed."

A Silly Topic for Debate: What's the explanation for the fact that the poet 11.1.5
starts his verse in the present tense and does not use the past, unlike, for example, the author of *The Thousand Lines on Grammar*,[47] God have mercy on him, when he writes, "Muḥammad, Mālik's son, *has said*. . . etc.?"[48] The Facetious Answer: It is the past tense of the verb, namely, *qāla*, from which the present tense, namely, *yaqūlu*, is generated, and from *yaqūlu* comes the verbal noun *qawl*, as already noted in tracing the origins of these verbs and nouns; thus the poet simply settled for using the derived rather than the base form. Or it may be that he wanted to enumerate the changes and vicissitudes of fate that had befallen him and, not having mentioned them earlier using past-tense forms, he determined to narrate them using the present-tense form, namely, *yaqūlu*, albeit this has past meaning formally speaking and present meaning in reality. As the poet says:

So *qāla*'s past, *yaqūlu*'s present,
Though the last is its past in reality.[49]

وقال أبو الطيب المتنبّي عفا الله عنه شعر [طويل]

إذا كانَ ما يَنويهِ فِعلاً مُضارِعًا   مَضَى قَبلَ أَن تُلقَى عَلَيهِ الجَوازِمُ

أي إذا نوى شيئاً مستقبلاً أمضى فعله قبل أن يدخل عليه ما يَجْزِمُه أي يمنعه عنه ويسكّنه عن الحركة عن فعله انتهى وأيضاً لو أتى بالماضي لاختلّ الوزن وإن كان المعنى باق على حاله فاتّجه الجواب وبان الصواب وقوله

(أبو شادوف) هذه كُنْيَته وغلبت عليه فصارت عَلَماً كما قالوا في مَعْدِي كَرِب وبَعْلَبَكّ ٦،١،١١
وبَرَق نَحْرُه ونحو ذلك وأمّا اسمه الحقيقي عُجَيْل تصغير عِجْل على ما قيل وسببه أنّ أمّه لمّا ولدته أَلْقَتْه في مَدْوِد البقرة فجاء العجل ولحسه فسمّي بذلك أيّاماً حتّى اشتهر بهذه الكنية وسبب اشتهاره بها أقوال أحدها إنّه لمّا مال عليه الدهر كما تقدّم أجّر نفسه لسقي الزرع بالآلة الّتي يجعلوها أهل الريف تسمّى أبو شادوف وصورة فعلها أنّهم يجعلوا ناطورَيْن من طين على جانب البحر ويحفروا بينهما نقرة مثل الحوض الصغير ويضعوا فوق الناطورين خشبة صغيرة ويعلّقوا فيها خشبة أيضاً بالعرض حكم قصبة الميزان يضعوا في طرفها الّذي من جهة البر شيئاً ثقيلاً والّذي من جهة البحر الدلو أو القَطْوة الّتي ينضحوا بها الماء ثمّ إنّ الرجل يقف إلى جهة البحر ويتّكي على طرف تلك القصبة فيقع الدلو أو القطوة في البحر ويغرف الماء ثمّ يتركه فيثقل طرفها الثاني ويصعد الدلو أو القطوة ويفرّغ في النقرة مع مساعدة الرجل له ويجري الماء إلى الزرع وهكذا حكم ما شاهدناه مراراً عديدة ويسموا مجموع الآلة والناطورين أبو شادوف وهو مشتقّ من الشدف وهو الغرف قال في القاموس الأزرق والناموس الأبلق شدف يشدف شدفاً بمعنى غرف يغرف غرفاً قال الشاعر [طويل]

إذا ما رَأَيتَ الماءَ فاشْدُفْ بِراحَةٍ   فَذلكَ لِلظَّمآنِ أَهنَى وَأَطيَبُ

And Abū l-Ṭayyib al-Mutanabbī,[50] may God excuse him his sins, says:

If what he intended were a present verb,
It would be past before any could negate it

—meaning, "If he intends to do something in the future, he completes the action before anything can 'negate' it," that is, can intervene between him and its doing and silence the vowels of his verb.[51] End. Also, if he were to introduce the past form, the meter would be broken, even if the meaning remained as before. Thus the answer now is right; the truth has loomed into sight.

Abū Shādūfi: this is his *kunyah,* but it took him over and became his primary name, as happened in the case of Maʿdīkarib, Baʿlabakk, Baraqa Naḥruhu, and so on.[52] His real name was ʿUjayl, diminutive of *ʿijl* ("calf"), or so it is reported, the reason for his being so named being that, when his mother gave birth to him, she threw him in the cow's trough, and then the calf came along and licked him, so they called him that for a few days, until he became known by the *kunyah* in question. The reason for his becoming known by the latter is variously explained. One version has it that when the times turned against him, as described above, he hired himself out to water the crops using the device made by the country people, called the Abū Shādūf.[53] The way this works is that they construct two pillars of mud next to the river and excavate a hole like a small pit between them; on the two pillars they place a small beam and also, at right angles, another, resembling the arm of a pair of scales; to the land end of the last they attach a weight, and to the river end, a bucket or scoop,[54] with which they raise the water. A man stands on the riverside and pulls the end of the crossbeam downward, and the bucket or scoop falls and scoops up the water; then he lets go, the other end descends under its weight, and the bucket or scoop rises and, with the aid of the man, empties into the pit; the water then runs on to the crops and so on, as we have ourselves observed on numerous occasions. The whole assemblage, consisting of the device itself with the pillars, is called *abū shādūf,* which is derived from *shadf,* which means "scooping" (*gharf*). It says in *The Blue Ocean and Piebald Canon*, *shadafa*, *yashdufu*, *shadfan* means *gharafa*, *yaghrifu*, *gharfan*. As the poet says: 11.1.6

If you see water, scoop (*ushduf*) carefully,
For that, to the thirsty, more comfortable is and more pleasant!

١١،١،٧ فالناظم لمّا لازم هذه الآلة وصار لا يفارقها في غالب الأوقات سُمّي باسمها من باب تسمية الحال باسم المحلّ وقيل إنّ أمّه ولدته عند أبو شادوف فسُمّي باسمه لكن يردّه ما تقدّم من أنّ اسمه الأصليّ عجيل وقد يُجْمَع بين الأقوال فيقال إنّ أمّه لمّا ولدته عند أبو شادوف أخذته ووضعته في المدود ولحسه العجل على ما تقدّم فسمّي عجيل ثمّ اشتهر بما ذكر فلا تعارض بين الأقوال وقيل سمّي بذلك لكثرة غرفه للماء بهذه الآلة فصار كلّ من سأل عنه يقال له عند الشدف أي الغرف ثمّ زادوا هذه الكلمة الألف والواو وقالوا شادوف ولكثرة تكرارها جعلوها حكم الولد والنواطير مثل الأب وقالوا أبو شادوف ووضعوها على ذات الناظم لكثرة مجاورته لتلك الآلة وعرّفوه بها فصارت علماً له يخاطَب بها كما سبق بيانه انتهى

١١،١،٨ (مسألة هباليّة) ما الحكمة في أنّ الدلو أو القطوة لا يفارق الخشبة التي هي في حكم قصبة الميزان وهل هي حكم الأب له كما سبق من أنّ النواطير في حكم مقام الأب للشادوف وأن الدلو أو القطوة إنّما لازما هذه الخشبة بالضرورة لها ومتى انفكّ عنها بطل عمله فهو مجاور لها في وقت الحاجة لا غير قلنا (الجواب الفشرويّ) أنّ الخشبة لا تستغني عن الدلو أو القطوة وهما لا يستغنيان عنها فكان كلاهما في حكم الولد للخشبة وكانت الخشبة في حكم الأب لما ذكر لأنّ كلاًّ من الدلو أو القطوة مرتبط بالخشبة فاتّجه المقال عن وجه هذا الهبال

١١،١،٩ (فائدة) الأب مشتقّ من آب إذا رجع قال ابن زُرَيْق رحمه الله في قصيدة له [بسيط]

Thus the poet, because he cleaved to this device and became almost insepa- 11.1.7
rable from it, came to be known by its name, according to the rule of "naming the condition after the position." Another version has it that his mother gave birth to him next to an *abū shādūf* and he was therefore named after it, but this is refuted by what has already been said, to the effect that his original name was ʿUjayl. The two versions may be reconciled by saying that after his mother had given birth to him next to the *abū shādūf*, she took him and placed him in the trough and the calf licked him and he became known as described above. Thus there is no contradiction between the accounts. It is also said that he was so named because he did so much scooping of water with this device—so much, indeed, that it got to the point that anyone who asked after him would be told, "he's busy *shadf*-ing" that is, "scooping"; then they added the *alif* and *waw* to the word and said *shādūf*.[55] With constant repetition, they have come to think of the crossbeam as though it were the child and the pillars as though they were the father, so that now they call the device "the father of the crossbeam (*abū shādūf*)"; and they applied the name to the poet himself because he was always next to the device and they identified him with it, and thus it became a proper name by which he was addressed, as already explained. End.

A Silly Debate: What is to be learned from the fact that the bucket or scoop 11.1.8
never leaves the beam, which resembles the arm of a pair of scales; and does the latter play the role of father to the former, just as, as pointed out earlier, the two pillars play the role of father to the crossbeam of the *shādūf*; and is it the case that the bucket or scoop adheres to the beam merely out of necessity and, once disconnected from it, ceases to perform its function; and, as such, may it be said to be attached to it only when needed and not otherwise? We declare: the fatuous response is that the beam cannot dispense with the bucket or the scoop and neither can dispense with the beam, and so together they play the role of child to the beam, and the beam plays the role of father for the reason given, since both of them—the bucket and the scoop—are in a stable relationship with the beam. Now the contention's straightened out, the silliness shown up for what it's about.

A Useful Note: the word *ab* ("father") is derived from *āba*, meaning "he 11.1.9
returned."[56] Ibn Zurayq,[57] God have mercy on him, says in an ode:

مـا آبَ مِن سَفَـرٍ إلّا وأَزعَجَـه   رأيٌ إلى سَفَـرٍ بالعَـزمِ يمنَعُـهُ

أي ما رجع من سفر إلّا وأزعجه رأيه إلى سفر ثاني وكذلك الأب لأنّه في كلّ ساعة يرجع إلى ولده ويفتقده وينظر إليه وقيل مشتقّ من الأُبُوّة كما أنّ الأخ مشتقّ من الأُخُوّة قال الشاعر [طويل]

أبو المرءِ مَن آبَ اشـتِقاقاً لإسمِهِ   وَاخو المَرءِ أَيضاً قَد أَتَى مِن أخوّه

ومصدره آب يأوب أَوْباً فهو آبٍ

وقال ابن سودون إنّ أبو هذا فعل ماض ناقص وأصله أبوس ويدلّ على ذلك قول الشاعر [بسيط] ١٠،١،١١

قَالوا حَبيبُكَ وارَى ثَغرَهُ صَلَفاً   ماذا تُحاوِلُ إِن أَبداه قلتُ أبو

أي أبوس وإنّما حُذِفت السين لوجهين الأوّل لقصد حصول اللبس على السامع إذ هو اللائق بهذا عند الأدباء والأقرب إلى السلامة من الواشين والرقباء والثاني حُذِفت السين لأنّها في الجُمّل بستّين والستّون في البوس إسراف عند البعض * هذا كلامه المصرَّح به في ديوانه انتهى

قلت وكلام هذا البعض الذي نقله ابن سودون مردود لأنّ المحبّ إذا ظَفِر بمحبوبه فلا يستَفي فؤاده بستّين قُبْلة ولا بمائة خصوصاً إذا كان ذلك المحبوب لطيف الذات * حسن الصفات * مطيع للعاشق * مصافياً مصادق * وانطبع بقدّه المأنوس * وانضمّ لعاشقه انضمام العروس * وتملّى المحبّ بالحبيب * وخلا المجلس من الواشي والرقيب * هنالك لا ينحصر البوس بعدّ * ولا يكون له غاية ولا حدّ * قال الشاعر [سريع] ١١،١،١١

He never returns (*āba*) from one journey but feels an urge
To be on his way again, that only his will can purge.

That is, "he never comes back from one journey but the urge to undertake a second disturbs him." It is the same with a father, because he is always coming back to his child and missing him and looking about for him. Others say that the word is derived from *ubuwwah* ("fatherhood"), just as *akh* ("brother") is derived from *ukhuwwah* ("brotherhood"). Says the poet:

A man's *ab* from *āba* derives,
And a man's *akh* from *ukhuwwah* likewise.

The paradigm is *āba, ya'ūbu, awban,* active participle *ābin.*[58]

Ibn Sūdūn[59] claims that *abū,* the construct form of *ab,* is really a perfect-tense defective verb,[60] being originally *abūsu* ("I would kiss"), and he cites as evidence the verse that says: 11.1.10

"They said, 'Your sweetie hides his mouth affectedly from view;
What would you attempt, if he should show it?' Said I, '*abū*. . .' [61]

"that is, *abūs* ('I would kiss'), the *s* having been dropped for two reasons, the first being to deceive the listener, this being the proper thing to do in literary opinion and the more conducive to safety from tattletales and nosy parkers, and the second because its numerical value is sixty,[62] and sixty kisses, according to some, is excessive."

These are his words as explicitly stated in his collected works. End.

Personally, I would say that the opinion of such people, as transmitted by Ibn Sūdūn, is invalid, because, once the lover succeeds in winning his beloved, his heart will never be satisfied with sixty or even a hundred kisses, especially if the beloved in question is graceful of form, comely of feature, to his lover obedient, sincere, and compliant, whose genial body has not been denied, and who to his lover has been gathered like a bride, the lover of his beloved being thus fully possessed, the place free of tattletale, nosy parker or other pest. Then for kissing there is no number firm—it knows no bounds nor any term. As the poet says: 11.1.11

سَأَلْتُ بَدرَ التّمّ في قُبلةٍ   أَجابَ أَنْ يوفي ومُنشي السّحابْ
لمّا اختلَينا واجتَمَعنا بِهِ   غَلِطتُ في العَدّ وضاعَ الحِسابْ

وقلت في المعنى [طويل] ١٢،١،١١

رَأيتُ لَه شَرطاً على الخدّ قد حَوى   جَمالاً وَقَد زانَ المَلاحَةَ بالقُرطِ
فَقُلتُ مُرادي اللّثمُ قالَ بخَلوَةٍ   فَقبّلتُهُ أَلفاً عَلى ذلك الشّرطِ

اللّهمّ إلّا أن يكون المحلّ غير قابل للمحبّ والحبيب * بأن يكون ثَمّ خوف من واشٍ أو رقيب * فيكون الضمّ في تلك الحالة والتقبيل * بحسب أمن العاشق في الكثرة والتقليل * ومنهم من لا يعتريه في ذلك وَهْمٌ ولا إلباس * ويقبّل محبوبه ولو بحضرة الناس * ولو نفر منه وفرّ * ربّما مال نحوه ومرّ * قال الشاعر [رمل]

لو تراني وحبيبي عِندَما   فَرَّ مِثلَ الظَبيِ مِن بَينِ يَدَيّ
وغَدا يَعدو وأعدو[١] خَلفَهُ   وكِلانا قَد طَوينا الأَرضَ طَيّ
قالَ ما تَرجِعُ عنّي قُلتُ لا   قالَ ما تَطلُبُ مني قُلتُ شَيّ
فَنأى عَنّي وَوَلّى خَجِلاً   وانثَنَى بالتّيهِ عنّي لا إليّ
كِدتُ بَينَ النّاسِ أنْ أَلْثِمَهُ   آهِ لَو أَفعَلُ ما كانَ عَلَيّ

ومن اللطائف أنّ أبا نواس مرّ يوماً في شوارع بغداد فرأى غلاماً جميلاً فقبّله عِياناً فترافع الغلام هو وإيّاه على يد القاضي يحيى بن أكثم وادّعى عليه بما وقع قال فأطرق القاضي ساعة وأنشد يقول [طويل] ١٣،١،١١

---

١ بي: يغدو وأغدو.

"One kiss!" I asked the full moon high in the sky.
"By Him who draped the clouds,"[63] he said, "I will comply!"
But when we met with none about,
I reckoned wrong and lost all count!

And I myself said on the same theme:[64] 11.1.12

I saw upon his cheek a stippled mark that beauty held—
He whom an earring had made yet sweeter to behold.
"I want a kiss," I said. Said he, "When we're alone!"
And on that "stipulation" I kissed a thousandfold!

—unless the place be unsuitable for a lover and the object of his adoration, in that there's a fear of tattletales or of observation, in which case any hugging and kissing will depend on how comfortable the lover feels—as to whether it be quite a lot or almost completely missing—though there are a few who have, in this regard, no doubt or fear and will kiss their loved ones in front of anyone who's there, and, even though the latter turn and flee, chase after him relentlessly. As the poet says:

Would that you'd seen me and my darling
When, like a deer, he from me fled
And ran away, and I gave chase;
Would you'd seen us when after hot pursuit he said,
"Will you not leave me be?" and I said, "No!"
And he, "What would you of me?" and I, "You know!"
And he then stayed aloof and shyly turned his back,
And proudly turned, not to me, but away—
For then I almost kissed him, right in front of everyone.
Ah, would I now could do what then I should have done!

An amusing story has it that Abū Nuwās was one day walking in the streets 11.1.13
of Baghdad when he saw a beautiful youth and kissed him in front of everyone. He and the youth were brought before the judge Yaḥyā ibn Aktham, and the youth brought charges against Abū Nuwās. After bowing his head in silence for a moment, the judge recited:[65]

إذا كنتَ للتَّجميشِ والبَوسِ مانِعا   فلا تَدخلِ الأسواقَ إلّا منقَّبا
ولا تُرخِيَ الأهدابَ مِن فَوقِ طُرّةٍ   ولا تُظهِرَنْ مِن فَوقِ صُدغِكَ عَقربا
فتَقتُلَ مِسكيناً وتُهجِرَ عاشِقاً   وتَترُكَ قاضِي المسلِمينَ معذَّبا

قال فأطرق الغلام ساعة وأنشد يقول [طويل]

وكُنّا نُرَجّي أن نَرَى العَدلَ بَينَنا[1]   فأَعقَبَنا بَعدَ الرَّجاءِ قُنوطُ
مَتى تَصلُحُ الدُّنيا ويَصلُحُ أَهلُها   إذا كانَ قاضِي المسلِمينَ يَلوطُ

وقوله (من عظم ما شكا) أي من عظيم أمر أو أمور يشكو منها وصرّح بشكواه راجياً ١٤،١،١١
من الله تعالى أن يفرّج عنه ويعيد له ما سلف من أيّام النعيم الّتي كان فيها فإنّ الأمر
إذا اشتدّ هان وإذا ضاق اتّسع قال الشاعر [كامل]

وَلَرُبَّ ليلٍ في الهُمومِ كَدُمَّلٍ   عالجتُهُ حتّى ظَفَرتُ بِفَجرِهِ
وَلَقَدْ تَمُرُّ النائِباتُ عَلَى الفتى   وتَزولُ حتّى لا تَجولُ بِفِكرِهِ

والشكوى على أقسام شكوى لله وهي محمودة وشكوى للمخلوق وهي مذمومة اللّهمّ إلّا أن يكون في حال شكواه معتمداً على الله تعالى متّكلاً عليه مستعيناً به في دفع ما نابه من الشدائد فلا بأس بذلك وإذا صبر واحتسب كان أولى وفرّج الله عنه قال تعالى ﴿وَبَشِّرِ ٱلصَّابِرِينَ﴾ وقال تعالى ﴿فَإِنَّ مَعَ ٱلْعُسْرِ يُسْرًا﴾ ومن كلام الأستاذ يحيى البهلول نفعنا الله تعالى بركاته [هزج]

---

[1] بي: وكنا إذا نرجوا انتهاء العدل بيننا؛ ب: وكنا اذا نرجوك للعدل بيننا؛ ك با م: وكنا اذا نرجوك انتها للعدل بيننا.

If you object to being groped and kissed
  Don't go to market without a veil;
Don't lower lashes o'er a forelock
  And don't display upon your temple a scorpion curl,
For as you are, you slay the weak, drive the lover to delirium,
  And leave the Muslims' judge in dire travail!

The youth in turn bowed his head in silence for a while and then recited:[66]

We had hoped to see justice between us,
  But after hope there followed despair.
When will the world and its people go right
  If the judge of the Muslims fucks boys in the rear?

min ʿuẓmi mā shakā ("from all that he has suffered"): that is, from the thing, or indeed the things, he has to complain of. He expresses his complaint out loud in the hope that the Almighty will release him from his sufferings and restore him to his former life of ease, for when things are at their worst they are not far from getting easier, and though the gate be strait, it opens onto larger spaces. Says the poet: **11.1.14**

How many a night of woes like ulcers
  I have tended, till I won through to day!
The blows of fate pass young men lightly by
  And dissipate, and in their thoughts they do not stay.

There are different categories of complaint. There is the complaint to God, which is praiseworthy, and the complaint to one of His creation, which is blameworthy, unless the complainer place his trust entirely in the Almighty and rely on Him, seeking His help to repel whatever misfortunes may have befallen him—in which case there is no harm, though it is preferable for him to have patience and resign himself to God's will, in which case God will grant him relief. The Almighty has said, «And give good tidings to the patient!»[67] and also, «Verily, along with hardship there shall be ease.»[68] Among the verses of Master Yaḥyā al-Buhlūl,[69] may the Almighty benefit us through him, are:

إِذا ضاقَتْ بِكَ الأَحوالْ   تَفَكَّرْ في ﴿أَلَمْ نَشْـرَحْ﴾
تَجِدْ يُسْرَيْنِ بينْ عُسْرَيْنْ   ولا تَحْزُنْ ولا تَفْـرَحْ

ثمّ إنّ الناظم أراد تعداد الأمور الّتي ترادفت عليه مبتدئًا بأعظمها وأهمّها فقـال ١٥،١،١١

(من القلّ) بكسر القاف وسكون اللام أي إنّ أهمّ شكواي وأعظمها أوّلًا من القِلّ وهي قلّة المأكل والمشرب حُذِفَتْ تاء الكلمة لضرورة النظم وأيضاً عدم الميسرة في اللبس وشدّة التعب والنصب في كدّ المعيشة وفي الحديث كاد الفقر أن يكون كُفْرًا أي قارب أن يُوقِع في الكفر لأنّه يحمل على عدم الرضاء بالقضاء وسُخُط الرزق وذلك يجرّ إلى الكفر وفي الفقر قال ابن دقيق العيد رحمه الله [طويل] ١٦،١،١١

لَعَمْري لَقَد قاسيتُ بالفَقرِ شِدَّةً   وَقَعتُ بِها فِي حَيرَةٍ وشَتاتِ
فَإِنْ بُحْتُ بالشّكوى هَتَكتُ سَريرَتي   وَإِنْ لم أَبُحْ بالفَقـرِ خِفْتُ مَماتي

(وقيل) وُجِدَ مكتوب على تاج كِسْرى أنوشِرْوان أربع كلمات وهي العدل إن دام عمّر * والظلم إن دام دمّر * والأعمى ميّت وإن لم يُقبّر * والفقر هو الموت الأحمر * وهذه الكلمة يعاير بها أهل الأرياف الرجل الفقير فيقولوا فلان في قِلّ وربّما زادوا كلمة أخرى فقالوا في قِلّ وعتّره أي في حالة كدّ وتعب وارتكاب أمور شنيعة وأحوال مكربة وهي من ألفاظ أهل الريف قال بعض شعرائهم [هزج]

أَبُو جَامُوسْ صِبِحْ حَالُو   يُبَكِّي ٱلنَّاسْ وَهُوْ شُهْرَهْ
بِيَجْرِي مَا بِيلْقَاشِي   وَفِي قِـلَّهْ وَفِي عَتْرَهْ

When things get tough,
Think on «Have we not dilated . . .?»![70]
Remember one "hardship" between two "eases"[71]
And neither mourn nor feel elated!

Next the poet decided to enumerate the things that had befallen him, one after another, beginning with the worst and the most important, so he says: **11.1.15**

min al-qilli ("of want"), with an *i* after the *q* and no vowel after the *l*;[72] that is, my gravest and greatest complaint is of *qill* ("want"), which is a paucity (*qillah*) of food and drink (the *ah* having being dropped for the meter)[73] and also of inadequate clothing and of the great toil and exhaustion required by the struggle to make a living. In the Tradition it says, "Poverty may bring one to the verge of denying one's faith," meaning that it may come close to forcing one to deny his faith because it leads to dissatisfaction with providence and displeasure with his material state and this may drag him into denying his faith. Ibn Daqīq al-ʿĪd, God have mercy upon him, said of poverty: **11.1.16**

By my life, poverty has dealt me a cruel stroke,
And reduced me with it to confusion and dismay.
If I go public with my plaint, I violate my privacy;
But if I don't confess my need, I fear I'll die!

And it is said that four sayings were written on the crown of Chosroes Anūshirwān: "Justice If It Lasts Brings Prosperity"; "Injustice If It Lasts Brings Ruin"; "The Blind Man Is as Dead Though He Be Not Buried"; and "Poverty Is the Red Death."[74] The people of the countryside use the word to cast aspersions on a poor man. They say that so-and-so is *fī qill* ("in a state of want"), and sometimes they add another word and say *fī qill wa-ʿatrah*, that is, in a state of struggle and exhaustion and the performance of foul deeds and awful doings. It is an expression used by the people of the countryside. One of their poets says:

Abū Jāmūs—his state
Makes people weep; he's quite lost face:
He runs around and finds nothing,
And lives in want and disgrace (*fī qillah wa-fī ʿatrah*).

١١،١،١٧ (والقلّ) على وزن الغِلّ أو الظِلّ مشتقّ من القَلْقَلة أو من القُلّة بضمّ القاف أو القولق وعَتْرَه بفتح العين المهملة وجزم الهاء في آخرها على وزن زُبْرَه فخذ زبره وَزِنْها على عتره لا تختلف أبداً ومعناها ارتكاب المفاسد وقلّة الدين ونحو ذلك ومن هذا المعنى قالوا فلان عتر أي مرتكب هذه الأمور وأمّا بالثاء المثلّثة فهي واحدة العثرات وهي اللغة الفصحى بمعنى أنّ المتلبّس بهذه الحالة عثراته كثيرة فالمعنى واحد وقد ورد لفظ القلّ في كلام العرب (وهو ما حكي) أنّ رجلاً حضرياً عزم على رجل بدويّ فأخرج له صحناً من الطعام وشيئاً يسيراً من الخبز فصار البدويّ كلّما أخذ لقمة يقول له الحضريّ قل بسم الله الرحمٰن الرحيم يا بدويّ ولم يزل يكرّر عليه التسمية فاستحى البدويّ وقام ولم يشبع من الطعام ومضى ثمّ بعد أيّام خرج البدويّ من منزله فرأى صاحبه الحضريّ فأخذه وأجلسه في داره وأخرج له قصعة كبيرة ملآنة من الثريد واللحم وقال له كل يا حضريّ وسفّ ما في القِلّة بركة أي ما فى قِلّة الطعام مع الشُحّ بركة ودَعْك تسمّي الله أو تترك التسمية وإن كان محلّ ذلك البركة فالمدار على سماحة النفس وإن كان صاحبها فقيراً فالكرم فيه راحة القلوب وستر العيوب قال الشاعر [وافر]

إذا كَثُرت عُيوبُكَ في البَرايا وسَرَّكَ أنْ يَكونَ لها غِطاءُ
تسـتَّرْ بالسَّخاءِ فكُلُّ عَيبٍ يُغَطّيـهِ كَما قيـلَ السَّخاءُ

وفي الأثر كلّ عيبٍ الكرم يغطّيه

١١،١،١٨ (مسألة هباليّة) ما الحكمة في اشتقاق القلّ من القولق أو من القُلّة أو من القَلْقَلة وما المناسبة لذلك وما معنى هذه الألفاظ (الجواب الفشرويّ) أنّ القولق اسم لشيء من الجلد يُصنَع لحفظ الدراهم ويُربَط في الحزام على الفخذ الأيمن يفعله بعض سقاة القهوة

The word *qill* is of the measure of *ghill* ("rancor, spite") or *ẓill* ("shadow") and derives from *qalqalah* ("agitation, convulsion") or from *qullah* ("water pitcher"), with *u* after the *q*, or from *qawlaq* ("leather money pouch"). The word *ʿatrah*, with *a* after the ʿ and no inflectional vowel at the end, is of the measure of *zubrah* ("small penis"); take a *zubrah* and weigh it against a *ʿatrah*, and you'll see there's no difference at all. The word means "the performance of acts of corruption and deficiency in religion" and so on. They say, "So-and-so is an *ʿitr*," that is, one who does such things.[75] As for *ʿathrah*, with *th*, it is the singular of *ʿatharāt* ("slips, mistakes, sins"), which belongs to the chaste language, in which case the meaning would be that the sins of one who is mired in such a state are many; thus the sense is the same. *Qill* occurs in the language of the Arabs, as in the anecdote that a city man invited a Bedouin to a meal, and brought him out a bowl of food and a little bread. As often as the Bedouin took a mouthful, the city man would say to him, "Say, Bedouin, 'In the Name of God, the Merciful, the Compassionate!'" and he kept repeating the same until the Bedouin was abashed and got up without eating his fill and left. Then, a few days later, the Bedouin left his dwelling and saw his city friend, so he took him and sat him down in his house and brought out a large bowl full of bread and meat with broth and said to him, "Eat, city man, and knock it back! There's no blessing in paucity (*qillah*)!" that is, "there's no blessing in paucity of food when accompanied by stinginess, whether you say 'In the name of God' or not, even though He be the source of that blessing, for what matters is an ungrudging spirit, even though its owner be poor," for generosity comforts the heart and covers many a flaw. As the poet says:[76] 11.1.17

If your flaws are become well known to men,
And you're inclined to find for them a cover,
Assume a mantle of liberality, for any flaw,
They say, by liberality may be covered over

—and, as the common saying has it, "Whatever the flaw, generosity covers it."

A Silly Debate: What is the wisdom in deriving *qill* from *qawlaq*, or from *qullah*, or from *qalqalah*, and how do they fit with one another, and what do these words mean? The Fatuous Response: *qawlaq*[77] is the name for a leather thing that is made to keep money in and tied onto the belt on the right thigh; some coffee waiters and others use it. The derivation of *qill* from *qawlaq* 11.1.18

وغيرهم فاشتقاقه منه لضيقه وعدم اتّساعه كما أنّ القلّ هو ضيق المعيشة وعدم اليسرة فناسب المعنى في ذلك وأمّا اشتقاقه من القُلّة بضمّ القاف فلأحد أمور إمّا لحصر الماء فيها فكذلك حكم القِلّة وعدم البركة حكم وجود الماء وعدمه أو أنّ المناسبة في ذلك لضيقها في حدّ ذاتها وأنّ الماء لا ينزل منها إلّا من خروم ضيّقة وأنّها إذا وُضِعَت في الماء بقبقت وصارت حكم الّذي يشكو إلى الماء قال الشاعر [بسيط]

ما بَقْبَقَ الكوزُ إلّا مِن تَأَلّمِهِ   يَشكو إلى الماءِ ما قاسَى مِنَ النّارِ

فكان في ذلك مشقّة وشدّة تعب فناسب اشتقاق القلّ من هذا المعنى والقول الثالث إنّه من القَلْقَلة فهو كذلك من قلقلة الأمور أي سرعة حركاتها وشدّتها وارتكاب المشقّات ونحو ذلك قال الشاعر [كامل]

قَلْقِلْ رِكابَكَ في الفَلا   وَدَعْ الغَواني في القُصورِ
القـاطِـنينَ بِأَرضِـهِـمْ   عِندي كَسُكّانِ القُـبورِ

أي حرّك ركابك في الفلا وهو الفضاء المتّسع والمعنى سر شرقًا وغربًا واكتسب ما يُغْنيك عن سؤال الناس ولا تكن عَيْلة عليهم ولا تذلّ نفسك لهم ودع الغواني جمع غانية وهي ذات الجمال أي اتركها ولا تشتغل بها عن طلب رزقك فربّما اشتغالك بها يتولّد منه البطالة والكسل فلا تجد ما تنفقه عليها فتميل نفسها إلى غيرك ويترتّب على هذا مفاسد كثيرة فإذا سعيت وتركتها وأتيت لها بما يسدّ جوعتها ويستر عورتها ممّا تحتاج إليه دامت معك على أتمّ مراد وأحسن حال وإن كان لا يفيدك من السعي والسفر إلّا اليسير فهو أَوْلى من عدمه بالكلّيّة قال الشاعر [طويل]

comes from the latter's crampedness and its lack of room, since *qill* denotes a cramped life and lack of ease; thus it fits the meaning from that perspective. As for its derivation from *qullah* ("water pitcher"), with *u* after the *q*, this could be for one of several reasons. It may be because water is retained within it, in which case want and lack of good fortune are analogous to the presence or absence of the water. Alternatively, the fit may lie in the actual narrowness of the *qullah* and the fact that the water has to pass through narrow holes in order to come out,[78] and that, when submerged in water, it makes a gurgling sound, as though it were complaining to the water. As the poet says:

> The mug makes a gurgle because it's in pain:
> It protests to the water what it suffered from the flame.

This process of firing implies distress and hardship, so it fits with the derivation of *qill* from that perspective. The third opinion states that it is derived from *qalqalah* ("agitation, convulsion"). From this point of view *qill* would be from the agitatedness (*qalqalah*) of events, that is, the speed with which they move, their intensity, and the distressing circumstances to which they give rise and so on. As the poet[79] says:

> Stir (*qalqil*) your stirrups in the steppes (*falā*)
> And leave the pretty girls at home.
> Like dwellers in the grave to me are those
> Who never from their homelands roam.

—that is, move your stirrups "in the *falā*," which means the wide-open spaces. The meaning is: "Go east and west, and acquire whatever will relieve you of having to beg from others, and be not a burden upon them, and do not humiliate yourself before them, and leave the *ghawānī*—plural of *ghāniyah*, which means 'a female possessed of beauty'; that is, abandon any such and do not allow yourself to be distracted by her from seeking your livelihood, for that distraction may lead to inactivity and idleness, in which case you will not find the wherewithal to spend on her and her heart will turn to someone else, with all sorts of evil consequences. If, on the other hand, you bestir yourself and leave her and then come back with all the things she needs to assuage her hunger and clothe her nakedness, she will stay with you just as your heart would desire and in perfect felicity. And even if you benefit little from your efforts and journeys, what you get will still be better for you than doing nothing." As the poet says:

عَـلى المَـرءِ أَنْ يَسعَى لِما فيـه نَفعُـهُ   ولَيسَ عَليـه أَنْ يُساعِدَهُ الدَّهـرُ

(وفي بعض الكتب المُنَزَّلة) يقول الله تعالى يا عبدي خلقتك من حركة تحرّك أَرْزُقْك وفي المثل الحركة فيها بركة وقال الإمام الشافعيّ رضي الله تعالى عنه شعر [طويل]

تَغَرَّبْ عَنِ الأوطانِ في طَلَبِ العُلَى   وسافِرْ ففي الأسفارِ خَمسُ فَوائِدِ
تفـرُّجُ[1] هَـمٍّ واكتسابُ مَعيشَةٍ   وعِـلْمٌ وآدابٌ وصُحبَـةُ مـاجِـدِ
فإنْ قيل في الأسفارِ ذُلٌّ وغُربَةٌ   وتَشتيتُ شَمْلٍ واجتِماعُ شَدائِدِ
فَموتُ الفَتَى خَيـرٌ لَه مِن حَيـاتِـهِ   بِدارِ هَوانٍ بَينَ واشٍ وحـاسَـدِ

فاتّضح الجواب باتّفاق * عن وجه هذا الاشتقاق * وقوله

١٩،١،١١ (جسْمو) الضمير راجع للناظم أي جسمه وهو ذاته مشتقّ من التَجَسُّم أو من المُجَسِّمَة وهم طائفة يقولون بالحلول والتجسيم قبّحهم الله تعالى أو من جسم العاشق إذا أنحله بُعْد الحبيب ولم يجد له دواء ولا طبيب وقوله

٢٠،١،١١ (ما يضال) كلمة ريفيّة ومعناها ما يزال كما تقدّم في الجزء الأوّل أي لم يزل جسمه من القلّ والتعب وعدم اليسرة

٢١،١،١١ (نحيف) على وزن رغيف وأصله نحيفا بالألف المقصورة وحُذِفَت لضرورة النظم والمعنى أنّ جسمه ضَعُفَ ورقّ من كثرة توارد الهموم عليه وتحمّل الأذى والكدّ في تعب المعيشة ونحو ذلك فإنّ الهمّ يُضْعِف الجسد ويُمْرِضه بخلاف الراحة وكثرة النعم ومن هنا يظهر أنّ أصحاب المال والرفاهيّة في الغالب أنّ أجسامهم في نضارة

---

[1] بي: تفريج.

Man must work for what he needs,
And Fate is not obliged to help.

In one of the Revealed Books, the Almighty says, "My slave, I created you from motion; move and I will provide for you!" and the proverb says, "In activity is blessing,"[80] and the Imam al-Shāfiʿī,[81] may the Almighty be pleased with him, says:

Leave your lands and seek advancement!
Go abroad, for there are five good things in travel:
Escape from care and a way to earn your living,
Knowledge, savoir faire, and the friendship of the noble.
Though some say travel means abjection in exile,
And loss of one's friends and meeting with trouble,
Still better a young man die than live
In ignominy 'midst jealousy and tittle-tattle.

Thus the answer now is clear, all can agree, and the nature of this derivation's plain to see.

jismū ("his body"): the pronoun suffix refers to the poet, that is, "his body" means "his person," the word being derived from *tajassum* ("corporeality") or from *al-mujassimah* ("the Corporealists"), which is a sect that holds to the doctrine of incarnation and corporealization,[82] may the Almighty disfigure them, or from *jism al-ʿāshiq* ("the body of the lover"), when the latter is worn thin by separation from the beloved and the poet can find neither medicine nor doctor for it. 11.1.19

mā yaḍāl ("is ever"): a rural phrase, meaning *mā yazālu*, as discussed in Part One.[83] That is, his body is never free of want, toil, and discomfort. 11.1.20

naḥīf ("thin"): of the measure of *raghīf* ("loaf"); it is properly *naḥīfan*, with an *alif* of prolongation, the latter having been dropped for the meter.[84] The meaning is that his body became weak and thin from the succession of cares that afflicted it, and the injury and hardship that it had to put up with in the course of making a living and so on—for care weakens and sickens the body, unlike ease and abundance of comforts, from which it will be evident that the bodies of the rich and affluent are in general vigorous, attractive, and graceful, because of the excellence of their food and drink and the cleanliness 11.1.21

وملاحة وطلاوة من حسن المآكل والمشارب ونظافة الملابس ورقّتها فلا يرون بذلك للهمّ تأثيرًا وقد قال الإمام الشافعيّ رضي الله تعالى عنه من نَظُفَ ثوبه قلّ همّه وفي الحديث الثوب يسبّح الله فإذا اتّسخ انقطع تسبيحه فالجسد مثل الزرع ما دام صاحبه يتعهّده بالسقي والإصلاح وتنظيف الغَلَت عنه دام في نضارة زائدة وملاحة زاهية ومتى تركه اعترته الآفات وتغيّرت عليه الأحوال وأمّا رقّة الجسد ورشاقته من غير مرض فهو ممدوح في النساء والرجال ويقال لصاحبه أهيف قال الشاعر [رجز]

وأَهْـيَفـانِ لعـبا   بالنَّـرْدِ أُنـثى وذَكَرْ
قالَتْ أنا قُـمْرِيَّـةٌ   قلتُ اسكُتي أنتِ قَمَرْ

وأبلغ من هذا قول بعضهم [بسيط]

هَيفاءُ لَو خَطَرَت في جَفْنِ ذي رَمَدٍ   لما أَحَسَّ له مِن وطـئِها أَلَمـا
خَفيـفَةُ الرُّوحِ لَوْ رامَت لِخِفَّتِها   رَقْصًا على الماءِ ما بلّت لها قَدَما

١١،١،٢٢ (مسألة هباليّة) لأيّ شيء قال الناظم نحيف ولم يقل سقيم لكونه أنسب في المعنى وأفصح في العبارة وقد وردت في القرآن العظيم في قوله تعالى ﴿فَنَظَرَ نَظْرَةً فِي ٱلنُّجُومِ فَقَالَ إِنِّي سَقِيمٌ﴾ أي من عبادتكم الأصنام (قلنا الجواب الفشرويّ) أنّ الناظم عدل عن هذه اللفظة لتضمّنها معنى اللفظة الّتي على وزنها وهي قطيم والقطيم بلغة الريّافة هو صاحب الأبنة وبلغة أخرى هو الخالي من الزواج فلو فرض أنّه أتى بها في النظم لربّما نسبوه أنّه كان به أبنة فيحصل من ذلك الضرر أو يقال إنّه راعى في ذلك قوافي الشعر فلا إشكال * فاتّضح المقول عن وجه هذا الهبال *

and fineness of their clothes, and they do not, as a result, suffer any of the ill effects of care. Imam al-Shāfiʿī, may the Almighty be pleased with him, said, "He whose garments are clean has few worries," and it says in the Tradition, "One's garments should give glory to God"; if they get dirty, this glorification is brought to a halt. The body, in fact, is like a crop of plants: so long as its owner is careful to water it and tend it and clean out the weeds, it remains full of vigor and glows with good looks, but when he ceases to attend to it, diseases attack it and things take a turn for the worse. In the absence of sickness, on the other hand, slenderness and trimness of the body are desirable characteristics in both women and men, and one possessed of such characteristics is referred to as *ahyaf* ("slender waisted"). As the poet[85] says:

Two slender-waisted creatures,
One girl, one boy,
At backgammon played.
Said she, "I am a turtledove!"
"Hush!" said I. "You are the moon above!"

—and even more expressive are the words of the poet who said:

A slender-waisted lass—should she tread on the lids of one with eyes inflamed,
No pain from her footfall would he feel.
Light-spirited—should she, of her levity, desire
To dance on water, not a drop would wet her heel.

A Silly Topic for Debate: "Why did the poet say *naḥīf* rather than *saqīm* **11.1.22**
('sick'), though the latter is more appropriate in meaning and more elegant in expression and is found in the Mighty Qur'an, in the words of the Almighty, «And he cast a glance at the stars, then said, 'Lo! I feel sick (*saqīm*)!'»[86] that is, 'I feel sick at your worship of idols'?" We declare, the fatuous response is that the poet avoided the latter word because it includes the meaning of the word that rhymes with it, namely, *qaṭīm*, and *qaṭīm* is, in the language of the country people, a passive sodomite, and, in another dialect, an unmarried man;[87] if he had used the word in the verse, they might have attributed passive sodomy to him, with harmful consequences. Or it may be said that, in this, he was following the rules of rhyme for poetry, so there is no problem. Our words are now clear, the silliness made to appear.

٢٣،١،١١ ثمّ إنّ الناظم أراد الإخبار عن بليّة ابتلى بها أيضاً نشأت من القلّ والعترة وعدم ما في اليد كما تقدّم فقال

ص

٢،١١ أَنَا ٱلْقَمْلُ وَٱلصِّيبَانُ فِي طَوْقِ جُبَّتِي   شَبِيهُ ٱلنُّخَالَهْ يَجْرُفُوهُ جَرِيفْ

ش

١،٢،١١ قوله (أنا) يعني أبو شادوف أخبركم أيضاً معاشر الأصحاب وأشكو إليكم

٢،٢،١١ وهو أنّ (القمل) المعروف المتداول بين الناس بخلاف الوارد في القرآن العظيم فإنّه نوع من السوس أو القراد كما ذكره بعض المفسّرين (فائدة) ذكر الدَميريّ في حياة الحيوان عن بعضهم أنّ القراد يعيش سبعمائة سنة وهذا من العجب انتهى والقمل يتولّد من العرق ومن أوساخ الجسد واشتقاقه من التقمّل أو من تقميل الغزل إذا صُبِغَ وبُوِّشَ ووُضِعَ في شدّة حرارة الشمس فيبس ويصير فيه نقط بيض تشبه القمل فلهذا يقال غزل مقمّل ومصدره قمل يقمل قملاً وهو اسم جنس الأنثى منه قملة وأمّا الذكر فلعلّه يسمّى قامل قال الشاعر شعر [طويل]

وما قامِلٌ في الثوبِ إلّا رأيتَهُ   يَدبُّ دبيبَ العُقْرُبانِ إذا مشى

(والعقربان) على لغة الثُّعْلُبان اسم للثَّعْلَب قال الشاعر [طويل]

أَرَبٌّ يبول الثُّعْلُبان بوجهِهِ   لقد ذَلَّ من بالت عليه الثعالبُ

Next the poet sought to tell of a further misfortune by which he was smitten and which was a product of the aforementioned want, abasement, and lack of wherewithal. He says: **11.1.23**

TEXT

anā l-qamlu wa-l-ṣībānu fī ṭawqi jubbatī **11.2**
shabīhu l-nukhālah yajrufūhū jarīf

Me, the lice and nits in the yoke of my gown
are like bran that they shovel willy-nilly

COMMENTARY

anā ("me"): meaning "Me, Abū Shādūf, I inform you in addition, good friends, and I complain to you" of **11.2.1**

(a)l-qaml ("lice")—the well-known type that makes the rounds among people, not the type mentioned in the Mighty Qur'an, for the latter is a type of worm or tick, according to some of the commentators.[88] (Useful note: al-Damīrī, in his *Life of Animals*,[89] mentions, on someone's authority, that the tick lives seven hundred years, which is remarkable. End.)[90] Lice are born from the sweat and dirt of the body. The word is derived from *taqammul* ("infestation with lice") or from the *taqmīl* ("licing") of yarn, when the latter is dyed and sized and placed in the hottest sun, so that it dries and develops white spots that look like lice; thus one speaks of "liced yarn." The paradigm is *qamila, yaqmalu, qamlan* ("to be infested with lice"); *qaml* is a collective noun, the female being a *qamlah* ("a louse");[91] the male is perhaps called a *qāmil*. The poet says: **11.2.2**

I never had a male louse (*qāmil*) in my clothes but it seemed to me
To creep like a male scorpion (*ʿuqrubān*) as it moved.

The word *ʿuqrubān* is of the pattern of *thuʿlubān*, which means "fox" (*thaʿlab*). As the poet says:

Is there a lord on whose face the dog-foxes pee?
Contemptible indeed is he on whom the foxes pee!

وخوطب بلفظ المُثنّى كما ورد في القرآن العظيم في قوله تعالى خطاباً لمالك خازن النار ﴿أَلْقِيَا فِي جَهَنَّمَ﴾ وقول الحجّاج يا غلام أضربا عنقه وأمّا قوله في البيت الأوّل يدبّ دبيب العقربان أي لأنهم شبّهوا القملة بالعقرب والبرغوث بالفيل وهذا لأنّها تلدغ والبرغوث يعضّ (فإن قيل) إذا كانت القملة تشبه العقرب والبرغوث يشبه الفيل فلأيّ شيء لم تكن كبيرة مثلها ولدغتها كلدغة العقرب وكذلك البرغوث لم يكن قدر الفيل وفعله كفعله (الجواب عن ذلك) أنّ القمل لمّا كان مُنْشَأة من جسد الإنسان وأنّه لا يفارقه لمنافع اقتضتها الحكمة الإلهيّة وهي مصّ الدم الفاسد وإن كان يتحصّل منه الأذى كان المناسب لحكمة الله تعالى أن يكون صغيراً ولدغته قليلة الألم إذ لو كانت القملة[1] قدر العقرب لَلَزِمَ أن يكون الآدميّ قدر الجمل ويكون دائماً في خوف من رؤيتها وتعذيب من لدغتها والله تعالى كرّم بني آدم وكذلك البرغوث لمّا جعله الله تعالى يسكن مخارق الثياب والمحلّات الضيّقة كان صغيراً مثل القمل إذ لو كان قدر الفيل للزم أن يكون الآدميّ قدر الجبل والبرغوث واحد البراغيث والأنثى منه برغوثة وهو مشتقّ من البِرّ والغَوْث قال الجلال السيوطيّ رحمه الله [سريع]

لا تَكرَهِ البُرغوثَ إنَّ اسمهُ　　بِرٌّ وغَوْثٌ لا بـه تدري
فَبِرُّه مَـصُّ دمٍ فـاسدٍ　　والغَوثُ إيقـاظُكَ للفَجرِ

واستغنى الناظم عن ذكره بذكر القمل لأنّه تابع له

---

١ بي: القمل.

The dual[92] may be used as a form of address, as it is in the Mighty Qur'an when the Almighty addresses the Guardian of the Fire, saying, «Throw (dual) into Hell . . .»[93] and as in the words of al-Ḥājjaj, "Boy, strike (dual) his neck!."[94] As for the poet's words in the first verse, "creep like a male scorpion," this is the case because the louse is conventionally likened to the scorpion and the flea to the elephant, because the former stings while the flea bites. If it be said, "If the louse resembles the scorpion and the flea resembles the elephant, why is the louse not as large as the scorpion and its sting like the scorpion's sting, and, by the same token, why is the flea not the size of the elephant and why does it not behave like one?" the reply would be that, because the louse is generated by and never leaves the human body for a specific beneficial purpose ordained by the Divine Wisdom, namely, the removal by sucking of corrupt blood, even though it may sometimes do harm too, it is in accord with the wisdom of the Almighty that it should be small and also that its sting should cause hardly any pain, because, were the louse the size of a scorpion, a human would have to be the size of a camel and would live in dread of seeing one and being tortured by its sting—but Almighty God is generous to mankind. Likewise, the flea, given that the Almighty has formed it to live in the creases of clothes and other tight places, is small like the louse because, if it were the size of an elephant, a human would have to be the size of a mountain. The word *burghūth* ("flea") is the singular of *barāghīth*, and the female is a *burghūthah*; it is derived from *birr* ("charity") plus *ghawth* ("help").[95] Al-Jalāl al-Suyūṭī,[96] God have mercy on him, said:

Hate not the flea—
  Its name is Charity,
And though you know it not
  It also helps a lot:
In sucking bad blood
  Its charity lies;
By rousing you at dawn for prayer
  Its help it supplies.

The poet's mention of the louse spares him the need to mention the flea, because the latter is subordinate to the former.

٣،٢،١١ (سؤال) ما الحكمة في أنّ البرغوث ينطّ والقملة لا تقدر على ذلك (الجواب) أنّ القملة لمّا نشأت من العرق وروائح الجسد كانت ضعيفة بهذا المقدار ولكونها أنثى والأنثى عاجزة عن الذكر وأمّا البرغوث لمّا كان مَنْشَأُهُ من التراب كانت طينته قويّة ولهذا تشبّه بالفيل وهو أعظم الحيوانات ذاتًا فكانت القوّة ناشئة فيه فصار ينطّ فاتّضح الحال عن هذا الإشكال

٤،٢،١١ وقال بعضهم إنّ أذى البرغوث أقوى من أذى القمل قال الشاعر [بسيط]

أشكو إليك براغيثا بُليتُ بها — قد جرّعوا القلب كأسات من الغَصَصِ
أصيد هذا يجي هذا يؤالمني — فتنقضي ليلتي في الصيد والقَنَصِ

وما أحسن ما قال بعضهم [طويل]

بَعُوضٌ وبُرْغُوثٌ وبَقٌّ لِزَمْنَني — حَسِبْنَ دمي خمرًا فطاب لها الخَمْرُ
فيرقص برغوث لزَمْرِ بعوضةٍ — وبَقُّهُمُ يسكتْ لِيَسْمَعَهُ الزَمْرُ

٥،٢،١١ وأفادني بعض إخواننا الحشّاشين أدام الله بأكل الحشيش أُنْسَهم * وأخمد بدخول الأرطال عند النوم حِسَّهم * أنّ الشخص إذا أسقط ما يتيسّر من الحشيش قبل النوم ودخلت عليه الأرطال ونام فلا يحسّ بأذى البراغيث ولا غيرها خصوصاً إذا استعمل الحَلْوَى بعد أكله فإنّه يفعل أفعالاً عجيبة ويُظهر مظاهر غريبة ولا يضرّه إلّا أكل الحامض كما قال بعضهم متضمّنًا كلام سيّدي عمر بن الفارض رضي الله عنه [طويل]

أَمُنْسَطِلٌ بالزَيْـهِ من فقد قهوةٍ — شَمولٍ على نيرانها يُجْمَعُ الشملُ
نصحتك إنْ أصبحتَ في سَطْلَةٍ فلا — تَذُقْ حامِضًا واختَرْ لِنَفسِكَ ما يحلو

٦،٢،١١ (وسمعت) من أمّي عفا الله عنها لُغزًا في البرغوث ولم أفهمه إلّا بعد زمن طويل

A Question: "Where is the wisdom in the fact that the flea can jump while the louse cannot?" The answer: "The louse, being born of the sweat and effluvia of the body, is correspondingly weak, and it is, moreover, female,[97] and the female is weaker than the male. The flea, however, being born of the earth, is of a stronger clay, which is why it resembles the elephant, which is the animal with the largest body. Thus, its strength is inborn, which allows it to jump." The situation's now revealed, the problem no more concealed. 11.2.3

Some say the flea is more harmful than the louse. The poet says: 11.2.4

I complain to you of certain fleas with which I am afflicted.
On my heart a choking cup these have inflicted.
While I chase one, another comes to bug me,
And so goes the night, in hunting and ven'ry.

And how well the poet put it, when he said:

Gnats, fleas, and bedbugs clung tight to me:
They thought my blood wine and held its taste most dear.
The fleas would dance to the piping of a gnat,
While the bedbugs kept mum so the others could hear.

One of our hashish-eating brethren—may God prolong through the eating of hashish their conviviality and stifle with a jar of wine on sleeping their raucous hilarity—informed me that, if one drops a little hashish before sleeping, followed by a few jars, and then sleeps, he doesn't feel the pain of fleas, or anything else, especially if he uses candy after eating the hashish, for hashish produces strange reactions and creates amazing effects, and the only thing that spoils it is eating sour things. As the poet says, incorporating words of Ibn al-Fāriḍ's, may God be pleased with him: 11.2.5

O you who're stoned on dope for lack of wine
(That vap'rous draft around whose fires men meet),
When you are high, I do advise you, Don't
Consume what's sour, do eat what's sweet!

My mother, may God excuse her sins, told me a riddle about fleas that I didn't understand until I had mastered the sciences and spent time among people with a command of the best language. It goes as follows: *yā shī min shī aḥmar ḥimmayr waraq al-jimmayr jarū warāh khamsah miskūh itnayn* 11.2.6

لمّا فهمت العلم ومارست الفصحاء وهو هذا (يا شي من شي أحمر حِمّيَّر ورق الجِمّيَّر جروا وراه خمسه مسكوه اتنين) وتفسيره (يا شي) يا حرف نداء أي يا رجل فسّر لنا اسم يخرج (من شيء) مُبْهَم وهو أحمر (حِمّيَّر) بتشديد الميم وكسر الحاء المهملة وسكون المثنّاة من تحت تصغير أحمر بمعنى شديد الحُمْرة (ورق الجمير) أي كورق الجمير في لونه تصغير جُمّار وهو قلب النخل وورقه الليف الملتفّ عليه (جروا وراه خمسة) وهي الأصابع (مسكوه اثنين) منهم وهو الشاهد والإبهام وبين حمير وجمير الجناس المصحف انتهى

٧،٢،١١ (وممّا يمنع أذى البراغيث) البخور بقشر النارنج الناشف عند النوم (وممّا يقتل القمل) الحِنّاء والزِئبَق إذا لُتّ منهما خيط صوف وعُلّقَ في العنق فعل ذلك (وأمّا منافع القمل) فذكر صاحب طبّ الفقراء أنّ صاحب الشقيقة إذا أخذ قملة من رأس سالمة من الوجع ووضعها في باقلاية مشويّة وسدّ عليها بشمع وعلّقها على موضع الشقيقة برئت بإذن الله تعالى

٨،٢،١١ (والصيبان) معطوف على القمل وهو بزره المتولّد منه فعطف الفرع على الأصل لأنّه لازمه وغالب كثرته في رؤوس الأطفال لرِقّة أجسادهم فيُعالَج بالأدهان والحناء وتسريح الشعر ونحو ذلك وله أكلان في الجسد بسهولة فهو أخفّ ضررًا من القمل لكونه أضعف منه وألطف جسمًا وأصله صُبَيّان بتقديم الموحّدة على الياء المثنّاة من تحت جمع صَبِيّ ثمّ إنّهم أرادوا العدول عن هذا الجمع لئلّا يشتبه بأولاد الآدميّين فقدّموا الياء المثنّاة من تحت على الموحّدة وقالوا صيبان وهو مشتقّ من الصابون لبياضه أو من المُصِيبة أو من قناطر الصابونيّ ومصدره صبين يصبين صبيانًا

٩،٢،١١ وسكت الناظم عن نوع آخر من أولاد القمل وهو النِمْنِم بكسر النونين وسكون الميمين لكونه من لوازمه أيضًا والفرع تابع للأصل كما تقدّم ونمنم على وزن سِمْسِم وهو

("Something from something else![98] Red as red can be, red as the leaves of the heart of the palm tree! Five ran after it, two caught it!"). It may be interpreted as follows: *yā shī* ("O thing"): *yā* ("O") is the vocative particle, that is, "O man, interpret to us a name that comes from something obscure and is" *aḥmar ḥimmayr* ("dark, dark red"): *ḥimmayr* (with double *m*, *i* following the *ḥ*, and no vowel on the *y*) being the diminutive of *aḥmar* ("red"), and meaning "of intense redness";[99] *waraq al-jimmayr* ("leaves of palm hearts"): that is, like the leaves of palm hearts in color, *jimmayr* being the diminutive of *jummār* ("palm hearts"), which are the core of the palm tree, while the "leaves" are the fibrous integument that is wrapped around them; *jarū warāh khamsah* ("five ran behind it"): namely, the fingers; *miskūh itnayn* ("two caught it"): two of the latter, namely, the index finger and the thumb. There is diacritical paronomasia between *ḥimmayr* and *jimmayr*.[100] End.

The noxious effects of fleas may be prevented by using incense mixed with dried bitter-orange peel on sleeping. Lice may be killed with a woolen thread pounded with henna and mercury and hung around the neck. As for the beneficial qualities of lice, the author of *The Book of the Physick of the Poor*[101] mentions that, if a migraine sufferer takes a louse from a head that is free of pain and puts it in a grilled bean and seals the latter with wax and hangs it at the point of the migraine, his head will get better, if the Almighty wills. 11.2.7

wa-l-ṣībānu ("and nits"): joined to *al-qaml* ("the lice") by the conjunction *wa-* ("and"), these being the seeds that are born of the latter; in other words, the poet joined the branch to the root, since the former is a concomitant of the latter. They are generally found in the greatest numbers on the heads of children, because children's bodies are tender and should be treated with fats and henna and by combing the hair and so forth. They are very prone to cause itching in the body but are less harmful than lice, because they are weaker and have softer bodies. The origin of the word is *ṣibyān* ("boys") (with the *b* before the *y*), plural of *ṣabī*.[102] Subsequently, they decided to avoid that plural, lest nits be confused with human children; so they put the *y* after the *b* and said *ṣibyān*. The word is derived from *ṣābūn* ("soap") because of the whiteness of the creatures, or from *muṣībah* ("disaster"), or from the Bridges of al-Ṣābūnī. The paradigm is *ṣabyana, yuṣabyinu, ṣibyānan*.[103] 11.2.8

The poet is silent on another form of the offspring of the louse, namely, the *nimnim* (with *i* after the two *n*'s and no vowel after the two *m*'s),[104] the latter, 11.2.9

مشتقّ من النَّمْنَمَة أو النَّمّام نوع من المشموم وأمّا إذا فتحنا نونيه فيكون مركّباً من فعل أمر فكأنّه يأمره بالنوم مرّتين ومن معناه قول الحريريّ عفا الله عنه [سريع]

سِمْ سِمَةً تُحْمَدُ آثارُها فاشكرْ لمن أعطى ولو سِمْسِمَهْ

وهذا يقرب من فنّ الأحاجي كقولهم طاجن وطافية والياسمين وقول بعضهم [بسيط]

إنّي رأَيتُ عَجيباً في دِيارِكُمُ شيخاً وجاريةً في بَطنِ عُصفورِ

وقول الآخر [مجتثّ]

وأحمرُ الخَدِّ قاني يُغْري إليه الخِضابُ
بِغَيرِ عَينٍ ونابٍ وفيه عينٌ ونابُ

١٠،٢،١١ ويطلق لفظ نمنم على كلام الطفل الصغير إذا اشتهى الأكل فيقول نمنم أو بُفّ بضمّ الموحّدة وسكون الفاء لأنّه ينطق بألفاظ تخالف ألفاظ الكبير كما هو شاهد وأمّا لغته قبل نطقه فقيل أنّها بالسريانيّة وإذا اشتهى الماء يقول أُنْبُوهْ بضمّ الهمزة وسكون النون و رفع الموحّدة وجزم الهاء وإذا أدنى بيده لنجاسة يتناولها ينزجر بلفظ كُخْ بالكاف والخاء المعجمة وإذا دنا لأخذ شيء يؤذيه ينزجر أيضاً بلفظ أَحّ بالألف والحاء المهملة وإذا أخذ شيئاً أعجبه ولعب به يقال له أو يقول عليه دَحّ بالدال والحاء المهملتين ويقال له أو يقول على المأكول إذا فرغ منه بَحّ بالموحّدة والحاء المهملة وإذا أرادت أمّه تخويفه وسكوته عن الصياح تقول له اسكت لا ياكلك البِعْبِع بكسر الموحّدتين أو رفعهما وجزم العينين المهملتين (والبعبع) مشتقّ من البَعْبَعة وهو

too, being a concomitant of the former and the branch being subordinate to the root, as previously stated. The word *nimnim* is of the measure of *simsim* ("sesame") and is a derivative of *namnamah* ("wren") or of *nammām*, a sweet-smelling plant.[105] If, on the other hand, we spell it as *namnam*, it would be a compound made of an imperative verb, as though one were ordering someone to go to sleep twice.[106] Al-Ḥarīrī,[107] God excuse him his sins, said in similar vein:

Perform an act for whose same seed you will be praised,
Thanking Him who gives, be it but a sesame seed!

This is close to the art of word puzzles[108] such as *ṭājin* and *ṭāfiyah* and *yāsamīn*[109] and the verse that says:

I saw a marvel in your houses—
An old man and a maiden in the stomach of a bird![110]

And another says:

Red of cheek, of a crimson
That all rouge to emulate must try;
Fangless, eyeless,
But with fang and eye.[111]

The word *namnam*[112] is used in the language of small children:[113] when a child wants to eat, he says *namnam*, or *buff* (with *u* after the *b* and no vowel after the *f*), for children utter different words from those used by adults, as may be observed. As for the language children use *before* they start to talk, some say it is Syriac. When a child wants water, he says *unbūh* (with *u* at the beginning, no vowel after the *n*, *ū* after the *b*, and no vowel after the *h*). If he puts out his hand to something dirty to take it, he is scolded with the word *kukhkh* (with *k* and *kh*), and if he is on the point of taking something that might harm him, he is rebuked with the word *aḥḥ* (with *alif* and *ḥ*). If he takes something that pleases him and plays with it, they call it (or he calls it) *daḥḥ* (with *d* and *ḥ*) with no following vowels.[114] They call (or he himself calls) food when he has had enough of it *baḥḥ* (with *b* and *ḥ*). If his mother wants to scare him or stop him from bawling, she says, "Quiet, or the *biʿbiʿ* ('bogeyman') will eat you!" (with *i* or *u* after the two *b*s and no vowel after the *ʿ*s). *Biʿbiʿ* is derived from *baʿbaʿah*, which is the sound of the camel.[115] Among *aḥḥ* and *daḥḥ* and *baḥḥ* there is mutational paronomasia of the first letter.[116] The child addresses his 11.2.10

صوت الجمل وبين أَحّ ودَحّ وبَحّ الجناس المتغيّر الأوّل ويخاطب أمّه بلفظ ماما وأبوه بابا وأخوه الصغير واوا ونحو ذلك وتغزّل بعضهم في صغير ببيت من المواليا جمع فيه هذه الألفاظ فقال [بسيط]

يا مَن سَلَبْ للحَشا والرُّوحِ واوا أَحْ   غيري يواصِلُكَ وأنا مِن وصالكْ بَحْ
البُفّ أُطْعِمك والنَّمْنِم وقولةْ بَحْ   بِعْبِعْ أنا كُخٍّ يا نِنّا وغيري دَحْ

وقال ابن سودون رحمه الله تعالى في معنى ذلك [هزج]

لموت آمي أرى الاحزانَ تَحْنيني   فطالما لحستنى لحس تَحْنينِ
وطالما دلّعتني حالَ تربيتي   حتّى طلعتُ كما كانت تربّيني
أقولُ نَمْنَمْ تجي بالأكلِ تُطْعِمُني   أقولُ انبُوهْ تجي بالماءِ تَسْقيني

وقوله (تحنيني وتحنيني) فيه الجناس التامّ الأوّل من الانحناء والثاني من التحنّن والشفقة كما لا يخفى

ويقال عِذارمُنَمْنِم أي يشبه في نبته بدبيب النمنم أو نبات النمام وقد قلت في تشبيهه ١١،٢،١١
بدبيب النمنم [بسيط]

دَبُّ العذار على خدّيه خُيِّلَ لي   بأنّه نَمْنِمٌ يمشي على مَهَلِ

(وبعضهم زاد نوعاً رابعاً) وسمّاه لِحِيس بكسر اللام وتشديد الحاء المهملة على وزن ١٢،٢،١١
بَعبيص أو لِقّيس مأخوذ من البعبصة وهي وضع الإصبَع في دُبُر الغير ولِقّيس من اللقاسة يقال لقس الكلب الإناء أي لَحِسَه بلسانه فيكون فيه نوع شبه بالحيس أو يكون على قياس فطيس واللحاسة والنجاسة على وزن واحد يقال فلان لحس

mother as *māmā*, his father as *bābā*, his little brother as *wāwā*,[117] and so on. A poet has gathered these expressions together in a verse from a *mawāliyā* in which he flirtatiously addresses a little boy:

You who stole my heart and soul, Ouch! It hurts!
You make friends with others, but when it's me, your love's "all gone!"?
I feed you din-dins and tidbits and you say "All gone!"
Am I a "Bogeyman"? Am I "Yuck," little baby, while another's "Yumyum"?[118]

And Ibn Sūdūn, may the Almighty have mercy on him, says, in similar vein:[119]

Because of my mother's death I find sorrows wring me (*taḥnīnī*).
How often she suckled me tenderly (*taḥnīnī*),
And, as she brought me up, how often she indulged me,
So that I turned out just as she made me.
If I said *namnam*, she'd bring food and feed me.
If I said *unbūh*, she'd bring water to give me.

The words *taḥnīnī* ("wring me")[120] and *taḥnīnī* ("tenderly") constitute "perfect paronomasia,"[121] the first being from *inḥinā'* ("bending"), the second from *taḥannun* ("tenderness") and "having pity" (*shafaqah*), as is clear.

One also speaks of *'idhār munamnim* ("creeping fuzz") on a young man's cheek, meaning that the down resembles the creeping of the *nimnim* or of the *nammām* plant as it sprouts. Comparing it to the creeping of the *nimnim*, I wrote: 11.2.11

The down crept o'er his cheeks; it seemed to me
To be *nimnim* moving lazily.

Some have added a fourth type of vermin and named it *liḥḥīs* (with *i* after the *l* and double *ḥ*), of the measure of *ba'bīṣ* or *liqqīs*, *ba'bīṣ* being taken from *ba'baṣah*, which is "the insertion of a digit between the buttocks of another," while *liqqīs* is from *liqāsah* ("licking"); one says, "The dog licked (*laqisa*) the dish," meaning "it licked it clean (*laḥisahu*) with its tongue."[122] Thus there is a kind of resemblance to the *liḥḥīs*; or it may be that the word is formed according to the analogy of Fuṭays.[123] The words *liḥāsah* and *najāsah* are of the same 11.2.12

أي مرتكب شيئاً يشبه النجاسة أو كثير الكلام بلا فائدة فتكون اللحاسة والنجاسة بمعنى واحد (قال) في القاموس الأزرق والناموس الأبلق لا فرق بين لقاسة ولحاسة والنجاسة فيها بلا شكّ فهذا أَصْوَب ويقال أنت تعيس لحس أي تشبه لحس الكلب للإناء أو أنك تلحس الخراء بلسانك أو تتلحّس بالكلام ولا تدري منطوقه من مفهومه والتعيس من معنى ذلك أيضاً فكلّها ألفاظ قريبة الشبه من بعضها البعض ولهذا اللِّحيس مزيد الضرر قال في القاموس الأزرق والناموس الأبلق [طويل]

ولي من أذى اللِّحيسِ في الرأسِ كُرْبَةٌ   وغَلْيٌ وأَكْلٌ في الثياب وفي الجسدْ

ومصدره لحّس يلحّس تلحيساً

١٣،٢،١١ (فإن قيل) إنّ هذا اللحيس الّذي زاده هذا البعض شيء تافه جداً فكان وجوده كالعدم ولهذا تركه الناظم كغيره فما الجواب (قلنا) نعم وإن سلّمنا أنّه لا وجود له إلّا بعُسْر لدقته ففي الجملة له محض أذيّة وضرر فصار من أتباع القمل بل من أولاده كالصيبان والنمنم كما تقدّم * أو يكون هذا قياساً على من زاد في الأقوال نوعاً رابعاً وسمّاه خالفة وعنى به اسم الفعل وهو صَهْ بمعنى اسكت فاتّضح الحال عن وجه هذا الهبال وقوله

١٤،٢،١١ (في طوق جبتي) أي كائن أو مستقرّ في طوقها والطَوْق على وزن الجَوْق كما يقال جوق الطبّالة وجوق المغاني ونحو ذلك وهو اسم لما طُوِّقَ به العنق من ثوب أو غيره كالحديد والفضّة والذهب والنحاس ونحو ذلك قال الله تعالى ﴿سَيُطَوَّقُونَ مَا بَخِلُوا بِهِۦ يَوْمَ ٱلْقِيَامَةِ﴾ أي المال الّذي كنزوه في الدنيا ولم يؤدّوا زكاته ولم يصرفوه في وجوه الخير يُجْعَل في عنقهم كالطوق ويعذَّبون به في النار والطوق مشتقّ من الطاقة أو من

pattern; one says, "So-and-so is *laḥis*," that is, "one who has committed something resembling impurity (*najāsah*) or who talks a great deal to no effect."[124] Thus *liḥāsah* and *najāsah* have the same underlying meaning. In *The Blue Ocean and Piebald Canon* it says, "There is no difference between *liqāsah* and *liḥāsah*, and undoubtedly *najāsah* enters into it too," and this is the more correct formulation. One also says, "You are *taʿīs laḥis*," that is, you resemble a dog licking a dish, or you lick shit with your tongue, or you talk raving nonsense (*tatalaḥḥas bi-l-kalam*) and cannot tell a thing from its name. *Taʿīs* has the same meaning, making all of them closely similar expressions, which is why the *liḥḥīs* are so harmful.[125] In *The Blue Ocean and Piebald Canon* it says:

And I suffer torments from the harm the *liḥḥīs* do to my head,
And a boiling and an itching in my clothes and in my body.

The paradigm[126] is *laḥḥasa, yulaḥḥisu, talḥīsan.*

If it be said, "This *liḥḥīs* added by the people you refer is insignificant, almost to the point of nonexistence, and this is why the poet, like others, leaves it out, so why do you raise the issue at all?" we would reply, "True. However, even if we grant that it is so minute that it barely exists, nevertheless it becomes, in bulk, unmitigated harm and injury and on this basis is to be associated with lice, and indeed it should be counted among the latter's offspring, just like the nits and the *nimnim* mentioned above. Alternatively, the issue is raised by analogy to those who add a fourth category to the parts of speech and name it 'the residual,' meaning by this the verbal substantive, namely, *ṣah* ('Hush!') in the sense of *uskut* ('Be silent!')."[127] Thus the situation now's revealed, the silliness no more concealed. 11.2.13

fī ṭawqi jubbatī ("in the yoke of my *jubbah*"): that is, I speak of those lice and nits that are existing or well established in its yoke. *Ṭawq* ("yoke") is of the pattern of *jawq* ("band of musicians"), as used in the expressions *jawq al-ṭabbālah* ("the band of drummers") and *jawq al-maghānī* ("the singing band") and so on. It is the name given to anything that encircles the neck, of a garment or of anything else, be it made of iron, silver, gold, brass, or the like.[128] The Almighty says, «That which they hoard will be their collar on the day of resurrection,»[129] meaning that the wealth that they store up in this world and on which they do not pay tithes and which they do not use for good works will be placed around their necks like a collar, and they will be tormented by it in the Fire. The word 11.2.14

الطواقي لتدويرهم أو من خان أبو طاقيّة بمصر ومصدره طوّق يطوّق تطويقاً ونساء الأرياف يجعلونه من فضّة ويسمّى عندهم ضامن أيضاً وهو أحسن الحُليّ عندهم وأمّا ما يوضع في أعناق الرجال في السجن فإنّه يسمّى ضامنة يقال فلان في الضامنة أي بمعنى أنّ هذه الآلة الحديد الّتي في عنقه ضامنة له لا يقدر أن ينفكّ عنها مثل الرجل الضامن للإنسان متى طُلِبَ منه أحضره وقوله

١٥،٢،١١ (جبتي) على وزن شختّي ولحيتي هذا إذا نسبتها لنفسك وأمّا إذا كانت لغيرك فتقول جبّتك على وزن شختّك ولحيتك مثلاً وإذا وصفتها وقلت جبّتك حمره فتكون بالتصحيف خَنَتَكَ حَمْزه أي ناكك رجل يسمّى حمزة والجبّة واحدة الجبب مشتقّة من الجَبّ وهو القطع لأنّ الخيّاط يجبُّها أي يقطعها ويفصّلها يقال جاب الفيافي بمعنى قطعها وقد قلت في المعنى [طويل]

أَجوبُ الفَيافي طامِعًا في وِصالكَ   وأَقطعُ أرضاً لَست مِنها بخابِرِ

ومصدره جب يجب جبا وجبة

١٦،٢،١١ وهي على قسمين ريفيّة وحضريّة فالريفيّة من صوف تخين غليظ مسدودة حكم الثوب ويجعلوا أكمامها متّسعة خصوصاً شعراؤهم فإنّهم يُعْرَفون بزيادة وسع الأكمام لأنّ كمّ الرجل منهم مُخْتَصَر زكيبة على شكل الشعراء في وسع الأكمام وزيادة وأمّا نساؤهم فإنّ كمّ المرأة منهنّ يسع الرجل يدخل منه ويخرج من الكمّ الثاني وربّما جامع الرجل زوجته من كمّها ولا يحتاج لرفع بقيّة الثوب كما وقع لي ذلك فإنّي تزوّجت منهنّ وكنت أجامع زوجتي في بعض الأحايين من كمّها فسبحان من خصّهم بقلّة الهندام* حتّى فى الثياب والأكمام* فهي أمور بينهم محبوبه* والمناسبة مطلوبه* (وفي المثل)

ṭawq is derived from *ṭāqah* ("aperture") or from *ṭawāqī* ("skullcaps"), because of its roundness, or from the Khān of Abū Ṭaqiyyah in Cairo. The paradigm[130] is *ṭawwaqa, yuṭawwiqu, taṭwīqan.* The women of the countryside make their neck rings of silver, calling them also *ḍāmin,* and they regard them as the best of ornaments. The type of collar that is placed on the necks of men in prison is called a *ḍāminah*; one says, "So-and-so is in the *ḍāminah*" meaning that this iron device that is on his neck is a guarantee (*ḍāminah*) for him that he will not be able to get away, just like the man who acts as a guarantor (*ḍāmin*) for another and produces him when he is summonsed.

jubbatī ("my *jubbah*"): of the measure of *shakhkhatī* ("my pissing") and *liḥyatī* ("my beard"), or so it is if the form refers to oneself; but, if it refers to someone else, you say *jubbatak* ("your *jubbah*") on the pattern of *shakhkhatak* ("your pissing") or *liḥyatak* ("your beard"), for example. If you were describing it and said *jubbatak ḥamrah* ("Your *jubbah* is red"), you could change the dots and it would become *khanatak Ḥamzah,* meaning "a man named Ḥamzah fucked you."[131] *jubbah* is the singular of *jubab,* derived from *jabb,* which means "cutting," because the tailor tailors (*yajubbu*) the *jubbah,* that is, cuts (*yaqṭaʿu*) it and pieces it together. One also says *jāba l-fayāfī* ("he traversed open country"),[132] meaning "he cut across it (*qaṭaʿahā*)," and in this vein I said: 11.2.15

I traverse (*ajūbu*) the open spaces, greedy for your arms,
And cross (*aqṭaʿu*) a land of which I have no knowledge.

The paradigm is *jabba, yajubbu, jabban,* and *jubbatan.*[133]

There are two types: the rural and the urban. The rural type is of thick, coarse wool, closed in front like a *thawb.* They make the sleeves wide, especially their poets. Indeed, they are known for the excessive width of their sleeves, for the men's sleeves are made of cut-off sacks and are as wide as those of poets, or wider.[134] As for their women, their sleeves are wide enough to accommodate a man, who can go in through one and come out by the other; thus a man may have intercourse with his wife via her sleeve without needing to raise the rest of her shift, as I myself have experienced, for I married one of these women and had intercourse with my wife via her sleeve on several occasions—so glory to Him who made them unkempt, even with regard to their sleeves and other raiment, for these are things by them desired, and consistency is required. As the proverb has it, "They saw an ape getting drunk on 11.2.16

رأوا قرد يسكر على خرّاره فقالوا ما للمُدام الرايق إلّا لهذا الشَبّ العايق ورأوا جاموسة منقَّبة بكِيب فقالوا ما للصبيّه القصّيفه إلّا للنقاب الرفيع قال الشاعر [وافر]

رَأيتُ مجذَّماً في قاعِ بيرٍ   وآخرَ أبرصَ يخرا عليهِ
فقلتُ تَعَجَّبوا مِن صُنْعِ ربّي   شَبيهُ الشَّيءِ مُنجَذِبٌ إليهِ

(وأمّا الحضريّة) وهي الّتي يستعملها أهل المدن خصوصاً العلماء والظرفاء وهي من الصوف الرفيع اللطيف يجعلوها محصورة الآباط مفتوحة ويقال لها جبّة مفرَّجة بتشديد الراء لكونها انفرجت من مقدَّم الشّخص وبان ما تحتها ويصنعوا لها السِجاف الحرير وغيرها حتّى تصير أعجوبة للناظرين * وبهجة للابسين * فسبحان من حلاّهم بطلاوة الملبوس * وزيّنهم بكلّ قدّ مأنوس * وجعل نساءهم زينة النفوس * (كما في المثل) الأساس بحسب بانيه * وكلّ شيء يشبه قانيه * فالإنسان ينشأ على الطبع الّذي جُبِلَ عليه * وشبه الشيء منجذب إليه * قلت في المعنى [وافر]

رأيتُ بِخَدِّهِ ماءً ونارًا   وذاكَ الوَردُ مُنتَثِرٌ عليهِ
فقُلتُ تَعَجَّبوا مِن صُنْعِ ربّي   شبيهُ الشَّيءِ مُنجَذِبٌ إليهِ

١٧،٢،١١ (ثمّ إنّ الناظم) لمّا علم أنّ القمل والصيبان وغيره الكائن في طوق جبّته لا يمكن حصره لكثرته أراد أن يشبّهه بشيء يناسبه في الكثرة واللون فقال

١٨،٢،١١ (شبيه النّخاله) وهي قشر البُرّ والشعير الّذي يعلو المُنْخَل عند النخل وسيأتي تعريفها واشتقاقها وهذا الشبه يعطي حكم المشبَّه به من وجهين الأوّل أنّ القمل أبيض والنخالة كذلك الثاني أنّه إذا تراكم على بعضه البعض يرى في العين كثيرًا كما ترى النخالة فكان تشبيهه بها هو المناسب وهي مشتقّة من النّخل أو المُنْخَل قال في القاموس الأزرق والناموس الأبلق شعر [بسيط]

a dung heap and said, 'For so pellucid a wine what better match than a youth so fine?' And they saw a buffalo blinkered with a reed mat and said, 'For so elegant a girl, what better match than so divine a veil?'"[135] As the poet says:

I saw a leper deep down in a well
And another with vitiligo whose shit on him fell.
Said I, "Behold what your Lord hath wrought—
The like of a thing attracts its own sort!"

The urban sort is the one used by the people of the cities, especially scholars and sophisticates. It is of soft, fine wool, and they make it tight at the armpits and open in front. They call it a *jubbah mufarrajah* ("an open *jubbah*") (with double *r*) because it has been opened (*infarajat*) at the wearer's front and what is beneath may be seen. They add a silk or other trimming, so that the beholder is amazed by the sight and the wearer finds it a true delight—glory be to Him who has embellished such people with elegant raiment, bestowed on them every kind of pleasant form as adornment, and made their women an embellishment! As the proverb has it, "The foundation is according to the builder, and all things resemble their owner," for men grow up according to their God-given natures to be as they ought, and the like of a thing attracts its own sort. In the same vein, I myself said:

I saw on his cheek both water and fire[136]
And, strewn about, those roses fair.
Said I, "Behold what my Lord hath wrought—
The like of a thing attracts its own sort!"

Next, the poet, realizing that the lice, nits, and other vermin present in the yoke of his *jubbah* were too many to be counted, decided to liken them to something resembling them in quantity and color, so he said: **11.2.17**

shabīhu l-nukhālah ("are like bran"), which is the husks of wheat and barley that come to the top of the sieve when they are bolted. More information on this, and the etymology, are to come. This simile yields the likeness of the comparator from two perspectives. The first is that lice are white, and so is bran. The second is that, when they accumulate in heaps, they appear to the eye to be a lot, just as bran does. In other words, this is an appropriate comparison. The word *nukhālah* is derived from *nakhl* ("palm trees") or from *munkhal* ("sieve"). In *The Blue Ocean and Piebald Canon* it says: **11.2.18**

اسمُ النُخالَةِ مُشتَقٌّ كَما ذكروا من مُنْخَلٍ ونَخيلٍ ثمَّ مِنْخالِ

ونخالة الشعير أقوى نفعاً لأنّها إذا نُقِعَت في الماء وسُخِّنَت بالنار وشربها من يشتكي وجع الصدر أبرأته بإذن الله تعالى

وقوله (يَجْرُفوه) أي القمل والصيبان وتوابعهما المتقدّمة ١١،٢،١٩

(جريف) أصله جرفا لأنّه مصدر حُذِفَتْ ألفها وزِيِّدَ فيها الياء لأجل الرويّ أو أنّها ١١،٢،٢٠
لغة ريفيّة فلا اعتراض وهو مشتقّ من الجَرْف أو المِجْرَفة أو الجرّافة (فإن قيل) كان حقّ الناظم أن يرجّع الضمير لأقرب مذكور وهي النخالة وكان هذا هو الأنسب (قلنا) لعلّه عدل من تأنيث الضمير لضرورة النظم إذ لو فعل ذلك لاختلّ الوزن أو يكون من باب الترخيم كقولهم [طويل]

أفاطمَ مهلاً بعضَ هذا التَدَلُّلِ وإِنْ أَنتِ قد أَصرَمْتِ حَبْلي فاجملي[١]

أو أنّه رجّعه إلى قشر البر والشعير المسمّيان بالنخالة فيكون على تقدير حذف المضاف فلا اعتراض عليه (فإن قيل أيضاً) إنّ كلام الناظم يُفهَم منه أنّ القمل والصيبان قد انحصروا في طوق جبّته فقط ولم يكن على بدنه منه شيء وإذا كان كذلك فما فائدة الشكوى منه (قلنا) يمكن الجواب بأن يقال إنّ قوله في طوق جبّتي أي غالب القمل يتراكم ويصعد إلى طوق جبّته حتّى يصير من كثرته يشبه النخالة في الجرف ولا يلزم من هذه العبارة أنّ بقيّة جسده سالم منه بل إذا كان في طوق جبّته بهذا المقدار فيكون شيء منه في الجسد من باب أَوْلى لأنّ الجسد محلّ معاشه وغذائه من مصّ دمه وشرب أوساخه وإنّما القمل من شأنه أن يسبح أوّلاً في الثياب ثمّ ينتشر على البدن يمتصّ الدم الفاسد وكلّ من شبع منه صعد إلى أعلى الجسد فيمكث فيه

١ بي (في جميع النسخ): فاحملي.

The noun *nukhālah* is derived, as they recall,
From *munkhal* and *nakhīl*[137] and, finally, from *minkhāl*.[138]

Barley bran is the best for one because, if it is steeped in water and heated and someone suffering from chest pains drinks it, it will cure him, if the Almighty so wills.

yajrufuhū ("they shovel"): that is, the lice and the nits and their aforementioned relatives. **11.2.19**

jarīf ("willy-nilly"): originally *jarfan*, because it is a verbal noun with the *alif* omitted, the *ī* being added for the sake of the rhyme; or it may be a rural form; in either case there can be no objection.[139] It is derived from *jarf* or from *mijrafah* ("shovel") or from *jarrāfah* ("shovel-sledge"). If it be said, "The poet ought to have referred the pronominal suffix of *yajrufuhū* to the nearest antecedent, namely, *nukhālah*,[140] and this would have been more appropriate," we say, "He may have avoided using a feminine pronominal suffix for the meter, because, if he had used one, the line would no longer have scanned;[141] or it may be a case of truncation,[142] as in the line[143] **11.2.20**

Gently now, Fāṭim![144] A little less disdainful:
Even if you would cut my rope, do it kindly!

"—or he may have been referring it to the 'husks of wheat and barley,' which are called collectively *nukhālah*, in which case it should be taken as an example of the suppression of the first term of a genitive construct,[145] so there can be no objection." And if it also be said, "One might understand from the poet's words that the lice and nits were confined exclusively to the yoke of his *jubbah* and there were none of them whatsoever on his body, in which case what would be the point in his complaining about them?" we would reply, "The answer may be that one might say that his words 'in the yoke of my *jubbah*' mean that *most* of the lice were accumulated in and had risen to the yoke of his *jubbah* and then, in their abundance, came to resemble bran when shoveled and that it does not necessarily follow from this wording that the rest of his body was free of them. Indeed, if they were present in the yoke of his *jubbah* in such quantities, then, a fortiori, there should be some on the rest of his body, for the body is where they live and derive their nourishment, by sucking blood and imbibing the body's wastes. In fact, it is the way of lice to spread first in the clothes,

ليستنشق الهواء ويرتاح كما أنّ الآدميّ إذا شبع يرتاح بسكونه ونومه مثلاً فهذا دأبه كما جرت به العادة فاتّضح الجواب

٢١،٢،١١ (سؤال) لأيّ شيء لم يتعرّض الناظم للشكوى من البقّ والنمل والبعوض ولم يذكر شيئاً منهم مع أنّ لكلّ منهم أذيّة وضرر شديد (الجواب) عن هذا السؤال من وجوه شتّى الأوّل أنّ البقّ وإن كان كثيراً كما في المثل إنّ البقّه تولد مِيّه * واتقول يا قِلّة الدُرّيّة * فإنّه في الغالب لا يهوى إلّا بلاد المدن لعلوّ أماكنها وكثرة أخشابها وطليها بالجصّ والجير لأنّه يعيش بها ويتولّد فيها وبلاد الأرياف ليس فيها شيء من البناء العالي المكلّف وإن وُجِدَ في القرية فيكون دار الشادّ بها أو دار الملتزم مثلاً والناظم لا يتوصّل إليها ولا ينام بها وإنّما بيوتهم غالباً من الكِرْس والوَحْل وربّما كان فيها الجلّة أيضاً فلهذا لا يعرفوا البقّ ولا يروه ولا يهوى أماكنهم (وأمّا النمل) فإنّه وإن كان موجوداً في بلاد الأرياف فإنّه لا يهوى إلّا المحلّ الّذي فيه بعض الأدهان كالسمن والزيت ويهوى الشيء الحلو كالعسل والسكّر فيأتي إليه ويشمّه ويكون قوّته الشمّ كما ذكره صاحب حياة الحيوان ومثله الكمّون فإنّ الوعد يُغْنيه عن سقي الماء قال الشاعر [بسيط]

لا تجعلنّي ككمّون بمزرعةٍ إنْ فَاتَهُ السَّقيُ أَغْنَتْهُ المَوَاعيدُ

(والناظم) لم ير للنمل أثراً في بيته لقلّة ما فيه من الحلوى والأدهان بل لعدمه بالكلّيّة فلهذا لم يكن للنمل عليه سبيل لا في ثوب ولا موضع فكان منعه عنه بهذا السبب (وأمّا البعوض) وإن كان موجوداً في بلاد الأرياف فإنّه يأتي أيّاماً ويذهب بخلاف القمل والصيبان فإنّ أذاهما دائماً مستمرّ في الثياب وغيرها كما تقدّم والشيء إذا كان

then expand throughout the body, sucking out the bad blood; and those that have had their fill climb up to the top of the body and stay there to take the air and rest, just as humans, for example, having eaten their fill, rest by keeping quiet and sleeping. This is their habitual way of behaving, according to custom, so the answer now is clear."

Question: How come the poet does not raise a complaint against bedbugs, ants, and gnats and omits all mention of them, despite the fact that each of these is responsible for great harm and injury? This question may be answered from several perspectives. The first is that bedbugs, though plentiful—as the proverb has it, "The bedbug gives birth to a hundred and says, 'So few children!'"—in general favor only cities because of their tall buildings, the large quantities of timber there, and the plaster and lime with which they are coated, because it is in these things that they live and breed; whereas the country villages have no tall, costly construction. If they were to be found in a village, it would be in the house of the bailiff or the tax farmer, for example, to which the poet would never have access and in which he would never sleep. In fact, their houses are mostly made out of slabs of dung mixed with urine and of daub, to which dung cakes are sometimes added. As a result, they are unacquainted with bedbugs and do not see them and tend not to frequent the same places. Ants, though found in the villages of the countryside, nevertheless favor only those places in which there are fatty things such as clarified butter and oil, and they like sweet things, such as honey and sugar; they come to these and feed off them simply by smelling them, as mentioned by the author of *The Life of Animals*,[146] resembling in this the cumin plant, which can live simply on the prospect of being watered. As the poet[147] says: 11.2.21

> Don't treat me like the cumin in its plot,
> Whom promises content though it be watered not!

Our poet never saw any trace of ants in his house because it contained so few fats and sweets, or, rather, because there were none of these whatsoever. As a result, ants would have no way of getting to him, whether via his clothes or his home, and this would be the reason for their failure to affect him. As for gnats, though these are found in the villages of the countryside, they come just on certain days and then go away again, unlike lice and nits, whose harm is constant and unremitting, in clothes and elsewhere, as mentioned above; and

يؤذي قليلاً ويغيب كثيراً فيكون وجود ضرره كالعدم فكان هذا سبباً لتركه الشكوى من الجميع فاتّضح الجواب

٢٢،٢،١١ (فائدة) إذا نُقِعَ الحَنْظَل في مقّة الغزل بعد استوائه ورُشّ بها في المحلّ وهي حارّة قتلت البقّ ولم يبق منه شيء وإذا ظهر النمل في محلّ فيه البقّ أكله قال الشاعر [وزن غير معروف]

أكل البق آلمـني جسمي ما حمل بقّـهْ
جبت النمل ساعدني مـا خلّى ولا بقّـهْ

(وأمّا النمل) فيمنعه رائحة القطران ويمنع البعوض دخان النخالة

٢٣،٢،١١ (مسألة هباليّة) ما الحكمة في أنّ الشخص إذا أكلته قملة أو قرصه برغوث أو شيء ممّا يؤذي يسري ذلك الأذى في جسده ظاهراً وباطناً حتّى يشمل الكبد والرئة والقلب ونحو ذلك مع أنّ القمل أو البرغوث ونحوه لا يتوصّل إلى باطن الجسد إلّا أن دخل من منفذ من المنافذ وإذا دخله نادراً ربّما مات في الحال قبل وصوله إلى باطن الإنسان وكثيراً ما يدخل البرغوث في أذني فيمكث قليلاً في حركة وأذيّة ويخرج بسرعة أو يموت فما وجه ذلك (الجواب الفشرويّ) عن هذا البحث الهباليّ أن يقال إنّ الجسم باطنه وظاهره في التألّم على حدّ سواء لأنّ الروح سارية فيه كسريان الماء في العود الأخضر فإذا حصل الأذى في ظاهره تألّمت الروح وسرى الألم في جميع الجسد ظاهراً وباطناً وأمثّل لك مثالاً فشرويّ وهو أنّ الشخص إذا حبس في خزانة صغيرة مثلاً وكانت لا تسع غيره وليس لها منفذ وطال سجنه فيها فإنّ جسمه يضعف ويتغيّر وتعتريه الأمراض ويتألّم ظاهراً وباطناً خصوصاً إذا حصره البول وبال فيها حتّى ملأها أو ضرط فيها أيضاً فتصعد تلك الروائح إلى العلوّ فلا تجد لها مصرفاً فتعود على لحيته وشواربه فتضرّه ضرراً بليغاً خصوصاً صاحب اللحية الطويلة العريضة ما لم يكن عرضها ضرّ

the harm done by something that hurts a little and is absent a lot is insignificant, and this may be the reason for his omitting to complain about the lot of them. Thus the answer's clear.

Useful Note: If colocynth is steeped in water in which yarn has been thoroughly soaked and the place is sprinkled with that water while it is hot, it will kill the bedbugs and not one will be left, and if ants appear in a place where there are bedbugs, they eat them. As the poet says: 11.2.22

My body couldn't take another bug,
Their bite was giving me such pain.
I brought the ants. They helped me out—
They spared not one and let not one remain.[148]

Ants are repelled by the smell of tar, gnats by the smoke made by burning bran.

A Silly Topic for Debate: What is the wisdom in the fact that, if a louse bites a man or a flea or any other harmful creature stings him, the pain spreads through the body, outside and in, until it comes to embrace the liver, the lungs, the heart, and so on, even though the louse, the flea, and the rest do not have access to the inside of the body, unless one of them should enter through one of the orifices; and if, on some rare occasion, it should enter, it usually dies immediately, even before it reaches the interior of the body, as indeed a flea has often entered my own ear and stayed a while moving about and doing damage and then quickly come out or died? What is the explanation for this? The fatuous reply to this silly enquiry is: it may be said that the body experiences pain to the same degree internally and externally because the spirit circulates within it the way sap circulates in a green branch. Thus, if any damage is done to the body's surface, the spirit feels pain and the pain spreads to the whole body, outside and in. Let me draw you a facetious example, to wit, if a man is imprisoned in a small closet, for example, that is too small to hold anyone else and has no outlet and the man is locked up there for a long time, his body weakens, changes, and sickens and he feels pain both externally and internally, especially if he is pressed by the urge to urinate and does so until he fills the place, or if he farts there too and the resulting odors rise upwards and then, finding no escape, come back down on his beard and mustache, causing him grievous harm, especially if he is the owner of a long, broad 11.2.23

طولها فيخفّ الضرر أو قلّ طولها فكذلك على كلّ من الحالتين فانكشف الحال عن وجه هذا الهبال

٢٤،٢،١١ ثمّ إنّ الناظم شرع في ذكرمصيبة أخرى ابتلى بها وهي في الجملة أشدّ ضرراً من القمل والصيبان لكونها من جهة الأقارب فقال

ص

٣،١١ وَلَا ضَرَّنِي إِلَّا ٱبْنُ عَمِّي مُحَيْلَبَهْ يَوْمٍ تَجِي ٱلْوَجْبَهْ عَلَيَّ يَحِيفْ

ش

١،٣،١١ قوله (ولا ضَرَّنِي) أي ضرراً زائداً على ما تقدّم

٢،٣،١١ (إلّا ابن عمّي) أخو والدي وهو مشتقّ من العموم لأنّ نفعه يعمّ أولاده وأولاد أخيه لأنّه في حكم الأب لهم إذا فقد والدهم ولهذا تسمّيه العرب أبا (قال) بعض المفسّرين في قوله تعالى ﴿وَإِذْ قَالَ إِبْرَاهِيمُ لِأَبِيهِ ءَازَرَ﴾ إنّ المراد به عمّه أو من العِمامة لعلوّها فوق الرأس حكم التاج كما في الحديث العمائم تيجان العرب فذلك العمّ له الرفعة على أولاد أخيه لكفالته إيّاهم وولايته عليهم وقوله

٣،٣،١١ (محيلبه) تصغير محلبة وهي إناء يعمل من فخّار أحمر مجوّف البطن محصور الرقبة لها أذن واحدة وتُعْمَل بأذنين أيضاً إذا كانت كبيرة سمّيت بذلك لحلب اللبن فيها من باب تسمية الظرف باسم المظروف

beard (as long as its breadth has not rendered its length odious, in which case the damage will be less, or it has not become less commode-ious, in which instance it is the same for both cases).[149] Thus the situation's now revealed, the silliness no more concealed.

Next the poet embarks on the description of another disaster that afflicted him—one yet more damaging, taken as a whole, than lice and nits, for it comes to him from the direction of his relatives. He says: 11.2.24

TEXT

wa-lā ḍarranī ʾillā-bnu ʿammī Muḥaylibah 11.3
yawmin tajī l-wajbah ʿalayya yaḥīf

And none has harmed me as much as the son of my paternal uncle,
Muḥayliba—
the day the *wajbah* comes, he heaps upon me more than my lot.

COMMENTARY

11.3.1 *wa-lā ḍarranī* ("and none has harmed me"): that is, harmed me over and above what has already been mentioned.

11.3.2 *ʾillā-bnu ʿammī* ("as much as the son of my paternal uncle"): that is, my father's brother, *ʿamm* ("paternal uncle"), being derived from *ʿumūm* ("generality") because his competence encompasses both his own children and those of his brother, for he is like a father to them, if their actual father is not present. This is why the Arabs call the paternal uncle "father." One of the commentators on the words of the Almighty «When Ibrahim said unto his father Āzar,»[150] says, "What is meant is 'his paternal uncle.'" Or the word is derived from *ʿimāmah* ("turban") because of the latter's being high above the head, like a crown—as it says in the Tradition, "Turbans are the crowns of the Arabs"—for the paternal uncle has an exalted position with regard to his brother's children because of his responsibility for and guardianship of them.

11.3.3 *Muḥaylibah*: diminutive of *maḥlabah,* which is a vessel made of red earthenware with a concave belly and a narrow neck; it has one handle but is sometimes made with two, if it is large.[151] It is so called because milk is milked (*ḥalb*) into it, according to the rule of "naming the container after the thing contained."

٤،٣،١١ (والحاصل) إنّ الأواني المُعَدّة للحلب على أقسام محلبة ومحلاب وهو على ثلاثة أقسام صغير وكبير ومتوسّط والمحلاب أطول من المحلبة وأوسع منها فماً وأضيق بَطْناً قعره يشبه قعر القادوس صغير جدّاً ورُبَع وهو إناء صغير يأخذ في الكيل قدر ربع المحلبة وقَرّوفهْ بفتح القاف وتشديد الراء المهملة وكسر الفاء وسكون الهاء في آخرها وهي تشبه المحلاب في صغر القعر إلّا أنّها محصورة الرقبة واسعة البطن جدّاً مثل المحلبة ولها أذنين أو أذن واحدة وأكبر أواني اللبن القِسْط وهو جرّة كبيرة وهناك إناء آخر يقال له الكوز يباع به اللبن في بلاد المدن كما شاهدنا ذلك وهو ثقيل في الجرم قليل في البركة ومحيلبة على وزن مدولبة ومحلاب على وزن دولاب وقِسْط على وزن قِبْط سمّي بذلك لكونه مقسّطا بالوزن أو الكيل وربع على وزن سُرَع وكوز على وزن بُوز لأنّه يشبه بوز البقرة أو العجلة في وسع فمه وهو مشتقّ من الكزّ وهو العَضّ يقال كزّت الأرض على المحراث إذا عضّت عليه وكزّ الطفل على إصبعه إذا عضّه هكذا رأيته في القاموس الأزرق والناموس الأبلق فالكوز إذا وضع فيه اللبن أو الماء بقبق وتألّم يشكو ما ناله من ألم النار وما قاساه من العناء حتّى صار فخاراً قال الشاعر [بسيط]

ما بَقبَقَ الكوزُ إلّا مِن تألّمِهِ يشكو إلى الماء ما قاسى من النارِ

فكان القياس الفطيسيّ من هذا القبيل فهذه الأواني معروفة عند أهل الريف هي وغيرها ومنها الزِير والتُمْنة وغير ذلك

٥،٣،١١ (فإن قيل) إنّ المحلبة والمحلاب ونحوهما كالقسط والربع والكوز تقدّم تعريف أسمائهم واشتقاق بعضهم فما معنى القرّوفه وما أصل وضع هذا اللفظ الغريب على هذا الإناء وما مناسبة ذلك (قلنا) يمكن الجواب من وجوه (الأوّل) أنّ هذا الإناء عُمِلَ

A Brief Overview: Vessels prepared for milking are of different sorts. There is the *maḥlabah*, and there is the *miḥlāb*, which is itself of three sorts—small, large, and medium; the *miḥlāb* is taller than the *maḥlabah* and has a wider mouth and more slender belly; its bottom is like that of the jar in which the water is raised on a waterwheel (*qādūs*),[152] being very small. There is also the *rubʿ*, which is a small vessel that holds, as a unit of measurement, one quarter of a *maḥlabah*. And there is the *qarrūfih* (with *a* after the *q*, double *r*, *i* after the *f*, and no vowel on the *h* at the end).[153] This resembles the *miḥlāb* in having a small base, but has a narrow neck and a very wide belly, like the *maḥlabah*; it has either one or two handles. The largest of the milk vessels is the *qisṭ*, which is a large jar. There is also another vessel, called the *kūz*, with which milk is sold in the cities, as we have observed; it is crudely made and holds little. *Muḥaylibah* is of the measure of *mudawlibah* ("causing to go round and round"), *miḥlāb* of the measure of *dūlāb* ("waterwheel"), and *qisṭ* of the measure of *qibṭ* ("Copts"). It is called a *qisṭ* because it is divided up (*muqassaṭ*) by weight or volume. The word *rubʿ* is of the pattern of *surʿ* ("reins"), and *kūz* is of the pattern of *būz* ("muzzle") because its wide mouth resembles the muzzle of a cow or a calf; *kūz* is derived from *kazz* which means "to bite" (*ʿaḍḍa*);[154] one says the earth "bit" (*kazzat*) on the plow, when it seizes (*ʿaḍḍat*) it with the share, and the child "bit" (*kazza*) on his finger, when it takes it between its teeth (*ʿaḍḍahu*); so I find in *The Blue Ocean and Piebald Canon*. If milk or water is put in the *kūz*, it gurgles and moans, complaining of the pain of the fire and all that it suffered when being turned into pottery. 11.3.4

The mug makes a gurgle because it's in pain:
It protests to the water what it suffered from the flame.

This would be according to the analogy of Fuṭays.[155] These vessels are well known to the people of the countryside, as are others, among them the *zīr* ("water jar")[156] and the *tumnah* ("one-eighth measure") and so on.

If it be said, "The definition and, in some cases, the etymologies of the names *maḥlabah* and *miḥlāb* and the rest such as *qisṭ*, *rubʿ*, and *kūz* have been given, but what is the meaning of *qarrūfih*, and how did this strange word come to be applied to this vessel and what was the occasion for that?" we reply that this question may be answered from a number of perspectives. The first is that this vessel was made at the time of the *qirr* (with *i* after the *q* and no vowel after the *r*),[157] which means "extreme cold"; then they completed (*wafaw*) its firing in 11.3.5

في زمن القِرّ بخفض القاف وجزم الراء وهو شدّة البرد ثمّ إنّهم وَفَوْا حرقه في زمن الصيف فصار يقال قرّوفه أي هذا الإناء وَفِيَ حرقه وتمّ أمره ثمّ إنّهم حرّكوا الراء من قرّ مع ضمها مشدّدة وجعلوا مجموع هذه الحروف علماً عليه وقالوا قرّوفه فصار مركّباً من اسم وفعل (الثاني) أنّه لمّا أُتِيَ به وهو جديد ووضعه الحلاّب بين رجليه وحلب فيه اللبن فصار يفور ويتحلّل منه رغوة كثيرة فخاف الحلاب من سيلان اللبن خارج الإناء فصار ينادي اللبن قرّ فيه قرّ فيه أي اسكن فيه واستقرّ ثمّ زادوا في هذا اللفظ واواً بين فعل الأمر والجارّ والمجرور وحذفوا الياء المثنّاة من تحت لثقلها في اللفظ وحرّكوا الواو وقالوا قرّوفه فسمّي بذلك (الثالث) أنّ طينته في الأصل أُخِذَت من محلّ قريب من قَرافة مصر فصاروا يقولوا إناء قرافيّ ثمّ إنّهم اشتقّوا له هذا الاسم من هذا المعنى وقالوا قرّوفه (الرابع) أنّه مشتقّ من القِرْفة بكسر القاف وهو نوع من البُهار زكيّ الطعم والرائحة يدخل في الأطعمة الفاخرة والمآكل النفيسة وكذلك اللبن عند حلبه يكون فيه طيّب الرائحة وحلو الطعم قال الله تعالى ﴿لَبَنًا خَالِصًا سَائِغًا لِلشَّارِبِينَ﴾ ثمّ زادوا فيه واواً وجعلوه علماً عليه (الخامس) أنّ الأسماء لا تُعَلَّلُ فلا نحتاج إلى هذه الأبحاث الفشرويّة وهذه الخرافات الهباليّة فاتّضح الجواب وبان الصواب

(وأمّا) سبب تسمية ابن عمّ الناظم بهذا الاسم فعلى أقوال (أحدها) أنّ أمّه لمّا وضعته سمعت إنساناً يقول لآخر هات المحلبة فسمّته بذلك تفاؤلاً بهذا اللفظ وصغّرته لكون الولد صغيراً (الثاني) أنّ أمّه أتت بولد قبله وسمّته محلاب فمات ثمّ ولدته وكرهت أن تسمّيه باسم أخيه فأنّثت اللفظ وصغّرته وقالت محيلبه واشتهر بذلك (الثالث) أنّ أمّه لمّا ولدته زارها إنسان بمحلبة جديدة ساعةَ ولادتها فتفاءلت بذلك وقالت محيلبه فهذا ما ظهر لي من هذه المباحث الفشرويّة والخرافات الهباليّة وقوله ٦،٣،١١

(يوم) بالتنوين وخفض الميم لضرورة النظم واليوم اسم لبياض النهار المضيء ٧،٣،١١

the summer, and so it was called *qirrwafih*, that is, the firing of this vessel was accomplished (*wafiya*) and it was finished; then they put a *ū* after the double *r* of *qirr* and made a name for it out of all these letters and said *qarrūfih*. In this case it would be composed of a noun and a verb.[158] The second is that, when it had just been invented and the milker put it between his legs and directed the milk into it, the milk started to rise and make a lot of froth, so the milkman became afraid that the milk would overflow the vessel and called out to the milk *qarr fīh qarr fīh* ("Stay in it! Stay in it!"), that is, "Remain in it and be settled!" Then they added a *w* to the word between the imperative verb and the prepositional phrase, omitted the *ī* because it was awkward to pronounce, realized the *w* as *ū*,[159] and said *qarrūfih*, and that became its name. The third perspective is that the clay of which it was made was originally taken from a place close to the Qarāfah ("cemetery") of Cairo, so they started saying "a *qarāfī* vessel,"[160] then derived this name for it from that sense and said *qarrūfih*. The fourth is that it is derived from *qirfah* ("cinnamon") (with *i* after the *f*), which is a spice with a delicious taste and smell that is used in fine dishes and sumptuous foods, for milk too, when fresh from the cow, has an appetizing smell and sweet taste—as the Almighty has said, «pure milk, palatable to the drinkers»;[161] then they added a *ū* to it and made that its name. And fifthly, names cannot be etymologized, so there is no need for these fatuous investigations and inane fabulations. Thus the answer now's clear, the truth made to appear.

Various accounts are given for how the poet's paternal cousin came by this name. The first is that, when his mother gave birth to him, she heard one person say to another, "Fetch the milk crock!" so she named him thus, taking a good omen from the word and making it into a diminutive, seeing that the child was small. A second version has it that his mother had borne another boy before him and called him Miḥlāb, but he died. When she gave birth to this child, she did not want to call him by his brother's name, so she made the word feminine[162] and made it a diminutive and said *muḥaylibah*, and by this he was known. A third account has it that someone visited her with a new milk crock (*maḥlabah*) at the moment when she gave birth, so she took this as a good omen and said, "I shall call him Muḥaylibah." This is the extent of what I have learnt from these fatuous investigations and inane fabulations. 11.3.6

yawmin ("on the day when"): with *in* following the *m*, for the meter.[163] *Yawm* ("day") is a name for the whiteness of daylight that is illumined by the rays of 11.3.7

المُشْرِق بسبب الشمس الّذي يُصام شرعاً كما لا يخفى وقوله

(تجي) من المجيء وهو الحضور ٨،٣،١١

(الوجبه) ووقت مجيئها وحضورها بمجرّد طلوع الشادّ أو الملتزم أو النصرانيّ إلى الكفر أو البلد فتوزعّ على الفلّاحين بحسب ما يخصّهم من الأرض من القراريط والفِدَن ونحو ذلك فمنهم من يكون عليه في الشهر يوماً ومنهم من يفعلها في كلّ جمعة مرّة ومنهم من يجعلها في كلّ ثلاثة أيّام وهكذا بحسب كثرة الفلّاحين وقلّتهم وحسب زيادة الأرض ونقصها فلا بدّ منها في كلّ يوم مدّة الإقامة فيقوم الرجل بكُلْفة الشادّ والنصرانيّ إن كان حاضراً وجميع من يكون من طائفة الملتزم بأكلهم وشربهم وجميع ما يحتاجوا إليه من عليق دوابهم وما يتمنّوه عليه من المأكل من اللحم والدجاج ولو كان فقيراً ألزموه بذلك قهراً عليه وإلّا حبسه الشادّ وضربه ضرباً موجعاً وربّما هرب من قلّة شيء يضعه فيرسل إلى أولاده وزوجته ويهدّدهم ويطلب منهم فربّما رهنت المرأة شيئاً من مصاغها أو ملبوسها على دراهم وأخذت بهم الدجاج أو اللحم وطبخته وأحرمت أولادها من الأكل منه خوفاً على نفسها من أنّه لا يكفيهم مثلاً وقد يربّي الفلّاح الدجاج فلا يأكل منه شيئاً ويحرم نفسه وعياله من خوفه من الضرب والحبس ومثل الدجاج والسمن[١] والدقيق يبقيه لأجل هذه البليّة ويطبخ بالسيرج ويأكل الخبز الشعير ويضع لهم القمح الزريع ويأكل الجبن القَرِيش المالح ويتكلّف لشري الجبن الطري الحلو ويرسله في الوجبة كلّ ذلك خوفاً على نفسه من هذه الأمور ٩،٣،١١

وسمّيت وجبة لكونها صارت على الفلّاحين حكم الأمر الواجب عليهم للملتزمين فلا بدّ من فعلها للشادّ بالقرية أو النصرانيّ أو الملتزم إذا حضر كما تقدّم بيانه وإذا ١٠،٣،١١

---

١ بي: السمن.

the sun and during which one may undertake a legally meaningful fast, as is well known.[164]

tajī ("comes"): from the verbal noun *majī'* ("coming"), which means arriving at a place. 11.3.8

al-wajbah ("the *wajbah*"): this takes effect from the moment of the coming, or arrival, of the bailiff or the tax farmer or the Christian in the hamlet or the village, at which time it is distributed among the peasants on the basis of how many carats or feddans, etc., of land each one works. Some are obligated to provide it one day a month, others once a week, and still others once every three days, etc., according to how many or few are the peasants and how extensive or limited is the land. It must be provided every day throughout the stay. Under this system, a man sees to the provisioning of the bailiff and the Christian, if the latter is present, and of all those belonging to the tax farmer's entourage, and undertakes to provide them with their food and drink and everything they need in the way of fodder for their animals and whatever dishes of meat or fowl they may have a liking for. If the man is poor, they impose this on him by force, or else the bailiff imprisons him and beats him severely. Sometimes a man will flee because he does not have enough to offer, and the bailiff then sends for his children and his wife and demands it from them with threats. A wife may pawn some of her jewelry or her clothes for a little money and use the proceeds to buy poultry or meat, and cook it and prevent her children from touching it for fear of what will happen to her if it is not enough for them. Sometimes a peasant will raise chickens and eat none of them and make himself and his children go without for fear of being beaten or imprisoned, and things such as chickens and butter and flour he will keep aside in readiness for this disaster, doing his own cooking with sesame oil and eating barley bread, and he may put his seed wheat aside for them and eat salty cottage cheese and put himself to the expense of buying sweet fresh cheese and send this with the *wajbah*, all for fear of what may happen to him because of these matters. 11.3.9

It is called *wajbah* because it has come to be like a duty (*wājib*) that the tax farmers impose on the peasants, for it has to be done for the bailiff in the village or the Christian or the tax farmer, if he comes, as stated above. While some tax farmers have waived it, they have replaced it with an agreed sum of money and added that to the land tax, forcing them to pay it to the bailiff in the 11.3.10

أسقطها بعض الملتزمين جعل في مقابلها شيئاً معلوماً من الدراهم وأضافه إلى المال ويلزمهم بدفعه إلى الشادّ بالقرية يؤخذ منهم كلّ عام فهي من أنواع الظلم والأكل منها حرام ما لم تكن من الفلاّحين عن طيب نفس وانشراح صدر بحيث أنّ الملتزم يرضيهم بشيء من الأرض أو غيرها في مقابل ذلك وبعض الملتزمين يتوقّف عنها بالكليّة ولا يجعل عليهم شيئاً لا للشادّ ولا لغيره إلّا إذا تبرّعوا بشيء من عند أنفسهم فعلى هذا لا تكون حراماً ويحِلّ الأكل منها ومثل الوجبة غرامة البطّالين واستخدامهم بغير أجرة ما لم يكن عن رضاء منهم في مقابل السكنى وترك الزرع ونحوه فكلّ ما كان فيه أضرار للناس فهو حرام قال الشاعر [بسيط]

كُنْ كَيفَ شِئْتَ فإِنَّ اللهَ ذو كرمٍ   وما عَليكَ إذا أذنبتَ مِن بَأْسِ
إلّا اثنَتَينِ فَلا تَقرَبهُما أَبداً   الشِّركُ باللهِ والإِضرارُ بالنّاسِ

١١،٣،١١ (فإن قيل) إنّ الأمير أو غيره إذا التزم بقرية وجد في دفاتر من التزم بها قبله الوجبة وغرامة البطّالين وغير ذلك ممّا هو من أنواع الظلم فيجعل ذلك على أهلها حكم الخوالي السابقة كما جرت به العادة فهل يكون الإثم عليه أو على من أحدث هذا قبله أو عليهما معاً (الجواب) ورد في الحديث عن النبيّ صلّى الله عليه وسلّم أنه مَنْ أحدث في أمرنا هذا ما ليس فيه فهو رَدّ أي من أتى بشيء لم يكن موجوداً في زمن النبيّ صلّى الله عليه وسلّم وهو المسمّى بالبدعة فهو ردّ أي مردود ومعناه باطل لا يُقتَدى به وفيه بيان على أنّه لا فرق بين أن يكون أحدثه بنفسه أو سبقه به غيره فالإثم على كلّ من فعله أو أمر بفعله إذ كلّ فعل لم يكن على أمر الشرع ففاعله آثم لقوله صلّى الله عليه وسلّم من أحدث حَدَثاً أو آوى مُحْدِثاً فعليه لعنة الله وفيما تناوله الحديث ردّ على ذوي

village, the money being taken from them annually. It is a form of injustice, and eating such food is forbidden by religion so long as the peasants do not give it of their own free will and cheerfully,[165] the tax farmer keeping them happy by granting them a little land or something else in return. Some tax farmers have given it up altogether and impose nothing on them, neither for the bailiff nor anyone else, although they may volunteer something of their own free will. In that case, it is not forbidden and it is permitted to eat it. Similar to the *wajbah* is the fine imposed on the landless and putting them to work without pay, as long as this is without their consent, in return for covering their lodging and compensation for leaving their crops and so on. Anything that involves injury to others is forbidden. The poet says:

Be as you wish, for God is kind—
No harm shall befall you if you sin.
Two things alone you must eschew in full—
Ascribing partners to God[166] and doing injury to men.

If it be said, "If an emir, or someone else, on assuming the right to farm the taxes of a village, finds the *wajbah* or the fine on the landless or any other form of injustice on the ledgers of those who held the tax farm before him and so imposes that on the people of the village as was done under earlier determinations by the surveyors according to established custom, is the sin then his or that of the person who introduced the practice before him, or both of theirs together?" the answer is to be found in the Tradition of the Prophet, upon whom blessings and peace, that says, "He who introduces into this affair of ours that which is not in it is rejected," meaning, whoever introduces something that was not present in the time of the Prophet, upon whom blessings and peace—such things being called "innovation"—is rejected, that is, refused, meaning invalid and not to be taken as an example. This shows clearly that there is no difference between someone's introducing the practice himself and someone else having preceded him in this. Thus the sin pertains to everyone who acts in accordance with this practice or orders others to act in accordance with it, for everyone who performs an act that is not stipulated by the Law is a sinner, as stated in the words of the Prophet, blessings and peace upon him, "He who introduces into it an innovation or provides accommodation for an innovator, upon him be the curse of God." The substance of the Tradition constitutes a response to those whose minds are corrupt and to government 11.3.11

العقول الفاسدة والحكم مع الجهل والجور ونحو ذلك ممّا لا يوافق الشرع فاتّضح الجواب وبان الصواب

وفي قوله (تجي الوجبه) نوع من أنواع البديع يسمّى التوزيع وهو أن يوزّع الشاعر حرفاً من حروف الهجاء في كلّ كلمة من ألفاظ البيت أو غالبه كقول الصَفيّ الحِلّيّ رحمه الله في بديعيّته [بسيط] ١٢،٣،١١

مُحمّدُ المُصطفى المُختارُ مَنْ خُتِمَتْ   بِمَجْدِهِ مُرْسَلو الرحمٰن للأُمَمِ

فإنّه كرّر حرف الميم في جميع كلمات البيت والناظم حُكِمَ له حرف الجيم في كلمتين فقط

(ويقرب من هذا المعنى) ما اتّفق أنّ رجلاً قلاّء سمك كان يهوى امراة جميلة وكان له غلام صغير في غاية من الحذق والفصاحة فأرسله يوماً إليها لتأتي إلى محلّه فذهب الغلام حتّى أتى محلّها وأخبرها أنّ معلّمه يريدها فامتثلت الأمر وأرادت الذهاب معه فحضر زوجها في ذلك الوقت فتنكّر الغلام ومضى ولم يشعر به أحد حتّى أتى إلى معلّمه فرآه يقلي السمك على جاري عادته والناس حوله يطلبوا منه فابتدره بكلام مقفّى موزون يفهّمه فيه القضيّة ويعمّي فيه على الحاضرين فقال (يا معلّمي فق لي من ذا السمك فاقلي جات تجي فجا لو لم يجي لجت ولكن ترتجي لمّا يروح تجي) ١٣،٣،١١

(وتفسير) هذه الكلمات أنّ قوله (يا معلّمي فق لي) أي تنبّه لقولي واستمع له وافهمه ١٤،٣،١١

accompanied by ignorance, oppression, and other things of the same sort that are not in accordance with the Law. Thus the answer now is clear, the truth made to appear.

The poet's words *tajī l-wajbah* contain an elegant literary device called "distribution," which consists of the poet's "distributing" one of the letters of the alphabet in each, or most of, the words of a line of verse, as in the following verse by al-Ṣafī al-Ḥillī, may God have mercy on him, from his *Embellished Ode in the Prophet's Praise* (*Al-Badīʿiyyah*):[167] 11.3.12

Muḥammadu l-muṣṭafā l-mukhtāru man khutimat
Bi-majdihī mursalū l-raḥmāni li-l-umamī

Muḥammad, the Named, the Nominated,
With whose majesty the messengers of the Merciful to men were made complete

—where he repeats the letter *m* in every word of the line. Our poet managed to work the letter *j* into just two words.

In the same vein is what happened once concerning a man who was a fryer of fish by trade. He was in love with a beautiful woman and had a young servant boy who was extremely quick-witted and a master of correct speech. One day he sent this boy to her to ask her to come to his home. The boy went to her home and told her that his boss wanted her. She accepted and was about to set off with him when her husband turned up. The boy made himself inconspicuous, took off without anyone noticing him, and made his way back to his boss, whom he found frying fish, as was his wont, with people all around him placing their orders. So as to make the man understand the situation while concealing it from those present the boy accosted him with words rhymed and metered. He said to him, *Yā muʿallimī fuq lī, min dha l-samak fa-qlī. Jat tajī fa-jā. Law lam yajī la-jat. Wa-lākin tartajī lammā yarūḥ tajī* ("Boss, hear my cry! Of this fish now fry! She was going to come, but he came. Had he not come, she would have come. But she hopes, when he goes, to come"). 11.3.13

These words are to be explained as follows: 11.3.14

yā muʿallimī fuq lī ("Boss, hear my cry!"): that is, "Boss, hearken to what I say, and listen well to it and understand it!"

(من ذا السمك فاقلي) أتى بهذا الكلام ليوهم الحاضرين أنّه يريد شيئاً من السمك أو أنّه ١٥،٣،١١
يطلب منه سرعة قليه وبيّن قوله (فق لي) و(فاقلي) الجناس المحرّف المزيد وقوله

(جات تجي) أي أرادت المجيء وامتثلت الأمر ١٦،٣،١١

(فجا) أي زوجها في وقت الإرادة للذهاب ثمّ قال ١٧،٣،١١

(لو لم يجي) أي زوجها ١٨،٣،١١

(لجت) أصله لجاءت سهّله للضرورة أي لحضرت إليك ولم تخالف أمرك ثمّ ١٩،٣،١١
استدرك الكلام بقوله

(ولكن ترتجي) أي حضورها من الرجاء وهو حصول الشيء على وفق إرادة الطالب ٢٠،٣،١١

(لمّا يروح) زوجها ويخلو مكانها ٢١،٣،١١

(تجي) إليك ويحصل المطلوب والشاهد في قوله جات تجي فجا إلى آخره فإنّه كرّر حرف ٢٢،٣،١١
الجيم في كلّ كلمة كما لا يخفى

(فإن قيل) إنّ النصرانيّ إذا نزل قرية لقبض مالها يحضر إليه الفلاّحون ويكرموه ٢٣،٣،١١
ويرسلوا له الوجبة ويتذلّلوا بين يديه ويطيعوا أمره ونهيه بل يكون غالبهم في خدمته
هل هذا حرام عليهم لتعظيمهم له وهل يكونوا آثمين بذلك أم كيف الحال (قلنا) الجواب
أنّ خدمة المسلم للكافر حرام وكذلك تعظيمه والخضوع له والتذلّل بين يديه ويكون
الفاعل آثماً بذلك ما لم يَخَفْ منه ضرراً أو أذيّة بأن يكون حاكماً عليه ومتولّي أمره

min dha l-samak fa-qlī ("Of this fish now fry!"): he came up with these words to make the people around think that he wanted a portion of fish or that he was asking him to hurry up with the frying (note the "augmentative consonantal paronomasia" between the words *fuq lī* ("hear my cry") and *fa-qlī* ("now fry")!).[168] 11.3.15

jat tajī ("She was about to come"): that is, she wanted to come and obey your summons 11.3.16

fa-jā ("but he came"): that is, her husband, at the moment that she wanted to go; then he said 11.3.17

law lam yajī ("Had he not come"): that is, her husband, 11.3.18

la-jat ("she would have come"), which is originally *la-jā'at*, which the boy elided for the meter; that is, she would have presented herself and not disobeyed your order. He continues by saying: 11.3.19

wa-lākin tartajī ("But she hopes"): that is, her coming will be in accordance with her hope (*rajā'*), which means the occurrence of a thing agreeably to the will of the one who requests it 11.3.20

lamma yarūḥ ("when he goes"), meaning her husband, and leaves the place free 11.3.21

tajī (ilayk) ("to come (to you)"); and what you want will come to pass. The relevant citation lies in his words *jat tajī fa-jā*, etc., for he repeats the letter *j* in every word, as you can see. 11.3.22

If it be asked, "Is it forbidden by religion for the peasants to honor the Christian by coming and entertaining him and sending him the *wajbah* when he comes to a village to collect its taxes, abasing themselves in front of him and obeying his every command and prohibition, most of them indeed being at his service, and are they sinning in so doing, or what is the situation?" we reply, "The response is that a Muslim is forbidden to serve an infidel, just as he is forbidden to honor him, submit to him, or abase himself before him, and the one who does so sins in that respect, unless he does so out of fear of some harm or injury from him as a result of the infidel's being set in authority over him and given charge of his affairs, or is compelled to have recourse to him in a matter such as the Christian's collection of taxes in the villages of the countryside 11.3.23

واضطرّ إليه في أمر كِبَاض المال من النصارى في بلاد الأرياف وغيرهم فإنّهم مالكون هذا الأمر بل إنّ بعض الملتزمين يولّي النصرانيّ أمر القرية فيحكم فيها بالضرب والحبس وغير ذلك فلا يأتيه الفلاح إلّا وهو يرتعد من شدّة الخوف

٢٤،٣،١١ (كما اتّفق أنّ في زمن الأستاذ العارف بالله تعالى الشيخ تقيّ الدين بن دقيق العيد) نفعنا الله به ولّى السلطان شخصاً من النصارى على إقليم مصر كلّه يقبض ماله فكان ينزل إلى الإقليم في موكب عظيم من الخدم والحشم ويمرّ على البلاد يقبض أموالها وهو راكب على فرسه ولا ينزل إلّا لضرورة الأكل والشرب والمبيت من شدّة أذيّته وقوّة ضرره وكان لفرسه رِكاباً من الفولاد مطليّ بالذهب وقد جعل فيه سَفُّوتَيْنِ من الحديد خارجين إلى الخلاء قدر شِبْر ثمّ يرسل خلف الرجل فلا يأتيه إلّا وهو يرتعد من شدّة الخوف فيقف بجانب فرسه وهو راكب فيغلظ عليه بالكلام القبيح ويقول له ادفع ما عليك من المال في هذه الساعة فإن أجاب وإلّا ضربه بالسفُّوتَيْن فيجرحه أو يخرق أجنابه فيموت وكان هذا دأبه مع المسلمين لعنة الله عليه فاتّفق أنّه طلع إلى قرية الشيخ ابن دقيق العيد رحمه الله وأرسل خلف رجل من أتباعه عليه بقيّة مال من خراج أرض يزرعها فلمّا حضر إليه قال له ادفع ما عليك فقال الرجل أمهلني بقيّة النهار فأراد أن يحرّك الركاب ويضربه بتلك السفافيت يقتله فولّى هارباً والنصرانيّ يتبعه على الأثر إلى أن ألقى بنفسه بين يدي الشيخ وهو يحرق في قَمِين جير لأنّها كانت صنعة الشيخ في ابتداء أمره فقال له ما الخبر فقصّ عليه الأمر فلم يشعر إلّا والنصراني واقف على رأسه فقال له الشيخ أمهله بقيّة النهار فأغلظ على الشيخ بالكلام فأخذ الشيخ الغضب والغيرة على المسلمين وقام إليه وجذبه من أطواقه فبقي في يده كالعصفور وقال له يا ملعون الأبعد طال عمرك واشتدّ ضررك على المسلمين والآن قد زال اسمك وانمحى رسمك ثمّ اتّكأ عليه حتّى قصف ظهره

and elsewhere, for they monopolize this business; indeed, some tax farmers hand control of everything to do with the village to the Christian, who rules it through beating and imprisonment and the like, so that the peasants are so frightened that they never come before him without trembling.

"As it happened in the days of the Master and Initiate of the Almighty, Shaykh Taqī al-Dīn Ibn Daqīq al-ʿĪd, God benefit us through him, when the sultan handed over control of the entire province of Egypt to a certain Christian for the collection of taxes. The latter used to visit the province with a great procession of servants and retainers and pass through the settlements collecting their taxes. He would ride his horse and dismount only when he had to eat and drink and stop for the night, so evil was he and so great the harm he brought. His horse had stirrups of steel plated with gold, to which he had attached two iron spikes that projected about a hand's breadth. He would summon someone and the man would come, trembling with fright, and stand next to his horse, while the Christian, from the back of his horse, would speak roughly and brutally to him, telling him, 'Pay the taxes you owe this minute!' If the man did as he was told that was that, but if he did not he would strike him with the spikes, stabbing him or slashing his sides, so that he died. Such was his way with Muslims, God's curse upon him! It happened that this same Christian went to the village of Shaykh Ibn Daqīq al-ʿĪd, God have mercy upon him, and summoned one of the shaykh's followers who had a balance to pay on the tax on land that he cultivated. When the man came before him, he said to him, 'Pay what you owe!' but the man replied, 'Give me till the end of the day.' The Christian was about to put his stirrups to work and strike him with the spikes and kill him when the man turned and fled, the Christian in hot pursuit, until he came to the shaykh and threw himself down before him. The shaykh, who at the time was burning lime in a kiln (for that was his profession when he was young), asked what was the matter and the man told him the story. Before he knew what was happening, the Christian was towering over him. 'Give him till the end of the day!' the shaykh told him. However, the Christian replied to the shaykh with angry words, at which the shaykh became filled with fury and zeal for the defense of the Muslims and attacked him, grabbing him by the neck of his garments, so that he became like a sparrow in the shaykh's hand. Then he said to him, 'Accursed wretch! Your life has been long and the harm you do to the Muslims has become excessive. Now your name is expunged and every trace of you obliterated!' and he bore down on him until his back 11.3.24

وألقاه في تنّور القمين فانحرق ثمّ نظر إلى جماعته نظرة الغضب فألقى الله الرعب في قلوبهم فولّوا الأدبار حتّى وصلوا إلى السلطان وأخبروه بالقضيّة فاشتدّ به الغضب وأرسل خلف الشيخ فسار إليه حتّى طلع الديوان فلمّا مثل بين يديه قال له ما حملك على حرق النصرانيّ فقال له الشيخ وأنت ما حملك على أن تولّيه على المسلمين وتأمره بأذيّتهم فزاد به الغيظ وأراد أن يَبْطِش بالشيخ فأشار الشيخ إلى الكرسيّ الذي هو جالس عليه فتحرّك من تحته فانكبّ إلى الأرض مغشياً عليه وصار للكرسيّ دَوَرَان وطَنِين في القلعة ودَوِيّ كالرعد وهاجت العسكر في بعضهم البعض وارتجّت القلعة بمن فيها من الجند فصاحوا الأمان الأمان فأشار الشيخ بيده فرجع كلّ شيء إلى حاله ثمّ أشار إلى الملك فصَحِي من غشوته فلمّا أفاق قبّل يديه وقال له العفو يا سيّدي تَمَنَّ عليّ ما تريد فقال له لا أريد منك شيئاً غير أنّك لا تولّي أحداً من النصارى على المسلمين وإلّا هلكت فقال السمع والطاعة ثمّ إنّ الشيخ نزل من عنده على غاية من الكرامة والمحبّة وسار إلى قريته ولم يزل هذا الأمر منقطعاً زماناً لا يتولّى أحد من النصارى أمر المسلمين في قبض المال ولا غيره إلى أن احتاجوا إليهم الحكّام لِحذْقهم وصحّة عقولهم في الحساب فولّوهم هذا الأمر إلى زماننا هذا وكذلك اليهود تعاطوا علم الطبّ حتّى يتصرّفوا الفريقين في الأموال والأرواح ولله درّ القائل حيث قال[كامل]

لُعِنَ النَّصارَى واليَهُودُ جَمِيعُهُمْ   نَالُوا بِمَكْرِ مِنهُمُ الآمالا
جُعِلُوا أَطِبّاءَ وحُسّاباً لِكَي   يَتَقاسَمُوا الأَرْواحَ والأَمْوالا

٢٥،٣،١١ فعلى هذا يجوز للشخص معاشرتهم والخضوع لهم إذا خشي على نفسه أو عياله ضرراً منهم في أمر دينيّ أو دنيويّ يتوقّف على ذلك وقد اضطرّ إليه فلا بأس

snapped and he threw him into the oven of the kiln, where he was consumed. Then he directed a look of fury at the men who were with the Christian and God cast terror into their hearts and they turned and ran till they reached the sultan and told him of the matter. Incensed, the latter sent for the shaykh, who proceeded until he reached the audience chamber. When he presented himself before him, the sultan said to him, 'What drove you to burn the Christian?' 'And what,' replied the shaykh, 'drove you to put him in authority over the Muslims and order him to do them harm?' At this the sultan's fury increased, and he was about to strike the shaykh a blow on the head, when the shaykh made a sign to the chair on which the sultan was seated and it moved beneath him and he was spilled onto the ground in a swoon, and the chair itself started to spin through the Citadel with a humming sound, rumbling like thunder. The soldiers leapt up in confusion and the Citadel with all the troops that were in it shook, while they cried, 'Spare us! Spare us!' Then the shaykh made a sign with his hand, and everything returned to its place, after which he gestured towards the king, who awoke from his swoon and, when he had revived, kissed the shaykh's hands and said to him, 'Pardon, My Master! Ask of me what you will!' The shaykh replied, 'All I want from you is that you never again set a Christian in authority over the Muslims. Should you do so, you will perish.' 'I hear and obey!' said the sultan. Then the shaykh descended from his presence, to the accompaniment of the utmost honor and love, and proceeded to his village. Thereafter, this practice remained in abeyance for a while, and no Christian was set in authority over the Muslims with regard to the collection of taxes or other matters, until the rulers were forced to have recourse to them for their acuteness and talent for accounting; so they put them in charge of these matters up to our day. Similarly, the Jews have taken over the practice of medical science, so that the two groups have come to hold sway over our money and our lives. How well the poet put it when he said:

A curse on both Christians and Jews!
They've got what they wanted by stealth:
They've made themselves doctors and clerks
To divide up our lives and our wealth!

"Thus one is permitted to associate with them and obey them if he fears that **11.3.25**
they might harm him or his dependents in any matter, religious or secular, that depends on such contact and that he is compelled to undertake. Under such

باستصحابهم من هذا القبيل وقد عوقب سيّدي عبد العزيز الديرينيّ نفعنا الله به بسبب تردّده على نصرانيّ بلدته فقال [طويل]

يَلومونَني في عِشرَةِ القُبطِ خُلَّتي   فواللهِ طُولُ الدَّهرِ ما حَبَّهُم قَلبي
ولكنَّني صيّادُ رِزقٍ بأرضهِمْ   ولا بدّ للصَّيّادِ مِن عِشرَةِ الكَلبِ

وأمّا إذا داخلهم الإنسان بالمحبّة والصحبة لا لغرض دنيويّ قد اضطرّ إليه ولا لخوف ضرر منهم فربّما دخل في ضمن قوله صلّى الله عليه وسلّم من أحبّ قوماً حُشِرَ معهم وقوله

(عليّ) يريد نفسه لا غيره ٢٦،٣،١١

(يحيف) أي يميل عليّ ويظلمني ويكلّفني ما لا أطيق فكان عليه هذا الضرر أشدّ ٢٧،٣،١١
من غيره الذي هو أذيّة القمل والصيبان ونحوهما كما تقدّم لكونه ناشئاً من الأقارب قال الشاعر [وافر]

أَقارِبُ كالعَقارِبِ فاجْتَنِبْهُمْ   ولا تَرْكَنْ إلى عَمٍّ وخالِ
فَكَمْ عَمٍّ أَتاكَ الغَمُّ مِنْهُ   وَكَمْ خالٍ مِنَ الخَيْراتِ خالِ

(فانظر) إلى هذا الشاعر اللبيب كيف أتى بالعمّ والخال وصحّف الأوّل بالغمّ واستخدم لفظ الثاني في كونه خالي من الخيرات وحكّم فيه الجناس وتورية اللفظ وقال بعضهم [رجز]

عَداوَةُ الأَهْلِ ذَوِي القَرابَهْ   كالنّارِ يومَ الرِّيحِ وَسْطَ غابَهْ

(وقال) عليّ كرّم الله وجهه العداوة في الأهل والحسد في الجيران والمودّة في ٢٨،٣،١١
الإخوان وأصل عداوة الأهل من قصّة قابيل لمّا قتل هابيل فصارت العداوة

circumstances, there is no harm in making friends with them. Master ʿAbd al-ʿAzīz al-Dīrīnī, God benefit us through him, was punished for frequenting the Christian of his village, and he said:

They blame me, my friends, for befriending Copts,
Though never, by God, did I love them in my heart!
But I'm one of those who hunts for his living in their land,
And hunter and dogs cannot live apart!

"On the other hand, the person who has intercourse with them on the basis of affection and friendship for no compelling worldly objective or fear of any harm that they might do should probably be counted among those referred to in the words of the Prophet, may God bless him and give him peace, 'He who loves a people shall be marshaled with them on the Day of Judgment.'"

ʿalayya ("to me"): meaning to himself and no other. **11.3.26**

yaḥīf ("he does wrong (to me)"): that is, he turns against me and treats me unjustly, charging me with more than I can bear. This injury was more severe for him than the others, namely, the previously described harm caused by the lice and the nits and so on, because it originated with his relatives. The poet says: **11.3.27**

Relatives (*aqārib*) are like scorpions (*ʿaqārib*), so avoid them,
And depend not on father's or mother's brothers.
How many of the first will bring you grief
And how devoid of good are the others!

Observe how this clever poet used *ʿamm* ("father's brother") and *khāl* ("mother's brother"), changing the letters on the first to make it into *ghamm* ("grief") and employing the second to mean that they are "devoid" (*khālī*) of boons, and how he managed to work in both paronomasia and punning.[168]

Another poet said:

The enmity of kith and kin
Is like a fire in a forest when there's wind.

ʿAlī,[170] God honor his face, said, "Enmity is among relatives, envy among neighbors, and affection among brothers." The origin of the enmity among relatives is to be found in the story of Qābīl's murdering Hābīl,[171] as a result **11.3.28**

بين الإخوة والأقارب إلى زماننا هذا ومنشأ هذا كلّه الحسد فالحسود لا يسود (وفي الحديث) لا حسد إلّا في اثنتين رجل آتاه الله مالاً فسلّطه على هَلَكَتِهِ في الخير ورجل آتاه الله عِلماً فهو يعلّمه الناس وقال الشاعر [بسيط]

إنْ يَحْسُدُوني فَإنّي غَيْرُ لائِمِهِمْ   قَبْلي مِنَ النّاسِ أَهلُ الفَضْلِ قد حُسِدُوا
فَدامَ لِي ولَهُمْ ما بِي وَما بِهِمُ   وَماتَ أَكْثَرُنا غَيْظاً بِما يَجِدُ

وقال آخر [سريع]

لا ماتَ أَعْداؤُكَ بَلْ خُلِّدُوا   حَتّى يَرَوا مِنْكَ الّذي يُكْمِدُ
وَلا خَلاكَ الدّهْرُ مِنْ حاسِدٍ   فَإنَّ خَيْرَ النّاسِ مَنْ يُحْسَدُ

٢٩،٣،١١ ثمّ إنّ الناظم انتقل من شكوى ابن عمّه محيلبه إلى شكواه من ابن أخيه خنافر لكونه أيشم عليه من ابن عمّه فقال

ص

٤،١١ وَأَيْشَمْ مِنُو إِبْنْ اَخُوهْ خَنافِرْ   يُقَرِّطْ عَلَى بَيْضِي بِخُلْبَةْ لِيفْ

ش

١،٤،١١ قوله (وأيشم) من الشؤم أو من التيشمة وأصله أشأم على وزن أبلم أو أقطم وفي المثل أشأم من طُوَيْس ويقال فلان ميشوم وذو تيشمة أي عنده قوّة وتجبّر وشدّة ظلم وسمّي

of which enmity among brethren and relatives has continued down to these days of ours, the root cause of it all being envy—and "may the envious not prevail!"[172] In the Tradition it says, "Two alone are to be envied: a man on whom God bestows wealth and who uses it to defeat his perdition through good works, and a man on whom God bestows knowledge and who instructs others in it." The poet says:

Though they envy me, I blame them not—
　Good men before me have felt the evil eye.
Let me keep mine and them keep theirs,
　And he who is the more vexed by what he finds can die!

And another said:

May your enemies not die but live
　Till you have had the chance to make them livid,
And may Fate not deprive you of an envier,
　For the best are those who've been envied!

Next the poet moves on from complaining about his paternal cousin Muḥaylibah to complaining about the latter's nephew Khanāfir, who brings him even more trouble than his cousin. He says: 11.3.29

TEXT

wa-ʾayshamu minnū ʾibnu-khūhu Khanāfir 11.4
　yuqarriṭ ʿalā bayḍī bi-khulbat līf

And more inauspicious than him is the son of his brother Khanāfir.
　He draws tight around my balls a palm-fiber knot

COMMENTARY

wa-ʾayshamu ("and more inauspicious"): from *shuʾm* ("calamity") or from *tayshimah*.[173] The word is originally *ashʾam*,[174] on the pattern of *ablam* ("more/most stupid") or *aqṭam* ("more/most given to passive sodomy"). The proverb says, "More of a jinx (*ashʾam*) than Ṭuways,"[175] and one says, "So-and-so is *mayshūm* ('possessed of the power to jinx')" or *dhū tayshimah*, that is, possessed of strength and tyrannical powers and capable of doing great harm 11.4.1

الخشب الشُوم شوماً لقوّته وصلابته والعرب تهجو بالشؤم واللؤم

(قيل) بنى جعفر البرمكيّ قصراً بديعاً وزخرفه بأنواع الحرير وغير ذلك وجلس فيه أيّاماً فبينما هو ينظر يوماً من شبّاك له إذ نظر إلى أعرابيّ يكتب على جداره بيتين من الشعر وهما [بسيط] ٢،٤،١١

يا قصرَ جعفرَ علاكَ الشومُ واللومُ　　حتّى يُعشِّشَ في أركانِكَ البُومُ
إذا يُعشِّشُ ذاكَ البُومُ من فَرَحي　　أكونُ أوّلَ مَنْ يَنعاكَ مَرغومُ

فقال عليّ بهذا الأعرابيّ فلمّا حضر بين يديه قال له ما حملك على ما فعلت وما سبب دعاءك على قصرنا بالخراب فقال له حملني على ذلك الفقر والفاقة وصِبيَةٌ خلّفتُها كأفراخ القَطا يتعاوون من ألم الجوع وجئت لأستمطر إحسانك وأرجو نوالك فمكثت شهراً على باب هذا القصر لا أتمكّن من الدخول إليك فلمّا أيست دعوت عليه بالخراب وقلت ما دام عامراً لا يفيدني منه شيء فإذا خرب ربّما أمرّ به فآخذ منه خشبة أو شيئاً من زخارفه فأنتفع به قال فتبسّم جعفر وقال عدم علمنا بك قد أطال وقوفك وأضرّ بعيالك أعطوه ألف دينار لقصده إيّانا وألف دينار لطول مكثه على باب دارنا وألف دينار لدعائه على قصرنا بالخراب وألف دينار لِحِلمنا عليه وألف دينار لصبية خلفها كأفراخ القطا فأخذ الأعرابيّ الخمسة آلاف دينار وارتدّ شاكراً

وقوله (منّو) بتشديد النون للضرورة أي أشدّ وأقوى منه في الضرر عليّ والظلم لي ٣،٤،١١

(إبن آخوه) أي أخو محيلبه شقيقه وكان الأَولى جرّه على الإضافة ولكن لم يساعده لسانه على هذا الوضع لكونه من أهل الريف ٤،٤،١١

to others. *Shūm* wood[176] is so called because of its strength and hardness. The Arabs use "jinxing and infamy" (*al-shu'm wa-l-lu'm*) in their flytings.

It is said that Ja'far al-Barmakī built a magnificent palace and embellished it with all kinds of silks and so on and stayed there some days. Gazing one day through one of its windows, he beheld a Bedouin writing on the wall of the palace two lines of verse, as follows: 11.4.2

Palace of Ja'far, may ill fortune and infamy engulf you,
Till the owls in your corners make their nest!
When the owls nest there, from sheer delight,
I'll be the first to offer condolences, if under protest![177]

—so Ja'far said, "Bring me that Bedouin!" When the man was in front of him, he asked him, "What has driven you to do as you have done, and what has made you call down ruin upon our palace?" The man told him, "Poverty and need have driven me to it, and a brood of young lads that I have sired, like the chicks of the sandgrouse,[178] that whimper from the pangs of hunger. I came to beseech your charity and plead for your favor and I have dwelt a month at the gate of this palace, unable to come in to you. When I despaired, I called ruin down upon it and said, 'So long as it remains prosperous, I shall benefit nothing by it. But if it turns to ruins, I may pass by and take from it a piece of wood or some of its embellishments that I can make use of.'" Ja'far smiled and said, "Our ignorance of your presence has prolonged your waiting and caused harm to your children. Give him a thousand dinars for seeking us out, and a thousand dinars for dwelling so long at our gate, and a thousand dinars for calling ruin down upon our palace, and a thousand dinars for our clemency towards him, and a thousand dinars for a brood of young lads that he has sired, like the chicks of the sandgrouse!" And the Bedouin took the five thousand dinars and retired, giving thanks.

minnū ("than he"): with double *n*, for the meter;[179] that is, "stronger and more extreme than him" in the harm he does me and his oppression of me. 11.4.3

'ibnu-khūhu ("is the son of his brother"): that is, of the brother of Muḥaylibah, the latter being his brother on both his mother's and his father's side. He should have said *akhīhi*, as a genitive construct, but his tongue gave him no help in producing such a form because he was from the countryside, and it would have broken the meter, too.[180] 11.4.4

ثمّ بيّن اسمه بقوله (خَنافِر) مشتقّ من الخنفرة على وزن الخرخرة أو البربرة يقال رقد فلان وخنفر بمعنى أنّه ردّد النَفَس في حَلْقه وأخرجه من خياشيمه حتّى صار نفساً عالياً بخنفرة وبربرة قال الشاعر [طويل] ٥،٤،١١

وَخَنْفَرَ عِنْدَ النَّوْمِ مِنْ خَيْشومِـهِ   فَصارَ بِهذا الإِسْمِ يُدْعَى خَنافِرا

وسمّي بذلك لكثرة خنفرته عند النوم ومصدره خنفر يخنفر خنفرةً فهو خَنْفور على وزن خَنْشور وخَنافر على وزن عَباير واحدتها عبورة وأمّا أخوه فاسمه قادوس على وزن بَعْبُوص وقادوس هذا خلّف ولدين محيلبه وفساقل وخنافر هذا ابنه فكان ضرر الناظم من ابن عمّه وابن أخي ابن عمّه

ثمّ بيّن الضرر الحاصل منه بقوله (يقرّط) بضمّ المثنّاة من تحت على وزن يضرّط ويضرط فيها لغتان كما تقدّم قال الشاعر [وافر] ٦،٤،١١

فَفِيها ضَرَطَ الواشُون جَمْعاً   فَصارَ ضُراطُهُمْ فيها يَفوحُ

وهو هنا بمعنى التقريط بالحبل بشدّة وقوّة وأمّا القَرْط بفتح القاف وجزم الراء فهو قرط الزرع وهو أخذ سنبله وإبقاء أصله في أرضه يقال فلان قرط زرع فلان وبضمّ القاف اسم لحَلَقة صغيرة من لُجَيْن أو فضّة تُعْمَل في أذن الصبيّ وهي ممدوحة خصوصاً الولد الجميل فإنّها تزيده حسناً وتكسوه حلاوة قال أبو نواس في مطلع قصيدة له [كامل]

وَمُقَرْطَقٍ يَسْعَى إلى النُّدَماءِ   بِعَقِيقَةٍ في دُرَّةٍ بَيْضاءِ

Next he states his nephew's name, by saying 11.4.5

Khanāfir: derived from *khanfarah* ("snoring") of the measure of *kharkharah* ("snorting") or *barbarah* ("jabbering"). One says, "So-and-so slept and snored (*khanfar*)," meaning that he stored up the breath in his throat and expelled it through his nostrils in such a way as to make a loud breath accompanied with snoring and snorting. Said the poet:

He snored on sleeping through his nostril
And thus he got this name—Khanāfir.

He was so called because he snored so much when sleeping. The paradigm is *khanfara, yukhanfiru, khanfaratan*, active participle *khanfūr*,[181] of the measure of *khanshūr* ("tough guy"), while Khanāfir is of the measure of *ʿabāyir*, plural of *ʿabūrah* ("sheep"). His brother's[182] name was Qādūs ("waterwheel jar"), of the pattern of *buʿbūṣ* ("goosing"); this Qādūs fathered two boys, Muḥaylibah and Fasāqil, and this Khanāfir was the latter's son, meaning the poet suffered harm from both his paternal cousin[183] and his paternal cousin's son.[184]

Next the poet makes plain the harm that he suffered from the latter by saying: 11.4.6
yuqarriṭ ("he draws tight"): with *u* after the *y*, of the measure of *yuḍarriṭ* ("he farts audibly and repeatedly").[185] *Yuḍarriṭ* has two forms, as already stated.[186]

As the poet has it:

There the snitches all farted together,
So their farts wafted everywhere about.

The word *yuqarriṭ* is used here in the sense of constricting (*taqrīṭ*) strongly and forcibly with a rope. *Qarṭ* with *a* after the *q* and no vowel after the *r* refers to the *qarṭ* of the crops, namely, taking the ears and leaving the roots in the ground. One says, "So-and-so cut off the ears of so-and-so's crop (*qaraṭa zarʿa fulān*)." With *u* after the *q*, it is the name of a small ring of silver that is put in the ear of a young boy—a praiseworthy custom, especially if the boy is beautiful, for it adds to his good looks and clothes him in cuteness. Abū Nuwās[187] says in the opening line of one of his odes:

An earringed[188] boy who hastens to the drinking companions
With a carnelian in a white pearl

أي إنّ هذا الجمال اللطيف والشكل الظريف الذي زانه هذا القرط واتّصف به صار يسعى على الندماء وبيده خمرة تشبه العقيق في لونها وهي في كأس يشبه الدرّة البيضاء من صفاء جوهره ولطف ذاته ويسقيهم ممّا في يده ويدير عليهم المدام ويلاطفهم برشاقة القدّ وحسن الكلام إلى آخر ما قال

١١،٤،٧ وقوله (على بيضي) أي بيض الناظم لا بيض المتكلّم ولا بيض غيره من الدجاج والطيور ونحو ذلك وسمّي بيضاً لشبهه بالبيض إذا انسلخ عنه الجلد وهو مشتقّ من البياض أو من أبو بيوض حيوان يشبه العنكبوت أو من بيضة القبّان

١١،٤،٨ (مسألة هباليّة) ما الحكمة في تسمية البيض بالخصيتين وما مشابهة الخصيّ لهما في الاسم وما اشتقاقهما وما معنى ذلك (الجواب الفشرويّ) وهو أنّ الخصيتين واحدتهما خِصْية بكسر الياء المعجمة وكذلك مثنّى الخِصا خِصْوَان واحدهما خِصي فإذا أخذت الخصي مثلاً وأضفت إليه آخر صرت آخذاً خِصْوَيْن بلا خلاف فافهم ذلك وقد يقال له خِصْو بالواو بدل الألف وهو اسم للذكر وهو في حكم الأب للخصيتين لأنّه لا يفارقهما وهما في حكم البنتين له فاشْتُقّ من اسم الفرع لعدم انفكاكه عنه ولهذا أنّ الخصيتين دائماً في مقام الخضوع للذكر وهو في مقام الرفعة عليهما وهما في مقام التدلّي وهو في مقام الترقّي وهما أيضاً في مقام الإضافة وهو في مقام الرفع والنصب وأيضاً له قوّة في فتح الأبواب المغلقة وهجم الحصون وقرع القُبَب المسطّحة وهما واقفان له على الباب تأدّباً معه وهذا من علامة البرّ بالوالد (كما اتّفق) أنّ بعض الشعراء قصد ملكاً يستمطر إحسانه فرآه في البستان فوقف على الباب وأراد الدخول فمنعه الحارس فنظر خلف حائط البستان فرأى جَدْوَل ماء يجري وينتهي إلى محلّ تحت

—that is, this graceful beauty and charming form, adorned with and characterized by this silver earring, now hastens towards the drinking companions, with a wine in his hand whose color resembles that of a carnelian, in a cup resembling in purity of substance and refinement of form a white pearl, and gives them to drink from what is in his hand and passes the wine among them, beguiling them with his slender figure and charming talk . . . and so on to the end of the poem.

ʿalā bayḍī ("around my balls"): that is, the poet's balls, not those of the person actually reciting the verse, nor the "balls" of anything else such as a chicken, a bird, or the like.[189] Testicles are called "eggs" because they resemble them if you peel the skin off them. The word is derived from *bayāḍ* ("whiteness") or from *abū buyūḍ* ("the one with the eggs"), an animal resembling a spider,[190] or from *bayḍat al-qabbān* ("the 'egg' of the steelyard", i.e., the counterweight). 11.4.7

A Silly Topic for Discussion: What is the wisdom in *bayḍ* ("balls") also being called *khiṣyatān* ("testicles (dual)"),[191] and what points of resemblance are there between the two in name, and what is their etymology and what does it mean? The Facetious Answer is that the singular of *khiṣyatān* is *khiṣyah* with *i* after the *kh*; and likewise the dual of *khiṣā* ("testicles (plural)") is *khiṣwān*, and one of them is a *khiṣy/khaṣī*,[192] and if you were to take one *khaṣiy*, for example, and add another, you would have taken a pair of balls (*khiṣwayn*), no doubt about it! Understand this well! The same thing may also be called *khiṣw*, with *w* instead of *a*, which is also a word for the penis,[193] for the latter is like a father to the two testicles, because it never leaves them, and they are as two daughters to it; thus its name is derived from that of the subordinate entity because it is never separated from the latter. From this it follows that the two testicles are in a position of permanent submission to the male organ, while the latter is in a position of high standing over them and they likewise are in a position of dependence while it is in a position of upward mobility; and, additionally, they are in the position of annexation, while it is in the position of the elevated and erected vowels.[194] Further, the male organ has the power to open locked doors, assault fortresses, and knock at smooth domes, while the testicles politely wait for him at the entrance, which is a sign of the filial piety due to a father. In illustration of which, it once came about that a certain poet sought out a king in order to plead for his charity and found him to be in his garden. The poet stood by the gate and tried to gain entrance, but the 11.4.8

الحائط ينصبّ في فِسْقية كبيرة ورأى الملك جالس عليها فأخذ ورقة وكتب فيها هذا البيت [بسيط]

النّاسُ كُلُّهُمُ كالأَيْرِ قَدْ دَخَلوا وَالعَبْدُ مِثْلُ الخِصا مُلْقىً[١] على البابِ

ثمّ طواها ووضعها في قصبة فارسيّة وسدّ عليها بشمع وألقاها في الجدول فأخذه الماء حتّى ألقاها بين يدي الملك فتناولها وفكّ ختامها وأخرج الورقة فلمّا قرأ البيت تبسّم وناداه ادخل يا خصا فقال الشاعر هذا منك عن وسع عظيم أطال الله بقاك فانسرّ الملك لمصادفة هذه النكتة وأنعم عليه وارتدّ شاكرًا

٩،٤،١١ (قلت) وبذكر مصادفة هذه الألفاظ ذكرت ما اتّفق أنّ السلطان قانصوه الغوريّ رحمه الله غضب على إنسان وأراد قتله فشفع فيه بعض الحاضرين وعمل عليه ثلاثة آلاف دينار ونزل من عند الملك ليأتي بهم فلقيه رجل من أصدقائه وهو على سُلَّم الديوان فقال له بلغني أنّ الملك عمل عليك ألف دينار فقال لا عليّ الطلاق ثلاثة قال فلمّا سمع الملك وقوع هذه الكلمة منه واستخدامها في معنى الطلاق والدراهم عفا عنه وسامحه من الثلاثة آلاف دينار وأنعم عليه ومضى إلى حال سبيله

١٠،٤،١١ (وقد يطلق) لفظ الخصا على الذكر أيضاً ويسمّى الدُلْدُول والذَنَب والزُبّ والأَيْر والغُرْمول وغير ذلك لكنّ أشهر أسمائه خمسة وقد ذكرتها في رسالتي رياض الأنس فيما جرى بين الزُبّ والكُسّ وهي [رجز]

لي عِنْدَهُم أَسْماءُ حَقًّا تُذْكَرْ أَيْرٌ وزُبٌّ دُلْدُلٌ وذَكَرْ
وَخامِسُ الأَسْماءِ أُدْعَى بِالخِصا إذا غَضِبْتُ خِلْتَني كَما العَصا

---

١ بي: (في جميع النسخ) واقف.

guard prevented him. The poet then looked behind the wall of the garden and found a water channel running towards, and ending at a point beneath, the wall, where it debouched into a large basin, next to which he beheld the king sitting. So he took a piece of paper and wrote on it this verse:[195]

Everyone else, like a penis, has gone in,
But this slave, like the testes, is left lying at the door.

Then he folded it and put it in a Persian reed, sealed it with wax, and threw it into the channel, whence the water carried it until it cast it at the feet of the king. The king picked it up, broke the seal, and pulled out the piece of paper. When he read the verse he smiled and called out to him, "Come in, testicles!" to which the poet replied, "This is just evidence of your great capacity, God preserve you!"[196] The king was well pleased with the aptness of the joke and rewarded him, and the poet retired, giving thanks.

Apropos of the aptness of these words, I am reminded of what happened once when Sultan Qānṣawh al-Ghawrī, God have mercy upon him, got angry with a man and wanted to kill him. Some of those present interceded on his behalf, and the sultan imposed on him instead a fine of three thousand dinars. The man left the sultan's presence to get them and one of his friends, encountering him as he was descending the steps from the audience chamber, said to him, "I hear that the sultan has fined you a thousand dinars." The other replied, "No, may I be divorced—times three!"[197] When the sultan heard of this bon mot of his and how he had used the same word to cover both divorce and money, he pardoned him, forgave him the three thousand dinars, and rewarded him, and the man went his way. 11.4.9

The word *khiṣā* may also be applied to the male organ, which is also called *duldūl* ("dangler"),[198] *dhanab* ("tail"), *zubb*,[199] *ayr*,[200] *ghurmūl*,[201] and other names too. However, the best known are five, which I have mentioned in my treatise *Meadows of Intimate Vim concerning What Transpired 'twixt the Prick and the Quim*, namely: 11.4.10

They give me different names, some quite popular:
Ayr, *zubb*, *duldul*,[202] and *dhakar* there are.[203]
The fifth of these names I'm called is *khiṣā*—
When I get stiff, you'd think I was a shillelagh!

ويُلَقب بالأعْوَر والأفْطَس والسدّاد والمدّاد وهادم الحصون وفاتح البروج ويُكْنَى أبو الحملات وأبو الصَدَمات وأبو الهيازع وأبو الزلازل ونحو ذلك وإذا أُطلق الإنسان عِنانه وأطاع هواه ألقاه في أشدّ المصائب قال ابن عروس رحمه الله [مجتثّ]

النّاسُ في الله تاهُوا والأجوادُ شاعَت تَناها
ما ضرّني غيرُ بطني والّي مدلّي حداها

وقد تُشبَّه الخصيتين بالدجاجتين قال بعضهم يهجو شيخه بهذين البيتين [رجز]

يا رَبِّ زوِّلْ غمّنا يا ربّا يا ربِّ إقْبِضْ شيخنا الأَدَبّا
كأنَّ خِصيَتَيهِ إذْ أكَبّا دَجاجَتانِ يلْقُطانِ حبّا

١١،٤،١١ فالخصا بالضمّ والكسر اسم مشترك بين الذكر والخصيتين وكذلك بإبدال الألف واوًا كما تقدّم ويكون من باب تسمية الشيء بما جاوره وخِصيَتَيْن على وزن ضَرطتين أو شَخّتين فيكون فيها الضرطة والشخّة بيقين واشتقاقهما من الخُصّ بضمّ الخاء المعجمة أو من قرية تسمّى الخُصوص أو من قولهم للكلب إخْصا مثلاً ومصدرهما خصا يخصو خصاءً قال الشاعر [وافر]

خَصا يَخْصُو مَصادِرُ خِصيَتَيْنِ خِصاءٌ صَحَّ في نَظْمِ الطُنَيْنِ

انتهى الجواب عن هذه المباحث الفشرويّة والإشكلات الهباليّة وقوله

١٢،٤،١١ (بخلبة ليف) أي ربطة قويّة دائرة على بيضه مرتّين بحبل مفتول من ليف النخل سمّي بذلك لكونه ملتفًا على أصول الجريد وسمّيت هذه الربطة بالخلبة لكونها تخلِب على الشيء فلا ينفكّ منها إلّا بعسر وفي اصطلاح الرُعيان أنّهم إذا أرادوا ربط شيء

It is given the nicknames the One-Eyed, the Snub-Nosed, the Plugger, the Extender, and the Demolisher of Donjons and Conqueror of Castles, along with the *kunyahs* of Father of Campaigns, Father of Collisions, Father of Disturbances, Father of Earthquakes, and so on. If a man gives it free rein and obeys its whims, it will propel him into the most terrible calamities. Says Ibn ʿArūs, God have mercy upon him:

The people in God are lost,
And praise of noble men spreads far and wide.
Naught hurts me but my belly
And this thing that's dangling by its side.

The testicles may be likened to two hens. A certain poet made up the following lines to make fun of his shaykh:

O Lord, relieve us of our woe—O Lord!
O Lord, seize upon our shaykh, of facial hair galore!
His testes when he's bended o'er
Are like two chickens pecking grain up off the floor.

To sum up, *khuṣā* with *u*[204] and *khiṣā* with *i*, and likewise with *w* instead of the *ā*,[205] are names common to the male organ and the testicles, this falling under the rubric of "naming a thing according to its neighbors." The word *khiṣyatayn* is of the pattern of *ḍarṭatayn* ("two audible farts") or *shakhkhatayn* ("two pisses"), so it contains both farts and pisses for sure. Both words[206] are derived from *khuṣṣ* ("hovel") with *u*, or from a village named al-Khuṣūṣ,[207] or, for example, from the word *ikhṣā* ("bad dog!") that they use for dogs. The paradigm is *khaṣā, yakhṣū, khaṣā'an*.[208] As the poet says: 11.4.11

Khaṣā, *yakhṣū* are the base forms of *khiṣyatayn*.
khaṣā' is correct in the verse of al-Ṭunayn.[209]

This brings these fatuous discussions and inane problems to an end.

bi-khulbat līf ("a palm-fiber knot"): that is, a strong knot going twice around his balls with a rope made of plaited palm fiber (*līf*), which is so called because it is wrapped (*multaff*)[210] around the bases of palm fronds. This knot is called a *khulbah* because it grasps (*takhlibu*) a thing that can then only be released from it with difficulty. In the jargon of shepherds, if they want to tie something 11.4.12

بمُكْنة يقولوا اخلب عليه خُلْبَة وَتد أي لُفَّ الحبل عليه مرّتين واربطه ربطة قويّة حتّى لا ينفكّ وهي مشتقّة من خلب الزرع أو من مخلاب الطير أو من البرق الخُلَّب بضمّ الخاء المعجمة وتشديد اللام وهو الّذي لا مطر فيه قال ابن العربيّ نفعنا الله به [كامل]

كُلُّ الّذي يَرْجُو نوالَكَ أُمْطِروا ... مَا كانَ بَرْقُكَ خُلَّبًا إِلّا مَعِي

١٣،٤،١١ ثمّ إنّ الناظم ذكر السبب الحامل لحدوث شَيْبه قبل أوانه فقال

ص

٥،١١ وَمِنْ نَزْلَةِ الكُشَّافِ شَابَتْ عَوَارِضِي ... وَصَارَ لِقَلْبِي لَوْعَةٌ وَرَجِيفُ

ش

١،٥،١١ قوله (ومن نَزْلَةِ) النزلة واحدة النزول وتطلق على الجماعة الكثيرة إذا نزلوا في محلّ واستمرّوا فيه زمناً كما يقال نزلة بني فلان ونزلة العرب ونزلة الغوازي ومن هذا القرية المعروفة بالنزلة وأمّا النزول فمعناه تدلّي الشيء من الأعلى إلى الأسفل وضدّه الصعود وهو الترقّي من الأدنى إلى الأعلى يقال صعد إلى أعلى الجبل ونزل إلى أدنى الأرض قال امرؤ القيس يصف فرساً شجاعاً [طويل]

مِكَرٍّ مِفَرٍّ مُقْبِلٍ مُدْبِرٍ مَعًا ... كَجُلْمُودِ صَخْرٍ حَطَّهُ السَّيْلُ مِنْ عَلِ

tightly, they say, "Secure it with a clove hitch (*khulbat watid*, literally, 'peg knot')", that is, wrap the rope around it twice and tie it tightly so that it cannot come undone. It is derived from the *khalb* ("reaping") of crops, or from the *mikhlāb* ("talon") of birds, or from "deceptive" lightning (*barq khullab*), with *u* after the *k* and double *l*, meaning lightning that brings no rain.[211] Says Ibn al-ʿArabī, God benefit us through him:

All those who seek Your favor have been granted rain;
Your lightning has failed in its promise to me alone.

Next the poet mentions the reason his hair has turned prematurely white. 11.4.13
He says:

TEXT

wa-min nazlati l-kushshāfi shābat ʿawāriḍī 11.5
wa-ṣāra li-qalbī lawʿatun wa-rajīf

And from the descent of the Inspectors, my side whiskers have turned white
and my heart is afflicted with pangs and trembling.

COMMENTARY

11.5.1 *wa-min nazlat* ("And from the descent of"): *nazlah*[212] is the instance noun from *nuzūl* ("descending") and is applied to a large company if it alights at a place and remains there a while. Thus one speaks of *nazlat banī fulān* ("the settlement of the tribe of So-and-so") and *nazlat al-ʿarab* ("the settlement of the Bedouin") and *nazlat al-ghawāzī* ("the settlement of the Ghawāzī"); hence also the village known as al-Nazlah.[213] *Nuzūl* means "the descent of something from higher to lower" and its opposite is *ṣuʿūd*, which means "ascent from lower to higher"; one says, "He ascended (*ṣaʿada*) to the top of the mountain and descended (*nazala*) to the lowest part of the land." Describing a mettlesome steed, Imruʾ al-Qays[214] says:

At once wheeling and turning, advancing and retreating,
Match for a boulder that the flood throws down from above.

وقوله (الكُشّافِ) جمع كاشف واتّصف بهذه الصفة لأنّه يكشف عن الإقليم المتولّي عليه ويزيل ما فيه من المفاسد والمظالم ويسدّ النهور ويمكّن الجسور ويزيل اللصوص وكان هذا عادة كلّ كاشف تولّى في قديم الزمان يسير سيرة حسنة ويمرّ على البلاد وإذا أقبل على قرية يَقْرَع الطبل فيخاف منه أهل البدع وأرباب المفاسد ويرتحلوا هاربين خوفًا منه وربّما وقعوا في يده فيعاقبهم بما يستحقّوه من قتل أو حبس أو ضرب أو أخذ دراهم ثمّ ينزل على القرية إن كان له عليها عادة بالنزول وتأتي إليه مشايخها ويقفوا بين يديه في أشدّ ما يكون من الرعب والخوف ويستخبرهم عن أحوالهم ويسألهم عن أرباب المفاسد وأصحاب البدع ويلزمهم بالقبض عليهم إذا لم يكونوا في القرية ثمّ بعد ذلك يسرعوا له في الأكل والشرب والتقادم ممّا جرت به العادة وإذا وقع في قرية فتنة فيما بينهم أو قتل أو خرجوا عن طاعة أستاذهم هجم عليهم بأمر الوزير وأخرب القرية وقتل منهم من يستحق القتل وأزال العصاة والجبابرة فعلى كلّ حال وجوده على الأقاليم رحمة وسُتْرة وكشف غمّة ما لم يحصل منه ومن عسكره الضرر على الناس من نهب متاعهم وأذيّتهم وتكلّفهم في المآكل والمشرب فوق طاقتهم وإلّا فيكون هذا من باب الظلم وهو حرام ويجب ردّه لأربابه إلّا إن سمحت نفوسهم بذلك فلا بأس وقوله ١١،٥،٢

(الكشاف) ولم يكونوا غير واحد فهو على حذف مضاف تقديره أي ومن تواتر نزول كاشف بعد كاشف مع ما يحصل لي منه من الرعب والخوف من قرع الطبول ودكدكة الخيول وهيبته عند السير والنزول ورجفان القلب من رؤية العسكر والمقدّمين والبلاصيّة وخوفي من هذا الأمر أن ينالني منه ضرر ١١،٥،٣

al-kushshāfi ("the Inspectors"): plural of *kāshif*, so called because he inspects (*yakshifu*) the region placed under his charge and does away with whatever corruption and unauthorized imposts may exist there, and dams the waterways, strengthens the dikes, and rids the place of robbers; such was the custom of every Inspector in former times. He would behave righteously and make a progress around the settlements, and when he approached a village the drums would beat and those who had introduced unsanctioned practices and the corrupt would feel frightened and run away in fear of him and sometimes fall into his hands, in which case he would punish them as they deserved, whether by execution, imprisonment, beating, or fines. Then he would descend on the village, if it was his custom to stop there, and its shaykhs would come and stand before him in the utmost terror and fear, while he interrogated them concerning their affairs and asked them who was corrupt and who had introduced unsanctioned practices, and enjoined them to apprehend the latter if they were not in the village. Afterward they would hurry to bring him the customary food, drink, and presents. If any conflict had arisen among them in a village, or any killing, or they had shown disobedience to their Master, he would attack them on the viceroy's orders, lay waste to the village, kill those of them who deserved to be killed, and destroy the rebels and tyrants.[215] However that may be,[216] his presence in charge of the provinces constitutes a mercy, a shield, and a discovery of afflictions, provided no injury is done to people at his hands or at the hands of his soldiers by way of seizure of their property, harassment, or commanding them to provide food and drink beyond their capacity to do so. Should such things occur, it should be considered injustice and, as such, forbidden by religion, and whatever is taken should be returned to its owner (unless he had provided it of his own free will in the first place, in which case there is no objection). 11.5.2

His saying "the Inspectors," even though there would not be more than one of them, should be taken as implying the suppression of the first term of a genitive annexation,[217] whose implied sense would be "from the continuous descents of inspector after inspector, accompanied by the terror and fear that afflict me as a result of the beating of the drums, the stamping of the horses' hoofs, the Inspector's awe-inspiring demeanor when on progress and descending on the village, and the thudding of my heart at the sight of the soldiers, the retainers, and the torturers, and my fear that he should cause me injury on this account." 11.5.3

(شابت عوارضي) لضعفي عن مقابلة الكشّاف وعجزي عن شيء يأخذوه من داري من جلّة للمطبخ أو غير ذلك فمن هنا تنزع الأعضاء وترجف الجوانح وينبت الشيب في غير أوانه والشيب كرامة من الله تعالى لعبده أكرمه به وأوّل من شاب إبراهيم الخليل عليه السلام شابَ نصف لحيته فقال يا ربّ ما هذا فقال هذا وقار لك في الدنيا ونور لك في الآخرة فقال يا ربّ زدني من هذا الوقار فأصبح وقد ابيضّت لحيته كلّها وفي الحديث إنّ الله يستحي أن يعذب شيبة شابت في الإسلام وللشيب فضائل كثيرة منها أنّه وقار للشخص كما تقدّم وهيبة له ويذكّره قرب حِمامه لأنّه نذير الموت قال بعضهم [طويل] ٤،٥،١١

إذا اِسْوَدَّ جِلْدُ المرءِ وابْيَضَّ شَعْرُهُ   وَطالَ عَلَيْهِ ثَوْبُهُ مِنْ أمامِهِ
وَقارَبَ عِنْدَ المَشْيِ في خَطَواتِهِ   هُنالِكَ بَشِّرْهُ بِقُرْبِ حِمامِهِ

وقال آخر وأجاد [سريع]

تَبَسُّمُ الشَّيْبِ بِوَجْهِ الفَتَى   أَوْجَبَ سَحَّ الدَّمْعِ مِنْ جَفْنِهِ
وَكَيْفَ لا يَبْكِي عَلَى نَفْسِهِ   مَنْ ضَحِكَ الشَّيْبُ عَلَى دَقْنِهِ

وفي هذين البيتين الطباق اللفظيّ كما لا يخفى والشيب مذموم عند النساء قال هارون الرشيد لزوجته ما تحبّون من الرجال فقالت من خدّه كخدّي * وأيره كزندي * قال فإذا التحا قالت يُطرق الحَدَقة * ويَعْجل بالنَفَقة * قال فإذا شاب قالت يصبر على الخناق * أو يبادر بالطَلاق * فهو عندهم مذموم * وصاحبه من أنس الغانيات محروم * خصوصاً إذا قلّ ماله * وساء حاله * قال بعضهم [طويل] ٥،٥،١١

shābat ʿawāriḍī ("my side whiskers have turned white"): because of my inability to face the Inspectors and my having nothing for them to take from my house such as dung cakes for the kitchen or anything else. Consequently, my limbs tremble, my heart flutters, and white hairs sprout before their time. White hairs are a sign of the Almighty's favor, with which He honors one of His slaves. The first to grow white hairs was Ibrāhīm the Beloved,[218] blessings and peace be upon him. Half his beard turned white, and he said, "Lord, what is this?" The Lord said, "It is a token of your venerability in this world, and a light for you in the next." So Ibrāhīm said, "Lord, give me more of this venerability!" and he awoke the next morning and the whole of his beard had turned white. In the Tradition it says, "Verily, God would feel ashamed to treat harshly hairs that had turned white in Islam." White hair has many virtues, among which are that it is a sign of venerability in a person, as already mentioned, and a sign of dignity for him, and that it reminds him of his approaching end, for it is the harbinger of death. A poet says: 11.5.4

When a man's skin turns black and his hair turns white,
And his robe's too long in front,
And he takes short steps as he walks along,
Tell him then that he's close to defunct.

And another, putting it excellently, said:[219]

The smile of white hairs on the young man's cheeks
Forced tears from his eyelids to race.
And who would not weep for himself
When white hairs laugh in his face?

The lines contain "antithesis" in the wording,[220] as you will have noticed. Women, however, dislike white hair. Hārūn al-Rashīd asked his wife, "What kind of men do you women find attractive?" She replied, "One whose cheek is like my cheek and whose member is like my forearm." "And if his beard grows?" he asked. "He should keep his eyes to himself, and be ready with his wealth!" she said. "And if his hair turns white?" he said. "He must either put up with strife, or offer to divorce his wife!" she said—for this is something they condemn and the company of pretty women is denied to such men, especially if their money's tight, in which case their outlook's not bright. As the poet[221] said: 11.5.5

سَلُونِي عَنِ ٱحوالِ النِّساءِ فإنّني خَبيرٌ بِأَحْوالِ النِّساءِ طَبيبُ
إِذا ابْيَضَّ شَعْرُ المَرْءِ أَو قَلَّ مالُهُ فَلَيْسَ لَهُ في وُدِّهِنَّ نَصيبُ

٦،٥،١١ فكيف بمن فيه النوعين الشيب والفقر فهو عندهنّ وجوده كالعدم وقال القاضي الفاضل رحمه الله [بسيط]

تَعَجَّبَتْ حينَ راحَ سَعْدي مِن بَعْدِ نَضْوِ الخِضابِ حالي
قالَتْ أَهذا الَّذي أَراهُ غُبارُ طاحُونَةٍ بَدا لي
فَقُلْتُ لا تَعْجِبي فَهذا غُبارُ طاحُونَةِ اللَّيالي

أي إنّها تكدّرت لمّا رأت هذا الشيب المشبّه بغبار الطاحونة قد لاح على وجهه وغيّر لحيته وتعجّبت من حدوثه بسرعة وتعجّبها منه يقتضي تكدّر صدرها وطيّ بساط أنسها فأجابها بقوله لا تعجّي من إسراع ظهوره فإنّ عجائب الليالي واستنتاجها المصائب المشبّهة عند دورانها بالطاحون أظهرت هذا الغبار الّذي ترينه فلا تلومي واصبري على ما بُليتي به وبعضهم شبّه حدوث الشيب في لحيته بالطائر المعروف بالنّسر لبياضه وشبّه بقيّتها في السواد بابن داية وهو الغراب الأسود فقال [طويل]

وَلَمّا رَأَيْتُ النَّسْرَ حَدَّ ابنِ دايَةٍ وَعَشَّشَ في وَكْرَيْهِ[1] ضاقَ لَهُ صَدْري

٧،٥،١١ (ومنهم) من شبّه حدوثه بظهور الصبح واشتعاله في السواد كاشتعال النار في الحطب الغليظ اليابس قال ابن دُرَيْد رحمه الله تعالى في أوّل مقصورته [رجز]

١ بي: وكرها.

Ask me how women are, for I'm
Well versed in women's ways, a physician.
When a man's hair turns white or his money runs out,
Let him abandon all hope of their affection.

How much worse, then, for the man who has both—white hair and poverty! Such a one might as well not exist, as far as they are concerned. Al-Qāḍī al-Fāḍil,[222] God have mercy on him, said: 11.5.6

She wondered, when my wealth took off
Right when my hair had lost its hue—
"This thing I see," she said, "what is't?
Is it dust from some mill that I have in view?"
Said I, "Be not amazed! This is
The powder that from time's mill does accrue."

—that is, her mood darkened when she saw that white hair resembling mill dust had appeared upon his face and altered his beard, and she wondered at its sudden onset, a wonderment that necessarily plunged her into gloom and "rolled up the carpet of her conviviality." Then he answered her by saying, "Be not amazed" at how fast it has appeared—for the wondrous events that the passing of time brings and the disasters that result from these, which may be likened in their turning to a mill, have caused the appearance of these flecks that you see; so do not blame me, and patiently endure this misfortune that has befallen you. A poet[223] has compared the onset of white hair in the beard to the bird called the vulture because of the latter's whiteness[224] and compared the remaining part, in its blackness, to the "Ibn Dāyah" ("Son of a Midwife"), which is the black crow. He says:

When I saw the vulture mourn Ibn Dāyah
And roost in its two nests,[225] my heart felt pain at his loss.

Others have likened its onset to the appearance of the light of morning and have said that the way it "catches fire" in the blackness is like fire catching in thick, dry firewood. Ibn Durayd, may the Almighty have mercy upon him, says at the start of his *maqṣūrah*:[226] 11.5.7

يا ظَبْـيَةً أشْـبَهَ شَيْءٍ بِالمَهَا   رَاتِعَـةً بَيْنَ العَـقِـيقِ واللِّوا
أمـا تـرَى رأْسِي حـاكَى لَوْنُـهُ   طُرَّةَ صُبْحٍ تَحْتَ أَذْيالِ الدُّجا
وَاشْـتَعَلَ المُبْيَضُّ فِي مُسْوَدِّهِ   مِثْلَ اشْتِعالِ النَّارِ في جَزْلِ الغَضا
فَكانَ كاللَّيْلِ البَهِيـمِ حَلَّ في   أَرْجائِهِ ضَوْءُ صَباحٍ فانْجَلَى

٨،٥،١١ والتشبيه للشيب من هذا المعنى كثير وهو مشتقّ من الشَّيْبَة الّتي تباع عند العطّار لبياضها ورقّة عروقها واشتباك الشعر بعضه ببعض ولهذا يقال رأوا في الشيبة نجاسة مثلاً ومصدره شاب يشيب شيباً وذِكْرُه الشيب في العارضين أوّلاً يدلّ على أنّه كان من الأماثل والكرماء لأنّ أوّل ما يشيب من الكرام العارضان ومن اللئام العَنْفَقة قال الشاعر [متقارب]

فَشَيْبُ الكِرامِ مِنَ العـارِضَيْنِ   وَشَيْبُ اللِّئامِ مِنَ العَـنْفَـقَهْ
وَشَـيْبُ الرُّؤوسِ بِما في النُّفوسِ   وَشَـيْبُ الصُّـدورِ مِنَ الزَّنْدَقَـهْ

٩،٥،١١ وقصره الشيب في عارضيه ليس على بابه وإنّما كان ابتداؤه في عارضيه ثمّ جرى في بقيّة لحيته بيقين فذكر الأصل والفرع تابع له وأمّا إلحاقه تاء التأنيث في الفعل فهو جرى على لغة الريّافة والناظم منهم وأيضاً لو قال شاب عارضي أو شابوا عوارضي لاختلّ الوزن فراعى لغته ووزن الكلام

١٠،٥،١١ (مسألة هباليّة) لأيّ شيء قال ومن نزلة الكشّاف ولم يقل ومن نزولهم لئلّا يتوهّم سامع بليد الطبع أنها النَزْلة الّتي تعتري الإنسان من حصول برد يحلّ به فينزل في رأسه ويتولّد منها العُطاس والأذى وغير ذلك ودواؤها أن تدهن الجبهة ببياض

Ah Gazelle, so like the oryx
'Twixt al-ʿAqīq and al-Liwā grazing,[227]
See you not how my head's color has mimicked
The dawn's gleam 'neath the skirts of darkness trailing,
And how the whiteness in the blackness has caught
Just as fire in a saxaul log breaks out blazing?
Methought it was some pitch-dark night
In whose expanse the morn, unloosed, turns all to light!

Similes of this sort for white hair are legion. The word *shayb* ("white hair") is derived from the *shaybah* ("artemisia") that is sold at the druggist's, because of its whiteness and the fineness of its roots and the way its hairs become entangled with one another, which is why they say, "They saw impurity in the artemisia" as a proverb.[228] The paradigm is *shāba, yashību, shayban* ("to turn white (of hair)"). The fact that he mentions that the sides of his beard turned white first is an indication that he was a man of stature and nobility, for the first thing to turn white on a noble man is the sides of the beard, and on an ignoble man the hair between the lower lip and the chin. The poet says: 11.5.8

White hairs on the noble start at the whiskers,
On the vile above the chin.
White hairs on the head by worry are fed
And white hairs on the chest are a sin!

However, his restriction of mention of white hairs to those on the sides of his beard is arbitrary: they would begin at the edges and then progress ineluctably to the rest of his beard. In other words, he stated the root and the secondary phenomena follow as a matter of course. As for his adding the feminine marker *-t* to the verb, he follows in this the language of the country people, of whom the poet was one; and, in addition, had he said *shāba ʿāriḍī* or *shābū ʿawāriḍī*, the meter would have been thrown off. Thus he acted in accord with both his own speech habits and the meter.[229] 11.5.9

A Silly Topic for Debate: What makes him refer to the *nazlah* ("descent") of the Inspectors instead of their *nuzūl*, when a slow-witted listener might imagine that the former refers to the *nazlah* that afflicts a person when he catches cold that is, "catarrh,"[230] and then descends (*yanzilu*) in the head and gives rise to sneezing and sickness and so on, the treatment for which is to anoint the 11.5.10

البيض ممزوجاً بالمصطكى فإنّه يخفّف ذلك وما الحكمة في أنّه أتى بعد العارضين بالقلب وهو بعيد عنهما وليس بينه وبينهما مناسبة وكان حقّه أن يأتي بالشاربين والعنفقة كقول الشاعر [رجز]

شواربكْ والعـنفقهْ في طيزِ كَلْبه مْطلّقهْ
والْحسْ خراها يا فَهِيمْ ومَـرْمِـزُهْ بالمِـلْعَـقهْ

(قلنا الجواب) أنّ النـزلة على وزن العجلة والنـزول على وزن العجول والعجول جماعة فاكتفى بالأقلّ دون الأكثر وأيضاً الأنثى ألطف من الذكر في الذات والصفات وإن كان الذكر أشرف وأيضاً الفلّاح عنده العجلة أو البقرة أكثر نفعاً من العجل والثور فعُلِمَ من هذا أنّ الناظم كان يهوى الأناث دون الذكر بخلاف مذهبنا نحن معاشر الفسّاق فإنّنا على حدّ قول أبي نواس [طويل]

عَجِبْتُ لِمَنْ يَـزْني وفي النّاسِ أَمْـرَدُ أَلَيْسَ رُكوبُ الفَحْلِ في الحَرْبِ أَجْوَدُ

١١،٥،١١ وأمّا ذِكْره القلب مع العارضين إنّما هو تغاير في اللفظ والمعنى واحد من حيثيّة أنّ الروح سارية في الجسد كلّه فإذا اهتمّ القلب وتعب سرى ذلك في الجسد ونشأ الشيب منه فيكون على معنى ما قارب الشيء يعطي حكمه أو على حدّ قولهم شاب القلب فيكون شيباً معنوياً فلا اعتراض فاتّضح الإشكال عن وجه هذا الهبال

١٢،٥،١١ والعارض مشتقّ من العرضيّ الّذي يُلَفُّ على الرأس أو من عارضة الباب أو من العَروض الّذي يعتري الإنسان من لمس الجنّ أو من العارض الّذي يأتي بالمطر أو من

forehead with egg white mixed with mastic, which alleviates it? And what is the wisdom in his immediately following a reference to the sides of the beard with one to the heart, which is located far from the former and has no meaningful connection with them? Should he not rather have talked about his mustache and the hair on his lower lip, after the manner of the poet who said:

Up the ass of an unleashed bitch
Shove your mustache, plus the tuft below your lip!
Then lick her shit, good Connoisseur,
And spoon it, sip by sip!?

We respond: the reply is that *nazlah* is of the measure of *ʿijlah* ("female calf") and *nuzūl* is of the measure of *ʿujūl* ("calves"), and *ʿujūl* is a plural, so he used the lesser to stand for the greater; likewise the female[231] is more refined in form and feature than the male (albeit the male is more honorable)—not to mention that, to a peasant, the female calf or cow is more useful than the male calf or the ox. From this it may be deduced that the poet loved females rather than males, in contrast to the school of reprobates like us—for we follow the words of Abū Nuwās:[232]

I wonder at one who has sex with girls
When there's a beardless boy in sight.
Aren't we all agreed from the start
Your stallion's the better mount in a fight?

As for his mentioning the heart in the same breath as the sides of the beard, **11.5.11**
this amounts to no more than a shift in wording while the meaning remains the same, from the perspective that the spirit diffuses itself throughout the body, so that, if the heart experiences anxiety and suffering, this is diffused throughout the body and white hairs sprout in response to it; in which case, it would be a matter of "what is in proximity to a thing lends it its own stamp." Or perhaps it should be taken in the sense that people use when they say "my heart's hairs turned white," in which case it would be a metaphorical whitening of the hair, and there would be no grounds for objection. Thus the problem is now revealed, such silliness no more concealed.

The word *ʿāriḍ* is derived from the *ʿarḍī* ("headcloth, turban")[233] that one **11.5.12**
wraps around the head or from the *ʿarīḍah* ("crossbar") of a door, or from the *ʿarūḍ* ("prosody, verse-making") that afflicts a person as a result of being

عارض الجبل قال بعضهم [كامل]

قِـفْ بِالقَرافَـةِ تَحْتَ ذَيْلِ العارِضِ وَقُلْ السَّلامُ عَلَيْكَ يا ابْنَ الفارِضِ

أو أنّه سمّي بذلك لتعرّضه في الوجه ومصدره عرض يعرض عرضاً فهو عارض وقوله

(وصار) على وزن فار من الصيرورة أو من صاري المركب أو من الصُرّ الّذي يُنْقَل ١٣،٥،١١
في كلّ عام إلى الحرمين

(لقلبي) المراد به قلب الناظم لا قلب غيره كما لا يخفى على صاحب العقل الفشرويّ ١٤،٥،١١
وقوله

(لوعة) وهي شدّة حرارة القلب وتلهُّفه من ألم العشق أو الخوف أو بُعد المحبوب ونحوه ١٥،٥،١١
كما قلت في معنى ذلك [بسيط]

أَوّاهُ وَاحَرَبَى مِنْ لَوْعَتي وكَفَى أَنّي أُكابِدُ زَفَراتٍ بِأَشْجاني

وقوله (ورجيف) على وزن رغيف أي رجفان لا يسكن ألمه ولا يهدأ تحرّكه من شدّة ١٦،٥،١١
ما نالني من رعب نزول الكشّاف وخوفي منهم كما تقدّم ومصدره رجف يرجف رجفاً مثل غرف يغرف غرفاً

ثمّ إنّ الناظم شرع في ذكر مصيبة أخرى ابتلى بها هو وإخوانه الفلاّحين وهي أشدّ ١٧،٥،١١
ما عليهم من الأمور المهمّة فقال

touched by the jinn,[234] or from the *ʿāriḍ* ("bank of clouds") that brings rain, or from the *ʿāriḍ* ("flank") of a mountain. As the poet says:

Halt in the Qarāfah[235] 'neath the flanks of al-ʿĀriḍ
And say, "Peace be upon you, O Ibn al-Fāriḍ!"

Or it may be so called because of its being spread sideways (*taʿarruḍ*) on the face. The paradigm is *ʿaraḍa, yaʿriḍu, ʿarḍan*, active participle *ʿāriḍ* ("to happen, to present, to expose").

wa-ṣāra ("and (my heart) is"): of the measure of *fāra* ("it boiled over"), from *ṣayrurah* (verbal noun of *ṣāra*), or from the *ṣārī* ("mast") of a boat, or from the *ṣurr* ("purse") that is transferred every year to the Two Sanctuaries.[236] 11.5.13

li-qalbī ("(to) my heart"): meaning the poet's heart and not anyone else's, as will be obvious to anyone with a fatuous mind. 11.5.14

lawʿatun ("pangs"): these are an intense burning and yearning of the heart from the agony of passionate love, or fear, or separation from the beloved and so on. As I said in the same vein: 11.5.15

Woe is me and alack for my pangs! Enough
That I endure deep wrenching sighs in my sorrows!

wa-rajīf ("and trembling"): of the pattern of *raghīf* ("loaf"); that is, a trembling, the pain of which cannot be stilled and the motion of which cannot be quieted, resulting from the terror that has afflicted me from the descending of the Inspectors and my fear of them, as previously described. 11.5.16

The paradigm is *rajafa, yarjufu, rajfan* ("to tremble"), like *gharafa, yaghrufu, gharfan* ("to ladle").

Next, the poet begins to talk of another disaster with which he and his fellow peasants are afflicted and which is the most severe of the grave matters that affect them. He says: 11.5.17

ص

وَيَوْمٍ يَجِي ٱلدِّيوَانُ تَبْطُلْ مَفَاصِلِي   وَٱهُـرُّ عَـلَى رُوحِي مِنَ ٱلتَّخْوِيف ٦،١١

ش

قوله (ويوم) بالتنوين ١،٦،١١

(يجي) وقت قبض مال ٢،٦،١١

(الديوان) وهذا من باب ﴿وَٱسْأَلِ ٱلْقَرْيَةَ﴾ أي أهلها وهو أنّ النصرانيّ إذا حضر إلى القرية أو الكفر وفرّد المال على الفلّاحين حُكْمَ الخوالي والقوانين الّتي جرت بها العادة وشرع في أخذها فيكثر الخوف والحبس والضرب لمن لا يقدر على غلاق المال فمن الفلّاحين من يقترض الدراهم بزيادة أو يأخذ على زرعه إلى أوان طلوعه بناقص عن بيعه في ذلك الزمن أو يبيع بهيمته الّتي تحلب على عياله أو يأخذ مصاغ زوجته يرهنه أو يتصرّف فيه بالبيع ولو قهراً عليها ويدفع الثمن للنصرانيّ أو لمن هو متولّي قبض المال وإن لم يجد شيئاً ولا يرى من يعطيه وخشي الملتزم أو الشادّ من خرابه من البلد أخذ ولده رهينة عنه حتّى يغلّق المال أو يأخذ أخاه إن لم يكن له ولد أو أحداً من أقاربه أو يوضع في الحبس للضرب والعقوبة حتّى تنفّذ فيه أحكام الله تعالى ومنهم من ينجو بنفسه فيهرب تحت ليله فلا يعود إلى بلده قطّ ويترك أهله ووطنه من همّ المال وضيق المعيشة كما قال بعضهم [كامل] ٣،٦،١١

هَمُّ المَعِيشَةِ فُرْقَةٌ   بَيْنَ الأَحِبَّةِ وَالوَطَنْ

TEXT

wa-yawmin yajī l-dīwānu tabṭul mafāṣilī 11.6
wa-hurru ʿalā rūḥī mina l-takhwīf

And on the day when the tax collectors come, my joints give way
and I void my loose bowels over myself from the terror they're creating

COMMENTARY

11.6.1 *wa-yawmin* ("and on the day when"): with nunation[237]

11.6.2 *yajī* ("comes"): the time for the collection of the taxes by

11.6.3 *al-dīwānu* ("the tax collectors"): This is one of those things of which they say, «And ask the village!»[238] that is, the people of the village. What happens is that, when the Christian arrives at the village or hamlet and divides up the tax into individual portions among the peasants according to the determinations made by the surveyors and the laws that are customarily followed and starts collecting them, fear, beatings, and the imprisonment of those who are unable to pay their taxes mount. A peasant may borrow money at excessive interest or take money against his crop before its ripening at a lower price than it will fetch when it is ripe, or sell his animal that provides milk for his children, or take his wife's jewelry—by force if need be—to pawn or sell, and pay the proceeds to the Christian or whoever is charged with collecting the tax. If he cannot come up with anything and cannot find anyone to give it to him, and the tax farmer or the bailiff fears that his impoverishment may lead to his land going to ruin and being lost to the village tax rolls, the latter will take the peasant's son and keep him as a pledge until he pays his taxes, or, if he has no son, his brother, or any of his relatives, or he may be put in prison to be beaten and punished so that the ordinances of the Almighty may be implemented against him. Some save themselves and flee under cover of night and never return to their homes, leaving their family and birthplace because of the oppressiveness of the taxation and the difficulty of their lives. As a poet said:

Life's bane is separation
From loved ones and from birthplace.

١١،٦،٤ فلا بدّ على كلّ حال * من تعليق المال * ولو حصل من ذلك الهمّ والغمّ * كما في المثل الّذي اشتهر وعمّ * مال السلطان يخرج من بين الظفر واللحم وما دام عليه شيء فهو في همّ شديد * ويوم السداد عند الفلّاح عيد *

١١،٦،٥ والحاصل أنّ الفلّاح على قسمين قسم ناجي ناجب * وقسم خائن خائب * (فأمّا الأوّل) فهو صاحب عقل وسياسه * وحسن تصريف ورياسه * عقله رزين * يلازم الصلاة والدين * والزرع والغيط * تارك السندة جنب الحيط * له على جماعته الحماسه * متجنّب الرذالة والخساسه * يباشر الزرع * ويقف عند الحصيدة والقلع * لا يتّكل على خولي ولا مُرابع * ولا يركن لتوّار ولا مُزارِع * بل يباشر الأمور كلّها * ويعرف مرضها وعِلَلها * ويلازم المَشَدّ والأستاد * ولا يسعى في خراب ولا فساد * فإن أخذ من مُعامِلٍ فلوس * لا يصرفها في أمر معكوس * بل على مصالح الزرع والبهائم * والأمر الّذي عليه لازم * وينوي السداد لصاحب الدين * ويشفق على الفقير والمسكين * ويفيق لأتواره * ويحفظ غيط جاره * وينوي سداد المال * ويتّكل على العليّ المتعال * ويترك نفش الشوارب * والجلوس على المصاطب * يبارك له الديّان * ويسدّ مال السلطان * وإن جاءه المعامل أوفاه * وإن طلب منه ثاني مرّة أعطاه * وترتاح أولاده * ويرضى عليه أستاده * ويعيش في راحة ودين * ويرضى عليه ربّ العالمين *

١١،٦،٦ (وأمّا القسم الثاني) لا عقل ولا معروف * عريان ومنتوف * لا صلاة ولا دين * ولا طاعة لربّ العالمين * ولا ذوق ولا معرفه * فائق للشرّ والمقرفه * بالنهار في لعب المَنَقَله * وبالليل ساحب العَتَلَه * لا يلازم غيط * يحبّ اللطعة جنب الحيط * نافش الشوارب * قليل المكاسب * عويل مِهْدار * شهلاط فشّار * إن دخل في ايده فلوس * فرّقها على العتورة والتيوس * لا يلازم مشدّ ولا

There is no escape, in any case, from paying the tax, even if that results in affliction and woe, for, as the well-known and widespread proverb says, "The sultan's taxes are extracted from between the nail and the quick," and the peasant remains in severe distress so long as he has any tax to pay, and the day he pays it off is, in his eyes, a feast day. 11.6.4

To sum up, peasants are of two sorts, one blameless and noble, one feckless and false. The first is intelligent and prudent, skilled at choosing to whom to entrust his affairs and at exercising leadership. Sober minded, he is as regular in his prayers and other religious duties as he is in attending to his crops and fields. He has no time for lounging by the wall and is eager to defend the interests of his family, while avoiding all that is base and mean. He supervises the planting himself and is present in person at the harvesting and picking. He resorts to neither surveyor nor sharecropper, and has recourse to neither cowman nor hired laborer. On the contrary, he directs all his affairs himself and knows the problems and underlying causes involved in each case. He pays regular visits to the bailiff and his Master and does not busy himself with destruction or corruption. If he takes money from a moneylender, he doesn't spend it on something perverse but rather on the well-being of his crops and animals and on servicing his obligations. He makes it his purpose to pay back his creditors and has compassion for the poor and the humble. He looks out for the well-being of his oxen, and respects his neighbor's field. He makes it his purpose to pay his taxes, and puts his trust in the High, the Exalted. He shuns the twirling of mustaches and sitting about on stoops, is blessed by the Divine Reckoner, and pays his taxes to the sultan. If the moneylender comes to him he pays him his due in full, and if he asks for a second loan, the moneylender gives it to him. His children live in comfort, and his Master is pleased with him. He lives in ease and piety, and the Lord of the Worlds is pleased with him. 11.6.5

As for the second sort, he is brainless and of service to none, naked and destitute. He neither prays nor observes any religious practices, nor is he obedient to the Lord of the Worlds. He lacks taste and understanding, is ever on the lookout for what's evil and disgusting, plays *manqalah* by day, and by night takes out his crowbar.[239] He spends little time in the fields, preferring to loaf by the wall. He is a mustache-twirler, a low earner, a scrounger, a ranter, a . . .,[240] and a braggart. Should any money come his way, he distributes it to blackguards and clods. He spends no time with bailiff or Master, but is sunk in perversity and corruption. His oxen starve, his horses waste away. He spends all his 11.6.6

أستاد * دائر في العكس والفساد * تيرانه جائعه * وخيوله ضائعه * لا يصرف إلّا في شياط وعياط * وزرعته ما فيها إلّا ضراط * يصرف من غير قانون * مشحوت منحوت مديون * ممقوت مع أستاده * دائر في غَيّه وفساده * لو ضربه مقارع أو كسّارات * ما يخلي النطّ في الدور والحارات * إن قال له إستاده على الصواب * ينوي على الرحيل والخراب * دائمًا في مقت وكرب * ولا يفيد فيه الحبس والضرب * قنف معكوس * مِحْراك شرّحرب البَسُوس * لا يقدر على وفاء دين * مكسور عليه الألف والألفين * فتنة في البلد * عمره في همّ ونَكَد * لا يوفي معامل * ولا له رأي كامل * أولاده عريانين * وأحواله أحوال المجانين * المقت منسكب عليه * وشبيه الشيء منجذب إليه * فلا خير في حياته * ولا يُبْكى عليه عند وفاته * لأنّه طويل الكمّ فشّار * قليل الفرح للدار * عَتْر أَكَّال خره * لا دنيا له ولا آخره * كما قيل [طويل]

فَهذا الّذي إِنْ عاشَ لا يُعتَنَى بِهِ   وَإِنْ ماتَ لا تَنْدَمُ عَلَيهِ أَقارِبُهُ

(وأوّل) من وضع الدواوين سيّدنا عمر بن الخطّاب رضي الله عنه وأوّل ديوان ١١،٦،٧
عُمِلَ في مصر على يد سيّدنا عمرو بن العاص لمّا فتح مصر ولم يُضْبَط على وتيرة واحدة وكان الخراج في زمانه يسيرًا ولهذا لمّا فتحها صلحًا أو عَنْوَة على ما قيل جمع منها أموالًا كثيرة تفوق عن الحصر من كنوز وغيرها * قال هشام بن رُقَيّة اللَخْمِيّ إنّ عمرو بن العاص لمّا فتح مصر قال لقبط مصر من كتمني كنزًا عنده فقدرت عليه قتلته وإنّ قبطيًا من أهل الصعيد يقال له بطرس ذُكِرَ لعمرو أنّ عنده كنزًا فطلبه وسأله فأنكر فحبسه في السجن وجعل عمرو يسأل عنه هل تسمعونه يسأل عن أحد فقالوا لا إنّما سمعناه يسأل عن راهب من الطور فأرسل عمرو إلى بطرس وأخذ خاتمه وكتب بالقبطيّة إلى

money on hubbub and hullabaloo, and his crops aren't worth a fart. He spends without logic and is broke, penniless, indebted, detested by his Master, sunk in his error and corruption. Though his Master were to whip him and break his bones, he would not leave off gallivanting in the houses and alleys. If his Master exhorts him to do what's right, he sets his heart on decamping, allowing his land to go to ruin. Forever caught up in spite and sorrow, imprisonment and beating have no effect on him. Haughty and perverse, an instigator of evil as great as the War of al-Basūs, incapable of paying what he owes, ever a thousand or two in arrears, a source of strife in his community, all his life he's in woe and misery. He does not repay the moneylender, and his judgment is unsound. His children are naked and his ways demented. He is the object of general loathing and "the like of a thing attracts its own sort." Thus his life brings no good, and no one weeps for him on his death, for his sleeves are long and he is a braggart, one who brings little joy to his household, a blackguard, a shit eater, without prospects in this world or the other. As it has been said:

> This is one who, alive, is of interest to none
> And who goes unmourned by his kin when he dies.

The first to establish apparatuses for the collection of taxes was Our Master 11.6.7
'Umar ibn al-Khaṭṭāb, may God be pleased with him, and the first such apparatus in Egypt was created at the direction of Our Master 'Amr ibn al-'Āṣ when he conquered Egypt,[241] though it was not organized in a uniform manner. In his time, the land tax was low and so, when he conquered it (whether by treaty or by force of arms, according to the different opinions),[242] he collected enormous wealth from it, beyond counting, in the form of treasures and other things. Hishām ibn Ruqayyah al-Lakhmī says[243] that when 'Amr ibn al-'Āṣ conquered Egypt he said to the Copts of Egypt, "I will kill anyone who conceals from me a hoard of treasure that he possesses and that I subsequently manage to obtain." He also mentions that 'Amr was told that a Copt from the Ṣa'īd called Buṭrus was in possession of a hoard, so he summoned and questioned him but the man denied it. Then he imprisoned him and every so often 'Amr would ask concerning him, "Have you heard him asking for anyone?" "No," they said. "But we have heard him ask about a monk from al-Ṭūr." So 'Amr sent to Buṭrus and took his seal and wrote to the monk in Coptic as though he were Buṭrus, urging him to tell him about his money and the place in which it was kept. He wrote what he wanted and sent it with a Copt whom he trusted.

الراهب على لسان بطرس يحرّضه على المال وعلى مكانه وذكر له ما شاء أن يذكره وجهّز الكتاب مع قبطيّ وثق به فجاء الرسول بقُلّة شاميّة مختومة بالرصاص ففتحها عمرو فوجد فيها صحيفة مكتوب فيها مالكم تحت الفسقيّة الكبيرة فحبس عنها الماء ثمّ قلع البلاطة الّتي تحتها فوجد فيها اثنين وخمسين إرْدَبّاً من الذهب الأحمر المضروب على سِكّة مصر فأخذ المال وضرب رأس بطرس عند باب المسجد انتهى

١١،٦،٨ وإطلاق الناظم لفظ المال المقبوض على الديوان لكونه آيلاً إليه من باب تسمية الشيء بما يصير إليه وسمّي ديواناً لإقامة الدين فيه بإظهار الحقّ وإنصاف الظالم من المظلوم أو لحضور ما دوّن الملك فيه أو لجمعه على أجناس مختلفة كما يقال للكتاب الجامع للقصائد والتوشيحات ومقاطيع الأشعار إذا أنشأه شخص ديوان فنزول الديوان في البلد على كلّ حال أمر مهول على الفلاّحين * ومصيبة على المِقلّين * والناظم رحمه الله كان من المُفلِسين المقلّين المنكسرين في مال السلطان كما سيأتي في قوله (يادوب عمري في الخراج وهمه) وإنّ الدهر والزمان مال عليه وصيّره في هذه الحالة كما تقدّم فلهذا قال عن نفسه إنّي إذا حضر الديوان أو قرب حضوره داخلني الخوف واعتراني الفزع ودهمتني الداهية الكبرى ولحقتني طَرْبة عظيمة لعدم شيء من الدراهم أورده في مال السلطان أو لخوفي من العقوبة والحبس فبسبب ذلك

١١،٦،٩ (تَبْطُلْ) أي ترتخي وتسكن ويقلّ نفعها

١١،٦،١٠ (مفاصلي) جمع مَفْصِل وهو فرجة يسيرة بين العظمين مستمسكة بالعروق فإذا سكنت تلك العروق وارتخت بطل عملها وقلّ نفع ذلك العضو وقد ذُكِرَ لفظ المفصل في قول أبي نواس لمّا احتضر [سريع]

The messenger returned with a Syrian pitcher sealed with lead, which ʿAmr opened, finding inside a sheet on which was written, "Your money is beneath the big fountain." He had the water blocked off and removed the tiles that were at the bottom, and there he found fifty-two sacks of red gold coined at the mint of Egypt. So he took the money and had Buṭrus beheaded at the door of the mosque. The End.

The poet's application of the term "the moneys collected" to the tax-collection apparatus (*dīwān*) because the latter is their destination is an example of "nomination by destination." It is called a *dīwān* because it is there that religion (*dīn*)[244] is upheld through the exposition of the Truth and the exaction of the rights of the oppressed from the oppressor; or because of the presence there of what the king has registered (*dawwanahu*); or because it brings together different types,[245] in the same way that a book bringing together the odes, strophic poems, and epigrams of an individual poet is called a *dīwān*. Whatever the case, the descent of the tax collectors on a village is a terrifying matter for the peasants and a disaster for the impoverished, and the poet, God have mercy on him, was one of the impoverished and penniless who are behind on the sultan's taxes, as will appear below in his words "Almost all my life on paying the taxes and their woes . . ." and Fate and Time had turned on him and driven him to this state, as already mentioned. Consequently, he says of himself, "If the tax collectors arrive, or are on the verge of arriving, fear enters into me, terror overwhelms me, the mightiest of disasters catches me by surprise, and a great agitation overtakes me because of my lack of any money to provide towards the sultan's taxes, or for fear of punishment and imprisonment." For this reason: **11.6.8**

tabṭul ("give way"): that is, go loose, cease to function, and become almost useless **11.6.9**

mafāṣilī ("my joints"): plural of *mafṣil*, which denotes a little gap between two bones, held together by sinews; should these sinews cease to function and go loose, they no longer do their job and the limb becomes nearly useless. The term *mafṣil* was employed by Abū Nuwās[246] in the verses he composed on his deathbed: **11.6.10**

لَمْ يَبْقَ إِلّا نَفَسٌ هـافِتٌ وَمُـقْلَةٌ إِنسانُها باهِتُ
ومُغْرَمٌ تَضْرَمُ أحشاؤُهُ بِالنّارِ إِلّا أَنّهُ ساكِتُ
ما فيهِ مِن عُضْوٍ ولا مَفْصِلٍ إِلّا وَفيـهِ أَلَمٌ ثابِتُ
رَثا لَهُ الشّـامِتُ مِمّا بِـهِ يا وَيْحَ مَنْ يَرْثِي لَهُ الشّامِتُ

١١،٦،١١ فمن هذا نبّه الناظم على هذا الأمر الّذي حصل له لعجزه عن دفع ما عليه من خراج الأرض ولكونه لم يُمهِله النصرانيّ ولا يرثي لحاله ولما كان يلزم من حدوث بُطلان مفاصله من شدّة الخوف والطربة وانطلاق البطن كما يقع غالباً لبعض الناس

١٢،٦،١١ قال (وَآهرّ على روحي) أي على ذاتي لا الروح السارية في الجسم من شدّة الطربة وهمّ

١٣،٦،١١ (التّخويف) أي تخويف جماعة النصرانيّ أو الشادّ والخوف الّذي يصيبني بمعنى أنّ الطبيعة تلين من انحصار هذا الهمّ وشدّة تلك الطربة الحاصلة فينزل الغائط ليّنا يشبه هِرار الطين بعد أن كان إذا ضربته في الحائط ردّ في وجهك من يُبْسه فيسيل على ذاتي وثيابي فلا أتمالك دفعه لأنّه يتدفّق بسرعة من شدّة الخوف والهرّ واحد الهِرار والهرار على وزن الجِرار واحده الجَرّة من قولهم هرّ عليك الحمار أو هرّت على لحيتك الكلبة أو هرّ على ذقنك مثلاً ويقال هرّ التراب وهرّ الرمل إذا تراكم على بعضه وسال لنفسه من الأعلى للأدنى فإنّك إذا نظرت إلى أكوام الرمل نظرت فيها الهرار بيقين أو هو مشتقّ من الهِرّة الّتي تصيد الفأر وتسمّى بلغة أهل الحجاز البُسّة بضمّ الموحّدة وبلغة أهل مصر القطّة ومصدره هرّ يهرّ هراراً

Naught remains but a faltering breath
  And an eye with pupil pale
And a passionate lover whose heart with fire
  Still burns, yet cannot tell the tale.
No limb has he, no joint (*mafṣil*)
  Without travail.
His elegy is spoke by those who revel in his state—
  Alas for him whose elegy the malign orate!

Moving on, our poet draws attention to what befell him as a result of his inability to pay the tax that he owed, of the Christian's refusal to grant him a delay or take pity on him, and of the inevitable consequences in terms of the weakening of his joints from the great fear and agitation and the loosening of his bowels, as generally happens to certain people. **11.6.11**

He says: *wa-ahurru ʿalā rūḥī* ("and I void my loose bowels over myself"): that is, over my own person, not over the spirit (*rūḥ*) that courses through my body,[247] from the great agitation and the affliction of **11.6.12**

al-takhwīf ("the terror they're creating"): that is, the terror being created by the followers of the Christian or the bailiff, and the fear that affects me, meaning that my bowels go soft as a result of the spasms caused by this affliction and the severity of the resulting agitation, so that the excrement comes out soft, like semi-liquid mud, when before it was so hard that if you flung it against a wall it would bounce back in your face. As a result, it runs over my person and my clothes, and my fear is so acute that it makes it spurt out too rapidly for me to control its eruption. *Hirr* ("tomcat") is the singular of *hirār*,[248] of the pattern of *jirār*, plural of *jarrah* ("jar"), deriving from the expressions *harr ʿalayka al-ḥimār* ("The donkey voided its loose bowels all over you!") or *harr ʿalā liḥyatika al-kalbah* ("The bitch voided her loose bowels all over your beard!") or *harr ʿalā dhaqinika* ("He voided his loose bowels all over your beard!"), for example. One also says *harr al-turāb* ("The dust piles collapsed") and *harr al-raml* ("The sand piles collapsed"), when they accumulate in heaps and flow spontaneously downward. Thus, if you look at piles of sand, you will observe *hurār* there for sure.[249] Or it may be derived from the *hirrah* ("she-cat") that hunts the mouse and which in the Hijaz they call *bussah*, with *u* after the *b*, and in the language of the people of Egypt, *quṭṭah*. The paradigm is *harra, yahirru, hirāran*.[250] **11.6.13**

ثمّ إنّ الناظم نبّه على أنّه لم يسعه من هذا الأمر بعد بطلان مفاصله وانطلاق ١٤،٦،١١
بطنه من شدّة خوفه إلّا الهروب من هذا الأمر الّذي دهمه والاختفاء منه فقال

ص

وَأَهْرَبْ حِـدَا ٱلنِّسْوَانْ وَأَلْتَفُّ بِالعَبَا   وَيَبْقَى ضُرَاطِي شِبْهَ طَبْلٍ عَنِيفْ ٧،١١

ش

قوله (وأهرب) أي أنا لا أحد غيري ١،٧،١١

(حدا) أصله بالمدّ والذال المعجمة واستُعْمِلَتْ بالدال المهملة جريًا على لغة الأرياف ٢،٧،١١
وقصّرها للضرورة وحذاء الشيء أي جانبه أو مقابله وقوله

(النسوان) أي عندهنّ أو محاذي لهنّ ويُجْمَع على نِساء ونِسْوة مشتقّ من التأنّس ٣،٧،١١
أو الأُنْس أو المؤانسة لأنّ آدم صلوات الله وسلامه عليه لمّا رأى حوّاء أَنِسَ إليها
وسعى لها فمن هذا أنّ الرجال تسعى إلى النساء وتميل إليهنّ لأنّهنّ غاية المطلوب
ورياحين القلوب قيل مرّ بعضهم بامرأة جميلة فأنشد يقول [بسيط]

إِنَّ النِّساءَ شَياطِينٌ خُلِقْنَ لَنا   نَعوذُ باللهِ مِن شَرِّ الشَّياطِينِ

فأجابته تقول [بسيط]

إِنَّ النِّساءَ رَياحِينٌ خُلِقْنَ لَكُم   وَكُلُّكُمْ يَشْتَهِي شَمَّ الرَّياحِينِ

Next, the poet calls attention to the fact that the only course left open to him after his joints have gone weak and his bowels loose because he is so scared is to flee from the events that afflict him and disappear. So he says: 11.6.14

TEXT

wa-ahrab ḥidā l-niswān wa-ʾaltaffu bi-l-ʿabā 11.7
wa-yabqā ḍurāṭī shibha ṭablin ʿanīf

And I flee next to the women and wrap myself in my cloak
and my farts are like a loud drum

COMMENTARY

wa-ahrab ("And I flee"): that is, I and no other person 11.7.1

ḥidā ("next to"): originally with long *-āʾ* and *dh*,[251] but used here in the form with *d* in accordance with the dialect of the countryside, but he has shortened it for the meter. To be *ḥidhāʾ* a thing means to be alongside it or facing it. 11.7.2

(a)l-niswān ("the women"): that is, with them or facing them. The word also has the plurals *nisāʾ* and *niswah*,[252] derived from *taʾannus* ("friendliness"), or *uns* ("friendliness"), or *muʾānasah* ("intimacy"), since, when Adam, God's blessings and peace be upon him, saw Eve, he felt friendly towards her (*anisa ilayhā*) and ran to her. Consequently, one finds that men run after women and are drawn to them, for they are the acme of desire, the fragrant nosegays of men's hearts. It is said that a man once passed a beautiful woman and recited: 11.7.3

Women are devils created for us—
God save us from those devils' ways!

To which the woman replied:

Women are nosegays created for you—
And all of you love to sniff nosegays!

(والنِسْوان) على وزن الجِرْوان والنِسْوة على وزن القَهْوة أو العَجْوة والنِساء على وزن الكِساء وقد يأتي فيها الفِساء أيضاً

٤،٧،١١ والمعنى أنّي أخشى على نفسي وأخاف ممّا دهاني فأمضي بسرعة وأنا في هذه الحالة وأهرب أي أنطلق بسرعة إلى النسوان وأختفي بينهنّ أو أجلس بجانبهنّ أو مقابلٍ لهنّ كما في المثل الهروب نصف الشطارة وقد هرب عنترة مع قوّته وشجاعته وقال أُعايَرُ بهذا ولا أُقْتَلُ فالشخص إذا خاف من ظالم أو أحد يؤذيه وتمكّن من الخلاص من بين يديه بالهروب له ذلك قال الله تعالى ﴿وَلَا تُلْقُوا بِأَيْدِيكُمْ إِلَى ٱلتَّهْلُكَةِ﴾

٥،٧،١١ (فإن قيل) لأيّ شيء اختار الناظم الهروب عند النساء دون الرجال مع أنّ النساء لا يقدرن على دفع الأذى والضرر ولا منع من يؤخذ من بينهنّ لضعفهنّ وعدم مقاتلتهنّ فما حكم ذلك (قلنا الجواب من وجهين) (الأوّل) أنّه لمّا دهمه هذا الأمر وأتاه الديوان على حين غفلة وارتخت مفاصله وحصلت له حالة الهرّهرّ عليها كما تقدّم ولم يستطع النهوض ولا المسير إلى أحد من الرجال يختفي عنده أو إلى محلّ بعيد عن القرية يتوارى فيه لشدّة خوفه وكثرة هراره على نفسه وضراطه عليها أيضاً إذ هو من لوازمه كما سيأتي ورأى هؤلاء النسوة قريباً منه أو من محلّه فتوارى بينهنّ (الثاني) يُفْهَمُ منه أنّه كان ضعيف القلب جبان لا يقدر على المخاصمة ولا المضاربة ولا على شيء من أمور الرجال وخشي أن يمضي إلى أحد من الناس أو من أقاربه فيدلّ عليه النصرانيّ فيأخذه ويشوّش عليه وينتقم منه لأنّ الفلّاحين ليس لهم أمان ولا عشرة حسنة مع بعضهم خصوصاً الأقارب كما تقدّم فكلّ شيء له من جنسه آفة كما قيل [كامل]

وَلِكُلِّ شَيْءٍ آفَةٌ مِنْ جِنْسِهِ   حَتّى الحَدِيدُ سَطا عَلَيْهِ المِبْرَدُ

Niswān is of the pattern of *jirwān* ("puppies"), *niswah* of the pattern of *qahwah* ("coffee") or *ʿajwah* ("pressed dates"), and *nisāʾ* of the pattern of *kisāʾ* ("clothes"); *fusāʾ* ("silent farting") may also be a contributing element.

11.7.4 The meaning is: "I am afraid for myself and am frightened at what has befallen me, so while in this state I go off quickly, and 'flee,' that is, make a quick departure, towards 'the womenfolk,' and hide myself among them" or "I sit next to them or facing them," as in the proverb "Half of valor is knowing when to flee." Even ʿAntarah, for all his strength and courage, fled, saying, "I would rather be reproached for this than be killed!" for if anyone is in fear of an oppressor or of one who might do him harm and he is able to free himself from his clutches by fleeing, he may do so. The Almighty has said, «Cast not yourselves into perdition!»[253]

11.7.5 If it be said, why did the poet choose to take refuge with the women rather than the men, even though women are incapable of fending off harm and injury or of protecting any person who might be taken from their midst because of their weakness and inability to fight, we would reply that the answer may be from either of two perspectives. First, that, when this disaster took him by surprise and the tax collectors arrived unexpectedly and his joints went loose and he suffered an attack of the trots, he shat all over himself, as explained above, and was unable to stand up or make his way towards any man with whom he might hide himself or towards any place far from the village in which he might conceal himself, because he was so scared and was shitting on himself so much—and indeed farting on himself, the latter being, as we shall see, a concomitant of the former—and when he saw these women near him, or near the place where he was, he concealed himself among them. Second, it may be understood from what he says that he was weakhearted and a coward, incapable of standing up to or trading blows with others, or of any other type of men's business, and that he was afraid that if he went to any of the people or to any of his relatives, they would direct the Christian to him, and the latter would take him and use him ill, and take his revenge on him; for the peasants give one another no quarter and do not maintain kindly relations among themselves, especially where relatives are concerned, as previously noted[254]—and everything has a foe of its own kind. As the poet says:

Everything has a foe of its own kind—
Even iron is attacked by the file!

٦،٧،١١ وأيضاً النساء غير متّهمين بهذا الأمر فإذا رآهنّ أحد قد اجتمعن في محلّ لا يشكّ أنّ بينهنّ رجل إلّا إن ظهرت له قرائن تدلّ عليه وربّما منعه الحياء منهنّ عن التفتيش وقد توارى سيّدنا حسّان رضي الله عنه عند النساء في بعض الغزوات لجبنه وقلّة شجاعته كما هو مذكور في السِيَر فاتّضح الجواب ثمّ إنّه لمّا كان هروبه عند النساء يحتاج إلى شيء يواريه من الأعداء ويستر عنه الأعين قال

٧،٧،١١ (وألتفّ بالعبا) أي وقت جلوسي بين النساء أو بجانبهنّ أو قبالتهنّ ألتفّ في العباء أو أرقد بعد لفّي فيها لأطرد عنّي الوهم بالتفافي بها فإنّ الخائف أيّ شيء رآه توارى فيه سواء كان عباء أو ثوباً أو شيئاً يواريه عن الأعين بل ربّما تزيّا بزِيّ النساء واختفى عن عدوّه ونجّاه الله تعالى

٨،٧،١١ (كما اتّفق) أنّ بعض الملوك كان كثير الطلب لرجل من العصاة ليقتله فقيل له هو في القرية الفلانيّة فأرسل له بعض الأمراء بطائفة من العسكر فدخلوا القرية وأحاطوا بها فلمّا عرف الرجل أنّهم يريدوا أخذه للملك تزيّا بزيّ النساء وخرج في جمع منهنّ ينوح ويبكي ويصيح فقال الأمير ما بال هؤلاء النسوة سَلُوهُنَّ عن حالهنّ فأقبلوا جماعة وسألوهنّ فقلن إنّه مات لنا ميّت في القرية الفلانيّة ونريد التوجّه إليه فخلّى سبيلهنّ فذهبن والرجل المطلوب بينهنّ ولم يعرف الأمير حاله إلى أن جاوز العسكر ومضى إلى حال سبيله ونجّاه الله تعالى

٩،٧،١١ (ومثل هذه الواقعة) ما اتّفق لي أنّي كنت في سفينة مسافراً من بلدي شِرْبِين لمصر فلمّا جاوزنا قرية تسمّى مَسِيد الخِضْر وإذا بغلام جميل الصورة عليه ملبوس حسن في زي خَدَمَة الأمراء وهو يصيح على رايس السفينة خذني ويتذلّل له ويتدخّل عليه

Additionally, women are not implicated in this business, so no one who saw them congregated in a place would suspect that they had a man in their midst, unless some circumstantial evidence should happen to give him away, and propriety would probably prevent anyone from searching them. Our Master Ḥassān,[255] God be pleased with him, hid among the women during certain raids because of his cowardice and lack of courage, as mentioned in the various biographies of the Prophet. Thus the answer now is clear. 11.7.6

Subsequently, since his taking refuge among the women required something to actually conceal him from his enemies and hide him from sight, he says:

wa-ltaffu bil-ʿabā ("and wrap myself in my cloak"): that is, "when I am seated in the midst of the women, or next to them, or opposite them, I wrap myself in my cloak (*ʿabā*), or I lie down after wrapping myself in it, in order by so wrapping myself to rid myself of my fears"—for one who is frightened will conceal himself in anything that he sees, be it a cloak or a robe or anything else that may hide him from sight. He may even go so far as to dress himself as a woman and so disappear from the sight of his enemies and be saved by the Almighty. 11.7.7

It once fell out that a certain king was searching everywhere for a rebellious subject in order to kill him and was told, "He is in such and such a village." So he sent one of his officers after him with a contingent of soldiers, who entered the village and surrounded it. When the man realized that they wanted to take him to the king, he put on women's clothing and went out among a throng of women, all of them wailing and weeping and shrieking. "What's the matter with those women?" asked the officer. "Ask them what they're doing!" So a company approached them and questioned them, and they replied, "A relative of ours has died in another village and we wish to go to him," and they allowed them then to pass and they proceeded—the fugitive, unknown to the officer, among them—until the man had passed through the soldiers and gone his way and the Almighty saved him. 11.7.8

A similar incident once befell me when I was in a ship traveling from my town, Shirbīn, to Cairo.[256] We were passing by a village called Masīd al-Khiḍr[257] when a good-looking youth appeared, handsomely dressed in the uniform of an emir's servant, who cried out to the ship's captain, "Take me with you!" and beseeched and implored him in great distress to take him on board. The captain, however, refused, fearing that someone might be coming 11.7.9

أنّه يأخذه وهو في كرب عظيم فامتنع ريّس السفينة من أخذه وخشي أن يكون خلفه أحد يفتّش عليه أو يأتي في أثره وكان في السفينة ثلاثة من النساء وفيهنّ امرأة كبيرة فقالت يا رايس غلام مكروب يسألك في أخذه فلم تجب دعوته ولا ترحمه ادخل البرّ وخذه وأنا أصنع له حيلة تواريه عمّن يطلبه وأخفيه بين بناتي ولا يعرفه أحد فسمع الريّس كلامها وأخذ الغلام فلمّا صار في السفينة أخبر أنّه كان في خدمة بعض الأمراء وأنّه استغفله وهرب ولا بدّ من مجيئه خلفه فقالت له هذه المرأة اقلع ثيابك فقلعهم فأخذتهم وأخفتهم في حوائجها وألبسته لبس النساء وأجلسته بجانبها فبينما نحن في هذه الحالة وإذا بأمير راكب على فرس وهو يركض بها ركضاً شديداً وخلفه رجال ومماليك حتّى صار قبالة السفينة وقال للرايس ادخل البرّ حتّى أفتّشك فإنّه هرب لي غلام في هذه الساعة ومعه ألف دينار سرقها فقالت له المرأة ادخل ولا تخف فدخل البرّ وصار كلّ من في السفينة في خوف من هذا الحال فطلع الأمير وأعوانه وفتّش السفينة والمرأة تقول هذا شيء ما رأيناه قطّ وإنّما رأينا غلاماً يجري من بعيد إلى الجهة الفلانيّة فمنعه الحياء وعدم الشكّ فطلع من المركب ولم يظفر بشيء وأمّا الغلام فإنّه مكث معنا في المركب إلى أن طلع مصر وذهب إلى أهله سالماً

١٠،٧،١١ والناظم لمّا رأى هذه العباءة اندرج فيها والتفّ بها واللفّ هو الاندراج في الشيء واللفّ به مراراً ويطلق على الأكل بلغة أهل الريف يقال فلان لفّ متردّ عدس أو متردّ بيسار بمعنى أنّه أكله ويقال داهية تلفك مثلاً فالناظم اندرج في العباءة المذكورة ليُوهِم من رآه أنّ هذه عباءة ملتفّة ولا يشكّ أنّ داخلها أحداً والعباءة كساء عريض طويل يعمل من الصوف له خطوط مختلفة الألوان يجعلوها أهل الريف فراشاً في الصيف وغطاء في الشتاء فهي مناسبة للفصلين وهي أفخر ما عندهم من الفراش والغطاء وقد ورد لفظ العباء في قول سيّدنا الحسين رضي الله تعالى عنه [رمل]

after him looking for him or following his tracks. At the same time, there were three women in the boat, one of them elderly. "Captain," said the last, "a young man in distress asks you to take him with you, and you do not accede to his plea or have mercy on him? Pull in to the shore, take him, and I'll come up with a trick to hide him from those who're looking for him. I'll conceal him among my daughters and no one will know who he is!" So the captain did as she said and took the youth on board. Once on the ship, he informed us that he was in the service of an emir and that he had duped him and fled and that he was certain to come after him. "Take off your clothes!" the woman told him, so he took them off. Then she took them and hid them among her things and dressed him in women's clothes and sat him next to her. While we were thus engaged, an emir appeared riding a horse, spurring it on for all he was worth, men and slaves behind him, till they drew abreast of the ship and he said to the captain, "Pull in to the shore so I can search you! A serving boy of mine has just now fled, taking with him a thousand dinars that he stole." The woman told the captain, "Pull in and don't be afraid!" so the captain pulled in to shore and everyone on the ship was frightened at what was going on. The emir and his helpers boarded and searched the ship, while the woman exclaimed, "We saw nothing of the sort! What we did see was a young man in the distance running in such and such a direction." Propriety and lack of grounds for suspicion prevented the emir from searching the women, so he left the boat empty-handed, but the young man stayed with us on the boat until it reached Cairo, and he went off to his family, safe and sound.

The poet, seeing this cloak (*ʿabāʾah*),[258] enveloped himself in it and wrapped it around himself. *Laff* ("wrapping") means enveloping oneself in something and wrapping it around oneself several times. In the language of the country people, the word is also applied to eating: one says, "So-and-so 'wrapped' (*laff*) a crock of lentils" or "a crock of *bīsār*," meaning "he ate it." And one says *dāhiyah taluffak* ("May a disaster consume you!"), for example. The poet enveloped himself in the aforementioned *ʿabāʾah* so as to trick anyone who saw it into thinking that it was just a folded cloak and not suspect that there was anyone inside it. The *ʿabāʾah* is a long, wide garment made of wool with varicolored stripes, which the country people use as something to lie on in summer and as a cover in winter.[259] Thus it is well suited to both seasons and is the most sumptuous bedding and covering that they have. The term *ʿabāʾ* is used in the verse of Our Master al-Ḥusayn, may the Almighty be pleased with him: 11.7.10

نَحْنُ أَصحابُ العَبا خَمْسَتُنا   قَدْ مَلَكْنا شَرْقَها والمَغْرِبَيْن

١١،٧،١١ والعباءة مشتقّة من عَبّ الماء لأنها تعبّه إذا أُلْقِيَت فيه أو من عبوب البحر أيّام النيل أو من أبو عُبَيّة كنية لبعض الفراريج الصغار يكنّوه نساء الأرياف بها ومصدرها عبّ يعبّ عبّاً وقوله

١٢،٧،١١ (ويقى) أي عند هذه الحالة الّتي أنا فيها وهي انسهال الطبيعة وسيلان الهرار على نفسي من عدم الأمن وشدّة الخوف وأنا ملفوف في هذه العباءة ومندرج فيها

١٣،٧،١١ (ضراطي) أي صوت الريح المتلائم في بطني من أكل العدس والبيسار عند خروجه من ضربات الأعضاء ورجفان القلب

١٤،٧،١١ (شبه) أي يشبه صوت قرع

١٥،٧،١١ (طبل) وهو جلدة مركّبة على خشب أو نحاس تُقْرَع عند المواكب والتحام الحرب له دَوِيّ شديد ورعب زائد وكلّه حلال إلّا الكوبة وهي طبلة صغيرة محصورة الرقبة وتسمّى أيضاً بالدَّرابُكّة وطبل الرَّقّ يستعملها أرباب الدخول وهي من آلات الملاهي وكذلك الزَمْركلّه حرام إلّا النفير وقوله

١٦،٧،١١ (عنيف) أي شديد الضرب يقال فلان عنّف فلاناً بمعنى أنّه ضربه أو أدّبه والمعنى أنّ صوت هذا الريح الخارج من بطنه المسمّى بالضراط يشبه صوت طبل يضربه رجل بقوّة وشدّة فالصفة راجعة للضارب لا لنفس المضروب أو أنّ مراده بالطبل العنيف هو الكبير مثل النُقّارة ونحوها لكونه لا يعرف غيرها

١٧،٧،١١ والحاصل من هذه العبارة أنّ الضراط فيها على أربعة أقسام (الأوّل) ضراط يخرج رقيقاً ضعيف الصوت ممتدّاً (الثاني) ضراط يجول في البطن بقرقرة ثمّ يخرج

Wearers of the *ʿabā* are we, the five of us;[260]
We hold sway over east and west!

ʿAbāʾah is derived from *ʿabb al-māʾ* ("he gulped the water") because it "gulps it up" (*taʿubbuhu*) if it is thrown into it, or from the *ʿubūb* ("billows") of the river in the days of the Nile flood,[261] or from the *abū ʿubayyah* ("the one with the little cloak"), a nickname that the women of the countryside give to certain small chicks. The paradigm is *ʿabba, yaʿubbu, ʿabban.* 11.7.11

wa-yabqā ("and (my farts) are"): that is, are while I am in this state in which I find myself, namely, that of having loose bowels and with my sloppy stools running all over me from the insecurity and the terror while I am wrapped and enveloped in that cloak . . . 11.7.12

ḍurāṭī ("my farts"): that is, the sounds made by the wind resounding harmoniously in the belly as a result of eating lentils and *bīsār,* when expelled by the pounding of my members and the shaking of my heart, are . . . 11.7.13

shibha ("like"): that is, resemble the sounds made by the beating of . . . 11.7.14

ṭablin ("a drum"): meaning a hide mounted on wood or copper beaten during processions and on joining combat; it makes a loud noise and creates great terror and is permitted by religion in all its forms except for the *kūbah,* which is a small drum with a narrow neck also known as the *darābukkah* ("goblet drum"), and the *ṭabl al-riqq* ("tambourine"), which is used by singers—these belong to the category of instruments employed for frivolous purposes. Likewise, all types of wind instruments, except the trumpet, are forbidden by religion.[262] 11.7.15

ʿanīf ("loud"): that is, beaten hard; one says someone "dealt harshly with" (*ʿannafa*) another, meaning that he beat him or disciplined him. The meaning is that the sound of that wind that exits from his belly and is called farting resembles the sound of a drum beaten vigorously and forcefully, according to which analysis the adjective would refer to the one beating rather than the thing beaten.[263] Or it may be that by "a loud drum" he means a big one, such as the kettledrum or the like, since he knows no other. 11.7.16

To give a brief overview of this word, farts fall into four categories: first, the fart that emerges delicately, with a feeble sound, and is of extended duration; second, the fart that circulates, rumbling, in the belly, then emerges as 11.7.17

ريحاً من غير صوت (الثالث) ضراط يخرج ممتزجاً بالغائط وصوته يشبه صوت قُلّة الماء عند امتلائها (الرابع) ضراط يخرج بعنف وله صوت عالي يفزع القلوب وهو الّذي نبّه عليه الناظم وصرّح به ولكلّ قسم من هذه الأقسام الأربعة سبب يتولّد منه

(فالأوّل) سببه أرياح لطيفة تتولّد في بطن الإنسان فتخرج على حسب حالها ١٨،٧،١١
وضعفها من بين الأليتين بصوت رقيق بحسب لطفها ورقّتها للطف المأكل قال الشاعر [كامل]

خَرَجَ الضُّراطُ مِنَ الحبيبَ بِرِقَّةٍ   وَلَطافَـةٍ لِوُجودِ لُطْـفِ المَـأكَلِ

وهذا ينشأ من أصحاب الأجسام اللطيفة وأرباب المآكل الخفيفة

(والثاني) ضراط يجول في البطن بقرقرة وربّما وقف في وسطها فلا يتحرّك حتّى ١٩،٧،١١
يكاد يهلك صاحبه ثمّ ينتقل في أركان البطن بقوّة انتفاخ وعلوّ قرقرة فيتولّد منه الضرر وهذا يسمّى عند الأطباء ضراطاً لا يَنْضَج وسببه من المآكل الغليظة وإذا نَضِجَ أسرع في الخروج وقبل نضاجه إذا خرج منه شيء يكون فساء وفي هذه الحالة يكون خروج الضراط فيها نادراً قال الشاعر [طويل]

يُخَلْبِطُ في المَـأكولِ طولَ نَهـارِهِ   وَفي اللَّيـلِ تلقى بَطنَـهُ يَتَقَـرقَرُ

(كما اتّفق أنّ رجلاً أتى إلى طبيب) فقال له أُحِسّ في بطني معمعة وقرقرة فقال له ٢٠،٧،١١
أمّا المعمعة فلا أعرفها وأمّا القرقرة فضراط لا ينضج وإذا كان الريح يجول في البطن من غير قرقرة مع شدّة وجع يقال له مَغَص يُعالَج بأكل شيء من الشِيح أو الصَعتَر المغليّ بالسكّر فطوراً وربّما مكث يوماً كاملاً أو ليلة كاملة (كما اتّفق لابن الراونديّ) عفا الله عنه أنّه أصابه هذا المغص ليلة كاملة فبات يسأل الله تعالى أن يفرّج عنه بفسوة تخرج

wind with no sound; third, the fart that emerges mixed with feces and makes a sound like a water pitcher when it is full; and fourth, the fart that emerges violently, with a loud noise that strikes terror into the heart, this last being the one to which the poet so frankly draws our attention. And each of these four categories has a cause by which it is occasioned.

The first is caused by refined airs that are generated in a person's belly, then **11.7.18**
emerge, as per their particular state and degree of feebleness, from between the buttocks, with a sound as delicate as they are refined, their delicacy being attributable to the refinement of the dish consumed. As the poet says:

The fart of the beloved emerged delicately
And with refinement, for his food was refined.

This type of fart emanates from people with refined bodies and from eaters of light foods.

The second is the fart that circulates, rumbling, in the belly, and sometimes **11.7.19**
comes to a stop right in the middle of it, not moving until the sufferer has almost perished, then proceeds with distentionary strength and loud rumbling to the extremities of the belly. This sort causes injury. It is known to physicians as an "unripened fart" and is generated by coarse foods. If it ripens, it emerges at speed, and if any part of it emerges before it has ripened, it does so as an inaudible fart, in which case the subsequent emergence of the audible fart is of rare occurrence. The poet says:

He eats any-old-how all day,
And at night you find his belly rumbles.

A man once went to a doctor and told him, "I feel the collywobbles and a **11.7.20**
rumbling in my belly." The doctor told him, "As to the collywobbles, I couldn't venture an opinion, but as to the rumbling, it's an unripened fart." If the wind circulates in the belly without rumbling but with acute pain, it is called colic and is treated by consuming a quantity of wormwood or thyme boiled with sugar for breakfast; it may last an entire day or an entire night. It happened that Ibn al-Rāwandī, may God excuse his sins, was afflicted by such a colic for an entire night and passed the time imploring the Almighty to send him relief in the form of a single fart, but such was not vouchsafed to him. First thing in the morning he went out supporting himself on a stick he had and heard a man saying, "Lord, send me a thousand dinars!" Ibn al-Rāwandī said to him, "You crass fool!

منه فلم يتيسّر له ذلك فخرج من الصباح يتوكّأ على عصاة له فسمع رجلاً يقول اللّٰهمّ ارزقني ألف دينار فقال له يا سقيع الذقن أنا طول ليلي أطلب منه فسوة فلم يعطها لي أيعطيك ألف دينار وتركه ومضى ولهذا يقال مغصة قليلة الفساء

(والثالث) ضراط يخرج ممتزجاً مع الغائط وسببه أنّ الأرياح عند قرب خروج ٢١،٧،١١
الخارج تمتزج به وتتلايم معه وتخرج هي وإيّاه عند قضاء الحاجة خصوصاً مع لين الطبيعة فيظهر منها أصوات متقطّعة غير ممتدّة كبقبقة قلّة الماء عند امتلائها وهذا يحصل من تساريح نفخ البطن ولين الطبيعة من تناول المآكل المهضمة وكثرة نزولها بسرعة قال الشاعر [طويل]

إذا ما خَلا الإِنسانُ في بَيْتِ غائِطٍ   فَلاحَتْ بِلا شَكٍّ تَسـاريحُ نَفْخَتِـهْ
فَمَنْ كانَ ذا عَقْـلٍ فَيَسْتِرُ ضـارِطًا   وَمَنْ كانَ ذا جَهْلٍ فَفي وَسْطِ لَحْيَتِهْ

وقد يخرج الضراط له صوت رقيق يشبه صوت دندنة المِرْدَن ورنّته وقت غزل ٢٢،٧،١١
النساء به وقد خرج من بعض الشعراء فلاموه فقال [سريع مع كسر]

ذي بنت بطني خرجت تعيّط   ضـاعَ لي مِـرْدَن ولا لقـيتُهْ
ومن يقل لي اكتم ضـراطك   أجـعل خـرايَ جوّا لحـيتُهْ

فجعل البطن مثل الأمّ وجعل الضرطة فيها مثل البنت لها الّتي فارقت أمّها وصارت تعيّط وتدندن كالمردن لمفارقتها إيّاها فمن هذا أنّه معذور ومن لم يعذره يكون جاهلاً بحاله ويكون خراه في لحيته

وقد يأتي الضراط على بَغْتَةٍ عند حمل شيء ثقيل أو وثبة فاحشة أو تحرّك للقيام ٢٣،٧،١١
بشدّة ولكن لا يمتدّ له صوت مثل غيره وهذا أخفّ ضرراً ممّا سبق (كما اتّفق أنّ أعرابيّاً ضرط على حين غفلة) فلاموه فأنشد يقول [طويل]

All night long I've been asking Him for a single fart and He didn't give it to me, and you think He's going to send you a thousand dinars?" Then he left him and went his way. For these reasons it is called "low-emission colic."

The third is the fart that emerges mixed with feces and is caused by the winds mixing and blending with the excreta just before they emerge, the two coming together as one relieves himself, especially if the bowels are loose. As a result, noises that are staccato and non-legato are to be heard, resembling the gurgling of a water pitcher when full. These are caused by emissions from the bloating of the stomach and relaxation of the bowels consequent to taking food that is too easily digested, followed by its copious, rapid descent. As the poet says: 11.7.21

When a man's in a shithouse all on his own,
The emissions of his bloat will surely be heard.
Thus the man of good sense will pretend he heard naught,
While the moron can have the farts up his beard!

Sometimes a fart will emerge with a delicate sound like the mewling and humming that a spindle makes as women spin with it. Such a sound once emerged from a certain poet and when his companions chided him for it he said: 11.7.22

This is a child of my belly who came out crying,
"I've lost me a spindle. It's quite disappeared."
And if anyone says to me, "Stifle your farts!"
I'll bury my shit deep in his beard!

The poet makes the stomach the mother and the fart within it the daughter who leaves her mother and who starts crying and mewling like a spindle on being separated from her. From this it is to be understood that he is to be excused, and he who does not excuse him is ignorant of his state and the poet's shit will be in his beard.

A fart may come without warning, as when one lifts something heavy, or makes a great leap, or stands up suddenly, but in such cases the sound is not as long as in the others, and such a fart is less harmful than the preceding. For instance, it happened that a Bedouin poet once let out a sudden loud fart, and his companions reproached him. The Bedouin then proceeded to recite the following: 11.7.23

ضَرَطْتُ فَمَا أَحْدَثْتُ فِي النَّاسِ بِدْعَةً   وَلَمْ يَأْتِ إِسْتِي مُنْكَرًا فَأَتُوبُ
إِذَا كَانَتِ الأَسْتَاهُ[1] تَضْرِطُ كُلُّهَا   فَلَيْسَ عَلَيَّ فِي الضُّرَاطِ رَقِيبُ

٢٤،٧،١١ (وأتى) رجلان إلى قاض فتقدّم أحدهما فتظلّم من صاحبه وشكا قصّته فبينما هو يتكلّم إذ ضرط فالتفت إلى استه وقال لها إمّا أن أتكلم أنا أو أنت

٢٥،٧،١١ (وحكى نِفْطَوَيْه) عن حكيم بن عيّاش الكلبيّ قال اجتمع عند عبد الملك وفود الناس من قريش والعرب فبينما هو في المجلس إذ دخل عليهم أعرابيّ كان عبد الملك يُعْجَب به فسُرّ عبد الملك وقال هذا يوم مسرور وأجلسه إلى جانبه ودعى بقوس رمى عنها وأعطاها مَن على يمينه فرمى عنها حتّى إذا صارت إلى الأعرابيّ فلمّا نزع فيها بقوّة ضرط الأعرابيّ فرمى بها مستحياً فقال عبد الملك دهينا في الأعرابيّ وكنّا نطمع في أنسه وإنّي لأعلم أنّه لا يسلّي ما به إلّا الطعام فدعا بالمائدة وقال تقدّم يا أعرابيّ لتضرط وإنّما أراد لتأكل فقال قد فعلت فقال إنّا لله وإنّا إليه راجعون لقد امتحنّا فيه اليوم والله لأجعلنّها مذكورة يا غلام ائتني بعشرة آلاف درهم فجاء بها فأعطاها للأعرابيّ فلمّا صارت إليه تسلّى وانبسط ونسي ما صدر منه فأنشد حكيم بن عيّاش الكلبيّ يقول [وافر]

وَيَضْرِطُ ضَارِطٌ مِنْ عَبْدِ قَيْسٍ   فَيَحْبُوهُ الأَمِيرُ بِهَا بُدُورَا
فَيَا لَكِ ضَرْطَةٌ جَرَّتْ كَثِيرًا   وَيَا لَكِ ضَرْطَةٌ أَغْنَتْ فَقِيرَا
يَوَدُّ القَوْمُ لَوْ ضَرَطُوا جَمِيعًا   وَكَانَ حِبَاؤُهُمْ مِنْهَا عَشِيرَا
أَيُقْبَلُ ضَارِطٌ أَلْفًا بِأَلْفٍ   فَأَضْرِطُ أَصْلَحَ اللهُ الأَمِيرَا

[1] بي: الأَسْتاتُ؛ ب ك با: الاستات؛ م: الاستان.

I farted but by that did nothing unknown to mankind,
Nor did my anus commit some sin of which I should repent.
Since all the world's anuses are given to farting,
Who can reproach me for such an event?

And once two men went before a judge, and one of them stepped forward and made his complaint against his companion and presented his story. While he was speaking, however, he farted, so he turned to his backside and said to it, "Either I speak or you do!" 11.7.24

Nifṭawayh relates, on the authority of Ḥakīm ibn ʿAyyāsh al-Kalbī, that delegations from Quraysh and the Bedouins met with ʿAbd al-Malik. While the latter was holding audience, a Bedouin of whom ʿAbd al-Malik was particularly fond came in. ʿAbd al-Malik was delighted and said, "A happy day indeed!" and seating the man next to him called for a bow, with which he took a shot. Then he passed it on to the next man on his right, who in turn took a shot, until it came around to the Bedouin. When the Bedouin pulled hard on the bow, he farted, and threw it down in embarrassment. ʿAbd al-Malik said, "The Bedouin has put us to shame! We were too greedy for his company, but I know that the only thing that will settle his problem is food." Then he called for the food tray to be brought and said, "Come forward, Bedouin, and fart!" though what he meant to say was "and eat!" The Bedouin said to him, "I have already done so!" to which ʿAbd al-Malik responded, "We belong to God and to God we shall return! We have indeed been tested today! By God, I shall make it something to remember! Page, bring me ten thousand dirhams!" The page brought them, and ʿAbd al-Malik gave them to the Bedouin, who, when he received them, was consoled and rejoiced and forgot what he had let slip. At this Ḥakīm ibn ʿAyyāsh al-Kalbī recited: 11.7.25

A farter from ʿAbd Qays lets one rip,
And the Commander gives him a ten-thousand-dinar tip?
Some fart, to net so much!
Some fart, to make a pauper rich!
We all would happily fart as one
If that fart would net one tenth of that sum.
If a thousand per thousand's the going rate,
Just hear me fart, God set the Commander straight!

قال فابتسم عبد الملك وأجاز حكيم بن عيّاش بمثلها

(وقيل) أقبل الصَغيري على مجلس بعض الأمراء وأراد أن يتكلّم فضرط فولّى خجلاً فأنشد بعض من سمعه يقول [بسيط] ١١،٧،٢٦

قُل للصغيريِّ إذ وَلّى على عَجَلٍ مِنْ ضَرطَةٍ أَشْبَهَتْ نايًا على عُودِ
فَإِنَّما هِيَ رِيحٌ لَسْتَ تَمْلِكُها إذ أَنتَ لَسْتَ سُليمانَ بْنَ داوُدِ

(وهذا) كلّه من باب الحلم والتستّر وإبداء العذر عن الجالس في الحضرة إذا ضرط فيها قهراً عليه لما يعتريه من الخجل والضحك عليه ممّن لا يعذره ولهذا يُلْغَز في الضرطة ويقال [طويل] ١١،٧،٢٧

ومَولودَةٍ لَمْ تَعرِفِ الطَّمْثَ أُمُّها ولَيسَ لَها رُوحٌ ولا تَتَحَرَّكُ
تُقَهْقِهُ مِنها القَومُ مِن غَيرِ نَظْرَةٍ وصاحِبُها مِن عارِها لَيسَ يَضحَكُ

وأمّا إذا كان الضراط باختيار الشخص لا لِعلّة ولا لمرض فإنّه يكون من القباحة وسوء الأدب والازدراء بالجالس في الحضرة فلا يليق بالضارط فيها أن يفعل ذلك ولو أراد به المزح مثلاً

(وقد شاهدنا في بلاد الأرياف) أنّ الشخص إذا ضرط في مجلس على حين غفلة يحصل له منهم غاية الأذيّة والضرر ويلزموه بطعام يفعله لهم وربّما جعلوا له علامة في الحائط الّذي جلس بجانبه من جِصّ أو جير حتّى يراها كلّ أحد ويعرف أنّه ضرط بهذا المكان وربما خرج من القرية بهذا السبب من كثرة ما يلوموه على ما فعل وكلّ هذا من كثافة طباعهم وسوء أخلاقهم وقلّة معذرتهم للضارط وعدم تستّرهم عليه فعلى كلّ حال إنّ الضارط من غير اختيار معذور وخصوصاً إذا كان كَتْمُ الريح يشوّش عليه وكان في جلسة فلا بأس بضراطه فيها وينبغي مسامحته لهذه العلّة ١١،٧،٢٨

ʿAbd al-Malik smiled and rewarded Ḥakīm ibn ʿAyyāsh with a like amount.

And it is said that al-Ṣaghīrī[264] approached an emir when the latter was holding a salon and wanted to speak but farted instead and turned away in embarrassment. One of those who heard him then said: 11.7.26

Tell al-Ṣaghīrī when he turns away fast
At a fart like a flute playing to the oud,
"'Tis but a wind you cannot control,
Since you're not Sulaymān son of Dāʾūd!"[265]

These are all examples of savoir faire and of how to draw a veil over the faults of others and find excuses for a member of a gathering if he farts unavoidably, to spare him the embarrassment and the ridicule of the unforgiving that he would otherwise have to endure. This is why they tell the following riddle about a fart: 11.7.27

One newly born, whose mother never bled,
Who has no life and does not stir.
All guffaw, though she's not seen,
But her owner doesn't laugh—he's too ashamed of her.

If, on the other hand, the farting is a deliberate act on someone's part and not because of an indisposition or an illness, then it's disgusting and bad-mannered and shows contempt for those sitting in the gathering, and the one who farts there behaves inappropriately even if he is trying, for example, to be funny.

We have observed in the villages of the countryside that, if a person farts unexpectedly at a gathering, he suffers enormously at the others' hands, and they force him to prepare them food. Sometimes they make him a mark in whitewash or lime on the wall next to where he was sitting so that everyone may see and know that he farted on that spot. On occasion he may even leave the village because of the reproach they heap on him for what he did, all of which arises from the coarseness of their natures, the worthlessness of their characters, their intolerance of farters, and their indifference to their embarrassment. However that may be, anyone who farts involuntarily is to be excused, especially if stifling the wind would cause him discomfort, even if he is in company. In such circumstances there is nothing wrong with his farting there, and he should be forgiven by reason of his indisposition. 11.7.28

(ورأيت في بعض الكتب) أنّ سبب ما لُقِّبَ حاتم نفعنا الله به بالأصمّ أنّ امرأة جاءت إليه تسأله عن حاجة فلمّا تكلّمت خرج منها ريح بصوت فخجلت وسكتت فقال لها حاتم أَعْلِي صوتك بالكلام فإنّي رجل أصمّ وكان كلامه لها من باب التستّر عليها ففرحت المرأة وظنّت أنّه لم يسمع منها الضراط فاشتهر بذلك رضي الله عنه ١١،٧،٢٩

(واتّفق لي أنّي كنت أهوى غلاماً جميل الذات) * لطيف الصفات * فصيح اللسان * رَطْب البَنان * بديع الجمال * رخيم الدلال * وأنا مشغوف بجماله * وراغب في وصاله * وكنت أترقّب أن أخلو به ساعة من الزمان * وأن يجمعني السعد أنا وإيّاه في مكان * إلى أن صدفته في روضة بالمشموم عابقه * ونخيلها باسقه * وطيورها بالتغريد ناطقه * يَرْفُلُ في ثياب العزِّ والإِمْداد * وكلّ صدفة خير من ميعاد * فباديته بالسلام * وأبديت له الغرام * وسألته الجلوس فأجاب * وما أحلى اجتماع الأحباب * فلمّا استقرّ بنا الجلوس * وأردت أن أتملّى بقدّه المأنوس * بين هاتيك الرياض الزاهره * والروائح العاطره * وأحظى بحديثه العذب الرائق * وبنطقه الشهيّ الفائق * إذ أقبل علينا جماعة من أرباب الذوات الكثيفه * وذوي الطباع العنيفه * وجلسوا من غير طلب * وخاضوا في الحديث من غير أدب * فخجل الغلام منهم وأطرق * واعتراه الوهم والحنَق * وأراد أن يتحرّك للنفار * فخرج منه صوت من غير اختيار * فضحكوا عليه وقاموا منصرفين * وعليه بالقول لائمين * فنظر إليّ بطرف كحيل * ووجه جميل * وقال ما تقول في لُؤْم هؤلاء الأراذل فأنشدت أقول ١١،٧،٣٠

[بين الكامل والرجز]

١١،٧،٣١ لاموا الحبيب وما دَرَوْا قَصْدَ الحبيب بما فَعَلْ
لمّا ازدرى جُلاّسَهُ ورأى بهم ذاك الثِّقَلْ
ورأى التفَوُّه معْهمو بلطيف لَفْظٍ كالعَسَلْ
فيه الخسارة إذ همو أهل الكثافة والمَلَلْ

I saw in a book that the reason that Ḥātim, God benefit us through him, was given the nickname "the Deaf"[266] is that a woman came to ask him about something and, when she spoke, an audible wind came out, so she was embarrassed and fell silent. Ḥātim told her, "Raise your voice when you speak, for I am deaf!" as a way of sparing her embarrassment. The woman rejoiced and was convinced that he had not heard her fart. Then he became known for that, God be pleased with him. 11.7.29

And once it happened that I loved a youth,[267] comely of person, refined of personality, honeyed of tongue, tender of limb, most wonderful in beauty, most winsome in coquetry. Infatuated with his charms, hankering for his arms, ever alert to be alone with him for a space and for fortune to cast us together in some place, I happened across him in a meadow whose fragrant plants exuded balm, whose birds filled the air with song under many a towering palm, where proudly he strolled in garments of glory with to his gait a delectable twist—and how much sweeter a chance encounter than any tryst! I greeted him in open fashion, revealed to him my passion, and asked him to sit down, with which request he complied—and ah, how sweet it is when lovers sit side by side! Then, after we'd settled ourselves and taken our place, and I wanted to take advantage of his compliant grace, among those meadows all in bloom, and all that fragrance and perfume, and to enjoy his converse sweet and pure, and accents of supreme allure, along came a bunch of those whose persons are coarse and natures gross, who sat down without invitation, and plunged without manners into conversation. The youth felt shy and hung his head, assailed by rage and dread, but as he made a move to flee a sound escaped, involuntarily. They mocked him then and left without more ado, making disparaging comments as they did so. He looked at me, his eye with kohl bright, his face a lovely sight, and said, "What say you to the chidings of those boors?" And thus did I recite: 11.7.30

They chided the beloved, unaware 11.7.31
 Of what he meant by what he did
When he displayed his scorn for his companions,
 Showing that from him their churlishness was no way hid,
And thought it best to speak sweetly with them,
 Employing a subtle utterance, like honey,
Though this was lost on them, since they
 Were men of coarseness and ennui.

ناداهـمُ مِنْ إسْته   بلطيفِ صوتٍ قد حَصَلْ
كَيْمَا يُناسِبَ حالَهُمْ   ومقامَهُمْ ذاكَ الأَقَلْ ٣٢،٧،١١
فتفـرّقوا عن مجلسٍ   حاوى الغـزال مع الغَزَلْ
فـلا عـدمنا ضرطـةً   فيهـا ذَهـابٌ للعِـلَلْ
رقّت وراق مَحلُّها   من العواذل والعَذَلْ
والحمد لله علـى   ذهاب هَمٍّ قد رَحَلْ
فاضْرِطْ وغنِّ[1] وانبسط   واشْطَحْ وطِبْ يا ذا البَطَلْ ٣٣،٧،١١
في روضـةٍ يا حُسْنَهَا   بهـا السرور قد وَصَلْ
فكلّما تـرضى بِـهِ   فالعبد عنه ما عَدَلْ
لكنْ بحقّ المصطفى   غيري فلا تأْخُذْ بَدَلْ

فتبسّم عن ثغر كأنّه عقود الجُمَان * ومال عليّ بقدّ كأنّه غصن البان * وقال لا وحقّ من فلق الحبّه * وغرس في فؤادك شجر المحبّه * لا أكون في يميني حانث * ولم يدخل بيننا مدى الدهر ثالث * ولم أزل أنا وإيّاه على هذا الحال * حتّى لحق بذي الجلال * ٣٤،٧،١١

(ومن اللطائف) أنّ السلطان قانصوه الغوريّ مرّ يوماً في شوارع مصر مختفياً هو والوزير فسمع رجلاً من أرباب الدخول يقول لآخر مثله تفتخر عليّ يا فلان وأنا أقدر أصوّر النغمات من طيزي فقال لوزيره عليّ بهذا الرجل فأحضره بين يديه فأخبره الملك بما سمع منه وقال له ليس الخبر كالعيان لا بدّ من فعل ما التزمت به فقال له تعفوني يا ملك الرجل في المخاصمة يقول ما شاء قال لا بدّ من صدق مقالتك وإلّا قتلتك فقال ٣٥،٧،١١

١ بي (في جميع النسخ): وغني.

He called out to them from his buttocks
    With a delicate sound, unpremeditated—
Something to match their condition 11.7.32
    And their most lowly state;
And so they left a gathering
    That gazelle and ghazal did unite—
May we ne'er be deprived of a fart
    That can put such ills to flight!
It came out sweetly, and cleared the place
    Of censors and their displeasure,
So praise be to God for getting rid
    Of a burden that's now gone forever!
So fart, sing, and be happy, 11.7.33
    And roam, brave lad, and be gay,
In a meadow, oh so lovely,
    Where joy has come to stay!
So long as you're willing to have him,
    Your slave will ne'er avert his face—
But, by the Chosen One, swear
    That you'll take none else in my place!

At this he smiled, revealing teeth like a pearly line, his willowy body close to 11.7.34 mine, and said, "Nay, by Him who split the grain[268] and planted in your heart love's tree, I'll never break this oath of mine—no third shall come between us till the end of time!" And so we remained, he with me, till he joined the Lord of Majesty.[269]

An amusing story relates how Sultan Qānṣawh al-Ghawrī was walking in 11.7.35 disguise one day with his vizier in the streets of Cairo when he heard one singer say to another, "You dare to boast of your superiority to me, So-and-so, when I know how to produce the musical modes from my ass?" The sultan said to his vizier, "Bring the man to me!" So the vizier brought him before him and the sultan related to him what he had heard him say and said to him, "Seeing is believing! Make good your claim!" "Please let me off, Your Majesty," the man replied, "for in the heat of an argument a man may say anything!" However, the sultan answered, "Prove your claim or I'll kill you!" "Will you grant me immunity from punishment?" said the man. "That is yours," said the sultan.

تعطيني الأمان قال لك ذلك فقال يكون في محلّ خال قال نعم فتحوّل الملك إلى قاعة الجلوس وأحضره وطاب معه في الكلام وقال له افعل ما بدا لك وكان السلطان الغوريّ له دراية بهذا الفن وألّف فيه بعض رسائل فقال له أيّ نغمة تريد فقال الحجاز مثلاً فحرّك أَلْيَتَيْهِ وصنعها ولم يزل يفعل نغمة بعد أخرى حتّى أتى على جميع النغمات ونهزاتها ولم يترك شيئاً يلام عليه فتعجّب الملك وقال له مثلك لا يكون إلّا ريّس مصر في هذا الفنّ ثمّ إنّه أجازه بألف دينار وجعله رئيساً على أرباب الدخول كلّهم ويقال إنّه جدّ أولاد العَتْر المشهورين الآن

٣٦،٧،١١ (وقد) اجتمعتُ برجل يقال له ماضي الضرّاط كان رحمه الله على غاية من الدين والورع واللطافة والدخول وكان يحفظ القرآن حفظاً جيّداً وضراطه كان مصنوعاً يفعله بإبطه إلّا أنّه كان يفعل به أيّ نغمة كانت ويعمل منه أشغالاً ونحو ذلك فكان بهذه المثابة أعجوبة لكلّ من رآه وسمعه يضحّك الجماد وكان مشهوراً عند الأمراء مقبولاً عند العظماء عفا الله عنه

٣٧،٧،١١ (فائدة فشرويّة) سمعتها من بعض أهل الخلاعة وهو أنّ إبليس لعنه الله يضرط في كلّ يوم خمس ضرطات يفرّقها على خمسة أنفار أوّلهم من يركّب زوجته ويزوّرها أضرحة الأولياء والمقابر والثاني من رأى اثنين يتسارروا وأدخل نفسه بينهما وهذا يسمّى عويل مصاحبة والثالث من رأى اثنين يتضاربا وأدخل نفسه بينهما فيقع غالب الضرب عليه كما في المثل ما ينوب المخلّص إلّا تقطيع الثياب والرابع من يمشي في الطريق ويلتفت من غير حاجة والخامس محبوس الزوجة وقِسْ على أمثالهم

٣٨،٧،١١ (فإن قيل) إنّ الضراط صوت وقد عرّفوا الصوت بأنّه هواء منضغط بين قالع ومقلوع أو قارع ومقروع وليس هنا قارع ولا مقروع إنّما هو يخرج من الاست عند

"Let it be in an empty place," said the man. "So be it," said the sultan. So the sultan decamped to the reception hall, had the man brought, spoke kindly to him, and told him, "Proceed at your leisure!" (Sultan al-Ghawrī was well-versed in this art and had written several treatises on it).[270] "What mode would you like?" said the man. "Ḥijāz,[271] for example," said the sultan. So the man worked his buttocks and produced it, and then continued to make one mode after another until he had run through them all, along with their transitions,[272] omitting none and leaving no room for criticism. The sultan was delighted and said, "Such as you must surely be the master of Egypt in this art!" Then he awarded him a thousand dinars and appointed him chief of all the singers of Egypt, and it is said that he is the ancestor of the Awlād al-ʿAtr Troupe that is famous today.

Once I met a man called Māḍī the Farter, God have mercy on his soul. 11.7.36
He was extremely meticulous in his religion and pious, as well as refined and musical, and he knew the Qurʾan very well by heart. His farts were made by artifice, in that he did them with his armpit, but he could still make any mode whatsoever that way and work variations and so on on them. He was a source of amazement to all who saw him and hearing him would make a stone laugh. He was famous among the emirs and received by the mighty, may God excuse him his sins.

A bit of facetious useful knowledge that I heard from a profligate: Satan, 11.7.37
God curse him, farts five farts every day and distributes them among five individuals. The first of these is the man who puts his wife on a mount and takes her around to visit the tombs of the saints and the cemeteries. The second is the man who sees two people delighting in one another's company and inserts himself between them; such people are known as a "parasites of friendship." The third is the man who sees two people fighting and inserts himself between them so that most of the blows fall on him, according to the proverb "The peacemaker gains nothing but torn clothes." The fourth is the man who walks in the highway looking this way and that for no reason. And the fifth is the man who is a prisoner of his wife. Many more could be added to the list.

If it be said that a fart is a sound, and sound has been defined as "air com- 11.7.38
pressed between what is pulled and what it is pulled out of," or "between what strikes and what is struck"—while, in this case, there is no striker and nothing struck, the fart merely emerging from the anus at the parting and articulation of the buttocks—so what is the explanation, we would reply that it may be said

انفتاح الألْيَتَيْن وتحرّكهما فما الحكم (قلنا الجواب) أن يقال إنّ هذا لا يتأتّى إلّا على التعريف الثاني وهو أنّ الصوت هواء يتموّج بتصادم جسمين فاتّضح الجواب

٣٩،٧،١١ (فإن قيل) إنّ في قول الناظم (ويبقى ضراطي شبه طبل عنيف) إشكال من حيث أنّه إذا كان ضراطه يشبه صوت الطبل الشديد يكون كلّ من سمعه أقبل عليه وعرفه وظهر حاله واستدلّ بهذه الحالة عليه النصرانيّ وغيره فلا فائدة في اختفائه بين النساء ولا في اندراجه في العباءة فما الحكم (قلنا الجواب) أنّ الناظم ما ذكر حصول الضراط له بهذه الصفة إلّا بعد لفّه في العباءة فهو وإن كان قويّاً وله صوت عالي فلقوّة اندراجه في العباءة لا يسمع منه شيء والمعنى أنّه لو كان خالياً عن اندراجه ولفّه ليُسْمَع منه الضراط كصوت الطبل وهذا مثل رجل محبوس في جُبّ عميق مثلاً ومعه طبل يقرعه فلا يُسْمَعُ منه إلّا قليلاً وإن كان ضربه شديداً فيكون سماعه قاصراً على نفسه أو من يكون واقفاً على باب الجبّ أو قريباً منه فالعباءة حكم الجبّ وهي أضيق لاندراجها ولفّها عليه ولو كان الضراط فيها قويّاً لا يظهر حسّه من الخارج إلّا ضعيفاً أو أنّه من باب الغلوّ في الشيء كما قال الصفيّ الحِلّيّ في بديعيّته [بسيط]

عَزيزُ جارٍ لَو اللَّيلُ استَجارَ بِهِ   مِنَ الصَّباحِ لَعاشَ النّاسُ في الظُّلَمِ

٤٠،٧،١١ أو يقال إنّ هذا الضراط وإن سُمِعَ منه بالصفة الّتي ذكرها لا يتوهّم أنّه رجل مختفٍ بل ربّما يُظَنُّ أنّه رجل أو امرأة يقضي حاجة فلا يكون فيه مظنّة للتهمة فعلى كلّ حال لا إشكال في كلامه فاتّضح الجواب (قلت) ولم أر من صرّح بهذه العبارة وجعل الضراط فيها على هذه الأقسام وعرّفه بهذه التعاريف غيري

that this phenomenon, namely, the fart, can be integrated only under a second definition, which is that sound is air that forms waves on the collision of two bodies. Thus the answer now is clear.

And if it be said that there is a problem with the poet's words, "and my farts are like a loud drum," to wit that, if his farts resembled the sound of heavy drumming, everyone who heard them would come to him and they would discover him, his presence would become known, and the Christian and others would be informed about it, so there would be no point in his hiding among the women or in wrapping himself in the *ʿabāʾah*, so what is the wisdom in this, we would reply that the poet mentions that he would fart in this manner only after wrapping himself in the *ʿabāʾah*. Thus, even if his farts were forceful and loud, nothing would be heard once he had wrapped himself in the *ʿabāʾah*. Thus the meaning is that, absent any envelopment and wrapping, his farting would be heard like the sound of drums. As it stands, however, the situation would be similar, for example, to that of a man imprisoned in a deep pit who has drums with him on which he beats: scarcely any of the sound would be heard, even if he were beating on them hard, for the ability to hear the sound would be confined to the man himself, or to those standing at the opening of the pit or close to it—the *ʿabāʾah* playing the role of the pit, albeit narrower, because he is enveloped and wrapped up in it—and even if the farting were strong on the inside, the noise would emerge only feebly to the outside. Or it may be that the whole thing should be treated under the rubric of "impossible rhetorical exaggeration," similar to the example given by al-Ṣafī al-Ḥillī in his *Embellished Ode in the Prophet's Praise* (*Al-Badīʿiyyah*), when he says:[273] 11.7.39

A champion so strong that were the night to seek his aid
Against the morn, mankind would live in darkness!

Or it may be said that, even if this farting were to be heard as described, no one would imagine that it was a man who was hiding; rather, it might be thought that it was a man or a woman relieving him or herself, in which case there would be no reason to think that there was anything suspicious. In any case, there is nothing problematic in the poet's words, and the answer now is clear. 11.7.40

And I would like to add that I am the only person to have set forth such an interpretation, made such a classification of farting, and defined it in such terms, so far as I am aware.

٤١،٧،١١ ثمّ إنّ الناظم نبّه على أنّ عمره قد انقضى وزمانه قد مضى فيما لا طائل تحته ولا فائدة فيه لشدّة فقره وقلّة كسبه فقال

ص

٨،١١ وَيَادَوْبَ عُمْرِي فِي ٱلْخَرَاجِ وَهَمِّهِ   تَقَضَّى وَلَا لِي فِي ٱلْحَصَادِ سَعِيفْ

ش

١،٨،١١ قوله (ويا دوب) الواو عاطفة بحسب ما قبلها والياء للنداء ودوب هذه لفظة لها اشتقاقات فشرويّة ومعاني مختلفة فإمّا أن تكون مشتقّة من دأب الإنسان وهو شأنه وحاله الّذي هو مهتمّ به والمعنى أنّكم تعلموا يا إخواني أنّ دأبي طول

٢،٨،١١ (عمري) مع ما حصل لي من الهموم سابقاً في حساب وفكر وتعب شديد ممّا عليّ من

٣،٨،١١ (الخراج) وما ينشأ من (همّه) أي خراج الأرض وهو المال المكتتب عليّ تحت زرع الأرض وما يخرج منها في كلّ عام فلا يغطّي ما عليّ من المال لزيادته وقلّة الزرع ولضعفي وشدّة فقري وقلّة من يُسعِفني في الزرع والقلع فلهذا

٤،٨،١١ (تقضّى) عمري وأنا في هذا الحال إلى آخره

٥،٨،١١ أو أنّه من الدَبّ ليلاً على الولد الأمرد إذا رقد بين جماعة ولم يتمكّن منه الفاسق فيصبر عليه حتّى ينام ويدبّ عليه على حين غفلة فما يشعر إلّا والأير قد دخل غالبه أو

Next the poet draws attention to the fact that his life has been expended in puerility and passed in futility, because he is so poor and earns so little. He says: 11.7.41

TEXT

11.8 *wa-yā dawba ʿumrī fī l-kharāji wa-hammihī*
taqaḍḍā wa-lā lī fī l-haṣād saʿīf

Almost all my life on the tax and its woes
Has been spent, and I have no helper when the harvest comes!

COMMENTARY

11.8.1 *wa-yā dawba* ("almost all"): *wa-* ("and") is the conjunction that coordinates the words with what goes before, *yā* is the vocative particle, and *dawb* is a term that has facetious etymologies[274] and a variety of meanings. It may derive from the *da'b* ("ongoing concern") of a person, that is to say, his affairs, and the circumstances in which he is involved. Thus the meaning would be, "You are aware, my brethren, that my ongoing concern, throughout

11.8.2 "*ʿumrī* ('my life'): has lain (in addition to the worries that afflicted me previously) in the computation of, worrying over, and great suffering concerning how much

11.8.3 "of *al-kharāji* ('the tax') and what springs from *hammihī* ('its woes'), that is, the land tax (*kharāj al-arḍ*), namely, the tax that is entered against my name in payment for cultivation of the land and for what it produces every year, for these do not cover the tax I owe, because the latter is great, while farming produces little, and because I am so weak and poor and have few to help me in sowing and harvesting. Consequently, my life

11.8.4 "*taqaḍḍā* ('has been spent'): in this state," etc.

11.8.5 Or it (*yā dawba*) may be from nocturnal "creeping up" (*dab*) on a beardless youth, when he lies down in the midst of a throng, meaning that the profligate has not been able to get at him; in such cases, the man bides his time until the boy is asleep and then "creeps up" on him unawares, the boy feeling nothing until most, or all, of the penis has entered.[275] Then the boy submits until

كلّه فيخشع خَوْفَ أحد يتحرّك أو خَشْيَةَ الفتنة حتّى يقضي الفاسق مراده وربّما عاتبه الأمرد عتاباً لطيفاً أو شتمه شتماً خفيفاً فيقول له قدّر الله وأنا عبدك مثلاً وإنّي هلكت في حبّك إلى أن تمضي القضيّة على أحسن حال قال بعضهم مواليا [بسيط]

دَبّيْتُ ليلاً على مَن للمَلاحَةِ حازْ بَقَيْتُ راكِبْ على ظَهْرُو شبيهَ البازْ
لما انْتَبَهْ من مَنامُو قالْ مَنْ دا فازْ بِوَصْلنا قُلْتُ أَعْمى جَسَّ بالعُكّازْ

١١،٨،٦ (والمعنى) أنّي أكون على حين غفلة فيدبّ عليّ همّ الخراج وتعبه والحساب فيه فيمنعني الراحة في معاشي والسرور في أوقاتي وهكذا طول زماني كما يدبّ الفاسق على الأمرد فما يشعر إلّا وقد علا ظهره ونال مقصوده كما تقدّم أو أنّه من دبيب سمّ العقرب بمعنى أنّ الحساب في هذا الأمر في الليل والنهار يتولّد منه غمّ يسري على القلب ويدبّ فيه دبيب سمّ العقرب في سائر الجسد أو أنّه مشتقّ من الدُبّ بضمّ الدال وهو حيوان غليظ الجسم غزير الشعر بليد الطبع ليس في الحيوان أبلد طبعاً منه إلّا أنّ عنده قوّة إدراك عن غيره كما في المثل (بلادة الدبّ غلبت فطانة القرد) وعجيب منه أنّه إذا رأى أيّ جماعة يريدون صيده يلصق شعره على صمغ الشجر فيمتزج الصمغ بشعره ثمّ يتمرّغ على الرمل حتّى يصير شعره يابس كالحجر فلا يؤثّر فيه ضرب النُشّاب ولا غيره ويكون وقاية له ففي التبلّد في الأمور ضرب من الراحة واختبار للعقول قال الشاعر [طويل]

تَبالَدْ تَرَنْ عَقْلَ الأَنامِ ويُظْهِروا إِلَيكَ أُموراً لَستَ مِنها بِخابِرِ

١١،٨،٧ والمعنى أنّ كثرة الهمّ من حساب المال ووزن الخراج صيّرتني في حالة تشبه بلادة الدبّ وعدم حركته في السعي لعدم المكاسب وقلّة البركة في الزرع وشدّة الفقر

the profligate has gotten what he wants, either for fear of anyone stirring or because scared of causing strife. Sometimes the boy will then reproach him gently, or chide him lightly, and the other will say, "God has decreed it so, and I am your slave," for example, or "I'm dying for love of you" and so on, until things are sorted out to everyone's satisfaction. A poet has said in a *mawāliyā*:

I crept up at night on a boy most cute
And rode like a hawk with his back in my clutch.
Waking, he asked, "Who's this who's won his suit?"
Said I, "A blind man, poking with his crutch!"

The meaning would be "at any time, the worry and fatigue associated with the land tax and the calculation of it may creep up on me and deny me any ease in my daily life or pleasure in my days and so on as long as I live, just as the profligate creeps up on the beardless boy, who feels nothing until the man is on his back and has had his way with him, as described above." Or it may be from the spreading (*dabīb*) of the poison of the scorpion, in the sense that preoccupation with making this sort of calculation night and day engenders a depression that diffuses itself to the heart and spreads itself there, just as the scorpion's poison spreads throughout the entire body. Or it may be derived from *dubb* ("bear"), with *u* after the *d*, an animal with a massive body, thick hair, and slow reactions, than which there is no more slow-witted beast, albeit its powers of comprehension are greater than others'—as the proverb says, "Better the slowness of the bear than the quickness of the monkey." One of its remarkable traits is that, if it sees a hunting party coming, it rubs its hair against gum from trees so that the gum mixes with the hair, then rolls in the sand until the hair becomes as hard as rock. Thereafter, neither arrow nor anything else has any effect on it, and the hair protects it. 11.8.6

There is a kind of ease and a way of testing people's thinking to be found in reacting slowly to things. As the poet says:

Affect slowness, weighing thus men's minds,
And these will reveal to you things you never knew!

In this case, the meaning would be "Excessive worry from calculating the money that I owe in tax and weighing out the tax in kind[276] have brought me to a state that resembles that of the bear in the slowness of its reactions and its sluggishness in bestirring itself, because of the low earnings and small profit 11.8.7

وتواتر الطلب عليّ في كلّ ساعة فأنا محروم من لذّات الدنيا ولم يفدني ما أنا فيه شيء
قال بعضهم [سريع]

أَصبَحتُ لا شُغلٌ ولا عُطلَةٌ   مِزيَدُنا مِن صَفقَةٍ خاسِرهْ
وحاصِلُ الأَمرِ وغايَتُهُ   أَنِّي لا دُنيا ولا آخِرهْ

فلا أرى في الزرع بركة في ابتدائه لقلّة التقاوي وضعفي عن إصلاح الأرض لأنّ الأرض لا يقوم بزرعها إلّا الفلاّح القويّ المتيسّر خصوصاً لما زاد عليها الآن من المظالم وزيادت الخراج والعوائد المكتتبة على الفلاّحين والمغارم فالزرع وإن ورد أنّ فيه تسعة أعشار البركة لا يفي بهذا المقدار من كثرة الظلم وإلّا في الزمن المتقدّم فلم يكن عليه عوائد ولا كُلَف ولا مغارم ولا شيء ممّا هو موجود الآن بل كان الشخص يزرع الأرض ويزن خراجها شيئاً يسيراً ولا يعرف وجبة ولا غرامة ولا شيء من ذلك قطّ وكانت البركة حاصلة بزيادة والأرض كلّها عامرة بالزرع والناس في غاية الخير وسعة الرزق والكسب

١١،٨،٨ (ولمّا دخل المأمون مصر) وسار في قراها كان يُبْنى له في القرية يوماً تَكّة يضرب عليها سُرادِقه والعساكر حوله وكان يقيم في كلّ قرية يوماً وليلة فمرّ بقرية يقال لها طا النمل فلم يدخلها لحقارتها فلمّا جاوزها خرجت إليه امرأة عجوز تُعْرَف بمارية القبطيّة صاحبة القرية وهي تصيح فظنّها المأمون مستغيثة متظلّمة فوقف لها وبين يديه التراجمة من كلّ جنس فذكروا له أنّ القبطيّة قالت أمير المؤمنين نزل في كلّ ضيعة وترك ضيعتي ولم ينزل بها والقبط تعايرني بذلك وأنا أسأل أمير المؤمنين أن يشرّفني بحلوله في ضيعتي ليكون لي الشرف ولعَقِبي ولا يشمت الأعداء بي وبكت بكاءً كثيراً فرقّ لها المأمون وثنى عنان فرسه إليها ونزل فجاء ولدها إلى صاحب المطبخ وقال له

that are to be gotten from farming and my extreme poverty and the unceasing demands upon me from one moment to the next, for I am denied the good things of this world and my situation benefits me nothing." As a certain poet[277] has said:

I'm left with neither work nor leisure—
  Our earnings are from a bargain vexed;
And the outcome of it all and the upshot
  Is naught in this life and naught in the next!

—for I can see no profit in farming, starting from the lack of seed and my inability to improve the land, for only the strong, affluent peasant can cultivate the land, especially in view of the abusive levies,[278] tax augmentations, and customary dues that are entered nowadays against the peasants, and the "obligations." For, though it is written that it is "nine-tenths of all blessing," farming falls short of such a yield because of the pervasive injustices. In earlier times, the peasant did not have "customary dues" or "charges" or "obligations" or any of the other things that exist today imposed upon him. On the contrary, a person would farm the land, the tax calculated on it would be light, and he would know nothing of the *wajbah*, the fine on the landless, and the rest. Blessing was unconfined, all the land was under cultivation, and the people enjoyed the greatest good fortune, affluence, and profit.

When al-Ma'mūn entered Egypt[279] and made a progress through its vil- **11.8.8**
lages, a foundation of crushed stone would be built for him in a day in each village on which his pavilion would be erected and this would be surrounded by troops, and he would stay a night and a day in each village. So he passed a village called Ṭā l-Naml[280] but did not enter it because it was so wretched. When he had gone by, an old woman known as Māriyah the Copt, the owner of the village, came after him, shouting. Al-Ma'mūn thought she was calling on him for help as a petitioner against some injustice, so he stopped for her. He had interpreters of every race on hand, and they told him that the Coptic woman said, "The Commander of the Believers has stayed at every estate and ignored mine and not alighted there, and the Copts are using this to mock me. I ask the Commander of the Believers to honor me by alighting at my estate, that he may honor me and my progeny, and that my enemies do not gloat over me," and she wept copiously. Al-Ma'mūn felt sorry for her, so he turned his horse back towards her and alighted. Her son came to the master of

كم تحتاج من الغنم والدجاج والفراخ والسمك والتوابل والسكر والعسل والطيب والشمع والفواكه والعلوفة وغير ذلك ممّا جرت به العادة قال كذا وكذا فأحضرت أمّه جميع ما ذكر وزيادة وكان مع المأمون أخوه المعتصم وولده العبّاس وأولاد أخيه الواثق والمتوكّل ويحيى بن أكثم والقاضي داود فأحضرت لكلّ واحد منهم ما يخصّه على انفراده ثمّ أحضرت هي للمأمون من فاخر الطعام ولذيذه شيئاً كثيراً حتّى أنّه تعجّب من ذلك فلمّا أصبح وقد عزم على الرحيل حضرت إليه ومعها عشرة وصائف مع كلّ وصيفة طبق مغطّى فلمّا عاين المأمون ذلك ورآها قال قد جاءتكم القبطيّة بهديّة الريف فلمّا وضعت ذلك بين يديه وكشفت الأطباق فإذا كلّها ملآنة بالذهب فاستحسن ذلك وأمرها بإعادته إلى بيتها فقالت لا والله هذا هديّة لك يا أمير المؤمنين فتأمّل الذهب فإذا هو ضَرْب عام واحد كلّه فقال هذا عجب ربّما يعجز بيت مالنا عن مثل ذلك فقالت يا أمير المؤمنين لا تكسر قلوبنا وتحقّر بنا فقال إنّ في بعض ما صنعتيه لكفاية ولا يجب التثقيل على أحد فردّي مالك عليك بارك الله لك فيه فأخذت قطعة من الأرض وقالت يا أمير المؤمنين هذا وأشارت إلى الذهب من هذا وأشارت إلى الطينة الّتي تناولتها من الأرض ثمّ من عدلك وإنصافك يا أمير المؤمنين وعندي من هذا شيء كثير فأمر به وأخذه منها وأعطاها عدّة ضِياع وأعطاها من قريتها طا النمل مائتي فَدّان بغير خراج وارتحل متعجباً من كبر مروءتها وسعة حالها فانظر إلى ما كانت الأرض في الزمن الماضي تعطي زرّاعها من الخير والبركة وسعة الرزق وكلّه من عدم المظالم وكثرة العدل وقلّة الحوادث

(وأوّل) من أحدث بمصر مالاً سوى الخراج أحمد بن المدبّر لمّا ولي خراج مصر ٩،٨،١١
فإنّه كان من دُهاة الناس ابتدع بدعاً كثيرة منها أنّه حجر على الأطرون بعد ما كان مباحاً لجميع الناس وقرّر على البهائم مالاً وسمّاه المراعي وقرّر على ما يُطعم الله من البحر

the kitchen and asked him, "What quantities of sheep and fowl and chickens and fish and spices and sugar and honey and perfume and candles and fruit and fodder and other customarily provided things do you need?" "Such and such amounts," he replied, and the man's mother provided everything he had mentioned, and more. Al-Ma'mūn's brother al-Muʿtaṣim, his son al-ʿAbbās, his nephews al-Wāthiq and al-Mutawakkil, Yaḥyā ibn Aktham, and Judge Dāʾūd[281] were with him, and each of these she provided with his own supplies. Then she personally brought al-Ma'mūn such a large quantity of superb and delicious food that he wondered at it. When the morning came and he was about to set off, she came to him accompanied by ten serving women, each carrying a covered dish. When al-Ma'mūn spotted this and saw her, he said, "The Coptic woman has brought you all a country present!" When she placed the dishes in front of him and uncovered them, each one turned out to be filled with gold. Impressed, he ordered her to take it all back to her house, but she said, "No, by God! This is a gift for you, Commander of the Believers." He looked at the gold, and behold, it was all of one year's minting. "This is a wonder," he said. "Our own treasury might not be able to come up with the like." She replied, "Commander of the Believers, do not break our hearts and treat us with contempt!"[282] He said, "You have done more than enough. There is no need to overburden anyone. Take your wealth back and keep it, and may God bless you in it!" Then she took a piece of the soil and said, "Commander of the Believers, this" (and she pointed to the gold) "is from this" (and she pointed to the earth that she had picked up from the ground) "and then from your justice and fairness, Commander of the Believers, and of the former I have much!" Then he gave an order and accepted the gold from her and awarded her many estates and exempted her from the tax on two hundred feddans of her own village of Ṭā l-Naml, and departed, wondering at her gallantry and affluence. See what bounty, blessing, and affluence the land used to give those who farmed it in the past, and all of it because of the absence of abusive levies, the abundance of justice, and the rarity of upheavals!

The first[283] to introduce a tax other than that on land was Aḥmad ibn al-Mudabbir, when he took charge of Egyptian taxation. He was a crafty rogue, who introduced many harmful innovations, among them a monopoly on caustic soda, which previously had been free for everyone to take. He also set a tax on animals, calling it "the pastures," and another on the food that God provides from the sea, calling it "the fisheries." From then on, the taxes of Egypt 11.8.9

مالاً وسمّاه المصايد فانقسم من حينئذ مال مصر إلى خراجيّ وهلاليّ وعُرِفَ المال الهلاليّ بالجديد وقوله

١٠،٨،١١ (ولا لي في الحصاد سعيف) أي ولا أرى من يُسْعِفني في حصاد الزرع عند انتهائه ولا من يعاونني على تحميله على الجمال ونزوله في الجُرُن ودرسه ودوارته وحصاد الزرع هو ضمّه بآلة من حديد أو قلعه من أصله إذا بلغ الاستواء ويبس حَبّه وطاب سنبله ونشف وآل إلى السقوط فيجلوا عليه بالحصاد وقد شُبِّه الآدميّ بالزرع فإنّه في ابتدائه يكون خضرًا نضرًا زاهيًا كذلك الشخص في حال نشأته وصباه إذا كبر وترعرع يكون على هذه الصفة فإذا طاب وآن أوان حصاده انتهى زمانه وكذلك الآدميّ إذا صار كَهْلاً ودهمه الشيب آن أوان انقضاء عمره فإنّ الشيب نذير الموت ولهذا يقال للرجل إذا دهمه الشيب طاب الزرع أي قرب الموت ودنا حصاده ويطلق الزرع على الحسّيّ والمعنويّ فالحسّيّ ما تقدّم ذكره والمعنويّ مثل فعل الخير مثلاً يقال زرع فلان الجميل أي فعله مع غيره قال الشاعر [بسيط]

اِزرَعْ جَميلاً وَلَو في غَيرِ مَوضِعِهِ ما خابَ قَطُّ جَميلٌ أَينَما زُرِعا
إِنَّ الجَميلَ وَإِنْ طالَ الزَمانُ بِهِ فَلَيسَ يَحصِدُهُ إِلّا الَّذي زَرَعا

(ومن الحِكَم) من فرش رقد ومن زرع حصد وكلّ زارع يحصد ما زرعه من خير أو شرّ

١١،٨،١١ (ثمّ إنّ الناظم) رحمه الله نبّه على مصيبة أخرى من أنواع الظلم ابْتُلِيَ بها هو وغيره من إخوانه الفلّاحين والبطّالين وغيرهم فقال

were divided into land-based and lunar, and the lunar taxes became known as "the new tax."[284]

wa-lā lī fī l-ḥaṣādi saʿīf ("and I have no helper when the harvest comes"): that is, "and I find no one to help me when the harvest is ready or to help me load it onto the camels and unload it on the threshing floor, thresh it, and winnow it." The harvesting of a crop consists of gathering it with an iron implement or pulling it up by the roots when it is ripe and the seeds have hardened and the ears are full and firm and about to fall; this is when they make haste to harvest it. Humans may be likened to a crop. When a crop starts to sprout, it is green, tender, and resplendent. Likewise, a person during his early childhood and youth grows larger and blossoms as described. And when the crop reaches maturity and the time comes for it to be harvested, its days are over; and likewise the human being, when he reaches maturity and gray hairs afflict him, has reached the end of his life, for gray hairs are the harbingers of death. This is why one says of a man afflicted with gray hairs "the crop has ripened," meaning death is approaching and the harvest is nigh. "Sowing a crop" may be used in both concrete and abstract senses: the concrete is that employed above; the abstract is, for example, the doing of good deeds. One says, for instance, "So-and-so 'sowed' good deeds," meaning he did good to others. The poet says: 11.8.10

Sow good deeds, though in a barren spot—
  No good deed is ever wasted, wherever it be sown.
In good deeds, though the wait be long,
  No man reaps any crop but his own.

And there is a wise saying that goes "As you make your bed, so shall you lie, and as you sow, so shall you reap," and every sower reaps what he has sown, be it of good or evil.

Next the poet, may God have mercy on him, draws attention to another of 11.8.11
the disastrous varieties of injustice with which he has been afflicted, he and others among his brother peasants and the landless, and says:

ص

٩،١١ وَيَوْمٍ تَجِي ٱلْعَوْنَهْ عَلَى ٱلنَّاسِ فِي ٱلْبَلَدْ تُخَبِّيُّنِي فِي ٱلْفُرْنِ أُمُّ وَطِيفْ

ش

١،٩،١١ قوله (ويوم) بالتنوين وعَدَمِهِ في هذا البيت

٢،٩،١١ (تجي العونه) وهو أوان حفر السواقي وضمّ الزرع وشيل القَنى ممّا يحتاج إليه في هذا المعنى والعونة إنّما تكون في بلاد الملتزمين الّتي فيها الأُوسَيَة وهو أنّ غالب الملتزمين إذا أخذ قرية أو كفراً من كفور الريف يزرع فيها أو في الكفر جانباً من الأرض والبقيّة يعطيها للفلّاحين بخراج معلوم ويسمّى هذا الجانب الّذي يزرعه زرع الأوسية فيرسل ثيراناً وأخشاباً ومحاريث وما يحتاج إليه ويجعل له على ذلك وكيلاً ومحلاً معدّاً لأخشابه وبهائمه ويقال لها دار الأوسية ويوكّل من يصرف على البهائم وغيرها بحساب وضبط فإذا احتاج الأمر لشيل الطين من الآبار أو حفر القنى أو ضمّ الزرع أمر الشادّ بالقرية أو الكفر رجلاً يقال له الغفير فينادي العونه يا فلّاحين العونه يا بطّالين فيخرجوا عند صَبِيحَةَ النهار جميعهم ويسرحوا للحفر أو الضمّ أو لكلّ ما يأمرهم به كلّ يوم من غير أجرة إلى أن يفرغ الحفر والضمّ وكلّ من تراخى أو تكاسل عن السروح أخذه الشادّ وعاقبه وغرّمه دراهم معلومة وبعض بلاد تكون العونة فيها على رجال معروفين بالبيوت مثلاً فيقولوا يخرج من بيت فلان شخص واحد ومن بيت فلان شخصين بحسب ما تقرّر عليهم قديماً وحديثاً فلا ينفكّ من عليه العونة منها وإن مات جعلوها على ولده وهكذا فهي داهية كبرى على الفلّاحين ومصيبة عظمى على البطّالين ولله الحمد أراح قريتنا منها إنّما هي قراريط معلومة على الفلّاحين لا يعرف

TEXT

wa-yawmin tajī l-ʿawnah ʿalā l-nāsi fī l-balad 11.9
tukhabbiʾunī fī l-furni ʾUmmu Waṭīf

And on the day when the corvée descends on the people in the village
Umm Waṭīf hides me in the oven

COMMENTARY

wa-yawmin ("And on the day when"): with or without nunation in this verse.[285] 11.9.1

tajī l-ʿawnah ("the corvée descends"): this occurs when activities that require 11.9.2 it, such as the excavation of pits for waterwheels, the gathering of crops, and the digging of canals, take place.[286] The corvée is found only in those tax farmers' villages that include demesne land. The system is that most tax farmers, when they take a village or one of the hamlets of the countryside, cultivate a parcel of land in the village or the hamlet and give the rest to the peasants against a fixed tax. This parcel cultivated by the tax farmer is called "the demesne." The tax farmer sends oxen, timber, plows, and whatever else is needed and appoints an agent to take charge of it and prepares a place for the timber and animals belonging to it, the latter being called "the demesne house." He also commissions someone to spend money on the upkeep of the animals, etc., and to keep careful accounts. If mud needs to be cleared out of the wells, or canals dug, or crops brought in, the bailiff of the village or hamlet gives an order to a man known as the watchman and the latter calls out, "Corvée, you peasants! Corvée, you landless!" and they leave in a body early in the morning and set off to dig or do whatever else he may order them to do, every day, without pay, until the digging or harvesting is done. Anyone who is slack or lazy about going to work is taken by the bailiff, who punishes him and takes from him a fine of a set amount. In some villages the corvée applies to a number of men, fixed by household, for example. Thus they say, "From such and such a household one man is to go, and from such and such two," according to the quota set for them in the distant or more recent past. A person subject to the corvée cannot be released from it, and if he dies they impose it on his sons, and so on. It is a great tribulation for the peasants and a huge disaster for the landless. Thank God that He has relieved our village of it! There the peasants are obligated for a fixed number of carats only and all the tax farmer concerns himself with is

الملتزم إلّا خراجها يأخذه في كلّ سنة على التمام والكمال وإن كان عليهم بعض عوائد ومظالم فليست كبلاد الأوسية لأنّهم دائماً في تعب وكدّ وغرامة وعونة وسخرة وهمّ زائد والناظم كان ساكناً ببلاد الأوسية فلهذا ذكر أنّه إذا حضرت العونة

٣،٩،١١ (على الناس في البلد) أي بلد الناظم والناس هم المخصوصون بها لا كلّ سكان القرية ولعلّ الناظم كان ممّن يسرح للعونة لقلّة زرعه وشدّة فقره وأنّه متى غاب ساعة عن عياله من غير كسب احتاجوا إلى ذلك فلا يقدر أن يترك العونة ويذهب لشغل يكتسب منه فلهذا قال

٤،٩،١١ (تخبّئني) أي تخبئني عن أعين الناس حتّى لا يراني أحد ولا يسمع بي

٥،٩،١١ (في الفرن) أي فرنه الكائن في داره المُعَدّ لخَبْز العَيْش ودَمْس الفطير وطبيخ البيسار والفول المدمّس ونحو ذلك

٦،٩،١١ (أمّ وطيف) أصله وطفه وذكره بلفظ المذكّر لضرورة النظم وهو مشتقّ من الطّيْف وهو الخيال الساري مناماً قال الشاعر [طويل]

سَرَى طَيْفُ سُعْدى طارِقاً يَستَفِزُّني سُحَيْراً وصَحْبي بالفَلاة رُقودُ
فَلَمّا انْتَبَهْنا للخَيالِ الّذي سَرَى أَرى الدّارَ قَفْرى والمَزارَ بَعيدُ

أو من الطوفان أو من أطواف الجلّة الّتي تفعلها نساء الأرياف فإنّها كانت كثيرة الشغل في لزق الجلّة وعملها أطوافاً فمن هذا كنّوها أمّ وطيف وأمّا اسمها على ما قيل زوبعة وقيل خطيطه أو معيكه وهي إمّا أنها أمّ الناظم أو زوجته أو أخته وسمّيت العونة عونة لاشتقاقها من المعاونة لأنّها جماعة يخرجوا معاونين بعضهم البعض في

the tax on these, which he takes each year in full. Although they do have to pay the customary dues and abusive levies, it is not like the villages with demesnes, which are constantly caught up in hardship and distress, levies on the landless, corvée, and excessive affliction. The poet lived in a village with a demesne, which is why he says that if the corvée descends . . .

ʿalā l-nāsi fī l-balad ("on the people in the village"): that is, the poet's village, the "people" here being the ones in the village singled out for the corvée, not every inhabitant. It may be that the poet was one of those who used to set off to work on the corvée because his own acreage was so small and he was so poor, and that when he had been away from his dependents for a while without earning anything, they found themselves in need, though he could not leave the corvée and look for paid work. Consequently he says, **11.9.3**

tukhabbiʾunī ("(she) hides me"): that is, hides me from people's eyes so that no one sees or hears me **11.9.4**

fī l-furni ("in the oven"): that is, the oven of his house that is used for baking bread and cooking flaky pastry in the ashes and stewing *bīsār* and fava beans and so forth. **11.9.5**

ʾUmmu Waṭīf: the name is properly Waṭfah, but he uses it in the masculine for the sake of the meter.[287] It derives from the *ṭayf*, which is the phantasm that appears in one's dreams—the poet says: **11.9.6**

Suʿdā's phantom came to me by night and woke me with a start
  At break of dawn, while my fellows in the desert sleeping lay;
But, by that night-phantom woken,
  I find the dwelling desolate, while the place of tryst is far away

—or from *al-ṭūfān* ("the Flood") or from the *aṭwāf* ("small domes") of dung that the women make in the countryside,[288] for Umm Waṭīf used to work a lot at mashing the dung into cakes and making them into *aṭwāf*, for which they bestowed on her this honorific. Some say her real name was Zawbaʿah ("Whirlwind"), others that it was Khuṭayṭah or Muʿaykah. She was the poet's wife, or mother, or sister.[289] The *ʿawnah* ("corvée") is so called because it derives from *muʿāwanah* ("helping one another") because it consists of a group who go out to help one another in the tax farmer's work and so on. Or it may be that it is the name for a group that cooperates in doing something, which is why they say,

شغل الملتزم ونحوه أو أنّها اسم للجماعة المتعاونين على الشيء ولهذا يقال ناكوا فلان الليله عونه أي تعاونوا كلّهم على نيكه دفعة واحدة في الزريبة أو الشونة ويعايروا بهذا الأمرد ويقولوا له أنت يا خور يا بقره دايماً عونتك مِيّه أي مائة نفس أو أنّها من الماعون اسم للزلعة الكبيرة ومصدرها عوّن يعوّن تعويناً أو عان يعين إعانة قال الشاعر [طويل]

فـعَوّنَ تَعوينًا وَعـانَ إعـانَةً وكُلٌّ لَه مَعْنىً صَحِيحٌ[1] وقد وَرَدْ

١١،٩،٧ (فإن قيل) إنّ كلام الناظم يُشعِرُ أنّه إذا اختفى في الفرن يتركوه ولم يَشْعُر به أحد وهذا بخلاف ما تقدّم من أنّ العونة لا بدّ من السروح إليها وخصوصاً إذا كانت مقرّرة على الشخص من قديم الزمان أو من زمن أجداده كما تقدّم فما الجواب (قلنا) الجواب أنّ الناظم لمّا مال عليه الزمان وبقي من ضعفاء الناس وفقرائهم صار وجوده كالعدم ولا أحد يفتكره وإنّما أراد الاختفاء خوفاً من أقاربه لا يسلّطوا عليه جماعة الملتزم يؤذوه أو يشوّشوا عليه وعلى هذا القول يدلّ على أنّ العونة لم تكن مقرّرة عليه لأنّه كان في ابتداء الزمان شيخ الكفر ومتصرّف فيه أو أنّه اعتراه الكِبَر وصار شيخاً عجوزاً فإذا حضر وقت العونة اختفى في الفرن سترًا على نفسه حتّى لا يراه أحد كما يقال (ابعد عن الشرّ وغنّي لُو) و(عين لا تنظر قلب لا يحزن) فاتّجه الجواب عن هذا الإشكال

١١،٩،٨ ولمّا فرغ الناظم من شكواه من القلّ والعترة والقمل والصيبان وعداوة أقاربه وما ناله من همّ الوجبة والخراج والعونة ونحو ذلك شرع في تمنّي جملة المآكل أو رؤيتها لشدّة ما هو فيه من عدم ذلك وكثرة فقره وأنّه لا يعرف هذا الطعام ولا يراه إلّا عند الناس فتمنّى أنّ الدهر يغلط معه ويرى ذلك أو يملكه ولو يسيرا قبل انقضاء عمره وابتدأ بالكِشْك لأنّه أفخر مأكول أهل الريف فقال

[1] بي (من جميع النسخ): صحيحًا.

"They fucked So-and-so last night *as a group* (*ʿawnah*)," that is, they all cooperated in fucking him at one go in the byre or the granary. Similarly, they mock a beardless boy by saying to him, "You, you faggot, you cow! You're always getting gangbanged by a hundred (*ʿawnatuka miʾah*)!" (meaning by a hundred persons). Or it is from *māʿūn,* a name for the big storage jar.[290] The paradigm is *ʿawwana, yuʿawwinu, taʿwīnan* or *ʿāna, yuʿīnu* , *iʿānatan.*[291] Said the poet:

> Thus *ʿawwana, taʿwīnan* and *ʿāna, iʿānatan—*
> Each has its true sense and attestation.

11.9.7 If it be said that the poet's words give the impression that, if he were to hide in the oven, they would leave him alone and no one would notice him, though this contradicts the preceding statement that there is no escaping going off to work on the corvée, especially if it has been imposed on a certain person since early times or since the days of his grandfathers, as explained above, so how do you explain this, we would reply that the explanation is that, when fate turned against the poet and he joined the ranks of the weak and the poor, he became as one who did not exist, and no one gave any further thought to him. The only reason he hid himself was for fear that his relatives should sic the tax farmer's followers on him to do him harm and beat him up. From this perspective, the words would indicate that the corvée was not applied to him because, in former times, he had been shaykh of the hamlet and administered its affairs, or because age had taken its toll on him and he had turned into an old man; thus, when the time for the corvée arrived, he hid in the oven simply for the sake of decorum and so that no one should see him, according to the maxims "Keep out of harm's way, and thumb your nose at it!" and "What the eye doesn't see the heart doesn't grieve for." The solution to this problem has now been correctly set forth.

11.9.8 When the poet is done with complaining about want, disgrace, lice, nits, the enmity of his relatives, and the distress caused him by the *wajbah,* the tax, the corvée, and so on, he turns his attention to longing for all kinds of foods, or at least to seeing them, because of the extreme straits he finds himself in as a result of the absence of such things and his great poverty and because he knows such victuals only from other people's houses and that is the only place he sees them. He longs that Fate might bungle his case and he might get to see such things and possess them, even in a small amount, before his life ends. He begins with wheat groats, as it is the country people's most sumptuous dish. He says:

ص

١٠،١١ وَلَا هَدَّنِي مِنْ بَعْدِ هَادَهْ وَهَادِهِ سِوَى ٱلْكِشْكِ لَمَا يَسْتَحِقُّ غَرِيفْ

ش

١،١٠،١١ قوله (ولا هدّني) أي هد حَيْلِي وقوّتي مأخوذ من هدّ الحائط وأصله الهَدْم بزيادة الميم حُذِفَتْ منه جريًا على اللغة الريفيّة أو أنّه من الاكتفاء كقول الشاعر [بسيط]

مَلِيكَةَ الحُسنِ جُودي بِاللِّقَا كَرَمًا لِمُغْرَمٍ قَلبُهُ قَدْ ذابَ فِيكِ أَذا
أَفسَدْتِ قلبي فقَالت تِلكَ عادَتُنا قد قالَ سُبحانَه إِنَّ المُلوكَ إذا

٢،١٠،١١ (وقيل) هد وهد مجموع هُدْهُد بضمّ الهاء فيكون اسم مركّب من فعلين والهدهد طائر معروف ذكره الله تعالى في القرآن الكريم في قوله تعالى حكاية عن سيّدنا سليمان عليه السلام ﴿وَتَفَقَّدَ ٱلطَّيْرَ فَقَالَ مَا لِيَ لَآ أَرَى ٱلْهُدْهُدَ أَمْ كَانَ مِنَ ٱلْغَآئِبِينَ﴾ لأنّه كان رسول الطير وكان يدلّه على الماء لأنّه يرى الماء تحت الأرض بخاصّيّة جعلها الله تعالى فيه (وسئل ابن عبّاس) رضي الله عنه ما الحكمة في أنّ الهدهد يرى الماء تحت الأرض ولا يرى الفخّ ويقع فيه فقال رضي الله عنه (إذا وقع القضاء عمي البصر) أو أنّه مشتقّ من الهَديّة لمقاربة اللفظ وفي الحديث تهادوا تحابّوا ويقال أصل المحبّة الهديّة وأصل العداوة الشكيّة وأصل البِغْضة الأَسِيّة فالهديّة لها موقع في النفس ولو كانت شيئًا يسيرًا وفي المثل (هديّة الأحباب على ورق السَداب) وقال بعضهم [بسيط]

TEXT

wa-lā haddanī min baʿdi hādah wa-hādihī 11.10
siwā l-kishki lammā yastaḥiqqu gharīf

And nothing has demolished me after this and that
but wheat groats when they're ready to ladle!

COMMENTARY

11.10.1 *wa-lā haddanī* ("and nothing has demolished me"): that is, nothing has demolished my stamina and my strength, taken from *hadd al-ḥāʾiṭ* ("he demolished the wall"), which is originally from *hadm* ("destruction"), with an additional *m*, which has been dropped from it in accordance with rural usage,[292] or as a case of "restraint," as in the verse:

"Queen of Beauty, grant a meeting of your kindness
To a lover whose heart melts for you in pain—
My heart you've ruined!" Said she, "Such is our way!
He to whom all glory says, «Lo! Kings, when . . .»"[293]

11.10.2 It is said that *hadd* combined with *hadd* makes *hudhud* ("hoopoe"), with *u* after the *h*, which would thus be a compound noun formed of two verbs.[294] The *hudhud* is a well-known bird mentioned by the Almighty in the Noble Qur'an when He says, quoting Our Master Sulaymān, upon whom be peace, «And he sought among the birds and said, "How is it that I see not the hoopoe, or is he among the absent?"»[295] referring to the fact that it is the messenger of the birds and guides them to water, for it can see water beneath the ground due to a special faculty created in it by Almighty God. Ibn ʿAbbās, may God be pleased with him, was asked, "What is the wisdom in the hoopoe's seeing the water beneath the ground but not seeing the trap, and falling into it?" and he replied, God be pleased with him, "When destiny falls, the eye is blinded." Or it may be derived from *hadiyyah* ("gift"), because it sounds similar.[296] In the Tradition it says, "Give one another gifts and you will love one another," and it is said that the source of love is a gift, the source of enmity a complaint, and the source of hatred maltreatment. A gift, even though small, touches the soul. In the proverb it says, "The gift of friends is on leaves of rue."[297] A poet says:

جاءَ سُليمانَ يومَ العَرْضِ قُنبُرَةٌ تُهْدي إِلَيهِ جَراداً كانَ في فِيها
وأَنشَدتْ بِلسانِ الحالِ قائِلَةً إِنَّ الهَدِيَّةَ عَلى مِقدارِ هادِيها
لَوكانَ يُهدى إِلى الإِنسانِ قيمتُهُ لَكانَ يُهدى لَكَ الدُّنيا وما فيها

١١،١٠،٣ (أو أنّه) من الهَذَيان بالذال المعجمة وهو الصحيح ومصدرها هد يهد هدًا أو هدم يهدم هدماً على اللغتين من قولهم هدّك الله هدًّا أو هدمك هدماً بمعنى أنّه يُضعِف قواك ويُبطِل حركتك كما يَبْطُل نفع الحائط إذا هُدِمَ ونحوه

١١،١٠،٤ قوله (من بعد هاده وهاده) بالهاء والألف والدال المهملة والهاء المربوطة فتكون كلمة محبوكة الطرفين أوّلها مثل آخرها إذا وقفتَ عليها وأصلها هذا اسم إشارة إلّا أنّ ألسنة أهل الريف غيّرتها والمعنى أنّ ما هدّ حيلي وأضعف قواي من بعد ما تقدّم أوّلاً وهوأكل القمل والصيبان والقلّ والعترة ونحوه والّذي أتى عقبه وهو الضرر من الأقارب وهمّ الخراج والوجبة والخوف من نزول الكُشّاف والعونة وطلب مال السلطان والطرد في الغيطان وغير ذلك ممّا تقدّم ذكره على حدّ قول الشاعر

[وزن غير معروف]

همّ الفِلاحـه حيـّرني وكلّ ساعـه في نقصان
ما انفكّ من هـمّ الوجبـه لما يجي مال السلطان

١١،١٠،٥ (فالفلّاح) إذا كان فقيرًا تجده دائماً معرّض للهلاك من ضرب وحبس وعدم لذّة المآكل والمشارب ولا يجد له راحة إلّا إن غلّق مال السلطان وأمّا إذا بقي عليه شيء يسير فإنّه دائماً في افتكار آناءَ الليل وأطرافَ النهار وطرد ونصب إلّا أن أعطاه الله تعالى البركة في الزرع فإنّه يأتي من القليل كثير بحسب نيّته وقت البذر في الأرض

The lark on parade day[298] came to Sulaymān
To give him a locust it had in its beak
And uttered the while these words, in nature's tongue:[299]
"Gifts are proportionate to the giver, be he mighty or meek.
If each according to his worth were given,
Your gift would be the World and all you therein seek!"

Or it is from *hadhayān* ("raving"), with *dh*, which is the correct form.[300] **11.10.3** The paradigm is *hadda, yahuddu, haddan* or *hadama, yahdimu, hadman* according to the two forms, deriving from the expression *haddaka Allāhuan* ("May God demolish you utterly!") or *hadamaka hadman* ("May He destroy you utterly!"), meaning that He should weaken your powers and immobilize you, as a wall becomes profitless when demolished, and so on.

min ba'di hādah wa-hādihī ("after this and that"): *hādah* being with *h* and *ā* **11.10.4** and *d* and final *h*,[301] which means that its ends are "knotted together,"[302] with its beginning being the same as its end, as you will notice if you look closely. The origin of the word is *hādhā*, a demonstrative, but the tongues of the country people have changed it. The meaning is that this has demolished my stamina and weakened my powers after all that went before (namely, being bitten by lice and nits, and want and disgrace and so on) and what came after (namely, the injuries done by relatives and worries over the tax and the *wajbah* and fears over the arrival of the Inspectors and the corvée and demands for the sultan's taxes and scurrying about in the fields and so on, as set out above). As the poet says:

The worry of farming has put me in a dither
And all the while I'm losing more.
No sooner I escape the *wajbah* 's worries
Than the sultan's tax is at the door.

Indeed, you will find the peasant, if poor, is always on the verge of perishing **11.10.5** from beatings, imprisonment, and a lack of delicious things to eat and drink, and finds no rest unless he has paid the sultan's tax; and, if he has a small balance owing, he will think about it all night long, and at daybreak and day's end, and exist in a state of frantic effort and exhaustion, unless the Almighty bless him in his planting—for much may come forth from little if his intentions at the time of sowing the land are good and if his purpose at the time be that

وقصده ذلك الوقت أنّه ينتفع به هو وغيره كأكل الطيور والدوابّ ونحو ذلك مع الاتّكال على الله تعالى في طلوعه وحفظه من الآفات فإنّ الله يبارك له فيه مع مزيد الثواب (لما رُوِيَ عن سيّدنا عمر) رضي الله عنه أنّه مرّ بجماعة جالسين من غير شغل ولا اكتساب يسألون الناس فقال من أنتم قالوا نحن المتوكّلون فقال لستم كذلك إنّما المتوكّل من وضع الحبّة بين الماء والطين اذهبوا فاكتسبوا فالزرّاع أقوى توكّلاً من غيره إن لاحظ ما تقدّم ذكره وقت البذر

(فائدة) يُستحبّ عند بذر الحبّ في الأرض أن يصلّي ركعتين ثمّ يقول إلهي أنا عبدك ضعيف إليك سلّمت هذا البذر فبارك لي فيه ثمّ يصلّي على النبيّ صلّى الله عليه وسلّم فإنّ الله تعالى يحفظ الزرع من الآفات ذكره الإمام الزاهديّ ولكن نحمد الله الّذي أراحنا من الفلاحة وهمّها ولم تكن لآبائنا ولا أجدادنا فنحن على حدّ قول البهلول رحمه الله [وافر] ١١،١٠،٦

إذا رَكِبَ المُلوكُ عَلَى الجِيادِ   وَقَد شَدّوا البُنودَ عَلَى القِصادِ[1]
رَكِبتُ قُصَيْبَتي ولَبِستُ مِسْحي   وسِرتُ كَسَيرِهِم في كُلِّ وادي
فَلا الأَجنادُ تَطلُبُني بِمالٍ   ولا الدّيوانُ يَغلَطُ في عِدادي

(فالفلاحة) على كلّ حال بليّة أعاذنا الله والمحبّين منها وقوله

(سوى الكشْكُ) وهو في أصله مركّب من البُرّ واللبن غليظ محرّك للأمراض قال الشاعر [مجتثّ] ١١،١٠،٧

الكِشْكُ فَظٌّ غَليظٌ   مُحرِّكٌ لِلسَّواكِنْ
الأَصلُ دَرٌّ وبُرٌّ   نِعْمَ الجدودُ ولكِنْ

١ بي (في جميع النسخ): الفِصادِ.

he and others should benefit by what he is doing, as by providing food for the birds and the animals and so on, and if he places his trust in the Almighty for its growth and preservation from pests. In such a case God will bless him in it, with great reward, as witnessed by the fact that it is related of Our Master ʿUmar,[303] God be pleased with him, that one day he passed by some people sitting without work or gain and begging. "Who are you?" he asked. They said, "We are those who place our trust in God." "That you are not," he said, "for those who place their trust in God are those who place the grain between the water and the soil. Go and be gainfully employed!" The cultivator is the person who puts the greatest faith in God, if he heeds what is prescribed above at the time of sowing.

A Useful Note: It is desirable that the cultivator should pray two prostrations at the time of sowing the grain in the earth and then say, "My God, I, Your feeble slave, have commended this seed to You, so bless me in it!" Then he should bless the Prophet, God bless him and grant him peace, for God will preserve the plants from infestations if he does so. Imam al-Zāhidī mentions this. **11.10.6**

For our part, however, we thank God that he has relieved us of farming and its woes; it was never our father's or our grandfathers' occupation, for we are of the sort described by al-Buhlūl,[304] God have mercy on him, when he said:

When kings mount steeds
  After fixing their standards to lances frail,
I mount my reedling and don my cassock
  And travel as they do in every vale.
Then never can troopers demand from me taxes
  Nor the collectors over my assessment fail.

Agriculture is, in any case, a tribulation from which we pray God to spare us and our loved ones.

siwā l-kishki ("but *kishk*"): *kishk* ("wheat groats") is at base a mixture of wheat and milk; it is Coarse[305] and stimulates sickness. The poet says: **11.10.7**

Kishk is Gross and Coarse.
  It activates what's still.
Its ingredients are milk and wheat—
  Noble forefathers, but still . . .[306]

أي ولكن بئس ما خلّفوا ففيه اقتباس واكتفاء

٨،١٠،١١ وصفته أن يؤخذ البرّ وهو القمح ويُغسَل غسلاً جيّداً ويُغمَر بالماء ويوضع على النار ويقاد عليه حتّى يلين ويغلظ الحبّ ويصير مصلوقاً ثمّ يُجفَّف في الشمس ويُدَشّ ويوضع في إناء ويُصبّ عليه اللبن والمِشّ الحصير ويُحرّك ثمّ يترك أيّاماً ثمّ يحرك ويوضع عليه اللبن وهكذا حتّى يتخمّر ويأخذ قوامها وتفوح له رائحة الحموضة ويصير على غاية من جودة الطَعْم ثمّ يزاد من اللبن لأجل خفة حموضته ثمّ يُقرّص أقراصاً صغاراً ويوضع في الشمس إلى أن يجفّ ويؤخذ ويخزّن لوقت الطبخ وهذه صفة كشك بلاد البحر وهو الأجود والأحسن في المأكول وأمّا كشك الكفور وبلاد المَلَق الّذي ذكره الناظم فلا أراك الله مكروهاً فإنّهم يصنعوه بالمشّ الحصير وقليل من اللبن ولهذا أنّه كثير الحموضة حريف الطعم غليظ الطبع عن غيره محرّك للضرورات وهو الّذي يضرب لونه إلى سمرة وكلّما كان أبيضاً نقيّ قليل رائحة الحموضة كان جيّداً وكذلك كشك الصعيد فإنّه يشبه كشك الكفور في عدم الجودة إلّا أنّهم يجعلوه مثل البنادق الكبار وفيه نوع جيّد لكثرة لبنه وحسن نظافته

٩،١٠،١١ وأمّا كيفيّة طبخه فعلى أقسام بحسب البلاد الّتي يعمل فيها فأهل بلاد البحر يطبخوه بالأرز واللحم السمين تارة وبالدجاج أو شيء من أصناف الطيور المأكولة أخرى أو يجعلوه بالأرز فقط ويصيّروه ثخيناً وأهالي المَنْزَلة ودمياط يطبخوه بالسمك البُوري السمين وأكلته بدمياط مراراً وأبناء الترك يجعلوه رقيقاً مائعاً بقليل من الأرز بحيث يُشْرَب بالملعقة ويقلّوا له بالخضرة والأدهان والسمن الطيّب ويجعلوه باللحم الضاني السمين فيكون له لذّة عظيمة في المأكل وتعتدل طبيعته خصوصاً مع لحوم الضأن المذكورة والدجاج والأرز ونحوه وأمّا القسم الرديء المحرّك للسواكن المذكور في الشعر المتقدّم فهو كشك أهل الكفور وبلاد الملق فإنّهم يتساهلون عند الطبخ في غسله وتصفيته ويضعوه في بوشة أو قِدْرة أو دِست على النار ويضيفوا إليه ملء كفّ من الفول المدشوش ويقيدوا عليه بالنار إلى أن يأخذ قوامه فينزّلوه ويخرطوا له بصلة

—that is, "but still, what a horrible child!" with "quotation" and "restraint."

The recipe is to take *burr* ("wheat"), synonym *qamḥ*, wash it well, and soak it in water.[307] Then it is placed on the fire and heated until it goes soft and the grain swells and it is well boiled. Then it is dried in the sun and husked and put in a pot, and milk and strained *mishsh* is poured onto it and it is stirred, then left for several days, then stirred again and more milk is added and so on until it ferments and thickens and acquires a sour smell and a most excellent taste. More milk is added to cut the sourness and it is formed into small cakes and put in the sun to dry, and taken and stored until it is to be cooked. This is how they make the groats of the villages by the river, which is the best in quality and the finest to eat. As for the groats of the hamlets and the villages of the swamplands, which is the type referred to by the poet, God spare you such a disgusting sight! They make it with strained cottage-cheese culture and just a small quantity of milk, which makes it extremely sour, sharp to the taste, gross in nature compared to other types, and laxative. This is the sort that is brownish, and the whiter, purer, and less sour-smelling it gets, the better it is. The groats of Upper Egypt is the same, for it resembles that of the hamlets in its poor quality, though in Upper Egypt they form it into small balls, and they also have a type that is of good quality because it has high milk content and is very clean. 11.10.8

As for how to cook with it, this varies according to the place where that is done. The people of the villages on the river sometimes cook it with rice and fatty meat, other times with chicken or one of the other types of edible fowl, or make it with rice alone, and they make it thick. The people of al-Manzalah and Dimyāṭ cook it with fat mullet, and I have eaten it in Dimyāṭ many times. The Turks make it thin and runny, with a small quantity of rice, and it is drunk with a spoon, and they make a garnish for it by frying greens and fats and good clarified butter, and they cook it with fat mutton. This makes it extremely delicious to eat. Its nature is Moderate, especially when eaten with mutton, chicken, and rice. The bad kind that "activates what's still," as mentioned in the verses above, is the groats of the people of the hamlets and the villages of the swamplands, for they neglect to wash it or strain it well when they cook it, and they put it in a crock or a kettle or a pan on the fire and add a handful of shelled fava beans and heat it until it thickens. Then they take it off the fire and mince an onion into it and add a little sesame oil and make it a fried garnish with these, and ladle it into earthenware kneading bowls or milk crocks and crumble maize or barley bread into it. Such people eat a crockful, chewing and gulping, and set 11.10.9

وشيء قليل من الشيرج ويقلّوا له بذلك ويغرفوه في متارد أو شوالي فُخّار ويفتّوا فيه خبز الدرة أو الشعير ويأكل الشخص منهم متردًا بالمضغ واللهط ويسرح الغيط إلى وقت المساء يرى ما بقي منه قد جمد وظهر فيه فصوص الفول فيلهط منه إلى أن يكتفي وهذا يسمّى عندهم هِراش العجائز وهو أعزّ المأكول عندهم وغالب ما يصنعوه في أعراسهم كما سبق بيانه في الجزء الأوّل من هذا الشرح ولا يعرفوا طبخه بالأرز ولا اللحم فإنّ الأرز لا يوجد عندهم إلّا نادرًا واللحم لا يأكلوه إلّا من العام إلى العام كما سيأتي بيانه ونوع آخر من هذا القسم يطبخوه من غير فول بل مجرَّد كشك لا غير ومن غير وضع شيء من التقالي عليه يسمّى عندهم نيرب وهذا وما قبله يولّد الأرياح ويحرّك السواكن ويضرّ بالمعدة لزيادة الفول فيه لأنّه غليظ الطبع وكذلك القمح فإنّه حار رطب والمشّ الحصير بارد رطب والفول غليظ ثقيل فيتولّد الضرر من مجموع هؤلاء الأربعة

وللكشك منافع قبل طبخه منها إذا أذيب بالماء وشربه المحرور نفعه وسكّن التهاب ١١،١٠،١٠
معدته وإذا توعّك الجمل من ألم الحرّ يُسّق منه يزول ما به ولهذا يستعمله المسافرون إذا أذاهم الحرّ وحصل لهم الضرر منه كالحُجّاج وغيرهم وينفع من ألم ضرب السياط طِلاء وله منافع أخرى مذكورة في كتب الطبّ وأمّا أهل الصعيد فإنّهم يطبخوه من غير تصفية فيكون مثل النخالة المطبوخة بالخلّ لا غير فهذا لا فائدة فيه ولا طعم ولا لذّة لأنّ نفعه لا يكون إلّا بعد تصفيته لكنّ غالب مأكولهم الوَيكة والمُلوخية كما شاهدناه في بلادهم (قيل) أتي رجل من أهل الصعيد من نواحي قِنا وقُوص إلى مصر ليشتري له جارية للخدمة فرأى جارية تباع بأغلى ثمن لمعرفتها بأنواع الطعام فوقف عليها وسألها هل تحسني الطعام مثل ما يقولوا فنظرت إليه وقالت له من أيّ البلاد أنت قال من الصعيد فقالت أنت لا تحتاج إلى طعام فاخر فان مأكول أهل الصعيد في كلّ سنة ستة أشهر ويكة وستة أشهر ملوخية فلا يحتاجوا إلى طعام فاخر غير هذا قال فتركها ومضى متعجبًا

off for the fields, where they stay until evening. By that time, what is left has gone hard, with bits of fava beans sticking out. This they gulp down till they are satisfied. This is what is called among them *hirāsh al-ʿajāʾiz* ("old women's butting")[308] and it is the most highly prized of their dishes. Most of them make it for their weddings, as stated above in Part One of this commentary.[309] They know nothing of cooking it with rice and meat, for rice is found among them only rarely and they only eat meat once a year, as we shall show. Another type in the same category they cook without fava beans and consists of just *kishk* and nothing else, without any kind of garnish; this they call *nayrab*, and that and the preceding generate wind and "move what is still" and are harmful to the stomach because they contain so many beans,[310] the latter being Gross in nature. Wheat is similar because it is Hot and Moist, and cottage cheese culture is Cold and Moist, and beans are Coarse and Heavy. Thus harm arises from the combination of these four.[311]

Groats, before it is cooked, has several beneficial qualities. For example, **11.10.10**
if dissolved in water and drunk by someone with heartburn, it brings relief and soothes the inflammation of the stomach. If a camel sickens from the heat and is given some to drink, it recovers. For the same reason, travelers such as pilgrims and others use it when the heat overcomes them and makes them feel unwell. As an ointment, it is good for the pain caused by whipping, and it has other beneficial properties mentioned in the medical books. The people of Upper Egypt cook it without straining it first, so that it resembles nothing so much as bran cooked with vinegar; there is no benefit to be had from it, and it has no taste or savor because their good properties are present only after they have been strained—but anyway their food consists mostly of okra and Jew's mallow, as we have observed in their villages. It is said that an Upper Egyptian from the region of Qinā and Qūṣ once came to Cairo to buy himself a girl to do the housework. He came across a girl who was for sale at an extremely high price because of her knowledge of different dishes. He stood in front of her and asked, "Do you cook well as they say?" She looked at him and asked him, "What country are you from?" "From Upper Egypt," he said. Then she said, "You have no need of fine food, for the diet of the people of Upper Egypt is six months a year okra and six months Jew's mallow. They have no need of finer foods than these." The man left her and went away amazed.

(مسألة هباليّة) ما معنى اسم الكشك وما اشتقاقه وما معنى اسم النوع المطبوخ منه هراش العجائز والنوع الآخر المسمّى بالنيرب وما معنى قول الناظم إنه هدّ حيله عند مشاهدته وقرب غرفه وشمّ رائحته فما الحكم (الجواب الفشرويّ) أنّ لفظة كشك هذه من الألفاظ المقلوبة الّتي تُقرأ طرداً وعكساً ومثلها كعك وشاش وباب ومثلها سِرْ فلا كبا بك الفرس وقِلع مركَّب بِبكَرِ معلَّق وحسَّك تتزوّج عجوز تتكسّح وقد ورد ذلك في القرآن العظيم في قوله تعالى ﴿وَرَبَّكَ فَكَبِّرْ﴾ ﴿كُلٌّ فِي فَلَكٍ﴾ وغير القرآن مثل كمالك تحت كلامك وكلب يبلّك وعِلَق تحت قِلَع (ومن النظم قول الحريريّ) [رجز] ١١،١٠،١١

أُسْ أَرْمَلاً إذا عَرا وَارْعَ إذا المَرْءُ أَسا
أَسِلْ جَناب غاشِمٍ مُشاغِبٍ إنْ جَلَسا

وأيضاً أنّ الكشك إذا قلبوه في الشمس يكون باطنه مثل ظاهره وأوّل الكشكة مثل آخرها فكان فيه بعض مناسبة من هذا المعنى أو أنّه عند وضعه في الشمس يكشّ وَيَنْضُمُر من حرارتها أو أنّه من قول بعضهم فلان كشّك عند فلان بمعنى أنّه أكل أكلاً كثيراً حتّى انتفخت بطنه وصارت مثل ماجور الكشك أو من قولهم للكلب كشكش إذا أرادوا أن يُلْقوا له شيئاً يأكله ينادوه بهذا اللفظ أو من الكُشُك بضمّ الكاف والشين وهو محلّ خارج من البناء المرتفع مركَّب على الأخشاب تجعله الأكابر للجلوس فيه أو أنّ الكشكة لمّا صارت مدوّرة كانت تشبه الكُسّ بالسين المهملة وهو الفَرْج

A Fatuous Question: What is the meaning of the name *kishk* and what is its etymology, and what is the meaning of the name of the cooked type that is called *hirāsh al-ʿajāʾiz* and the other type called *nayrab*, and what does the poet mean when he says that it "demolished" his stamina when he beheld it as it was about to be ladled out and he smelled its aroma? The Facetious Answer is that *kishk* is one of those back-to-front words that can be read forward and backward. Similar are *kaʿk* ("a type of short pastry"), *shāsh* ("muslin"), *bāb* ("door"), etc.[312] Similar too are *sir fa-lā kabā bi-ka al-faras* ("Go, and may the mare not stumble with you!") and *qilʿ murakkab bi-bakar muʿallaq* ("A sail set with a pulley suspended") and *ḥissak tatazawwaj ʿajūz tatakassaḥ* ("Mind you don't marry an old woman who hobbles!"). The same is also found in the Mighty Qurʾan in the words of the Almighty «*(wa-)rabbaka fa-kabbir*[313] ("(and) thy Lord magnify"),» «*kullun fī falak*[314] ("each in an orbit"),» and elsewhere, as in *kamālak taḥta kalāmak* ("Your words are the offspring of your perfection") and *kalb yabulluka* ("May a dog wet you!") and *ʿilq taḥta qilʿ* ("A faggot under a sail"). An example in verse is the words of al-Ḥarīrī:[315] 11.10.11

*Us armalan idhā ʿarā * wa-rʿa idhā l-marʾu asā*
*Uslu janāba ghāshimin * mushāghibin in jalasā*

Give to the pauper when he passes by
and stay friends with one who does you harm.
Avoid the abode of an unjust
scoundrel when he's at home!

Also, when they turn groats over in the sun, their bottoms are just like their tops, and the beginning of each ball of groats is the same as its end; from this perspective there is a certain appropriateness in their being a palindrome. Or the name may derive from the fact that when it is put in the sun it shrinks (*yakishshu*) and shrivels from the heat; or from the saying they have, "So-and-so 'ate *kishk*' (*kashshaka*) at So-and-so's house," meaning he ate a lot, so that his belly swelled till he looked like a crock full of *kishk*; or from *kishkish*, which they say to a dog—when they want to throw it something to eat, this is the word they use to call it. Or from *kushuk* ("kiosk, gazebo"), with *u* after the *k* and the *sh*, which is a place outside a large building, mounted on timbers, that the great erect to sit in. Or from the fact that the *kishkah* ("cake of *kishk*"), once formed into a ball, would resemble the *kuss* ("cunt"), with *s*, which is the

ثمّ إنّهم غيّروا السين المهملة بالشين المعجمة لقبح اللفظ وأضافوا إلى الكلمة كافًا وقالوا كشك ومصدره كشّك يكشّك تكشيكًا

١٢،١٠،١١ (وأمّا تسمية النوع منه بهراش العجائز) فالهراش في الأصل النطاح يقال مهارشة التيوس ونقار الديوك ونسب إلى العجائز لأنّهم في الغالب يطبخوه شهوة ويتهارشوا عنده مهارشة تضيق منها النفوس * ويظهر منها الهمّ والعكوس * وناهيك بعجائز أهل هذه البلدان * فإنّهن قسم من غيلة الجان * فلأجل مهارشتهنّ على هذا المأكول سمّي بذلك الاسم أو أنّه من باب هَرْش المعدة

١٣،١٠،١١ (وأمّا تسمية النوع الآخر نيرب) فلعلّه من النيروب على وزن الديلوب أو أنّه نسب إلى رجل يقال له نيرب أو إلى الأرنب حيوان يحلّ أكله فخشوا الالتباس في اللفظ فقالوا نيرب أو أنّه فُعِلَ في زمن النَيْروز فقالوا أوّلًا نيروز فالتبس الأمر في اسمه واسم الزمن فأبدلوا الزاي الّتي في آخره بالباء الموحّدة وقالوا نيرب

١٤،١٠،١١ وقول الناظم إنّه هدّ حيله وقد شاهده ورآه وشمّ رائحته فمن عدم ملكه له وقلّة طبخه عنده وإنّما كانت رؤيته له عند الجيران فمن هذا إذا رآه قد استحقّ الأكل تحسّر وتأسّف وخصوصًا

١٥،١٠،١١ (لمّا يستحِقُّ غَريفْ) أي لمّا ينتهي طبخه ويريدوا غرفه وتفوح رائحته عند غرفه وأصله لمّا يستحق الغرف بآلة التغريف لكن حذفها وزاد الياء المثنّاة من تحت لأجل النظم وغريف على وزن كَنيف وهي نقرة معدّة للخراء فيها بيقين فعند مشاهدته لهذه الحالة وشمّ الرائحة ينهدّ حيله لأنّ همّة الشخص طول عمره بطنه وفَرْجه كما قال ابن عروس رحمه الله في ديوانه [مجتثّ]

vagina; later they changed the *s* (without dots) to the *sh* (with dots) because of the ugliness of the expression and added a *k* and said *kishk*.[316] The paradigm is *kashshaka, yukashshiku, takshīkan* ("to form *kishk* into balls").

As to the naming of one type, *hirāsh al-ʿajāʾiz, hirāsh* originally means the same as *niṭāḥ* ("butting"). One speaks of the *muhārashah* ("butting contests") of rams and the *niqār* ("pecking contests") of cocks.[317] It is known as "old women's" because it is generally they who cook it with relish and butt one another to get at it in a fashion most distressing that seems both perverse and depressing, not to mention that the old women of villages such as these belong to the ghoulish jinn species. Thus, the dish was given this name because of their butting one another to get at it. Or it may fall under the rubric of "wear and tear" (*harsh*) on the stomach. **11.10.12**

And as to the other type being called *nayrab*, this may be because it derives from *nayrūb*, of the pattern of *daylūb*,[318] or because they trace it to a man called *nayrab*,[319] or to the *arnab* ("rabbit"), an animal that it is permitted to eat, but were afraid of confusion in the pronunciation, so they called it *nayrab*. Or because it is made at the season of Nayrūz, so first they said *nayrūz* and then its name and that of the season got mixed up, so they exchanged the letter *z* at the end of the word for a *b* and said *nayrab*. **11.10.13**

The poet's statement that it demolished his strength when he beheld it, saw it, and smelled its aroma is attributable to the facts that he did not possess any, that it was so infrequently cooked at his house, and that he used to see it only at his neighbors' houses. Consequently, whenever he saw it ready for eating, he would grieve and mourn, especially . . . **11.10.14**

lamma yastaḥiqqu gharīf ("when it's ready to ladle"): that is, when it's done cooking and they want to ladle it out, and its aroma, as it is being ladled, wafts here and there. It is originally "when it's ready for ladling (*gharf*) *with a ladling instrument*," but he shortened it and added the *ī* to *gharf* for the sake of the meter.[320] *Gharīf* is of the pattern of *kanīf* ("latrine"), the latter being a hole for shitting in, for sure. When he observed this situation and smelled that smell, his strength was demolished, for a person's greatest zeal, all his life long, is for his belly and his privates; as Ibn ʿArūs, God have mercy on him, says, in his collected works: **11.10.15**

النَّـاسُ ــفي اللهِ تاهُوا   والأَجوادُ شاعَتْ تَناها
مـا ضَـرَّني غيرُ بَطني   وــإلّي مـدلّي حَـداها

وقال بعضهم مواليا [بسيط]

يا دنية الشوم طول عمري وأنا أشتدّ
في هـمّ دي البطنِ إلّي ما تريّح حـدّ
أضـالُ أبني وآجي بعد العشـا أنمـدّ
وآقومُ ألصبحَ ألقى مـا بنـيتو انهـدّ

(فمن هذا) لم يقنع الناظم لأنّه لا يقضي مراده ولا هو من قسم النمل يعيش بالشمّ بل من الآدميّين وخصوصاً من أهالي كفور الريف يفطر الشخص منهم على المترد أو المتردين من الكشك أو البيسار أو الفول المدمّس كما سيأتي فلا لوم عليه في هدّ حيله

(وبذكر هذا المعنى) ذكرتُ ما اتّفق لبعض الأطبّاء أنّه جلس في بعض الأسواق ينظر في أمراض الناس فأتى إليه رجل لطيف الذات من أبناء النعم وذوي الرفاهيّة وجلس بين يديه ومدّ يده إليه وقال له انظر ما بي فجسّ نبضه وقال له ما أكلت اليوم فقال شيئاً يسيراً من الفول الحارّ على الفطور فقال له تاخذ لك يسيراً من الزبيب والسَنا المكّي ويسيراً من السكر وتستعمل ذلك فإنّ فيه الشفاء ثمّ قام من عنده وإذا برجل من أهل الريف كأنّه في الشكل هِبَل * أو سارية فوق الجبل * أقبل على ذلك الطبيب * وهو يخّ نخ الديبيب * وقال له انظر ما بي من المرض بلطف * فأنا باحسّ في بطني ضعف * وقدّم له يداً كأنها خشبه * وساعداً كأنّه حطبه * فجسّ الطبيب يده وقال له ما الّذي دهاك * وما أكلت اليوم في فطورك وغداك * فقال له أنا احكي لك وحقّ النبيّ عليه السلام * وتربة ابو معيكه بن ابو جعرام * أنا لمّا قمت من النوم لقيت امراتي امّ معيكه عملت بوشة بيسار كبيره وكنت اسحب العيش ولهطت منها مترد متردين قل تلاته فقال الطبيب وغير ذلك فقال ورحت لجارتنا امّ دعموم لقيت عندها فول ١١،١٠،١٦

The people are lost in God,
　　And praise of the noble spreads far and wide.
Nothing does me harm but my belly,
　　And that thing dangles on its underside.

And another poet says in a *mawāliyā*:

Ah wretched world—all my life hard pressed,
　　By the woes of this belly that lets none rest!
All day I build, then sup, go lie me down;
　　Mornings I rise, find what I built knocked down![321]

For the same reason, the poet is not content just to look, because he cannot satisfy his desire that way, and he is not of the species of the ant that he should live by smell alone;[322] on the contrary, he belongs to the human species and, moreover, to that of the people of the country hamlets, any of whom would consume a crock, or two crocks, of wheat groats or *bīsār* or stewed beans for breakfast, as we shall see—so he is not to be blamed if his strength collapsed.

In the same vein, I am reminded that it happened that a doctor was sitting in **11.10.16** a market examining people's ailments when a young man of refined physique, a child of the wealthy and well-to-do, came to him and sitting down before him stretched out his hand to him and said, "See what ails me!" The doctor felt his pulse and asked him, "What have you eaten today?" "A few beans with linseed oil for breakfast," he said. The doctor told him, "Get a few raisins and senna pods plus a little sugar and take these, for therein lies your cure." So the young man rose and left him. Then up came a countryman, a real hulk, like a mast on a mountain in bulk, and to the doctor his proximity he increased, puffing like some crawling beast, and said to him, "Gently see what sickness ails me, for I feel my belly fails me!"—holding out a hand like a clog, with a forearm like a log. The doctor took his pulse and asked, "What delivered you such a punch, and what did you eat for breakfast and for lunch?" The other said to him, "I'll tell you now, by the truth of the Prophet, to whom we salaam, and by the grave of Abū Muʿaykah, son of Abū Juʿrām! When I got up from sleeping, I found my wife, Umm Muʿaykah, had put out a big pot of *bīsār*, and I pulled out the bread and tossed down a crock or two . . . say three." "And what else?" said the doctor. The man said, "I went to our neighbor, Umm Daʿmūm, and found stewed beans at her place. I ate a crock or two of them . . . say three."

مدمّس اكلت منه مترد متردين قل تلاته قال الطبيب نعم وغير ذلك فقال وسرحت غيط الفول اكلت منه ِشمال شمالين قل تلاته ورحت من الغيط رايت عند مشدّ الكفركشك لهطت منه مترد متردين قل تلاته ورايت عندنا عرس في الحاره وعزموني ودخلت عندهم طبخوا طبيخ كتير اكلت من داك الطعام مترد متردين قل تلاته ورايت عندنا خيار اصفر ينباع اكلت منه كوم كومين قل تلاته وجيتك تنضرحالي فإنّي باحسّ في نِفْسي ضعف (فقال له الطبيب) خذ لك من الزبيب قنطار قنطارين قل ثلاثة ومن السنا المكيّ قنطار قنطارين قل ثلاثة ومن السكّر قنطار قنطارين قل ثلاثة فقال له أنا سمعتك بتوصف للّي جالك قبلي شي يسير من السنا المكى والسكر والزبيب وبتوصف لي قناطير فقال له يا أخسّ الفلاّحين وهل يصلح هذه الأكلات إلّا هذه القناطير وهذه الشربات ثمّ أخذ خُرجه على كتفه وحلف أنّه لا يجلس بقيّة يومه في السوق لأجل هذا الفلاّح فاتّجه المقال *عن معنى هذه الأحوال * واتّضحت العبارات *عن هذه الخرافات *

(ثمّ إنّ الناظم) لمّا فرغ من ذكر هذا الطعام تشوّق إلى شيء أغلظ منه مستعملاً ١٧،١٠،١١
عند أهل الريف في غالب مأكولهم فقال

ص

وَلَا شَاقَنِي إِلَّا ٱلْمُدَمَّسْ وَرِيحَتُو عَلَى مَنْ جَتُو جَفْنَهْ وَنُصّ رَغِيفْ ١١،١١

ش

وقوله (ولا شاقَني) من الشوق وهو رقة القلب وميله للمحبوب قال ابن الفارض نفعنا ١،١١،١١
الله به (ولولاكم ما شاقني ذكر منزلي) وشاق على وزن قاق وهو صوت الإوَزّ

"Indeed," said the doctor, "and what else?" "I went off to our field of beans, and ate a bundle or two of them . . . say three. And I left the field and, at the house of the bailiff of the hamlet, I saw some *kishk* and tossed down a crock or two of it . . . say three. And I saw there was a wedding in our alley, and they invited me over, so I went into their house. They cooked lots, and I ate a crock or two of that food . . . say three. And I saw someone selling yellow cucumbers by our house, so I ate a heap or two . . . say three. Then I came to you to see what's wrong with me, because I feel my appetite is failing me." The doctor told him, "Take of raisins a hundredweight or two . . . say three, and of senna pods a hundredweight or two . . . say three." The man said to him, "I heard you prescribe a little senna, sugar, and raisins for the man who came to you before me, and you want to prescribe them for me by the hundredweight?!" The doctor replied, "Vilest of peasants! Could anything deal with such meals as those but hundredweights of purges such as these?" Then he slung his bag over his shoulder and swore that he would not sit in the market anymore that day because of that peasant. Now the record's straight as regards the import of such a state, and the explanation's plain as regards such tales inane.

Next the poet, having done with talk of that particular food, felt a desire **11.10.17** for something coarser that is used by the people of the countryside in most of their dishes. So he said:

TEXT

wa-lā shāqanī illā l-mudammas wa-rīḥatū **11.11**
ʿalā man jatū jafnah wa-nuṣṣu raghīf

And nothing has made me yearn like stewed beans and their smell!
Happy is he to whom comes a bowl with half a loaf!

COMMENTARY

wa-lā shāqanī ("And nothing has made me yearn"): from *shawq* ("yearning, **11.11.1** desire"), which is the softening of the heart and its inclination towards the beloved. ʿUmar ibn al-Fāriḍ, God benefit us through him, says, "Were it not for you, the mention of my home would not make me yearn (*mā shāqanī*) . . . ."[323]

ومصدره شاق يشوق شوقاً مثل قاق يقوق قوقاً والمعنى أنّه يقول لمّا كثر شوقي وزاد هيامي عن جميع المأكولات

٢،١١،١١ (إلّا المدمّسْ) مأخوذ من الدِمِس لكونه يُدَمّس في النار كما سيأتي ومصدره دمّس يدمّس تدميساً فهو دامس ومدموس وهو نوعان ريفيّ وحضريّ وإن كان الأصل واحد وهو الفول لأنّ الشيء يَشْرُفُ بشرف الأماكن تارة وبالصناعة الجيّدة أخرى

٣،١١،١١ (فأمّا الحضريّ) وهو ما يباع في مصر وغيرها من المدن فإنّهم يأخذوا الفول النقيّ الأبيض ويتركوا منه الرديء ويضعوه في قدور كبار واسعة البطون ضيّقة الأفواه بقدر ما تسع يد الرجل يتناول منها ثمّ يصبوّا عليه ما يغمره من الماء الرائق العذب ويسدّوا فم القدرة بشيء من الليف النظيف أو إناء طاهر سدّاً مُحكَماً ويُدَمّس في نار قويّة نظيفة خالية عن الأدخنة والروائح الكريهة مثل جورة الفرّان ونحوها ويتعهّدوه بالسقي كلّما نشف ليلة كاملة حتّى يطيب طعمه ويعتدل وتزكو رائحته ويصير على غاية من جودة الطعم وحسن الاستواء يشبه في لونه الذهب وفي استوائه العَجْوة مثلاً بحيث كلّ من رآه يشتهيه فإذا أرادوا أكله اشترى الشخص ما يكفيه أو المرأة إذا اشتهت ذلك وأضافوا إليه السمن البقريّ أو الزيت الطيّب أو قشطة اللبن وأحضروا الخبز الأبيض النظيف وربّما كان مصحوباً بالكُرّاث الأخضر والليمون أو الخلّ فمن هذا يصير غذاء جيّداً تكتسب منه الأعضاء وتمتلئ به المعدة ويصلحه قليل من الصعتر وخصوصاً إذا شرب عليه القهوة بعد ذلك فيكتفي الشخص به عن غيره إلى المساء

٤،١١،١١ (وأمّا النوع الثاني) وهو مدمّس أهل الريف الّذي اشتاقه الناظم فلا أراكَ الله مكروهاً إن كنت ما ذقت الخراء تأكل منه فإنّهم يأخذوا الفول دَعْه جيّداً أو رديء على سائر أوصافه وربّما أخذته زوجة الفلّاح من مدود البقرة أو الثور ونحّت ما عليه من آثار التبن ووضعته في إناء يقال له البَوْشة وغمرته بماء كدر متغيّر الرائحة

Shāqa ("it caused yearning") is of the measure of *qāqa* ("it honked"), which is the sound a goose makes. The paradigm is *shāqa, yashūqu, shawqan*, like *qāqa, yaqūqu, qawqan*, and what he means to say is, "My yearning has not grown and my thirst has not increased for any dish . . ."

illā l-mudammas ("like stewed beans"):[324] *mudammas* being taken from *dims* ("bedding straw for cattle") because the beans are cooked in a fire fueled with *dims*, as will be explained. The paradigm is *dammasa, yudammisu, tadmīsan*, active participle *dāmis*, passive participle *madmūs*.[325] There are two kinds, the rural and the urban, even though the origin is the same, namely, fava beans, the difference being due to the fact that things are ennobled at times by virtue of place and at others by virtue of excellence of manufacture. 11.11.2

To make the urban kind, which is that sold in Cairo and other cities, they take clean white beans, discard any bad ones, and put them in large broad-bellied kettles with narrow mouths just wide enough for a man to insert his hand into when he serves from them. Then they pour enough sweet, pure water over them to cover them and they plug the mouth of the kettle tightly with some clean palm fiber or a clean vessel and they cook them in a strong, clean fire of threshings that makes no smoke or unpleasant odors, such as that of a baker's pit or the like. For a whole night they watch over them, adding water whenever they dry out, until the taste is good, the consistency just right, the aroma enticing, and they taste wonderful and are beautifully cooked. At this point the beans take on a golden color and the consistency of, for example, pressed dates, so that any who sees them wants to eat them. When they want to eat some, a man, or a woman if she so desires, will buy enough for him or herself, and add clarified cow's butter or olive oil or clotted cream, and bring clean white bread. They may also be eaten accompanied by green leeks and limes or vinegar. All this makes them excellent nourishment, sustaining for the limbs and filling for the stomach. A little thyme balances them,[326] especially if coffee is drunk immediately afterward. A man can go from morning to night on this alone. 11.11.3

As for the second kind, namely, the *mudammas* of the country people—which is what the poet craves—God spare you such a disgusting sight! If you've never tasted shit, try this! They take the beans, be they good or bad, as is. The peasant's wife may well take them from the cow's or the ox's feeding trough and blow the remnants of straw off them, and put them in a vessel 11.11.4

من ماء البرك أو من مقاطع النيل الّتي تبقى في بلادهم أو ماء الآبار وتسدّ فم البوشة بساس الكتّان أو بخرقة فيها الدناسة وتضعها في مِحماة الفرن الملآنة من الدمس والجلّة وربّما وضعت ذلك عليها أيضاً وتسدّ عليها باب المحماة المذكورة إلى الصباح تخرجها وقد امتزج الفول بروائح الزبل والجلّة وذلك الماء المتغيّر واسودّ وصار مثل زبل الغنم وظهرت له رائحة كريهة ثمّ تأتي بالمترد وتهزّ البوشة وتفرغ الفول فيه ويجلس الشخص منهم مثل الكلب الكاشر وتحضر له بخبز الدرة اليابس أو خبز الشعير ويقطع ويبلع حتّى تمتلئ بطنه فإذا أكلت منه فكأنّك تأكل من زبل الغنم مثلاً ومنهم من يأكله بالكرّاث أو البصل وربّما أضافوا عليه شيئاً من القمح أو الحِمّص والأكابر منهم يجعلون عليه شيئاً يسيراً من الزيت الحارّ ومنهم من لا يكون عنده خبز فيسفّ منه عند الصباح من غير صلاة ولا غسل وجه إلى أن يكتفي ثمّ يشرب فوقه الماء حتّى يصير كالزِقّ المنفوخ ويسحب النبّوت ويسرح مثل النعوت فهذا مدمّسهم وصفة مأكولهم أعاذنا الله من ذلك وقوله

٥،١١،١١ (وِرِيحتو) أصله ورائحته حذفت الهمزة للضرورة أو جرياً على اللغة الريفيّة أي شاقني رائحته الممتزجة بالروائح المتقدّمة للذّتها عندي إذا اشتهيتها فأشتاق إليها وإلى الأكل من الفول ولكن لا أجد ذلك لشدّة فقري والريحة مشتقّة من الريح أو من الرواح أو من أبو رِياح الذي تلعب به الصبيان أو من الراح وهو من أسماء الخمرة قال الشاعر [بسيط]

وَالرَّاحُ كَالرِّيحِ إِنْ مَـرَّتْ عَلَى عِـطَرٍ   أَرَكَتْ وَتَخْبُثُ إِنْ مَرَّتْ على الجِيَفِ

أو من قولهم [وزن غير معروف]

called a *bawshah* ("earthenware pot") and cover them with dirty, foul-smelling water drawn from the ponds or from the cut-off stretches of Nile water that remain in their villages after the flood recedes, or from the wells. She plugs the mouth of the pot with flax straw mixed with dung or with a filthy rag and puts it into the fire chamber of the oven, which is filled with bedding straw and dung cakes, which may also be heaped on top of it, and she closes the door of the fire chamber on it tightly till the morning. Then she takes it out, by which time the beans will have mixed with the odors of the droppings and the dung cakes and that foul-smelling water and turned black and become like goat droppings and developed a foul smell. Next she gets the crock, shakes the pot, and empties the beans into it. The countryman then sits down, like a snarling dog, and she brings him dry sorghum or barley bread, and he cuts and swallows till his belly is filled. If you were to eat it, you would think you were eating sheep droppings or something of the sort. Some of them eat it with leeks or onions, and sometimes they add some wheat or chickpeas, and their great men put a little linseed oil on it. Some of them have no bread, and such a one gulps it down in lumps in the morning without saying a prayer or washing his face, until he has had enough. Then he washes it down with water until he is like a swollen waterskin, and takes his cudgel and sets off like a . . . .[327] Such is their *mudammas* and the nature of their food, God preserve you from it!

wa-rīḥatū ("and their smell"): originally *wa-rā'iḥatuhu*, the glottal stop being omitted for the meter, or in accordance with rural usage;[328] that is, "its smell, mixed with the aforementioned odors, caused me to yearn for it, because I think it so delicious when my appetite yearns for it; consequently I crave it, and beans, but I find none of these things because I am so poor." *Rīḥah* is derived from *rīḥ* ("wind") or from *rawāḥ* ("going") or from the *abū riyāḥ* ("windmill toy") that boys play with or from *rāḥ*, which is one of the words for wine. The poet says: 11.11.5

> Wine (*rāḥ*) is like the wind (*rīḥ*): if it passes a perfume
> It turns sweet, and it turns bad if it passes a corpse.

Or it, *rīḥah*, may be from the words of the poet:

المعدّيه رايحه جيّه تنسحب بالخيط
يا ابو جبّه إلّا أنا رزليت

ومن هذا المعنى قال بعضهم مواليا لُغزًا [بسيط]

وآيْش قُلْتَ يا صاحِبي في رايِحَهْ جَيَّهْ
مِنْ تحْتِ حَيْطْ وَهِيا مَيّتَةٌ حَيَّهْ
وقاعِدهْ واقِفهْ عالأرضِ مَرْمِيَّهْ
وجايِزهْ راقِدهْ فَوْقْ حَيْطِ مَبْنِيَّهْ

٦،١١،١١ (ثمّ إنّ الناظم) لمّا ذكر اشتياقه إلى المدمّس ورائحته وأن من لازم ذلك الأكل منه لأنّ النظر والشمّ لا يقوم مقام الأكل والمضغ فتمنّى ذلك وقال

٧،١١،١١ (على) هذا من حروف الجرّ إلّا أنّه وقع هنا فِعْلاً والمعنى علي وارتفع قدر (من جَتو جَفْنَهْ) أو علي جسمه وقَوِيَ جنانه وشبع جوفه واشتهر بالقوّة بعد الجوع قال الشاعر [طويل]

عَلَى زَيْدُنا يومَ اللِّقا رأسَ زَيدِكِمْ بِأَبيَضَ ماضي الشَّفرَتَيْنِ يَماني

أو يكون حرف الجرّ على بابه ويكون المعنى على كلّ حال أن

٨،١١،١١ (من جَتو) أي حصلت له

٩،١١،١١ (جَفْنَهْ) ملآنة من هذا الفول المدمّس ولوكانت هديّة أو صدقة (و) حصل له معها

١٠،١١،١١ (نُصّ رَغيفْ) حذفت الفاء من نصف جريًا على اللغة الريفيّة كقولهم نصّ فضّه أو من قبيل الاكتفاء أو من جهة الترخيم كقولهم (أَفاطِمَ مهلاً بعض[١] هذا التدلّل[٢]) فيكون

١ بي: بعد. ٢ بي (في جميع النسخ): التذلل.

The ferryboat's going and coming (*rāyiḥah jayyah*),[329]
By a thread[330] it's jerked along.
You in the open-fronted cloak,
See where my foot stepped wrong!

And with the same meaning a poet says in a *mawāliyā*, as a riddle:[331]

What make you, my friend, of something going and coming
From beneath a wall, both dead and living,
On the ground thrown down, yet standing and sitting,
Moving, well-built, yet atop a wall reclining?

Next, the poet, having mentioned his craving for *mudammas* and its smell, and the eating thereof that follows naturally from that—for seeing and smelling cannot take the place of eating and chewing—desires to do just that, and says: 11.11.6

ʿalā ("happy is he"): this is a preposition, though used here as a verb,[332] the meaning being "May the standing of him to whom comes a bowlful be exalted (*ʿalā*) and raised up!" or "May his body be exalted (*ʿalā*), his soul invigorated and his belly satisfied, and may he become renowned for strength after hunger!"—as the poet says: 11.11.7

Our Zayd rose high above (*ʿalā*) your Zayd's head, on the day of battle,
With a white sword of Yemen, sharp on both edges!

—or perhaps the preposition is used in its original function, the meaning being "in any case (*ʿalā kulli ḥāl*), verily . . ."

man jatū ("he to whom comes"): that is, he who acquires . . . 11.11.8

jafna(h) ("a bowl"): full of the aforementioned stewed beans, even if it be a gift, or alms, *wa-* ("and") who acquires along with it . . . 11.11.9

nuṣṣu raghīf ("half a loaf"): (the *f* of *niṣf* having been elided in accordance with the rural language,[333] as when they say *nuṣṣ fiḍḍah* for *niṣf fiḍḍah*), or as an example of "restraint,"[334] or by way of apocopation, as when the poet says, "Gently now, Fāṭim! A little less disdainful . . . ,"[335] should such a thing befall him, then it would be the most blessed and happiest of days. The fact that he asks for half a loaf and not a whole one is an allusion to the fact that stewed 11.11.10

يومه أبرك الأيّام وأسرّها إن حصل له هذا الأمر وطلبه نصف رغيف ولم يطلب رغيفاً كاملاً فيه إشارة إلى أنّ الفول المدمّس حامي الطبيعة فلا يحتاج إلى خبز كثير فيكون النصف رغيف كاف له مع كثرة الأكل من نفس الفول من غير خبز مثلاً أو من باب سدّ الجوعة

١١،١١،١١ والجفنة إناء كبير معدّ لوضع الطعام فيه وقال الله ﴿وَجِفَانٍ كَٱلْجَوَابِ﴾ جمع جابية وهي الحوض الكبير (قال بعضهم) يصف قوماً بكثرة الأكل واتّساع البطن [رمل]

كُلُّ جِلْفٍ بَطنُهُ جابِيَهْ[١] وإِذا صُحِّفَتْ كانت خابِيَهْ

١٢،١١،١١ (وفي نسخة أخرى) بالحاء المهملة أي حفنة من الفول المدمّس والحفنة ملء كفّي الإنسان مع انضمام الأصابع بعضها لبعض لكنّها بالجيم المعجمة أَوْلى وبين جفنة وحفنة الجناس المصحف وهي مشتقّة من جَفْن العين لكونها حافظة للطعام كما أنّ الجفن حافظ للعين ولما وُضِعَ فيها من كحل وغيره فيسري في أجفانها وتنطبق عليه وتحفظه حتّى يوئّر في قوّة النظر وكمال حسن الخِلْقة بذلك قال الشاعر [وافر]

أَقولُ لِمُقْلَتَيهِ حِينَ نامَتْ وكُحْلُ العَينِ في الأَجفانِ ساري
تَبارَكَ مَن تَوَفّاكُمْ بِلَيلٍ ويَعلَمُ ما جَرَحْتُمْ بِالنَّهارِ

(ومصدره) جفن يجفن جفنة

١٣،١١،١١ (ثمّ إنّ الناظم) تمنّى مأكولاً آخر من غالب مأكول قريته أغلظ طبعاً من المدمّس فقال

---

١ بي: خابية.

beans are Hot and do not call for a lot of bread; thus half a loaf will be enough for him, when combined with all the beans he is going to eat without bread, for example. Or it may be a case of just asking for any little thing to satisfy his hunger temporarily.

The *jafnah* is a large vessel made to hold food. The Almighty has said, «*wa-jifānin ka-l-jawābī* ("and basins like reservoirs"),»[336] the latter being plural of *jābiyah*, which means a large tank. Describing a people as being much given to eating and as having capacious bellies, a poet says: 11.11.11

Every lout has a belly like a vat (*jābiyah*),
  Which, if you change the dots, comes out as "twat" (*khāyibah*).

In another copy, the word occurs with *h*, that is, as a *ḥafnah* ("handful"), of stewed beans. A *ḥafnah* is what fills a man's two cupped hands, when the fingers are brought close together. However, it is more appropriate with *j*. Between *jafnah* and *ḥafnah* there is "orthographic paronomasia." *Jafnah* is derived from the *jafn* ("lid") of the eye, because the former protects the food just as the *jafn* provides a protective covering for the eye and whatever kohl or anything else may be put on it, such things suffusing the lids, which close over them and preserve them, allowing them to affect the eyesight[337] and perfect the charm of the face. As the poet[338] says: 11.11.12

I say to his eyes when closed in sleep,
  The lids with kohl suffused,
"Blessed be He who grants you rest at night,
  When He knows how cruelly by day you're used!"

The paradigm is *jaffana, yujaffinu, jafnatan* ("to hollow out (a bowl)").

Next the poet desires another dish, one of those most often eaten in his village and coarser in nature than stewed beans. He says: 11.11.13

ص

عَلَى مَنْ رَأَى ٱلْبِيسَارَ فِي ٱلْجُرْنِ جَالُو وَيَدْعَسْ وَلَوْكَانْ بِٱلْقُلَنْجِ ضَعِيفْ ١٢،١١

ش

قوله (على) تقدّم معناه في البيت الذي قبله ١،١٢،١١

(من رأى) رؤية بصريّة ٢،١٢،١١

(البيسارَ) وهو نوعين ريفيّ وحضريّ كما تقدّم في غيره (فالريفي) مركَّب من شيئين الملوخيّة الناشفة والفول المدشوش لا غير وكيفيّة طبخه عند الريّافة أنّهم يضعوا في البوشة الملوخيّة الناشفة وشيئاً من الفول المدشوش ويغمروه بالماء ويضعوا البوشة في الفرن إلى قرب الاستواء يخرجوها منه ويفركوها بالمفراك إلى أن يأخذ ما فيها قوامه وينهري الفول وتفوح رائحته فيعيدوها في الفرن يسيراً إن احتاج إلى ذلك ويزيدوها ماء إن افتقر إليه حتّى استوى ثمّ يُقلّوا له بشيء يسير من الشيرج بالبصل ويغرفوه في شالية أو مترد ويفتّوا فيه الخبز الشعير أو فطير الدرة حتّى يصير مثل قطع الكرس ويأكلوه بالبصل الأخضر أو الناشف يأكل الشخص منهم المترد الفتّ أو المتردين في الغداء والمترد في العشاء ويسحب نَبّوته وحِذوته خلف قفاه ويسرح بالبهائم أو للضمّ أو المحراث وهذا غالب مأكولهم خصوصاً في رمضان وقت الفطور والسحور حتّى يصير الشخص منهم كأنّه الزقّ المنفوخ كما تقدّم ثمّ ينضجع على الفرن بالجلّة والوحل على رجليه هو وزوجته من غير صلاة ولا عبادة فتدور الروائح في بطونهم وتخرج من بينهم مثل الزوابع فيكون هذا بخورهم طول ليلتهم فلا يقوم الشخص منهم إلّا وجُبّته قد فاحت رائحتها من كثرة الفساء فيها والضراط وإن جامع زوجته تلك الليلة فيكون ٣،١٢،١١

TEXT

ʿalā man raʾā l-bīsāra fī l-jurni jā-lū 11.12
wa-yadʿas wa-law kān bi-l-qulinji ḍaʿīf

Happy is he who sees *bīsār* come to him on the threshing floor
and bolts it, though he be by colic enfeebled!

COMMENTARY

ʿalā ("Happy is he"): the meaning of *ʿalā* is explained in the preceding verse. 11.12.1

man raʾā ("who sees"): visually. 11.12.2

(a)l-bīsāra: *bīsār* is of two kinds, rural and urban, as was previously seen to be 11.12.3
the case with regard to other dishes. The rural is composed of two things—dry Jew's mallow and pounded beans, nothing more. The way the people of the countryside cook it is to put the dry mallow and a small quantity of pounded beans in the pot, cover with water, and put the pot in the oven until it is almost done. Then they take it out and break up the lumps with a wooden whisk until it reaches the right consistency and the beans have crumbled and their smell permeates the air. After this they return it, if necessary, to the oven, adding water, if required, until it is done. Next they make it a garnish by frying onion in a little sesame oil and ladle it out into a crock or a milk pot and crumble some barley bread or flaky sorghum pastry into it until it turns into something like slabs of dung mixed with straw, and they eat it with green or dry onions. One of them will eat a crock or two, mixed with crumbled bread or pastry, for lunch, and a crock for dinner, and pick up his stick, with his leather sandals slung behind his neck, and set off with the animals, or to reap or plow; and this is the greater part of their food, especially in Ramadan at the time of the breaking of the fast or just before dawn, so that the peasant ends up looking like a swollen waterskin, as previously noted. Then he lies down on top of the oven with the dung and the daub on his legs, he and his wife, without a prayer or any other act of worship, and the flatulence goes around and around in their bellies and erupts like a hurricane, and this serves as their incense all night long. None of them gets up in the morning but the stink of his *jubbah* wafts about from the quantity of farts, audible and inaudible, therein. Should he have intercourse that same night with his wife their fate will be farting and fracas, and

حظّهم ضراط وعياط * وفساء وشياط * فهذا حالهم في الأكل والنكاح * فنعوذ بالله من طباع الفلّاح *

٤،١٢،١١ (وأمّا النوع الحضريّ) فما أَلَذّه وأَشْهاه * وما أَطْيَبه وأَهْناه * وهو أنّ الشخص من أكابر مصر أو غيرها من المدن الّتي تُجْلَب إليها الملوخيّة أو تُزْرَع فيها إذا اشتهى فعلها فعلى أصناف منهم من يأخذها ناشفة نقيّة من العيدان قريبة العهد من زمن تنشيفها أو ربّما نشّفها في بيته ويسلّمها لمن يتعاطى طبخها من زوجة أو خادم فتضعها في دست نحاس مبيّض أو طنجرة رومي عليها غطاء مُحْكَم وتضع عليها الماء العَذْب الزُلال الرائق ويقاد عليها بالحطب الروميّ حتّى تأخذ قوامها في الاستواء ثمّ تفركها فركًا لطيفًا ثمّ تقلّي لها بالثوم الشاميّ أو البلديّ ممزوجًا بالسمن البقريّ وتضيف إليه دهن الِليَة وتلقي عليها شيئًا من الحرارات كالفلفل وما أشبهه وشيئًا من الكَمُّون لدفع ضررها ومنهم من يضيف إلى هذا شيئًا يسيرًا من الفول المدشوش ولكن يزيد في الدهن والسمن حتّى يستهلك طعم الفول ويغلب طعم الدهن والسمن والحرارات ونحو ذلك ومنهم من يجعل مكان الفول صغار الكَبَاب من لحم الضأن ويسمّى هذا النوع بجمع الأحباب (ونوع آخر) وهو أنّها أي الملوخيّة تؤخذ وهي خضراء نضرة بنت يومها وتخرط خرطًا جيّدًا وبعض أبناء الترك يفعلها من غير خرط ثمّ يقاد عليها بالنار كما تقدّم ويُقَلَّى لها بالأدهان والسمن والحرارات كما تقدّم ذكره فيصير لها لذة عظيمة وبعضهم يحشيها باللحم ويسمّى هذا النوع مليّن الطبائع لما فيه من البرودة ولطافة المأكل وسرعة الانهضام وحصول الخفّة في الجسد (ونوع آخر) وهو ألذّ وأشهى ممّا تقدّم وأقوى نفعًا وأشهى مأكولًا وهو أخذ الملوخيّة وهي صغيرة في ابتداء طلوعها وخرطها جيّدًا وطبخها بالفراريج أو الإوزّ مع كثرة الأدهان والحرارات أو باللحم الضأن وأهل مصر يرغبون في هذا النوع ويفعلوه كثيرًا حتّى أنّ الشخص منهم ينفق على طعام الملوخيّة في ابتداء أمرها جملة من الدراهم ويدعو أعزّ أصحابه يأكل منها وتكون عندهم ألذّ من طعام الأعياد ويتحدّثون بهذه النعمة ويقول الضيف فلان أطعمني الليلة الملوخيّة بركة السنة وربّما أكلوها بالخبز النظيف المقطّف المقمَّر المخبوز

gas and tintamarre. Such is their condition with regard to eating and coition—we seek shelter with God from the peasant's disposition!

As for the urban kind, how delicious it is, and how toothsome, good, and wholesome! What happens is that, should one of the great men of Cairo or one of the other cities to which Jew's mallow is brought for sale or in which it is grown have an appetite to make it, he may do so in a variety of fashions. One of them will take it dry and cleaned of stems, shortly after it has been dried, or perhaps dry it in his own house and entrust it to whoever, wife or servant, will see to the cooking of it. The latter then places it in a tinned copper basin or Anatolian-style casserole with a tight-fitting lid and adds pure, cold, sweet water and heats it over wood[339] until it reaches the right consistency. Then she gently breaks up the lumps and makes it a garnish of Syrian or local garlic mixed with clarified cow's butter and adds the fat from the tail of a sheep and throws in some seasonings such as pepper and so on, plus a little cumin to get rid of its harmful attributes. Another may add to this a few crushed beans but also increase the fat or clarified butter until the latter absorbs the taste of the beans and the taste of the fat, butter, seasonings, and so on predominates. Yet others use small mutton kebabs in place of the beans, this form being called "the Gathering of Loved Ones."[340] Another way is to take it, that is, the mallow, when green and fresh, gathered that day, and chop it well (though some Turks do it without chopping), then heat it as before and make a garnish for it with fats, clarified butter, and seasonings, as described above; it is then very delicious. Some stuff it with meat, and this kind is called "the Softener of Constitutions" for its Coldness, the ease with which it is eaten, the speed with which it is digested, and the lightness that results in the body. Another kind is yet more delicious and appetizing than the preceding and more beneficial and makes a more delicious dish. This consists of taking the mallow when small, when it is starting to sprout, chopping it well, and cooking it with chicken or goose, with a lot of fats and seasonings, or with mutton. The people of Cairo are very fond of this type and make it often, so much so that one of them may spend large amounts of money on mallow when it first appears and invite his closest friends over to eat it. They consider it more delicious than the feast-day foods, and talk of this treat, and the guest will say, "Tonight So-and-so fed me mallow, the first of the year!" Sometimes they eat it with clean toasted bread made of finely sieved flour and baked with fennel-flower seed or fennel, which 11.12.4

بالحبّة السوداء أو الشّمَر فيفتّوا فيها حتّى تتشرّب بتلك الدسومات العظيمة وروائح تلك اللحوم السمينة

٥،١٢،١١ وهذا من جودة رأيهم وزكاوة عقولهم وحبّهم للشيء عند ابتداء طلوعه كما يقال (كلّ جديد له لذّة وكلّ قديم له هِجران) ويقرب من المعنى قول ابن عروس رحمه الله تعالى ونفعنا به [مجتثّ]

أولْ زمانكْ يعزّوكْ غالي وقعْ في آيدْ غالي
وآن دُبْتَ يا شاشْ يرموكْ وآلّي جرى لكْ جرى لي

٦،١٢،١١ (فإنّ الشيء) في ابتداء طلوعه له لذّة عظيمه * وفرحة عند العيال عميمه * (ونوع) يسمّى بورانيّ وهو أنّه تُقْطَف أوراق الملوخيّة ثمّ يقلوها بالسمن ثمّ يفعلوا بها كما مرّ

ولهذا ذكر سيّدي عبد الوهّاب الشعرانيّ نفعنا الله به أنّه يُسْتَحَبّ الأكل من الشيء عند ابتداء طلوعه مثل الخضروات وغيرها من الفواكه فإنّ نَفْعه في ابتدائه أكثر من نفعه في انتهائه وأهل مصر على هذا القدم يتفاءلوا في أخذ الشيء في ابتدائه ولا يكترثوا به في انتهائه فجزاهم الله خيراً عن مروءتهم * وأدام سرورهم بنسائهم وطيب معاشرتهم * وأعاذنا الله من الريف وجهله * وغلظ مأكوله وطباع أهله *

٧،١٢،١١ (سؤال) ما الحكمة في تسمية الملوخيّا بالفول بيسار وأيضاً تسميتها ملوخيّا وما اشتقاقها وما معنى ذلك (الجواب الفشرويّ) على وجهين (الأوّل) أنّ الذي اخترع البيسار في الأصل كان أبوه فلّاحاً يزرع الملوخيّا وكان بينه وبين ولده مشاحنة فذهب هذا الرجل إلى غيط أبيه المذكور وسرق شيئاً من تلك الملوخيّا المذكورة وأتى به إلى زوجته فقالت له ما تريد بهذا فقال لها قصدي أصنعه طعاماً ثمّ أخذ ورقها ووضعه

they crumble into it, so that it absorbs those wonderful fats and the flavors of the fatty meats.

This follows from their excellent judgment, intelligence, and love of things when they first appear, as exemplified by the proverb that says, "Everything new is delicious and everything old distasteful" and, in the same vein, the words of Ibn ʿArūs, God have mercy upon him and benefit us through him: **11.12.5**

They hold you high on your debut—
Something dear for a dear hand to hold.
But Muslin, when you fade, they toss you out—
And so it was for me, when I grew old.

—for everything, when it first appears, holds an appeal of a special kind, and, for children, joy unconfined. There is also a kind called *būrānī*[341] made by tearing up the mallow leaves and making a garnish for them with clarified butter; then they prepare it as previously described.

This is why Master ʿAbd al-Wahhāb al-Shaʿrānī, God benefit us through him, mentions that it is desirable to eat things such as vegetables and fruit and the like at their first appearance, for their health benefits when new are greater than when old. The people of Cairo are of this school and think it auspicious to obtain things when they are still new, and care nothing for them when they are old—may God reward them for their doughtiness, granting them everlasting pleasure in their womenfolk and seasoning to perfection their togetherness, and God protect us from the countryside and its stupidities, the coarseness of its food and of its people's proclivities! **11.12.6**

Question: What is the wisdom in calling mallow with fava beans *bīsār*, and what is the wisdom in calling mallow *mulūkhiyyā*, and what are the etymology and the meaning of the latter? The Facetious Answer may take two forms. The first is that the father of the man who originally invented *bīsār* was a peasant who used to grow *mulūkhiyyā*. However, there was bad blood between him and his son, and the latter went to the field of his aforementioned father and stole some of the aforementioned *mulūkhiyyā* and took it to his wife, who said to him, "What do you want with this?" He replied, "I intend to have it made into food," and he took its leaves and placed them in a pot and put it on the fire. Then along came his young son, who threw into the pot a few stewed fava beans that he had taken from the donkey's trough, and the *mulūkhiyyā* **11.12.7**

في بوشة وحطّها على النار فجاء ولده الصغير وألقى في البوشة شيئاً من الفول المدمّس أخذه من مدود الحمارة فامتزج الفول بالملوخيا ثمّ إنّه أخذ البوشة بعد استواء ما فيها وغرفه في مترد وجلس يأكل منه فدخل أبوه وقال له ما هذا الشيء الأخضر فدلّس عليه القول وقال له هذا حشيش جئنا به من الغيط ثمّ بان الأمر أنّه سرق الملوخية من غيط أبيه فتضارب هو وإيّاه وحلف أبوه لا يمكث في البلد وركب حماره وسار إلى بلد أخرى فصار ابنه ينادي أبي سار أبي سار فحذفوا الألف من أبي وجعلوا هذا اللفظ المركّب من اسم وفعل عَلَماً على هذا الطعام وقالوا بيسار (وأفادني) بعض إخواننا اللطفاء رحمه الله (وجهاً آخر) وهو أنّه لمّا وضع فيها الفول نادى لسان حاله بي سار[1] أي سارطعمي بهذا الفول طيّب (والوجه الثالث) أنّه مركّب من البُسْر أو من البيسارة من قولهم في معنى ذلك [مجتثّ مع كسر]

سعيدَه كانت مِـزارهْ تحب طبيخ البـيسارهْ

(وأمّا الملوخيّا) فقد عرّفها ابن سودون رحمه الله بهذا اللفظ الموضوع عليها بقوله في ديوانه [وافر] ١١،١٢،٨

أبو قُـرْدانْ زَرَعْ فَدّانْ
مُـلوخِيّـا وَبادِنْجـانْ

إنّ هذا اسم لنبات أخضر نضر وأصله يا ملوخي فأخّر حرف النداء وأبو قردان أوّل من سمّاه بذلك على ما قيل وسبب ذلك أنّه لمّا زرعه في فدّانه وصلح للطبخ ملَخ منه شيئاً وتركه في مكان وذهب لبعض شأنه فجاء بعض أولاده وأخذه فلمّا رجع لم يجده فناداه بحذف حرف النداء لظنّ قربه منه وقال ملوخي فلم يجبه بشيء فأتى بحرف

---

١ : بي: بيسار.

mixed with the beans. Next, after what was in the pot had cooked, he took it and ladled it into a crock and sat down and ate from it. Then his father came in and said, "What's that green stuff?" and the man spoke deceitful words to him and said, "It's grass we brought from the field." Later it came out that he had stolen the *mulūkhiyyā* from his father's field, and the two of them fought, and his father swore that he would stay no longer in the village and mounted his donkey and went off to another village, with the result that the son took to crying out, "*Abī sār! Abī sār!*" ("My father has gone off! My father has gone off!"). Finally, they dropped the *a* from *abī* ("My father") and constructed this compound term out of a noun and a verb as a name for that dish, calling it *bīsār*. And one of my refined brethren, God have mercy upon him, informed me of another possible answer, which is that when the beans were placed in the pot they called out, "*Biya sār*," using their "natural tongue," that is, "through me (*biya*) it has become (*sār*)," meaning "through these beans my taste has become"[342] good. A third possibility is that the word is formed from *busr* ("fresh, juicy plants"), or from *bīsārah*,[343] on the basis of the verse on the same topic:

Happy was Mizārah—
She loved to cook *bīsārah*!

As for *mulūkhiyyā*, Ibn Sūdūn, may the Almighty have mercy on his soul, **11.12.8**
defines it by means of the following term coined for it in his *Works*, when he says on the topic:[344]

Abū Qurdān[345]
Sowed a feddan
Of *mulūkhiyyā*
And *bādinjān*.[346]

This is a name for a green tender plant. It was originally *yā mulūkhī*. Then they put the vocative particle *yā* at the end. Abū Qurdān was the first to call it so, or so they say. It came about as follows: when he sowed it in his feddan and it became ready for cooking, he tore some of it out and left it where it was and went off on some other business. Then one of his children came along and took it. When Abū Qurdān came back he could not find it, and he called out for it, omitting the vocative particle because he thought it must be somewhere close to him, and he said, "*Mulūkhī*!" ("My tearings!"). However, it answered

النداء وقبل أن يقول ملوخي أتاه ولده وأعلمه بأخذه فتحصّل من ملوخي بيا وأُدْغِمَتْ الياء في الياء فصارت ملوخيّا انتهى الجواب

٩،١٢،١١ وتُلَقَّب بالخضيرة وتُكنّى بأمّ الأدهان وأمّ الأفراح وليس في الأطعمة ألطف منها ولا أقوى نفعاً وقد صنّف بعض العلماء في منافعها كتاباً جليلاً وأمّا نهي الحاكم بأمر الله عنها فلميل سيّدنا معاوية رضي الله عنه إليها لأنّها كانت أحبّ الأطعمة إليه خصوصاً عند ابتداء طلوعها وقوله

١٠،١٢،١١ (في الجُرُن) وهو محلّ معدّ لدرس الفول والقمح ويطلق على الحجر المنقور الّذي يدقّ فيه بنّ القهوة يقال جرّن اليوم فلان زرعه بمعنى أنّه نقله من الغيط ووضعه في هذا المحلّ على بعضه البعض كالكوم وصار يأخذ من حواليه شيئاً بعد شيء ويدرسه بالنورج وهذا المأخوذ يقال له عند الفلّاح رَمْية وقيل أصل الجرن الجرم بالميم بدل النون مأخوذ من جَرْم اللحم وهو أخذه بالسكّين من على العظم أبدلت الميم نوناً لقربها في المخرج والمناسبة لهذا المعنى أنّ النورج يجرم القمح أو الفول أو ما أُلْقِيَ إليه من الحبوب ويخلّصه مثل ما تخلّص السكّين اللحم من عظمه ويطلق هذا اللفظ على الجرم الّذي يعمل من الخوص وقوله

١١،١٢،١١ (جالو) بالتخفيف أي جاء إليه والضمير راجع للبيسار أي على من رأى البيسار جاء إليه وهو في الجرن يدرس القمح وهو راكب النورج أو بيقلب في الرمية أو يحرس مثلاً لأنّه يكون في هذه الحالة تعبان جيعان ولهذا قال

١٢،١٢،١١ (ويَدْعَس) أي يأكل بحُرْقة وعَجَلة من غير تأنّي في المضغ والبلع والدعس لفظة ريفيّة استعملت بهذا المعنى ومصدرها دعس يدعس دعساً فهو داعس لأنّ الأكل

not a word. Then he introduced the vocative particle, but before he could say *mulūkhī* a second time, his son came to him and informed him that he was the one who had taken them, so the net result was *mulūkhī yā*,[347] and then the second *yāʾ* was joined to the first and the word became *mulūkhiyyā*.[348] End of answer.

It is nicknamed Little Greeny and given the *kunyah*s "Mother of Fats" and "Mother of Joys." There is no food more refined or more beneficial to the health. A certain scholar has composed a wonderful book on its virtues. As for al-Ḥākim bi-Amri-llāh's having banned it, this was because Our Master Muʿāwiyah, may the Almighty be pleased with him, was greatly attached to it, it being his favorite food, especially at the start of the season.[349] **11.12.9**

fī l-jurni ("on the threshing floor"): this is the place prepared for threshing fava beans and wheat, and the word is also applied to the hollowed-out stone in which coffee beans are pounded. One says, "Today So-and-so brought his crop to the threshing floor (*jarrana zarʿahu*)," meaning that he transported it from the field and put it there, one bit on top of another, in the form of a pile, and started taking it little by little from the edges and threshing it with the threshing sledge, the quantity so taken being what the peasants call a *ramyah*. It is said the origin of *jurn* is *jarm*, with *m* instead of *n*, taken from *jarm al-laḥm*, namely, "the removal of the meat from the bone with a knife"; the *m* got changed into an *n* because of the closeness of the points of articulation. The appositeness of this sense comes from the fact that the threshing sledge "bones" (*yajrimu*) the wheat, or the beans, or whatever grains are thrown to it, from the ears, and frees it, just as the knife frees the meat from the bone. The same term (*jurn*) is also applied to the *jarm* that is made out of palm fronds.[350] **11.12.10**

jā-lū ("come to him"): with suppression of the glottal stop, that is, *jāʾa ilayh*.[351] The subject pronoun refers to the *bīsār*, that is, happy is he to whom *bīsār* comes while he is on the threshing floor threshing wheat and riding the threshing sledge, or while he is turning the wheat so that it passes under the blades of the sledge, or standing guard, for example, because when so engaged he will be weary and hungry. For this reason he says . . . **11.12.11**

wa-yadʿas ("and bolts it"): that is, gulps it down at agonizing speed without taking any time to chew and swallow. *Daʿs*[352] is a rural expression used in this sense,[353] and the paradigm is *daʿasa, yadʿasu, daʿsan*, active participle *dāʿis*. **11.12.12**

المطلوب تصغير اللقمة وتطويل المضغة وفي المثل (صغّر لقمتك وطوّل مضغتك يبارك الله لك في أكلتك)

١٣،١٢،١١ (مسألة هباليّة) وهي أنّ الناظم نسب المجيء للبيسار وهو طعام والطعام لا يمكن مجيئه بنفسه ولا يتأتّى ذلك فما الحكم (الجواب الفشرويّ) أنّ هذا على تقدير حذف مضاف أي جاء به رجل حامله حتّى أوصله كما يقال جاءت السفينة مثلاً أي جاء بها الملّاح وكما تقول جاءني الليلة صحن ملآن عدس أو بيسار فهذا ممكن فعلى هذا لا إشكال في كلام الناظم وقوله

١٤،١٢،١١ (ولو كانْ) أي هذا المتمني لهذا الطعام الذي هو الناظم بمرض

١٥،١٢،١١ (القُلِنْج ضَعيفْ) أي سقيم والقلنج ريح يابسة تمنع البخار أن يجري في الأعضاء فتكبّ الإنسان عند هيجانها وتمنعه الشمّ حتّى تكاد تخرج روحه فمنها حار ومنها بارد فعلامة الحار هيجان العلّة عند ملاقاة الحرارة والسمائم والانتباه من النوم وعلاجه أكل الصَبِر الأخضر على الريق دائماً فإنّه يقطع هذه العلّة من الجوف ويحلّلها وعلامة البارد هيجان العلّة عند ملاقاة البرد الشديد والغَيم والأمطار والرياح الباردة ونحو هذا وعلاجه أن يؤخذ صبر سُقُطْرِيّ وحَبّ الرَشاد وفلفل وزنجبيل يابس أجزاء سواء ويُدَقّ الجميع مع مثله سكّر أبيض دقّاً ناعماً ويُعْمَل سَفوفاً يُفْطَر عليه على الريق وعند هيجان العلّة فإنّه نافع ويجتنب صاحب هذه العلّة الحارّة أكل الأشياء الحارّة وصاحب العلّة الباردة أكل الأشياء الباردة وخصوصاً عند هيجان العلّة فإنّه نافع إن شاء الله تعالى

١٦،١٢،١١ والمعنى أنّ الناظم لشدّة فقره وجوعه وعدم شيء يصنع به هذا الطعام تمنّى مجيئه إليه ويشبع منه ولو كان مبتلى بمرض القَوْلَنْج ولو كان في أكله زيادة ضرر عليه اذ هو

This way of eating is unacceptable, because the proper way to eat is to make the size of the mouthful as small as possible and take a long time chewing. As the proverb says, "Make your mouthfuls small and take time over your chewing, and God will bless you in your eating."

A Fatuous Problem. The poet attributes the coming to the *bīsār*, which is a **11.12.13**
food, and it is inconceivable that a food should come on its own, so what is the wisdom in that? The Facetious Answer is that this should be taken as an example of "the omission of the first element of a genitive construction,"[354] that is, *a man* came with it, carrying it until he handed it over, in the same way that one says for example, "The ship came," that is, the navigator brought it, and in the same way that one says, for example, "Tonight a dish full of lentils or *bīsār* came to me." On this basis there is nothing problematic in the poet's words.

wa-law kān ("though he be"): that is, though the one who desires this food, **11.12.14**
namely, the poet, be, by the sickness called . . .

al-qulinji ḍaʿīf ("colic enfeebled"): that is, though he be indisposed. Colic is **11.12.15**
a dry flatulence that prevents vapor[355] from circulating through the limbs. It prostrates the sufferer when it breaks out and prevents him from inhaling, to the point that he almost gives up the ghost. It has Hot and Cold forms. The sign of the Hot is that the sickness breaks out on exposure to heat and hot winds and on sudden waking from sleep. The treatment is to eat green aloes, always on an empty stomach, for this denies the sickness access to the stomach cavity, and dissolves it. The sign of the Cold form is the eruption of the sickness on exposure to extreme cold, clouds, rain, cold winds, and so on. The treatment is to take aloes of Socotra, seeds of garden cress, pepper, and dry ginger in equal parts, and pound all these with an equal quantity of white sugar till smooth. This is made into a powder, which is taken at breakfast on an empty stomach, when the sickness breaks out. It is effective. The sufferer from the Hot form of this sickness should avoid eating hot things and the sufferer from the Cold form should avoid eating cold things, especially when the sickness first breaks out. This is effective, if the Almighty wills.

The meaning is that the poet was so poor and hungry and so lacking in the **11.12.16**
wherewithal to prepare this food that he wished that it would come to him and that he might eat his fill of it, even if he were to be stricken with the colic and even if eating it should cause him further harm, for it is a crude, vile food,

من الأطعمة الرديئة المغلّظة خصوصاً إذا استعمله صاحب هذا المرض فإنّه يؤذيه أذيّة بالغة (فإن قيل) لأيّ شيء ذكر الناظم هذا المرض دون غيره وما حكم معرفته له مع أنّه من أهل الريف وما اشتقاق اسمه (الجواب الفشرويّ) أنّه إنّما ذكر هذا المرض لكونه أرياحاً منعقدة فيكون من باب المبالغة في الشيء والبيسار يضرّ صاحب الأرياح ضرراً بالغاً خصوصاً إذا أكل البصل الأخضر أو الناشف فتمتلئ البطن أرياحاً ويكثر فيها الفساء والضراط فيكون مرضاً على مرض فتمنّى ذلك لشدّة جوعه ولو كان يحصل له هذا الأمر أو يموت في الحال وأمّا حكم معرفته له فلعلّه سمعه من بعض الأطبّاء وهو يصفه أو من غيرهم وأمّا اشتقاق اسمه فلعلّه من القَوق أو القُوَيقة وهي طائر قدر الحمامة كبير الرأس ويقال لها البومة تأوي الأماكن الخراب وفي المثل (اتبع البوم يؤدّيك الخراب) وقد يشبّه الشيب ببياضها كما يشبّه سواد الشعر بالغراب الأسود ومن هذا المعنى قول الإمام الشافعيّ رضي الله عنه [طويل]

أَيا بُومَة قَد عَشَّشَتْ فَوقَ هامَتي ... عَلَى الرَّأسِ مِنِّي حينَ طارَ غُرابُها
رَأَيتِ ذَهابَ العُمرِ مِنّي فَزُرتِني ... وَمأْواكِ مِن كُلِّ الدِّيارِ خَرابُها

١٧،١٢،١١ (وبذكر البومة) وأنها تأوي الخراب ذكرت ما اتّفق لبعض الملوك أنّه ظلم رعيّته ظلماً فاحشاً وكان له وزير فطن عارف فشكوا الناس إليه وتضرّر من ظلمه بهم فأراد أن يتحيّل عليه ويمنعه عن الظلم ويرشده إلى العدل فخرج هو وإيّاه يوماً يريد التَنَزُّه خارج المدينة إلى أن مرّوا على أماكن خربة فسمع الملك ذكر بوم يصيح على بومة فقال للوزير ما أحسن صياح هذا الطائر على هذه البومة فقال الوزير يا ملك أتدري ما يقول لها فقال لا وهل تعرف يا وزير لغة الطيور قال نعم فقال ما يقول لها قال يا ملك هذا عاشق لها ومشغوف بحبّها ويقول لها يا ستّ الطيور وبهجة الأحباب

especially if used by someone suffering from this sickness, to whom it will do great injury. If it be asked why the poet mentions this particular illness and not others, and how come he is acquainted with it when he is from the countryside and what is the etymology of its name,[356] the Facetious Answer would be that he only mentions this illness because it consists of complex gases, this thus falling under the rubric of hyperbole. *Bīsār* does immense harm to the sufferer from flatulence, especially if he eats green or dry onions with it, for it causes his belly to fill with wind and farts, silent and audible, and these multiply in it, so that the latter becomes a second illness on top of the first. Nevertheless, he is so hungry that he longs for it even though he should fall victim to these things or die on the spot. As for how he came to be acquainted with the sickness, it may be that he heard of it from a doctor who was describing it, or from anyone else. As for the etymology of the name, it may be from *qawq* ("screeching") or from the *quwayqah*, which is a bird the size of a dove with a large head, also called the *būmah* ("owl"), which inhabits ruined places. The proverb says, "Follow the owl, and it will lead you to the ruin." White hairs are sometimes likened to it, just as black hair may be likened to the black crow. Imam al-Shāfiʿī, may the Almighty be pleased with him, said on this topic:[357]

O owl, who made your nest above my crown,
Atop my head, after the crow had taken flight—
Seeing my life depart, you came a-visiting,
For the ruin, above all abodes, is where you love to light.

Apropos of the owl and its preference for inhabiting ruins, I am reminded **11.12.17** that once a certain king oppressed his subjects outrageously. Now, he had a minister who was sagacious and wise, and to him the people brought their troubles and complained of the king's tyranny. The minister then decided to play a trick on the king to turn him aside from his oppressive ways and guide him to justice. One day he and the king went out to relax outside the city. They proceeded until they passed by some ruins, and the king heard a male owl calling to a female. He said to the minister, "How lovely is the call of this bird to the female owl!" and the minister replied, "Sire, do you know what he is saying to her?" "No," said the king, "but do you, minister, know the language of the birds?" "I do," he replied. So the king asked, "What was he saying to her?" The minister responded, "This bird, sire, is in love with her and is smitten with desire for her, and he was saying to her, 'Mistress of Birds and Lovers'

مرادي وصالك والتقرّب إليك في الحلال فقالت له لن تقدر على صَداقي ولو أشغلك حبّي واشتياقي فقال لها وما صداقك فقالت له عشر مدائن خراب فقال لها أَبْشُرى فإن دام ملكنا هذا على حالته مع الرعيّة إلى آخر العام خذي مائة مدينة خراب قال فتفطّن الملك لكلام الوزير وعلم أنّه في غفلة عن الرعيّة وأنّهم في ظلم وبليّة وأنّه نصحه وأرشده للعدل على لسان الطير فقال له جزاك الله خيراً ثمّ إنّه أظهر العدل في الرعيّة وأزال عنهم ما هم فيه من المظالم والبليّة وعدل من وقته وساعته وارتاحت الناس من تغيير حالته فاتّضح المقال عن وجه هذا الإشكال

(ثمّ إنّ الناظم) اشتاق إلى مأكول آخر يصنع في الريف وغيره فقال ١٨،١٢،١١

ص

عَلَى مَنْ قَشَعْ جَفْنَةْ بِلِيلَهْ مَلَانَهْ   وَلَوْكَانَتْ بِلَا قُلْقَاسِ يَا دَنْدِيفْ ١٣،١١

ش

قوله (على من قَشَعْ) أي نظر بلغة الريّافة يقال قشعتك أي رأيتك وقشعت المحلّ الفلانيّ أي رأيته ويطلق على ميل الشيء يقال انقشع السحاب أي مال وانكشف إلى محلّ آخر ١،١٣،١١

(ومن العجائب) أنّ شخصاً سمع هذه اللفظة من طائر في بعض بساتين الشام وذلك إنّه دخل يوماً يتفرّج في بستان ويأكل ممّا أسقطته الأشجار من الفواكه فسمع قائلاً يقول شفتك قشعتك روح فخرج هارباً وظنّ أنه صاحب البستان يصيح عليه فلقيه رجل ٢،١٣،١١

Delight, I wish to be one with you and be joined with you in holy matrimony.' And she replied, 'You will never be able to afford my dowry, even though love and yearning for me exercise you.' 'And what is your dowry?' he said to her. Said she, 'Ten ruined cities.' 'What joyful news,' said he, 'for if this king of ours continues to treat his subjects until the end of the year as he is treating them now, you may have a hundred ruined cities!'" The king took in the meaning of the minister's words and realized that he had been neglectful of his subjects and that they were living in parlous injustice and that the minister had given him advice and guided him towards justice through the language of the birds. "God reward you well!" he said to him, and from then on he manifested justice towards his subjects and relieved them of the abuses and catastrophes from which they had been suffering, and from that day and hour he behaved with righteousness and the people found comfort in his change of state. Our words are now clear, the answer to the problem has appeared.

Next the poet longed for another dish that is made in the countryside and **11.12.18** elsewhere, and said:

TEXT

ʿalā man qashaʿ jafnat balīlah malānah **11.13**
wa-law kānat[358] *bi-lā qulqāsi yā dandīf*

Happy is he who sees a bowl with *balīlah* filled,
though it be without taro, you good-for-nothing!

COMMENTARY

ʿalā man qashaʿ ("Happy is he who sees"): that is, *qashaʿ* means "to see" in the **11.13.1** language of the country people: one says *qashaʿtak*, that is, "I beheld you" and *qashaʿtu l-maḥalla l-fulānī* ("I saw such and such a place"), that is, "I beheld it."[359] The same word is used in the sense of something's "turning away": one says *inqashaʿa l-saḥāb* ("the clouds were scattered"), that is, they turned aside and were borne away to another place.[360]

An Amazing Thing: one day a man heard a bird say the same word in an **11.13.2** orchard of Damascus. What happened is that he entered an orchard one day to look around and eat some of the fruit that had fallen from the trees and he heard someone say, "I see you (*shuftak*)! I spy you (*qashaʿtak*)! Go!" so the

وهو خارج من البستان فقال له ما بالك تجري فقال سمعت من داخل البستان إنساناً يقول لي كذا وكذا قال فضحك الرجل وقال له ارجع وكل ما تشتهي ولا تختش من أحد هذا طائر وليس هو إنسان وهذه لغته يخوّف بها من يدخل البستان قال فتعجّب الرجل وأكل حتّى اكتفى ومضى إلى حال سبيله (وقد سمعت) وأنا متوجّه إلى الحجّ في البحر من الصعيد على بندر القُصَيْر سنة خمس وسبعين وألف طائراً في غيط قمح يقول طاب دقيق السنبل سبحان القديم الأزليّ وسمعه كلّ من في السفينة (وذكر الحلبيّ) في السيرة النبويّة أنّ غراباً كان يحفظ سورة السجدة فإذا سجد قال سجد لك سوادي وآمن بك فؤادي

١١،١٣،٣ (ومن العجائب) أنّه أُهْدِيَ لبعض الملوك طائر له أربعة أجنحة على شكل ظريف فإذا جاء وقت صلاة الفجر ذكر الله تعالى بلسان فصيح ثمّ يقف على رأس الملك ويقول الصلاة خير من النوم مرّتين ثمّ يصلّي على النبيّ صلّى الله عليه وسلّم ويسكت ومثل هؤلاء كثير فسبحان القادر على كلّ شيء ﴿وَإِنْ مِنْ شَيْءٍ إِلَّا يُسَبِّحُ بِحَمْدِهِ﴾ وقوله

١١،١٣،٤ (جَفْنَةْ) تقدّم معناها

١١،١٣،٥ (بَليلَهْ) اسم للقمح المصلوق المضاف إليه بعض الحِمِّص وهذا يباع أيضاً ببلاد المدن وله لذّة ولذّته من إضافة الملح عليه والحمص عليه فإنّه يعدّل طبعه والحمص أزكى الطعام كما ذكره بعض المفسّرين في تفسير سورة الكهف وأمّا البليلة المذكورة هنا في النظم فإنّ أهل الريف يصنعوها طعاماً وهو إنّهم يضعوا القمح في بوشة فخار وربّما أضافوا عليه ما يتيسّر من الحمص ويغمروه بالماء ويجعلوه في النار حتّى يستوي يأخذوه ويأكلوه بخبز درة أو شعير أو يقطعوا ويبلعوا من غير خبز لأنّهم يجعلوه يابساً يقطع الشخص بالكف ويبلع ويقلّوا له بالبصل وشيء من الشيرج والأكابر منهم يجعل فيه بعض قُلْقاس وسمّي بليلة لِبَلّه بالماء في حال صلقه أو لرخاوته وطراوته ولهذا يقال للرجل

man fled, thinking that the owner of the orchard was shouting at him. As he was leaving the orchard, a man met him and asked him, "Why are you running?" so he said, "In the orchard I heard a person say such and such to me." The man laughed and said, "Go back and eat what you like and fear no one! It is a bird, not a man, and that is its language, with which it frightens those who enter the orchard." The man was amazed and ate until he had had enough, and went his way. And I myself, while heading for the port of al-Quṣayr on my way to make the pilgrimage by sea from Upper Egypt in 1075,[361] heard a bird in a wheat field say, "The flour has ripened in the ear, glory to the Ancient, the Eternal!" and everyone on board the ship heard it. Al-Ḥalabī, in his biography of the Prophet, mentions a raven that memorized the Chapter of the Prostration,[362] and when he prostrated himself would say, "To You my blackness has bowed down, in You my heart has placed its faith."

Another Amazing Thing: A certain king once received a gift of a bird with four wings, pleasingly formed. When the time came for the dawn prayer, it would utter the name of the Almighty with clear tongue and then stand by the king's head and say, "Prayer is better than sleep"[363] twice, then pronounce blessings on the Prophet, God bless him and grant him peace, and fall silent. Such things are numerous, so glory be to God who is capable of anything—«and there is not a thing but glorifies His praise.»[364] 11.13.3

jafna(t) ("a bowl"): defined above.[365] 11.13.4

balīlah ("with *balīlah*"): a name for boiled wheat with some chickpeas added. 11.13.5
This is sold in the cities too and is delicious, its tastiness lying in the addition of salt and chickpeas, for the latter adjusts its humors. Chickpeas are the purest food there is, according to a commentator writing on the Chapter of the Cave.[366] As for the *balīlah* that is mentioned here in the verse, the country people make it into a dish, the method being to put the wheat in an earthenware pot, to which they may add a few chickpeas, and then cover it with water and place it on the fire till done. Then they take it and eat it with sorghum or barley bread, or break off bits and swallow them without bread, for they make it dry, and one just breaks off a piece with his hand and swallows it. They garnish it with fried onions and a little sesame oil, and their great men put in a little taro. It is called *balīlah* because of the wetting (*ball*) in water it receives when it is boiled, or because of its sloppiness and moistness, which is why any

الهايف المرخي الأكمام البارد القلب بليلة لعدم اكتسابه وقلّة بركته وبليلة على وزن هبيلة أو عويلة ومصدرها بلّ يبلّ بليلة وقوله

(ملانهْ) راجع للجفنة ١١،١٣،٦

(ولوكانت) البليلة الّتي في الجفنة ١١،١٣،٧

(بلا قُلْقاسِ) أي فلا حاجة له به إنّما مراده شيء يسدّ الجوعة يقال له طعام والقلقاس من مأكولات فصل الشتاء وهو ألذّ طعام أُكِلَ في هذا الفصل لأنّه حارّ يابس مناسب لبرودة الزمن خصوصاً عند ابتداء ظهوره إذا أُكِل باللحم الضأن وأضيف إليه السمن مع الخضراوات ونحو ذلك فإنّه يعتدل ويصير له لذة عظيمة في المأكل وتذهب حرارته ويعتدل طبعه وأَجْوَده الرؤوس الأناثي وكذلك الصوابع وهي الرفيعة الّتي تشبه أصابع الآدمي لأنّ ذلك كلّه سريع الاستواء وأرداه الأحمر لكونه بطيء الهضم بطيء الاستواء وإذا أُكِلَ القلقاس مشويًّا منع ألم الكَبِد وسكن ضربان البواسير وأكله نيئاً ليس فيه فائدة ولا منفعة ١١،١٣،٨

(فائدة) أربع قافات تستعمل في فصل الشتاء وهي ما تقدّم ذكره والقُشْطة والقَصَب والقَسْطَل ١١،١٣،٩

وسمّي قلقاساً لاشتقاقه من القلقسة لأنّه يشبه الطين المقلقس أي اليابس لأنّه إذا قُلِعَ من أرضه فيكون حكم قِطَع الطين اليابسة المقلقسة وهو مركّب من فِعْلين ماض وأمر قال بعضهم [وافر] ١١،١٣،١٠

فَإِنْ سَألوكَ عَن قَلبي وما قاسا فَقُلْ قاساً وَقُل قاساً وَقُل قاسا

(فائدة أخرى) قيل لمّا ادّعى فرعون الألوهيّة لاموه وقالوا له إنّ الإله لا يبول ولا يتغوّط فاصطنع الموز وصار يأكله فصار لا يتغوّط إلّا نادرًا وما ذاك إلّا أنّه أخذ القلقاس من أرضه وهو صغير وصار يفلق القلقاسة ويملؤها سكرًا ويعيدها في ١١،١٣،١١

futile, slack-twisted,[367] slothful man is referred to as a *balīlah* for his inability to earn a living and his failure as a breadwinner. *Balīlah* is of the measure of *habīlah* ("stupid") or *ʿawīlah* ("parasitic, sponging"), and the paradigm is *balla, yabullu, balīlatan* ("to wet").[368]

malānah ("filled"): referring to the bowl **11.13.6**

wa-law kānat ("though it be"): as though the *balīla* which is in the bowl be . . . **11.13.7**

bi-lā qulqāsi ("without taro"): that is, he has no need of the latter, and all **11.13.8**
he desires is anything that can be called food, to satisfy his hunger. Taro is a winter food, the most delicious thing eaten in that season, since it is Hot and Dry, which fits the coldness of the period, especially when it first appears on the market. If eaten with mutton and the addition of clarified butter with greens and so on, its nature is tempered and it acquires a most delicious flavor, its Hotness being dissipated and its nature tempered. The best parts of it are the female heads and the "fingers"—which are the thin bits that look like human fingers—because these all cook quickly. The worst is the red part because it is slow to digest and slow to cook. If taro is eaten grilled, it stops liver pains and relieves throbbing piles. There is no value or benefit to eating it raw.

A Useful Note: Four things beginning with *q* are used in winter: the above, **11.13.9**
qushṭah ("clotted cream"), *qaṣab* ("sugarcane"), and the *qasṭal* ("water pipe").

It is called *qulqās* because it derives from *qalqasah* ("colocassation"),[369] **11.13.10**
since it resembles "colocassated," that is, dry, mud, because when it is pulled out of the ground it is like lumps of "colocassated," dry, mud. It is formed of two verbs, one in the perfect tense, the other imperative. A poet says:

> If they ask you of my heart and what it suffered,
> Say, "It suffered tarobly, tarobly, tarobly!"[370]

Another Useful Note: It is said that, when Pharaoh claimed divine status, **11.13.11**
they reprehended him, telling him, "A god neither urinates nor defecates!" So Pharaoh invented the banana and started eating it and reached a point at which he defecated only rarely. He did this by taking some taro plants from the ground when small, splitting each tuber in half, filling it with sugar, and putting it back in the soil by a method he devised, so that the sweetness mixed with the taro, and the banana grew from it and took on its form. This is why

الطين بحكمة دبّرها فامتزجت الحلاوة بالقلقاس ونشأ منه الموز وصار على هذا الشكل ولهذا ترى أوراقه قريبة الشبه من ورق القلقاس في العرض إلّا أنّه طويل الشكل عنه هكذا في بعض كتب الحكمة وقوله

١٢،١٣،١١ (يا دَنْديفْ) أصله يا دندوف على وزن يا بعبوص قُلِبَت الواو ياءً لضرورة النظم والدندوف هو الّذي يروح ويغدو من غير فائدة يقال فلان يدندف أي لا فائدة في ذهابه وإيابه ولا بركة في سعيه وكسبه أو أنّه عَلَمٌ على شخص من أهل قرية الناظم كما هو معدود من أسمائهم وهو مشتقّ من الدندفة أو من أحمد الدَنَف أو من نَدْف القطن

١٣،١٣،١١ (ثمّ إنّ الناظم) تشوّق إلى قصعة ملآنة من أيّ طعام كان فقال

ص

١٤،١١ عَلَى مَنْ جَتُو قَصْعَهْ وَهُوَّ بِيحْرِتْ   وَيَقْعُدْ يُجَرِّفْ لِلْحَنَكْ تَجْرِيفْ

ش

١،١٤،١١ قوله (على من جتو) أصله جاءته

٢،١٤،١١ (قَصْعَهْ) أي جاء بها واحد من الناس لا هي بنفسها كما تقدّم فالضمير راجع إلى المحذوف والقصعة إناء من خشب مدوّر معدّ للطعام وغيره وأمّا الّذي على شكل الحوض يقال له مَنْسَف وفي الحديث علّم الله آدم الأسماء كلّها حتّى القَصْعة والقُصَيْعة والفَسْوة والفُسَيْوة وسمّيت قصعة لأنّ الشخص إذا جلس يأكل منها يَقْصَعُ ظَهْرَه

you will notice that its leaves are close in shape to those of the taro in terms of breadth, though the banana's are longer than the taro's. So it is written in one of the books of wisdom.

yā dandīf ("you good-for-nothing"): originally this is *yā dandūf*, of the measure of *yā buʿbūṣ* ("you little bump"), the *ū* having been turned into an *ī* for the sake of the rhyme. A *dandūf* is a person who comes and goes and achieves nothing. One says, "So-and-so *yudandifu*,"[371] that is, there is no benefit in his comings and goings or blessing in his efforts and earnings. Or it may be that it is the proper name of someone from the poet's village, seeing that it is counted among their names.[372] It is derived from *dandafah* ("acting ineffectually"),[373] or from Aḥmad al-Danaf, or from the *nadf* ("carding") of cotton.[374] 11.13.12

The poet then goes on to long for a basin full of any food whatsoever and says: 11.13.13

TEXT

ʿalā man jatū qaṣʿah wa-huwwa bi-yaḥrit 11.14
wa-yaqʿud yujarrif li-l-ḥanak tajrīf

Happy is he to whom comes a basin while he's plowing
and sits and shovels away into his gob!

COMMENTARY

ʿalā man jatū ("Happy is he to whom comes"): the origin of the second word is *jā'athu*.[375] 11.14.1

qaṣʿah ("a basin"): that is, someone brought it to him; it did not come of its own accord, as previously explained,[376] the subject pronoun of the preceding verb referring to the omitted agent. The *qaṣʿah* is a wooden vessel, round in shape and made for food and other things.[377] The vessel that is made in the form of a watering trough, on the other hand, is called a *mansaf*.[378] In the Tradition it says, "We taught Adam all the names, even the *qaṣʿah* and the *quṣayʿah* and the *faswah* ('silent fart') and the *fusaywah*."[379] It is called a *qaṣʿah* because, when one sits and eats from it, he bows his back (*yaqṣaʿu ẓahrahu*), that is, he bends over and eats. Thus it falls into the category of "naming a thing after the 11.14.2

أي ينخي ويأكل فيكون من باب تسمية الشيء باسم صفة الآكل منه أو من قَصَعَ القَملَ والبراغيثَ وقوله

١١،١٤،٣ (وهوّ) بضمّ الهاء وتشديد الواو لضرورة النظم أو جريًا على اللغة الريفيّة وقوله

١١،١٤،٤ (يِحَرِتُ) على وزن يِبَضرِطُ فيها ذلك بيقين أي في وقت الحرث من أيّ طعام كان من عدس أو بيسار أو غير ذلك

١١،١٤،٥ (ويَقْعُدْ) قعدة جيعان تعبان ممّا قاسى من مشقّة الحرث وغيره

١١،١٤،٦ و(يُجَرِّفْ) على وزن يخرّف أو يغرّف أي يكون كفّه حكم المجرفة الّتي تجرف الشيء

١١،١٤،٧ (للحَنَكْ) من التحنيك على وزن التحكيك أو التديك ويطلق على الفكّ الأعلى والفكّ الأسفل من الإنسان وقد ورد أنّ النبيّ صلّى الله عليه وسلّم حنّك بعض الأطفال بالتمر فيكون من باب تسمية الشيء بما طرأ عليه ويطلق على الفم والفاه أيضًا يقال فتح فمه أو فتح فاه قال صاحب البديعيّة رحمه الله [بسيط]

فَمِي تَحَدَّثَ عَن سِرِّي فَمَا نُطِقَتْ سَرائِرُ القَلْبِ إِلّا مِن حَديثِ فَمِي

١١،١٤،٨ وقوله (تَجْرِيفْ) أصله بالألف لأنّه مصدر وسكّن لأجل الرويّ أي يجرّف للحنك الّذي هو فمه تجريفًا زائدًا متتابعًا بسرعة وعجلة حتّى يكتفي ويشبع الشبع المُفرِط لما ناله من ألم الجوع وشدّة التعب وكثرة المشقّة فيقضي مراده وينشرح صدره ويقوى جنانه على الحرث وغيره

properties of the one who eats from it."[380] Or it may be from *qaṣaʿa l-qamla wa-l-barāghīth* ("he squashed the lice and fleas between his fingernails").

wa-huwwa ("while he"): with *u* after the *h* and double *w*, for the sake of the meter, or according to the language of the countryside.[381] 11.14.3

bi-yaḥrit ("is plowing"): of the measure of *bi-yaḍriṭ* ("is farting audibly"), which is something that happens in plowing, for sure; that is, at the time of plowing, happy is he to whom comes any food whatsoever, be it lentils or *bīsār* or anything else. 11.14.4

wa-yaqʿud ("and sits"): as one sits who is hungry and tired out from the labor of plowing and so on that he has endured. 11.14.5

and *yujarrif* ("shovels"): of the measure of *yukharrif* ("he talks twaddle") or *yugharrif* ("he ladles"), that is, his hand would perform the function of the shovel that shovels things . . . 11.14.6

li-l-ḥanak ("into his gob"): from *taḥnīk* ("to make worldly-wise"), of the measure of *taḥkīk* ("to rub") or *tadkīk* ("to pass a drawstring through a waistband"). The word is applied to the upper and lower jaws of a human being, and it is reported that the Prophet, God bless him and grant him peace, "stuffed the jaws of" (*ḥannaka*) a child with dates, in which case it would fall into the category of "naming a thing after what drops into it." It is also applied to the mouth (*al-fam* and *al-fāh*);[382] one says either *fataḥa famahu* or *fataḥa fāhu* ("He opened his mouth").[383] The author of the *Badīʿiyyah*,[384] may the Almighty have mercy on his soul, says: 11.14.7

> My mouth (*famī*) speaks of my secrets, and naught reveals
> The secrets of my heart but the speech of my mouth (*famī*).

tajrīf ("*away*, used as an intensifier"): properly *tajrīfan* because it is a verbal noun, but the *an* has been dropped for the sake of the rhyme.[385] That is, because of the pangs of hunger, the severe exhaustion, and the great hardship he has suffered, he shovels food into his "gob" (that is to say, "his mouth") with an intemperate, continuous shoveling, conducted at speed and with haste, until he is satisfied and stuffed to the limit. By so doing, he achieves his desire, his good humor is restored, and he acquires renewed vigor for plowing and what have you. 11.14.8

(ثمّ إنّه اشتهى) مأكولاً آخر خارجاً عن الطعام المطبوخ من مأكول أهل الريف فقال ١١،١٤،٩

ص

عَلَى مَنْ دَعَسْ بِٱلْعَزْمِ فِي ٱلْمِشّ بِٱلْبَصَلْ وَلَوْكَانَ بِٱلْكُرَّاتِ كَانَ ضَرِيفْ ١١،١٥

ش

قوله (على من دَعَسْ) تقدّم معناه ١١،١٥،١

(بالعَزْمِ) أي بالقوّة والشدّة لأنّ العزم على الشيء هو الإقدام عليه بجراءة وشدّة يقال فلان صاحب عزم شديد أي قوّة زائدة ١١،١٥،٢

(في المِشّ) أي مشّ الجبن القريش الأزرق الّذي مضى عليه زمان مستطيل حتّى صار يقطع ذنب الفأر من شدّة حرارته وقوّة ملوحته لأنّ هذا غالب مأكول أهل الريف في الغداء وربّما أكلوه في العشاء أيضاً فيأتي الشخص منهم بالمترد المشّ والخبز الشعير اليابس والبصل الأخضر أو الناشف ويأكل حتّى تَدْمَع عيناه من حرارة ذلك المشّ ورائحة ذلك البصل ويشرب عليه الماء ويسرح الغيط يحرث أو يدرس والأكابر منهم تضع عليه شيئاً يسيراً من الزيت الحارّ ويعصر عليه الليمون خصوصاً ١١،١٥،٣

(بالبَصَلْ) المخروط فإنّه ألذّ من أكله خارجاً عنه وبعضهم يأكله بالكرّات أبو شويشة فيكون أقوى في جمع الأرياح خصوصاً إذا كان في دويرة ضيّقة فإنّ الفساء يتراكم فيها حتّى يملأها من أوّلها إلى آخرها ١١،١٥،٤

(والمشّ) على أقسام مشّ حصير وتقدّم معناه ومشّ بخيره وهو المستعمل في بلاد ١١،١٥،٥

Next he longs for another of the dishes of the country people, but this time one that is uncooked. He says: 11.14.9

TEXT

ʿalā man daʿas bi-l-ʿazmi fī l-mishshi bi-l-baṣal 11.15
wa-law kāna bi-l-kurrāti kāna ḍarīf

Happy is he who gobbles energetically at *mishsh* with onions—
and were it with leeks, that would be nice!

COMMENTARY

ʿala man daʿas ("Happy is he who gobbles"): defined above.[386] 11.15.1

bi-l-ʿazmi ("energetically"): that is, with strength and vigor, for to approach something with *ʿazm* ("determination, resolution, energy") is to approach it with boldness and vigor. One says, "So-and-oso has great *ʿazm*," that is, abnormal strength. 11.15.2

fī l-mishshi ("at *mishsh*"): that is, the *mishsh* of blue skimmed-milk cheese that has been left to age till it has become sharp and salty enough to cut the tail off a mouse, for this is the thing the country people most often eat for lunch and sometimes for dinner, too.[387] One of them will get the *mishsh* crock and dry barley bread and green or dry onions and eat until his eyes weep from the sharpness of the *mishsh* and the smell of the onions, and wash it down with water and set off for the fields or to plow or thresh. The great ones among them put a little linseed oil on it and squeeze lime over it, especially . . . 11.15.3

bi-l-baṣal ("with onions"): that is to say, with chopped onions, for it is tastier to eat it thus than to eat it on its own. Some of them eat it with leeks, which makes it more likely to generate flatulence, especially if it is eaten in a confined space, in which case the farts will accumulate there until they fill it from top to bottom. 11.15.4

Mishsh is of various kinds. There is strained *mishsh*, which has been defined above,[388] and full-fat *mishsh*, which is the kind used in the cities and is lighthearted and delicious. One speaks of *ḥālūm*-cheese *mishsh* and of 11.15.5

المدن وله فكاهة ولذّة ويقال له مشّ جبن حالوم ومشّ جبن قريش وهو مشّ الرِّيافة المتقدّم ذكره ويقال مشّ جبن التَنّور والمشّ على وزن الوشّ بلغة الرِّيافة فإنّ الشخص منهم إذا شتم آخر يقول له (دمّ اهدم وشّك) مثلاً وهو مشتقّ من المَشَش وهو داء يعتري الخيل والحمير يقال (جاك المشش) أي أبلاك الله به والأوّل الّذي هو المشّ الحصير ينفع من الجرب شرباً والثاني ينفع السُدَد ويقوّي المعدة والثالث ليس به نفع بل هو محض الضرر لا غير أو أنّه مشتقّ من المشي لأنّه إذا صُبَّ على الأرض صار يمشي عليها أي يسيح فيها

١١،١٥،٦ (والبصل) حارّ يابس وقيل رَطب يقطع البلغم إلّا أنّه يثير الشقيقة وصداع الرأس ويولد أرياحاً ويظلم البصر وكثرة أكله يورث النسيان ويفسد العقل (وأمّا منافعه) فإنّه يطرد الوباء لما رُوِيَ عن رسول الله صلّى الله عليه وسلّم أنّه قال إذا دخلتم بلداً وبئة فخفتم وباءها فعليكم ببصلها وينفع من تغيير المياه ويَفتُق الشهوة ويهيج الباه ويزيد في المَنِيّ ويحسن اللون وإذا سُحِقَ وعُجِنَ بعسل ووُضِعَ على الكَلَف الغليظ والقوابي والبَهَق الأسود قلع ذلك وإذا دُقّ ناعماً وطُلِيَ به موضع الشعر ينفع داء الثعلب وهو مَعْط شعر الرأس والاكتحال بمائه يُذهِب الغشاوة ويُصلِحه الخلّ واللبن إذا أُكِلَ به

١١،١٥،٧ (ولو كانَ بالكُرّاتِ كانَ ضَريفْ) أي لأنّه حارّ ليّن يفتح المَريء والدم إلّا أنّه مثل البصل في ظُلمة البصر وتولّد الأرياح كما تقدّم لكنّه يشدّ القضيب وينفع البواسير ويصلحه الأكل بالشيرج وأكل البصل والثوم والكرات نيئاً مكروه لداخل المسجد إن لم يُزِلْ رائحة فمه بشيء لقوله صلّى الله عليه وسلّم مَنْ أكل الثوم والبصل والكرات فلا يقربنّ مسجدنا فإنّ الملائكة تتأذّى ممّا يتأذّى منه بنو آدم وقِسْ على ذلك بقيّة المساجد فاللفظ خاصّ أُرِيدَ به العموم (فائدة) رأيت في بعض الكتب أنّ جميع البقول نزلت في مائدة سيّدنا عيسى عليه السلام إلّا الكرّاث (وأمّا بصل العُنصُل) فله

cottage-cheese *mishsh,* which is the *mishsh* of the country people referred to previously. One also speaks of oven-cheese *mishsh. Mishsh* is of the measure of *wishsh* ("face") as that word is pronounced in the language of the country people.[389] When one of them insults another, he says, "*Damm ihdim wishshak*" ("Blood destroy your face")![390] for example. It is derived from *mashash* ("splint"), a disease of horses and donkeys. One says, "*Jāk mashash* ('Get splint')!" that is, may God afflict you with it. The first kind, that is "strained *mishsh,*" is good against mange, if drunk; the second is good against blockages and strengthens the stomach; and the third is good for nothing—on the contrary, it is pure harm, no more, no less! Or it may be derived from *mashy* ("walking"), because, if poured on the ground, it will "walk" on, that is, spread over, it.

Onions are Hot and Dry (and, some say, Moist). They inhibit phlegm but 11.15.6
provoke migraines and headaches, cause wind, and weaken the eyesight. Overconsumption results in forgetfulness and disorders the mind. As for their good qualities, they drive away pestilence, for it is related concerning God's Messenger, God bless him and grant him peace, that he said, "If you enter a land where there is pestilence, and are afraid of catching the disease, eat of its onions!" They are good against foul waters, release the carnal appetite, provoke sexual excitement, increase the semen, and improve the complexion. They get rid of coarse freckles, tetters, and black vitiligo when powdered, kneaded with honey, and applied to these. Pounded smooth and applied to the roots of the hair they are good against "fox disease," which is hair loss. The juice, used as an ointment, revives one who has fainted, and vinegar and milk balance its humors if it is eaten with either.

wa-law kāna bi-l-kurrāṭi kāna ḍarīf ("and were it with leeks, that would be 11.15.7
nice!"): that is, because they are Hot and Soft, and stir up the stomach and the blood, though, like onions, they weaken the eyesight and cause wind, as previously noted. However, they tighten the phallus and are good for piles. They are best eaten with sesame oil. Eating raw onions, garlic, and leeks is disapproved of for one entering a mosque unless he take something to rid his mouth of the smell, in accordance with the words of the Prophet, God bless him and grant him peace, "The eater of garlic, onions, and leeks, let him not approach our mosque; for the angels suffer from those things from which men suffer"—by analogy, this extends to all mosques, for the wording is specific but

خواصّ جيّدة مذكورة في كتب الطبّ ومن العجائب أنّ الذئب إذا وطئه مات لوقته ولهذا أنّ الثعلب إذا خاف على نفسه من الذئب يأتي بالبصلة منه ويضعها على باب جحره فإذا رآها الذئب وشمّها هرب ولم يأت إليه فتكون وقاية له فسبحان من ألهمه هذه الحكمة وقوله

(ضَريفْ) أصله ظريف بالظاء المشالة لا الضاد المعجمة أتى بهذا اللفظ جريًا على اللغة الريفيّة أي كان فيه الظرافة بمعنى أنّه يكون أخفّ ضررًا من البصل وإن كان أقوى أرياحًا فإنّه أجلّ شهوةً وألذّ أكلًا فلا بأس به إذا حضر فيكون هو المراد ٨،١٥،١١

(ثمّ إنّ الناظم) اشتهى شيئًا من الألبان يشربه فقال ٩،١٥،١١

ص

عَلَى مَنْ شَرِبْ مَتْرَدْ مَلَانَ مُطَنبَرْ مِنَ ٱللَّبَنِ ٱلْحَامِضْ يَرِفْ رَفِيفْ ١٦،١١

ش

قوله (على من شَرِبْ) الشرب هو مجاوزة الماء وغيره من المائعات الفم إلى داخل الجوف قال الله تعالى ﴿وَكُلُوا وَٱشْرَبُوا﴾ وقال ﴿فَشَرِبُوا مِنْهُ إِلَّا قَلِيلًا مِنْهُمْ﴾ لا ما وُضِعَ في الفم وأخرجه الإنسان كالدخان المستعمل الآن فلا يسمّى شربًا حقيقةً إلّا من باب المجاز وقوله ١،١٦،١١

(مَتْرَدْ) والمترد إناء من فُخّار أحمر أصغر من الشالية وهو غالب أواني الريّافة خصوصًا في أعراسهم وأصله مركّب من فعلين مات وردّ لأنّه لمّا عُمِلَ في ابتدائه وكُسِرَ عملوا ٢،١٦،١١

the intention is general. A Useful Note: I have seen in a book that all edible green plants found their way onto the table of Master Jesus, peace be upon him, except leeks.[391] As for the squill, it has excellent properties that are mentioned in works on medicine. It is a remarkable fact that, if a wolf steps on one, it dies instantly. This why if a fox is in fear for his life from a wolf, it gets a squill tuber and puts it at the entrance to its hole; when the wolf sees it and smells it, it runs away and never comes back, and it thus acts as a protection for the fox, glory be to Him who inspired it with this wisdom!

ḍarīf ("nice"): originally, *ẓarīf*, with *ẓ* and not with *ḍ*; his use of the first form is in accordance with rural usage. That is, it would be a pleasant thing, meaning that they would be less injurious than onions (albeit more likely to cause flatulence), for leeks are far more appetizing and tasty; there would be no harm therefore if they were present, and this, indeed, is what he wants. 11.15.8

Next the poet desires some milk product to drink. He says: 11.15.9

TEXT

ʿalā man sharib matrad malāna muṭanbir 11.16
mina l-labani l-ḥāmiḍ yariffu rafīf

Happy is he who drinks a crock, full to the brim
of sour milk that flutters!

COMMENTARY

ʿalā man sharib ("Happy is he who drinks"): drinking is the passing of water and other fluids via the mouth into the belly. The Almighty says, «Eat and drink»[392] and He says, «But they drank thereof, all but a few of them.»[393] It does not cover what a man puts in his mouth and then expels, like the tobacco that is used nowadays: when people refer to this as "drinking," they do so not in a real but in a figurative sense.[394] 11.16.1

matrad ("a crock"): this is a vessel of red pottery, smaller than the *shāliyah*. It is the vessel most in use among the country people, especially at their weddings. The word was originally composed of two verbs, *māt* ("it died") and *radd* ("it returned") because, when it was first made and broke, they made 11.16.2

بدله فقالوا رَدَّ أي بعد ما مات ثمّ حذفوا الألف وجعلوه علماً وقالوا مَترَد وهو على وزن مَقْعَد أو مَسْنَد فتمنّى اللبن الّذي داخله لا نفس المترد لأنّه ظرف لما حواه فلا يتصوّر شرب المترد بعينه وقيل سمّي بهذا الاسم لتردّد الخبز فيه ووضع الطعام عليه فيكون من باب تسمية الظرف بمعنى المظروف أو أنّه عمل بمدينة تسمّى ماتريد الّتي ينسب إليها الشيخ الماتريدي نفعنا الله به وقوله

(مَلانَ) أي غير ناقص حتّى يكون فيه القناعة من جهة الشبع والرؤية لأنّ الناقص ربّما استقلّه الإنسان ولم يَقْنَعْ برؤيته فتمنّى أن يكون ملآناً وقوله ١١،١٦،٣

(مُطَنبَرْ) على وزن مُزَنبَر أو مُطَرطِر يقال كُسّ مُزَنبَر وزُبّ مُطَرطِر أي عالي عن حوافيها لشدّة حموضته ويُبْسه يقال فلان بطنه مطنبر أي منفوخ[١] أو مات واطّنبر أي انتفخ كما يقال دمّ يطنبر بطنك مثلاً أي تموت وتنتفخ ويقال للشَّدّ الحجازيّ المعمول بالحرير الأصفر والأبيض شدّ مطنبر وعلى قياسه الشدّ البلديّ ولعلّه وُصِفَ بهذا الوصف لكونه إذا لفّه الإنسان على رأسه صار كبيرًا عاليًا مطنبرًا كما يعلو اللبن الحامض عن حوافي المترد وهو مشتقّ من الطنبرة وهي التحكيك للأولاد الصغار قال الشاعر [طويل مع كسر] ١١،١٦،٤

إذا كنتَ آلاتي وطَبْعُكَ رِقّي   طَنبِرْ برِقّة واعتبر بالمشنوقِ

(وأصل) هذا الكلام أنّ شخصاً من الفسّاق أخذ ولداً صغيراً وأراد أن يحكّك له فزَلَقَ العِيار فدكّه فمات الولد وشُنِقَ الرجل فقيل فيه كلاماً كثيرًا لم يحضرني منه غير هذا المطلع أو إنّه من الطنبورة على وزن العصفورة قال الشاعر [وزن غير معروف]

---

١ بي: منفوج.

another one instead, and said, "It returned (*radd*) after it died (*māt*)." Then they omitted the *alif* and made it a proper name and said *matrad*.[395] It is of the measure of *maqʿad* ("seat") or *masnad* ("cushion"). What the poet wants is the milk that is within it, not the crock itself, for it is just a container for what it holds, and the idea of drinking the crock itself is not to be entertained. Some say that it was given this name because bread is frequently found in it (*li-taraddud al-khubzi fīh*) and food is placed upon it, in which case it would belong to the category of "naming the container after the thing contained"; or that it was named after a city called Māturīd from which Shaykh al-Māturīdī, God benefit us through him, took his name.

malāna ("full"): that is, not lacking, so that it be satisfying to both the stomach **11.16.3**
and the eye, for a person may well reckon something that is less than full to be too little, and not be satisfied when he sees it. This is why he wants it to be full . . .

muṭanbir ("to the brim"): of the measure of *muzanbir*[396] or *muṭarṭir* ("raised"); **11.16.4**
one speaks of a *kuss muzanbir* ("an engorged cunt") and a *zubb muṭarṭir* ("a stiff prick"); that is, one that is high above its surroundings, referring here to the extreme sourness and stiffness of the milk. One says, "So-and-so's belly is 'brimful' (*miṭṭanbar*)" that is, inflated (*manfūkh*), or "He died and became brimful (*iṭṭanbar*),"[397] that is, "became inflated" (*intafakh*), and one says, "Blood fill your belly to the brim! (*damm yiṭanbar baṭnak*)" for example, that is, "May you die and inflate!"; and similarly one speaks of the Hijazi turban made of white and yellow silk, on which the local turban is modeled, as "brimming over" (*miṭṭanbar*), this description being used perhaps because, when one wraps it around his head, it becomes large, high, and "brimming over" (*miṭṭanbar*) in the same way that sour milk rises above the edges of the crock. It is derived from *ṭanbarah*,[398] which is frottage with young boys. The poet says:

> If you're into your "instrument" and your nature's "tamborine-ish,"
> Rub away gently and remember the one they hung![399]

—the background to these words being that a certain reprobate took a young boy intending to practice frottage with him, but he "misfired" and rammed it home. The boy died, the man was hung, and a lot of verse was composed, of which I recall only this opening line. Or it may be from *ṭunbūrah* ("tambourine"), of the measure of *ʿuṣfūrah* ("sparrow"). The poet says:

أيا عصفورة البستان كم ذا تنبشي بايدك ورجلك ما في الأرض شي

ثمّ إنّه بيّن هذا الشيء المطنبر بقوله ١١،١٦،٥

(من اللبَنْ الحامضْ) قيّده بالحموضة لعدم وصوله إلى اللبن الحليب فلأجل هذا قال أشتهيه ولوكان حامضاً لأنّ غيره بعيد عليّ وخصوصاً إذاكان في شدّة الحرّ فإنّ شربه يسكّن عطشه ويروي فؤاده إذاكانت حموضته معتدلة فإنّه بارد رطب وأمّا إذا خرج عن الحدّ في الحموضة ضرّ وكلام الناظم يدلّ على أنّه إنّما اشتهى ما خرج عن حدّ الحموضة بدليل قوله الآتي يرفّ رفيف وأجود الألبان لبن البقر لأنّه موافق لسائر الأدوية وفي الحديث لحمها داء وألبانها شفاء وقوله

١١،١٦،٦ (يَرِفُّ رَفِيفْ) أي صار من الحموضة الشديدة يرفّ كما يرف جناح الطائر بمعنى أنّه يسمع له غليان وبقبقة تحاكي رفّ الجناح ويرفّ على وزن يَسِفّ أو يَلُفّ ورفيف مصدر حذفت ألفه كما سبق في نظائره وهو مشتقّ من رَفّ الخشب الّذي يُعْمَل في البيوت أو من الرفرافة الّتي يعملوها قبل رمضان أو آخر شعبان من الدجاج والإوزّ وغير ذلك

١١،١٦،٧ (ثمّ إنّه تمنّى شيئاً آخر تستعمله أهل القرى القريبة من البحر المالح أو من البحائر المالحة ونحوها) فقال

ص

١١،١٧ عَلَى مَنْ جَتُو أُمُّ ٱلْخُلُولِ لِدَارُو وَيَعْـزِمْ عَلَى أَهْـلِ ٱلْبَلَدْ وَيَضِيفْ

Garden sparrow, how you scratch around
With hand and foot, when nothing's on the ground!

Next he reveals what this thing that is "brimming over" is by saying 11.16.5

mina l-labani l-ḥāmiḍ ("with sour milk"): he specifies that it is sour because he is unable to obtain fresh milk, which is why it is as though he were saying, "I desire it even though it be sour, anything else being beyond my reach." This would be especially true if it were the hot season, for, if he were to drink it then, it would quench his thirst and refresh his heart, as long as it were only moderately sour, for it is Cold and Moist. However, it is harmful if excessively sour, and, in fact, the poet's words indicate that he wants precisely the milk that has gone excessively sour, as evidenced by the following words: "that flutters." The finest milk is cow's milk because it is good for all medicines and all diseases. In the Tradition it says, "Its flesh is a disease,[400] a medicine its milk and cheese."

yariffu rafīf ("that flutters"): that is, it is so sour that it has started to flutter, 11.16.6
just as a bird's wing does, meaning that it makes boiling and bubbling sounds like those of a wing fluttering. *Yariffu* is of the measure of *yasiffu* ("he gulps") or *yaluffu* ("he bolts").[401] *Rafīf* is the verbal noun, with the *-an* dropped, as in similar cases.[402] It is derived from the wooden *raff* ("shelf") that is put up in houses, or from the *rafrāfah*[403] that they make of chicken, goose, and other ingredients before Ramadan or at the end of Shaʿbān.

Next the poet wants something else, which the people of the villages close 11.16.7
to the sea or the saltwater lakes and such-like areas make use of. He says:

TEXT

ʿalā man jatū ʾummu l-khulūli li-dārū 11.17
wa-yaʿzim ʿalā ʾahli l-balad wa-yaḍīf

Happy is he to whom mussels come, to his house
and who invites the people of the village and plays host!)

ش

قوله (على من جتو) أي جاءته بواسطةٍ وحضرت إليه ١،١٧،١١

(أُمّ الخُلولِ) وهي حيوان يتكوّن من داخل المحَار الصغير الّذي يشبه اللوز يوجد على ساحل البحر المالح وجوانب البحائر المالحة وله سرعة الحركة فإذا مسّه إنسان سكَن ولم يتحرك وصار كالحجر حتّى يفارقه وهذا الحيوان منطبق عليه محارتين صغيرتين ولونه أبيض ثخين يشبه لون المَنِيّ أو المُخاط فيأخذوه وينزِعوه من هذه المحائر أو القوقع ويضعوا عليه الملح والخلّ والليمون ويأكلوه وربّما أخرجوه وهو طري ولتّوه بالملح وأكلوه وهذا أقبح المأكول وأرداه وأخبثه نعوذ بالله منه ولله الحمد والمِنّة على عدم الأكل منه لأنّ الطبائع السليمة تمجّه وتأباه وتَعافُه الأنفس وأمّا طباع أهل الريف فلا تطالبنا بها فإنّها خبيثة ولا تطلب إلّا الخبيث وله عندهم لذّة عظيمة وموقع في نفوسهم الذميمة فمن له طبع سليم لا يمكن أن يأكل منه بل ولا يراه لأنّ رؤيته ترث القرف فضلاً عن أكله وكُنِيَتْ بأمّ الخلول لتواتر الملح والخلّ والليمون عليه عند الأكل وقوله ٢،١٧،١١

(لِدارو) أي دار الناظم بمعنى أنّه لا يتعب في مجيئها بصيد ولا شراء بل يصبح يراها في داره أتى بها شخص على سبيل الصدقة أو الهديّة وقوله ٣،١٧،١١

(ويَعْزِمْ على أَهل البلدْ[١]) أي يجمعهم لهذا المأكول النفيس الّذي يشبه عفّ الكلاب ويضيفهم في داره أي يكْرِمهم به يقال فلان عزم على فلان أي عزم في نِيّته وجزم في يقينه أنّه يأخذه ويكرمه أو عزمه بمعنى أذِن له أن يأتي إلى داره ويكرمه بطعام أو غيره ٤،١٧،١١

(ويَضيفْ) معطوف على يعزم وهل هو مغاير له أو المعنى واحد لأنّ العزم خلاف ٥،١٧،١١

١ بي: البلد ويضيف.

COMMENTARY

ʿalā man jatū ("Happy is he to whom (mussels) come"): that is, come to him by the agency of another,[404] and reach him. 11.17.1

ummu l-khulūli ("mussels"): a creature that forms inside the small shells resembling almonds that are found on the shore of the sea and the saltwater lakes. It moves quickly, but if one touches it, it goes still and does not move, remaining like a stone until he leaves it. This creature is enclosed within two small shells and has a thick white color, like semen or mucus. They take it and extract it from these shells and put salt and vinegar and lime on it and eat it. Sometimes they take it out while still alive and knead it with salt and eat it, this making the most disgusting, vile, and revolting dish—we seek shelter from it with God and give praise and thanks to Him that we have never eaten it, for sound natures spit it out and refuse it, and the appetite turns from it in disgust! As for the natures of the people of the countryside, on the other hand, do not ask us to speak of them, for they are revolting and seek only what is revolting, and they find this dish most delicious and their miserable souls hold it in high esteem. No one who has a sound nature will eat it or even look at it, for the very sight of it, not to mention its consumption, gives rise to revulsion. They are given the nickname *umm al-khulūl* ("mother of vinegars") because salt and vinegar and lime are put on them continually while they are being eaten. 11.17.2

li-dārū ("to his house"): that is, the poet's house, meaning that he would not have to exert himself to get them by hunting for them or buying them; on the contrary, he would look and find them in his house, someone having brought them as charity or a gift. 11.17.3

wa-yaʿzim ʿalā ahli l-balad ("and who invites the people of the village"): that is, gathers them to eat of this precious dish that resembles dog's vomit and hosts them in his house, that is, honors them there. One says, "So-and-so invited (*ʿazama ʿalā*) So-and-so," that is, he determined (*ʿazama*) inwardly[405] and resolved with certainty that he would take him and honor him, or "invited him" (*ʿazamahu*),[406] meaning, give him permission to come to his house, and honor him with food and so forth. 11.17.4

wa-yaḍīf ("and plays host"): *yaḍīf* is joined to *yaʿzim* by the coordinating conjunction *wa-*, in which case the questions becomes, "Does the former contrast 11.17.5

الضيافة فيكون قد عزم بالنيّة أوّلاً على أنّ هذا الشخص لا بدّ من حضوره وأنّه ينضاف إليه أي يتبعه إلى المحلّ الذي يريد كرامته فيه فيكون من إضافة الشيء إلى غيره ومصدره ضاف يضيف ضيافة أو ضيوفاً وسمّي الضَيْف ضيفاً لأنّه ينضاف إلى من يكرمه بمعنى أنّه يكون هو وإيّاه حكم الكلام المضاف لا ينفكّ عنه حتّى يدخل عليه التنوين فيفصله عن الإضافة قال الشاعر [طويل]

أَراني تَنوِيناً وأَنتَ إِضافةً   إِذا ما اجتَمَعْنا لَم تُخَلِّ مَكانِيا

فاتّجه المعنى الفشرويّ عن هذا البحث الهبالّي

٦،١٧،١١ (ثمّ إنّه انتقل) من تمنّيه إلى شيء آخر يقرب في الخباثة من أمّ الخلول فقال

ص

أَنَا آنْ شُفْتُ عِنْدِي يَوْمَ طَاجِنْ مُشَكْشِكٍ   فَهٰذَاكَ يَوْمُ ٱلْبَسْطِ وَالتَّقْصِيفْ ١٨،١١

ش

١،١٨،١١ وقوله (أنا) يعني أبو شادوف لا غيري

٢،١٨،١١ (انْ شُفْتُ) الشوف ضدّ العمى أو من الشيافة بمعنى رأيت

٣،١٨،١١ (عندي) في منزلي أو في المحلّ الّذي أنا فيه أو الغيط والجرن مثلاً

with the latter, or is the meaning the same?" for "the determination to invite (*ʿazm*)" is different from "(the actual provision of) hospitality (*ḍiyāfah*)." In the former case, the meaning would be "he first determined inwardly that this person must come to him," it being understood that he would then be "annexed to him" (*yanḍāfu ilayh*), that is, follow him to the place in which he wished to provide him with hospitality. Thus understood, it would be a matter of "annexing a thing (*iḍāfat al-shayʾ*) to something other than itself."[407] The paradigm is *ḍāfa, yaḍīfu, ḍiyāfatan*, or *ḍuyūfan*.[408] A guest is called a *ḍayf* because he is "annexed to" (*yanḍāfu ilā*) the one who hosts him, meaning that he and the other are in a relationship analogous to a possessive annexation—the one cannot be detached from the other until a nunation comes between them, in which case it separates it from the relationship of annexation.[409] The poet says:

> It seems to me that I'm a nunation, you an annexation:
> Whenever we meet, you leave no place for me to be!

Through this fatuous investigation, the facetious meaning has now been revealed.

Next, the poet moves on from this desire to something else almost as revolting as mussels. He says: 11.17.6

TEXT

anā-n shuftu ʿindī yawma ṭājin mushakshikin 11.18
fa-hādāka yawmu l-basṭi wa-l-taqṣīf

> If I see next to me one day a casserole of fish skins
> then that is a day of happiness and one on which of one's clothes to make boast!

COMMENTARY

anā ("I"): meaning Abū Shādūf and no one else. 11.18.1

in shuftu ("if I see"): seeing (*al-shawf*) is the opposite of blindness (*al-ʿamā*), or it may be from *shiyāfah* ("eye medicine"). The meaning is, if I behold it . . . 11.18.2

ʿindī ("next to me"): at home, or in the place in which I happen to be, or in the field and on the threshing floor, for example. 11.18.3

٤،١٨،١١ (يوم) أي في يوم من الأيّام غلط به الدهر ويسّر الله تعالى لي فيه

٥،١٨،١١ (طاجن) اسم لإناء فُخّار مدوّر واسع الجوف يطبخ فيه السمك والأرز واللحم والطير وغير ذلك يستعمل في سائر البلاد لكن لا يكون استواء الطعام فيه إلّا في الفرن وهو مشتقّ من التطجين أو من الطجانة أو من وَطْءِ الجِنّ لأنّ لفظة طاجن من ألفاظ المُعَمّيات بمعنى أنّ إنسانًا وطئ جِنًّا أي داس جماعة من الجنّ فيكون تركيبه من جملة فعل وفاعل ومفعول والفاعل محذوف تقديره أنت أي طأ أنت جنًّا ومثله طافية أي طافية من الناس

٦،١٨،١١ وقسم آخر من المعمّيات غير ما تقدّم كقول بعضهم في اسم حماد خذ فارغ واملاه ماء ومن النظم قولي في اسم شحاته [رمل]

سلَبَ النـاسَ دلالا والِفُـــ من بعدِ شُحْ
قلت بَدْري تِهْ كمالا تـمّ معناكَ بشرحْ

ولم أر في المعمّيات أرقّ من قول بعضهم في اسم أحمد [طويل]

وراكِعَـةٍ في ظِـلِّ بانٍ تَعَـلَّقَتْ بلُؤلُؤةٍ نِيطَتْ بِمِنقـارِ طـائِرِ

٧،١٨،١١ (مُشَكْشِكٍ) على وزن محكّك اسم للطعام الّذي تمنّى رؤيته والأكل منه وهو جلود الفسيخ يأكلوا لحمه ويأخذوا جلوده فيغسلوها بالماء ويضعوها في طاجن ويخرّطوا عليها بصل وشيء يسير من الزيت الحارّ ويدخّلوها الفرن حتّى تستوي ويأكلوها بالخبز وربّما وضعوا عليها شيئًا من الكُسْب المذاب بالماء يجعلوه بدل الطحينة وهذا له موقع عندهم وعند نسائهم كأنّه خاروف شوي ولهذا قال

yawma ("one day"): that is, one day when Fate has bungled and the Almighty is looking kindly on me 11.18.4

ṭājin ("a casserole"): name for a round earthenware vessel with a wide belly, in which fish, rice, meat, fowl, and other things are cooked, which is used throughout the country, though food can only be cooked in it in the oven. It is derived from *tatjīn* ("speaking harshly") or from *ṭijānah* ("the art of cooking in a casserole") or from *waṭ' al-jinn* ("treading on the jinn"), for *ṭājin* is a puzzle word,[410] deriving its hidden meaning from the fact that some person *waṭi'a jinnan*, that is, "'stepped on' (*dāsa*) a company of jinn," the word being constructed, from this perspective, from the combination of a verb, a subject, and an object, the subject (which is omitted) being "you"; thus the meaning is "(You there,) tread on some jinn! (*ṭa' anta jinnan*)"[411] A similar word is *ṭāfiyah*, that is, a *ṭā'ifah* ("group, company") of people.[412] 11.18.5

There is further category of such puzzle words, different from the preceding, exemplified by someone's saying that the name Ḥammād means "Take something empty and fill it with water";[413] and, for verse, my own lines on the name Shaḥātah: 11.18.6

He wreaked havoc on folk with his cute ways,
Making nice (*wālif*) after being tightfisted (*shuḥḥ*).
Long ago said I, to be done, "Get lost (*tih*)!—
My commentary's got your meaning untwisted."[414]

But the most exquisite word puzzle I have seen is a poet's words on the name Aḥmad, which go:

How many a one bends in prayer in the ban tree's shade,
Joined to a pearl in a bird's beak displayed![415]

mushakshikin ("of fish skins"): of the measure of *muḥakkik* ("rubbing"), the name of the food that he wants to see and of which he wants to eat. It consists of the skins of salt-cured fish: they eat the flesh and take and wash the skins in water and put them in a casserole with sliced onions and a little linseed oil, then put it in the oven until it is done and eat it with bread. Sometimes they put some cotton-seed cake dissolved in water on top of it as a substitute for sesame paste. This is highly regarded by them, and especially by their womenfolk, as much as if it were grilled mutton, which is why he says . . . 11.18.7

(فهداكَ) بالدال المهملة جريًا على اللغة الريفيّة كقول بعضهم مواليا [بسيط] ٨،١٨،١١

لَكْ وردَتَيْنِ على الخَدَّيْنِ يا هـادالـكْ
وـالِّ بلاني بِعِشْـقَكْ آهِ لو أبلالـكْ
وحقِّ من سبّحَتْ لوُ في السَّما الأملاكْ
لو ماتَ لي كلَّ يومْ أخّينِ ما أسلالـكْ

وقوله (يومُ) أي فهذا اليوم الّذي يأتيني فيه هذا الطاجن المشكشك هو يوم ٩،١٨،١١

(البَسْطِ) ضدّ القبض أي بسط النفس وانشراح الصدر لحصول المُنى وتيسير المطلوب وحضور المرغوب فيه وسدّ الجوعة وسرور أهل المنزل والجماعة الحاضرين معي وقت مجيئه إليّ قال الشاعر [وزن غير معروف] ١٠،١٨،١١

إنّ من اطيب اوقـاتي حين اكون مبسوط في ذاتي

(والتَّقْصيفْ) عطف على البسط مشتقّ من القصافة يقال فلان اليوم قصّيف بتشديد الصاد المهملة أي مسرور فرحان ماشي مشية الخيلاء متحزّم بسير وسكين راخي صنائف البردة تنجرّ على الأرض أو أنّه لبس اليوم قميص جديد وأرخى فوقه البردة وهو اليوم قصّيف الكفر بمعنى أنّ ما هناك أحد في الكفر أشلب منه ولا أعيق أو أنّه مشتقّ من قَصْف العود وهو كسره أو من قولهم (قَصْفه تجيك) أو (قصفه نقاوه) أو (فلان جتو قصفه) مثلاً ١١،١٨،١١

(مسألة هباليّة) لأيّ شيء سمّي هذا الطعام مشكشك وما معنى هذا اللفظ وما مناسبته لجلود الفسيخ (الجواب الفشرويّ) أن يقال إنّ هذا الطعام لمّا كان يشبه في طعمه المشّ والكشك إذا خُلِطَا معاً ركّبوا اسمه من مجموع الاسمين مع تغيّر الحركات وقالوا مشكشك أو إنّه مأخوذ من شكشكة المرأة له بعود أو بالملعقة عند قرب ١٢،١٨،١١

fa-hādāka ("then that"): with *d*, in accordance with rural usage,[416] as the poet says in a *mawāliyā*: 11.18.8

> You there (*yā hādāk*), on your cheeks you've roses twain,
> And would you could feel your lover's pain!
> By Him to whom the angels in Heaven raise their paean,
> Though I lose two brothers a day, your memory will forever remain!

yawmu ("is a day"): that is, then that day on which this casserole of fish skins comes to me is a day of... 11.18.9

al-basti ("happiness"): the opposite of *qabḍ* ("being unhappy"; literally "constriction"); that is, the *basṭ* ("unfolding") of the soul and the relaxing of the heart consequent on the acquisition of the object of desire, the easing of access to what is sought, the presence of what is wanted, the satisfaction of hunger, and the pleasure of the members of my household and all those who are with me when it comes to me. The poet says: 11.18.10

> Verily, among the best of my days are those when I'm happy (*mabsūṭ*) in myself!

wa-taqṣīf ("and one on which of one's clothes to make boast"): connected to *basṭ* by the coordinating conjunction *wa-*; derived from *qaṣṣāfah* ("clippers"). One says, "Today So-and-so is *qaṣṣīf*," with double *ṣ*, that is, happy, joyful, and walking proudly, belt and knife at his waist, letting the fringes of his mantle trail along the ground; or that today he is wearing a new shift and has draped his mantle over it; and one says, "Today he's the *qaṣṣīf* of the hamlet," meaning that there is no one more elegantly dressed or more dashing. Or it may be derived from the *qaṣf* ("snapping") of a stick, that is, the breaking of it, or from their expression *qaṣfah tajīk* ("May a snapping afflict you!") or *qaṣfah naqāwah* ("a snapping 'with your name on it!'") or *fulān jatū qaṣfah* ("So-and-so got snapped!"), for example. 11.18.11

A Fatuous Discussion. Why is this food called *mushakshik*, what is the meaning of this word, and why is it appropriate for the skins of salt-cured fish? The Facetious Answer: it is said that in view of its similarity of taste to *mishsh* and *kishk* mixed together, they made its name by combining those two names, with different vowels, and said *mishakshik*. Or it may be taken from a woman's pricking (*shakshakah*) of it with a stick or a spoon when it is almost done, to 11.18.12

استوائه لتختبر حاله أو من قولهم شكشكه بالإبرة أو إنّه من اللفظ المقلوب وهو شمّ كشك فيكون الّذي اصطنعه أوّلاً لمّا طبخه شمّه فقالوا ما شمّ هذا فقال بعضهم شمّ كشك أي شمّ طعاماً رائحته في الحموضة كرائحة الكشك ثمّ إنّهم قدّموا الميم على الشين المعجمة وجعلوه عَلَماً وقالوا مشَكْشِكْ بفتح الشين الأولى وكسر الثانية وجزم الكافين فاتّجه المقال عن هذا الهبال

(ثمّ إنّ الناظم) اشتهى شيئاً آخر من الخضروات يطبخ ويؤكل عند أوانه وهو أطيب مأكول أهل الريف فقال ١٣،١٨،١١

ص

مَتَى أَنْضُرُ ٱلْخُبَّيْزَ فِي ٱلدَّارِ عِنْدَنَا وَأَنْدِفُ مِنْهَا بِٱلْعُوَيْشِ نَدِيفْ ١٩،١١

ش

قوله (متى) أي أجزم وأنوي أنّي متى ١،١٩،١١

(أَنْضُرُ) بالضاد المعجمة جرياً على اللغة الريفيّة والظاء المشالة على اللغة الفصحى أي أنظر بعيني لا بأذني ولا بفمي لأنّ النظر خاصّ بالعين قال الشاعر [وزن غير معروف] ٢،١٩،١١

عيني نظرتْ وآفتي من عيني

(الخُبَّيْزَ) جمع خبائز بضمّ الخاء المعجمة وتشديد الموحّدة وتُجْمَع الخبيز على خُبوز وخبايز وخبّازين من هذه الجموع الفشرويّة وتأنيثه خبيزة وهي المراد بقول الناظم لرجوع الضمير إليها كما سيأتي في قوله (وأندف منها) وهي مشتقّة من الخبز لأنّ ورقها في التدوير يشبه أقراص الخبز وهي تنبت في أطراف الزرع من كثرة الأمطار وفي ٣،١٩،١١

test it, or from the expression *shakshakahu* ("he pricked it") with a needle. Or it may be from *shamma kishk* ("he smelled *kishk*") backward, in which case its inventor, when he cooked it, smelled it, and they said, "What has this man smelled?" and one of them said *shamma kishk* ("he smelled *kishk*"), that is, he smelled some food whose smell is as sour as *kishk*; then they put the *m* in front of the *sh* and made it a proper name and said *mishakshik*, with an *a* after the first *sh*, an *i* after the second, and no vowels after the *k*s. The contention's now straightened out, the silliness exposed for what it's about.

Next the poet longs for another vegetable that is cooked and eaten in its season and which is the country people's most delicious dish. He says: **11.18.13**

TEXT

matā 'anḍuru l-khubbayza fī l-dāri ʿindanā **11.19**
wa-'andifu minhā bi-l-ʿuwayshi nadīf

When shall I see mallow in the house at home
and cram it down with a little piece of bread?

COMMENTARY

matā ("when"): that is, I resolve and intend that when I . . . **11.19.1**

'anḍuru ("see"): with *ḍ*, in accordance with rural usage, its pronunciation with *ẓ* belonging to the classical language;[417] that is, (when) I see with my eye, and not with my ear or my mouth, for seeing is specific to the eye (the poet says: **11.19.2**

The eye did see and my sickness is from my eye) . . .

al-khubbayza ("mallow"): with *u* after the *kh* and double *b*: plural *khabā'iz* . The plural of *khubbayz* may be *khabbūz*, or *khabāyiz* or *khabbāzīn*, or what have you, to choose from among the possible facetious plurals.[418] In the feminine, it is *khubbayzah*, which is what is intended in the poet's verse, since the pronoun refers to it, as we shall see in the discussion of his words *wa-'andifu minhā*.[419] The word is derived from *khubz* ("bread") because the leaves, in their roundness, resemble rounds of bread. It sprouts on the edges of the cultivated land following heavy rains, and in low-lying and other lands. The best sort is that **11.19.3**

الأراضي المنخفضة وغيرها وأجودها ما كان ساقه طويل وورقه عريض وهو النابت في جوانب الزرع شديد الخضرة أو النابت بالبِزْر وأرداها القصيرة الساق المائل ورقها لزرقة وهي البعيدة عن الزرع والماء وهي كثيرة تنبت في المقابر وفي منخفض الأرض المسبَّخة وهي باردة رطبة تليّن الطبيعة وتفتح السدد وتسكّن الحرارات وهي قريبة في اللطف من طعام الملوخيّة إذا عملت بالشروط الآتية ثمّ إنّ أهل الريف يأخذوا ورقها ويخرّطوه مثل الملوخيّة ويضعوا عليه الكُزْبَرَة الخضراء ويقلّوا لها بالبصل والشيرج ويفتّوا فيها الخبز الشعير ويأكلوها وهي غالب طعامهم مدّة إقامتها عندهم لأنّها لا تكلّفهم شيئاً ما عدا البصل والشيرج ويسير من الكزبرة كما تقدّم فهي غالب مأكولهم زمن الشتاء وأهل بلاد البحر يطبخوها بالإوزّ والدجاج وغيره وأهل المدن يطبخوها باللحوم الدسمة كالضأن وغيره وبالدجاج ويضيفوا عليها الأدهان والسمن البقريّ والخضر والحرارات ونحو ذلك فلا تؤكل إلّا بهذه الكيفيّة فتكون بهذا الحكم خفيفة لذيذة الطعم وأمّا فعل الريّافة لها كما تقدّم فوجوده كالعدم وكذلك أهل بلاد البحر فإنّهم ولو عملوها بالدجاج لا يضيفوا لها سمناً ولا دسماً إلّا الأرزّ والشيرج ولا خضر ولا غيرها بل هي بمفردها وعلى كلّ حال فهي أرقى من طعام الريّافة المتقدّم ذكره وألذّ مأكولها في بلاد المدن لأنهم يكلّفوها فيصير لها خفّة في المأكل ولذّة عظيمة وقالوا (إنّ الطعام كُلْفة كَلِّفْ تَجِدْ)

(قيل) لمّا نزل السلطان قايتباي لدمياط اجتمع بالعينيّ الّذي بنى العينيّة وهي مسجد على سِمة مساجد الملوك فعمل للسلطان ضيافة عظيمة وخصّه بصحن من الذهب فيه دجاجتين ووضعهم بين يديه فأكل السلطان منهما فلم ير طول عمره ألذّ طعاماً منهما فقال له من صنع لك هاتين الدجاجتين فقال له جارية عندي فقال هل من سُلُوّ عنها فقال هي ومولاها في خدمة الملك فأهداها له فلمّا أتى بها إلى مصر أمرها أن تصنع له دجاجتين ففعلت فلم يقعا الموقع ولم يجد لهما لذّة مثل اللّتين أكلهما في دمياط فعاتبها الملك فقالت له يا سيّدي كلّف ترى إنّ سيّدي الّذي صنع لك ٤،١٩،١١

with a long stalk and broad, dark-green leaves, which is the kind that sprouts next to cultivated plants, or sprouts from seed. The worst sort is that with a short stalk, whose leaves are bluish in color, which is the kind that is far from cultivated crops and water. This kind is plentiful and sprouts in graveyards and in the low-lying parts of salt-logged land. It is Cold and Moist, eases the bowels, opens obstructions, and reduces fevers. It is as easy to digest as Jew's mallow, providing it is prepared according to the instructions given below. The people of the countryside take the leaves, chop them like Jew's mallow, put fresh coriander on them, garnish them with fried onions and sesame oil, crumble barley bread onto them, and eat them. This is the thing they eat most of for as long as it is available, because it costs them nothing but the onions, the sesame oil, and a little coriander, as mentioned. It is the thing they eat most of during the winter. The people of the villages on the river cook it with goose and chicken and so on, and the people of the cities cook it with fatty meats such as mutton or the like, and chicken, and they add fats, clarified cow's butter, greens, spices, and similar things, and this is the only way it should be eaten, for this way it is light and tasty. The way the country people do it, however, as described above, is worthless, and the same goes for the people of the villages on the river, for these, even if they do make it with chicken, add no clarified butter or fat, just rice and sesame oil, without greens or anything else; on the contrary, they eat it on its own. The latter is, nevertheless, more refined than the recipe of the country people referred to above. The best place to eat it, however, is in the cities, because they go to some trouble over it, which makes it light to eat and very tasty. They say, "Food is an expense: you get what you pay for."

It is said that, when Sultan Qāyitbāy stayed in Dimyāṭ and met with **11.19.4** al-ʿAynī, who built the ʿAyniyyah,[420] which is a mosque built in the style of a royal mosque, al-ʿAynī prepared for him a great banquet and prepared him his own plate of gold, containing two chickens, and placed these before him. The sultan ate some and had never in all his life tasted anything more delicious. "Who prepared you these chickens?" he asked al-ʿAynī. "A slave girl of mine," he responded. "Could you spare her?" asked the sultan. "She and her master," returned al-ʿAynī, "are the sultan's to command," and he made him a gift of her. When the sultan brought her back to Cairo, he commanded her to prepare him two chickens, and she did so, but they did not turn out as before, and he did not find them as tasty as the two he had eaten in Dimyāṭ. When the sultan reproached her for this, she said to him, "My Lord, you get what you

الدجاجتين طبخهما في إناء من ذهب وكان ماؤهما ماء الورد والخلاف والحطب من العود القَماريّ وحشاهما بحرارات كثيرة مع المسك والعنبر الخام وغرفهما في صحن فيروزج فمن هذا حصل هذا فتعجّب الملك ممّا صنع رحمه الله تعالى وقوله

(في الدارِ عندنا) أي في دار الناظم لا غيره لأنّه هو الّذي تمنّاه ولهذا قال عندنا أي في محلّنا لا محلّ غيرنا لأجل ما تأكل منه العيال ويتسرّوا بوجوده وسمّيت الدار لتدويرها بالطوب الآجرّ والحجر الكذّان وغير ذلك وهذه صفة دور بلاد المدن وأمّا دور بلاد الأرياف فإنّها تبنى بالكِرْس وربّما يكون فيها الوحل والجلّة أيضاً أو لأنّ الشخص يدور ويرجع إليها أو أنّها مشتقّة من لعب الدارة الّتي يلعبوها أولاد الريّافة بعد الغروب يقعد ولد منهم على قرافيصه ويقعد ولد آخر ويجعل ظهره في ظهره وتدور الأولاد حولهما ويضربونهما فإذا مسك واحد منهما ولداً أجلسه مكانه وهكذا فيتعلّموا من ذلك خفّة الأيدي وسرعة الضرب والمشي ونحوه وقوله ١١،١٩،٥

(وأَندِفُ مِنها) أي من طعام الخبيز ومعناه يأخذ منه بسرعة ويحشي في بطنه فصار يشبه ندّاف القطن إذا أخذه بالقوس وحشاه في الطَرّاحة ومن هذا يقال فلان الليلة ندف متردين عدس أو بيسار أي أكلهم بسرعة أو أنّه مشتقّ من أحمد الدَنَف من شُطّار مصر الّذين تقدّموا وسيرته مشهورة عند المخرّفين وقوله ١١،١٩،٦

(بالعُوَيْشِ) تصغير عَيْش سمّي بذلك لأنّ به قيام المعيشة قال الشاعر [كامل] ١١،١٩،٧

لا تَرْكَنَنَّ إلى الثّيابِ الفاخِرهْ   واذكُرْ عِظامَكَ حينَ تُمسي ناخِرهْ
وإذا رأيتَ زَخارفَ الدُّنيا فَقُلْ   لا هُمَّ إنّ العَيشَ عَيشُ الآخِرهْ

pay for. My master who prepared you those two chickens cooked them in a vessel made of gold, and the water he used was rosewater and such like, and the firewood was aloe wood, and he stuffed them with many spices as well as musk and ambergris, and ladled them into a dish made of gold. That exquisite taste was from this costly preparation." The sultan marveled at what al-ʿAynī, may the Almighty have mercy on his soul, had done.

fī l-dāri ʿindanā ("in the house at home"): that is, in the poet's house, not someone else's, because he is the one who desires it; and for the same reason he says "at home," that is, at our place and no one else's, so that the children can eat some of it and rejoice that it is there. A house is called a *dār* because of its being encircled (*li-tadwīrihā*) with baked brick, limestone, and so on, this being the way that city houses are. The houses of the countryside, on the other hand, are built of slabs of dung mixed with straw, sometimes including daub and dung cakes. Or the *dār* is so called because one goes about (*yadūru*) and then returns to it. Or it is derived from the game of *dārah* that the children of the country people play after sunset: one boy squats on his haunches and another boy does the same with his back to him and the rest circle round them and hit them; if one of the first two catches one of the others, he sits him in his place, and so on. From this they learn dexterity and how to strike and move quickly, and so forth. 11.19.5

wa-ʾandifu minhā ("and cram it down"): that is, cram down the mallow, the meaning being that he takes a little of it quickly and stuffs it into his belly, thus resembling the cotton teaser (*naddāf al-quṭn*), when he works the cotton with his bow and stuffs it into the mattress.[421] This gives rise to such statements as, "Last night So-and-so 'crammed down' (*nadaf*) two crocks of lentils, or of *bīsār*," that is, he ate them fast. Or it may be derived from Aḥmad al-Danaf, one of the clever rogues of Cairo of former times, whose life is well known to storytellers. 11.19.6

bi-l-ʿuwayshi ("with a little piece of bread"): diminutive of *ʿaysh* ("bread"), so called because it is on this that livelihood (*maʿīshah*) depends. The poet says: 11.19.7

Put not your faith in fine clothes
But think of your bones when bored by the worm;
On seeing the fripperies of this world, declare
"Dear God, the true life is the life the world to come!"[422]

أو أنّه مشتقّ من عُشّ الطائر لتدويره مثل تدوير العيش وأمّا تسميته خبز فهو من التخبيز وهو التنضيج بالنار يقال فلان ضرب فلان حتّى خبّز أضلاعه أي صار الضرب فوقها مثل نضج الخبز أو كسرها كما أنّ الخبز آيل للتكسير مثلاً أو يكون خبّز أضلاعه بمعنى فكّها من بعضها البعض وقوله

(نَديفْ) على وزن نتيف وهو الّذي ينتف ذقنه لأجل الخنات أو كان به مرض الأُبْنة أعاذنا الله منها فإنّها داء يَغْلي في الدبر بحرقة كغَلي الدود في العفن قال الشاعر [بسيط] ٨،١٩،١١

فَـإِنَّـهُ مَـرَضٌ كالنَّـارِ مُشْعَـلَـهُ   في الدُبْرِ يَغلي كغَلْيِ الدّودِ في العَفَنِ

وأكبر دوائها ما ذكره الشعرانيّ نفعنا الله به أن يُحْتَقَن بماء الفسيخ السائل منه مراراً فإنّه يبرأ بإذن الله تعالى وأصله نَدَفاً سُكِّنَ وصُغِّرَ لأجل الرويّ أي أندف من الخبيز ندفاً كثيراً حتّى أشبع شبعاً مفرطاً ليس بعده جوع بقيّة اليوم أو بقيّة الليلة

ثمّ انتقل من الطعام إلى الباقلّة الخضراء فقال ٩،١٩،١١

ص

مَتَى أَنْضَرُ ٱلْفُولَ ٱلْمُشَيْوِي بِفُـرْنِنَا   وَٱلْفُو بِقِشْـرُو وَٱلْعُـروقِ لَفِـيفْ ٢٠،١١

ش

قوله (متى أَنْضَرُ) يعني كما تقدّم في البيت الّذي قبله ١،٢٠،١١

—or it may be derived from the *ʿushsh* ("nest") of a bird because the latter has the same round shape as bread. As for why bread is also called *khubz*, this comes from *takhbīz* ("baking"), which is the process of bringing something to a state of maturation by fire. One says, "So-and-so beat So-and-so until he 'baked (*khabbaza*)' his ribs," that is, until the beating on them produced an effect similar to the thorough cooking of bread, or he broke them, for example, bread being easily broken. Or it may be that "he baked his ribs" means that he separated them one from another.

nadīf (used as an intensifier):[423] of the measure of *natīf* (literally "plucked"), **11.19.8** which is someone who plucks his beard in order to make himself effeminate or who has a morbid craving for passive sodomy—God protect us from it, for it is an affliction that squirms hotly in the anus as worms squirm in carrion. The poet says:

Indeed, it is a sickness like a fire ignited
  In the anus, squirming as worms in carrion squirm.

The surest cure for it is that mentioned by al-Shaʿrānī, God benefit us through him, namely, the repeated administration of an enema made from the liquid from salt-cured fish.[424] The sufferer will then recover, the Almighty willing. The word was originally *nadfan*, but the final *an* was dropped and it was turned into a diminutive for the sake of the rhyme;[425] that is, "I will stuff myself so full with mallow that I am utterly sated and feel no more hunger for the rest of the day, or the rest of the night."

Next the poet moves on from food to the green pulses, and says: **11.19.9**

TEXT

matā ʾanḍuru l-fūla l-mushaywī bi-furninā **11.20**
  wa-luffū bi-qishrū wa-l-ʿurūqi lafīf

When shall I see grilled beans in our oven
  and bolt them down with their skins and stalks in a manner
    uninhibited?

COMMENTARY

matā ʾanḍuru ("when shall I see"): with my eye, as in the preceding line . . . **11.20.1**

(الفولَ) الأخضر إذا أُتِيَ به من الغيط ووُضِعَ في الفرن وصار مشوياً والمطلوب أن يكون هذا الفول ١١،٢٠،٢

(المُشَيْوِيّ) تصغير مَشْويّ على وزن عطيويّ أو خريويّ وخريويّ فيها بيقين التصغير والوزن ١١،٢٠،٣

(بفُرَيْنِنا) لا بفرن غيرنا ١١،٢٠،٤

(وَأُلُفّو) أصله وأَلُفُّهُ بالهمز تركه للضرورة من اللفّ وهو حشو الفم وسرعة البلع والمضغ من غير تأمّل ولا تفتيش في المأكول ولهذا قال ١١،٢٠،٥

(بِقشْرِو) أي آكله من غير نزع قشره من فرحتي به ومن شدّة الجوع ١١،٢٠،٦

(والعروقِ) معطوف على القشر أي وألفّ عروقه أيضاً ١١،٢٠،٧

(لَفيفْ) أي لفّاً زائداً بحرقة قويّة وشهوة بهيميّة حتّى أكتفي منه ولا أنظر إلى خشونة بلعه لكونه بالقشر والعروق على حاله ولا أنظر لهذا المعنى كما فعله غيري من أنّه يخرجه من الفرن ويضع عليه الملح ويبقيه حتّى يبرد ويقشر منه ويأكل فأنا لشدّة اشتياقي إليه وكثرة الجوع والقِلّة والعَتَرة ألفّه بجميع ما عليه ١١،٢٠،٨

(فائدة) الفول الأخضر قيل شَيِّه بارد رطب وقيل بارد يابس ويُعَدّ له الأكل بالملح والصعتر ونفع أكله حارّاً أو مشوياً نزعه من قشوره جميعاً وأكله بالسكّر وفي بعض كتب الطبّ من أكل الباقلا أربعين يوماً وأصابه مرض الجُذام فلا يلومنّ إلّا نفسه ومتى أكلت المرأة الباقلّا أربعين يوماً لم تحبل أبداً وقد عدّوه من موانع الحمل ١١،٢٠،٩

ثمّ إنّه اشتهى شيئاً ممّا يُخْبَز ويتمنّى حصوله فقال ١١،٢٠،١٠

al-fūla ("beans"): meaning green fava beans brought from the field and put in the oven and grilled. What he wants is that these beans should be . . . 11.20.2

al-mushaywī ("grilled"): diminutive of *mashwī* of the measure of *ʿuṭaywī* ("little gift") or *khuraywī* ("little turd"), the latter containing both diminution and weight, for sure. 11.20.3

bi-furninā ("in our oven"): not in someone else's oven. 11.20.4

wa-luffū ("and bolt them down"): originally *wa-ʾaluffuhu* with a glottal stop, which he omitted for the sake of the meter;[426] from *laff* (verbal noun), which is cramming the mouth and swallowing and chewing fast without looking at or examining the food, which is why he says . . . 11.20.5

bi-qishrū ("with their skins"): that is, I will eat them without removing the skins, out of joy at having them and because I am so hungry. 11.20.6

wa-l-ʿurūqi ("and stalks"): joined to the *qishr* ("skins") by the coordinating conjunction, that is, and I bolt their stalks down too 11.20.7

lafīf ("'in a manner uninhibited,' used as an intensifier"[427]): that is, in an intemperate way, with great agony and bestial lust until I have had enough of them, and I will give no thought to the roughness of the swallowing that follows from their being as is, with skins and stalks, and I will not do as others do, that is to say, take them from the oven, put salt on them, leave them until they cool, and then skin some and eat them, for I have such a longing for them and am in such a hungry, poor, and wretched state that I will bolt them down with all that is on them. 11.20.8

A Useful Note: Green fava beans before grilling are Cold and Moist (or, according to others, Cold and Dry). They are prepared for eating by adding salt and thyme. The benefit to the health of eating them hot or grilled lies in completely removing the skins and eating them with sugar. In one of the books of medicine it says, "Whoever eats pulses for forty days and then contracts leprosy has only himself to blame, and if a woman eats pulses for forty days, she will never get pregnant." They considered them a contraceptive. 11.20.9

Next, the poet desires something baked and longs to obtain it. He says: 11.20.10

ص

١١،٢١ مَتَى أَنْضُرُ ٱنْ طَحَنَ ٱلطَّحِينَ وجِبْتُو وَٱبَطِّطُ مِنُّوفَطِيرَ رَهِيفْ

ش

١١،٢١،١ قوله (متى أَنْضُرُ) تقدّم معناه

١١،٢١،٢ (انْ طَحَنَ) أحد من الطحّانين

١١،٢١،٣ (الطحينَ) الّذي وضعته في الطاحون ورحت إليه ورأيته

١١،٢١،٤ (وجِبْتو) أي وجئت به بعد أن أعطيت الطحّان أجرته إلى منزلي

١١،٢١،٥ (وٱبَطِّطُ) على وزن وَضَرِّطُ وَبَرِّبُطُ وضرّط وربرط فيها بيقين المناسبة وهو مشتقّ من البطّ وهو طير يُربَى في الدور يشبه الإوزّ إلّا أنّه صغير عنه وأرجله قصيرة جدًّا أو من البطبطة أو من البِطَط الّتي يوضع فيها السمن وغيره أو هو من الهلفطة لا كلام

١١،٢١،٦ (مسألة هباليّة) لأيّ شيء سمّي مجموع القمح طحين وهل هذا اللفظ صفة أو عَلَم عليه (قلنا الجواب الفشرويّ) أنّه كان في الأوّل قمحًا لا كلام ثمّ طرأ عليه الطحن فنقله من حالة إلى حالة أخرى فيكون من تسمية الشيء بما طرأ عليه من الوصف الّذي قام به ونقله من حال إلى حال ومثله الإنسان في حال حياته إذا مات فإنّه لمّا طرأ عليه الموت صار يقال له ميّت فلذلك لمّا كان في قوّته قبل الطحن كان حكم الإنسان في حال حياته فكان أوّلًا معروفًا بالقمح فلمّا دارت عليه الطاحون وطحنته اندرس اسمه الأوّل وصار

TEXT

matā ʾanḍuru-n ṭaḥana l-ṭaḥīna wa-jibtū 11.21
wa-baṭṭiṭu minnū faṭīrah rahīf

When shall I see that he's ground the flour, and I've brought it
and pat myself out from it a pastry that's crumbly?

COMMENTARY

matā ʾanḍuru ("when shall I see"): explained above . . . 11.21.1

an ṭaḥana ("that he's ground"): referring to one of the millers . . . 11.21.2

(a)l-ṭaḥīna ("the flour"): which I put in the mill, and which I subsequently 11.21.3
have gone to and seen . . .

wa-jibtū ("and I've brought it"): that is, and after giving the miller his fee, I 11.21.4
have brought it to my house . . .

wa-baṭṭiṭu ("and pat myself out"): on the pattern of *wa-ḍarriṭu* ("and I fart 11.21.5
repeatedly or loudly") and *wa-barbiṭu* ("and I splash"),[428] both of which are certainly appropriate; derived from *baṭṭ* ("ducks"), which are fowl raised in the houses that resemble geese but are smaller and have very short legs, or from *baṭbaṭah* ("flattening" or "splashing"), or from the *biṭaṭ* ("vessels") in which clarified butter and other things are put, or, quite possibly, from sheer stuff and nonsense.

A Fatuous Point for Discussion: Why is wheat en masse called *ṭaḥīn,*[429] and 11.21.6
is the latter term an adjective or a proper noun belonging to the former? We declare the Facetious Answer to be that in its original form it was wheat, without a doubt; then, all of a sudden, the process of milling descended unexpectedly upon it, which converted it from one state to another. Thus it is a question of "the naming of a thing after what fate may bring" via the attribute that comes to exist in it and converts it from one state to another. Similarly, a man, when he dies, and after death unexpectedly descends upon him, is referred to as "dead." This being the case, this substance, enjoying its strength to the full before the milling, was then analogous to a man while alive, and was therefore known as "wheat," but when the mill turned upon it and ground it up, its first name was obliterated, and it became *ṭaḥīn*. Likewise, when mortal

طحيناً فكذلك الإنسان لما تدور عليه المَنِيّة خفي اسمه وصار ميتاً وطحنته الأرض ومضى أمره إلى أن يُبعث فاتّجه الجواب عن هذه الأبحاث الفشرويّة

٧،٢١،١١ وفي بعض نسخ المتن (ان طحنتُ الطحين) بإثبات التاء المثنّاة من فوق فيكون هو الّذي طحنه بنفسه وهذا هو الأَوْلى لأنّ أهل الريف يجعلوا في الدار أو في الكفر طاحونة مشتركة بينهم وإن كان عند الرجل منهم طحين يأخذ ثوره ويعلّقه ويطحن عليه وأمّا بلاد البحر فإنّهم يطحنون بالأجرة وطواحينهم كلّها بالخيل حكم بلاد المدن ولا يفعل ما تقدّم إلّا أهل الكفور والقرى الصغيرة ولا شكّ أنّ الناظم منهم كما تقدّم في ذكر قريته فلهذا قال ان طحنتُ الطحين وجبتو وَبَطّطُ أي أعجنه بالماء أو بشيء من اللبن وآخذ القطعة العجين وأضعها على خرقة أو رَدّة أو قرص جلّة مثلاً وأخبطها بالكفّ حتّى ترقّ وآخذ غيرها فيتحصّل لي

٨،٢١،١١ (مِنّو) أي من هذا العجين

٩،٢١،١١ (فَطيرَ) مشتقّ من الفطور لكونهم يفطرون به أو من الفُطْرة أو من عيد الفِطْر

١٠،٢١،١١ (رهيفْ) صفةً للفطير أي طريّ رقيق وفي كلامه اكتفاء فإنّه ذكر الفطير وكيفيّة عمله ولم يذكر أكله فيُفْهَم من الكلام أنّه لمّا بطّط الفطير خبزه في الفرن أو في الجورة الّتي يصنعوها في الزريبة ويحطّوا عليها الزبل وفي بعض الأحيان الجلّة أيضاً وأكل منه حتّى اكتفى

١١،٢١،١١ ثمّ إنّه قال

fate turns upon a man, his name disappears and he becomes "dead" and the ground grinds him up and he is no more, until he is resurrected. Thus we conclude with the right answer to these fatuous investigations.

In some copies of the text we read *an ṭaḥantu l-ṭaḥīn* ("that I have ground"), with the *t* clearly written, in which case he would be the one who milled it, by himself, which is the more appropriate, for the people of the countryside make a common mill in the house or in the hamlet, and when one of their men has wheat to mill, he takes his ox and hitches it up and grinds it. In the villages by the river, however, they pay a fee for milling, and all their mills are operated by horsepower, as in the cities. The previously described process takes place only in the hamlets and small villages, to which the poet, without doubt, belongs, as was made clear earlier, when his own village was mentioned. He says, "When shall I see that I've ground the flour and I've brought it, and pat myself out, that is, knead it with water or a little milk and take each piece of dough and place it on a rag or some bran or a dung cake, for example, and strike it with the palm until it is thin, and then take another, by which means I will obtain" . . . **11.21.7**

minnū ("from it"): that is, from this dough . . . **11.21.8**

faṭīra ("a pastry"): from *faṭūr* ("breakfast"), because they eat it for breakfast, or from *fuṭrah* ("fungus"), or from ʿĪd al-Fiṭr ("The Feast of the Breaking of the Fast").[430] **11.21.9**

rahīf ("(that's) crumbly"): an adjective modifying "pastry," that is, moist and thin. His words contain "restraint," since he mentions the pastry and how to make it without mentioning eating it; it is thus to be inferred from his words that, after patting out the pastry, he baked it in the oven or in the pit that they make in the barn and on top of which they put droppings and sometimes dung cakes too, and ate of it till he had had enough. **11.21.10**

Then the poet says: **11.21.11**

ص

أَيَا مَطْيَبَ ٱلْجُلْبَانَ وَٱلعَدْسَ ٱذَا ٱسْتَوَى   وَشِرْشُ بَصَلْ حَوْلُو وَمِيِّتْ رَغِيفْ ٢٢،١١

ش

قوله (أيا) ناس ١،٢٢،١١

(ما أطيب) في الطعم واللذّة ٢،٢٢،١١

(الجُلْبَانَ) على وزن الجِذْيان أو الخِرّفان مشتقّ من جِلْبَة النبّوت أو أنّ الّذي زرعه سقاه في الأصل على ثور جَلَب أو من جَلَبَة العبيد والجلبان نبات يُزْرَعُ حَبُّه يشبه حَبّ الملوخيّة وله قرون صغار مثل قرون الملوخيّة مشتبك في بعضه البعض مثل البرسيم يزرعوه أهل الريف ويأكلوه مثل الفول الأخضر وربّما طبخوه بالعدس وأكلوه كما قال الناظم ويزرعوه كثيراً وتأكل منه البهائم أيضاً وقوله ٣،٢٢،١١

(والعَدْس) معطوف عليه أي وما أطيب العدس معه والعدس معروف لا يحتاج إلى بيان ٤،٢٢،١١

(إذا استوى) فإنّه لا يؤكل نيئاً بخلاف الجلبان بل يؤكل مطبوخاً وهو بارد يابس ثقيل يشبه الدُخْن في فعله يُمسِك إطلاق البطن ومَرَقُه أنفع من حَبّه وأكله يرقّ القلب (وفي زهر الكِمام) أنّ بعض الأنبياء شكا إلى الله تعالى قسوة قلوب قومه فأَوحى الله إليه (مُرْهُم فيأكلوا العدس فإنّه يرقّ قلوبهم) (وفي الحديث) عليكم بالعدس فإنّه يُرِقّ القلب ويكثر الدمعة وقد بارك فيه سبعون نبيّاً والإكثار من أكله يخاف منه الضرر ٥،٢٢،١١

TEXT

a-yā maṭyaba l-julbāna wa-l-ʿadsa-dhā-stawā 11.22
wa-shirshu baṣal ḥawlū wa-miyyat raghīf

Ah, how good is vetch and lentils when cooked
with a bunch of onions around it and a hundred loaves!

COMMENTARY

a-yā ("Ah"): [431] meaning "Ah, you people" . . . 11.22.1

maṭyaba ("how good"): in taste and scrumptiousness . . . 11.22.2

(a)l-julbānah ("is vetch"): of the pattern of *jidyān* ("young goats") or *khirfān* ("sheep"), derived from the *jilbah* ("ferrule") of a staff, or from the fact that the person who sowed it watered it originally with a draft ox (*thawr jalab*), or from *jalabat al-ʿabīd* ("traders in slaves"). *Julbān* is a plant that is grown from seed, the latter resembling that of Jew's mallow, and it has small pods resembling the pods of Jew's mallow and grows intertwined with itself like clover. The country people grow it and eat it as they do green fava beans, and sometimes they cook it with lentils and eat it, as described by the poet. They grow it in large quantities, and the animals eat it too. 11.22.3

wa-l-ʿadsa ("and lentils"): joined to the preceding by the coordinating conjunction, that is, and how good lentils are with it! Lentils are too well known to require comment. 11.22.4

(i)dhā-stawā ("when cooked"): since lentils, unlike vetch, cannot be eaten raw but indeed must be eaten cooked. They are Cold, Dry, and Heavy, resembling millet in their effect and impeding the release of the bowels. The broth is more beneficial than the grain, and eating it softens the heart. In *The Flowers in the Calyces*,[432] it says that one of the prophets complained to the Almighty of the hard hearts of his people and God inspired him to "command them to eat lentils, for that will soften their hearts!" And in the Tradition it says, "You are enjoined to eat lentils, for they soften the heart and cause copious tears!" and seventy prophets have given them their blessings. At the same time, it is to be feared that excessive consumption thereof will cause harm: in *The Canon*,[433] it says that excessive consumption thereof leads to leprosy and damages the nerves 11.22.5

وفي القانون الإكثار منه يرث الجذام ويضرّ بالعصب ويولّد الأخلاط السوداويّة (وقال) بعض الأطباء يُعَدّ له السَلَق الأخضر وطعامه على نوعين مدشوش وهو أخفّ من غيره وغير مدشوش ويسمّى عدساً بجُبّته فأهل الريف يضعونه في بوشة فخّار ويحطّوه في محماة الفرن أو في الفرن ويغمروه بالماء حتّى يستوي ويفركوه بالمفراك ويقلّوا له بما يتيسّر من الشيرج والبصل مثل البيسار (وأمّا أهل المدن) فإنّهم يطبخوه طبخاً جيّداً ويضعوا عليه دهن الليّة والسمن الخالص والحرارات خصوصاً أبناء الترك فإنّهم يُكْثِروا فيه الأدهان وربّما فعلوه باللحم الضأن ولهذا يأتون به رأس السِماط فهو عندهم له موقع عظيم وربّما عُمِلَ بالقلقاس إذا كان مدشوشاً وهو ألذّ وأطيب وبلاد البحر يطبخوه بالأرزّ ثخيناً يدشوه ويضيفوا عليه الأرزّ ويسمّوه بَغْلِيّة بفتح الموحّدة وسكون الغين المعجمة وكسر اللام وتشديد الياء المثنّاة تحت وسكون الهاء المربوطة في آخره وهذا النوع ثقيل جدّاً يشبه البِسِلّة في ثقلها وربّما أكلوه بالبصل من غير خبز وكذلك البسلة يصنعوها أيضاً بالأرزّ

وكلّ هذا يولّد الأرياح ويضرّ بالمعدة خصوصاً البسلّة فإنّها أشدّ في الضرر وبعضهم استطرد حرف الباء في اسمها في وصفين منها فقال بسلة باردة بايتة ثمّ استطرد حرف التاء في مضرتها فقال تُعَشّي تُفَسّي تُنْسي فيكون لفّ ونشر مرتَّب ومعناه بسلّة تعشّي باردة تفسي بايتة تنسي ثمّ قال ٦،٢٢،١١

(وشِرْشُ بَصَلْ) اسم لِلحزمة المربوطة منه فإنّه يقال لها شرش ويطلق على أوّل خروج الفساء أيضاً فهو لفظ مشترك بين الفساء وشرش البصل ولهذا يقال (في لحيتك شرش) مثلاً وهو من الألفاظ الّتي تُقرأ طرداً وعكساً أوّلها مثل آخرها وقوله ٧،٢٢،١١

(حَوْلو) أي حول العدس بعد وضعه مغروفاً في المترد أو الشالية ويكون البصل موضوعاً حوله كما جرت به العادة في بلاد الريف وغيرها أنّهم يضعوا البصل حول ٨،٢٢،١١

and engenders melancholic humors. According to one physician, it should be taken with fresh chard. It may be prepared in two ways: husked, which is the easier to digest, and unhusked, which is called "lentils in their jackets." The country people put them in an earthenware pot and put that in the stokehole of the oven or in the oven itself, covered with water, until they are cooked. Then they whisk them with the wooden whisk and make a fried garnish for them with a little sesame oil and onions, like *bīsār*. The city people, on the other hand, and especially those of Turkish descent, cook them well and put fat from a sheep's tail, clarified butter, and spices on them, for they like to eat them with a lot of fat. Sometimes they make them with mutton, which is why they give them the place of honor on the dining cloth, for they hold them in the greatest esteem. Sometimes they are done with taro, if they are husked, and this is the most delicious and tasty way. The villages on the river cook them with rice, making them thick; they husk them and add rice and call it *baghliyyah* (with *a* after the *b*, no vowel after the *gh*, *i* after the *l*, double *y*, and nothing after the final *ah*).[434] This kind is very heavy, a feature in which it resembles peas. Sometimes they eat them with onions without bread, and peas likewise they prepare with rice.

All these cause flatulence and do harm to the stomach, especially peas, for 11.22.6
they are the most harmful. One person built on the letter *b* in the noun *bisillah* and used it to form two appropriate adjectives: *bisillah bāridah bāyitah* ("postprandial perishing peas"), then went on to build on the letter *t* to describe the harm they do, saying *tuʿshī tufsī tunsī* ("turn me blind at night, turn into farts, and turn my memory into a blank!"), which constitutes a display of "sequential rolling and unrolling,"[435] the meaning being, "peas turn me blind at night, being perishingly cold enough to turn into farts, and postprandially turn my memory into a blank!" Then he says . . .

wa-shirshu baṣal ("with a bunch of onions"): *shirsh* is a name for a tied bundle 11.22.7
of onions; it is called a *shirsh*. The word is also applied to the beginning of the emergence of a silent fart. Thus it is a term common to both farts and bunches of onions, which is why one says *fī liḥyitak shirsh* ("A *shirsh* in your beard!"), for instance. It is one of those words that read the same forward and backward, the beginning being the same as the end.[436]

ḥawlū ("around it"): that is, the bunch of onions will be arranged around the 11.22.8
lentils, after they have been ladled into the small or medium-sized milk crock, because it is the custom in the country villages and elsewhere to place the

العدس والبيسار والمش أو غير ذلك ويأخذ الرجل البصلة يقطم منها مثل الخيارة وأمّا أهل المدن فيقشّروه ويفلقوا البصلة أربع فلقات ويضعوها حول السُفْرة ولكلّ شيء مناسبة وإذا عُصِرَماء البصلة ذهبت حرارتها واعتدلت في الأكل وقوله

٩،٢٢،١١ (ومِيّة رَغيف) أصله ومائة سهّله لضرورة النظم أي من خبز الشعير وذكر هذا العدد لأجل ما يشفي غليله من الأكل أو ربّما يعزم على أحد بالأكل مثلاً أو يأتيه أحد ضيف على غفلة فتكون المائة رغيف فيها المحتمل للأكل منها والتفرقة وكذلك الشرش البصل وهي الحزمة الّتي تملأ الكفّ كما تقدّم تكون الأخرى تكفيه للأكل منها وتفرقتها إن شاركه أحد

١٠،٢٢،١١ ثمّ إنّه استطرد شيئاً آخر واشتهى حصوله فقال

ص

٢٣،١١ أَيَا مَحْسَنَ ٱلْخُبْزَ ٱلْمُقَمَّرَ عَلَى ٱلنَّدَهْ   وَفَوْقُو مِنَ ٱلسَّرْسُوبِ حَلْبُ نَضِيفْ

ش

١،٢٣،١١ قوله (أيا) ناس

٢،٢٣،١١ (ما أحسن) أي ما أظرف وألطف وألذّ مأكول

٣،٢٣،١١ (الخُبْزَ) النظيف الأبيض

٤،٢٣،١١ (المُقَمَّرَ) بالنار لا بالشمس

onions around the lentils or the *bīsār* or the *mishsh* or whatever else there may be and for a man to take an onion and break pieces off it as though it were a cucumber. City people, on the other hand, peel it first and chop the onion into four segments and place them around the dining tray, and consistency is maintained. If the juice is squeezed out of the onion, it loses its piquancy and makes a balanced food.

wa-miyyat raghīf ("and a hundred loaves"): the origin is *wa-mi'ah*, but he drops the glottal stop for the sake of the meter; that is, a hundred loaves of barley bread. He specifies this number as being sufficient to satisfy his craving for food, or because he might invite someone to eat with him, for example, or a guest might turn up unexpectedly. A hundred, under such circumstances, would be enough to eat from and to hand around. Similarly, the bunch of onions, which is a bundle large enough to fill the hand, as explained above,[437] would also be enough for him to eat from and to hand around, if anyone should join him. **11.22.9**

Next he proceeds to another thing and longs to obtain it. He says: **11.22.10**

TEXT

a-yā maḥsan al-khubza l-muqammar ʿala l-nadah **11.23**
wa-fawqū mina l-sarsūbi ḥalbū naḍīf

Ah, how fine is toasted bread first thing
and on top of it, of milk-and-beestings, one milking's-worth that's clean!

COMMENTARY

a-yā ("Ah"): that is, Ah, you people . . . **11.23.1**

maḥsana ("how fine is"): that is, how delightful and refined and delicious is the food called . . . **11.23.2**

(a)l-khubza ("bread"): that is, clean white bread . . . **11.23.3**

al-muqammar ("toasted, crisped"): by fire, not by the sun . . . **11.23.4**

(على النَدَهْ) أي على الفطور عند نزول الندى وهو الماء اللطيف الّذي ينزل وقت الصبح إلى طلوع الشمس سمّي بذلك لأنّه يندّي الأرض أي يبلّها بللاً خفيفاً وفيه منافع كثيرة للزرع وغيره وفيه بركة عميمة ويشبَّه بالسخاء والكرم يقال (كَفُّه نَدِيّ) ويقال (فلان ما عنده ندى) مثلاً والندى قرين الجود قال بعضهم يمدح السلطان زيد والي مكة المشرّفة رحمه الله تعالى [طويل] ٥،٢٣،١١

سَأَلْتُ النَدى والجودَ من عَهْدِ آدَمٍ　　لَقَدْ عِشْتُما دهراً وَقَدْ مُتُّمَا أحيانا
فقالا نَعَمْ مُتْنا زَمانا وعِنْدَما　　أَتى زيدُ والي كَعْبَةِ الله أحيانا

فالفطور في هذا الوقت على الخبز المقمّر فيه منفعة عظيمة وفي كلام الحكماء الكَسْرة اليابسة مَرْهَم البدن ورأيت في بعض كتب الطبّ أنّ المعدة يعلوها شيء يشبه الشعر فإذا فطر الإنسان على الكسرة اليابسة نزلت على هذا الشعر حكم الموسى فحلّقها فعلى كلّ حال الفطور على الخبز اليابس المقمّر أنفع من غيره ٦،٢٣،١١

(و) خصوصاً إذا كان ٧،٢٣،١١

(فوقو) أي فوق الخبز المقمّر بعد تكسيره ووضعه في الإناء ٨،٢٣،١١

(مِنَ ٱلسَّرْسُوبِ) على وزن الجعبوب وهو اللبن الّذي يوضع فيه شيء يسير من اللبن الّذي ينزل عقب ولادة البهيمة ويسمّوه مسماراً يأخذوه ويضعوه في طاجن فخّار أحمر ويضعوا عليه شيئاً من الملح لإصلاحه ومكثه لحاجتهم فإذا أرادوا السرسوب يضعوا اللبن في الدست ويصبّوا عليه من هذا الّذي يسمّوه المسمار ويفوّروه على النار فيقال له مفوّر ويقال له سرسوب ويفتّوا فيه الخبز المقمّر مع العجوة ويأكلوه وله لذّة عظيمة ويجعلوه أيضاً في طواجن ويضعوه في الفرن بعد وضع المسمار فيه فيجمد ويسمّوه لِبّه بخفض اللام والباء الموحّدة ويأكلوه وله لذّة عظيمة ٩،٢٣،١١

ʿalā l-nadah ("first thing"):[438] at breakfast, at the descent of the dew, which is the fine moisture that descends in the morning until the sun rises, so called because it "bedews" (*yunaddī*) the ground, that is, it wets it lightly. It has many beneficial properties for crops and other things. It contains general blessing and is used figuratively to stand for liberality and generosity. One says, "So-and-so's hand is 'like dew'" and "So-and-so 'has no dew,'" for example, and "dew is the companion of excellence."[439] A poet said in praise of Sultan Zayd, governor of Mecca the Ennobled, may the Almighty have mercy on his soul: 11.23.5

I asked of Generosity (*al-nadā*) and Munificence, "From Adam's time
Have you not lived long years, and many a time have you not died?"
Said they, "Indeed, for long we were quite dead, but when
Zayd came to rule God's House, we were revived!"

Thus to break one's fast, at that time of day, with toasted bread has many benefits. In the words of the doctors, "A dry crust is the body's balm." In a book of medicine I saw that the stomach is coated with something resembling hair. When a person breaks his fast with a dry crust, it comes down on the hair like a razor and shaves it off. However that may be, the healthiest way to break one's fast is with dry, toasted bread. 11.23.6

wa- ("and"): especially if there be . . . 11.23.7

fawqū ("on top of it"): that is, on top of the toasted bread, after it has been broken into pieces and put in the vessel . . . 11.23.8

mina l-sarsūbi ("of milk-and-beestings"): *sarsūb* being of the measure of *juʿbūb* ("black part of a wick"). It is milk into which a little of the milk that descends immediately after an animal is born and which they call *musmār* ("beestings") has been put. They take this and put it in a red earthenware casserole, with a little salt to season it and make it last till they need it. When they want *sarsūb*, they put milk in a basin and pour into it some of that milk that they call *musmār* and boil it over the fire. It is called both *mufawwar* ("boiled") and *sarsūb*. They crumble toasted bread into it, along with pressed dates, and eat it, and it is extremely delicious. They also make it in a casserole and put it in the oven after adding the beestings. This makes it solidify and they then call it *libbih*, with *i* after the *l* and after the *b*,[440] and they eat it, and it is extremely delicious. 11.23.9

١٠،٢٣،١١ وأفضل الألبان لبن الأنعام وأجودها لبن البقر لقوله صلّى الله عليه وسلّم (عليكم بألبان البقر فإنّ لبنها شفاء وسمنها دواء ولحمها داء) (وأجودها) ما شرب من تحت الضرع أو كما حلب وإذا خلط بالسكّر خضّب البدن وصفّى اللون وليّن الطبيعة وزاد قوّة في الباه وسمّي اللبه لبه لأنّه مشتقّ من اللُبّ أو من اللَبْوة أو من قولهم (لبّك واحد بفَرقَلّه) مثلاً أو من لَبَّ الجَدْي الصغير أمّه إذا أراد شربها قال الشاعر

[بسيط]

فأنت كالجـدي لما أن يَلُبّ وكـ . . . . الجرّ و المطوّق إسراعاً إلى اللبنِ

١١،٢٣،١١ وقوله (حَلْبُ) أي قدر حلب وهو اسم لما يملأ المحلاب أو المحلبة أو أنّه مشتقّ من حلب الرجل بيده فيكون اسم لما حُلِبَ من البهيمة والمعنى أنّه يكون فوق هذا الخبز ما يعمّه من لبن السرسوب المحلوب حلباً

١٢،٢٣،١١ (نَضيفْ) أصله نظيفاً ذكره بالضاد المعجمة جرياً على اللغة الريفيّة وسكّنه لضرورة النظم أي ليس فيه شيء يدنّسه من أثر جلّة أو غبار يلحقه ونحو ذلك كما أنّهم إذا تعاطوا الحلب لا يتحاشوا عن مسك جلّة وغيرها من أنواع النجاسات بل ربّما أنّ دِرّة البقرة أو الجاموسة يلطّخوها جلّة فتحلب اللبن بسرعة فطلب الناظم أن يكون هذا السرسوب طيّباً نظيفاً خالي من هذه الأمور وإن كان معفوّاً عنها

١٣،٢٣،١١ ثمّ بيّن كيفيّة الأكل منه فقال

The most beneficial milk is that of ewes, and the finest is cow's milk, on the basis of the words of the Prophet, God bless him and give him peace, "You are enjoined to drink the milk of the cow, for its milk is a cure, its butter is a remedy, and its flesh is a disease"; and the finest of that is what is drunk straight from the udder or as it is milked. When mixed with sugar, it brings color to the body, purifies the complexion, eases the bowels, and increases sexual potency. *Libbih* is so called because it is derived from *lubb* ("intelligence"), or from *labwah* ("lioness; sexually voracious woman"). Or it may be from the expression "Someone *labbaka* ('struck you hard on the chest') with a drover's whip," for example, or from "The young kid *labba* ('butted') its mother" when it wanted to drink from her. The poet says: 11.23.10

You're like the kid when it nuzzles and like
The collared puppy in their haste for the milk.

ḥalbū ("one milking's-worth"): that is, the amount of a *ḥalb* ("a milking"), which is as much milk as it takes to fill a *miḥlāb* or a *maḥlabah* ("earthenware milk pitcher"), or it is derived from "the man milked (*ḥalaba*) with his hand"—being, in either case, a name for what is milked from an animal. The meaning is that there should be, on top of the aforementioned bread, enough milk, mixed with beestings and extracted by milking, to cover it with a portion of milk . . . 11.23.11

naḍīf ("that's clean"): the word is originally *naẓīfan*, but he gives it with *ḍ* in accordance with rural usage[441] and drops the *an* for the rhyme; that is, containing nothing in the way of traces of dung or adherent dust or the like that might sully it, since they feel no shame about touching dung and similar impurities while they are handling milk—on the contrary, sometimes they smear the cow or buffalo's udder with dung so that it gives milk faster. The poet therefore requests that this *sarsub* be good and clean and free of such things, even though he might be excused if it were not. 11.23.12

Next he explains how he will eat it. He says: 11.23.13

ص

وَأَقْعُدْ على رُكْبَهْ وَنُصّ وَٱشَمِّرْ عَنِ ٱلْكَفّ بِيَدِي مَا أَخَافُ مُخِيفْ ٢٤،١١

ش

قوله (وأَقْعُدْ) متأهّب للأكل من هذا الخبز بالسرسوب تأهُّب الجيعان الشديد الشهوة لهذا المأكول ١،٢٤،١١

(على رُكْبَهْ ونُصّ) وهي قعدة القويّ الشديد الّذي يريد الأكل الكثير أو الّذي عنده شَرَه في الطعام مثلاً وأمّا جلسة الأدب فإنّها بخلاف ذلك بأن يجلس على الركبتين ولا يلتفت يميناً ولا يساراً ويأكل ممّا يليه ولا يمدّ يده إلى طعام بعيد عنه مدّاً عنيفاً (كما اتّفق أنّ شخصاً قال لآخر وهما في وليمة يأكلان) يا فلان أقرّب لك هذا الصحن فقال أنا ايدي تجيب من مكّه ومدّ يده بعنف فضرط فقال له الرجل بلغ البياض في مكّه كام الكورجة فخجل وقام من غير أكل وللأكل آداب مذكورة في بعض الكتب وقوله ٢،٢٤،١١

(وَٱشَمِّرْ[١]) من التشمير وهو رفع كمّه ٣،٢٤،١١

(عن الكَفّ) أي كفّه يقال شمّر ذيله بمعنى رفعه عن النجاسة وشمّر عن ذَكَره أي أراد عطفة يبول فيها والتشمير المعنويّ هو الكفّ عن الذنوب قال الشاعر [بسيط] ٤،٢٤،١١

شمّرْ فَإِنَّكَ ماضي العَزْمِ شِمِّيرُ ولا يَهولُكَ أَحوالٌ وتَكديـرُ

---

١ بي: وَشَمَّرْ.

TEXT

wa-ʾaqʿud ʿalā rukbah wa-nuṣṣin wa-shammir 11.24
ʿani l-kaffi b-īdī mā ʾakhāfu mukhīf

And I'll sit with one knee crooked and roll up my sleeves
from my hand, with my hand, and fear no frightener.

COMMENTARY

11.24.1 *wa-ʾaqʿud* ("And I'll sit"): in preparation for the consumption of this bread with *sarsūb*, as does one who is hungry and seized by great appetite for the dish.

11.24.2 *ʿalā rukbah wa-nuṣṣin* ("with one knee crooked"):[442] this being the sitting posture of a strong, vigorous person who intends to eat a lot or who is ravenous for food, for example. The polite way of sitting, on the other hand, is quite different and consists of the person sitting with both his knees tucked beneath him, not looking to the right or the left, eating what is in front of him, and not stretching out his hand roughly to food that is far from him. As once it happened that one man said to another, as they were eating at a banquet, "So-and-so, may I move this dish closer to you?" and the other replied, "My hand can fetch from Mecca!" and he stretched his hand out roughly and let out an audible fart. The first man said to him, "And how much does a grab bag of catfish fetch in Mecca?" at which the other was overcome by embarrassment and got up and left without eating. It is a fact that eating has its own etiquette, which is described in a number of books.

11.24.3 *wa-shammir* ("and roll up my sleeves"): from *tashmīr*, which is the act of pulling the sleeve back.

11.24.4 *ʿani l-kaffi* ("from my hand"): that is, from his hand. One says, "He raised (*shammara*) the skirts of his robe," meaning he raised them out of the way of something filthy, and "He lifted his skirts to expose (*shammara ʿan*) his member," that is, he wanted to find a back alley in which to make water; used figuratively, *tashmīr* means "holding back" from sinful acts.[443] The poet[444] says:

Tuck up your robe, for you are resolute and bold,
And changing times and trouble cannot affright you!

لكنّ الناظم مراده التشمير الحسّي وهو رفع الأكمام ومنه الشِمار الّذي تصنعه أولاد الأرياف من الصوف ويضعوه في أكتافهم يرفعوا به أكمامهم وله هُدّاب سائل إلى كَفَل الأمرد وفيه نوع من الجمال وهو عندهم أمر عظيم حتّى أنّ بعض الأولاد يعمله ويجعل[1] فيه من الخزّ والحرير الأصفر والأحمر والأخضر والأسود حتّى يُرْغِب العاشق فيه وغالب أولاد الطبّالة به يجعلوه حكم أعقصة النساء ويجعلوا له عُقَداً صغاراً في رؤوس الهداديب ويزيّنوه بها وقوله

١١،٢٤،٥ (بايدي) أصله بيدي لا بيد غيري فلا أحتاج إلى أحد غيري يشمّر لي بل أنا أتعاطى تشميره بنفسي لأجل خلوص يدي عن شيء يمنعها من تناول الطعام وهذا يدلّ على أنّ كمّه كان طويلاً حتّى احتاج لتشميره أو أنّ مراده بالتشمير رفع يده وخفضها في حالة الأكل بسرعة وقوّة من غير التفات لأحد ولهذا قال

١١،٢٤،٦ (ما أخافُ) أي وآكل من هذا السرسوب ما أخاف من أحد يأتيني أو يمنعني عنه

١١،٢٤،٧ (مُخيفْ) أصله مخيفاً أي مخوِّفاً يمنعني عن شهوتي بل لا أبالي إذا حصل لي وظفرت به من أحد أبداً ولا يعتريني خوف ولا فزع حتّى أكتفي وأشبع منه الشبع المفرط ولا أختشي من تُخمة ولا غيرها

١١،٢٤،٨ ثمّ إنّه اشتاق مأكول آخر من ألذّ مأكول أهل الريف فقال

ص

١١،٢٥ عَلَى مَنْ قَشَعْ رُوحُو حِدَا ٱلرُّزِّ بِٱللَّبَنْ وَيَقْطَعْ وَيَبْلَعْ مِنْ تَقِيلْ وَخَفِيفْ

---

١ بي: ويلظم.

What our poet has in mind, however, is a physical raising, namely, the lifting up of the sleeves, which involves the use of the *shimār*,[445] which the boys of the countryside make from wool; they place it round their shoulders and raise their sleeves with it, and it has a fringe that hangs down to the buttocks of the beardless boy and has a kind of beauty. It is a matter of great importance to them, to the degree that some boys attach yellow, red, green, and black silk-wool and silk to it to make themselves attractive to their lovers. Most drummers' boys make them in imitation of women's braids, with little knots on the ends of the fringes to decorate them.

b-īdī ("with my hand"): originally *bi-yadī*;[446] with *my* hand and not with anyone else's, for I do not need anyone else to roll up my sleeves for me—on the contrary, I will take care of rolling them up myself in order to free my other hand of anything that might prevent it from taking food. This indicates that his sleeve was long, or he would not have needed to roll it up, and that what he wanted to achieve by rolling up his sleeves was the rapid and vigorous upward and downward motion of his hand while eating and paying attention to no one. This is why he says . . . **11.24.5**

mā ʾakhāfu ("and fear no"): that is, and eat of these beestings, having no fear that anyone will come to me or hold me back from it. **11.24.6**

mukhīf ("frightener"): originally *mukhīfan*, that is, no scarer will get between me and my appetite—on the contrary, I will have no cares at all if it reaches me and I manage to acquire it from anyone, and no fear or terror will seize me until I have had enough and sated myself with it to excess, nor will I fear indigestion or anything of that sort. **11.24.7**

Then he felt a yearning for another dish, one of the most delicious of those made by the people of the countryside. He says: **11.24.8**

TEXT

ʿalā man qashaʿ rūḥū ḥidā l-ruzzi bi-l-laban **11.25**
wa-yaqṭaʿ wa-yablaʿ min taqīl wa-khafīf

Happy is he who finds himself next to rice pudding
and cuts off pieces and swallows them, heavy and light!

ش

١،٢٥،١١ قوله (على من قَشَعْ روحو) أي على من نظر روحه أي ذاته لا ذات غيره

٢،٢٥،١١ (حِدا الرُزّ باللبَنْ) أي حذاءه بالذال المعجمة أي مُحاذِيَهُ بمعنى أنه جالس بجانبه والأرزّ باللبن هذا طعام لذيذ وهو غالب مأكول بلاد البحر لكثرته عندهم وكثرة الأرزّ أيضاً وهو حار رطب ينفع من احتراق المعدة وما ألذه وأطيبه إذا وضع عليه السمن البقريّ في وقت نزوله من على النار ويؤكل بالعجوة المَخَصيّة أيضاً إلّا أنه بالسمن أطيب وأشهى للأكل وكلّما كان لبنه كثيراً كان جيّداً وكلّما قلّ أرزّه كان أجود وأرداه الكثير من خلط الماء والأرزّ كما تفعله أهل الأرياف فإنّهم يجعلوه ثخيناً جدّاً يقطعوا منه اللقمة مثل ما يقطع الشخص من الطين اليابس وأمّا أبناء الترك فإنّهم يصنعوه باللبن الخالص من غير ماء ويجعلوا فيه شيئاً يسيراً من الأرزّ حكم الشرب ولهذا يشربوه بالملاعق فيصير حلواً لذيذاً وهذا النوع أجود طعامه وأطيبه وطبيخ اللبن على كلّ حال أطيب من العدس والبيسار وما شابههما قال الشاعر [طويل]

طَبيخ اللبَنْ أَحْسَنْ من الّي بكُزْبَرَهْ وأَلْعَدْسُ والبيسارْ يجيبوا الحوادرْ

٣،٢٥،١١ (وأمّا النوع الّذي تمنّاه الناظم) أن يكون بجانبه هو الّذي تقدّم ذكره وهو الثخين الّذي يشبه الطين في يبسه لأنّه المشهور عندهم وفي بلاده وأمّا بلاد البحر فيفعلوه حالة وسطى لا ثخين ولا مائع إلّا في الغالب يضعوا عليه شيئاً من الماء وأمّا الناظم فلا يعرف إلّا ما في بلده ولهذا قال

٤،٢٥،١١ (ويَقْطَعْ) والقطع لا يكون إلّا من الطعام اليابس أي يقطع بكفّه وقوله

٥،٢٥،١١ (ويَبْلَعْ) من البلع وهو جواز الأكل من الحلق يقال (فلان بلعه الحوت) بمعنى أنّه دخل جوفه ووصل إلى بطنه ومنه سميّت البلاّعة لأنها تبلع الماء في جوفه والقطع هو فصل

COMMENTARY

ʿalā man qashaʿ ("Happy is he who finds himself"): that is, sees himself, that is, his own person, not some other person's person . . . 11.25.1

ḥidā l-ruzzi bi-l-laban ("next to rice pudding"): that is, *hidā* is equivalent to *ḥidhāʾahu*, with *dh*,[447] that is, *muḥādhiyahu* ("adjacent to"), meaning that he is sitting next to it. This rice pudding is a delicious dish and is what they eat most of in the villages on the river, because there is so much milk and rice there. It is Hot and Moist and good for heartburn, and how delicious and tasty it is if clarified cow's butter is put on it as it is taken off the fire! It is eaten with pitted pressed dates, too, but is tastier and more appetizing with clarified butter. The more milk it has the better, and the less rice the better still. The worst sort is when a lot of water has been mixed with the rice, which is how the people of the countryside make it: they make it very thick and cut pieces off it as one would chunks of hard mud. People of Turkish descent make it with milk alone, without water, and add just a little rice, so that it is like a drink, which is why they eat it with spoons. This makes it sweet and delicious, and this kind is the best tasting and most appetizing. In general, milk dishes are more appetizing than lentils, *bīsār*, and the like. The poet says: 11.25.2

Dishes cooked with milk beat those with coriander,
And lentils and *bīsār* cause dropsy.

The kind the poet desires to be next to, however, is that mentioned above, namely, the thick sort that is as hard as a rock, for this is what is known to them and in his village. The villages on the river, on the other hand, make it halfway, neither thick nor runny, though they do usually add a little water. The poet, of course, knows only what is to be found in his village, which is why he says . . . 11.25.3

wa-yaqṭaʿ ("and cuts off pieces"): cutting can apply only to dry food; that is, he cuts off pieces with his hand 11.25.4

wa-yablaʿ ("and swallows"): from *balʿ*, meaning "swallowing," which is the passing of food down the throat; one says, "So-and-so was swallowed by the whale," meaning that he entered its insides and reached its belly. From the same one also gets *ballāʿah* ("drain"), because the latter "swallows" water inside itself. *Qaṭʿ* ("cutting") means the severing and separating of one thing 11.25.5

الشيء من الشيء وبعده عنه يقال (فلان قطع فلاناً) مدّة بمعنى أنّه هجره وبعد عنه وقوله

١١،٢٥،٦ (من تقيل) أي من قِطَع وافية عن اللُقَم المعتادة بحيث يكون قطعاً وافراً فتكون اللقمة ملأ الكف بحيث تُدْمِع العين من كبرها (كما ذكرتُ ذلك في خطبة) كنت ألّفتها سابقاً في المأكولات وهي هذه

١١،٢٥،٧ (الحمد لله) مستحقّ الحمد على التحقيق * الّذي وفّق بين الفَرَج والضيق * وأمرنا بالحجّ إلى بيته العتيق * وجعل السمن البقريّ للعسل النحل رفيق * أحمده حمد من عنده من الجوع دسيسه * وأغاثه الله بقصعة من البسيسه * بالفطير الرقيق فملأ منها بطنه * وأحسن بالله ظنّه * ونام على راحة من الله وتوفيق * وأشكره شكر عبد تقلّع عن الحوامض والمشّ العتيق * وأشهد أنّ لا إله إلّا الله وحده لا شريك له شهادة تنجي قائلها من الضيق * وأشهد أنّ سيّدنا محمّداً صلّى الله عليه وسلّم عبده ورسوله الناطق بالحقّ والموصوف بالصدق والتصديق * وعلى آله وأصحابه أهل الكشف والتحقيق * وسلّم تسليماً كثيراً

١١،٢٥،٨ أيّها الناس مالي أراكم عن الزَرْدة بالعسل النحل غافلون * وعن الأرزّ المفلفل باللحم الضاني تاركون * وعن البقلاوة في الصواني مُعْرِضون * وعن الإوزّ السمين والدجاج المحمّر لاهون * فما هذا يا إخواني إلّا أحوالَ المُفْلِسون * وأفعال الفقراء المِقْلّون * فجِدّوا رحمكم الله في تحصيل الدراهم لتغتنموا المآكل النفيسه * والمطاعم اللذيذه * فقد قال الإمام سيّدنا عليّ كرّم الله وجهه صاحب العلم والفهم لذّة الدنيا ثلاث أكل اللحم وركوب اللحم وإدخال اللحم في اللحم فمن أنعم الله عليه فليشكر * ومن أحرمه فليصبر *

١١،٢٥،٩ وعليكم بالأرزّ باللبن * فإنّه طعام جيّد حسن * وصباحه أبرك الصباح * خصوصاً عند الفلّاح * إذا جاء وحلب بقرتُهْ * وأتت زوجته بالدست وعلّقتُهْ * وصبّت فيه اللبن وقادت عليه وحرّكتُهْ * وبالأرزّ الأبيض طبّختُهْ * وفي الصحون

from another; one says, "So-and-so 'cut' So-and-so" for a while, meaning that he shunned him and kept his distance from him.

11.25.6 *min taqīl* ("heavy"): that is, pieces larger than the normal mouthful, meaning that this would be a major cutting, meaning that the mouthful would fill the hand and be big enough to make the eyes water. I made reference to this in a sermon on different dishes I composed a while ago, which goes as follows:[448]

> 11.25.7 Praise be to God, to whom for sure all praise is owed, who hands out ease and care in measured load, who has adjured us to be pilgrims to His Ancient House,[449] and who has made honey companion to the ghee of cows! Him I praise as one by hunger waylaid, whom God with a basin of *basīsah* (made with fine pastry) saved, one who thereon ate his fill, and thought of Him with no ill will but slept in God-given ease and reconciliation. And Him I thank as a mortal slave who has made renunciation of all things sour plus cheese well aged after fermentation, bearing witness that there is no god but God alone, companionless—testimony that spares its maker deprivation! And I bear witness that our Master and Prophet Muḥammad, God bless him and grant him peace, is His slave and messenger, speaker of sooth, endowed with truth and approbation! God, bless and grant peace and benison to Our Master Muḥammad, his Kith and Companions, the people of disclosure and confirmation, and make this blessing abundant!
>
> 11.25.8 Good people, why do I behold you of sweet rice with honey all unaware? Showing for fluffy rice with mutton never a care? Baklava on its platters shunning? From fat geese and roasted chickens running? What are these, my brethren, but the doings of the indigent and the deeds of the financially incontinent? Apply yourselves then, God have mercy upon you, to acquiring cash that you may carry off dishes precious and victuals delicious! Our Master, the Imam ʿAlī, master of knowledge and understanding, God honor his visage, has said[450] that the joys of this world are three: the eating of flesh, the riding of flesh, and the insertion of flesh into flesh. So he to whom God has given much, let him be thankful, and he to whom God has given little, let him be stoical.
>
> 11.25.9 To eat rice pudding you are commanded, for it is a dish both excellent and commended, and the day that starts with it is the most blessed day, to the peasant especially—when he goes to his cow and milks it, and his wife brings the basin and hangs it, and pours the milk in and lights a fire beneath

غرفتُهُ * وجاء الشيخ الكبير وقعد وثنى ركبتُهُ * فعند ذلك يا إخواني * انصفّت الأواني * ولاذ كلّ إنسان بإنسانٍ * فلا ترى إلّا أيادي تقطع * وألسنة تبلع * وزراديم تفرقع * وحلق يتقلقع * والعين من كبر اللقمة تَدْمَع * والبطن من شدّة الوجد تتّسع * بل تزيد افتعالاً * وهي تقول جلّ ربّنا وتعالى * إن سبقك أخوك المؤمن بلُقمه * فبادر على جدع رقبته بلَكْمه * واغتنموا رحمكم الله هذه المَوْعِظه * ودعوا المآكل المغلّظه * كالعدس والبيسار * والمدمّس والفول الحار * والبسلّة والكشك بالفول * وجبن التنُّور المعمول * فإنّهم يورثوا الأرياح * وليس في أكلهم صلاح *

١٠،٢٥،١١ وعليكم بالأطعمة الفاخره * كاللحم الضاني فإنّه سيّد طعام الدنيا والآخره * وعليكم بالشراب الحلو البارد * ففيه حديث عن النبيّ صلّى الله عليه وسلّم وارد * واحمدوا الله أيّها الأغنياء المتنعّمون * واصبروا أيّها الفقراء المقلّون * نسأل الله أن يمنّ علينا وعليكم بالأطعمة الفاخره * ويرزقنا وإيّاكم الراحة في الدنيا والآخره * وأن يجعلنا وإيّاكم من الآكلين المتنعّمين * ويجنّبنا وإيّاكم موارد الجيعانين المقلّين * وأن يغفر لنا ولكم ولجميع المسلمين * آمين * ﴿فَٱسْتَغْفِرُوهُ﴾ يغفر لكم فيا فوز المستغفرين *

١١،٢٥،١١ (رُوِيَ) عن سهلب * بن مهلب * عن زنطاح * بن النطّاح * بن قليل الأفراح * أنّه قال كان رجل من العرب قام من منامه ولذيذ أحلامه وأكل في فطوره فصيلاً ابن عامين وصبر إلى ضحوة النهار فأكل أربعين دجاجة محشيّة باللحم الضاني محمّرة بالسمن البقريّ وشرب زِقّين من الخمر ونام في الشمس فمات ولقي الله شبعان سكران ريّان

١٢،٢٥،١١ (الحمد لله) مزيل الحزن * ومزين الأرزّ باللبن * وأشهد أنّ اللحم الضاني سيّد الأطعمة ومُصلِح للبدن * واعلموا أنّ القشطة لا تُترَك * وأنّ المَهَلَّبيّة أحسن وأبرك * فتهيّأوا لأكلكم وشربكم واعلموا أنّكم غداً بين يدي الله موقوفون * وبأعمالكم محاسَبون * وعلى ربّ العزّة تُعرَضون * وسيعلم الّذين جاعوا ﴿أَيَّ مُنقَلَبٍ يَنقَلِبُونَ﴾ * اللّهمّ وارض عن

and stirs it with white rice, and cooks it, and into dishes spoons it, and the aged shaykh comes and crooks one leg and sits upon it—at this, my brother, the vessels are set out next to one another, and each man draws close to the other, and nothing can be seen but hands tearing and tongues at work, epiglottises jumping and throats a-jerk. Eyes water at the size of the bite, and the belly from excess of passion grows ever less tight; nay, it gets ever more flighty, exclaiming, "Glory to Our Lord, the Almighty!" If your brother Muslim beats you to a munch, knock his head off with a punch! And seize, God have mercy on you, upon this edifying discourse, and have nothing to do with foods that are coarse, such as lentils and *bīsār* (which is beans with mallow brought to a boil), or stewed beans and beans with linseed oil, or groats with beans and peas, and stuffed oven-cheese—all these cause gas, and eating them is truly crass.

Next, to the use of sumptuous foods, such as Mutton, you are bidden, for **11.25.10** he is Lord of Foods[451] in This World and the Hidden, and to drinks that are sweet and cold, for of these a Tradition from the Prophet (God bless him and give him peace) is told, and praise God, you who are rich and blessed, and be patient, you who are poor and hard-pressed! We beseech God to bestow upon us all such sumptuous foods and provide us all with ease both before and after our decease, and to number us all among the blessed, and save us all from the haunts of the ravenous hard-pressed, and forgive our sins and yours and those of all who Islam have professed. Amen. «Seek forgiveness of Him»[452] and He will grant you forgiveness, and how great is the triumph of those who seek forgiveness!

It is related on the authority of Sahlab, who had it from Mahlab, who had **11.25.11** it from Zinṭāḥ, son of Naṭṭāḥ, son of Qalīl al-Afrāḥ,[453] that he said, "A certain Bedouin arose from his slumbers and sweet dreams and ate a two-year-old camel for breakfast, then endured till the middle of the day, ate forty chickens stuffed with mutton and roasted in clarified ghee, drank two skins of wine, went to sleep in the sun, and died, thus meeting his Maker sated, intoxicated, and irrigated!"

Praise be to God, embellisher of rice with milk and dispeller of grief! **11.25.12** I bear witness that Mutton is Lord of Foods and the body's relief! And know that clotted cream is not something to shun or of which to be suspicious, and that blancmange is better still and even more auspicious! Prepare yourselves, then, to eat and drink, knowing that soon in God's sight you'll stand and that

الأربعة الأعيان * الّذين ذكرهم الله تعالى في القرآن * التين والزيتون والخوخ والرمان * وارض عن الستة الباقين من العشره * الأطعمة المفتخره * الماوَرديّة والمهلّبيّه * والشّعيريّة بالزغاليل المربّيه * والأرزّ المفلفل باللحم الضاني المحشيّ المحمّر * والكُنافة المتبّلة بالسمن والعسل النحل والسكّر * والقطايف الغارقة بالسمن والعسل * والقَرْع المحشيّ باللحم والبصل * والبقلاوة الموصوفه * وخرفان القمـمة المعلوفه * والبخني والقِرمِزيّة باللحم السمين * متّعنا الله وإيّاكم بهم أجمعين *

١١،٢٥،١٣ اللهمّ وأَدِمْ النصر والتأييد والثبات * ولمّ الشمل بعد الشتات * ببقاء السلطان السكّر النبات * ابن القنانيّ * مَنْ أصله من القصب الملّوانيّ * اللّهمّ وأيّده بأرماح القصب * وبسبائط الرُطَب * وبعناقيد العنب * وأجمعنا عليه من أوّل النهار وفي وسطه وآخرُهْ * وأنصر عساكُرهْ * في الدنيا تنتفع به يا ربّ العالمين واهلك اللّهمّ الثلاثة الفُجّار * العدس والبسلّة والبيسار * عبادَ الله من أراد خِلَع القبول أن تَفاضَ عليه * فليأكل الموز بين والديه * وتفكّهوا قبل الطعام * واقتدوا بسُنّة خير الأنام * ولا تتضاربون ولا تتخابطون وكونوا عبادَ الله إخوانًا إنّ الله يأمركم بأكل الحلال ممّا تشتهي العقول * وينهى عن أكل الحرام ولو من أطيب المأكول * ﴿وَٱلْبَغْيِ يَعِظُكُمْ لَعَلَّكُمْ تَذَكَّرُونَ﴾ * وقوله

١١،٢٥،١٤ (وخَفيفٌ) أي ويأكل من خفيف اللقم وكبيرها ليحصل التعادل ولا يغترّ بقول من قال [طويل]

كُلوا أَكْلَةً مَن عاشَ يُخْبِرُ أَهْلَهُ   وَمَن ماتَ يَلقَى اللهَ وَهْوَ بَطِينُ

١١،٢٥،١٥ (فسبيل الإنسان) أن يجعل البطن ثلاثة أثلاث ثلث للأكل وثلث للشرب وثلث للنفس فلا يفرط في الأكل ولا يفرط في الجوع كما قال صاحب البردة رحمه الله [بسيط]

by your works you'll be saved or damned, and that the Lord of Might will soon review what you have earned, and that those who went hungry will come to know «by what a great reverse they have been overturned.»[454] Be pleased, O God, with the four leaders great,[455] by the Almighty in the Qur'an designate—the fig, the olive, the peach, and the pomegranate![456] And be pleased, O God, with those that remain of the ten,[457] in number six, of foods deluxe, namely, blancmange and rosewater jelly, and fattened squabs with vermicelli, and fluffy rice stuffed with mutton and fried, and bee's honey, almonds, sugar, and *kunāfah* drenched in butter clarified, and little pancakes that in syrup and butter swim, and squash that's stuffed with meat and onions to the brim, as well as the baklava earlier described, and stall-fed sheep, and hot-pot and *qirmiziyyah*[458] with fatty meat—may God bestow them on us all to eat!

O God, bring us, after dispersal, all together, and grant victory, support, and safety to Sultan Sugar-Candy, may he rule for ever—son of Flagon, Mallawī sugar's noble scion! Aid him, O God, with sugarcane spears and thrusters, and sticky dates and grapes in clusters! And unite us with him at day's beginning, middle, and end, and to him and to his soldiers victory send, that we may benefit from him in This World, O Lord of All. And destroy, O God, the reprobates three, namely, *bīsār*, lentils, and the pea! Slaves of God, whoever wishes to wrap himself in the robes of God's pleasance, let him eat bananas in his parents' presence! Before eating, unwind, and follow the example of the Best of Mankind.[459] Neither fight one another nor fall to blows, O Slaves of God, but brethren be! God commands you to eat of what your minds desire only what His religion declares to be good and forbids you to eat what is forbidden, though it be the tastiest of food, and forbids you «wickedness. He exhorteth you that you may reflect!»[460] 11.25.13

wa-khafīf ("and light"): that is, and he will eat light mouthfuls as well as large ones, to achieve a just balance and not be misled by the words of the poet[461] who said: 11.25.14

Eat hearty! If you survive, you can tell your folks,
And if you die, you'll meet your God with your stomach full!

One should divide his stomach into three equal parts: one third for food, one third for drink, and one third for appetite; on this basis he will neither eat excessively, nor hunger excessively. As the author of *The Mantle*,[462] God have mercy on his soul, says:[463] 11.25.15

واخشَ الدَّسائِسَ مِنْ جُوعٍ ومِن شِبَعٍ   فرُبَّ مَخْمَصةٍ شرٌّ من التُخَمِ

ثمّ إنّ الناظم انتقل إلى نوع من الأُدْم قد تمنّاه فقال ١٦،٢٥،١١

ص

عَلَى مَنْ مَلاَ قَحْفُو جُبَيْنَهْ طَرِيّهْ   وَرَاحَ وَرَا ٱلْجَامُوسِ يَرْعَى ٱلنِّيفْ ٢٦،١١

ش

قوله (على من ملا قَحْفو) القَحْف شيء طويل يعمل من الصوف أو الشعر يلبس على الرأس وليس له زيّ ولا هِندام تستعمله بعض الفقراء وغالب الخلابيص ويلبسوا شيئاً يشبهه يقال له الطرطور ويختلف عنه القحف بكونه واسع من جهة الرأس وضيّق من أعلاه قصير عن الطرطور وكان استعمال ذاك في سابق الزمان كثيرًا واستعمال اللِبَد على أصناف شيء يشبه القحف وشيء يشبه البرانيط والآن طائفة تلبس هذه اللبد الّتي تشبه البرانيط وهم صلحاء متصوّفون ثمّ ظهرت القواويق القطيفة وصار لها بهجة ورونق وأُنس وظَرْف فبطل لبس اللبد وغيرها وصار لا يلبسها إلّا بعض الفقراء المتصوّفين المتقشّفين ولهذا يقال اخفي يا فلان خِفّوة اللبد ومن هذا قيل في تركها كلام كثير منه (يا لبده مالك في السوق يا لبده إلّا خازوق) (وسمّي) قحفاً لقحافته ويبسه ولهذا يشبَّه به الرجل السيّء الخُلُق فيقال هذا قحف أي سيء الطبائع قال الشاعر [كامل] ١،٢٦،١١

إنَّ اللَّطافَةَ لَمْ تَزَلْ   بينَ الأَكابِرِ فاشِيَهْ
فَهَل رَأَيتُم في الوَرَى   قَحْفًا رَقِيقَ الحاشِيَهْ

And fear hunger's traps as those of satiety,
For an empty stomach may be worse than dyspepsia!

Next, the poet moves on to a kind of condiment that he felt a longing for. **11.25.16**
He says:

TEXT

ʿalā man malā qaḥfū jubaynah ṭariyyah **11.26**
wa-rāḥa warā l-jāmūsi yarʿā l-nīf

Happy is he who fills his cap with a moist little cheese
and goes behind the buffaloes to graze on *nīf*!

COMMENTARY

11.26.1 *ʿalā man malā qaḥfū* ("Happy is he who fills his cap"): the *qaḥf* ("cap") is a tall thing made of wool or hair that is worn on the head and lacks both elegance and style. Some dervishes and most buffoons use it. They also wear another thing that resembles it, called the *ṭurṭūr*,[464] from which the *qaḥf* differs in being wide where it meets the head and narrow at the top,[465] and in being shorter than the *ṭurṭūr*. The *ṭurṭūr* was much used in the past. Felt caps (*libdah*, plural *libad*) are used in a number of ways: some resemble the *qaḥf*, and some the European hat; nowadays there is a sect that wears the *libdah*s that resemble European hats—they are righteous people, Sufis. Subsequently the velvet *qāwūq*[466] made its appearance, and came to be seen as chic and glamorous, appealing and sophisticated, and the wearing of the *libdah* and other similar hats was abandoned, the only people continuing to wear them being certain shabbily ascetic Sufi dervishes. This is why they say, "Hey you, go to hell like the *libad*!" Much has been said about their fall from favor, including the saying, "*Libdah*, if to market you come, all you'll get is a spike up your bum!"[467] It is called a *qaḥf* because of its coarseness (*qaḥāfah*) and stiffness, which is why a man of bad character is likened to it, and one says, "He's a *qaḥf*," that is, evil-natured. The poet says on this topic:

Refinement is ever among the great diffused,
But did you ever see a *qaḥf* of polished views?

٢،٢٦،١١ وهو مشتقّ من قحف الحوت أو من أنّ الرجل الذي صنعه أوّلاً كان من قُحافة وهي قرية معروفة موقوفة على سيّدي أحمد البدويّ نفعنا الله به وقوله

٣،٢٦،١١ ‹جُبَيْنَهْ› تصغير جبنة على وزن أُبَنة وهي واحدة الجبن

٤،٢٦،١١ ‹طَرِيَّهْ› أي كما عُمِلَتْ قبل يبسها أي في وقت نزولها من على الحصير الّتي يعملوا فيها الجبن فاشتهى أنّ الله يمنّ عليه بملأ قحفه جبناً طريّاً ولو كان هديّة أو صدقة تصدّق به عليه أحد أو سرقة فإنّ الرزق ما ينفع ولو حراماً قال صاحب الزُبَد رحمه الله والرزق ما ينفع لو محرّماً وقال أبو نواس رحمه الله [وافر]

يَقولُ لِيَ العَذولُ وَليسَ يَدري   دَعِ المالَ الحَرامَ وكُنْ قَنوُعا
إِذا أَنا لَمْ أَجِدْ مالاً حَلالاً   ولَمْ آكُلْ حَرامًا مُتُّ جُوعا

٥،٢٦،١١ ‹فإن قيل› لأيّ شيء تمنّى الناظم ملأ قحفه من الجبن مع أنّ القحف لا يعدّ لشيل الجبن فيه وخصوصاً وقد قال جبينه طريّه فإذا وضعه في قحفه ففيه ضرر من وجهين الأوّل أن يحصل لقحفه التقذير من جهة الجبن والثاني ماء الجبن يبلّ قحفه ويشوّش عليه ‹قلنا الجواب الفشرويّ› من وجوه إمّا أنّه تمنّى شيئاً من الجبن بحيث لو وضع في قحفه لملأه لكون قحفه كبيرًا طويلاً حتّى يكفيه للأدم بقيّة الجمعة أو الشهر لكونه مفتقرًا لذلك ومحتاج إليه بخلاف ما إذا أتاه شيئاً يسيرًا لا يكفيه ولا يقوم بأولاده أو أنّ الكلام على حقيقته وأنّ أهل الريف إذا أعطاهم أحد شيئاً من مأكول أو غيره يأخذوه في أطراف بردهم وأرديتهم وفي أكمامهم وعلى شدودهم الّتي على رؤوسهم وكانوا في الزمن السابق يضعوا الشيء في قحوفهم فإنّهم في الغالب كانوا يضعوها على رؤوسهم من غير شيء يلفوه حولها فكان الشخص منهم إذا أخذ شيئاً من السوق

The word is derived from the *qaḥf* ("head") of a fish or from the fact that the man who first fashioned such caps was from Quḥāfah, which is a well-known village held as an endowment for the benefit of Master Aḥmad al-Badawī, God benefit us through him. 11.26.2

jubaynah ("with a moist little cheese"): *jubaynah* is the diminutive of *jubnah* ("piece of cheese"), of the measure of *ubnah* ("passive sodomy"), and is the unit noun from *jubn* ("cheese"). 11.26.3

ṭariyyah ("moist"): that is, as it was made and before it got hard, that is, at the moment of its removal from the reed strainer in which they make the cheese. He fantasizes that God will bestow on him enough moist cheese to fill his cap, even if he acquire it as a gift, or as alms given him by someone else, or by theft—for one's God-given means of subsistence are whatever one is sustained by, even if it be ill-gotten. The author of *The Most Pleasing Portions*,[468] God have mercy on his soul, says, "One's God-given means of subsistence is whatever provides sustenance, even if it be something forbidden," etc., and Abū Nuwās,[469] God have mercy on his soul, says: 11.26.4

"Leave ill-gotten gain and pull your belt still tighter!"
So my critics (but what do they know?) said,
But if I find no gains well-gotten,
And eat nothing forbidden, I'll just drop dead!

If it be said, "Why does the poet want to fill his cap with cheese, when a cap is not designed for carrying cheese; especially given that he says 'moist cheese,' which means that, were he to put it in his cap, the latter would suffer in two ways, the first being that the cheese would soil the cap, the second that the liquid from the cheese would soak, and thus spoil, it?" we respond that a facetious answer may be given from various angles. On the one hand it may be that he wants enough cheese that, were it to be placed in his cap, it would fill it, his cap being large and tall, so as to provide him with something to eat with his bread for the rest of the week, or of the month, because he lacks any such and is in need of it; while in contrast if he got only a little, it would not suffice him or take care of his children. Or it may be that what he says should be taken literally, because, if one gives country people food or anything else, they take it in the skirts of their cloaks or robes, and in their sleeves, and in the turban cloths that are on their heads, and in the past they used to place it in their caps, 11.26.5

ولم يكن معه مَقْطَف أو صحن مثلاً يضعه في قحفه وأمّا تلويث القحف وتقذيره فالناظم كان لا يبالي بهذا الأمر فإنّ غاية قحفه كان يساوي نصفاً أو نصفين ومن كثرة استعماله وتداول الأيّام عليه وطروء العرق والحال الّذي هو فيه يبس وصار مثل الخشب فصار لا يؤثّر فيه رطوبة الجبن ولا غيرها فينزل الكلام على حقيقته فاتّضح الإشكال عن هذا الهبال وقوله

١١،٢٦،٦ (وراحَ) أي وسار وهو مشتقّ من الرَوحَاء وهو محلّ بأرض الحجاز أو من الراحة أو من الريح أو من أبي رِياح الّذي يُصْنَع على غابة طويلة وهو أربع ورقات ملصوقة على أربع قطع من الغاب تلعب به الأولاد الصغار مشهور في بلاد المدن وغيرها وقوله

١١،٢٦،٧ (ورا) أي خلف

١١،٢٦،٨ (الجاموسِ) نوع من البقر فإنّ اسم البقر يشمل الجاموس وغيره وهو كبير ضخم غليظ الجلد أسود وسمّي البقر بقراً لأنّه يَبْقُر الأرض أي يشقّها وواحدته بقرة وأهل الريف يعايرون الولد الأمرد بذلك ويقولون له أنت بقرة يعني ياكثير الخنات

١١،٢٦،٩ (مسألة هباليّة) لأيّ شيء لم يقولوا للولد الأمرد يا جاموسه مثلاً مع أنّها في حكم البقرة مع أنّ الفحل يطلع عليها ويضربها فهي في هذا الأمر مثل البقرة من غير خصوصيّة لذلك (قلنا الجواب الفشرويّ) من وجوه (الأوّل) أنّ الجاموس داخل تحت اسم البقر كما تقدّم بيانه فصار شاملاً للنوعين (والوجه الثاني) أنّ لفظة جاموسة مركّبة من اسم وفعل فإذا قال الشخص للولد الأمرد أنت يا جاموسه ربّما يفهم منه أنت يا ولد جاء رجل اسمه موسى مثلاً فكأنّه يستفهم منه فتندفع المَعْيَرة عن الولد الأمرد ولا

for they would generally wear these on their heads without anything wrapped around them; so if one of them got something from the market and had no basket or plate, for example, he would put it in his cap. As for the soiling and dirtying of his cap, the poet would pay no heed to such a thing, for his cap would have cost at most one or two *nuṣṣ*, and with his constant use of it and the passage of time and its getting soaked in sweat and its general condition, it would have turned as hard as wood, and neither the moisture of the cheese nor anything else could make any difference to it. Thus his words turn out to be literally true, and the problem's now revealed, its silliness no more concealed.

wa-rāḥa ("and goes"): that is, and proceeds, *rāḥa* being derived from *al-Rawḥāʾ*, a place in the Hijaz, or from *rāḥah* ("rest, ease; palm of the hand"), or from *rīḥ* ("wind"), or from the *abū riyāḥ* (literally "father of winds, wind thing") that is made on a long cane and which consists of four blades stuck onto four pieces of cane; small children play with it and it is well known in the cities and elsewhere. **11.26.6**

warā ("behind"): that is, following . . . **11.26.7**

(a)l-jāmūsi ("the buffaloes"): a sort of cattle, for the word "cattle" (*baqar*) encompasses the buffalo and other sorts; it is enormously large and has a thick black hide. Cattle are called *baqar* because they "cut open" (*yabquru*), that is, furrow,[470] the earth; the unit noun is *baqarah* ("cow"). The country people use the word as a term of abuse for a beardless boy, saying, for example, "You're a cow!" meaning "How effeminate you are!" **11.26.8**

A Silly Topic for Debate. "Why don't they say to a beardless boy, 'You she-buffalo! (*yā jāmūsah*)' for example, when the latter is analogous to the ordinary cow in that the bull buffalo mounts her and serves her, the she-buffalo thus resembling the cow in this respect, with nothing to distinguish her?" We respond that the facetious answer may be from any of various points of view. The first is that the buffalo is covered under the name "cattle," as explained above, so that the same name embraces both species. The second point of view is that the term *jāmūsah* is a compound formed of a proper name and a verb. Thus, should someone say to a beardless boy *anta yā jāmūsah* ("Hey there, you buffalo-cow!"), it might be understood, for example, as "Hey there, boy! Has a man called Mūsā come (*jā(ʾ) . . . Mūsā*)?" as though he were questioning him about him, in which case the calumny would be deflected from the boy, **11.26.9**

يتوهّم ذلك كما يُلغَز ويقال امرأة ولدت جاموسه أي وقت ولادتها جاء رجل يقال له موسى (الوجه الثالث) أنّ اسم الجاموس مشتقّ من التجميس وهو التحسيس يقال فلان يجمّس في الظلام بمعنى أنّه يحسّس على شيء يأخذه واسم البقر مشتقّ من بَقَرَ الأرض أي شَقّها بالمحراث فكان مثل وضع الذكَر في الكُسّ مثلاً لأنّه يشقّه أي يدخل فيه ومثله الأمرد فإنّه يُدخَل الزب في استه مثلاً فكان مشبّهاً بالفعل وأمّا التجميس فهو مشبّه بمقدّماته والفعل أقوى لأنّ التحسيس والتقبيل زرع والنيك حصاده فكان النيك أبلغ من التحسيس فلهذا صار يعاير بذلك ويقال له يا بقره فاتّضح الإشكال عن وجه هذا الهبال وقوله

(يَرعى النِيفْ) أي يسوق الجاموس لأجل ما يرعى لا أنّه هو يرعى بنفسه وإنّما الرعي ١٠،٢٦،١١
راجع للجاموس أي إنّه يسوق الجاموس إلى المحلّ الّذي ينبت فيه الحشيش المسمّى بالنيف وهو يرعى أي يأكل يقال (الجاموس أو البقر بيرعى في المحلّ الفلانيّ) بمعنى أنّه يأكل منه وأمّا قولهم للّذي يسوقه ويتعهّد مصالحه من حلبه وسوقه وربطه في الغيط ومباشرته وحراسته ونحو ذلك راعي لأنّه من ملازمه وتحت كَنَفه فعليه أن يراعيه بالشفقة عليه والرحمة به وفي الحديث كلّكم راع وكلّ راع مسؤول عن رعيّته أي يوم القيامة يُسأَل عمّن هو من لوازمه من حيوان وغيره والنيف حشيش ينبت في الأرض بنفسه من آثار نزول المياه على الأرض وأكثره في الأراضي الّتي لا تزرع وهو مشتقّ من النِيفة الّتي تعمل في بلاد المدن وهو لحم يُشْوى في التنّور ويؤكل وله لذّة عظيمة أو من النُوف الّتي توضع على رقاب الثيران وقت استعمالهم في الساقية أو المحراث وذكر الجبن ولم يذكر الخبز والظاهر أنّه كان موجوداً عنده ومضى عليه مدّة

and he would have no idea what was meant. Similarly, there is a riddle that says *imra'atun waladat jāmūsah* ("A woman gave birth to a buffalo"), that is, at the time of her giving birth came a man called Mūsā (*jā(')* . . . *Mūsā*). The third point of view is that the name *jāmūs* is derived from *tajmīs*, which means "groping around, feeling with the hand, etc." (*taḥsīs*). One says, "So-and-so is groping around (*yujammisu*) in the dark," meaning that he is feeling about (*yuḥassisu*) for something to take hold of. The name *baqar* ("cattle") is derived from *baqara* ("to cut open") the earth, that is, to furrow it with the plow, from which perspective it resembles the placing of the penis in the cunt, for example, since the former "furrows," that is, enters, the latter, and the same is true of the beardless boy, for the prick is inserted into his anus, for example. Thus, it is as though an analogy were drawn between the verb *baqara* and the associated term of abuse to a boy and the act itself, while *tajmīs* ("groping") would be analogous to the preliminaries. The verb, of course, is stronger than the noun, as witness the fact that groping and kissing are like sowing, while fucking is reaping, implying that fucking is stronger than groping, which is why they abuse the beardless boy with the former and say to him, "You cow (*yā baqarah*)!"[471] The problem's now revealed, its silliness no more concealed.

yarʿā l-nīf ("to graze on *nīf*"): that is, he drives the buffaloes so that *they* may **11.26.10**
graze, not so that he may graze, the verb "to graze" referring to the buffaloes; that is, he drives the buffaloes to the place where the plant called *nīf* grows, and they graze, that is, eat. One says "The buffaloes or the cattle are grazing (*bi-yarʿā*) in such and such a place," meaning they are eating there. The word they use for the person who drives them and takes care of their needs by way of milking, driving, tethering in the field, tending, guarding, and so on, is *rāʿī* ("herder") because he stays with them all the time and they are under his wing; he must therefore look after them (*yurāʿīhim*) with kindness and compassion. In the Tradition it says, "Every one of you is a shepherd, and every shepherd shall be questioned about his flock," that is, on the Day of Resurrection everyone will be asked concerning those under his charge, be they animals or anything else. *Nīf* is a plant that sprouts on its own in the earth, a consequence of the descent of waters thereon, and is found mostly in uncultivated lands. It is derived from the *nīfah* that is made in the cities, which consists of meat grilled in a clay oven and eaten, and is very delicious, or from the *nūf* ("yoke") that is placed on the necks of oxen when they are being used for the waterwheel or the plow.

وهو يأكل منه من غير أُدْم فاشتهى ملأ قحفه جبناً لأجل ما يكفيه مدّة من الزمان

١١،٢٦،١١ ثمّ انتقل لتمنّي شيء آخر من الأطعمة الّتي تفعل اشتهاء عند أهل الريف وغيرهم فقال

ص

٢٧،١١ عَلَى مَنْ قَشَعْ لَقَّانَة ٱمُّو مَلَانَهْ   مِنَ ٱلْهَيْطَلِيَّه ٱلّي لِهَا تَرْصِيفْ

ش

١،٢٧،١١ قوله (على من قَشَعْ) أي نظر نظرًا حقيقيًا

٢،٢٧،١١ (لَقّانة ٱمّو) أو زوجة أبيه أيضاً واللقّانة تأنيث اللقّان على وزن الخِرْفان ويقال لها القَصْرِيّة أيضاً وهي إناء من الفخّار متّسع دون الماجور وفوق الشالية سمّيت لقّانة لأنّ الشخص إذا أراد أن يشرب منها يَلُقّ بلسانه أو بفمه الماء لأنّه لا يقدر على حملها أو أنّ الّذي صنعها في الأصل من لقّانة قرية مشهورة أنتج الله منها علماء أجلاّء وفضلهم مشهور وينتفع الناس بعلومهم إلى يوم القيامة نفعنا الله ببركاتهم وإضافة اللقّانة إلى أمّه لكونها كانت لها ولم يكن يعرف غيرها ولا له شيء سواها فتمنّى رؤيتها بحيث أنّها تكون

٣،٢٧،١١ (ملانَهْ) لا ناقصة وسهّل الهمزة لضرورة النظم ثمّ بيّن الشيء الّذي تمنّاه فقال

٤،٢٧،١١ (من الهَيْطَلِيّه) وهي طعام يُعْمَل من نشاء القمح واللبن ولها لذّة عظيمة في المأكل وهي أخفّ من الأرزّ باللبن خصوصاً إذا أضيف إليها العسل لأنّ النشاء بارد يابس

He mentions cheese but not bread, and it appears that he had some with him, which he had been eating for a while with nothing to go with it. Consequently, he fantasizes about filling his cap with enough cheese to last him a good while.

Next, he proceeds to yearn for another dish that the country people, and others, love to eat. He says: **11.26.11**

TEXT

ʿalā man qashaʿ laqqānata-mmū malānah **11.27**
mina l-hayṭaliyya-llī lahā tarṣīf

Happy is he who sees his mother's bowl full
of *hayṭaliyyah* that gleams

COMMENTARY

ʿalā man qashaʿ ("Happy is he who sees"): that is, sees in reality and not figuratively . . . **11.27.1**

laqqānata-mmū ("his mother's bowl"): or, equally, that of his father's wife; *laqqānah*[472] is the feminine form of *laqqān*,[473] of the measure of *khirfān* ("sheep"), and is also called *qaṣriyyah*. It is a vessel made of earthenware that holds less than a kneading bowl and more than a middle-sized milk crock. It is called a *laqqānah* because, if one wants to drink from it, he has to lap up (*yaluqqu*) the water with his tongue or his mouth, because it is too heavy for him to lift;[474] or because the first person to make one was from Laqqānah, a famous village from which God has produced outstanding scholars who are celebrated for their virtues and from whose learning the people will continue to derive benefit to the Day of Resurrection, may God benefit us through their blessings! He designates the *laqqānah* as belonging to his mother because it was hers and the only one he knew and he had nothing else. Then he desired to see it . . . **11.27.2**

malānah ("full"): not short-measured. He drops the glottal stop for the meter.[475] Then he specifies the thing that he desires, and says . . . **11.27.3**

min al-hayṭaliyyah ("of *hayṭaliyyah*"): which is a dish that is made out of wheat starch and milk and is extremely good to eat.[476] It is lighter than rice pudding, especially if honey is added, for starch is Cold and Dry and sweet things **11.27.4**

ويعدّله الحلو واللبن تقدّم أنّه رطب وقيل معتدل الحرارة والرطوبة والأرزّ حارّ يابس فيكون النشاء أقلّ درجة منه وإن كان الأرزّ موافقاً لكلّ طعام وفي كلام بعضهم لو كان الأرزّ رجلاً لكان حليماً لأنّه موافق على ما يُفعَل به وسمّيت هيطلية من هَطَل السحاب وهو المطر لكونها تشبه ببياضه أو من هطل الثياب وهو طولها وجرّها على الأرض ولمعانها ولهذا قال الناظم

(ٱلّي) بتشديد اللام يعني الّتي وهي لغة ريفيّة ١١،٢٧،٥

(لها تَرْصيفْ) أي من حسنها وشدّة بياضها ولمعانها ترصّف أي تضيء ويُشْتَهى أكلها ويُلْتَذّ بها يقال (فلان عليه مَلّوطة بيضاء ترصّف) أي تلمع وتضيء مشتقّ من الرُصافة قرية معروفة بنواحي العراق (ومن اللطائف) أنّ رجلاً مرّ بين الجِسْر والرصافة فرأى جارية حسناء بديعة الحسن والجمال وهي تمشي فقال صدق أبو العتاهية في ما قال ولم يذكر ما قال فهزّت رأسها وقالت بل صدق أبو العلاء المعرّيّ ولم تذكر هي أيضاً ما قال فاعترى الرجل الخجل وتركها ومضى وكان بالقرب منهما رجل سمع ما قالاه فلحق المرأة وقال لها أخبريني ما أردت وما أراد وإلّا أعلمت بكما أمير المؤمنين فقالت له إنّه عنى بقوله صدق أبو العتاهية قوله [طويل] ١١،٢٧،٦

عُيونُ المَهـا بَينَ الرُّصـافَةِ والجِسْـرِ   جَلَبْنَ الهَوَى مِن حَيثُ أَدري ولا أَدري

وأنا عنيت بقول أبي العلاء المعرّيّ قوله [طويل]

أَيا دارَهـا بالخَيْـفِ إِنَّ مَـزارَهـا   قَريبٌ ولكـنَّ دونَ ذلك أَهوالُـــــ

فأفهمته أنّ الدار قريبة ولكنّها بجوار أمير المؤمنين فلا تقدر إلى الوصول لمطلوبك فانظر إلى قوّة حذق الجارية ومعرفتها المقصود وإلى شدّة فصاحة الآخر وفهمه المقصود أيضاً

moderate these qualities. Milk is Moist, as explained earlier (though some say that it is Moderately Hot and Moist) while rice is Hot and Dry, making the starch a degree less heavy, though it is also true that rice goes with all foods; as someone said, "If rice were a man, he would be tolerant and clement," because it accepts whatever is done to it. It gets its name, *hayṭaliyyah*, from the *haṭl* ("downpouring"), namely, the raining, of clouds, because it resembles their whiteness, or from the *haṭl* of clothes, which is their being long, and dragging on the ground, and being shiny. This is why the poet says . . .

(i)llī ("that"): with double *l*, meaning *allatī*;[477] a rural form. **11.27.5**

lahā tarṣīf ("gleams"): that is, because of its beauty and intense whiteness and **11.27.6** shininess, it gleams, that is, radiates light, and one longs to eat it and savor it. One says, "So-and-so is wearing a white overgown that gleams (*turaṣṣif*)," that is, shines and radiates light. The word is derived from al-Ruṣāfah, a well-known village in Iraq. An amusing story has it[478] that a man was going between al-Jisr and al-Ruṣāfah when he saw a lovely slave girl, outstandingly comely and beautiful, walking along. Said he, "Abū l-ʿAtāhiyah spoke the truth!" without specifying what the latter had said, at which she shook her head and said, "Not so! It was Abū l-ʿAlāʾ al-Maʿarrī who spoke the truth!" and did not specify what he had said either. The man was overcome with embarrassment, let her be, and went his way. Nearby was another man, who overheard what they said, and he chased after the woman and said to her, "Tell me what you meant and what he meant, or I'll report the two of you to the caliph!" She answered, "When he said, 'Abū l-ʿAtāhiyah spoke the truth,' he had in mind his verse:

> The eyes of the wild antelope between al-Ruṣāfah and al-Jisr
> Summoned love from places I know and know not!

"—while by the words of Abū l-ʿAlāʾ al-Maʿarrī I meant,

> Ah, her abode in al-Khayf! Within easy reach,
> But before it lie terrors!"

In other words, she had communicated to him that her abode lay nearby but was close to that of the Commander of the Faithful, "so you will not be able to attain your desire." Observe the slave girl's quickness of wit in grasping what was meant, and the man's command of the language and his understanding likewise of what was meant!

ثمّ إنّه بيّن كيفيّة الأكل من الهيطليّة فقال ١١،٢٧،٧

ص

وأَقْعُدْ لَهَا بِٱلْعَزْمِ فِي رَايِقِ ٱلضُّحَى وَأَسْحَبْ لَهَا مَصْبُوبَةً ٱمّ وَطِيفْ ١١،٢٨

ش

قوله (وأَقْعُدْ) أي أجلس من غير استعجال بل أقعد قعدة متمكّنة من غير خوف ولا فزع ولا أحد يشوّش عليّ ١١،٢٨،١

(لها) إمّا أنّ الضمير راجع للقانة الّتي فيها الهيطليّة فإن كان للقانة يكون قوله وأقعد لها بمعنى أنّي آكل ممّا فيها وهو الهيطليّة لا نفس اللقانة وإن كان الضمير راجع لنفس الهيطليّة فلا إشكال ورجوعه لها أصوب فاتّضح الجواب عن هذه الأبحاث الفشرويّة وقوله ١١،٢٨،٢

(بالعَزْم) أي بالقوّة والشدّة أو أنّه يقعد لها عازم على الأكل منها مثلاً ١١،٢٨،٣

(في رايق الضحى) أي وقت ارتفاع الشمس وقت جواز صلاة الضحى فيه ويقال ضَحْوَة النهار وقت احتكام الغداء وخلوّ الباطن واشتداد الجوع ١١،٢٨،٤

(وأَسْحَبْ) أي يأخذ أخذاً سريعاً مرّة بعد أخرى لأنّ السحب هو جرّ الشيء بحبل أو غيره جرّاً سريعاً قال الشاعر ١١،٢٨،٥

المعدّية رايحه جيّه تنسحب بالخيط

فيكون سحبه يطلق على الأخذ من غير عدد وقوله

Next he explains how he will eat of the *hayṭaliyyah*, saying: 11.27.7

TEXT

wa-ʾaqʿud lahā bi-l-ʿazmi fī rāyiqi l-ḍuḥā 11.28
wa-ʾasḥab lahā maṣbūbata-mmi Waṭīf

And I'll sit down to it with ardor in the clear forenoon
and keep snatching away at the pancakes of Umm Waṭīf

COMMENTARY

11.28.1 *wa-ʾaqʿud* ("and I'll sit down"): that is, I will seat myself unhurriedly, nay, I will adopt a firm posture without fear or alarm, and none will do me harm.

11.28.2 *lahā* ("to it"): the pronominal suffix refers either to the bowl that contains the *hayṭaliyyah*, in which case his words "and I'll sit down to it" mean I will eat of it while it is in it, the thing that he eats thus being the *hayṭaliyyah*, not the bowl itself, or the suffix refers to the *hayṭaliyyah* itself, in which case there is no problem (the latter being the preferred referent). The outcome of these facetious investigations now is clear.

11.28.3 *bi-l-ʿazmi* ("with ardor"): that is, forcefully and vehemently, or it means that he will sit down to it determined (*ʿāzim*) to eat of it, for example . . .

11.28.4 *fī rāyiqi l-ḍuḥā* ("in the clear forenoon"): that is, when the sun is high, at the time at which the forenoon prayer is permitted.[479] This time of the morning is called *ḍaḥwat al-nahār* and is the right time for lunch, when the belly is empty and hunger extreme.

11.28.5 *wa-ʾasḥab* ("and keep snatching away at"): he will take them quickly and repeatedly, for *saḥb* means pulling a thing quickly with a rope or anything else. The poet says:

The ferryboat's going and coming
By a thread it's pulled back and forth (*yansaḥib*).

Thus, *saḥb* may be applied to taking a thing over and over again.

١١،٢٨،٦ (لها مصبوبة أمّ وطيف) أي من المصبوبة الّتي تعملها أمّ وطيف وطيف ولدها وسمّي بهذا اللفظ لكونه كان يصنع الجلّة أطواقاً وقيل كان له دُوَيرة يحطّ فيها الجلّة طَوقاً بعد طوف وقيل من طوافه حول البقرة في صغره وأمّا اسمه الّذي سمّي به عند ولادته على ما قيل دعموم لكن اشتهر بهذا الاسم وغلب عليه فصار عَلَماً واشتهرت أمه به فصار يقال لها أمّ وطيف

١١،٢٨،٧ وأمّا المصبوبة فإنّها تعمل من نوعين من دقيق الحنطة ومن دقيق الأرزّ فأهل الكفور والبلاد الّتي لم تزرع الأرزّ يصنعوها من الحنطة وأهل بلاد الأرزّ يصنعوها من دشيش الأرزّ ويقال للّتي تصنع من القمح قطايف وربّما صنعوها من الأرزّ خالصاً والفقراء يصنعوها من الدُنَيْبة الّتي تخرج من الأرزّ عند بياضه مع خلط شيء عليها من دشيش الأرزّ وسمّيت مصبوبة لأنّهم يجعلوا عجيناً مائعاً مثل عجين الكنافة ويحمّوا الفرن ويأخذوا نصف قرعة ناشفة أو جوزة هند فارغة ويثقبوها ويجعلوها في عصا طويلة ويغرفوا من هذا العجين ويصبّوا في الفرن أقراصاً على قدر أرغفة الخبز وعندها رخاوة وطراوة فسمّيت بذلك لكونها تُصَبّ على هذا الحال وأمّا القطايف فإنّها تُعْمَل في بلاد المدن من الدقيق الأبيض الخالص المقطّف وتصبّ على صواني صغار يقال لها الرُقَع من الحديد أو من النحاس إلّا أنّها صغيرة مثل القرصة وهي ألذّ هذه الأنواع وأطيبها خصوصاً إذا قُلِيَتْ بالسمن وصُبّ عليها العسل النحل ولله الحمد أكلناها مراراً وتلذّذنا بها ونسأل الله تعالى أن يطعمها لإخواننا الفقراء ويُنعِمهم بأكلها لكنّ هذه بعيدة عن مقصد الناظم بل ولا يعرفها بالكلّيّة وإنّما اشتهر في بلده مصبوبة أمّ وطيف هذه قيل إنّها زوجته على ما تقدّم وقيل كانت امرأة تصنعها في قريته مشهورة بذلك وسمّيت قطايف لأنّ الدقيق الّذي تعمل منه مقطّف أي منخول من مُنْخَل رفيع فيكون من باب تسمية الشيء باسم الصفة الّتي تطرأ عليه

١١،٢٨،٨ وتمام الكلام أنّه إذا سحب المصبوبة ورأى الهيطليّة فيقعد ويأكل منها حتّى يكتفي

lahā maṣbūbata-mmi Waṭīf ("the pancakes of Umm Waṭīf"): that is, snatch from the pancakes that Umm Waṭīf makes, Waṭīf being her son, so called because he used to make dung cakes into *aṭwāf*,[480] some saying that he had a little enclosure in which he would place the dung cakes, course upon course, while others claim that the name comes from his circumambulating (*ṭawāf*) of the cow when he was little. The name that he was given when he was born was Daʿmūm, but he became known by the former, and that is the one that stuck to him and was turned into a proper name, and it was by that that his mother became known, people referring to her as Umm Waṭīf ("Mother of Waṭīf"). 11.28.6

Pancakes (*maṣbūbah*) are made in two kinds, one from wheat flour, the other from rice flour. The people of hamlets and villages that have not planted rice make them of wheat, and the people of the rice villages make them of hulled rice. Those made from wheat are called *qaṭāyif*. Sometimes they make them from rice alone, while the poor make them from the barnyard grass that appears among the rice plants when they turn white, adding to it a quantity of hulled rice. It is called *maṣbūbah* ("poured") because they make a runny dough like that for *kunāfah*, heat the oven, take half a dried gourd or empty coconut, make holes in it, attach it to a long stick, scoop up some of the dough, and pour it out inside the oven in floppy soft disks the size of loaves of bread; in other words, it is so called because it is "poured out" (*tuṣabbu*) in this way. *Qaṭāyif* are made in the cities of special finely sieved white flour and poured out onto small iron or copper sheets called "patches," but they are small, the size of the disk-shaped loaf of bread called a *qurṣah*. They are the most delicious of all the different types and the tastiest, especially when fried in clarified butter and drenched in honey. Praise God, we have eaten them many a time and enjoyed them thoroughly, and we beseech the Almighty to feed them to our brethren the dervishes and grant them the luxury of tasting them! These, however, are a far cry from what the poet has in mind and are, indeed, totally unknown to him. What was known in his village were the pancakes of Umm Waṭīf, who is said to have been the poet's wife, as mentioned earlier,[481] though others claim she was another woman in his village who was well known for making them. *Qaṭāyif* are so called because the flour of which they are made is *muqaṭṭaf*, that is, bolted with a fine sieve, in which case it would be an example of "naming a thing by the name of the attribute that fate may bring." 11.28.7

In essence, what he is saying is that, when he snatches at the pancakes and beholds the *hayṭaliyyah*, he will sit down and eat of them until he has had 11.28.8

لئلّا يفهم أحد أنّ ما مراده إلّا النظر وهذا محال كما قال بعضهم [رمل]

النَّظَرُ بالعَينِ لا يَقضي مَلامهْ غَيرَ مَصِّ الرّيقِ ولَثْمِ الخالْ وشامهْ
النَّظَرُ بالعَينِ ما يَشفي غَليلَكْ إلّا أنْ واصَلتَ في بَيتِكْ خَليلَكْ
واجعَلِ الفِضّهْ لِمَحبوبِكْ رَسولَكْ وادخُلِ القُبّهْ تَرَى لِلشَّيخْ كَرامهْ

إلى آخر ما قال ويجري هذا المعنى في الأبيات الّتي صرّح فيها بالرؤية جميعاً فإنّ ما مراده إلّا الرؤية مع الأكل وليس المراد النظر إلى الطعام لأنّه ما يكفيه ذلك خصوصاً مع كثرة شهوته له وشدّة جوعه

٩،٢٨،١١ ثمّ إنّه التفت إلى مأكول آخر قال

ص

٢٩،١١ أَلَا يَا تَرَى ٱشْحَالُ ٱللَّبَنْ بَعْدَ غَلْوِهِ وَلَوْكَانَ بِٱلْخُبْزِ ٱلسُّخَيْنِ رَدِيفْ

ش

١،٢٩،١١ قوله (ألا يا ترى) يريد أن يستفهم ويختبر ويسأل ويتحقّق عن شيء بعيد عنه لم يره ولم يشاهده مثل ما يسأل الإنسان عن صديقه الغائب عنه مدّة طويلة ولهذا قال

٢،٢٩،١١ (ٱشْحال) يعني ما حال هذا الشيء الغائب كما يقول الرجل إذا لاقى صديقه بعد مدّة وأوحشه أيش حالك اليوم وما حالك اليوم مثلاً

٣،٢٩،١١ (اللبن) الحليب

enough, lest anyone should think that all he wants to do is to look at them, which would be an absurdity. As the poet says:

Looking alone no blame involves—
  Only sucking saliva and kissing moles.
Looking alone will not put out your fire—
  Only consummation at home with the one you desire.
Let silver then as messenger to your beloved race,
  Then enter the dome and the shaykh will show you his grace[482]

—and so on to the end of the poem, the same stipulation holding for all verses in which he speaks of "seeing," for his sole object is to see while eating and not just to look at the food, as this would never satisfy him, especially in view of his enormous appetite and huge hunger.

Next he turns to another dish, and says: 11.28.9

TEXT

alā yā tarā-shḥālu l-laban baʿda ghalwihī 11.29
  wa-law kāna bi-l-khubzi l-sukhayni radīf

Now I wonder, how is milk after it's boiled
  (and were it with bread, nice and hot, riding pillion, that would be better still)?

COMMENTARY

ʿalā yā tarā ("Now I wonder"): he seeks to inquire, test, query, and ascertain the truth concerning something far distant from himself, which he has not seen or witnessed, as though he were someone asking after a friend who has been away from him for a long time, which is why he says . . . 11.29.1

(i)shḥālu ("how is"): meaning, "What is the state of this absent thing?" just as a man says, on meeting his friend after a period during which he has missed him, "How are you (*aysh ḥālak* and *mā ḥāluka*) today?" for example. 11.29.2

(a)l-laban ("milk"): is the same as *ḥalīb*.[483] 11.29.3

(بعد) وضعه في الدست ١١،٢٩،٤

و(غَلْوِه) أصله وغَلْيِهِ أُبدِلَت الياء المثنّاة من تحت واوًا جريًا على اللغة الريفيّة أي غليه بالنار يعني هل له لذّة في المأكل وحلاوة في الطعم ١١،٢٩،٥

(و) خصوصاً ١١،٢٩،٦

(لوكانَ) أي هذا اللبن المغليّ ١١،٢٩،٧

(بالخُبْز) وتقدّم تعريفه ١١،٢٩،٨

(السُخَيْنِ) تصغير سُخْن وصغّره لحلاوة اللفظ مثل قول بعضهم [دوبيت] ١١،٢٩،٩

ما قلتُ حُبَيِّبي من التَّحقيرِ بل يَعْذُبُ إسم الشيء[١] بالتَّصغيرِ

فلهذا قال السخين على وزن الطُنَيْن أي المسخَّن بالنار وقوله

(رَديفٌ) على وزن كَنِيف مشتقّ من الرَدْف وهو ركوب الشخص على الدابّة خلف آخر والسخين مشتقّ من السخونة وهي الحُمّى لحرارتها وشدّة ضررها فكان الخبز إذا سُخِنَ يشبه الحمّى في حرارتها وسخونة الجسد إذا اعترته أعاذنا الله منها وجعل الخبز رديفاً للبن بمعنى أنّه لا يفارقه ولا ينفكّ عنه حتّى يؤكل معه فهو مثل الرجل الرديف خلف آخر لا يفارقه ولا يزايل ظهر الدابّة فهو وإيّاه على ظهرها لا يفترقا أو ينزلا إلّا سَوِيّةً أو يفارق أحدهما صاحبه وقوله ١١،٢٩،١٠

هذا من باب تلذّذ إحدى الحواسّ الخمس وهو السمع فكأنّه يقول أخبروني عن حال اللبن وعن أكله بالخبز وهل هو على هذه الحالة لذيذ المأكل ولذّذوا سمعي بذكره فلعلّي أن أراه حقيقةً وآكل منه يقيناً كما قال أبو نواس رحمه الله [طويل] ١١،٢٩،١١

أَلا فَاسْقِني خَمرًا وقُلْ لي هِي الخمرُ ولا تَسقِني سِرًّا إذا أَمكَنَ الجهرُ

---

١ بي: المليح.

baʿda ("after"): putting it in the basin and . . . 11.29.4

ghalwihī ("it's boiled"): the word is originally *ghalyihi*, the *y* being changed to a *w* in accordance with rural usage;[484] that is, its being boiled with fire. In other words, "Is it delicious to eat and sweet to taste?" 11.29.5

wa- ("and"): especially . . . 11.29.6

law kāna ("were it"): referring to this boiled fresh milk . . . 11.29.7

bi-l-khubzi ("with bread"): explained above[485] 11.29.8

(a)l-sukhayni ("nice and hot"): diminutive of *sukhn* ("hot"), used for the sweetness of the form,[486] in the spirit of the verse of the poet who says: 11.29.9

> I didn't say my "little" darling in deprecation—
> Rather, a cute thing's name grows sweeter with diminuation.

This is why he said *sukhayn*, of the measure of *ṭunayn* ("little sheaf of sugarcane"); that is, "heated (*musakhkhan*) with fire."

radīf ("riding pillion"): of the measure of *kanīf* ("latrine"); derived from *radf*, which is the riding of one person behind another on the same mount. *Sukhayn* is derived from *sukhūnah*, which is "fever," because fever is hot and very dangerous, and bread when heated is like fever in its hotness and the way it heats the body when it afflicts it, God preserve us from it! He makes the bread the "pillion rider" of the milk in the sense that it is inseparable from it and not to be detached from it, in order that it may be eaten with it; thus, it is like the man who is mounted behind another—he never leaves him nor parts company with the back of his mount: the two of them are on its back and never separate or dismount unless together and neither ever parts from his companion. 11.29.10

The line in question is an example of the pleasuring of one of the five senses, namely, the hearing, for it is as though he were saying to them, "Inform me as to how milk is, and what it is like to eat it with bread, and whether it is tasty eaten in this fashion, and pleasure my ears by saying its name, for then perhaps I will see it in reality and eat of it truly!" As Abū Nuwās, God have mercy on him, says:[487] 11.29.11

> Come fill my cup, and tell me, "This is wine!"
> And serve it to me openly that all may so divine!

الشاهد في قوله وقل لي هي الخمر أي لأجل ما ألتذّ بسماع اسمها وتلتذّ أُذنايَ بذكرها فإنّ الحواس الأربع قد التذّت وبقي حاسّيّة السمع وكقول ابن الفارض نفعنا الله به

[طويل]

أَدِرْ ذِكرَ مَن أَهوى ولو بمَلامِ   فإنَّ أحاديثَ الحبيبِ مُدامي

ليشهد سمعي إلى آخر ما قال

١٢،٢٩،١١ (ثمّ لمّا أراد) تلذيذ سمعه باللبن المغليّ مع الخبز المسخّن أراد أن يلذّذ سمعه أيضاً بمفروكة اللبن حتّى يريد الله له بالأكل من الجميع ويقضي مراده وما ذلك على الله بعزيز فإنّ الله سبحانه وتعالى عند المنكسرة قلوبهم فقال

ص

٣٠،١١ أَلَا يا تَرَى إِشْحالُ مَفْرُوكَةُ ٱللَّبَنْ   عَلَى رَنْطِهَا قَلْبِي يَرِفُّ رَفِيفْ

ش

١،٣٠،١١ معنى هذا البيت مثل الّذي قبله فقوله (ألا يا ترى) أي يا ترى أحداً يخبرني خبراً شافياً

٢،٣٠،١١ (إِشْحالُ) أي أسأل عن حال

٣،٣٠،١١ (مفروكة اللبَنْ) أي الفطير الّذي يُفرَك باللبن بمعنى أنّه يعمل من الدقيق الأبيض الناعم ويخبز في الفرن أو الجورة ويفرك أي يكسر بالأيدي وهو حارّ ويوضع في زبديّة أو مترد ويصبّ عليه اللبن الحليب حتّى يغمره ويمتزج به ويصير مثل الثريد لين ناعم في

—the probative authority lying in the words "and tell me, 'This is wine!'"; that is, "Tell me this is wine, so that I may feel pleasure at hearing its name and my ears may feel pleasure at hearing it spoken," for the other four senses have had their pleasure and now it is the turn of the hearing—as Ibn al-Fāriḍ, God benefit us through him, says:

Pass my beloved's name around, though it be with blame:
My wine is hearing tales that contain his name

—"That my hearing may witness" and so on, to the end of the poem.[488]

Next, after wanting to indulge his hearing with mention of boiled milk with heated bread, he wants to indulge it further with "flaky-pastry-in-milk," in the hope that God might perhaps grant his wish and allow him to eat of all of these things, which would not be something difficult for God, for "God Almighty is with the meek." So he says: **11.29.12**

TEXT

alā yā tarā ʾishḥālu mafrūkatu l-laban **11.30**
ʿalā zalṭihā qalbī yariffu rafīf

Now I wonder, how is flaky-pastry-in-milk?
At the thought of its gulping my heart beats violently!

COMMENTARY

The meaning of this verse is similar to the one before. **11.30.1**

alā yā tarā ("Now I wonder"): that is, I wonder if anyone can give me a satisfying report on . . .

ʾishḥālu ("how"): that is, I am asking about the state of . . . **11.30.2**

mafrūkatu l-laban ("flaky-pastry-in-milk"): that is, flaky pastry that is crumbled (*yufraku*) with milk, or, in other words, made with fine white flour and baked in the oven or the cooking pit and crumbled, that is, broken up with the hands while hot, and put into a butter pot or crock. Then fresh milk is poured over it until it covers it and is absorbed by it and it turns into something like *tharīd* ("crumbled bread moistened with broth"), that is to say, something soft **11.30.3**

البلع والزلط لأنّ الثريد فيه اللذّة وهو أفضل الطعام (وفي الحديث) فضل عائشة على النساء كفضل الثريد على سائر الطعام (وورد أيضاً) أثردوا فإنّ في الثريد بركة

ثمّ قال (على زَلْطِها) وكثرة شوقي إليها وحسرتي على بعدها ١١،٣٠،٤

(قلبي يرِفُّ رَفِيفْ) أصله رفيفاً لأنّه مصدر حذفت ألفه للضرورة أي يَخْفِق خَفَقاناً زائداً يشبه في خفقانه رَفّ جناح الطائر وتحرّكه من شدّة الوجد على زلط هذه المفروكة ١١،٣٠،٥

والزَلْط مشتقّ من الزلَط بفتح اللام جمع زَلَطة وهي حجارة صغيرة ملساء تتكوّن في الرمال وسواحل البحر وسمّي زَلْط الطعام به لملوسته واندفاعه من غير مضغ أو لأنّ اللقمة تحاكي الزلطة الكبيرة لأنّ الزلطة لها قوّة وسرعة في رميها من اليد كما يقال (زلطه في راسك) مثلاً يعني أتى لك ضربة زلطة في رأسك بسرعة حتّى يؤثّر ضربها فيها فشبّهت بذلك لأنّه يأخذ اللقمة منها بسرعة ويحدفها في حلقه ويزلطها كما يحدف الرجل الزلطة بشدّة وقوّة وأيضاً الفطير لين واللبن رطب فلا يحتاج لمضغ أسنان ولهذا تأسّف على فراق هذا المأكول وصار من شدّة وجده عليه يرفّ قلبه ويخفق كالغصن الّذي عليه طائر يتحرّك ويرفرف بجناحيه وهذا من كثرة الشوق ودواعي الشهوة وانتظار حصول المقصود والمطلوب فإنّك تجد العاشق دائماً قلبه يخفق على فراق محبوبه فلا يسكن إلّا أن اجتمع به وتحدّث معه ولاطفه في الحديث وآنسه في المسامرة فهناك يزول ما به وتسكن حواسّه بأنسه بحبيبه واجتماعه به قال سيّدي عمر بن الفارض نفعنا الله به [كامل] ١١،٣٠،٦

and smooth to swallow and gulp down, for *tharīd* is delicious and the best of foods:[489] in the Noble Tradition it says, "The superiority of ʿĀʾishah over all other women is as that of *tharīd* over all other foods," and a further Tradition is cited that says, "Eat *tharīd*, for in *tharīd* is blessing."

Next he says: **11.30.4**

ʿalā zalṭihā ("at the thought of its gulping"): and at the height of my desire for it and my agony at its inaccessibility . . .

qalbī yariffu rafīf ("my heart beats violently"): the last word is originally *rafīfan* **11.30.5**
because it is a verbal noun, the *an* being dropped for the meter;[490] that is, it palpitates very hard, its palpitation resembling the fluttering motion of a bird's wings, because it so desperately wants to gulp down this flaky-pastry-in-milk.

The word *zalṭ* ("swallowing without chewing, gulping") derives from *zalaṭ* **11.30.6**
("pebbles"), with *a* after the *l*, plural of *zalaṭah*, meaning small smooth stones that are formed in sand and on the seashore. The *zalṭ* ("gulping") of food is named after the latter because of the smoothness and quickness of the action, which occurs without chewing; or because the piece of food that is gulped down resembles a large pebble, for a pebble, when thrown from the hand, gains force and speed, as witness the expression "A pebble in your head!" for example, meaning, "May a blow from a pebble strike your head at speed so that the striking impacts upon it!" The action is thus likened to the throwing of a pebble because he takes a piece of food quickly, tosses it down his throat, and gulps it down in just the same way that a man throws a pebble—hard and with force. In addition, flaky pastry is soft and milk is moist, so they do not need to be chewed with the teeth. This is why he expresses his sorrow at his separation from this dish and why his heart, being so overwhelmed by desire for it, takes to fluttering and palpitating like a branch on which sits a bird that is moving and fluttering its wings. All of this is due to the enormity of his longing, the promptings of his appetite, and the delay in attaining the object of his longing and desire—for you will find that the lover's heart is always palpitating at its separation from its beloved and only quiets down when he meets with him and talks to him, whispering sweet nothings to him and delighting him with nocturnal discourse. When this happens, what ails him disappears and his senses are lulled by the comfort that the presence of the beloved and being united with him bring him. Master ʿUmar ibn al-Fāriḍ, God benefit us through him, says:[491]

وَمُشَبَّهٍ بالغُصنِ قَلْبِي لا يَزالُ عَلَيه طائِرْ
حُلْوُ الحديثِ وإنّها لَحلاوةٌ شَقَّتْ مرائِرْ
أَشكُو وأَشكرُ فِعلَهُ فاعجَب لِشاكٍ منه شاكِرْ

إلّا أنّ كلام الأستاذ نفعنا الله به ومَشْرَبه ليس ممّا نحن بصدده

١١،٣٠،٧ ثمّ إنّه آلى على نفسه أنّه متى رأى لقّانة ابن عمه الآتي ذكره ملآنة من الفتّ أكله كلّه لشدّة شهوته وكثرة جوعه وانتظاره لذلك فقال

ص

١١،٣١ أَنَا آنْ شُفْتُ لَقّانة ابنِ عَمِّي مُخَيْمِرْ مَلَانَهْ مِنَ ٱلتَّفْتِيتِ مَلْوَ طَفِيفْ
أَقَشَرْتُو جَمِيعُو مَا تَرَكْتُ بَقِيَّتُو لِغَيْرِي وَلَا عِنْدِي بِدَا تَوْقِيفْ

ش

١١،٣١،١ قوله (أَنَا) يعني أبو شادوف لا أحدًا غيري

١١،٣١،٢ (ان شُفْتُ) أي رأيت بعيني لا بأذني كما تقدّم تعريفه

١١،٣١،٣ (لَقّانة) تقدّم بيانها واشتقاقها وتعريفها

١١،٣١،٤ (ابنِ عمّي) أخو والدي

١١،٣١،٥ (مُخَيْمِرٍ) سمّي بذلك لأنّه كان له نقرة كبيرة يخمّر فيها الجلّة وربّما بال فيها أيضًا أو لإتيانه

And a boy like a bough
    On which my heart forever is descending.
Sweet his speech but
    With a sweetness heartrending.
I both protest and praise its work—
    Marvel, then, at one complaining and commending!

—albeit the words of the Master, God benefit us through him, and his ilk have nothing in common with the matter at hand.

Next he promises himself that, when he sees the bowl of his cousin (of whom more later) full of bread-in-broth,[492] he will eat it all up, so great is his appetite, so enormous his hunger, and so long his wait for it. He says: 11.30.7

TEXT

anā-n shuftu laqqānata-bni ʿammī Mukhaymirin 11.31
    malānah mina l-taftīti malwa ṭafīf
qashartū jamīʿū mā taraktu baqiyyatū
    li-ghayrī wa-lā ʿindī bi-dā tawqīf

Should I see the bowl of the son of my uncle Mukhaymir
    full of bread-in-soup brimming over,
I would polish it off completely and leave nothing over
    for others, and would not pause!

COMMENTARY

Anā ("(Should) I"): meaning Abū Shādūf and no one else . . . 11.31.1

(i)n shuftu ("see"): that is, should I perceive with my eye, not with my ear, as previously explained . . .[493] 11.31.2

laqqānata ("the bowl of"): previously described, etymologized, and explained . . .[494] 11.31.3

(i)bni ʿammī ("the son of my uncle"): the latter being the brother of my father . . . 11.31.4

Mukhaymirin: so called because he had a large hole in which he would ferment (*yukhammiru*) dung and in which perhaps he would also urinate, or because 11.31.5

بخميرة العيش لوالدته قبل خبزه أو لأكله من العجين المخمَّر قبل تقريصه أو لأنّ وجهه كان يشبه الخميرة المشقّقة لبشاعته ويعاير بذلك ويقال (يا وجه الخميره المشقّقه) وقوله

٦،٣١،١١ (ملانه) أي تلك اللقانة

٧،٣١،١١ (من التفتيتِ) جمع فتّ وهو تكسير الخبز لقماً صغاراً أو كباراً وأحسنها الصغار ويصبّ عليه العدس أو البيسار حتّى ييبس ويصير كقطع الحجارة وقوله

٨،٣١،١١ (مَلْوَ طَفيفْ) أي ملواً كاملاً مطفّفاً بمعنى أنّه زائد على حوافي الإناء مشتقّ من تطفيف الكَيْل قال الله تعالى ﴿وَيْلٌ لِلْمُطَفِّفِينَ﴾ أو من طَفّ الماء على الجروف إذا ارتفع عليها أو من الطَفّ محلّ بنواحي العراق من نواحي كَرْبَلاء قُتِلَ فيه سيّدنا الحسين رضي الله عنه

٩،٣١،١١ (وملخَّص قصّته) أنّ معاوية رضي الله عنه لمّا مات أخرج يزيد إليه من يأخذ بيعته فامتنع وخرج إلى مكّة فأتت كتب العراق بأنّهم بايعوه بعد موت معاوية فأشار عليه ابن الزُبَيْر بالخروج وابن عبّاس وابن عمر وجماعة من الصحابة بعدمه فلم يفد ذلك وأرسل إلى أهل العراق ابن عمّه مسلم بن عَقِيل يأخذ بيعتهم فأخذها وأرسل إليه يستقدمه فخرج الحسين من مكّة قاصداً للعراق فعلم يزيد بخروجه فأرسل إلى عُبَيْد الله بن زِياد واليه على الكوفة يأمره بطلب مسلم وقتله ولم يبلغ حسيناً ذلك حتّى صار بينه وبين القادسيّة ثلاثة أميال فلقيه الحُرّ بن يزيد التميميّ فقال له ارجع فإنّي لم أَدَعْ لك خلفي خيراً وأخبره الخبر ولقي الفَرَزْدَق فسأله فقال له قلوب الناس معك وسيوفهم مع بني أُمَيّة والقضاء ينزل من السماء وهَمّ أن يرجع وكان معه أخو مسلم فقال له

he used to bring the yeast (*khamīrah*) for the bread to his mother before it was baked, or because he used to eat the leavened (*mukhammar*) dough before it was shaped into loaves, or because his face was so ugly it looked like cracked yeast, for they use this as a term of abuse and one says, "You with the face like cracked yeast" (*yā wajh al-khamīrah al-mushaqqaqah*)! . . .

malānah ("full"): that is, referring to the bowl in question . . . **11.31.6**

mina l-taftīti ("of bread-in-broth"): *taftīt* is the plural of *fatt*, which is the crumbling of bread into small or large morsels, the small being better; on this lentils or *bīsār* are poured and it is then left until it dries and comes to resemble rocks. **11.31.7**

malwa ṭafīf ("brimming over"): that is, completely full and brimming over, meaning that it is too much to be contained within the rims of the vessel; derived from *taṭfīf al-kayl* ("the scanting of the measure")—the Almighty says, «*waylun li-l-muṭaffifīna* ("Woe to the defrauders")!»[495]—or from *ṭaffa l-mā' 'alā l-jurūf* ("the water overflowed the dikes") when it rises above them, or from al-Ṭaff, a place in Iraq in the area of Karbalā', where Our Master and Our Lord the Imam al-Ḥusayn, God be pleased with him, was martyred. **11.31.8**

The brief version of his story[496] is that, when Mu'āwiyah died, Yazīd dispatched someone to al-Ḥusayn to take his oath of allegiance, but he refused and left for Mecca. Then letters came from Iraq saying that they had sworn allegiance to him there after Mu'āwiyah's death. Ibn al-Zubayr advised him to leave and return to Iraq while Ibn 'Abbās, Ibn 'Umar, and several Companions advised him not to, but to no avail, and he sent his cousin Muslim ibn 'Aqīl to the people of Iraq to obtain their oath of allegiance. This Muslim did, and he sent word to al-Ḥusayn to join him. Our Master al-Ḥusayn then left Mecca, making for Iraq. Yazīd learned of his departure and sent word to his governor of al-Kūfah, 'Ubayd Allāh ibn Ziyād, ordering him to seek out Muslim and kill him, but news of this did not reach al-Ḥusayn until he was three miles from al-Qādisiyyah. There al-Ḥurr ibn Yazīd al-Tamīmī met him and said to him, "Go back, for what I left behind me does not bode well for you," and he told him the news. He also met al-Farazdaq and questioned him, and al-Farazdaq told him, "The hearts of the people are with you but their swords are with the Umayyads, and the decision will come from Heaven." At this, al-Ḥusayn made ready to turn back, but the brother of Muslim was with him and said to him, "We shall not go back until we have taken our revenge for him or been killed!" **11.31.9**

لا نرجع حتّى نأخذ بثأره أو نُقتَل وكان ابن زياد جهّز أربعة آلاف وقيل عشرين ألفاً لملاقاته فوافاه بكربلاء فنزل ومعه خمسة وأربعون فارساً ونحو مائة راجل فلقيه الجيش وأميرهم عمر بن سعد بن أبي وَقّاص وكان ابن زياد ولاّه الريّ وكتب له بعَهده عليها أن حارب الحسين ورجع

١٠،٣١،١١ فلمّا التقيا وأرهقته السلاح قال له الحسين اختر منّي إحدى ثلاث إمّا أن ألحق بثغر من الثغور وإمّا أن أرجع إلى المدينة وإمّا أن أضع يدي في يد ابن معاوية فقبل عمر ذلك منه وأرسل إلى ابن زياد فكتب إليه لا أقبل منه حتّى يضع يده في يدي فامتنع الحسين فتأهّبوا لقتاله وكان أكثر مقاتليه الكاتبين إليه والتابعين له فلمّا أيقن أنّهم قاتلوه قام في أصحابه خطيباً فحمد الله وأثنى عليه ثمّ قال (قد تروا) من الأمر ما ترون وأنّ الدنيا تغيّرت وتلوّنت وأدبر معروفها واستمرّت حتّى لم يبق منها إلّا صُبابة الإناء وإلّا خسيس عيش كالمرعى الوبيل ألا ترون الحقّ لا يُعمَل به والباطل لا يُتَناهى عنه ليرغب المؤمن في لقاء الله تعالى فإنّي لا أرى الموت إلّا سعادة والحياة مع الظالمين إلّا جُرماً فقاتلوه فكان آخر الأمر أن قتل وقتل معه سبعة عشر شاباً من أهل بيته وذلك بكربلاء في خبر رواه الطبرانيّ

١١،٣١،١١ (قال العلاّمة سيّدي عبد الرؤوف المُناويّ) نفعنا الله به في طبقاته (فإن قلت) ينافيه ما ورد عن الطبرانيّ أيضاً عن عائشة أنّه عليه الصلاة والسلام قال أخبرني جبريل أنّ الحسين يقتل بأرض الطَفّ وجاءني جبريل بهذه التربة وأعلمني أنّ فيها مَضْجَعه ورواية سعد عن أمير المؤمنين عليّ رضي الله عنه قال دخلتُ على المصطفى ذات يوم وعيناه تفيضان فسألته فقال أخبرني جبريل أنّ حسيناً يُقتل بشاطئ الفُرات

Ibn Ziyād had mustered four thousand, or, as some say, twenty thousand, to oppose him, and caught up with him at Karbalā'. So al-Ḥusayn set up camp, and there were with him forty-five horsemen and about one hundred infantry, and the army met him under the command of ʿUmar ibn Saʿd ibn Abī Waqqāṣ, whom Ibn Ziyād had made governor of Ray with a letter of appointment executable upon his return from fighting al-Ḥusayn.

When they met in battle, al-Ḥusayn, exhausted by the fight, said to him, "Allow me one of three choices. Let me either reach a border town, or return to Medina, or turn myself in to the son of Muʿāwiyah." ʿUmar accepted his conditions and sent word to Ibn Ziyād, who wrote to him, "I will accept nothing of what he asks for until he turns himself in to me." Al-Ḥusayn refused and they prepared to do battle with him, and most of those ranged against him were men who had pledged him their allegiance and been his followers. When he was certain that they were going to fight him, he rose among his companions to address them. He praised God and lauded Him and then said, "You have seen how the matter stands, how the world has turned and become fickle and withdrawn its favor, and it has come to a point at which all that is left is to drink the dregs of the cup or live a life of abasement—like tainted grazing. Do you not see that the truth is not acted upon and that falsity is not refrained from? Let the Muslim then desire to meet the Almighty, for in death I see only happiness and in life among the wrongdoers only sin." Then they fought him, and the end of the matter was that he was martyred and seventeen youths of his house were martyred with him. This was at Karbalā', as related by al-Ṭabarānī.[497] **11.31.10**

The eminent scholar Master ʿAbd al-Ra'ūf al-Munāwī, God benefit us through him, says in his *Biographical Dictionary*:[498] **11.31.11**

> If you say this is contradicted by what is reported on the authority of al-Ṭabarānī also, on the authority of ʿĀ'ishah, that the Prophet, blessings and peace be upon him, said, "Jibrīl informed me that al-Ḥusayn would be killed in the land of al-Ṭaff, and Jibrīl brought me this earth and told me that in it would be his resting place,"[499] and by what Ibn Saʿd relates on the authority of ʿAlī, Commander of the Believers, God be pleased with him, who said, "I went in one day to the Chosen One, blessings and peace be upon him, and his eyes were brimming with tears, and I asked him why and he said, 'Jibrīl has informed me that al-Ḥusayn will be killed on the bank of the Euphrates,'"[500] I would say that there is no discrepancy, because the Euphrates debouches

قلت لا تعارض لأنّ الفرات يخرج من آخر حدود الروم ثمّ يمرّ بأرض الطَف وهي من بلاد كربلاء فالتأم الكلام واستقام على أحسن نظام هذا كلامه نفعنا الله به

١٢،٣١،١١ ولمّا قتلوه حزّوا رأسه ثمّ أتوا به إلى ابن زياد فأرسله ومن معه من أهل بيته إلى يزيد ومنهم عليّ بن الحسين كان مريضاً وعمّته زينب فلمّا قدموا على يزيد سُرَّ سروراً كثيراً وأوقفهم موقف السَبِيّ بباب المسجد وأهانهم وبالغ في إهانتهم ولمّا وضعوا الرأس الشريف بين يديه صار يضرب على ثناياه بقضيب كان معه ويقول لقيت بعينك يا حسين وبالغ في الفرح ثمّ ندم لما مقته المسلمون على ذلك وأبغضه العالم وقد أخرج أبو يَعلى عن أبي عبيدة مرفوعاً لا يزال أمر أمّتي قائماً بالقِسط حتّى يكون أوّل من يثلِمه رجل من بني أميّة يقال له يزيد وقد صحّ عن إبراهيم النخعيّ أنّه كان يقول لو كنت ممّن قاتل الحسين ثمّ أُدخِلتُ الجنّة لاستحيت أن أنظر إلى وجه المصطفى صلّى الله عليه وسلّم وسُمِعَت الجنّ تنوح عليه كما أخرجه أبو نعيم وغيره

١٣،٣١،١١ وقُتِلَ يوم عاشوراء يوم الجمعة سنة إحدى وستّين وكسفت الشمس وقت قتله كسفة أبدت الكواكب نصف النهار واحمرّت آفاق السماء مدّة ستة أشهر يُرى فيها كالدم ومكثت الدنيا سبعة أيّام كأنّها عَلَقَة والشمس على الحيطان كالملاحف المعصفرة تضرب بعضها بعضاً وقيل إنّه لم يُقلَب حجر ببيت المَقدِس يومئذ إلّا وُجِدَ فيه دم عبيط وصار الوَرس الّذي في عسكرهم رماداً ونحروا ناقة في عسكرهم فصاروا يرون في لحمها النيران وطبخوها فصارت كالعلقم ثمّ ساروا برأسه إلى ابن معاوية فقعدوا في أوّل مرحلة يشربون الخمر فخرج عليهم قلم من حديد من حائط وصار يكتب بدم [وافر]

أَتَرجو أُمَّةٌ قَتَلَت حُسَينًا شَفاعَةَ جَدِّهِ يَومَ الحِسابِ

> from the farthest borders of al-Rūm, then passes through the land of al-Ṭaff, which is a dependency of Karbalā'. Thus the discrepancy we repel; the reports agree and hang together well.

These are his words, God benefit us through him.

After they had killed him, they severed his head and carried it to Ibn Ziyād, **11.31.12**
who sent it to Yazīd, along with the members of his family who were with him. Among these were 'Alī, the son al-Ḥusayn, who was sick, and his paternal aunt, Zaynab. When they were presented to Yazīd, he was overjoyed and stood them like prisoners at the door of the mosque and insulted them viciously; and when they placed the noble head before him, he started knocking at its front teeth with a rod he had in his hand, saying, "So, Ḥusayn, I meet you face to face!" and gave his joy free rein. Later, when the Muslims detested him for that and everyone hated him, he repented. Abū Ya'lā has published, on the authority of Abū 'Ubaydah, a Tradition attributed to the Prophet: "The affairs of my nation will be maintained in justice until they are spoiled for the first time by a man of the Banū Umayyah called Yazīd."[501] And it is reliably reported on the authority of Ibrāhīm al-Nakha'ī that he said, "Were I one of those who fought al-Ḥusayn, then entered Heaven, I would be ashamed to look into the face of the Chosen One, God bless him and grant him peace." The jinn were heard to lament for him, according to reports published by Abū Nu'aym[502] and others.

He was killed on 'Ashūrā',[503] a Friday, of the year 61. At the moment of his **11.31.13**
killing, the sun was eclipsed entirely so that the stars appeared at midday, and for six months the horizons of the heavens were red and blood was seen in them, and the earth stayed seven days like a clot of blood, while the rays of the sun appeared on the walls as though they were draperies dyed with safflower beating against one another. It is said that not a stone was overturned in Jerusalem that day but fresh blood was found beneath it, and the turmeric that was with their soldiers turned to ashes; and they slaughtered a she-camel among the soldiers and beheld fires in her flesh, and they cooked it and it tasted bitter as colocynth. Then they set off with his head, making for the son of Mu'āwiyah,[504] and they made camp at the end of the first day's march and drank wine, and a pen of iron came out towards them from a wall and wrote in blood:

> Can a nation that killed al-Ḥusayn expect
> his grandsire's intercession on the Day of Account?

١٤،٣١،١١ ثمّ إنّ يزيد ابن معاوية أمر بردّ أهله إلى المدينة وأن يطاف برأسه الشريفة في البلاد (و روى) ابن خالَوَيْه عن الأعمش عن مِنْهال بن عمرو الأسديّ قال والله رأيت رأس الحسين حين حُمِلَ وأنا بدمشق وبين يديه رجل يقرأ في سورة الكهف حتّى بلغ ﴿أَمْ حَسِبْتَ أَنَّ أَصْحَابَ ٱلْكَهْفِ وَٱلرَّقِيمِ كَانُوا مِنْ ءَايَاتِنَا عَجَبًا﴾ فنطق الرأس بلسان عربيّ فصيح فقال جهاراً أَعْجَبُ من أصحاب الكهف قتلي وحملي (وقال ابن حَجَر) و رد من طريق رواه عن عليّ عن المصطفى عليه السلام قاتل الحسين في تابوت من نار عليه نصف عذاب أهل الدنيا (واختلفوا) في رأس الحسين بعد مصيره إلى الشام إلى أين صار وفي أيّ موضع استقرّت فذهبت طائفة إلى أنّه طيف به حتّى انتهى إلى عسقلان فلاقاه أميرها فدفنه بها فلمّا غلبت الفرنج على عسقلان افتداها منهم الصالح طلائع وزير الفاطميّين بمال جزيل ومشى إلى لقائها من عدّة مراحل ثمّ بنى عليها المشهد المعروف بالقاهرة (وذكر آخرون) أنّه حُمِلَ إلى المدينة مع أهله ودُفِنَ بالبَقيع والّذي عليه طائفة من الصوفيّة أنّه في المدفن القاهريّ رضي الله عنهم أجمعين

١٥،٣١،١١ ثمّ إنّ الناظم نبّه على عدم الاكتفاء برؤيته وأنّه لا يكفيه إلّا أكله جميعه فقال

١٦،٣١،١١ (قَشَرْتو جميعو) والقَشْر في الأكل وغيره أخذ الشيء جميعه أو إتلافه ويُتفاءل به ويقال (كعب فلان أقشر) و(كعبك أقشر) ومنه يقال (أكعاب وأعتاب ونواصي) ويقال (امرأة قشراء) و (رجل أقشر) يعني أنّه قليل البركة قليل الرزق تأتي قلّة البركة والرزق عند حلوله ودخوله على الشخص ونحو ذلك (وكان في قريتنا) رجل قصّاب يقال له سُكَيْكَرعشق امرأة جميلة يقال لها كعب الخير فلمّا شغف بحبّها ماتت فقال فيه بعض الأدباء [بسيط]

Then Yazīd the son of Muʿāwiyah ordered that his family be returned to Medina and that his Noble Head be paraded from town to town. Ibn Khālawayh recounts, on the authority of al-Aʿmash, on the authority of Minhāl ibn ʿAmr al-Asadī, that the latter said, "By God, I saw the head of al-Ḥusayn as it was being carried, when I was in Damascus, and before it was a man reciting from *Sūrat al-kahf*, and when he came to «Or deemest thou that the people of the Cave and the Inscription are a wonder among our portents?»[505] the head uttered words in faultless Arabic and cried out loud, 'More wonderful than the people of the Cave are my killing and my carrying!'" Ibn Ḥajar, giving a chain of authority that goes back to ʿAlī, says that the Chosen One, God's blessings be upon him, said, "The killer of al-Ḥusayn lies in a sarcophagus of fire and bears half the torment of mortal man." People differ over where the head of al-Ḥusayn ended up after it went to Syria, and where it came to rest. One group tends to the belief that it was paraded until it ended up at ʿAsqalān, where the commander received it and buried it, and that when the Franks conquered ʿAsqalān, al-Ṣāliḥ Ṭalāʾiʿ, the Fatimid minister, ransomed it from them for a huge sum and went out many days' march to meet it, then built over it the famous shrine in Cairo.[506] Others state that it was borne to Medina along with his family and buried in al-Baqīʿ. The view endorsed by a certain party among the Sufis, may God be pleased with all of them, is that it is in the Cairo tomb. **11.31.14**

Next the poet draws attention to the insufficiency of seeing the bread-in-broth and to the fact that only eating it all will satisfy him. He says: **11.31.15**

qashartū jamīʿū ("I would polish it off completely"): with regard to eating and other things, *qashara* means "to take the whole of a thing" or "to devour it entirely." The word is also used in connection with luck: one says, "So-and-so has a jinxing ankle" (*kaʿbun aqshar*) and "Your ankle brings jinxes" (*kaʿbuka aqshar*), and in the same vein one speaks of "ankles and thresholds and horses' forelocks"; and one speaks of "a jinxing woman" (*imraʾah qashrāʾ*) and "a jinxing man" (*rajulun aqshar*), meaning that he is ill-fortuned and poor and brings ill fortune and poverty with him when he stays with or calls upon a person, and so on. In our village there was a butcher, called Sukaykar ("Little Sugar"), who fell in love with a beautiful woman, called Kaʿb al-Khayr ("Ankle of Good Fortune"). When he was in the midst of his throes of love for her she died and a man of letters said of him: **11.31.16**

صُحبَة سُكَيكَر لِكَعبِ الخَيرِ كانتْ فالْ
لُوكَعبُ أَقْشَرْ قَشَرها بالعَجَلْ في الحالْ
لَوْشارَني الموتُ أو شفتو على الإِمهالْ
قلتُ اقْتَلِعْ بو وخلّي كعبَ في الْخَلْخالْ

(ومنه) قصّة طُوَيْس المذكورة في الكتب وكلّها أسباب يُجْرِيها الله تعالى على يد من يشاء من خير أو شرّ وإلّا فالحديث الشريف لا عَدْوى ولا طِيرَةَ ولا فَأْل ونعق غراب فقال رجل خير إن شاء الله فسمعه بعض العارفين فنهر الرجل وزجره وقال له لا تقل هذا هل الخير والشرّ إلّا بيد الله وقوله

١٧،٣١،١١ (قشَرْتو جميعو) أي أكلته جميعه ولا أبقي منه شيئاً لغيري لأنّي مشتهيه وعندي مجاعة شديدة فمتى رأيته لا أبقي منه شيئاً وهذا من قبيل قلّة البركة لأنّ الشخص إذا شَرِهَ في الطعام وأرخى نفسه عليه وأكل منه زائداً عن القدر المعتاد ضرّه وآذاه وتولّد منه الأمراض ولهذا قيل (وأكثر موت الناس بالتّخَم) قال الشاعر [طويل]

إذا شِئتَ أَن تَحيَى صَحيحاً مُنعَّماً فكُل مِن طَعامٍ تَشتَهيهِ قَليلا
كَما قالَ بُقْراطُ الحَكيمُ وغَيرُهُ إِذا قَلَّ أَكْلُ المَرءِ عاشَ طَويلا

١٨،٣١،١١ (قيل) اجتمع عند ملك الهند ثلاثة من الحكماء هنديّ وروميّ ومصريّ فقال لهم ليصف لي كلّ واحد منكم دواء لا داء معه فقال الهنديّ الدواء الّذي لا داء معه أن تفطر كلّ يوم على شيء من بزر الهِندِباء وقال الروميّ الدواء الّذي لا داء معه أن تفطر كلّ يوم على ثلاث جرعات من الماء الساخن وقال المصريّ الدواء الّذي لا داء معه أن لا تأكل إلّا بعد الجوع وأن تقوم وأنت تشتهي الطعام فإنّك لا ترى علّة إلّا علّة الموت فقالوا كلّهم صدق المصريّ (ولمّا أرسل المُقَوْقِس) ملك مصر إلى النبيّ صلّى

Sukaykar's thing with the Ankle was doomed—
His ankle was a jinx, polished her off at one go.
Had Death asked me, "Shall I wait?" or had I seen him,
I'd have said, "By all means take him. Just leave the Ankle in the shoe!"

The story of Ṭuways that is told in the books belongs in the same category. All these things are, however, merely occasions that the Almighty brings about through the agency of whomever He pleases, for good or evil; were it not so, it would not say in the Noble Tradition, "No contagious disease, no evil omens, and no good augurs!"[507] Once a crow cawed and a man said, "May it be well, God willing!" One of God's initiates heard him and rebuked him, saying, "Do not say that! Are good and ill in any hands but the Almighty's?"

qashartū jamīʿū ("I would polish it off completely"):[508] that is, I would eat it all and leave none of it for anyone else, because I crave it and I am extremely hungry; consequently, when I see it, I will leave none of it. This is a typical sign of bootlessness, for if one is greedy and indulges his appetite for food and eats a more than normal amount, it will harm him and do him injury, and illnesses will arise therefrom, which is why it has been said, "Most people die of overeating." The poet says: **11.31.17**

If you want to live healthy and be at ease,
Eat sparingly of your favorite victual.
As Dr. Hippocrates and others have said,
He lives long who eats but little.

It is said that three physicians met at the court of the king of India: an Indian, a Greek, and an Egyptian. The king said to them, "Let each of you prescribe for me a medicine that prevents all disease!" The Indian said, "The medicine that prevents all disease is to breakfast every day on a few wild chicory seeds." The Greek said, "The medicine that prevents all disease is to breakfast every day on three sips of hot water." The Egyptian said, "The medicine that prevents all disease is to eat only when you feel hungry and to get up in the morning with an appetite; do this, and you will suffer no sickness but the sickness of death." All of them said, "The Egyptian is right!" And when al-Muqawqis, king of Egypt, sent the Prophet, may God bless him and give him peace, the two slave girls, Māriyah and Sīrīn (who were from the city of Anṣinā, which is now a **11.31.18**

الله عليه وسلّم الجاريتين مارية وسيرين وكانتا من مدينة أَنْصِنا الّتي الآن خراب على شاطئ بحر النيل من إقليم الصعيد وأرسل له البغلة المسمّاة بالدُلْدُل وأرسل له عسلاً من بَنْها قرية بإقليم مصر بنواحي القَلْيوبيّة أرسل معهم حكيماً وقال إن قبل الهديّة وردّ الحكيم فهو نبيّ فلمّا وصلت الهديّة والحكيم إلى النبيّ صلّى الله عليه وسلّم قبلها وردّ الحكيم وقال نحن قوم لا نأكل إلّا بعد الجوع وإذا أكلنا لا نشبع فلا نحتاج إلى حكيم فلمّا بلغ المقوقس ما قاله النبيّ صلّى الله عليه وسلّم قال يا له من نبيّ جمع الحكمة في كلمتين (وفي الحديث الشريف) جوعوا تَصِحّوا فالجوع محلّ النشاط للعبادة ويتولّد منه صحّة الجسم وعدم الأمراض خصوصاً أصحاب الرياضات وأرباب الخلوات فإنّ نتيجتهم في ذلك الجوع كما ذكر العارف بالله تعالى البونيّ في بعض كتبه أنّها لا تصحّ رياضة من أحد وفي قلبه مثقال حبّة من شبع

وأمّا كثرة الأكل فإنّه ينشأ من أمور إمّا من شدّة الشره على الطعام أو يكون ذلك ١١،٣١،١٩
عادة (فقد رأينا) مَنْ أكل الماجور الطعام ولم يشبع (ورأينا) مَنْ أكل المائة بيضة مشويّة بالخبز ولم يشبع (وكان) بعض الجبابرة يأكل الفصيل مشويّاً في غدوته فأكله يوماً وأراد أن يجامع زوجته فامتنعت فعاتبها فقالت كيف تصل إليّ وبيني وبينك فصيل (وذكر) سيّدي محيي الدين ابن العربيّ نفعنا الله به في مواقع النجوم أنّ عبد الملك كان أكولاً مرّ برجل معه زَنْبيلَيْن بيض مشويّ وتين فأكلهما جميعاً فمرض ومات بذلك (وكان الوليد) من ملوك بني أميّة جبّاراً عنيداً وكان يشرب الزقّ الخمر ويأكل الفصيل وفتح يوماً المصحف فرأى ﴿وَٱسْتَفْتَحُوا وَخَابَ كُلُّ جَبَّارٍ عَنِيدٍ﴾ فمزّقه وأنشد يقول [وافر]

تُهدِّدُني بجبّارٍ عنيدٍ وإنّي ذاكَ جبّارٌ عنيدُ
إذا ما جئتَ ربّكَ يومَ حشرٍ فقُلْ يا ربِّ مزّقني الوليدُ

ruin on the banks of the river Nile in the region of Upper Egypt), and the mule called al-Duldul and honey from Banhā (a village in the region of Cairo, belonging to al-Qalyūbiyyah), and with them a physician, he said, "If he accepts the gift and sends the physician back, he is a prophet." When the gift and the physician reached the Prophet, may God bless him and give him peace, he accepted the gift and sent back the physician, and said, "We are a people that eats only when hungry, and when we eat, we do not eat until we are full. Thus we have no need of a physician." When the words of the Prophet, may God bless him and give him peace, reached al-Muqawqis, he said, "How mighty a prophet he is! He has put all wisdom into a couple of words!" And in the Noble Tradition it says, "Go hungry and be healthy!" for hunger is the source of vigor in worship and produces a healthy, disease-free body. This is especially true of those who perform spiritual exercises and practice seclusion, for the outcome of this for them is hunger. As the Initiate of the Almighty the Imam al-Būnī[509] states in one of his books, "No one can perform a spiritual exercise correctly so long as there is so much as a grain's weight of satiety within him."

Overeating may spring from several causes. It may be from excessive greed **11.31.19**
for food or from habit. We have seen people eat a crock of food and not be satisfied, and we have seen people eat a hundred roasted eggs with bread and not be satisfied. A certain tyrant used to eat a ewe, roasted, for lunch. One day he ate and then wanted to have intercourse with his wife, but she refused. When he reproached her, she said, "How can you reach me when there is so much of ewe between us?"[510] And Master Muḥyī l-Dīn ibn al-ʿArabī, God benefit us through him, states in *The Positions of the Stars*[511] that ʿAbd al-Malik[512] was a glutton who one day passed a man who had with him two baskets, of roasted eggs and of figs. ʿAbd al-Malik ate everything that was in them and got sick and died as a result. Al-Walīd,[513] one of the kings of the Banū Umayyah, was a stubborn tyrant who would drink a skin of wine and eat a young camel. One day he opened a copy of the Qur'an and saw, «And they sought help from their Lord and every stubborn tyrant was brought to naught!»[514] and he ripped up the book and recited:

Threatenest thou me with "stubborn tyrant"?
Well, that I am indeed!
When thou seest thy Lord on Doomsday say,
"The one who ripped me was Walīd!"

وهذا كلّه من تعنّته وشدّة تجبّره (وكان المأمون) يأكل كثيرًا فاصطنع له بعض الحكماء المأمونيّة فصار يأكل منها فانسدّت معدته وقلّ أكله لأنّ قليلها يغذي الشخص ولهذا نسبت إليه (وأمّا ما اتّفق) لبعض الأولياء من أنّه كان يأكل الطعام الكثير الّذي يكفي الجماعة الكثيرة إنّما هو من باب التصريف وإظهار الكرامة

(قيل مرّ رجل أكول) في سفره واجتاز بقرية فأضافه إنسان وأجلسه وكانت زوجته في الفرن تخبز العيش فأتاه بجانب من الخبز وذهب يأتي بالأدْم فلمّا رجع وجده قد أكل الخبز جميعه فوضع عنده الأدم وذهب يأتي له بخبز آخر ورجع فوجده أكل الأدم ولم يزل على هذه الحالة حتّى أكل جميع ما خبزته زوجة الرجل والأدم فقال له الرجل يريد معه المداعبة والمباسطة لمّا رأى منه هذه الحالة إلى أين تمضي فقال إلى مصر قال ألك حاجة فيها قال نعم قال له وما هي قال وُصِفَ لي بها طبيب حاذق فقصدت الذهاب إليه قال لأيّ شيء قال أنا رجل قلّ أكلي وانسدّت معدتي ومرادي شيء يصفه لي لعلّي أقطع في الأكل فقال له الرجل أنا بقي لي عليك إحسان وسألتك بالله إذا قضيت حاجتك من الطبيب ورجعت فلا تمرّ على منزلي إن كان هذا فعلك ومعدتك مسدودة فكيف إذا اتّسعت ثمّ إنّه أخرجه من منزله وتوجّه إلى حال سبيله وقوله ١١،٣١،٢٠

(ما تركتُ بَقِيَّتو لغيري) أي لأحد غيري قريب أو بعيد ١١،٣١،٢١

(وَلا عِنْدي بِدا تَوَقيفْ) أي لا أتوقّف في الأكل ولا أستحي من أحد إذا كان مارًّا ولا أعزم ولا أطعم غيري منه ولا أنظر فيه إن كان باردًا أو حارًّا أو طيّبًا أو مُقارَبًا أو من حلال أو من حرام فعلى كلّ حال لا أنظر لهذا المعنى ولا التفت لهذا الأمر ١١،٣١،٢٢

—all of which was due to his obduracy and excessively tyrannical ways. Al-Ma'mūn used to eat a lot, and a certain physician concocted for him the dish called *ma'mūniyyah.*[515] He tried eating it and found that his stomach was filled and his consumption of food decreased, for a little of it is enough to nourish a person. This is why it was named after him. On the other hand, the case of the *walī* who used to eat large amounts of food, enough to satisfy a great multitude, is an example of divinely granted freedom of action and a demonstration of God's miraculous grace.

It is said that a glutton once passed by a village on a journey and a man **11.31.20**
invited him in and sat him down. At the time, his wife was at the oven baking bread, so the man brought his guest a quantity of bread and went off to get something to go with it. When he returned, he found that the man had eaten all the bread, so he put the condiments in front of him and went to get him more bread, and returned, and found that he had eaten the condiments, and so it went on until the guest had eaten all the bread the host's wife had baked and the condiments too. When he saw this, the host asked, in an attempt at cordiality, "Where are you on your way to?" "Cairo," said the man. "Do you have business there?" asked the host. "Indeed," said the man. "And what is that?" asked the host. "A clever doctor was recommended to me there," said the man, "so I decided to go to him." "Why?" asked the host. "I am a man," said the guest, "who eats little, and my bowels are obstructed. I want him to prescribe me something, lest I give up eating altogether." Then the host said to him, "I have a favor to request of you: I beseech you in God's name, if you complete your business with the doctor and come back, don't pass by my house! If this is how you behave when your bowels are obstructed, what will you do when they've been opened up?" Then he expelled the man from his house and he went his way.

mā taraktu baqiyyatū li-ghayrī ("and leave nothing over for others"): that is, for **11.31.21**
anyone other than myself, be they near or far.

wa-lā ʿindī bi-dā tawqīf ("and I would not pause"): that is, I would not pause **11.31.22**
in my eating or feel ashamed before anyone who might pass by, or invite him, or feed from it anyone other than myself; nor would I look at it to see whether it was cold or hot, or tasty or only so-so, or permitted or forbidden. In no case would I bother with such questions or pay any heed to such things.

ثمّ إنّه تشوّق إلى مأكول من السمك المالح يقال له الفسيخ وتمنّاه واشتهاه فقال ١١،٣١،٢٣

ص

أَنَا خَاطِرِي أَكْلَةْ فِسِيخ[1] عَلَى ٱلنَّدَهْ   أَضَالُ عَلَيْهَا بَاكِيًا وَأَسِيفْ ١١،٣٢

ش

قوله (أنا) يعني أبو شادوف لا غيري كما تقدّم معناه في أبيات غير هذا ١١،٣٢،١

(خاطري) أي مرادي ودائماً يخطر ببالي ذلك وأنا متشوّق إليه ومشتهيه ومنتظره وهو ١١،٣٢،٢

(أَكْلَةْ فِسِيخ) والأكلة واحدة الأكل والفسيخ نوع من السمك يقال له البوري ونوع آخر يقال له الطوبار يأخذوه ويرصّوه على بعضه البعض بعد أن يضعوا على كلّ رصّة الملح فيتنقع ثمّ يسيل منه ماء ثمّ يَضْمُر ويُصلِحه الملح ويشدّه ثمّ إنّهم يأخذوه ويبيعوه ويأكله أهل الريف وغيرهم يأخذوا الفسيخة منه ويشقّوا بطنها ويضعها الرجل أو المرأة على يده اليسار أو في يديه الاثنين ويعصر عليها الليمون ويَنْتِش منها لُقْمة بلقمة يأخذ بفمه القطعة اللحم ويأخذ عليها اللقمة الخبز فيصير مثل الكلب الّذي يَنْهش في رِمّة مثلاً ويعلو فمه ويديه القذارة والرائحة الخبيثة ويأكلوه حتّى في الأسواق وأغرب من هذا أنّه أخبرني من أثق به من أهالي سَمَنُّود[2] أنّه دخل مطهرة مسجد وليّ على البحر يقال له العَدَويّ نفعنا الله به فرأى شخصاً من الأرياف قاعداً في بيت الخلاء ومعه فسيخة ورغيف يأكل منهما فقام عليه وقال له تأكل في بيت الخلاء فقال له أنت تطردني من بيت الله فضحك عليه وتركه ١١،٣٢،٣

---

١ بي: فَسيخ. ٢ بي (في جميع النسخ): سمانود.

Next he felt a desire to eat a dish made of salt fish, called *fisīkh*, and hoped and yearned for it. He says: 11.31.23

TEXT

anā khāṭirī ʾaklat fisīkhin ʿalā l-nadah 11.32
ʾaḍālu ʿalayhā bākiyan wa-ʾasīf

Me, my wish is for a meal of *fisīkh* first thing.
I shall ever weep for it and grieve!

COMMENTARY

11.32.1 *anā* ("Me"): meaning me, Abū Shādūf, and no one else, as previously explained in relation to other verses.

11.32.2 *khāṭirī* ("my wish"): that is, my desire, and what constantly occurs (*yakhṭiru*) to my mind, and what I am longing and waiting for, is . . .

11.32.3 *ʾaklat fisīkhin* ("a meal of *fisīkh*"):[516] an *aklah* ("meal") is a single instance of *akl* ("eating"), and *fisīkh* is a kind of fish called *būrī*, and another kind called *ṭūbār*; they take these and stack them one on top of one another, having first put salt on each layer. The salt is absorbed, water leaches out, the fish shrinks, and the salt preserves and hardens it. Then they take them and sell them. The country people and others eat them: they take a fish and slit its belly and then the man or the woman takes the fish in his left hand, or in both hands, and squeezes lime over it and picks at it, morsel by morsel, taking a bit of the flesh in his mouth and then a morsel of the bread, like a dog worrying at a piece of carrion, the filth and vile stench all over his mouth and hands. They eat it even in the marketplaces and, stranger still, I was told by someone I trust from Samannūd that he entered the ablutions area of a riverside mosque dedicated to a saint called al-ʿAdawī, God benefit us through him, and saw an individual from the countryside sitting in the latrine with a piece of *fisīkh* and a loaf from which he was eating. My friend went up to him and said, "Would you eat in the latrine?" and the man replied, "And would you drive me from the House of God?" The man laughed at him and let him be.

٤،٣٢،١١ ولكن له عند نساء الأرياف موقع عظيم وشهوة لا يعدّلها شيء خصوصاً أهالي الكفور وبلاد المَلَق فإنّهم لا يروه إلّا زمن النيل يُجْلَب لهم من دمياط ورشيد في المراكب ويباع عندهم بالقُمح والدراهم ولهم فيه رغبة زائدة ويجلب لبلاد الصعيد وغيرها وهو مشهور ببلاد مصر وأمّا البَطارِخ فإنّهم يبقوه في الهواء إلى أن يجمد ويصير يابساً عن الفسيخ وهو مأكول الأكابر وسمّي بطارخ لأنّ جوفه ملآن بطروخ بخلاف الفسيخ فإنّه خالي عن ذلك ويأكلوا لحمه بالخلّ والزيت وربّما أضافوا إليه الثوم والبصل المخروطين والحرارات وهو شهوة عظيمة في بلاد المدن وغيرها يكلّفوا الأكل منه كُلْفة زائدة ويأكلوه وحده ويسمّوه صِرِص بكسر الصاد الأولى ويجعلوا البطارخ التي في جوفه في إناء ثاني ويضعوا عليه الشيرج وكلّ هذا له لذّة عظيمة لكنّه حارّ يابس واعتدال أكله في الشتاء

٥،٣٢،١١ وسمّي الفسيخ فسيخاً لتفسّخه عند الأكل أو أنّ الذي صنعه في الأوّل خرج منه ريح عند أكله فشمّه آخر فقال فِسي إخّ فركّبوا هاتين الكلمتين وجعلوها علماً وقالوا فسيخ (قيل) سمع بعض أهل الريف قارئاً يقرأ قوله تعالى ﴿وَفِيهَا مَا تَشْتَهِيهِ ٱلْأَنفُسُ وَتَلَذُّ ٱلْأَعْيُنُ﴾ فقال له يا شيخ وفيها فسيخ فقال نعم وفيها ما تشتهي نفسك الخبيثة وقوله

٦،٣٢،١١ (على النَدَه) أي وقت نزول النداء لأجل برودة الزمن لأنّ الفسيخ حارّ يابس فإذا كان في أوّل النهار ربّما اعتدل أكله هذا إذا كان في زمن الصيف وأمّا زمن الشتاء ففي أي وقت كان ويستحبّ أن يشرب عليه شراباً حلواً أو يأكل[1] عليه تمراً فإنّه يُذْهِب ضرره وأذاه وقوله

٧،٣٢،١١ (أضالُ) تقدّم معناه

٨،٣٢،١١ (عليها) أي على هذه الأكلة من الفسيخ لشدّة شهوة نفسي الخبيثة إليها

---

١ بي: يؤكل.

Amazingly, it is highly prized among the women of the countryside, who find it delicious beyond all comparison, especially those of the hamlets and the villages of the swamplands, for they set eyes on it only when the Nile is high, when it is brought to them in boats from Dimyāṭ and Rashīd and sold by the grain and the gram. They have an enormous liking for it, and it is taken for sale to Upper Egypt and elsewhere and is famous throughout Egypt. Roe-bearing gray mullet (*fisīkh al-baṭārikh*), on the other hand, they leave out in the air until it hardens and turns drier than *fisīkh*, and this is a dish of the great. It is called *baṭārikh* because its belly is full of *baṭrūkh* ("roe"), unlike ordinary *fisīkh*, which has none. They eat the flesh with vinegar and oil, sometimes adding chopped garlic and onions, and spices. It is considered a great delicacy in the cities and elsewhere, and they go to great lengths to eat it. They also eat it on its own, calling it *ṣirṣ*, with *i* after the first *ṣ*, after setting aside the roe from its internal cavity in another container, with sesame oil. All of this is extremely tasty but is Hot and Dry, and the proper time to eat it is in the winter. 11.32.4

Fisīkh is so called either because of its disintegration (*tafassukh*) when eaten, or because the first person to make it broke wind while he was eating and someone smelled it and said, "He farted! Yeccch!" (*Fisī! Ikhkh!*) and they put these two words together and made them into a name, saying *fisīkh*. It is said that a countryman heard a reciter of the Qur'an say the words of the Almighty, «And therein is all that souls desire and eyes find sweet»[517] and he said to him, "And is there *fisīkh* too, Shaykh?" to which the man replied, "Indeed, and everything else that your disgusting appetite desires!" 11.32.5

ʿalā l-nadah ("first thing," literally "at the dew"): that is, when the dew descends, for it is cool then, and, *fisīkh* being Hot and Dry, eating it at the beginning of the day may moderate its effect, if it be summer, though in the winter it may be eaten at any time whatsoever. It is preferable that one drink something sweet afterward or eat some dates, for this eliminates any harmful side effects. 11.32.6

ʾaḍālu ("I shall ever"): explained above . . .[518] 11.32.7

ʿalayhā ("(weep) for it"): that is, for this meal of *fisīkh* because of my disgusting soul's excessive longing for it. 11.32.8

(باكيا) أي على عدم حصول هذه الأكلة باكيًا والبكاء هو غرغرة الدموع وسقوطها على الخدود ويقال بكت السماء إذا نزل منها المطر قال تعالى ﴿فَمَا بَكَتْ عَلَيْهِمُ ٱلسَّمَآءُ وَٱلْأَرْضُ﴾ قال الشاعر [طويل] ٩،٣٢،١١

بَكَيتُ فأَبكاني بُكاها صَبابَةً   عَلَيها فكانَ الفَضلُ للمُتَقَدِّمِ

وهو مشتقّ من بكّ الجرح إذا خرج منه الدماء

وقوله (وأَسيفْ) سكّنه لضرورة النظم لأنّ أصله أضال أسيفًا على هذه الأكلة حتّى تحصل لي فلا ينفكّ عنّي الحزن حتّى آكل منها وأشبع والأسف هو شدّة الوجد على فقد الحبيب وبعد الصديق قال الشاعر [طويل] ١٠،٣٢،١١

ومـا أَسَفي إلا على مَنْ أَوَدّهُ   ومَنْ لا أَوَدّو ما عليه مَـلامُ

ثمّ إنّه انتقل من شهوة الخبيث إلى الطيّب فقال ١١،٣٢،١١

ص

عَلَى مَنْ نَضَـرْ فِي فُـرْنِ دَارُو طَوَاجِنْ   زَغَـالِيلَ مِنْ بُـرْجِ ٱبْنِ ابُو شَعْـنِيفْ ٣٣،١١

ش

قوله (على من نَضَرْ) بالعين ١،٣٣،١١

(في فُرْنِ) وهو ما تُضرَم فيه النار ويُخبَز فيه الخبز وتقدّم تعريفه في الجزء الأوّل من هذا الكتاب ٢،٣٣،١١

bākiyan ("weep"): that is, I shall go on weeping over the nonappearance of this meal. Weeping consists of the shedding of tears and their falling onto the cheeks; one also says "the heavens wept" when it rains, and "the clouds wept"; the Almighty says, «And the heaven and the earth wept not for them.»[519] The poet[520] says: 11.32.9

I wept, for her tears made me weep for love
Of her; and the credit goes to the one who wept first!

The word *bukā'* ("weeping") is derived from *bakka l-jarḥ* ("the wound oozed"), when blood comes out of it.[521]

wa-'asīf ("and grieve"): the word is shortened for the meter, the original form being *aḍālu asīfan* ("and I shall ever . . . grieve") for this meal until I get it, and sorrow will not leave me until I eat my fill of it. Grief is the extreme passion experienced at the loss of a beloved and separation from a friend. The poet says: 11.32.10

I grieve for none but the one I love,
And he whom I do not love need bear no blame.

Next he moved from a desire for something disgusting to a desire for something wholesome. He says: 11.32.11

TEXT

'alā man naḍar fī furni dārū ṭawājin 11.33
zaghālīla min burji-bn-Abū Sha'nīf

Happy is he who has seen in the oven of his house casseroles
of squabs from the dovecote of the son of Abū Sha'nīf!

COMMENTARY

'alā man naḍar ("happy is he who has seen"): with the eye . . . 11.33.1

fī furni ("in the oven of"): the oven is the thing in which fire is kindled and bread is baked and has been described in Part One of this book . . .[522] 11.33.2

١١،٣٣،٣ (دارو) أي دار الناظم فالضمير في داره راجع إليه يعني لا يكون في دار غير داره ولا تكون الطواجن في فرن غير فرنه لأجل ما يصير مطمئنّ الخاطر منشرح الصدر إذا حصل له ذلك وقوله

١١،٣٣،٤ (طواجنْ) جمع طاجن وتقدّم تعريفه ملآنة

١١،٣٣،٥ (زغاليلَ) وهي أفراخ الحمام البرّي المتّخذة من الأبراج ويقال له الحمام الغيطيّ لأنّه يرعى في الغيطان ومحلّات الزرع والأجران وأكلها نافع يقوّي الباه إذا أضيف لها الحرارات والسمن البقريّ فلا تسأل عن جودة طعمها ولذّة أكلها والحمام اسم شامل لكلّ ما عبّ وهدَر ثمّ إنّه بيّن أنّ الزغاليل الّتي أشار إليها لا تكون إلّا

١١،٣٣،٦ (من بُرُجِ) لا من الزغاليل المتولّدة من حمام البيوت والبرج واحد البروج ويطلق على برج القلعة وبرج الكواكب والكلام هنا على برج الحمام وهو بناء مستدير حول بعضه البعض فيه قواديس فخّار يأتي إليه الحمام البرّيّ ويَبيض في تلك القواديس ويفرّخ ويخرى فيها أيضاً ويسمّوه عندهم رسمالاً يأخذوه لزرع البطّيخ والنخل ويطعموه به وأمره عندهم مشهور ويأخذوا من أفراخه ويبيعوا ويذبحوا وهكذا في سائر البلاد واسم الزغاليل مشتقّ من الزَغَلَنْته وهو نبات أزرق اللون شُبِّهَتْ به الزغاليل لزرقة ريشها أو أنّه مشتقّ من الزُغَليّة طائفة يصنعوا الفضّة الزَغَل ويسمّوا الأنصاف الفضّة العصافير ويسمّوا القِرش فرس والفحم الّذي يصنعوا به زبيب والكِير الّذي ينفخوا به الشيخ ولهم اصطلاح في هذه الصنعة لكن تراهم دائماً في شدّة خوف من الحكّام وفقر زائد وقلّة بركة (وسئل الإمام الشافعيّ) رضي الله عنه عن الكيمياء فقال أعرف من افتقر بها لا من استغنى فكذلك الحمام في كلّ قليل يدخلوا عليه ويأخذوا أفراخه ويذبحوهم ويبيعوا منهم فهم دائماً في خوف مثل الزغلية وواحد الزغاليل زُغْلول كما أنّ

dārū ("his house"): that is, the house of the poet, the pronominal suffix of *dār* referring to him, meaning that he would not see them in anyone's house but his, and that the casseroles are not to be found in anyone's oven but his, so that, should this indeed befall him, he might be easy in his mind and of good cheer. 11.33.3

ṭawājin ("casseroles"): plural of *ṭājin*, described above,[523] full of . . . 11.33.4

zaghālīla ("squabs"): these are the chicks, taken from the dovecotes, of the free-ranging pigeons, which are also called "field pigeons" because they feed in the fields and where crops are sown and on the threshing floors. They are nutritious and act as an aphrodisiac if spices and clarified cow's butter are added. They are too delicious for words. *Ḥamām* ("pigeons, doves") is a generic term for everything that sips[524] and coos. Then he specifies that the squabs to which he is referring must be . . . 11.33.5

min burji ("from the dovecote of"): and not from squabs born to house-raised pigeons. *Burj* (literally "tower") is the singular of *burūj* and is also used of the Citadel (Burj al-Qalʿah)[525] and of a "mansion" of the zodiac (*burj al-kawākib*). Here the reference is to the dovecote (*burj al-ḥamām*),[526] which is a round building in which waterwheel jars[527] are set, the pigeons coming to these jars and laying their eggs and raising their chicks in them and dunging in them too. The peasants call their manure "capital" and use it for sowing watermelons and palm trees, which they feed with it; it is something with which they are extremely familiar. They also take the chicks and sell and slaughter them; so it is in all villages. The name *zaghālīl* is derived from *zaghalantah* ("ranunculus"), which is a plant, bluish in color, to which squabs are likened because their feathers are blue, or it may be derived from the *zughaliyyah*, a class of people who make counterfeit silver coins, which they call "sparrows"; they call the piaster coin a *faras* ("mare"), the charcoal that they use *zabīb* ("raisins"), the bellows that they blow with *al-shaykh* ("the old man"), and they have a whole jargon for their craft, but they appear to live in constant terror of the police and great poverty and from hand to mouth. The Imam al-Shāfiʿī, God be pleased with him, was asked about alchemy and said, "I know people who have been impoverished by it but none who have been enriched." Pigeons are in a similar state, at frequent intervals the peasants enter their houses, take their chicks, slaughter them, and sell some of them, so that they are in constant fear, like the *zughaliyyah*. The singular of *zaghālīl* is *zughlūl*, just as the singular of *habābīl* 11.33.6

واحد الهبابيل هِبَّوْل والبرج مشتقّ من التبرّج وهو المباهاة بالزينة قال تعالى ولا ﴿مُتَبَرِّجَاتٍ بِزِينَةٍ﴾

٧،٣٣،١١ (مسألة هباليّة) هل بين الحَمام الطائر والحمّام المعروف ببلاد المدن المُعَدّ للغسل ونظافة الأجساد مناسبة مع أنّ اللفظ واحد لا يختلف إلّا بتشديد الميم الأولى أم كيف الحال (قلنا الجواب الفشرويّ) أنّ المناسبة يمكن حصولها من وجهين وجه قياسيّ ووجه طبيّ (فالأوّل) أنّ الحمّام فيه ازدحام الناس وكثرتهم على الحيضان والمغاطس وائتلافهم مع بعضهم البعض وانبساطهم بالكلام والمنادمات ونحو ذلك وكذلك برج الحمام فيه ازدحام الحمام على بعضه البعض وائتلافه ودخوله القواديس لأفراخه وتغريده وهديره وغير ذلك فكانت قواديسه تشبه الحيضان والمغاطس ودخوله لأفراخه يشبه الخلاوي والاجتماع بالأولاد المرد لأجل التكبيس والتكييس ونحوه وصعوده بعد ذلك إلى أعلى البرج وذهابه لاكتسابه رزقه مثل خروج الناس من الحمّام يكتسبون أرزاقهم ومعاشهم كما في الحديث لو أنّكم توكّلتم على الله حقّ التوكّل لرزقكم كما يرزق الطَّيْرَ تغدو خِماصاً وتعود بِطاناً فكان هذا هو وجه القياس الفطيسيّ (والوجه الثاني) أنّ الحمّام حارّ رطب ينفع جميع الأعضاء إذا كانت حرارته معتدلة وأحسن الحمّامات ما قَدُمَ بناؤه واتّسع فِناؤه وفيه منافع كثيرة حتّى قيل إنّه الطبيب الأبكم وكذلك لحم الحمام فإنّه مسخّن محرّك للباه وإن كان في أفراخه الرطوبة والغلظ لا سيّما إذا أضيف إليها الحرارات كما تقدّم فإنّ نفعها يكون تامّاً وأجودها الحمام البرّيّ وأمّا المربّى في البيوت فإنّ المداومة على أكله يتولّد منها الحمّى وزيادة الدم فكان في ذلك المناسبة للحمّام من هذا المعنى فاتّجه الجواب عن هذا الهبال

٨،٣٣،١١ (أمّا اسم الحمام الطائر) فهو مشتقّ من الحَوْم وهو التردّد في الطَيَران يقال حام الطائر يحوم إذا فعل ما تقدّم ومصدره حام يحوم حوماً (وأمّا الحمّام المبنيّ) فإنّه مشتقّ

("idiots") is *hibbawl*. *Burj* is derived from *tabarruj*, which means "showing off one's finery"; the Almighty used the term when He said, without «displaying their finery (*mutabarrijātin bi-zīnah*).»[528]

A Silly Topic for Debate: Is there any connection between the bird called *ḥamām* ("pigeon") and the *ḥammām* ("bathhouse") that is well known in cities and is designed for ablutions and personal cleanliness, bearing in mind that the word is the same, except for the doubling of the *m*, or what is the situation? We reply, the Facetious Answer is as follows: a connection may be discerned from two perspectives, one analogical, the other medical. The first is that, in a bathhouse, people are crowded together and throng around the basins and tanks, mingling intimately with one another and indulging in pleasant converse and so forth.[529] Similarly, in a dovecote the pigeons crowd together and mingle intimately and go into the jars to see their chicks and twitter and coo and so forth. From this perspective, the jars are the basins and tanks and the going in to the chicks is reminiscent of the private booths and of meeting with beardless boys for massage and scrubbing with a rough cloth and so on;[530] and the ascent of the pigeons afterward to the top of the dovecote, whence they go off to find their food, is similar to the people leaving the bathhouse to gain their daily bread and their livelihood. As it says in the Tradition, "If you were to put your trust in God as you should, He would provide for you as He provides for the birds, which set out in the morning with their stomachs empty and return in the evening with their stomachs full." This is the gastronomical-analogical perspective. The other perspective is that the bathhouse is Hot and Moist and does good to every member, so long as the temperature is moderate. The best bathhouses are those of ancient construction, with spacious halls and sweet water; they have so many beneficial qualities that they are called "the silent doctor." The flesh of pigeons is the same, in that it is heating and stimulates the sexual appetite—even though the chicks are both Moist and Coarse—especially if spices are added, as noted earlier; when this is done, the benefit they confer is complete. The best of their meat is from wild pigeons. Long-term consumption of those raised indoors causes fever and excess of blood. The connection with bathhouses would be along these lines. Our response is now transparent, the silliness apparent. 11.33.7

The name *ḥamām* for the birds is derived from *ḥawm* ("hovering"),[531] which is "hesitating in flight"; one says, "The bird hovers (*yaḥūmu*)" when it 11.33.8

من الحُمَّى وهي السخونة لأنّ الشخص إذا دخله صار كأنّه متلبّس بالحمّى لما يعتريه من الحرارة وحدوث العرق أو من الحموم وهو الغطوس في الماء من قولهم فلان استحمّى في البحر بمعنى أنّه سبح فيه وغطس أو من الحميم وهو الماء الشديد السخونة والحرارة ومن ذلك قوله تعالى ﴿يُصَبُّ مِن فَوْقِ رُءُوسِهِمُ ٱلْحَمِيمُ﴾ ويطلق على الصديق المحبّ لما في المحبّة من شدّة الحرارة والشوق ومنه قوله تعالى ﴿مَا لِلظَّالِمِينَ مِنْ حَمِيمٍ وَلَا شَفِيعٍ﴾ أي محبّ يشفع لهم ولشدّة حرارته وقوّة أفعاله شُدِّدَتْ ميمه الأولى (وأمّا الحِمام) بكسر الميم فهو الموت فإنّ حاءه ما كُسِرَت إلّا لأنّ الشخص يكون في حال حياته في قوّة وشدّة فإذا مات انخفض حاله ومضى حكمه ولم يبق إلّا أثره قال الشاعر [خفيف]

هـذه آثارُنا تَـدُلُّ عَلَيـنا   فانظُروا بعدَنا إلى الآثارِ

وهو مشتقّ من الشدّة يقال حمّ الأمر إذا اشتدّ ولا شكّ أنّ الموت شدّة عظيمة في معالجة طلوع الروح وخلوصها من الجسد ونحو ذلك انتهت الأبحاث الفشريّة والمصادر الهباليّة وقوله

٩،٣٣،١١ (أَبْن) ويطلق عليه ولد ونَجْل يقال ولد فلان ونجل فلان

١٠،٣٣،١١ (أَبو شَعْنيفْ) أصله أبي ولكن لم يساعده لسانه لعجرفته في الكلام وهذه كنيته وأمّا اسمه الأصليّ فهو عفلق أو بحلق على ما قيل وابنه المذكور في النظم اسمه فلحس وهو من أسماء الكلب واشتهر بهذه الكنية لأنّه كان يسرق الحشيش المسمّى بالنيف المتقدّم ذكره ويضعه للبهائم فشاع خبره بالسرقة وصار يقال في البلد شاع بالنيف أي بسرقة النيف ثمّ إنهم حذفوا الجارّ والمجرور وأبقوا الفعل والاسم وركّبوه تركيباً

does the preceding, the paradigm being *ḥāma, yaḥūmu, ḥawman*. As for the building *ḥammām*, it is derived from *ḥummā*, meaning "fever", since, when a person enters it, the heating and the sweating that overcome him make him appear as though he were suffering from a fever; or from *ḥumūm* ("bathing"), which is plunging into water, from the expression *fulānun istaḥammā fī l-baḥr* ("So-and-so bathed in the river"), meaning he swam in it and immersed himself in it; or from *ḥamīm*, which is "extremely hot water," whence the words of the Almighty, «Boiling water (*ḥamīm*) will be poured down on their heads.»[532] The same word is applied to a loving friend, because of the great heat and desire that love contains, whence the words of the Almighty, «There will be no friend (*ḥamīm*) for the evildoers, nor any intercessor,»[533] that is, no friend to intercede for them. The first *m* of *ḥammām* is double because the thing itself is so hot and has such a strong effect. *Ḥimām*, with *i* after the *ḥ*, on the other hand, is "death." It gets the *i* after the *ḥ* because when a man is alive he enjoys vigor and strength, but when he dies he is diminished,[534] his wisdom is gone, and nothing is left but his remains. As the poet says:

> These are our remains that bear witness to us;
> So look, when we are gone, to our remains.

It is derived from the notion of "extremity, crisis" (*shiddah*). One says *ḥumma l-amr* ("things reached a critical point") when things get tough—and there can be no doubt that death is a major crisis in terms of its effect on the escape of the vital spirit and its release from the body, etc. This concludes our facetious investigations and silly references.

(i)bn- ("son of"): also called "boy" (*walad*) and "scion" (*najl*). One may say either "So-and-so's boy" or "So-and-so's scion." **11.33.9**

Abū Shaʿnīf: the first word is, in genitive construct,[535] properly *abī*, but his tongue was too awkward to allow him to say that. Abū Shaʿnīf is his *kunyah*. His original name was ʿAflaq, or, according to some reports, Baḥlaq, and the name of his son mentioned in the verse was Falḥas, which is a dog's name. He became known by this *kunyah* because he used to steal the grass called *nīf* (mentioned above)[536] and put it down for his animals; thus stories of his thievery became widespread, and people in the village took to saying *shāʿa bi-l-nīfi* ("he became well known for the *nīf*"), that is, for stealing the *nīf*. Then they dropped the preposition and the gentive case,[537] retained the verb and the **11.33.10**

مزجياً وقالوا شعنيف مشتقّ من الشعنفة على وزن القلحفة ولعلّها معناها ومصدره شعنف يشعنف شعنفة

ثمّ إنّه بيّن كيفيّة مأكوله في الزغاليل وأنّهم يؤكلوا بالفطير ١١،٣٣،١١

ص

وَفَطّرٍ[١] فَطَايِرْ مِنْ طَحِينِ ٱبْنِ عَمُّو   وَيَقْعُدْ لَهَا قَعْدَةْ غُلَامٍ حَسِيفْ ٣٤،١١

ش

١،٣٤،١١ قوله (وفَطّرٍ[٢]) على وزن وشمّر قال الشاعر [طويل]

وَشَمّرَ عن أَيْرٍ وطَرْطَرَ عامدا   عليها ببولٍ فَهْيَ في البَول تَغْرَقُ

ومعناه أنّه يقول إذا حصلت لي هذه الطواجن الزغاليل وأشفى الله مرادي بحضورها عندي لا يلذّ لي أكلها إلّا بالفطير فلهذا قال

٢،٣٤،١١ (وَفَطّرٍ[٣] فطايرْ) مصدرٍ مثل عمل عمايل أو مثل قشر قشاير ومعناه بطط أو صنع فطيراً والفطاير جمع فطيرة وتُجْمَع على فطير مثل خَمِيرة وخَمِير أو حمارة وحَمِير والفطير قيل إنّه ثقيل غليظ لا يوافق الآدميّ لأنّه يولّد الأرياح هذا إذا أُكِلَ وحده وأمّا مع غيره فلا بأس به هذا كلّه في فطير الريف الّذي أراده الناظم يأخذوا الدقيق لا غير ويعجنوه بالماء من غير خمير ويضعوه في الفرن أو يدمّسوه في الجورة ويقال له فطير دَمّاسيّ ثمّ إنّهم يأخذوه ويأكلوه فهذا هو الثقيل المنهيّ عنه (وأمّا الفطير) الّذي تفعله الأكابر

---

١ بي: وٱفَطّرْ. ٢ بي: وٱفَطّرْ. ٣ بي: وٱفطّرْ.

noun, put them together as a compound, and made it *Shaʿnīf*. The word *shaʿnīf* derives from *shaʿnafah*,[538] of the measure of *qalḥafah* ("dessication"), and the meaning may be one and the same. The paradigm is *shaʿnafa, yushaʿnifu, shaʿnafatan*.

Next he explains how he eats squabs, and that they are eaten with flaky pastry. **11.33.11**

TEXT

wa-faṭṭar faṭāyir min ṭaḥīni-bni ʿammū **11.34**
wa-yaqʿud lahā qaʿdat ghulāmin ḥasīf

And made *faṭāyir* cakes from the flour of his cousin
and sits down to them like a lovelorn adolescent!

COMMENTARY

wa-faṭṭar ("and made"): of the measure of *wa-shammar* ("and hitched up his skirts"). The poet says: **11.34.1**

And he hitched up his skirts to reveal a prick, and pissed down on her
Quite deliberately, till she was drowning in piss.

His words mean that "if these squab casseroles fall to my lot and God fulfills my wish through their arrival where I am, eating them will bring me no pleasure unless they are accompanied by flaky pastry," which is why he says . . .

wa-faṭṭar faṭāyir ("and has made *faṭāyir* cakes"): a verbal noun[539] like *ʿamal ʿamāyil* ("he did (terrible) deeds"), or like *qashshar qashāyir* ("he peeled peelings"); the meaning is "he patted out, or manufactured, *faṭīr*." *Faṭāyir* is the plural of *faṭīrah*, though this may also take the plural *faṭīr*,[540] like *khamīrah* ("yeast cake") and *khamīr* ("yeast"), or *ḥimārah* ("she-donkey") and *ḥamīr* ("donkeys"). *Faṭīr* is said to be Heavy and Coarse and unsuitable for human consumption because it generates flatulence; however, this is only true if it is eaten alone. When eaten with other things it does no harm. The preceding refers exclusively to the *faṭīr* of the countryside, which the poet wants. They take plain flour and knead it with water without any yeast and put it in the oven or stew it in the cooking pit, this latter type being called "slow-cooked *faṭīr*" (*faṭīr dammāsī*). Then they take it and eat it, and this is the Heavy type **11.34.2**

فهو من الدقيق العَلامة ويَبُسّوه بالسمن والعسل النحل فهذا لا بأس به أو الّذي يصنعوه وقت عجنه بالسمن ويخبزوه للفطور ونحوه فهذا هو المطلوب وأمّا الكلام فيما تقدّم وقوله

٣،٣٤،١١ (من طحينِ ابْنِ عمّو) واسمه غنداف أي يكون ابن عمّه يتبرّع له به من غير مُقابِل أو يعيره الدقيق حتّى يفتح الله عليه ويردّه له أو يهبه إيّاه أو يتمكّن من سرقته ويخبزه في الفرن أو الجورة ويخرّج الطواجن الزغاليل من الفرن ويفتّ في مرقها الفطاير المذكورة ويتأهّب للأكل منها

٤،٣٤،١١ (ويَقْعُدْ لها) أي للزغاليل أو لمجموع ذلك

٥،٣٤،١١ (قَعْدَةْ) أي مثل قعدة

٦،٣٤،١١ (غلامٍ) وهو الذي أطرّ شاربه قال الشاعر [بسيط]

مِنّا الغُلامُ الّذي أَطرّ شاربُهُ   والعَانِسون ومِنّا المُرْدُ والشِّيبُ

وقيل الغلام من بلغ تسع سنين من حين الفطام وقيل من حاز الكمال والشدّة وقوله

٧،٣٤،١١ (حَسيفْ) صفة لغلام أي عنده حسافة أي تفكّر وكآبة وشدّة جوع وحزن فأكون مثله عندي تفكّر وشدّة جوع فما أصدّق أن أرى هذا الطعام وهذا الفطير وآكل منه حتّى أكتفي ويذهب جوعي وتنقضي شهوتي مثل الغلام الّذي اعتراه الحزن والأسف وقعد متفكّرًا حتّى يُذْهِب الله حزنه ويجمعه على أحبابه وفرح وانسرّ بلقائهم فإنّ اجتماع الأَحِبّة عيد

٨،٣٤،١١ (كما اتّفق) أنّ بعض العارفين مرّ برجلين يأكلان في رمضان فقال لهما ما أمركما قالا نحن محبّين صادقين فرّقنا الدهر مدّة ثمّ اجتمعنا في هذا اليوم واجتماع المحبّين عيد

that is discommended. The *faṭīr* that is made by the great, on the other hand, is prepared with the finest flour, into which they work clarified butter and honey, and this type does no harm. Or there is the type to which they add clarified butter while kneading and bake for breakfast and so on; this is the desirable kind.

min ṭaḥīni-bni ʿammū ("from the flour of his cousin"): whose name was Ghindāf; that is, his cousin would have donated it to him for nothing, or lent him the flour till such time as his circumstances should improve and he could give it back to him, or given it to him as a present, or the poet was able to steal it and bake it in the oven or the cooking pit. He would then remove the squab casseroles from the oven and crumble the aforesaid *faṭāyir* into the broth and prepare himself to eat of it. **11.34.3**

wa-yaqʿud lahā ("and sits down to them"): that is, to the squabs, or to the thing as a whole . . . **11.34.4**

qaʿdat ("like"): with the demeanor of one sitting like . . . **11.34.5**

ghulāmin ("an adolescent"): a *ghulām* is one whose moustache has started to sprout. The poet[541] says: **11.34.6**

Among us are the lad whose lip has just begun to sprout,
The spinster, and beardless boys, and white-haired men.

Some define a *ghulām* as anyone who has lived nine years since being weaned, others as one who has reached maturity and strength.

ḥasīf ("lovelorn"): an adjective qualifying *ghulām*, that is, afflicted with *ḥusāfah*, that is, worries and gloom and great hunger and sorrow. The poet is saying, "I too, like him, will be afflicted with worries and great hunger, for I cannot believe that I shall ever behold this dish and this *faṭīr*, and eat of it till I have had enough and my hunger disappears and my appetite is satisfied, like an adolescent boy who, afflicted with sorrow and grief, sits absorbed in thought till God drives away his sorrow and reunites him with his loved ones and he is overjoyed and filled with happiness at finding himself once more with them—for 'the lovers' meeting is a feast.'" **11.34.7**

Apropos of which, an Initiate of God once passed two men eating during Ramadan and asked them, "What do you think you are doing?" to which they **11.34.8**

وصوم العيد حرام فقال ما علامة محبّتكما فقال أحدهما اجرح ذراعي فجرحه فخرج الدم من ذراع الآخر من غير جرح فصارت أرواحهما وأجسادهما كأنّهما روح واحدة في جسد واحد كما قال الشاعر [رمل]

نَحنُ جِسمَيْنِ بِجِسمٍ واحدٍ   نَحنُ روحَيْنِ حَلَلْنا بَدَنا

وقال ابن العربي نفعنا الله ببركاته [طويل]

ولمّا التقَينا للوَداعِ حَسِبتُنا   لدى الضمِّ والتَّعنيقِ حَرفًا مُشَدَّدا
ونَحنُ وإنْ كُنّا مُثنّى شُخوصُنا   فَما تُبصِرُ الأَبصارُ إلّا موحَّدا

ومن هذا المعنى كثير من مشرب المحبّين ومطلب العارفين نفعنا الله بهم أجمعين

ثمّ إنّ الناظم انتقل إلى شهوة أخرى فتمنّاها وقال ٩،٣٤،١١

ص

عَلَى مَنْ نَضَرْ طَاجِنْ سَمَكْ فِي فُرَيْنِهِ[١]   وَلَوْ كَانَ يَا ٱخْوَانِي بِلَا تَنْضِيفْ ٣٥،١١

ش

قوله (على من نَضَرْ) بعينه لا سمع بأذنه ١،٣٥،١١

(طاجنْ) ملآن ٢،٣٥،١١

(سمكْ) والسمك اسم جنس شامل لأنواع كثيرة أحلّ الله تعالى أكله هو والجَراد حيًّا وميتًا قال رسول الله صلّى الله عليه وسلّم أُحِلَّتْ لنا ميتتان ودمان السمك والجراد ٣،٣٥،١١

١ بي: فُرَيْنو.

replied, "We are two true lovers whom fate had separated for many a year. Then we met today, and 'the lovers' meeting is a feast' and to fast on a feast is a sin!" "And what," said the other, "is the mark of your love?" One of the two replied by saying, "Cut my arm!" and held it out to him, and the man cut it and the blood came out of the other's arm, without a wound, for their two souls and two bodies had become as one soul in one body. As the poet[542] says:

> We are two bodies as one body.
> We are two souls that have become a single form.

And Ibn al-ʿArabī,[543] God benefit us through his blessings, says:

> When we met to say good-bye, and hugged and hung,
> I reckoned us one single, doubled, sign;
> And though as selves we may be twain,
> To outside eyes we must appear as one.[544]

There is much in the same vein on the inclination of lovers and the quest of Initiates, God benefit us through them every one!

Next, the poet moves on to another tasty dish for which he longed. He says: 11.34.9

TEXT

ʿalā man naḍar ṭājin samak fī furaynihī 11.35
wa-law kāna yā-khwānī bi-lā tanḍīf

> Happy is he who sees a casserole of fish in his little oven
> though it be, my brothers, uncleaned!

COMMENTARY

ʿalā man naḍar ("Happy is he who sees"): with his eye, not hears with his ear . . . 11.35.1

ṭājin ("a casserole"): full of . . . 11.35.2

samak ("fish"): a name for a whole category, consisting of many different sorts, which the Almighty has permitted to be consumed, along with locusts, both dead and alive.[545] The Prophet, God bless him and grant him peace, said, "Two dead things and two things containing blood have been permitted to 11.35.3

والكبد والطحال والكبير من السمك بارد رطب غليظ والصغير بارد رطب لطيف وأجوده الطريّ وإذا طُبِخَ بالسمن والبصل والكوامخ الحارّة اعتدل وزاد في الباه والمالح أحرّ من الطريّ وأيبس ونفع الكبير منه أن يؤكل مع شراب عتيق وزبيب ونفع الصغير أن يؤكل بشراب عتيق وفالوذَج خصوصاً إذا كان متّخذاً من ماء عذب جاري والمفلَّس منه أَوْلى من غيره (قال بعض الحكماء) كُلْ منه ما تفلّس واترك منه ما تملّس والمتفلّس منه مثل البوري والقَجّاج والبنّيّ فإن كلّ واحد منهم له لذّة عظيمة ويتفاوتوا في الطعم واللذّة أمّا البوري فيُحْشَى بالبصل والحرارات ويعمل على الأرزّ المفلفل ويعمل أيضاً في الطواجن مَرَقَةً وغيرها وله لذّة عظيمة ويعمل بالكشك أيضاً وأكلتُه بدمياط مراراً ويعمل أيضاً بأرزّ لكن قليل عن المفلفل ويضيفوا إليه ماء الليمون ويسمّوه فقاعية وأكلتُه وله لذّة عظيمة وطعميّة لطيفة وأمّا القجّاج فإنّه أرقى رتبة وأطيب طعماً من البوري وهو يشبه الشَبار الكبير وفي المثل إذا عَدِمَ الدجاج كلّ القجّاج * ويتنوّع في الأطعمة مثل البوري (وأمّا السمك البِنّيّ) ألذّ في الطعميّة من الكلّ ولا يوجد إلّا في قاع البحر العذب يتحيّلوا على صيده ويأخذوه ويهادوا به الأكابر والأمراء والوزراء وهو جيّد الطعم كثير النفع عن غيره خصوصاً إذا قُلِيَ وحُشِيَ فلا تسأل عن لذاذة طعمه فإنّك تودّ أن تأكل أصابعك من حسنه وفي المثل يقول لسان حال البنّيّ (إن رأيت أحسن مني لا تأكلني) ونوع من السمك يقال له شَبار له مرارة في الطعم ولذاذة في المأكل وقد ورد أنّه يأكل من حشيش الجنة

٤،٣٥،١١ وكلّ هذا بعيد عن مقصد الناظم وإنّما مراده السمك الّذي يصيدوه من بلاده لمّا ينزل عنها ماء النيل وتصير بِرَك ونُقَر ملآنة بالماء فيتولّد فيها سمك قراميط سود وشبار صغير وصِير ونحو ذلك فتنزل أولادهم ويصيدوا منه فيأتوا به وينظّفوه ويضعوه في الطواجن ويضعوا عليه شيئاً يسيراً من الزنجار وبعض بصل مخروط ويضعوه في الفرن يأخذ قوامه فيأكلوه بخبز الدرة أو الشعير ويصير له زفرة ورائحة

us: fish and locusts, and the spleen and the liver." Large fish are Cold, Moist, and Coarse, and small fish are Cold, Moist, and Subtle. The best is fresh fish, whose humors may be adjusted by cooking with clarified butter, onions, and hot spices; they also increase sexual appetite. Salted fish are Hotter than fresh, and Drier. Large fish are most nutritious when eaten with old wine and raisins, and small fish when eaten with old wine and *fālūdhaj*, especially if taken from sweet running water. Those with scales are to be preferred to those without; a doctor says, "Eat of them what is scaly and leave of them what is slimy." The scaly ones are those such as the mullet, the bream, and the barb, each of which is very delicious and has its own particular taste and tastiness. Mullet, for example, is stuffed with onions and spices and prepared with fluffy rice and is also used in casseroles to make a broth and in other ways and is very delicious. It may also be made with groats, and I have eaten it this way many times in Dimyāṭ. It may be made with rice, but this has to be slightly sticky. To this they add lime juice and call it *fuqāʿiyyah*; I have eaten it, and it is very delicious and has a subtle flavor. Bream is considered more of a delicacy and better tasting than mullet and resembles a large perch; in the proverb it says, "If there's no chicken to be seen, eat bream!" It is prepared in various ways, like mullet. As for the barb, it is the best tasting of all, and is found only on the riverbed. They have special tricks for catching it, and they get it and present it to great men, emirs, and viceroys as a gift. Its taste is outstanding, and it is more nutritious than any other kind, especially if fried and stuffed, in which case words cannot describe how tasty it is—you want to eat your fingers, it's so good! The proverb says, putting the words into the mouth of the barb, "If you find better than me, don't eat me!" There is also a kind of fish called perch, whose taste is slightly bitter but makes delicious eating, and is said to feed on the plants of Paradise.

All of this, however, is far from what the poet has in mind. What he means is **11.35.4** the fish that he catches from his village when the water of the Nile retreats and the ponds and holes are left full of water; black catfish are generated therein, and little perch and small fry and the like, and their children go down and fish in them, then bring the fish, clean them, and put them in casseroles with a little linseed oil and some chopped onion and put them in the oven until they are done, and eat them with maize or barley bread, the whole thing having a cloying stench and a foul smell, though to them it is the most delicious of foods. The small black catfish they take and bury in the cooking pit until they are a

كريهة وهو عندهم ألذّ المأكول ويأتوا بالقراميط السود الصغار ويدفنوها في الجورة إلى أن تنضج يسيرًا ويأكلوها ودمها سائل أعاذنا الله من ذلك

٥،٣٥،١١ وبذكر السمك ذكرت (ما اتّفق أنّ رجلاً كان يهوى امرأة بديعة الحسن والجمال) وكان زوجها من إخواننا المطاعيم المغفّلين فمرّ عليها يوماً وقال لها طال الموعد فقالت له في غد تأتيني أخير النهار ثمّ إنها أصبحت وقالت لزوجها قد اشتهينا السمك أطبخه في هذا اليوم ونأكله فمضى إلى السوق وأتى به فنظّفته وأصلحت شأنه ووضعته في طاجن كبير وقالت له خذه وامض به إلى الفرّان وأَرِحْنا من طبيخه وقل للفرّان أن يرسله مع غلامه أذان العصر فأخذه زوجها وذهب به إلى الفرّان وأعلمه بما قالت زوجته فقال له سمعاً وطاعة ثمّ إنّ الفرّان طبخه وأرسله لها في الوقت المعلوم فبينما هي جالسة وإذا بصاحبها الّذي أوعدته يطرق الباب ففتحت له وطلع وأكل من ذلك السمك وتملّى بحسنها وجمالها وقضى منها مراده فبينما هو معها في الحديث إذ طرق زوجها الباب فارتعب الرجل فقالت له لا تخش من شيء والزم الصمت ولا تتكلّ ثمّ إنّها فتحت لزوجها الباب وأظهرت له الحزن والبكاء فقال لها ما الّذي أصابك فقالت له أتاني غلام الفرّان بالطاجن السمك فلمّا كشفته وأكلت منه طلع لي رجل فجلست خائفة مرعوبة ولم يزل في البيت جالس قال فطلع زوجها يجري بسرعة فرآه جالساً فقال له من وضعك في الطاجن هل هو الفرّان أو غلامه قالت له خذه وامضي إلى الفرّان يخبرك بحقيقة الحال وقل له من اليوم لا بقيت توضع لنا في طاجننا أحداً يخوّفنا ويشوّش علينا قال فمسك الرجل من يده وتوجّه به إلى الفرّان وأعلمه بالقصة فعرف الفرّان الأمر وحقيقة الحال فقام وضرب الرجل وقال له أنا وضعتك في طاجن اللحم خالفتني ونزلت في طاجن السمك إن بقيت تخالفني شوّشت عليك فقال الرجل للفرّان يا سيّدي ما عدت أخالفك أبداً الطاجن الّذي توضعني فيه لا أطلع منه أبداً ثمّ إنّ الفرّان قال لزوجها أخبر زوجتك أنّي شوّشت عليه ولا بقى ينزل لها في طاجن

little ripe, and then they eat them while the blood is still running, God protect us from such things!

Speaking of fish, I am reminded that a man once loved a woman of surpassing comeliness and beauty, whose husband, God bless him, was one of our more dim-witted and credulous brethren. One day her lover passed her and said, "It's ages since we met!" and she replied, "Come to me tomorrow at the end of the day!" On the morrow she said to her husband, "I feel like cooking fish today for us to eat," so he went to the market and brought some. She cleaned it and prepared it and put it in a big casserole, and told him, "Take this, go with it to the baker, and spare me the effort of cooking it. And tell the baker to send it with his boy at the time of the afternoon call to prayer." So her husband took it and went with it to the baker and gave him his wife's instructions, and the baker said, "To hear is to obey!" The baker cooked the fish and sent it to her at the agreed time, and while she was sitting and eating, her friend with whom she had made the tryst knocked on the door. She opened it and he went up and ate some of the fish and made free with her comeliness and beauty and had from her what he desired. While he was talking with her, her husband suddenly knocked on the door. The man was terrified but she told him, "Fear nothing but stay silent and do not say a word." Then she opened the door to her husband and made a show of sorrow and tears, so that he asked her, "What has befallen you?" to which she replied, "The baker's boy brought me the fish casserole, and when I took the cover off and started to eat, a man jumped out at me, so I sat down in fear and trembling, and he's still sitting in the house." The husband ran quickly upstairs, where he found the man sitting, and said to him, "Who put you inside the casserole? Was it the baker or his boy?" His wife told him, "Take him and go to the baker, and he'll tell you the truth of the matter! And tell him, 'From this day on, don't ever put anyone in our casserole again to scare us and put us through hell!'" So he took the man by the hand and went with him to the baker and told him what had happened. The baker realized what was going on and how things really stood, so he got up and struck the man, and told him, "I put you into the meat casserole, and you disobeyed me and got into the fish! If you go on disobeying me, I'll give you hell!" at which the man replied to the baker, "Master, I'll never disobey you again! The casserole you put me into I'll never get out of!" Then the baker said to the husband, "Tell your wife that I gave him hell and she'll never find him in a casserole again." The husband then went off and reported to her what had 11.35.5

أبدًا قال فمضى زوجها وأخبرها بالقصّة ففرحت وقالت إن عاد يوضع[1] لنا أحدًا في طاجن ما بقينا نطبخ عنده شيئًا أبدًا ثمّ تركها زوجها ومضى إلى أشغاله فانظر إلى هذا الطمع الحيدريّ وإلى هذا التغفّل العظيم

٦،٣٥،١١ (ومن العجائب) أنّ بعضهم صاد سمكة فرأى مكتوبًا على جانبها بقلم القدرة لا إله إلّا الله محمّد رسول الله فأطلقها كرامةً لكلمة الشهادة (وأعجب من هذا) أنّ بعض الأولياء كان في سفينة فهاجت الريح وأشرفت السفينة على الغرق فقال هذا الوليّ اسكن أيّها البحر فما على ظهرك إلّا بحر مثلك أي بحر من العلوم فسكن البحر وبطل الريح بإذن الله تعالى فخرج من البحر سمكة عظيمة وخاطبت هذا العارف وقالت له تزعم أنّك بحر علوم ومعرفة ولكن أنا أسألك عن مسألة تردّ جوابها قال قولي فتكلّمت السمكة بلسان فصيح وقالت له إذا مُسِخَ الرجل هل تَعْتَدُّ زوجته عدّة الأحياء أم عدّة الأموات فتحيّر الشيخ في أمره ولم يردّ جوابًا فقالت له السمكة أين دعواك فقال إنّي استغفر الله ممّا قلت فأرشديني إلى الصواب فقالت له إن مسخ جمادًا تعتدّ عدّة الأموات وإن مسخ حيوانًا تعتدّ عدّة الأحياء ثمّ إنّها غابت في البحر فتاب الوليّ من دعواه ورجع إلى الله سبحانه وتعالى ومن كرمه أنّه يقبل التوبة عن عباده فسبحان القادر على كلّ شيء فعجائب البحر لا تُحصى

٧،٣٥،١١ وبذكر قصّة الفرّان والسمك تذكّرتُ أنّ حفظ الوداد قليل في الناس ويعجبني قول بعضهم [طويل]

لَقَد كانَ لي خِلٌّ عَلِمْتُ وَلاءَهُ　　وَكانَ صَدوقًا في المَقالَ خَليلا
فَخانَ وِدادي ثُمَّ أَنكَرَ صُحْبَتي　　فَيا لَيتَني لَم أَتَّخِذْهُ خَليلا

وقال بعضهم [وافر]

---

[1] بي: توضع.

happened, and the woman was delighted and said, "If he puts anyone in our casserole after this, it'll be the last time we ever have anything cooked at his place!" Then the husband left her and went about his business. Observe this Ḥaydarian[546] trickery and that amazing credulity!

An Amazing Thing: Someone caught a fish and found written on its side, with the pen of God's omnipotence, "There is no god but God, Muḥammad is the Messenger of God!" He let it go, out of respect for the testament of faith. And more amazing than this, one of God's Friends was in a ship, and the wind rose and the ship was about to sink, and that holy man said, "Be still, Ocean, for on your back is an ocean like you!" meaning an "ocean of knowledge," and the ocean grew still and the wind dropped, by the will of the Almighty. Then a great fish emerged from the waters and addressed the Initiate and said to him, "You claim that you are a Friend of God and an ocean of knowledge and understanding, but should I ask you a question, would you know the answer?" "Speak!" said the man. Then the fish spoke in accents clear, saying, "If a man is transformed into some other shape, is the period that his wife must wait before remarriage that set for a dead man or that for a living?"[547] The shaykh was confounded and at a loss to answer, so the fish said to him, "Where now is your claim?" The man said, "I seek God's forgiveness for what I said! Guide me to the truth!" and the fish told him, "If he be transformed into something inanimate, the period to be observed is that for a dead man, and if he be transformed into an animal, the period is that for a living."[548] Then it disappeared into the waters. At this the holy man repented of his claim and turned back to God, Glorious and Mighty, who, in His magnanimity, accepts the repentance of His slaves—glory to Him who is capable of all things! The wonders of the ocean are beyond counting. 11.35.6

Apropos of the story of the baker and the fish, I am reminded that devotion is a rare thing among men. I find admirable the words of the poet who said: 11.35.7

I had a bosom friend, whose love I'd learned to trust,
Sincere in all he said, a lover true,
But he betrayed my love, then spurned my company—
Now how I wish his love I never knew!

And a poet[549] said:

وإخوانٍ حَسِبتُهم دُروعًا فكانوها ولكنْ للأعادي
وخِلْتُهمُ سِهامًا صائباتٍ فكانوها ولكنْ في فؤادي
وقالوا قد صَفَتْ مِنّا قُلوبٌ لقد صَدَقوا ولكنْ عن وِدادي
وقالوا قد سَعَينا كُلَّ سَعْيٍ لقد صَدَقوا ولكنْ في فسادي

وقال آخر [بسيط]

لأضرِبَنَّ رجائي ألف مَقْرَعَةٍ حدًّا وأَنْصُبُ آمالي على خَشَبَهْ
لِعِشْرَتي لأُناسٍ لا خِلاقَ لَهمْ بِيضُ الثِّيابِ وأقفالٌ على خَرِبَهْ

ومن كلام الإمام الشافعيّ رضي الله عنه [بسيط] ٨،٣٥،١١

أُبْعُدْ عَنِ النّاسِ كُلَّ بُعْدٍ ما لم تكنْ بينَهُم مجمَّلْ
ولا تقُلْ كانَ لي أيادٍ عَليهِمُ في الزَّمانِ الأوّلْ
المرءُ بَينَ أهلِهِ كُلَيْبٌ إذا رأوا ذَيلَهُ مُهَلْهِلْ

وقال أيضا رضي الله عنه [وافر]

لِقاءُ النّاسِ لَيس يُفيدُ شيئًا سِوى الهَذَيانِ من قيلٍ وقالِ
ألا فاقْلِلْ لِقاءَ النّاسِ إلّا لأَخذِ العِلمِ أو إصلاحِ حالِ

وقال بعضهم [بسيط] ٩،٣٥،١١

ما في زَمانِكَ مَن ترجو مَوَدَّتَهُ ولا صَديقٌ إذا جارَ[١] الزَّمانُ صَفا
فعِشْ فَريدًا ولا تَركَنْ إلى أحدٍ إنّي نَصَحتُكَ فيما قد جرى وكَفى

---

١ بي: جاز.

Many brothers I had whom I thought shirts of mail—
And so they were, but for my foes.
I thought them shafts shot straight—
And so they were—'twas at my heart they bent their bows.
They said, "Our hearts are pure!"
And they spoke true—but of all love for me, I must suppose.
They said, "We've tried so hard!"
And so they had—but only to increase my woes.

And another said:

Let me flog my hopes in punishment
And nail my longings to a cross
For being friends with those who have no worth—
White are their garments, but inside all is dross.

And Imam al-Shāfiʿī,[550] may God be pleased with him, said: 11.35.8

Stay far from men
If by them no respect to you is paid,
And do not say, "I did them many a favor
In the good old days!"
People will treat a man like Little Dog
If they see his tail's Frayed.

And he also said,[551] may God be pleased with him:

Meeting men will gain you nothing
But drivel and gossip
So make your meetings few, unless
To acquire knowledge or bestow profit.

And another said:[552]

11.35.9

None there is these days whose love you would desire,
No friend whose heart, when time is unjust, proves true.
So live alone and visit none,
And a word to the wise will do!

ولابن عروس قطب بلاد المغرب [مجتثّ]

النّاسُ بحرٌ عَميقٌ والبُعدُ عَنهُمْ سفينهْ
إني نَصحتُكَ فَانْظُرْ لِنَفْسِكَ المِسْكينهْ

١٠،٣٥،١١ وقوله (في فُرَيْنه[١]) أي فرن الناظم وصغّره لأجل النظم بمعنى أنّه يأتي من الغيط أو الجرن فيراه في الفرن حاضراً مطبوخاً من غير أن يتكلّف لصيده وتحويجه من الزيت الحارّ والبصل ونحو ذلك وقوله

١١،٣٥،١١ (ولوكانَ) هذا السمك الّذي أتمنّاه

١٢،٣٥،١١ (يَا ٱخْوَانِي) يخاطب به أصحابه وأحبابه والإخوان هم الأصدقاء والمحبّون وكلّ المؤمنين إخواناً في الله تعالى قال الله تعالى ﴿إِنَّمَا ٱلْمُؤْمِنُونَ إِخْوَةٌ﴾ (وفي الحديث) المؤمنون كالبنيان يشدّ بعضهم بعضاً وقال بعضهم من فقد إخوانه فقد مروءته

١٣،٣٥،١١ (قيل) أتى رجل إلى المأمون فقال له أنا أخوك أعطني من بيت المال ما يكفيني فقال له من أين أنت أخي فقال من قوله تعالى ﴿إِنَّمَا ٱلْمُؤْمِنُونَ إِخْوَةٌ﴾ فقال صدقت أعطوه درهما فقال ما هذا عطاء الملوك فقال له المأمون لو فرض أنّي فرّقت بيت المال على إخوتك ربّما يحصل لك أقلّ من ذلك فمضى الرجل ولم يظفر بشيء سوى الدرهم وقيل زاده عليه وارتدّ شاكراً (وكان المأمون) رحمه الله يحبّ الحِلم والعفو حتّى أنّه كان يقول حُبِّبَ إليّ الحلم حتّى ظننت أنّي لم أثاب عليه (ومن حلمه) أنّ جارية من جواره قدّمت إليه لحماً مشويّاً في أسياخ من الحديد فوقع منها سيخ على خلعته فخرقها وأتلفها فنظر إليها فقالت ﴿وَٱلْكَاظِمِينَ ٱلْغَيْظَ﴾ فقال قد كظمت غيظي فقالت وَالْعَافِينَ عَنِ النَّاسِ فقال قد عفوت عنك فقالت ﴿وَٱللَّهُ يُحِبُّ ٱلْمُحْسِنِينَ﴾ فقال أنت حرّة

[١] بي: فُرَيْنو.

And Ibn ʿArūs, Pole of the Maghrib, has it that:

Men are a deep, deep sea,
  Distance from them an ark—
So look to your pitiful soul
  And these words of mine do mark!

fī furaynihī ("in his little oven"): that is, in the poet's oven, using the diminutive for the meter, the meaning being that he should come from the field or the threshing floor and find it in his oven ready and cooked, so that he should not have to concern himself with catching it and flavoring it with linseed oil and onions and so on. 11.35.10

wa-law kāna ("though it be"): that is, though this fish that I long for be . . . 11.35.11

yā-khwānī ("my brothers"): he uses this word to address his companions and friends. One's "brothers" are one's friends and loved ones, and all believers are brothers in the Almighty. The Almighty has said, «The believers are indeed brothers,»[553] and in the Tradition it says, "The believers are to one another like a building whose parts hold each another up." And someone said, "He who loses his brothers has lost his manhood." 11.35.12

It is said that a man went to al-Ma'mūn and said to him, "I am your brother, so give me enough from the treasury to support me!" "By what logic are you my brother?" asked al-Ma'mūn. "By the logic of the words of the Almighty, «The believers are indeed brothers»," said the man. "You speak truly," said al-Ma'mūn. "Give him one penny!" "This is not the gift of a king!" said the man. Al-Ma'mūn responded, "Were I to divide up the treasury among your brothers, you might well get less!" Then the man left and got nothing but the one penny (though some say he gave him more and the man retired giving thanks). Al-Ma'mūn, God have mercy on his soul, loved clemency and forbearance so much that he used to say, "Clemency has been made so dear to me that I am afraid that I shall not be rewarded for it!" As an example of his clemency, one of his slave girls once was serving him grilled meat on iron skewers when one of the skewers fell from her hand onto his robe, burning it and ruining it. When he looked at her, she said, «Those who control their wrath!» "I have controlled my wrath," he replied. «And are forgiving of mankind!» she said. "I forgive you," he said. «And God loves those who do good works!» she said. "I set you free, for the sake of the Almighty," he replied.[554] His was an 11.35.13

لوجه الله تعالى وهذه مَلَكَة عظيمة في الحلم والعفو لا يقدر عليها أحد رحمه الله وقوله

(بِلا تَنْضيفْ) أي ولوكان يجد هذا السمك في طاجن في فرنه من غير غسيل ولا تنظيف بالماء بل يرصّوه في الطاجن بعظمه وبحوفه حتّى يصير مثل المشويّ في الجورة فتمنّى الأكل منه ولو على هذه الحالة لشدّة فقره وقلّة ما بيده وقوّة شهوته لرؤياه والأكل منه وفي المثل (الغريق يستند على القَشّ) وفي مثل آخر (بطينه ولا غسيل البِرَكْ) فعلى كلّ حال إنّه سدّ جوعه وقضي شهوة فالشخص إذا اشتهت نفسه شيئاً ولو أنّه حقير متى وجده كان عنده عظيماً وأكل منه أكلاً زائداً فإنّ الشهوة البهيميّة ترمي صاحبها على أخبث المأكول فكلّ من أطاع نفسه وهواه خسر (قال سيّدنا عيسى) عليه الصلاة والسلام لن تنالوا ما تطلبون إلّا بترك ما تشتهون وقال صاحب البردة رحمه الله تعالى [بسيط] ١٤،٣٥،١١

وخالِف النَّفسَ والشَّيطانَ واعْصِهما وإنْ هما مَحَضاكَ النُّصحَ فاتَّهِمِ

فمخالفة النفس فيها النجاة والراحة للإنسان والثواب في المعاد (قيل مكث سيّدي عمر بن الفارض) نفعنا الله به مدّة يشتهي أكل الهريسة ويخالف نفسه ويصبر إلى أن حصلت له يوماً وهو في الخلوة فمدّ يده ليأكل منها فانشقّ حائط الخلوة وخرج منه شخص وقال له أُفٍّ عليك يا عمر فقال إنْ أكلتها ثمّ إنّه تركها ولم يأكلها بقية عمره وخالف نفسه

(ومن النكت المضحكة) أنّ بعض الفقراء كان له تلميذ وكان دائماً يقول له خالف نفسك إذا قالت لك كل هذا فخالفها وكل غيره ولا تُطِعْها أبداً فأتى لشيخه يوماً طعام مفتخر ووُضِعَ بين يدي التلميذ صحن عدس وكان الّذي وُضِعَ بين يدي شيخه أرزّ مفلفل بلحم ضاني محمّر فمدّ التلميذ يده أخذ الصحن من قدّام شيخه ووضعه مكان صحن العدس فقال له شيخه أنا ما قلت لك خالف نفسك فقال له يا سيّدي حدّثتني نفسي أنّي آكل من هذا العدس فخالفتها وأكلت من هذا اللحم الضاني بالأرزّ المفلفل ١٥،٣٥،١١

outstanding capacity for clemency and forbearance that no one else could be capable of, God have mercy on his soul.

bi-lā tanḍīf ("uncleaned"): that is, if he were to find this fish in a casserole in his oven unwashed and uncleaned with water—and, truth to tell, they stack them in the casserole bones, heads, and all, just like grilled beans in the cooking pit—he would want to eat it even in that state, because he is so poor, so indigent, and so keen to see and eat it. The proverb says "The drowning man rests his weight on straw," and another says "Better with its own mud than washed in a pond!" In any case, it would stop his hunger and satisfy his craving, for if anyone finds something for which he has a craving, however vile, he holds it dear and eats an excessive amount of it, for an animal appetite will drive men to the most disgusting of foods, and all who obey their carnal appetites and cravings suffer. Master Jesus, blessings and peace upon him, said, "You will never attain what you want until you abandon what you crave."[555] And the author of *The Mantle*, may the Almighty have mercy on his soul, says:[556] 11.35.14

Oppose your appetite and Satan! Defy them both!
No honest counselors are they, so hold them in suspicion!

Denying the appetites brings salvation and ease, and reward on the Day of Judgment. It is said that Master ʿUmar ibn al-Fāriḍ, God benefit us through him, long craved *harīsah*, refusing to give in to his appetite and persevering until one day some appeared before him in his cell. But when he stretched out his hand to eat of it, the wall of the cell was rent, and a figure emerged from it and said to him, "Faugh on you, ʿUmar!" "I have not eaten of it," he said, and thereafter he gave it up and went the rest of his life without touching it, denying his appetite.[557]

An amusing joke is told, to the effect that a certain dervish had a disciple to 11.35.15
whom he was forever saying, "Deny your inclinations! Should they say to you, eat this, then deny them and eat something else, and never give in to them!"[558] One day a luxurious dish came to the shaykh, while a bowl of lentils was placed in front of the disciple (what was placed in front of the shaykh was fluffy rice with fried mutton). The disciple stretched out his hand and took the dish from in front of the shaykh and put it in place of the bowl of lentils. His shaykh said to him, "Have I not told you, 'Deny your inclinations?'" but the disciple responded, "Master, my inclinations told me to eat from the bowl of lentils, so

وكان لشيخه غلام جميل فدخل الشيخ يوماً الخلوة فوجد التلميذ يلوط به فقال له ما هذه الفعال فقال له يا سيّدي حدّثتني نفسي وقالت لي نِيك الشيخ فخالفتها وفعلت في هذا الغلام فقال له الشيخ اخرج قاتلك الله ما أشقاك وما أخبثك فخرج من عنده ولم يعد إليه

١٦،٣٥،١١ ثمّ إنّ الناظم اشتهى شيئاً لم يُرَ في بلده إلّا يوم عيد النحر فقال

ص

٣٦،١١ عَلَى مَنْ رَأَى فِي ٱلتَّـلِّ كِرْشْ مُـلَقَّحْ ‌ ‌ وَمِنْ فَوْقِـهِ ٱلدِبَّانْ يِعِـفُّ عَفِـيفْ

دَآنَا آنْ شُفْتُهُ[١] خَدْتُو بِحَالُو سَلَقْتُو ‌ ‌ وَكَلْتُو بِتِـفْـلُو مَـا أَرَى تَقْنِـيفْ

ش

١،٣٦،١١ قوله (على من رأى) أي رؤية بصريّة كما تقدّم في غير هذه الأبيات

٢،٣٦،١١ (في التَّلّ) أي تل بلده وهو الكوم العالي ويكون في الغالب حول البلد لأنّ كلّ من كان عنده تراب أو رماد يكبّه قدّام داره برّا البلد قصاد بيته وجاره مثله وهكذا إلى أن يتّصل ببعضه البعض ويعلو ويكبر من كثرة ما يُلقوا فوقه من القمامات وغيرها حتّى يصير كوماً عالياً يُرَى من بعيد وبجانبه أيضاً محّلات خالية يشخّوا فيها جميعاً نساء ورجال وأولاد وغالبهم يخروا فيها أيضاً ثمّ إنّ النساء والرجال يصعدوا إليه وقت الشخاخ وتحصل لهم المنادمة فيه والمحادثة عن الغيط والزرع والقلع والعجول

---

١ بي: شُفتو.

I denied them and took this mutton with fluffy rice!" Now the shaykh had a beautiful serving boy, and, coming in one day to the place of retreat, he found the disciple sodomizing him, so he said to the disciple, "What monstrous acts are these?" The disciple replied, "Master, my inclinations told me, 'Fuck the shaykh!' so I denied them and did this boy instead!" The shaykh told him, "Get out, God strike you dead! How wicked and vile you are!" So he left and never went back.

Next the poet craved something that is only seen in his village on the Feast **11.35.16**
of the Slaughtering.[559] He says:

TEXT

ʿalā man raʾā fī l-talli kirsha mulaqqaḥ **11.36**
wa-min fawqihi l-dibbān yiʿiffu ʿafīf
d-anā-n shuftuhū khadtū bi-ḥālū salaqtū
wa-kaltū bi-tiflū mā arā taqnīf

Happy is he who sees in the refuse dump tripes tossed away
even if the flies have settled on them in swarms!
If I saw them, I would take them all, boil them and eat them
with the undigested matter that's on them, and feel no revulsion.

COMMENTARY

ʿalā man raʾā ("happy is he who sees"): that is, sees visually, as explained above **11.36.1**
with reference to other verses . . .

fī l-talli ("on the refuse dump"): that is, the refuse dump of his village, which **11.36.2**
is a high mound that generally forms around the village, for anyone who has dust or ashes dumps them outside his dwelling on the outside of the village in front of his house and his neighbor does likewise, and so it continues until the mounds join and rise and grow larger from the quantities of garbage and so on that are thrown on top of them and turn into one tall mound that can be seen from far away. Next to it are deserted places where they all piss, men, women, and children, and where most of them shit too. The men and the women climb up to it when they piss and engage in friendly chats and conversations about the field, the crops, and the harvest, the calves and the buffaloes, and so forth. Sometimes quarrels break out while they are pissing and one of them attacks

والجاموس وغير ذلك وربّما وقع بينهم الشرّ عند الشخاخ فيقوم الشخص لخصمه وشخاخه في جبّته أو يسيل على ردائه حتّى يغرقها أي جبّته ويضارب رفيقه ورداؤه عليها الخراء وهكذا ثمّ يؤول أمرهم إلى الصلح أو القتل ونساؤهم على شكلهم عند قضاء الحاجة لا يتحاشوا عن الكلام في غزل الصوف والفلّ وغير ذلك لأنّهم لا يعرفوا المراحيض ولا تُبْنى عندهم ولا يقدروا عليها إلّا أن تكون في دار الشادّ بالكفر له ولجماعته يشخّوا فيها قال الشاعر [طويل]

سَألتُ بَني الأريافِ ما لِبُيوتِكمْ   مَراحيضُ قالوا لا مَراحيضَ للقَوم
فقلتُ فماذا تَصنَعوا في نِسائِكمْ   فقالوا جَميعاً نَحنُ نَخرا على الكَوم

فالتلّ والكوم عندهم بمعنى واحد ويسمّى عندهم أيضاً العِلِّيّة بكسر العين المهملة وتشديد اللام مع كسرها قال الشاعر [وافر] ١١،٣٦،٣

أتيتُ الكَفْرَ في ضَحْوَهْ   رأيتْ أهلو جميعْ شالوا
وراحوا فوقَ عِلِّيّهْ   عليها الكلّ قد بالوا

أي طلعوا كلّهم فوقها وشخّوا عليها جميعاً نساء ورجال وأطفال

وتطلق العلّيّة عندهم على الغرفة المبنيّة من الطين غير الطوب ولهذا يقال فلان اليوم في العلالي أي إنّه صار يجلس عالي عن الناس وبقي له في الكفر حرمة وقيمة على غيره ومن هذا المعنى قال شاعرهم [وزن غير معروف] ١١،٣٦،٤

جوز غزلان يا مَحْلاهم   شاقني على القَدَم حِنّاهم
متى يا زمان تجمعنا   في العلالي أنا وإياهم

ولا يكون التلّ أو الكوم مختصّاً لقضاء الحاجة عندهم بل ربّما اتّخذوا ذلك للمحادثة والمنادمة والمسامرة فيما بينهم ولغزيل الفلّ والصوف ونحو ذلك

his opponent, the piss all over his jubba or running down his outer garment till it—that is, his *jubbah*—is soaked, and trades blows with his comrade with the shit on his clothes, and so on, until the matter turns either to reconciliation or killing. Their women are the same when defecating: they feel no embarrassment at talking about spinning wool or jute and so on, for they are ignorant of latrines, which are not built in their houses and which they cannot afford, unless it be in the house of the bailiff in the hamlet, for him and his people to piss in. The poet says:

I asked the countrymen, "No latrines have your houses?"
Said they, "Not one!"
"What do you, then," I asked, "with your spouses?"
Said they, "All of us shit on the dump as one!"

Thus the refuse dump (*tall*) and the mound (*kawm*) to them are the same 11.36.3
thing, which they call also the *ʿilliyyah*, with *i* after the ʿ, double *l*, and *i* after it. Says the poet:

I came to the hamlet of a forenoon
And found it of people free—
They'd all gone up an *ʿilliyyah*,
And there they'd taken a pee.

—that is, they had all gone up on top of it and then collectively—women, men, and children—had pissed.

They also use the word *ʿilliyyah* of a room built of mud, as distinct from 11.36.4
brick, which is why they say, "So-and-so today is *fī l-ʿalālī*," that is, he now sits higher than other people and has acquired higher status and value than the rest.[560] On the same topic, their poet says:

Two gazelles—what could be cuter!
How the henna on their feet stirs my desire!
When, O Time, will you unite us,
That to the upper rooms we may retire?

The refuse heap or mound is not used by them exclusively to relieve themselves. It may be used for conversation, friendly chats, and evening talk among themselves, as well as for spinning jute and wool and so forth.

١١،٣٦،٥ (فإن قيل) إنّ الناظم قال (في التلّ) فيُفْهَم منه أنّه يرى الكرش في جوف التلّ فيكون متواري عنه وأكّد الرؤية بقوله (ومن فوقه الدبّان) والدبّان لا يسقط إلّا على شيء ظاهر لا على شيء مغطّى مستور كما تقول فلان في الدار أي في داخلها فما الجواب (قلنا الجواب الفشرويّ) أنّ في بمعنى على أي كرش ملقّ على التلّ أو الكوم كما يقال فلان في الجبل أي فوقه لا داخله لأنّه لا يستطيع أن ينفد الجبل ويدخل فيه أو أنّ حرف الجرّ على بابه ويكون قوله (في التلّ) بمعنى أنّ في جوف التلّ نقرة يشخّوا فيها ويرموا فيها الكروش مثلاً فصدق عليه أن الكروش في جوفه وإن كان ظاهرًا يُرى للناس فاتّجه الإشكال عن وجه هذا الهبال وقوله

١١،٣٦،٦ (كِرْشَ مُلَقَّ) أي كرش البهيمة التي يذبحوها يوم عيد النحر لأنّهم لا يروا اللحم إلّا في ذلك اليوم ولا يمكن أنّهم يلقوا الكرش على التلّ بل يأخذوه ويلقوا ما فيه من التِفْل ويغسلوه ويطبخوه مع بقيّة حوائج البهيمة ويسمّوه جغل مغل وله عندهم موقع عظيم (وأمّا في بلاد المدن) فإنّه من الضأن ويضيفوا إليه الرأس والكوارع ويسمّوه سَقَط ويصنعوه بالحرارات والسمن والكزبرة ويصبّوا عليه الخلّ ويصير له لذّة عظيمة فيبيعوه بالرأس تارة مدروجة في الكرش مغسولاً نظيفاً وتارة بغيرها والرؤوس يبيعوها مشويّة وحدها والكوارع تُصْنَع تسقية يبيعوها ويصبّوا عليها الخلّ والدهن والثوم ولها لذّة عظيمة كما هو مشهور في بلاد المدن وأمّا أهل الريف فإنّهم يصنعوا جميع ذلك في الدست أو البِرام ويضيفوا عليه الكزبرة وقليلاً من الشيرج ويقلّوا له بشيء من البصل أو الثوم ويأكلوه ولا يعرفوا السمن ولا الحرارات ولا شيئاً من ذلك وربما سلقوا ذلك بالماء وأكلوه حكم المرقة

If it be said, "The poet's use of the preposition *fī* in the phrase *fī l-tall* might lead one to understand that he saw the tripes *inside* the refuse dump, where they ought to be hidden from him, even though he confirms that he actually saw them by saying 'on which the flies' (for flies settle only on exposed things and not on things that are covered over and protected)—just as one uses the same preposition in the phrase *fulānun fī l-dār* ('So-and-so is in the house') that is, 'inside it'—how answer you?" we would reply that the Facetious Answer is that *fī* ("in") here is used in the sense of *ʿalā* ("on"), that is, he saw tripes discarded on the refuse dump or mound (*ʿalā l-tall awi l-kawm*), just as one says *fulānun fī l-jabal* ("So-and-so is on the mountain"), that is, on top of it, not inside it, since it would be impossible for him to penetrate the mountain and go inside it.[561] Or that the preposition is to be taken in its literal sense, and the words *fī l-tall* mean that there was indeed inside the refuse dump a hole into which they would piss and into which they would throw tripes, for example—in which case his claim that the tripes were *inside* the refuse dump would be correct, even though they might be exposed and visible to people. Thus the problem's now revealed, this silliness no more concealed. 11.36.5

kirsha mulaqqaḥ ("tripes tossed away"): that is, the tripes of the animal that they slaughter on the day of the Feast of the Slaughtering, for that is the only day on which they see meat, and in fact they would never throw the tripes on the dump. On the contrary, normally they would take them and remove the remaining food particles from them and wash them and cook them with the animal's offal; this they call *jaghl maghl* and hold in the highest esteem. In the cities, on the other hand, the tripes would be sheep's and they would add the head and the trotters, and this they call *saqaṭ*; they make it with spices, clarified butter, and coriander and pour vinegar over it, all of which makes it extremely tasty. Sometimes they sell it with the head, which they roll up in the clean, washed tripes, and sometimes without. They also sell the heads on their own, grilled. The trotters are made into a dish of broth and bread, which they sell with vinegar, fat, and garlic poured over them, which makes them very tasty, as is well known in the cities. The country people, however, put all of these things into a basin or an earthenware casserole and add coriander and a little sesame oil, garnish it with a little fried onion or garlic, and eat it, and they know nothing of clarified butter or spices or anything of that sort. Sometimes they boil the tripes in water and eat them as a broth. 11.36.6

١١،٣٦،٧ والكرش مشتقّ من التكرّش وهو البروز والظهور أي إنّه كرش بارز ظاهر كما يقال للحائط إذا برزت منه حجارته عن سَمْتها المعتاد وآلت للسقوط حائط مكرّش أي آيل للسقوط وفلان صاحب كرش أي كرشه ظاهر كبير خصوصاً إذا كان رجلاً سميناً جسيماً فإنّ كرشه يظهر كبيرًا خارجًا وفي الحديث إنّ الله يكره الحَبْر السمين لكن هو ممدوح في الغنم والبقر يقال كبش سمين ممتلئ شحمًا ولحمًا فإذا ذبح على هذه الحالة وأُدْرِجَتْ رأسه في كرشه فيكون سقطه لذيذ عن غيره لسمنه وكثرة شحمه

١١،٣٦،٨ (ومن المناسبة) أنّ السلطان قِرِلْبَاشْ أرسل إلى السلطان الغوريّ يهدّده بهذه الأبيات [سريع]

السَّيفُ والخنجرُ رَيحانُنا   أُفٍّ على النَّرجِسِ والآسِ
شَرابُنا مِن دَمِ أَعدائِنا   وكأسُنا جُمجُمةُ الرَّاسِ

فأجابه السلطان الغوريّ يقول [سريع]

لله في عالَمِه خاتمٌ   تجري المقاديرُ على نَقشِهِ
لا تَنبُشِ الشرَّ فتُبلَى بِهِ   واحذَرْ على نَفسِكَ من نبشِهِ
مَصارِعُ البَغْيِ لها صَوْلةٌ   تُنكِّسُ السلطانَ عن عرشِهِ
لما طغى الكبشُ بشحم الكُلى   أُدرِجَ راسُ الكبشِ في كرشِهِ
ونحن إن لم نَرْجُ أو نبتغي   كالميّتِ محمولاً على نعشِهِ

١١،٣٦،٩ فلم يرتدع بما أرسله له السلطان قانصوه الغوريّ بل سار إليه بخيله ورَجْله فتلقّاه نائبه وردّه خائباً وألقى الله كيده في نحره ولم يفده ما وعظه به السلطان قانصوه

Kirsh is derived from *takarrush* ("buckling, warping"), which means being protuberant and conspicuous; that is, the stomach (*kirsh*) is protuberant and conspicuous in the same way that one says of a wall whose stones project beyond the true and which is on the verge of collapse that it is *mukarrash* ("buckling"), that is, about to fall, or "So-and-so is *ṣāḥib kirsh* ('a big-bellied man')," that is, his stomach is conspicuously large, especially if he be a fat, big-bodied man, in which case his stomach will appear large and protruding. In the Tradition it says "God detests the fat scholar," though fatness is a desirable quality in sheep and cattle. One speaks of a "fat ram, bursting with fat and flesh." When it is slaughtered in this condition and its head is rolled up in its tripes, the *saqaṭ* made from it is tastier than anything else, because of the butter and the fat. 11.36.7

Apropos of which, Sultan Qizilbāsh once sent a message to Sultan 11.36.8
al-Ghawrī, threatening him in the following verses:[562]

Sword and dagger are sweet basil to us—
With narcissus and myrtle we have no truck!
Our drink is the blood of our foes
And the skulls of our foes are our cup!

—to which Sultan al-Ghawrī responded:[563]

God has a ring for His creatures,
By whose inscription their fortunes are sealed:
"Let sleeping dogs lie lest they bite,
And beware what you yourself may reveal!"
The battlegrounds of injustice are tyrants
That may drive a sultan from throne and from field.
When the ram's kidneys' fat overflows
Its head's rolled up in its tripes and concealed.
And, like it or not, we're like a dead man
When he's borne on his bier from the field!

However, Sultan Qizilbāsh was not deterred by Sultan Qānṣawh al-Ghawrī's 11.36.9
message; on the contrary, he marched against him with his horses and his foot soldiers. Al-Ghawrī's deputy did battle with him and drove him back discomfited, and God brought the consequences of his deceitfulness down upon his own head, and the advice that Sultan Qānṣawh al-Ghawrī gave him in the

الغوريّ بقوله ﴿لمّا طغى الكبش بشحم الكلى﴾ الخ وهذا مثال الرجل الظالم إذا طغى وتجبّر ربّما أخذه الله تعالى بَغْتَةً وفي الحديث إنّ الله لَيُمْهِلُ الظالم ولا يُهْمِلُهُ فإذا أخذه لم يُفْلِتْهُ

١٠،٣٦،١١ فالناظم تمنّى من الله تعالى وترجّى من كرمه وحلمه أن يرى كرشاً مرمياً على التلّ أي الكوم غفَلوا عنه أصحابه وتركوه نسياناً أو أنّ الشادّ بالكفر ذبح كبشاً وألقى كرشه على التلّ فإنّ أهل الريف إذ ذبحوا بهيمة يوم العيد لا يتركوا منها شيئاً ويأخذوا كرشها وجميع حوائجها يطبخوه ويأكلوه فالناظم ترجّى أنّ الدهر يغلط يوماً ويرى هذا الكرش الّذي تمنّاه وطلبه واشتهاه لكونه لم يقدر على مشاركة أهل الكفر في بهيمة

١١،٣٦،١١ ﴿و﴾ لو كان

١٢،٣٦،١١ ﴿من فوقِهِ الدِّبّانْ﴾ وهو الذبّان وإنّما استعمله العوام بلفظ الدِبّان لثقل الذبّان على ألسنتهم ومفرده دبّانة ودبّون مفرد الذكور منه والدبّان على وزن الخرفان أو الجديان والدبّون على وزن المحون أو المأبون قال بعض شعراء أهل الريف مواليا [بسيط]

فِي خاطري يا مليحْ لو كنتُ دبّانهْ
وَاحطّ فوقْ شَفَتَكْ وتْنِشّ اَقولْ دانهْ
علَيَّ ويابو حَسَنْ لكْ عينُ نعسانهْ
غيري تواصلْ وَاناجي لكْ تقولْ نانهْ

١٣،٣٦،١١ وللذباب خواصّ كثيرة ومنافع مذكورة في بعض الكتب منها أنّه إذا أُخِذَت ذبابة ورُبِطَت وهي حيّة في شرموط بحيث أن يكون واسعاً عليها بحيث لا تموت وعُلِّقَت على من يشتكِ الرمد خُفِّفَت عنه ﴿وسئل﴾ بعض الفضلاء لأيّ شيء خلق الله الذباب فقال ليُذِلّ به الجبابرة لأنّه يقع على تاج الملك فلا يقدر على منعه عنه

words "When the ram's kidneys' fat overflows," etc., did him no good. These are examples of what happens to the unjust man when he goes too far and behaves tyrannically: God will sometimes take him off all of a sudden. In the Tradition it says, "God grants the tyrant time but does not forget him, and when He takes him, He does not let him escape."

Thus the poet begs the Almighty and beseeches Him of His bounty and His graciousness that he might see some tripes tossed away on the refuse dump, meaning the mound, that his companions, out of forgetfulness, had overlooked and left behind, or that the bailiff of the hamlet might have slaughtered a ram and thrown his tripes on the refuse dump, for if the country people themselves slaughter an animal on the day of the feast, they leave nothing of it behind, and they take its tripes and all its offal and cook and eat them. The poet therefore prays that Fate will one day slip up and he will see these tripes that he longs, asks, and lusts for, because he is unable to join the people of the hamlet in the price of an animal.[564] **11.36.10**

wa- ("even if"): even if it be that . . . **11.36.11**

min fawqihi l-dibbān ("the flies (have settled) on them"): *dibbān* being the same as *dhibbān*,[565] the common people using it in the form *dibbān* because *dhibbān* is too heavy for their tongues; the singular is *dibbānah* and *dibbūn* is a single male.[566] *Dibbān* is of the measure of *khirfān* ("sheep") or *jidyān* ("kids") and *dibbūn* is of the measure of *mamḥūn* ("sluttish") or *ma'būn* ("passive sodomite"). One of the poets of the country people says in a *mawāliyā*: **11.36.12**

How I wish, sweet thing, I were a fly—
  I'd settle on your lip,
You'd swat at me, and I'd say, "Hi!"
  And "Hey there, good looking, you with the drowsy eye!
How come you give others favors,
  But when I come, you tell me 'Fie!'?"

Flies have numerous peculiarities and useful qualities that are mentioned in certain books. These include the fact that, if a fly is taken and tied alive inside a piece of cloth large enough to keep it from dying and is hung on one suffering from inflammation of the eyes, he will recover. And a virtuous man was once asked why God created flies, and he said, "To humiliate tyrants, for a fly may settle on a king's crown, and there is nothing he can do to prevent it." **11.36.13**

(وكان المشركون) يَطلوا أصنامهم بالزعفران وغيره فيقع عليهم الذباب فأنزل الله تعالى توبيخًا لهم ولأصنامهم ﴿إِنَّ ٱلَّذِينَ تَدۡعُونَ مِن دُونِ ٱللَّهِ لَن يَخۡلُقُوا ذُبَابًا وَلَوِ ٱجۡتَمَعُوا لَهُۥ وَإِن يَسۡلُبۡهُمُ ٱلذُّبَابُ شَيۡـًٔا لَّا يَسۡتَنقِذُوهُ مِنۡهُ ضَعُفَ ٱلطَّالِبُ وَٱلۡمَطۡلُوبُ﴾ (والذباب) له أعداء كثيرة منها حيوان صغير يقال له ضبع الذباب يشبه العنكبوت الصغير إلّا أنّ فمه واسع وأرجله قصيرة عن أرجل العنكبوت يأخذ الذبابة بسرعة في فمه ويلقيها في شيء يخرجه من فمه كنسيج العنكبوت فلم تزل معلّقة فيه إلى أن تموت (وذكر العارف بالله تعالى سيّدي عبد الوهّاب الشعرانيّ في المِنَن) أنّ زوجته أمّ عبد الرحمن أصابها مرض شديد أشرفت به على الهلاك فدخل يوماً بيت الخلاء فسمع هاتفاً يقول له خلّص الذبابة من ضبع الذباب ونحن نخلّص لك زوجتك من مرضها فالتفت الشيخ إلى الحائط فسمع حسّ الذبابة فتحايل وخلّصها فخلّصت زوجته في الحال وشفاها الله تعالى وقوله

١٤،٣٦،١١ (يِعِفّ عَفيفْ) أي يتراكم على بعضه البعض من كثرة نزوله عليه يمتصّ منه الرطوبة ونحوها ويِعِفّ بكسر الياء المثنّاة من تحت وكسر العين المهملة يقال عفّ الذباب على الشيء إذا سقط عليه وكثر وتراكم بعضه على بعض وأمّا بفتح المثنّاة وضمّ العين فمن العِفّة يقال عَفّ الرجل عن الشيء بمعنى كَفّ عنه وقوله

١٥،٣٦،١١ (دنا انْ شُفْتُهْ[١]) أي إذا منّ الله عليّ ورأيته ملقىً على التلّ

١٦،٣٦،١١ (خَدْتو) يعني أخذته وحذف الهمزة وأبدل الذال دالاً مهملة جرياً على اللغة الريفيّة

١٧،٣٦،١١ (سَلَقْتو) بمعنى أنّي أُلقيه في الدست أو البِرام وألقي عليها الماء لا غير وأسلقه من غير تقلية وشيرج وغير ذلك لشدّة فقره وعدم ما في يده وقوله

---

١ بي: شُفْتُو.

The polytheists used to anoint their idols with saffron and so on, and the flies would settle on them, so the Almighty sent down the following verses as a rebuke to them and to their idols: «Lo! Those on whom ye call besides God will never create a fly though they combine together for the purpose. And if the fly took something from them, they could not rescue it from him. So weak are the seeker and the sought!»[567] Flies have many enemies, among them a small animal called the "hyena of the flies" that resembles a small spider except that its mouth is wide and its legs are shorter than those of a spider. It takes the fly quickly in its mouth and casts it into something that it extrudes from its mouth like a spider's web, where the fly remains caught until it dies. The Initiate of the Almighty, Master ʿAbd al-Wahhāb al-Shaʿrānī, mentions in his *Blessings*[568] that his wife, Umm ʿAbd al-Raḥmān, was afflicted by a severe illness that had brought her to the point of death. One day, he went into the lavatory and he heard a voice say to him, "Release the fly from the hyena of the flies, and We will release your wife from her illness!" So the Shaykh turned to the wall and heard the sound of the fly and carefully released it, and his wife was released from her illness immediately and the Almighty cured her.

yiʿiffu ʿafīf ("have settled in swarms"): that is, the flies pile up one on top of another from the sheer quantity that descend on the tripes to suck the moisture from them and so on. *Yiʿiffu* is with *i* after the *y* and after the *ʿ*.[569] One says, "The flies settled (*ʿaffa*) on a thing in swarms" when they descend on it in large numbers and pile up on top of one another. When it is with *a* after the *y* and *u* after the *ʿ*, it is from *ʿiffah* ("abstinence").[570] One says, "The man abstained from the thing" (*ʿaffa ʿan al-shayʾ*), meaning he drew back from it. **11.36.14**

d-anā-n shuftuhū ("If I saw them"): that is, if God granted me the sight of some tripes tossed away on the refuse pile . . . **11.36.15**

khadtū[571] ("I would take them"): that is, *akhadhtuhu*,[572] with omission of the initial *a* and change of *dh* to *d*, in keeping with rural usage. **11.36.16**

salaqtū ("boil them"): meaning "I would throw them in the basin or the cooking pot and throw water on them and nothing else and boil them without garnish or sesame oil and so on," he is that poor and indigent. **11.36.17**

(وكَلْتو بِتفْلو) أي بما في جوفه من المرعى ولو أنّه نجس مبالغةً في الاشتهاء له وشدّة الحاجة وهذا يعايَر به الرجل الأكول عندهم فيقال (فلان ياكل الكرش بخراه) مثلاً ومن ذلك (ما اتّفق أنّ رجلاً من أهل الريف طلع مصر) يبيع جانباً من البيض لأجل غلاق ما عليه من مال السلطان فباعه وتوجّه إلى بلده فرأى بين القصرين كروشاً تباع فقال خذ لأمّ معيكه بجديد وكل أنت الآخر بجديد ولو انكسر عليك مال السلطان فأعطى بيّاع الكروش الجديدين فأخذ يقطع له ممّا يباع للقطط وهو يأكل من غير ملح وأخذ بالجديد الثاني قطعة كبيرة وأَزْوَدَ عليها كبدة ورُوَيّة ولفّ ما أخذه في شَدّه الّذي فوق رأسه وربط عليه وكانت الفلوس الّتي باع بها البيض مربوطة أيضاً على الشدّ ثمّ إنّه سافر إلى أن مرّ على قرية في الطريق فرأى شجرة فجلس يستريح تحتها فضربه الهواء فرقد فجاء كلب وشمّ رائحة اللحم الّذي على رأسه فخطف الشدّ باللحم وطلع إلى سطوح القرية فقام يجري خلفه ويصيح ودخل الدار الّتي طلع فوق سطحها الكلب فلمّا رأوه النسوان مكشوف الرأس في هذه الحالة قالوا هذا لصّ سارق فمسكوه وسلّموه للشادّ في القرية فضربه وحبسه يومين حتّى شفع فيه أهل الخير فأطلقوه فمن عدم ذوقه وشدّة جهله ضيّع الفلوس وأكل الضرب ورجع الكفر خائب نائب وقوله ١١،٣٦،١٨

(ما أرى تَقْنيفْ) بمعنى أنّي ما أتعفّف عن أكله لكون أنّ فيه التفل أو لأنّ جوانبه فيها النجاسة مثلاً فإن نفسي تطيب لأكله ولا تمتنع عنه (وفي القاموس الأزرق والناموس الأبلق) أنّ التقنيف مشتقّ من القَنْف وهو المنع عن الشيء كما يقال أنت قِنِف أو فلان يتقنّف أو من القُنَافة بضمّ القاف وهي الّتي توضع في خَرْق الناف الّذي على رقبة الثور ويعايَر بها الرجل الخفيف العقل فيقال له يا قنافة قال الشاعر [طويل] ١١،٣٦،١٩

wa-kaltū bi-tiflū ("and eat them with the undigested matter"): that is, with the fodder that is in the stomach, even though it be defiling, as a way to emphasize his longing and great need. This is something that gluttons are reproached for among them: one says, for example, "So-and-so eats tripes with the shit on!"—apropos of which, it happened that a man from the countryside went up to Cairo to sell a quantity of eggs so as to pay off the taxes that he owed, and he sold them and set off back for his village. When he was in Bayn al-Qaṣrayn, he saw tripes for sale and said to himself, "Buy a copper's-worth for Umm Muʿaykah and eat a copper's-worth yourself, even if you have to go into debt on your taxes!" So he gave the tripe seller two copper pieces, and the man cut him off the bits they sell for cats, which he ate without salt, and for another copper he took a large hunk to which he added liver and lights, and wrapped everything up in his headcloth that was on his head and tied it up, and the money that he had made by selling the eggs was tied to the headcloth too. Then he journeyed until he passed by a village on the road and noticed a tree, beneath which he sat down to rest, and the breeze caressed him, and he lay down. Along came a dog, which smelled the meat that was on his head and grabbed the headcloth with the meat and climbed up onto the roofs of the village. The peasant got up and ran after it shouting, and entered the house onto whose roof the dog had climbed. When the women saw him, bare headed and in this state, they said, "A thief, in the act!" and they seized him and handed him over to the bailiff in the village, who beat him and imprisoned him for two days, till men of goodwill interceded on his behalf and they let him go. Thus, as a consequence of his lack of manners and his ignorance, he lost the headcloth and the money and took a beating and returned to the hamlet a hopeless case. 11.36.18

mā arā taqnīf ("and feel no revulsion"): meaning "I would not abstain from eating it because it had the undigested matter on it, or because it had filth around the edges, for example, for my carnal appetite relishes the eating of it and does not hold back." In *The Blue Ocean and Piebald Canon* it says that *taqnīf* is derived from *qanf*, which is refraining from something: one says, "You are 'finicky' (*qinif*)" or "So-and-so 'recoils' (*yataqannafu*) in disgust." Or it may be from *qunnāfah* with *u* after the *q*, which is the thing that is inserted in the hole in the yoke on an ox's neck. A mental lightweight may be chided with the same word: one says to him, "You yoke peg!" The poet says: 11.36.19

لَقَد خَفَّ مني العَقلُ حتى كأنّني أُحاكِي في الأفعالِ قُنافة البَقرِ

ثمّ لمّا أنّه لم يتيسّر له كرش ملقّح على التلّ أو الكوم ترجّى من الله تعالى أن يبلغه ٢٠،٣٦،١١ مناه وأنّه بعد مدّة إن طال عمره يروح المدينة ويشبع فيها كروش وغيرها من الترمس والمقلي فقال

ص

أَنَا ٱنْ عِشْتُ لَاروحُ ٱلْمَدِينَهْ وَأَشْبَعُ كُرُوشَ وَلَوْ أَنِّي أَمُوتُ كَفِيفْ ٣٧،١١
وَآخذْ مَعِي غَزْلَ ٱلْعَجُوزِ وَٱبِيعُو وَآكُلْ بِحَقُّو يَا ٱبْنَ بِنْتِ عَرِيفْ

ش

قوله (أَنَا ٱنْ عِشْتُ) من المعيشة وهي قوام الجسد وانتعاشه من المأكل والمشرب أي ١،٣٧،١١ إن طال عمري وكان فيه تأخير في علم الله تعالى

(لاروحُ المدينهْ) والمراد بها مصر حرسها الله تعالى وأدام سرورها بأهلها * وأبّد ٢،٣٧،١١ نعيمها بسكّانها وحرس علماءها الأعلام * وأمراءها الكرام * لأنّها مدينة الأنس والصفاء * والسرور والوفاء * وخصّ الله نساءها بالحسن والجمال * والبهاء والكمال * وطيب المعاشره * ولطف المذاكره * كم عاشق بحسنهنّ افتتن * ومن لم يتزوّج مصريّة ليس بمُحْصَن * وملاحها الولدان * كأنّهم الغزلان *

My mind has grown so silly, I trow,
I've started behaving like the yoke peg of a cow!

Next, finding no easy access to tripes tossed away on the dump or mound, he beseeches the Almighty to grant him his desire and that, after a while, should he live so long, he might go to the city and eat his fill of tripes and other things such as lupine and *muqaylī*. He says: **11.36.20**

TEXT

anā-n ʿishtu lā-rūḥu l-madīnah wa-ʾashbaʿū **11.37**
kurūsha wa-law annī amūtu kafīf
wa-ʾākhudh maʿī ghazla l-ʿajūzi wa-bīʿū
wa-ʾākul bi-ḥaqqū yā-bna binti ʿarīf

If I live I shall go to the city and eat my fill
of tripes, though I should die "impaired"
And I'll take with me the old woman's yarn and sell it
and eat with the proceeds, O son of the daughter of *ʿarīf*

COMMENTARY

11.37.1 *anā-n ʿishtu* ("if I live"): *ʿishtu* being from *maʿīshah* ("living"), which is the sustaining of the body and its refreshment with food and drink. That is, "if I live long and if the Almighty has ordained sufficient days for me" . . .

11.37.2 *la-rūḥu l-madīnah* ("I shall go to the city"): by which he means Cairo—may the Almighty protect it and grant its people eternal pleasure, let its inhabitants continue in the enjoyment of its luxuries forever, and protect its eminent scholars and noble commanders, for it is the city of conviviality and amusement, of pleasure and fulfillment, whose women God has distinguished by making them comely and handsome, full of loveliness and perfection, sweet in their social relations, refined in their conversations. How many a lover by their charms has been beguiled, and he who does not marry a Cairene cannot hope to keep his reputation undefiled! And its cute young boys, like gazelles, whose grace the ben tree's branch excels—they have no like in Iraq or on Anatolia's

أو قضبان البان * لم يوجد مثلهم في الروم والعراق * ولم يُرَ ألطف منهم في العشرة والاتّفاق * كما قلت في معنى ذلك [رجز]

يا من يُـرِدْ عِشْق الجمالْ   شـدّ إلى مصرَ الرحالْ ١١،٣٧،٣
كمْ من جمالْ حازَ الكمالْ   في مِـصْرَ أَرْخى لُو دَلالْ
مـلاحُهـا لم يوجـدوا   في الرومْ ولا أرض العراقْ
ولا بلادْ أرض العجَمْ   وَمَنْ رَقى السَبْعَ الطِباقْ
اللطـفُ فيهـمْ منطبعْ   وريقهـمْ حـلو المـذاقْ
من حـادَ عنهـم بالميَالْ   حُرِّمْ عليهِ طِيب الوِصالْ ١١،٣٧،٤
كمْ من جمالْ حازَ الكمالْ   في مِـصْرَ أَرْخى لُودلالْ
يا حُسنَهـمْ يا لطفَهمْ   يا ظَرْفَهـمْ كمْ ذا تـرى
من كلِّ أغْيَدْ حينْ يميسْ   تقولْ لعـقلكْ لا يَـرى
مـثلو تَرى غيرو يفوقْ   سبحـانَ خـلاّق الورى
فـعش بهـم دَوْمَ الليالْ   فحُبُّهـمْ عندي حـلالْ ١١،٣٧،٥
كمْ من جمالْ حازَ الكمالْ   في مِـصْرَ أَرْخى لُودلالْ
وأمّـا العجَبْ ثـمّ العجبْ   في يوم الاعياد والفـرَجْ
كم ظَبْيَ يَرْفُلْ في الحُـلَلْ   والخالُ فوقْ خَدُّو عـرَجْ
تقولْ جِنانْ رضوانْ حقيقْ   قد فُـتِحَتْ وقـد خـرَجْ
منها يريـدْ قتل الرجالْ   بحسن قَدُّو والميـالْ ١١،٣٧،٦

ground, and none more refined in company and compliance may be found! As I said on this subject:

You who the love of beauties would know, 11.37.3
Break camp and off to Cairo go!
How many a beauty with perfection aglow
In Cairo puts his charms on show!
Its cute young boys are nowhere else to be found,
Not in Anatolia, nor in Iraq,
Nor in the cities of the Persian lands—
No, by him who climbed the seven heavens' arc![573]
By nature with refinement they're graced
And their saliva is sweet to the taste.
Whoever turns aside from them in disinclination 11.37.4
Let him forever forgo the joy of consummation!
How many a beauty with perfection aglow
In Cairo puts his charms on show!
How comely they are and how refined!
How elegant! How many you see!
With every stripling swaggering by
You say, "This one's the apogee,"
Then see another better still—
Glory to the Maker of Humanity!
So live with them as long as nights shall last 11.37.5
For love of them, I think, is no trespass!
How many a beauty with perfection aglow
In Cairo puts his charms on show!
Wonder, then wonder yet again—
On the days of feasts and fun,
Everywhere gazelles in gorgeous garments strut,
While aslant each cheek a mole doth run.
Truly, you'd think the garden of Riḍwān[574]
Had op'ed and out they'd come!
Some of them desire to bring men low 11.37.6
With beauty of form and curves on show.

كم من جمال حاز الكمال   في مصر أرخى لو دلال
والله والله العظيم   ومن له انشق القمر
من عشقهم صبري فنى   وزاد وجدي والسهر
وقد بقيت صفر اليدين   وليس أقنع بالنظر
٧،٣٧،١١ ما حيلتي في كل حال   إلّا الدعا أراه محال
كم من جمال حاز الكمال   في مصر أرخى لو دلال
يوسف سميت أدع الإله   يغفر ذنوبي كلّها
وبلدتي شربين عظيم   بين المدائن قدرها
بلد الفخار من العلا   والعلم مشهور ذكرها
ثم الصلاة بالاتصال   على النبي باهي الجمال
كم من جمال حاز الكمال   في مصر أرخى لو دلال

٨،٣٧،١١ فسبحان من خصّهم برشاقة القدود * واحمرار الخدود * ورقّة الكلام * وقلّة الملام * وحسن الانطباع * وقلّة الامتناع * لفظهم ألطف من النسيم * ورُضابهم أحلى من التسنيم قال الشاعر [رجز]

ما مِثلُ مصرَ في الورى بلدةٌ   سُكّانُها ترتَعُ في نعيمها
نسيمُها ألطفُ شيءٍ في الورى   وأهلُها ألطفُ من نسيمها

٩،٣٧،١١ وقوله (وأَشْبَعُ) الشِبَع هو امتلاء المعدة من الطعام والشراب والشبع الزائد مضرّ ويطلق على الحسّيّ وهو ما تقدّم وعلى المعنويّ وهو الغناء بعد الفقر يقال (فلان اليوم

How many a beauty with perfection aglow
  In Cairo puts his charms on show!
By Mighty God I swear, and swear again
  By him for whom the moon was split in twain,[575]
From love of them my patience has worn out,
  While passion's put all hope of sleep to rout!
I'm left without a penny to spend
  And looking alone will not make my longing end.
In any case, what can I do 11.37.7
  But pray, and even that's no go—
How many a beauty with perfection aglow
  In Cairo puts his charms on show!
Yūsuf I'm called—I pray God
  To forgive my every sin.
Shirbīn's my town, mighty
  Among cities is its standing!
A town of pride in rank
  And brains, whose fame all men do hymn![576]
So now let constant blessings flow
  And to the prophet of dazzling beauty go—
How many a beauty with perfection aglow
  In Cairo puts his charms on show!

Glory then to Him who gave them figures chic and ruddiness of cheek, Who made their way of talking delicate and their behavior immaculate, and Who endowed them with dispositions kind, rarely to demurral inclined. Their speech is gentler than the breeze, in sweetness their saliva heaven's nectar exceeds. As the poet has it: 11.37.8

There's no city in the world like Cairo—
  Its people revel in its life of ease.
Its breeze is the gentlest thing in the world,
  Its people yet gentler than its breeze.

wa-'ashba' ("and eat my fill"): *shiba'* ("satiation") is the filling of the stomach with food and drink. Excessive satiation is harmful. The word may be used concretely, that is, in the sense just given, and abstractly, in which case it 11.37.9

شبعان) أي استغنى بعد فقره وشبع بعد جوعه خصوصاً إذا ذاق التعب والنصب أوّل زمانه وأفاض الله عليه فيكون شديد الحرص على الدنيا كثير الشحّ ويقال لمثل هذا (مُحْدَث نِعْمة) لأنّه لم يعرف قدرها ولم يصرفها في مصارفها وإنّما جُنَّ به الدهر حتّى نال هذا الأمر قال الشاعر [رجز]

مُسْتَحْدِثُ النَّعْمَةِ مُسْتَوْدِعُها عــيناه مــملوءتا فــقْــر
جُنَّ به الدهـرُ فنال الغِـنى يا ويلَهُ إن عقَـل الدهْــر

(وأمّا) إذا عرف الشخص ما أنعم الله به عليه وشكره على هذه النعم ولازم فعل الخير وأحسن وتصدّق فهذا هو المطلوب والأمر المحبوب وقوله

(كُروشَ) جمع كرش أي إن بلغت المدينة لا أشبع من الكروش الّتي تُسْلَق وتباع فيها وأقضي مرادي منها ١١،٣٧،١٠

(ولو أنّيَ) بعد شبعي من الكروش المذكورة وقضاء شهوتي ١١،٣٧،١١

(أموتُ كَفيفْ) أي أعمى يقال كَفّ بَصَرُه إذا حصل له العمى (وفي الحديث القُدْسيّ) يقول الله تعالى إذا أخذتُ كريمتَيْ عبدي فصبر فما جزاءه عندي إلّا الجنّة وقال الأبو صيريّ الأديب [طويل] ١١،٣٧،١٢

إذا رمِدتْ عينايَ قلّ مُسامِري وقلّت أحبّائي من الحيّ والحِمى
يقولون إنْ عُوفِي مَلِقْناه ساعـةً وإنْ كَفَّ جئـنا نهـنّيه بالعمى

لأنّ الأرمد مريض لا يزار فإذا عمي يقولون له أنت بقيت من أهل الجنّة وحصل لك الخير ونحو ذلك ممّا هو مُشاهَد بين الناس الآن وفي الحقيقة إنّ الأعمى مسكين

means wealth after poverty. One says, "Today So-and-so is 'full' (*shab'ān*)," that is, has become rich after he was poor and filled his stomach after he was hungry, especially if he tasted hardship and sickness at the start of his career and God was generous to him later—in which case he will be extremely tight in worldly matters and very stingy. Such people are known as "newly blessed" as they have no comprehension of the value of such wealth and do not use it for its appointed purposes,[577] Fate merely having gone mad enough to allow them to acquire it. The poet says:

> One newly blessed with wealth is a sinkhole for it—
> His eyes with want still burn.
> Fate went mad, and he got rich—
> Woe to him, should Fate to its senses return!

On the other hand, should the individual acknowledge God's blessings and thank Him for that wealth and be diligent in doing good works and giving charity and alms, then that is recommended and commended.

kurūsha ("of tripes"): plural of *kirsh* ("stomach, craw"); that is, "if I reach the **11.37.10**
city, I will indubitably eat my fill of the tripes that are boiled and sold there and achieve my goal and my desire with respect to them . . ."

wa-law annī ("though I"): after eating my fill of the aforementioned tripes and **11.37.11**
satisfying my appetite . . .

amūtu kafīf ("should die 'impaired'"): that is, blind: one says of someone, **11.37.12**
"His sight was 'impaired'" if he was afflicted with blindness. In a Divine Tradition[578] the Almighty says, "If I take the eyes of My slave in this world, and he is patient, his reward with Me shall certainly be Paradise." The great man of letters al-Būṣīrī[579] says:

> When my eyes are inflamed, night companions disappear,
> And friends of hearth and home no longer pay me mind.
> They say, "If he gets better, we'll be nice to him then.
> If he's 'impaired,' we'll wish him well for going blind!"

—because a person with inflamed eyes is an invalid who is not to be visited, and if he goes blind they tell him, "Now you are one of the people of Paradise!" and "Good fortune is yours!" and so on, as one observes people doing nowadays.

والشفقة عليه فيها أجر عظيم * وفضل جسيم * خصوصاً إذا كان فقير الحال * فإنّه في حكم الميت لا مَحال * (قيل وُجِدَ مكتوب على تاج كِسْرَى هذه الكلمات) العدل إن دام عمّر * والظلم إن دام دمّر * والفقر هو الموت الأحمر * والأعمى ميّت وإن لم يُقْبَر * ومن لم يخلّف الذكر لم يُذْكَر * وما ابتلى الله عباده بشيء أضرّ من العمى والأعور على النصف من ضرر الأعمى كما في المثل (أعمى شكا لأعور فقال نصف خبرك عندي) وفي مثل آخر (الأعور الممقوت بين أهله أحسن من الأعمى على كلّ حال) وقوله

١١،٣٧،١٣ (كَفيف) على وزن نَتيف صفة الأمرد إذا طلعت ذقنه وكان يشتهي الخنات أو يكون به أُبْنَة والعياذ بالله تعالى فإنّه دائماً يحلق ذقنه ويُحْسن للفاسق نفسه ويَنْتِف أصول شعره بأظافيره أو يلقُطه بالملقاط فإنّ الأمرد ما دام خالي العِذار النفس تميل إليه وإذا التحى قلّ منه الوفاء * وصار وجهه كالقفاء قال الشاعر [خفيف]

الْتَحى الأَمْـرَدُ الّذي كانَ في التِيه مُسْرِفـا
حَسَـناً كانَ وَجهُـهُ وسـريعـا تصحّـفـا
سُـرَّ والله ناظـري مذ رأى ذاكَ واشتفا
شَـكَـرَ الله لِحْـيَةً صَـيَّرَتْ وَجْـهَهُ قَفـا

وقال آخر [خفيف]

سَلَبَ الناسَ بالمحاسن حتّى أذهب الله حُسْنَه والجمالا
طَلَعَتْ ذَقْنُهُ وراحت عليه وكفى الله المؤمنين القتالا

١١،٣٧،١٤ ومن العشاق الوقحاء من يميل إلى أصحاب اللحاء قال الشاعر [طويل]

But in truth, the blind man is to be pitied, and kindness to him brings great remuneration, and solid compensation, especially if he be poor, for then he's as good as dead for sure. It is said that the following words were found written on the crown of Chosroes: "Justice, If It Lasts, Brings Prosperity," "Injustice, If It Lasts, Brings Ruin," "Poverty Is the Red Death," "The Blind Man Is As Dead Though He Be Not Buried," and "He Who Leaves No Sons Will Not Be Remembered." God has afflicted his slaves with nothing more injurious than blindness, and the one-eyed man is half as badly off as the blind man; as the proverb says, "A blind man complained to a man with one eye, 'How bitter the cup of blindness!' The one-eyed man replied, 'My story is half of yours!'" And, in another proverb, it says, "A one-eyed man hated by his family is still better off than a blind man."

kafīf ("impaired," that is, "blind") is of the measure of *natīf* ("plucked"), **11.37.13**
a word used to describe a young boy if his beard has grown and he wants to play the role of a girl or has a morbid craving for passive sodomy (God Almighty save us from such things!) for such always shave their beards and doll themselves up for the profligate and pluck out the roots of their hairs with their fingernails or pull them out with tweezers—for when a young boy has no down on his cheeks he is found attractive but with the growth of his beard his charms evaporate, and his face turns ugly as his nape.[580] As the poet says:[581]

Bearded now is the lad who once
With himself was so smitten.
"Comely" once was his face,
But soon it got rewritten.
How my sight was gladdened
When it saw him thus and was cured!
Thanks be to God for a beard
That nape from face procured!

And another said:

He plundered us all with his charms, till
God put his beauty to sack.
His beard appeared and that was it—
"God spared the Believers attack."

Some brazen lovers prefer men with beards. The poet says: **11.37.14**

بلوطيٍّ يُدْعى عاشق المرد في الورى ويُدْعى بزانٍ من يحبّ الغوانيا
فملت لأصحاب اللحاءِ تعففا فما أنا لوطيّا وما أنا زانيا

(وبعضهم) يميل طبعه إلى الشيوخ * ويرى أن قول العَذول فيهم منسوخ * قال الشاعر [كامل]

أهواه طفلا في القِماط وأمردا وبلحيةٍ وإذا علاه مَشِيبُ

وقال آخر [طويل]

تعشقتُه شيخا كأنّ مَشِيبُهُ على وجنتيه ياسَمينٌ على وردِ
أخا العَذْل يدرى ما يراد من الفتى أَمِنْتُ عليه من حسودٍ ومن ضِدِّ

والعشق مراتب * وللناس فيما يعشقون مذاهب * قال الشاعر [طويل] ١١،٣٧،١٥

تعشقتُها شمطاء شاب وليدها وللناس فيما يعشقون مذاهبُ

وكلّ هذا من الانهماك على الشهوة والخمول في العشق والمحبّة وإلّا فالعاشق الظريف * لا يهوى إلّا الشكل اللطيف * المناسب للتعنيق والبوس * وكلّها غرامة فلوس * وقوله

(وآخُذْ معي غَزْل العجوزِ وَبيعو) والمراد به غزل زوجته وكان اسمها قطيعة وقيل اسمها بعرة بنت قلّوط وإذا كان اسمها بعرة بنت قلّوط فيها مناسبة لأنّ البعرة قريبة من القلّوط لأنّها بنته والبعرة فيها بيقين المعنى الصحيح والقلّوط أبوها فهو ملازم لها ولفظ العجوز يطلق على المرأة الكبيرة وعلى الخمرة يقال لها العجوز أيضاً والعذراء ولها أسماء كثيرة قال العارف بالله تعالى الحكّاك في وصفها من جملة أبيات [متقارب] ١١،٣٧،١٦

A fornicator they call the one who loves cute girls
While the lover of smooth boys they call a bugger,
So chastely to bearded men I turned,
For I'd rather be neither one nor t'other!

To others' fancies old men have appealed, these holding that censure of such things is repealed. As the poet says:

I love him as a babe in swaddling clothes and as a beardless boy,
And with a beard, and covered in gray hairs.

And another[582] says:

I came to love him as an aged man whose white hairs
On his cheeks were like jasmine over roses.
Censurer, it's known what boys are wanted for—
With him I'm safe from any who envies or opposes.

Degrees in love may be discerned, and one man's meat in love is by another **11.37.15**
spurned. As a poet[583] said:

I loved her as a gray-haired hag, whose own son's hair had turned—
For one man's meat, in love, is by another spurned!

—all of which comes of delivering oneself over to lust and wallowing in passion and affection. The sophisticated lover, on the other hand, is attracted only to the more refined brand that's fit to kiss and embrace—though it'll cost you money in either case.

wa-ākhudh maʿī ghazla l-ʿajūzi wa-bīʿū ("And I'll take with me the old woman's **11.37.16**
yarn and sell it"): by which he means his wife's yarn, her name being Qaṭīʿah, or, as others claim, Baʿrah bint Qallūṭ ("Dropping, daughter of Big Turd"); and if her name were indeed Baʿrah bint Qallūṭ it would be appropriate, because the dropping is related to the big turd, being its daughter. Baʿrah certainly must contain the true meaning, with Big Turd being the latter's father, as it always sticks to her. The word *ʿajūz* ("old woman") may be applied both to an aged woman and to wine, which may be called "old woman" but also "virgin" and many other names. In a description he gives of it among a number of verses the Initiate of the Almighty al-Ḥakkāk[584] says:

عجوزٌ وعـذراءُ فاعْجَبْ لها   تنادى بإسمَيْنِ من كل واسِمْ

وفي الكلام تقديم وتأخير ومعناه إذا عشت لأروح المدينة وآخذ معي غزل العجوز وأبيعه فيها

١٧،٣٧،١١ (واكُلْ بحقو) كروش وغيرها ولو أنّي بعد ذلك أموت كفيف لأنّي إذا قضيت مرادي وعشت بقيّة العمر أعمى لا أبالي بعد قضاء شهوتي وحصول ما كنت أرجوه من الله تعالى وقوله

١٨،٣٧،١١ (يَا ٱبْنَ بنتِ عَرِيفْ) يخاطب رجلاً من أهالي الكفر قيل إنه من أقاربه وقيل من أصدقائه والمعنى أنّه يبثّ إليه الشكوى ممّا ناله ويقول له لا بدّ أنّك تفرح لي إذا طال عمري ورحت المدينة وشبعت فيها كروش وأرجع إليك وهذا يدلّ على أنّه صديق له وصداقته مؤكّدة حتّى أنه خاطبه من دون أهالي الكفر فإنّ الشخص لا يشكو حاله إلّا لصديق يفرح لفرحه ويحزن لحزنه ويتحمّل عنه الهموم أو يواسيه إذ كان متيّسرًا من الدنيا ويسلّيه بالمحادثة ونحو ذلك قال الشاعر [طويل]

ولا بدّ من شَكوى إلى ذي مُروءةٍ   يواسيكَ أو يُسَلِيكَ أو يتوجعُ

وقال ابن عروس [مجتث]

أوْصيكَ إن صادفكْ ضَيْمْ   اشكيهْ للّي يـريدكْ
الحِمْلْ إذا تفَرَّقْ انشالْ   وانْ تمَّ راقِدْ يكيدكْ

١٩،٣٧،١١ وابن بنت عريف هذا اسمه على ما قيل خرا الحس واسم والده فسا التيران وأصل ما سمّي فسا التيران لأنّه كان كلّما ربطوا التيران على الطُوالَة يقف في وسطها ويفسي فيها لأنّه كان كثير الفساء فيشمّ من يقربه الفساء فيقول له أنت فسيت فيقول له هذا

Crone and virgin both! Wonder at her!
By two names she's known by all who give her names.

The words constitute "advancement and deferment."[585] The meaning is "If I live long enough, I will go to the city and take with me some of the old woman's yarn and sell it there . . . .

11.37.17 "*wa-ākul bi-ḥaqqū* ('and eat with the proceeds'): tripes and other things, even if later I should die 'impaired,' because, if I realize my dream, I will not care if I live the rest of my life blind, so long as I have satisfied my appetite and obtained what I wanted from the Almighty."

11.37.18 *yā-bna binti ʿArīf* ("O son of the daughter of ʿArīf"): he addresses one of the male inhabitants of the hamlet, said by some to have been a relation and by others a friend. The meaning is that he directs to this man his complaint against what afflicts him and says to him, "You must share my joy if I live long enough and go to the city and eat my fill of tripes there, and then come back to you!"—which indicates that he was a friend, a fact confirmed by his addressing him rather than any of the other inhabitants of the hamlet; for one complains of his case only to a friend, who feels joy at his joy and sorrow at his sorrow and takes on the burden of his anxieties or helps him materially if he be well off, and distracts him by talking to him and so on. As the poet[586] says:

Complaints must be to a stalwart man
Who can help you, distract you, or share your pain.

And Ibn ʿArūs says:

When trouble strikes, I do advise you,
Make your complaint to those who love you.
A burden shared is easily borne,
But if left lying around will surely trip you!

11.37.19 This "son of the daughter of ʿArīf" had the name Kharā Ilḥas ("Lick-Shit"), according to report, and his father's name was Fisā l-Tīrān ("Ox-Fart"), a name he acquired because, whenever they tethered the oxen to the feeding trough, he would stand in their midst and fart, a thing he was much given to doing; then those close by would smell the farts and ask him, "Did you fart?" and he would reply, "It's ox farts!" so they named him "Ox-Fart." As for his maternal

فساء التيران فسمّوه بذلك (وأمّا جدّه لأمّه) سمّي عريف لأحد أمور قيل إنّه كان يعرّف الأولاد المحلّات الّتي تحت التلّ يشخّوا ويخروا فيها وقيل كان يعرّف تغريبة بني هلال وما وقع بينهم وقيل كان له معرفة ودراية في ضرب الفَرْقَلة ونقر الطبلة والعمل على الزُمّارة ونحو ذلك وقيل كان يعرّف الشادّ أمور البَلَص ويقول له خذ من هذا كذا ومن هذا كذا صورة عواني فصار يقال له عريف من هذا القبيل كما أنّه يطلق هذا اللفظ على من يقيمه مؤدّب الأطفال في الكُتّاب يعرّف الأولاد أحوال القراءة ويعلّمهم ويعرّف أيضاً الفقيه عن أحوالهم في غيبته ممّا هو مشهور في بلاد المدن وغيرها فإنّ كلّ كُتّاب لا بدّ له من عريف على ما جرت به العادة

٢٠،٣٧،١١ وقوله

ص

٣٨،١١ وَأَسْرِقْ مِنَ ٱلْجَامِعْ زَرَابِينَ عِدَّهْ   وَآكُلْ بِهِمْ مِنْ شَهْوَتِي فِي ٱلرِّيفْ
وَأَشْبَعْ مِنَ ٱلتُّرْمُسْ وَآكُلْ مُقَلِّي   وَأَلْفُو بِقِشْرُو مَا أَرَى تَوْقِيفْ

ش

١،٣٨،١١ هذا الكلام كلّه من بقيّة كلامه لابن بنت عريف المتقدّم ذكره أي إنّه يقول إنّي إذا طلعت المدينة وبعت غزل العجوز وأكلت بحقّه كروش وقضيت شهوتي من الكروش المذكورة ورأيت الترمس والمقلي واشتهيته ولم يكن معي شيء من الدراهم فحينئذ أدخل بعض الجوامع الّتي في أطراف حارات المدينة الّتي يصلّوا فيها الريّافة لأنّ

grandfather being called ʿArīf, this could be for any of several reasons. Some say that he used to teach (*yuʿarrifu*) the children the way to the places at the foot of the refuse dump where they could piss and shit, while others say that he used to teach "The Westward Migration of the Banū Hilāl"[587] and their doings; others again say that he possessed knowledge (*maʿrifah*) and understanding in cracking drover's whips, beating drums, and tootling on pennywhistles and so on, and yet others that he used to instruct (*yuʿarrifu*) the bailiff in matters of extortion, telling him, "Take so much from this one and so much from that," like an unpaid servant, and that this is why he came to be called ʿArīf.[588] The word is also used of the person whom the schoolmaster at the *kuttāb* puts in charge of teaching (*yuʿarrifu*) the children to read and the instruction and also to inform (*yuʿarrifu*) the teacher of how they behave in his absence, as is common in the cities and elsewhere—for every *kuttāb*, by custom, must have an *ʿarīf*.

Next the poet says: **11.37.20**

TEXT

wa-ʾasriq mina l-jāmiʿ zarābīna ʿiddah **11.38**
wa-ʾākul bi-him min shahwatī fi l-rīf
wa-ʾashbaʿ mina l-turmus wa-ʾākul muqaylī
wa-luffū bi-qishrū mā arā tawqīf

And I'll steal from the mosque slippers in great number
and eat of them, such an appetite I have, in the countryside,
And eat my fill of lupine, and eat *muqaylī*
and eat it with the skin, and never stop

COMMENTARY

All the preceding is the continuation of what he said to the aforementioned **11.38.1** "son of the daughter of ʿArīf." That is, he says, "If I go to the city and sell the 'old woman's' yarn and, with the proceeds, eat tripes and thus satisfy my appetite for the aforementioned tripes, and see the lupine and *muqaylī* that I long for but have no money on me, then I will go into one of the mosques that are on the outskirts of the city quarters, where the people from the countryside pray," for *zarābīn* are found only on the feet of country people, the meaning being

الزرابين لا تكون إلّا بأرجل أهل الريف لأنّ المراد بها المراكيب جمع زَرْبُون على وزن محون أو مأبون وهو المركوب الّذي يمشي به الفلّاح ويسمّوه أيضاً جواد وترجيل

(وأَسْرِق) والسرقة حرام منهيّ عنها قال الله تعالى ﴿وَٱلسَّارِقُ وَٱلسَّارِقَةُ فَٱقْطَعُوا أَيْدِيَهُمَا﴾ أي إذا سرق السارق النِصَاب وهو ربع دينار ما لم يكن له فيه شبهة فيمتنع عنه القطع كما هو مذكور في كتب الفقه فأباح الله تعالى قطع يد السارق نكالاً له ولتركه الأمانة وعزّها وارتكابه الخيانة وذلّها كتب رجل لبعض العلماء ما لفظه شعر [بسيط] ٢،٣٨،١١

يدٌ بخمس مائِينَ عَسْجَدٍ فُدِيَتْ   ما بالها قُطِعَت في ربع دينارِ

فأجابه بقوله [بسيط]

عِزُّ الأمانة أَغلاها وأَرخَصها   ذُلُّ الخيانة فَٱفْهَمْ حِكْمَةَ الباري

أي إنّ هذه اليد لمّا أنّها تعدّت على مال الغير وأخذته وخانت الأمانة أرخص الله قدرها وأباح قطعها ذُلُّ الخيانة فهي حكم للباري جلّ وعلا وحدود أوجبها على خلقه من أمر ونهي وغير ذلك وقوله

(من الجامعْ) والمراد به المسجد وسمّي جامعاً لأنّه يجمع الناس للصلاة والعبادة ونحو ذلك ومسجد للسجود فيه ٣،٣٨،١١

(زرابينَ) وتقدّم أنّ المراد بها المراكيب والتراجيل ٤،٣٨،١١

(عِدّهْ) يعني كثير لأنّ سَرّاق المراكيب يحتاج إلى معرفة فى السرقة وقلّة دين بزيادة فأمّا المعرفة فإنّه يتقرّب من صاحب المركوب ويوهمه أنّه يريد الصلاة بل ربّما وقف بجانبه ٥،٣٨،١١

the same as *marākīb* ("slippers"). The singular is *zarbūn*, on the measure of *mamḥūn* ("sluttish") or *ma'būn* ("passive sodomite"); they are the slippers that the peasants walk in, and they also call them *jawād* and *tarjīl.*

wa-'asriq ("and I'll steal"): theft is a sin and prohibited. The Almighty has said, «As for the thief, both male and female, cut off their hands,»[589] meaning, do so if the thief has stolen at least the minimum amount necessary to incur this punishment, which is a quarter of a dinar, and so long as there is no doubt as to his guilt; if there is doubt, amputation is not practiced, as the books of jurisprudence state.[590] The Almighty has allowed the amputation of the hand of the thief as a warning to him and because he has broken faith and betrayed its high worth and committed treachery and dishonored it. A man once wrote to a scholar in verse as follows:[591] 11.38.2

A hand may be ransomed for five hundred gold pieces—
How come it's severed for a quarter dinar?

The scholar replied by saying:

The dearness of trust makes the hand itself dear,
While the baseness of treachery makes it cheap—see how wise the Creator!

—that is, when this hand trespassed on others' property and took it and betrayed its trust, God reduced its value, and its base treachery made its amputation permissible; and this is an instance of the wise ways of the Creator, Glorious and Sublime, and an example of the rules that He has made incumbent on His creation,[592] in terms of obligations and prohibitions and so forth.

min al-jāmiʿ ("from the mosque"): meaning the place of prostration (*masjid*); 11.38.3
it is called a *jāmiʿ* because it gathers (*yajmaʿu*) the people for prayer and worship and so on, while the *masjid* is so called because of the prostration (*sujūd*) that takes place there.[593]

zarābīna ("slippers"): it has been explained above that what is meant by this is 11.38.4
"slippers" (*marākīb*) or *tarājīl.*

ʿiddah ("in great number"): meaning "many" because the slipper thief needs 11.38.5
to be possessed of great expertise in stealing and a total lack of religion. The expertise lies in his getting close to the slippers' owner and making him

وصبر عليه إلى أن يَخِرّ للسجود لعلّام الغيوب يشتال هو الآخر بالمركوب وأمّا قلّة الدين فإنّه لا يعرف الصلاة ولا يدخل الجامع إلّا للسرقة فقط وربما كان جُنُباً وثيابه فيها النجاسة كما هو عادة الفلّاحين أنّهم لا يتحاشوا عن هذا الأمر ولا يعرفوا دين ولا عبادة ولا يدخل غالبهم الجامع إلّا لغزل الصوف والفَلّ أو لحساب المال أو يتظلّل فيه أوان الحرّ وربّما ربط فيه العجلة أو البقرة ويجعلوه في الغالب محلّاً لمحادثتهم في الغيط والحيط والزرع والقلع ويصير لهم فيه هجّة وضجّة وصياح وعياط وغارات كأنّهم في زريبة بقر والناظم كان منهم ومتلبّس بأحوالهم فلهذا نسب نفسه للسرقة وقال لابن بنت عريف المتقدّم ذكره إنّي إذا طلعت المدينة وأكلت بحقّ الغزل كروش ولم يبق معي شيء أتلصّص وأتجسّس وأسأل عن بعض الجوامع الّتي بأطراف حارات مصر وأسرق منها المراكيب

٦،٣٨،١١ (وأكلّ بهم) في كلامه هذا تورية إمّا أنّه يبيعهم ويأكل بثمنهم أو أنّهم يَصْدِفوه حال خطفه فيمسكوه ويطعموه بالمركوب الّذي خطفها عَلْقة فيكون هذا أكل معنويّ فإنّ في الغالب أنّ سرّاق الزرابين إذا وقع في أيديهم يقطعوها على أحبال رقبته يقال (فلان أكل علقة اليوم بالزرابين) و(فلان سرق مركوب ومسكوه وقطعوه على أحبال رقبته) فسرقة المراكيب تحتاج لخفّة ودراية في الأمور وإن كانت أرذل السرقات

٧،٣٨،١١ (قيل مرّ بعض الحذّاق من اللصوص على بعض التجّار) وهو جالس في حانوته وبجانبه نعاله فأراد هذا اللصّ أخذها فجانبه بخفّة وحطّ رجله اليمنى في واحدة وأراد أن يضع رجله اليسرى في الأخرى فالتفت التاجر فهرب اللصّ وتوارى بعيد بحيث لا يراه التاجر ولم يأخذ سوى فردة من نعاله ثمّ إنّ التاجر أراد القيام فلم يجد غير فردة

think that he just wants to pray; indeed, the thief may stand next to the man and wait until he bends over in prostration to the Knower of Secrets, then make off with his slippers.[594] The lack of religion lies in his not knowing how to pray and entering the mosque for no reason other than to steal. He may even be in a state of major ritual impurity,[595] and his clothes may be befouled, since it is usual for most peasants to know no shame in such matters, and they know nothing of prayer or worship, and the only reason most of them go into the mosque is to spin wool and jute or to calculate their taxes or take refuge in its shade when the weather is hot. Sometimes they tie up their calves or cows inside it, and usually they turn it into a place where they talk about the field and the wall and the sowing and the reaping, and they make a rumpus and a ruckus there and as much fuss, bother, and disturbance as though they were in the cattle barn, and our poet was one of this sort and implicated in their doings. This explains why he calls himself a thief and why he says to the aforementioned "son of the daughter of ʿArīf," "If I go to the city and eat tripes out of the proceeds of the yarn and run out of money, I will play sneak thief and snoop around and ask about some of the mosques that are on the outskirts of Cairo's quarters and steal slippers from them."

wa-ʾākul bi-him ("and eat of them"): this contains a pun: it may mean either that he will sell them and eat from the proceeds, or that people will come across him red-handed in the act of snatching them and seize him and make him "eat" a drubbing with the slippers that he stole, the latter constituting a figurative eating. In fact, it is generally the case that if a slipper thief falls into their hands, they thrash him on the back of his neck with the slippers till they fall to pieces. One says, "Today So-and-so 'ate' a drubbing with slippers" and "So-and-so stole a pair of slippers and they caught him and thrashed them to pieces on the back of his neck." In short, stealing slippers requires a deft hand and savoir faire, even though it is the lowest form of theft. 11.38.6

It is said that a sharp-witted thief passed a merchant sitting in his shop with a pair of shoes by his side, which the thief decided to take. Quietly sidling up to the man, he placed his right foot in one of the shoes and was about to put his left foot in the other when the merchant turned around, so the thief, having gotten just one of the pair, ran off and hid himself at a distance where the merchant could not see him. Then the merchant wanted to leave and, failing to find one of his shoes, he asked his servant, "Where's the other one?" 11.38.7

من نعاله فقال لغلامه أين الثانية قال له لا أدري قال قد سرقت خذ هذه وامض إلى فلان وقل له يصنع واحدة مثلها فأخذها الغلام ومضى فسبقه اللصّ حتّى عرف الرجل الّذي دفعها له فلمّا رجع الغلام إلى سيّده أتى اللصّ ومعه الفردة الّتي أخذها وقال للرجل لا تصنع للتاجر شيء فإنّه لقي الفردة الثانية وأوراها له وقال له هات الأخرى فأعطاه إيّاها فأخذ الأولى بالسرقة والثانية بالحيلة فلمّا جاء غلام التاجر يطلبها أخبره بالقضية فرجع وأعلم سيّده فتعجب من حذق هذا اللصّ

٨،٣٨،١١ (وقيل) طلع الأبوصيريّ الأديب إلى مصر وذهب إلى سوق المراكيب تحت الركن يشتري له مركوب أحمر فوقف على دُكّان فقال له بيّاع المراكيب عندي مركوب أحمر مثل وجهك يا شيخ العرب والثاني من البيّاعين قال له عندي مركوب مليح واحياة راسك وصار الجميع ينكّتوا عليه فصبر لهم حتّى فرغوا من كلامهم وقال لهم يا مشايخ السوق أنا رجل غريب وأنتم توصّوا بي فإنّهم قالوا لي جماعةُ المراكيب اليوم كثير ومن رُخصها على أقفية أصحابها فقالوا الكلّ خلص ثأره منّا جميعاً بما قال باللطافة ثمّ قالوا له بالله أنت الأبوصيريّ قال نعم فأكرموه وأعطوه مركوب أحمر مليح من غير شيء فأخذه ومضى ودخل على البدريّ العوديّ رحمه الله تعالى وكان ريّس مصر في الدخول فلمّا رآه وفي رجله المركوب قال له وجهك أحمر يا أبوصيريّ فقال له نِكّت بدريّ ودخلت الحمّام فكان الجواب أظرف من السؤال وممّا مُدِحَ به البدريّ قول الأبوصيريّ المذكور حيث قال [وزن غير معروف]

البـدري كمـل بالدخول   وفيه انـطوى واندرج
بوّابـه حـلف بالطـلاق   من يوم دخـل ما خرج

and the servant told him, "I don't know." So the merchant said, "It must have been stolen. Take this one and go to So-and-so and tell him to make me another like it." The servant took the shoe and went off, and the thief went ahead of him so that he could see to whom he gave it. Then, when the servant went back to his master, the thief brought the shoe he had taken and told the man, "Don't make anything for the merchant. He has found the missing shoe," and he showed it to him and told him, "Give me the other one." The man gave it to him, and that way he got the first shoe by thievery and the second by trickery. When the merchant's servant came back to ask for the shoe, the man told him what had happened, and he informed his master, who marveled at the thief's quick wits.

The tale is told too that the great man of letters al-Būṣīrī[596] once visited Cairo and went to the slipper market at Taḥt al-Rukn[597] to buy himself a pair of red slippers. He stopped at a shop and the slipper seller said to him, "I have a pair of slippers as red as your face,[598] Shaykh of the Arabs!" and the next shopkeeper said to him, "By the life of your head, Shaykh of the Arabs, I have a lovely pair of slippers!" and they started making jokes at his expense. He waited patiently until they were done and then said to them, "Shaykhs of the market, I am a stranger, and you have to give me a special deal on a pair, for people have told me that 'slippers are a glut on the market today and so cheap they're "on their makers' necks"!'"[599] They said, "He's taken his revenge on us all with his polite words!" and they asked him, "Pray tell, are you al-Būṣīrī?" "I am," he said. Then they honored him and gave him a pair of nice red slippers free of charge, and he took them and went to visit al-Badrī, the lutenist, who was Cairo's leading musician, may the Almighty have mercy on him. When al-Badrī saw him coming towards him wearing his new slippers, he said to him, "How come your face is so red, Būṣīrī?" to which the latter replied, "I fucked early (*badrī*) and went to the baths!"—a response that was wittier than the question. The following, by the same aforementioned al-Būṣīrī, is one of his pieces written in praise of al-Badrī:[600] 11.38.8

Al-Badrī got perfect at singing
And learned it inside out.
His doorman swears on his wife
That after he first "went in," he never again "went out"![601]

والعرب يشبّهون المَداس بالراحلة وقد جاء هذا في شعر المتقدّمين والمتأخّرين واستعمله المتنبّيّ في مواضع من شعره (قال ابن خَلِّكان) رحمه الله تعالى جاءني صاحبنا جمال الدين الإِرْدَبِلِيّ الأديب المجيد في صناعة الألحان وغيرها وأنا في مجلس الحُكم بالقاهرة المحروسة وقعد عندي ساعة وكان الناس مزدحمين لكثرة أشغالهم حينئذ ثمّ نهض وخرج فلم أشعر إلّا وغلامه حضر وفي يده رقعة مكتوب فيها هذه الأبيات [كامل] ٩،٣٨،١١

يا أيها المولى الّذي بوجوده ... أبدت محاسنَها لنا الأيّامُ
إني حججت إلى مقامك حجّة الـ ... ـأَشْواقِ لا ما يوجب الإسلامُ
وأَنَخْتُ بالحرم الشريف مطيّتي ... فتشرّفتْ واشتاقها الأقوامُ
فطلبتُ أُنْشِدُ عند نَشْداني لها ... بيتا لمن هو في القريضِ إمامُ
وإذا المطيّ بنا بلغْن محمّدا ... فظهورهنّ على الأنام حرامُ

فوقفت عليها وقلت لغلامه ما الخبر فذكر لي أنه لمّا قام من عندي وجد مداسه قد سُرِقَ فاستحسنت منه هذا التضمين انتهى كلام ابن خلكان

والبيت الأخير الذي تمثل به هذا القائل لأبي نواس من قصيدة مدح بها الأمين محمّد بن هارون الرشيد أيّام خلافته وأوّلها يقول [كامل] ١٠،٣٨،١١

يا دارُ ما صنعتْ بك الأيّامُ ... لم يبق فيك بَشاشةٌ تُستامُ

ويقول من جملتها في صفة ناقة

The Arabs compare a shoe to a riding camel, and this occurs in the poetry of both the ancients and the moderns, and al-Mutanabbī uses it in various places in his verse. Ibn Khallikān, may the Almighty have mercy on his soul, once said:[602] 11.38.9

> Our friend Jamāl al-Dīn al-Irdabīlī,[603] that great man of letters and wonderful composer of tunes and so on, came to me while I was in the government offices in Divinely Protected Cairo and sat with me for a while at a time when there were people with business to conduct crowding around me. Then he got up and went out. Before I knew it, his servant arrived with a piece of parchment in his hand on which were written the following verses:[604]
>
> Master, through whose presence
> The days have made their virtues manifest,
> My pilgrimage to your abode I made as one by passion drawn,
> Not one who carries out the rite at God's behest,
> And there I caused my mount to kneel within the sacred space—
> Thus was she ennobled and men desired of her to be possessed;
> And as I sought for her I tried to find a verse
> For him whose prosody leads the rest:
> "And if the mounts to Muḥammad bring us,
> Their backs thenceforth to no man's service may be pressed."
>
> I studied it and asked the servant, "What's the story?" He told me that when al-Irdabīlī left me he found his slippers had been stolen. I thought the way he worked in the line from another poem was very clever.

Here ends the quotation from Ibn Khallikān. 11.38.10

The final lines, which the poet quotes, are from a eulogy by Abū Nuwās dedicated to al-Amīn Muḥammad, son of Hārūn al-Rashīd, and were written when the former was caliph. The first line goes:

> Campsite, what has time wrought upon you?
> No smiling face remains to draw me to your rest!

Elsewhere in the same poem, describing his she-camel, he says:

وتجشّمتْ بي هولَ كلّ تنوفةٍ هَوْجاءُ فيها جُراةٌ قُدّامُ
تَذَرُ المطيّ وراءها فكأنها صفٌّ تَقدَّمهُنَّ وهيَ إمامُ
وإذا المطيّ بنا بلغن محمّدا فظهورهنّ على الأنام حرامُ

١١،٣٨،١١ (قيل) سرق رجل مركوب وأعطاه لولده يبيعه فسرق من الولد فرجع إلى أبيه فقال له أبوه بعت المركوب قال نعم قال بكم قال برسماله فقال هذا رسماله السرقة فقال الولد وقد سرق منّي لا خسرت ولا كسبت فضحك عليه أبوه وخلّى سبيله

١٢،٣٨،١١ (وقيل) سرق باب دار أبي سالم القاضي فجاء إلى باب المسجد فقلعه فقالوا له ما الّذي تصنع فقال أقلع هذا الباب فإنّ صاحبه يعرف من قلع بابي (وقيل) كان أبو جُحا معه زوجتين وكانت أمّ جحا ماتت فخرج أبوه يريد سفرًا فلمّا خرج من باب الدار تذكّر أنّه نسي مركوبه فصاح على ولده يا جحا هات المركوب فسمعوا زوجاته الصياح ولم يعرفوا ما الخبر فقالوا له يا جحا ما يقول أبوك فقال يقول نك زوجات أبيك في غيابي فشتموه وقالوا له هذا كلام باطل فقال اسمعوا أنتم منه وصدّقوا ثمّ قال له الواحدة يا أبي وإلّا الاثنين يعني أجيب فردة من المركوب وإلا الاثنين فقال له بل الاثنين فقال صدقتم الكلام فظنّوا أنّه يقول له بل نك الاثنين وما مراد أبوه إلّا المركوب فولع فيهم بالنيك إلى أن حضر أبوه

١٣،٣٨،١١ (وقيل) جلس العينيّ في محل يشرف على الطريق وكان عنده رجل من الشام من أعيان الناس فقال له يا سيّدي يقولوا إنّ أهل مصر عندهم الحذق واللطافة بخلاف بلدنا ومرادي أرى الأمر عِيانا فبينما هو يكلّمه إذ مرّ بيّاع فول حارّ وهو ينادي عليه فقال العينيّ لصاحبه هل في مصر أحقر من هذا قال لا قال اصبر حتّى أبيّن لك حذقه ثمّ إنّ العينيّ ناداه فطلع إليه ومعه الفول والخبز فقال له مرادي فول حارّ

She braved every desert terror with me,
Reckless, of dash and daring much possessed,
The others running behind her as though
She an imam were, they in line behind her dressed—
And if the mounts to Muḥammad bring us,
Their backs thenceforth to no man's service may be pressed.

The story is told that a man stole a pair of slippers and gave them to his son to sell, but they were stolen in turn from the boy. The latter went back to his father, who asked him, "Did you sell the slippers?" "Yes," he said. "How much did you get for them?" The son replied, "The same as you paid." "But they were stolen!" said the father. "And they were stolen from me," said the boy, "so you lost nothing and you gained nothing." The father laughed at his son's joke and let him go. 11.38.11

And the story is told that the door of Judge Abū Sālim's house was stolen, so he went to the mosque and had its door removed. When they asked him, "What are you doing?" he replied, "I'm taking this door because its owner knows who took mine!" And the story is told that Juḥā's father had two wives, Juḥā's own mother having died. One day his father left to set off on a journey, but as he went out the door he remembered that he had forgotten his slippers, so he shouted to his son, "Juḥā, fetch my slippers!" Now his wives heard him shouting but didn't know what about, so they said to Juḥā, "What's your father saying?" He replied, "He says, 'Fuck your father's wives while I'm away!'" The wives cursed him out and said, "Nonsense!" "Listen for yourselves," he said, "and you'll see that it's true!" Then he said to his father, "One of them, father, or both?" meaning, "Shall I bring one of the slippers or the pair?" "Both, of course!" answered his father. "Now do you believe me?" said Juḥā. The wives thought that he had told him, "Fuck them both," though all his father meant was "both slippers." So Juḥā fucked them to his heart's content until his father returned. 11.38.12

And the story is told that al-ʿAynī was sitting with a grandee of Damascus in a place that overlooked the highway. "Sir," said the latter, "they say that the people of Cairo are distinguished from those of our city by their quick-wittedness and sophistication, but I would like to see this for myself." While he was talking, a seller of beans in linseed oil went past, crying his wares. Al-ʿAynī said to his friend, "Is there any viler wretch in Cairo than this?" "No," said the 11.38.13

ولكن ما عندي دراهم وما عندي إلّا فردة مركوب تعطيني بها فقال له يا سيّدي كلّ شيء جئته أطعمناك به قال فضحك العينيّ وتعجب الشاميّ من حذقه وأنعما عليه ومضى إلى حال سبيله

ومن التورية قول بعضهم هجوًا في رجل اسمه عِوَض [رجز] ١٤،٣٨،١١

سـرموجتي قد سُرِقَتْ   وضاق بي رُحْب الفضا
أتيتُ للسِّرْوضُحًا   أخذت عنها عِوَضا

وقوله (من شهوتي في الريفْ) أي من شهوتي الّتي اشتهيتها وهي أكلي من الكروش وشبعي منها لأنّي ما وجدتها في الريف فإذا طلعت المدينة وفعلت ما تقدّم قضيتها وحصل لي المراد وقوله ١٥،٣٨،١١

(وأَشْبَعْ من التُّرْمُسْ) المراد به المملّح بعد نقعه في الماء أيّاما فإنّ لأهل الريف فيه رغبة لأنّه نُقْلهم أيّام الأعياد ويهادوا به بعضهم البعض وله عندهم موقع عظيم ويباع في بلاد المدن دائما وهو فاكهة الريّافة إذا طلعوا المدينة يفتخروا بأكله هو والمقلي وفي الترمس خاصية عظيمة ذكرها العلاّمة الشيخ شهاب الدين القليوبيّ رحمه الله تعالى وهو أن من داوم كل يوم على مِلْءِ كفّه من الترمس بقشره على الفطور نار بصره وزاد فيه قوّة وقوله ١٦،٣٨،١١

(وآكلْ مُقَلّي) أي وأشبع من المقلي وهو الفول المنبّت المقليّ بالنار ومن هذا سمّي مقلي وهو مشهور لا يحتاج لمعرفته[١] وقوله ١٧،٣٨،١١

(وَلُفّو بِقِشْرو) أي هو والترمس من شدّة شوقي إليه لأنّني متى أردت تقشير الترمس ١٨،٣٨،١١

---

١ بي: للمعرفته.

Damascene. "Wait, then," said al-ʿAynī, "while I show you how quick-witted he is." Then al-ʿAynī called to the man, who came over to him bringing his beans and bread. "I want some beans," said al-ʿAynī, "but I have no money. All I have is a single slipper—can I get some with that?" "My dear sir," said the man, "I'll feed you with whatever you give me!" Al-ʿAynī laughed and the Damascene marveled at the man's quick wit, and they rewarded him well, and he went his way.

And there is a riddling rhyme by a poet that makes fun of a man called ʿIwaḍ that goes: 11.38.14

> My slippers were stolen from me
> And everything seemed bad.
> I went to al-Sirw of a morning
> And from there I took ʿIwaḍ![605]

min shahwatī fī l-rīf ("out of my appetite in the countryside"): that is, "out of the appetite that I experience, namely, for eating tripes and filling my belly with them, for I find none in the countryside; but if I go to the city and do as mentioned above, I will satisfy my appetite and attain my goal." 11.38.15

wa-ʾashbaʿ mina l-turmus ("and eat my fill of lupine"): by which he means lupine that has been salted after being steeped in water for several days. This is something the people of the countryside have a liking for because it is their equivalent of nuts, that is, it is something they nibble on on feast days and make presents of to one another. It has high status among them, is always on sale in the cities, and is the equivalent of fruit to the country people: they take pride in eating it if they go to the city, along with *muqaylī*. Lupine has an important property, mentioned by the learned scholar Shihāb al-Dīn al-Qalyūbī, may the Almighty have mercy him, which is that, if one eats a handful of lupine with the skin regularly every day for breakfast, his eyesight will grow stronger. 11.38.16

wa-ʾākul muqaylī ("and eat *muqaylī*"): that is, "and I'll eat my fill of *muqaylī*," which is sprouted beans fried on the fire, which is how it gets its name.[606] It is too well known to require description. 11.38.17

wa-luffū bi-qishrū ("and eat it with the skins"): that is, "that and the lupine together because I am so hungry for them, since, were I to peel the lupine and the *muqaylī*, it would seem to me to take forever, because I would need to peel 11.38.18

والمقلي طال عليّ الأمر لأني أحتاج أن أقشّره واحدة بعد واحدة وهذا لا يشفي خاطري ولا مرادي وأيضاً فإنّ الناظم من أهل الريف والأرياف يأخذوا بالكَبْشة ويسفّوه ولا يعرفوا التقشير ولا غيره

١٩،٣٨،١١ (ومن المناسبة) أنّ رجلاً جلس هو وغلامه في محلّ ظلام يأكلوا زبيباً فقال له سيّده كل زبيبة زبيبة وأنا الآخر مثلك فلمّا فرغوا من الأكل قال له سيّده يا عبد الخير أنا طمعت عليك بقيت آكل اثنتين اثنتين فقال له يا سيّدي إن كنت أكلت اثنتين اثنتين أنا بقيت أسفّه سفّة والعرب من عاداتهم أنهّم يأكلون الزبيب بالكبشة والتمر بالخمسة ويجدوا في هذا الفعل اللذّة وهناوة الطعم والانبساط بذلك قال الشاعر [طويل]

هنيئا لسكّان البيوتِ بيوتُهُمْ   وللآكلين التمر أخماسَ أخماسا

(وبعضهم) يقشّر الترمس والمقليّ واحدة واحدة والأرياف بخلاف ذلك ولهذا قال

٢٠،٣٨،١١ (ما أَرى تَوْقِيفْ) يعني ما أتوقّف في لفّه بقشره ومراده باللفّ الأكل يقال فلان لفّ مترد عدس بمعنى أنّه أكله كلّه وينصرف اللفّ لغير الأكل كالعمامة ولفّ البردة و(داهيه تلفّك) مثلاً ونحو ذلك

٢١،٣٨،١١ ثمّ إنّه قال

ص

٣٩،١١ وَآخُذْ لِي لِبْدَهْ وَكَرّْ مُشَنْيَرْ   وَأَنْزِلْ كَمَا كَلْبِ ٱبْن ابو جَغْنِيفْ

them one by one and that would not assuage my desire." The poet, after all, is a countryman, and in the country they take them by the handful and toss them down without swallowing and know nothing of peeling or anything of that sort.

Apropos of which, a man once sat with his servant in a dark place eating 11.38.19
raisins. The master said to the man, "Eat them one by one, and I shall do the same." When they had done eating, the master said, "My good man, I was too greedy to bother with you and started eating them two by two!" to which the servant replied, "Sir, you may have been eating them two by two, but I was tossing them down my throat by the handful!" It is the custom of the Arabs to eat raisins by the handful and dates in fives, and they find this the tastiest, pleasantest, and most relaxing way to eat. The poet says:

> May the tents bring good health to their masters,
> And the dates to those who eat them five by five!

Some people peel lupine and *muqaylī* one by one, but the country people do the opposite. Thus he says . . .

mā arā tawqīf ("and never stop"): meaning "I'll not stop eating them with the 11.38.20
skins on." By *laff* he means "eat."[607] One says "So-and-so ate up (*laffa*) a crock of lentils," meaning that he ate them all. The same verb is also used for things other than food, such as the turban, and wrapping a cloak, and one also says *dāhiyah taluffak* ("May a disaster consume you!"), etc.

Next he says: 11.38.21

TEXT

wa-ʾākhudhu lī libdah wa-karra mushanyar 11.39
wa-ʾanzil ka-mā kalbi-bn-Abū Jaghnīf

And I'll get me a felt cap and a *mushanyar* headcloth
and go back like the dog of the son of Abū Jaghnīf

ش

قوله (وآخذُ لي لِبَدَه) هذا أيضاً من جملة قوله لابن بنت عريف السابق ذكره والمعنى ١١،٣٩،١
أنّه يقول إذا أسعفني السعد في سرقة الزرابين وبعتهم وأكلت من ثمنهم أكل حِسّيّ أو معنويّ كما تقدّم وبقي معي شيء ولو خمسة أنصاف أخذت لي لبدة جديدة بنصف من الخمسة

(و) أخذت بالأربعة ١١،٣٩،٢

(كَرَّ مُشَنْيَر) أي شدّا حواشيه غزل أحمر فإنّه يسمّى عند أهل الريف مشنير ولا ١١،٣٩،٣
يلبسه إلّا الأكابر منهم يقال (فلان اليوم لابس لبده وكرّ مشنير) يعني أنّه بقي من أكابر الكفر فالناظم تشوّق إلى هذا الأمر إذا طلع المدينة وهوّن الله عليه بسرقة الزرابين يأخذ ما في مراده وينزل بلبدة وكرّ مشنير في قوة وشهامة مثل الكلب الآتي ذكره ولهذا قال

(وأنْزِلْ كما كلبِ ابْنِ ابو جَغْنيفْ) وكلب ابن أبو جغنيف هذا كان مشهوراً في الكفر ١١،٣٩،٤
بالقوّة والشجاعة والنطّ على الكلاب وخطف العيش وأكل البيض فكان الشخص من أهالي الكفر إذا أنعم الله عليه بلبدة وكرّ مشنير يقولوا فلان اليوم أصبح مثل كلب ابن أبو جغنيف أي في القوّة والشطارة والسرقة حتّى ستر نفسه وكسا روحه وبقي من الأكابر كما أنّك تشبّه الإنسان في الخِسّيّة بالكلب أو الخنزير فتقول أنت مثل الكلب مثلاً وأبو صاحب الكلب كُنِيَ بأبي جغنيف أو جغناف أو جغنوف على ما قيل لثقله وكثرة كلامه يقال فلان جغناف بمعنى ثقيل الدم مهدار كلام من غير فائدة كما رأيته في القاموس الأزرق والناموس الأبلق

(ومن المناسبة) لثقالة الدم وكثرة الكلام الحكاية المشهورة في ألف ليلة وليلة ١١،٣٩،٥
(وهي ما اتّفق) أنّ رجلاً من أكابر الشام صنع وليمة وخرج يدعو الناس لها فرأى

COMMENTARY

wa-'ākhudhu lī libdah ("And I'll get me a felt cap"): this too is a continuation of what he said to the aforementioned son of the daughter of 'Arīf. The meaning of his words is, "If luck is on my side, when I steal the slippers, and I sell them and eat with the proceeds, either literally or figuratively, as explained above, and I have anything left over, even five *nuṣṣ*, I'll get myself a new felt cap with one of the five." 11.39.1

wa- ("and"): "with the remaining four I'll get" . . . 11.39.2

karra mushanyar ("a *mushanyar* headcloth"): that is, a head wrapper with fringes of red yarn, for this is what the country people call *mushanyar*, and it is worn only by their great men. One says, "So-and-so is wearing a felt cap and a *mushanyar* head cloth today," meaning that he has become one of the great men of the hamlet. Consequently, the poet longs for the same, meaning that, if he goes to the city and God is merciful to him in the matter of stealing slippers, he will get what he wants and go back to the hamlet with a felt cap and a *mushanyar* headcloth, in power and glory, like the dog mentioned below. He therefore says . . . 11.39.3

wa-anzil ka-mā kalbi-bn-Abū Jaghnīf ("and go back like the dog of the son of Abū Jaghnīf"): this dog belonging to Abū Jaghnīf 's son was well known in the hamlet for strength and courage and for jumping on the other dogs and snatching loaves of bread and eating eggs, so that, if one of the people of the hamlet was blessed by God with a felt cap and a *mushanyar* headcloth, they would say, "Today So-and-so is like Abū Jaghnīf 's son's dog," that is, strong, audacious, and larcenous, to the point that he has gained enough to dress himself decently and clothe himself respectably and become one of the great, just as one might compare a person in terms of baseness with a dog or a pig and say, "You're a dog!" for example. The father of the dog's owner was given the *kunyah* Abū Jaghnīf (or Jaghnāf or Jaghnūf) according to report, because of his obnoxiousness and loquacity. One says, "So-and-so is a *jaghnāf*," meaning that he is an obnoxious prattler of useless words, or so I find in *The Blue Ocean and Piebald Canon*. 11.39.4

The famous story from *The Thousand and One Nights* provides a pointed example of obnoxiousness and loquacity.[608] It tells how one of the great men 11.39.5

شاباً ظريف الشكل لطيف الذات بديع الحسن إلّا أنّه أعرج فدعاه إلى الوليمة فأجاب ودخل إلى الجالسين في منزله فقاموا له إجلالاً وتعظيماً لأجل صاحب المنزل فلمّا أراد هذا الشابّ أن يجلس رأى بين القوم إنساناً صنعته مُزَيِّن فامتنع من الجلوس وأراد أن يخرج من المجلس فمسكه صاحب الدعوة وحلف عليه وقال له ما سبب مجيئك معي ودخولك إلى منزلي وما سبب رجوعك قبل فراغ دعوتي فقال له الشاب بالله يا مولاي لا تعترض عليّ فإنّ سبب هذا كلّه رؤيتي لهذا الشيخ النحس المزيّن قاتله الله تعالى فإنّه ذميم الخصال * قبيح الفعال * تعيس الحركه * قليل البركه * فلمّا سمع صاحب الدعوة والحاضرون كلام الشابّ في حقّ المزيّن كرهوا مجالسته وقالوا للشابّ والله ما بقينا نأكل حتّى تذكر لنا ما وقع لك مع هذا المزيّن فإنّا كرهناه من وصفك فيه

فقال الشابّ يا جماعة جرى لي مع هذا الشيخ التعيس في بغداد بلدي حكاية عجيبة لو كتبت بالإبر على آماق البصر لكانت عبرة لمن اعتبر وهو سبب عرجي وكسر رجلي فحلفت أنّي لا أجالسه في مكان ولا أسكن مدينة هو فيها وسافرت من بغداد من أجله وسكنت هذه المدينة وهي أقصى البلاد وقد نظرته عندكم وأنا الليلة ما أبات إلّا مسافراً فقالوا له حدّثنا ما جرى لك معه وألحّوا عليه هذا والمزيّن قد اصفرّ وجهه وأطرق برأسه إلى الأرض وأمّا الشابّ فإنّه قال اسمعوا يا جماعة إنّ والدي كان من مياسير بغداد ولم يُرْزَق ولداً غيري فلمّا كبرت وبلغت انتقل والدي إلى رحمة الله وخلف لي مالاً عظيماً وخدماً وحشماً فصرت ألبس وأتنعّم وأنا في أهنأ عيش فبينما أنا ذات يوم من الأيّام ماشي في زُقاق من أزقّة بغداد إذ رأيت مَصْطَبَة فجلست عليها أستريح وإذا بصبيّة كأنّها الشمس المضيئة لم ترعيني أجمل منها طلّت من الطاق وكان لها زرع تسقيه فلمّا نظرت إليها تبسّمت ثمّ إنّها أغلقت الطاق ومضت فانطلق في قلبي النار وشغفت بحبّها ومكثت قاعداً على المصطبة غائب ١١،٣٩،٦

of Damascus once prepared a banquet and went out to invite people and came across a youth who was charming in appearance, refined in person, and outstandingly comely, but lame. The man invited the youth to the banquet, and the youth accepted and went into the house where the guests were seated, and these all rose to greet him out of respect and regard for their host. As the youth was about to seat himself, however, he caught sight of one among the guests whose profession was that of barber, and thereupon he refused to sit down and attempted to leave the gathering. The host, however, took hold of him, abjured him with oaths, and said to him, "What makes you come with me and enter my house and then leave before my hospitality is complete?" "By God, My Master," said the youth, "do not stand in my way! The cause of it all is that I caught sight of that ill-omened wretch of a barber, may the Almighty strike him dead! He is a man of despicable vices and hateful devices, of stumbling gait and unlucky fate!" When the host and the guests heard the youth's words against the barber, they were revolted to be sitting in the same gathering with the man and said to the youth, "By God, we will not eat another bite till you have told us what this barber did to you, for we have come to hate him just from hearing you describe him!"

"My friends," said the youth, "I suffered with this wretched old man in my 11.39.6
home city of Baghdad a story so amazing that it should be written with needles on the pupils of men's eyes, there to serve as admonition for the wise. He is the cause of my lameness and my broken leg, and I have sworn that I will never sit with him in the same place, or live with him in the same city. I left Baghdad because of him and came to live in this, the farthest of cities from there, and now that I see him among you, I shall not stay here this night but be on my way!" "Tell us what you suffered from him!" they said, and he demurred, but they insisted, while the barber's face turned pale and he hung his head low.

The youth, however, said, "Listen, my friends! My father was a rich man of Baghdad, and he was given no son but me. When I grew up and reached the years of discretion, my father passed into the mercy of God, leaving me great wealth and servants and followers. I started dressing well and indulging myself and was living in great felicity, when one day I was walking in one of the alleys of Baghdad and I saw a bench and sat down to rest. Suddenly a young girl like the radiant sun, more beautiful than any I had ever set eyes on, put her head out of a casement to water her flowers. When I looked at her, she smiled. Then she closed the casement and disappeared. Fire burned in my heart, and I

الصواب إلى المغرب وإذا بقاضي المدينة راكب على بغلة وقدّامه العبيد والخدم حتّى أقبل على هذا البيت الّذي فيه الصبيّة ودخله فعرفت أنّه أبوها فجئت إلى بيتي وأنا مكروب وزاد عليّ العشق والهيام واعتراني الضنى فمرضت بحبّها واستمرّيت على هذا الحال أيّاماً وأهلي يبكون عليّ ولم يعرفوا حالي حتّى دخلت عليّ عجوز فلم يخفاها أمري فقالت لي يا ولدي أطلعني على قضيّتك وأنا أبلغك مرادك فأثّر كلامها في قلبي وجلست وأخبرتها الخبر فقالت لي ما صفة الموضع الّذي رأيتها فيه فوصفته لها وقلت لها أبوها قاضي بغداد فقالت لي يا ولدي أعرفها وأعرف أبوها وأنا أدخل عليها كثير لكن عليها حَجْر من أمّها وأبيها ولكن أنا أسعى في اجتماعك عليها ولا تعرف هذا الأمر إلّا منّي فطِبْ نفسا وقَرّ عينا

١١،٣٩،٧ فلمّا سمعت حديثها طابت نفسي للأكل والشرب وقلت لها اسعي وجميع ما تطلبيه خذيه منّي فقامت من عندي وتوجّهت إليها وجاءتني ثاني مرّة ووجهها متغيّر وقالت لي كلّمتها فشتمتني وأغلظت عليّ فلمّا سمعت ذلك ازددت مرضاً على مرضي وصارت العجوز في كلّ يوم تعودني فجاءتني يوماً وهي تضحك وقالت لي البشارة قد طاب خاطر الصبيّة عليك لمّا ذكرت لها أنّك مرضت بحبّها ومن أجلها فقالت لي اقرئيه منّي السلام وطيّبي قلبه وقولي له إنّ عندي أضعاف ما عنده فإذا كان يوم الجمعة قبل الصلاة يجيء إلى الدار وأنا أنزل أفتح له الباب وأطلع به إلى عندي في الطَبَقة وأجتمع أنا وإيّاه ساعة ويخرج قبل ما يعود أبي فلمّا سمعت كلام العجوز زال عنّي ما كنت أجده من الألم وفرحوا أهلي ولم أزل مترقّباً يوم الجمعة حتّى أتى وإذا بالعجوز دخلت عليّ وقالت لي هيّء نفسك واحلق رأسك والبس أحسن ثيابك وامض في الميعاد وأزل ما عليك من الأوساخ في الحمّام فإنّ معك في الوقت فسحة وخرجت من عندي

١١،٣٩،٨ فقلت لغلام من غلماني امض إلى السوق وائتني بمزيّن يكون عاقلاً جيّداً قليل الفضول فغاب ساعة وأتاني بهذا الشيخ النحس لا كان الله له في عون فلمّا دخل سلّم

was overcome with love for her, and I remained sitting on the bench in a daze till sunset. At this point, the judge of the city appeared riding on a mule with slaves and servants before him and came to the girl's house and went in. Thus I discovered that he was her father, and I returned to my house sad at heart, and my passion and lovesickness increased and I started to pine away and grow sick for love of her. I continued in this state for several days, my relatives weeping over me and understanding nothing of my state, till one day an old woman came to see me to whom my case was no mystery. 'My son,' she said to me, 'Tell me your story and I will get you what you want!' Her words stirred my heart, and she sat down and I told her what had happened. 'Describe to me the place where you saw her,' she said, so I did so, and I told her, 'Her father is the judge of Baghdad.' 'My son,' said she, 'I know her and I know her father, and I visit her often. Her mother and father keep a close eye on her. Nevertheless I will try and arrange for you to meet her, which is something no one else can do for you; so recover your spirits and be happy!'

"When I heard her words, my appetite for food and drink returned, and I told her, 'Go to work, and whatever you need from me, take!' So she left me and went off to her and came back to me grim-faced, telling me, 'I spoke to her, but she insulted me and gave me harsh words.' When I heard this, my illness grew worse than ever. The old woman would come to visit me every day, and one day she came to me smiling and said, 'Give me a tip for my news! The girl's heart softened towards you when I told her that you had grown sick with love of her and for her sake, and she told me, "Give him my greetings, and offer him comfort and tell him I suffer a thousand times more than he! Let him come to the house on Friday before the evening prayer and I will come down and open the door for him and take him to my rooms in the private apartments where we can be alone together for an hour, and he can leave before my father comes back."' When I heard the old woman's words, the pain I had been feeling disappeared and my family rejoiced and I was left waiting until Friday should finally come. On that day the old woman came to me and said, 'Get yourself ready, shave your head, put on your finest clothes, and be on your way to your tryst. And get cleaned up at the baths, for you have plenty of time!' and she left me. 11.39.7

"I told one of my servants, 'Go to the market and get me a barber—one who is intelligent, skilled, and lacking in curiosity!' He absented himself for a while and then brought me this wretched old man, may God not help him! 11.39.8

عليّ فرددت عليه السلام فقال لي يا سيّدي إنّي أراك ناحل الجسم فقلت له إنّي كنت مريضاً فقال أذهب الله عنك البؤس والأحزان وجميع الآلام * وأماط عنك الأسقام * ولا زلّت بك الأقدام * وعافاك الله وشفاك * وهنّاك * بما أعطاك * فقلت له تقبّل الله منك دعاءك * فقال لي ابْشِرْ يا سيّدي فقد جات العافية إن شاء الله ثمّ قال تريد يا سيدي أن تقصر شعرك أو تنقص دماً فإنّه قد روي عن ابن عبّاس رضي الله عنهما أنّه قال مَنْ قصّر شعره يوم الجمعة صرف الله عنه سبعين داء من البلاء وروي عنه أيضاً أنّه قال من احتجم يوم الجمعة لا يأمَن ذهاب بصره فقلت له يا هذا قم الآن * واحلق رأسي ودع عنك الهذيان * ولقلقة اللسان * فإنّي ضعيف من أثر المرض فأدخل يده في حَرَمْدانه وأخرج منه منديلاً كان معه وفتحه فإذا فيه أَصطلابات سبع صفائح مطعَّم فأخذه ومضى إلى وسط الدار ورفع رأسه إلى شعاع الشمس ونظر فيه ساعة وتأمّل طويلاً وقال اعلم يا سيّدي وفقك الله * ورعاك وعافاك وشفاك * ودلّك وهداك * أن مضى من يومنا هذا وهو يوم الجمعة ثامن عشر صَفَر سنة ثلاث وخمسين وسبعمائة من هجرة سيّدنا محمّد صلّى الله عليه وسلّم بعد سبعة آلاف سنة من تاريخ آدم عليه السلام وثلثمائة سنة وعشرين من تاريخ إسكندر الرومي وأربعمائة سنة للتاريخ الفارسي والطالع في يومنا هذا المذكور على ما وجب في الحساب من المِرّيخ ثماني درجات وستّ دقائق اتّفق ربّ الطالع عُطارد وهو في ثلث الأصطرلابات[1] والمرّيخ معه في الطالع وهو داخل معه في تسديسه وذلك يدلّ على أنّ أخذ الشعر جيّد ويدلّ أيضاً يا مولاي على أنّك تريد الاجتماع بنفس والطالع فيه مفسود والحال فيه مذموم

٩،٣٩،١١ فقلت له يا هذا والله لقد أضجرتني وضيّقت منافسي وأصغرت روحي وفوّلت عليّ بفأل غير مليح وما دَعَوْتُك للنجامة ولا لشيء من كثرة الكلام فيما لا يعنيك وإنّما دعوتك لتأخذ شعري فافعل ما دعوتك من أجله ودع عنك ما لا أريد وإلّا فاذهب

---

١ بي: الأصطلابات.

When the latter entered, he greeted me and I returned his greeting. Then he said, 'Sir, your body looks wasted.' 'I was sick,' I told him. 'God chase harm, grief, and every ill away,' he replied, 'and keep every sickness at bay, and let your feet never give way; and may God heal you and anneal you, and please you in all He gives you!' to which I replied, 'May God accept your prayers!' Then he said to me, 'Rejoice, my dear sir, for surely good health is yours, if God wills!' Then he asked me, 'Do you wish me, my dear sir, to cut your hair or to let your blood? For it is reported on the authority of Ibn 'Abbās, God be pleased with them both,[609] that the Prophet said, "God relieves him of seventy calamitous ills who cuts his hair on a Friday," and it is reported on the same authority, too, that he said, "He who is cupped on a Friday may not be spared the loss of his sight."' 'Get on with it, you,' I said. 'Shave my head and leave this much ado and all this claptrap too, for I am still sick from my illness.' So he put his hand into his barber's sack and pulled out a cloth and opened it to reveal an astrolabe of seven sheets, all inlaid. This he took and, going to the center of the house, raised his head towards the sun's rays, observed for a while, thought long and hard, and then said, 'Know, my dear sir—may God grant you every success, and heal you and cure you and guard you from bad cess, and ever guide you and never let you digress!—that there has elapsed of this day[610] (it being Friday the eighteenth day of Ṣafar[611] of the year seven hundred and fifty-three after the Migration of Our Lord Muḥammad,[612] God bless him and grant him peace, which took place seven thousand years after the era of Our Lord Adam,[613] peace be upon him, three hundred and twenty years after the era of Alexander the Greek, and four hundred years from the start of the Persian reckoning) with the ascendant on this aforementioned day of ours being eight degrees and six minutes from Mars, according to the calculation, the lord of the ascendant, as it happens, being Saturn, which is in the third of the astrolabe, Mars being with it in the ascendant and entering with it into its sextile . . . all of which indicates that it is excellent for the removal of hair and also, my master, that you intend to meet some soul, though the ascendant in that respect is bad and the undertaking not recommended.'

"'By God,' I said to him, 'you've vexed me, suffocated me, depressed me, 11.39.9
and jinxed me with these nasty prognostications! I didn't summon you to read the stars or to talk a lot of nonsense to me about things that are none of your business. I summoned you to cut my hair, so do what I summoned you to do and leave well alone what I haven't asked you to do, or go your way and let

عنّي ودعني أحضر لي مزيّن غيرك فقال يا مولاي احمد الله أنت طلبت مزيّن فمنّ الله عليك بمزيّن ومنجّم وطبيب وعارف بصنعة الكيمياء والسيمياء والنحو واللغة والمنطق والمعاني والبيان والفقه والتواريخ والحساب وعلم الحديث وقد قرأت الكتب ودرستها * ومارست الأمور وعرفتها * ودبّرت جميع الأشياء وركبتها * وإنّما كان سبيلك أن تحمد الله على ما أعطاك * وتشكره على ما أولاك * فقد قال الله تعالى ﴿فَسْأَلُوا أَهْلَ ٱلذِّكْرِ إِنْ كُنتُمْ لَا تَعْلَمُونَ﴾ وقال رسول الله صلّى الله عليه وسلّم العلماء ورثة الأنبياء وما أنا بحمد الله عاجز عن الفضيلة حتّى تقول لي هذا القول وأنا أشير عليك اليوم أن تعمل ما أقول لك عليه في حساب الكواكب فإنّي ناصح لك ومشفق عليك وأودّ لو كنت في خدمتك سنة لأنّ حقّي عليك واجب وعلى أبيك من قبلك واجب ولا أريد منك أجرة ولو فعلت ذلك لكان أسرّ الأشياء إلى قلبي وكلّ هذا لأجل منزلتك عندي وإكراماً لوالدك رحمة الله عليه لأنّ له عندي أيادي متقدّمة وله عليّ فضل لا يحصى لأنّه كان يحبّ خدمتي وما كان يخدمه أحد غيري لما رأى من كثرة أدبي وقلّة كلامي وحسن صنعتي وخفّة يدي فلهذا كانت رغبته فيّ وكان يحبّني كثيرًا لقلّة فضولي فخدمتي لك وعليك فرض قال فلمّا سمعت ذلك منه قلت أنت اليوم قاتلي لا محالة من كثرة كلامك وهذيانك فيما لا يعنيك فقال لي يا مولاي ومثلي من ينسب إلى الهذيان وكثرة الكلام فوالله لقد كان والدك رحمه الله إذا حضرت إليه يتمنّى أن أتكلّم بين يديه سنة واحدة ليقتبس من علمي ويلتقط من درر نظمي وفهمي وينظر إلى حسن صناعتي ونحن سبعة إخوة الأوّل اسمه بقبوق والثاني اسمه الهدّار والثالث اسمه بقيبق والرابع اسمه الكوز الأسوانيّ والخامس اسمه الفشّار والسادس اسمه الزعقوق وأنا لقلّة كلامي سمّوني الصامت وإن أردت أن أحكي لك عن أصلي وفصلي ونسبي وحسبي وما جرى لإخوتي الستة من أوّل الزمان إلى آخره فاستمع ما أقول

١٠،٣٩،١١ فلما أكثر عليّ الكلام وأطاله بلا فائدة أمرض قلبي وحسّيت أنّ مرارة قلبي انفطرت فقلت لغلامي يا غلام ادفع له أربعة دنانير ودعه يروح عنّي لوجه الله تعالى فما بقيت

me get another barber!' 'My dear sir,' he replied, 'you should thank God that you called for a barber and He sent you someone who is barber, astrologer, and physician, knowledgeable in alchemy and magic, grammar and philology, logic, motifs and imagery, jurisprudence and history, arithmetic and the science of Traditions! I have read books and studied them, and had experience of affairs and understand them, and managed all manner of things and mastered them. You ought rather to praise God for what he has given you and thank Him for the favor He has done you, for the Almighty has said, «Ask those who are acquainted with the Scriptures if you know not!»[614] and the Prophet, God bless him and grant him peace, has said, "The scholars are the heirs of the prophets." Praise the Almighty, I am not some incompetent that you should talk to me that way! I am telling you that today you should take into account what I say about the planets, for I am offering you good advice out of compassion. If only I might be in your service for just one year, for it is my duty to serve you, just as it was my duty to serve your father before you. I seek no reward—just to be of service to you would be the dearest thing to my heart, for the sake of the high esteem in which I hold you and to honor your father, God rest his soul, for he did me many kind deeds in the old days and showed me generosity beyond calculation, because he loved the way I served him. He would allow no one but me to serve him because he found me so well-mannered and sparing of words, such a good worker and so dexterous. For these reasons he liked me well, and he loved me too for my lack of curiosity. It is, therefore, my sacred duty to serve you!' When I heard him speak thus, I told him, 'Today you will surely kill me with your prattling and rambling about things that do not concern you!' 'My dear sir,' he replied, 'are such as I to be accused of rambling and prattling? By God, your father, God rest his soul, when I attended him, would have wished that I could talk in front of him for a whole year that he might borrow from my knowledge, sample the pearls of my verse and my wisdom, and observe the excellence of my art! Now, we are seven brothers, the first called Burbler, the second Bellower, the third Burbelino, the fourth the Aswan Mug,[615] the fifth Braggart, and the sixth Screecher. Me they call the Silent because I speak so little. If you want me to tell you all about who I am and where I'm from, and everything that happened to my six brothers, from beginning to end, listen well!'

"As he kept on talking and stretching everything out to no purpose, my heart sickened and I felt as though my spleen had burst, so I said to my servant, **11.39.10**

أحلق رأسي في هذا اليوم فقال لي هذا النحس الخبيث لمّا سمع كلامي للغلام أيش يا مولاي هذا الكلام أيمان المسلمين تلزمني لا آخذ منك أجرة حتّى أحلق لك ولا بدّ لي من خدمتك فإنّها واجبة عليّ وإصلاح شأنك لازم لي ولا أبالي بعد ذلك إن أخذت منك شيئاً أو لم آخذ فإن كنت يا مولاي لا تعرف قدري وحقّي فأنا أعرف حقّك وقدرك لمقام والدك عندي فالله تعالى يرحمه ويطوّل عمرك فوالله لقد فُجِعَ الناس فيه كان والله جواداً عظيماً كريماً حليماً سخياً محبّاً لإخوانه أرسل خلفي مرّة في نهار جمعة مثل هذا النهار المبارك فدخلت عليه وكان عنده جماعة من أصحابه فقال أنقص لي دماً فأخرجت الأصطرلابات[١] وأخذت الارتفاع فوجدت الطالع مذموماً لإخراج الدم فأعلمته بذلك وقلت له يصبر المولى ساعة حتّى يتغيّر هذا الطالع وأقضي حاجة مولانا ففرح بكلامي وقال والله إنّ عندك فضيلة ولوكان أحد غيرك كان قد أخرج الدم وشكرني لجماعته وحكيت لهم حكايات ظريفة فأعجبته وطربوا جماعته منها غاية الطرب وأنشدت أقول [طويل]

أَتيتُ إلى المَولى لأنقصَ لهُ الدمَ ... فَلَم أَرَ وقتاً يَقتَضي صِحّةَ الجسمِ
جَلستُ أُحدِّثهم بكلِّ عجيبةٍ ... وبَينَ يَديهِ أنشُرُ العِلمَ مِن فهمي
فأَعجبَه مِنّي السَّماعُ وقال لي ... تَجاوزتَ حَدَّ الفَهمِ يا معدنَ العلمِ
فقلتُ له يا سيّدِ الكلِّ والوَرى ... أَفَضتَ عليّ الفَضلَ لا زلتَ في حلمِ
لأنّكَ ربُّ الفَضلِ والجودِ والعطا ... وكَنزُ العُلا في الحِلمِ والجُودِ والعِلمِ

(فلمّا سمع أبوك) رحمه الله حكايتي وشعري طرب وصاح على الغلام وقال أعطه مائة دينار وخلعة فأعطاني فأخذت الطالع فوجدته جيّداً فأخرجت له الدم

---

١ بي: الأصطلابات.

'Boy, give him four dinars and let him leave me and go to perdition, for I shall not shave my head today.' But when he heard what I said to my servant, the miserable wretch said to me, 'What words are these, my dear sir? I simply cannot allow myself, as a Muslim, to take a penny from you till I have shaved you. It is my duty to serve you and my obligation to make you presentable. Once I have done so, I care not whether I am paid or not. You, my dear sir, may know nothing of my worth and merit, but I know yours, because of the high esteem in which I held your father, may the Almighty rest his soul, and grant you long life! How people missed him! God only knows, he was generous and great, openhanded and wise, liberal and loving to his friends! Once on a Friday just like this blessed day he sent for me, so I went in to where he was and found that he had a party of guests with him. "Let my blood!" he said. So I got out my astrolabe and took the elevation and found that the ascendant was inauspicious for the letting of blood. I informed him of this and told him, "Let my lord be patient for an hour until this ascendant changes and I may relieve him!" He was delighted and said, "By God, what a competent fellow you are! Anyone else would just have let my blood!" and he praised me to his guests and I told them all sorts of marvelous stories and he was very impressed and his guests were ecstatic. I recited the following:

I came to my lord to let his blood,
But couldn't find a good time for phlebotomization.
So I sat down and told them of marvels galore
And scattered before him pearls of learning, fruits of my very own lucubration.
He listened, amazed, and said to me,
"You pass all understanding, you mine of information!"
Said I to him, "Lord of all men and mankind,
You've flooded me with kindness, may you never discontinue your consideration!
For you are lord of kindness, generosity, and giving,
You sublime treasure of toleration, magnanimation, and education!"

"'Your father, God rest his soul, hearing my narration and versification, was greatly moved and shouted to his servant, "Give him a hundred dinars and a robe of honor!" and he gave them to me. Then I took the ascendant and found it to be excellent, so I let his blood.'

١١،٣٩،١١ ثمّ إنّ هذا النحس صار يزيد في كلامه وهذيانه فقلت لا رحم الله والدي الّذي عرف مثلك قال فضحك هذا النحس من كلامي وقال لا إله إلّا الله سبحان من يغيّر ولا يتغيّر ما أظنّ إلّا أنّ المرض غيّرك لأنّي أرى عقلك ناقص والناس كلّما كبر سنّهم زاد عقلهم وما أظنّ إلّا أنّك خَرِفْتَ من المرض والله تعالى يقول ﴿وَٱلْكَاظِمِينَ ٱلْغَيْظَ وَٱلْعَافِينَ عَنِ ٱلنَّاسِ﴾ وقال تعالى ﴿وَوَصَّيْنَا ٱلْإِنسَانَ بِوَالِدَيْهِ حُسْنًا﴾ وروي عن أَنَس بن مالك أنّه قال من أرضى والديه فقد أرضى الله ومن أسخط والديه فقد أسخط الله وقال الشاعر [بسيط مع كسر]

وَاسِ[١] الفقيرَ إذا ما كنتَ مقتدراً … على الزمان وللإحسان فاغتنمِ
الفقر داء دفين لا دواء له … والمال زين يَزِين المنظر الشَّيِمِ
وافْشِ السلام إذا ما كنت في ملأٍ … والوالدين فكن عونا لبِرِّهِمِ

لكن يا سيّدي أنت معذور والله تعالى يقول ﴿لَيْسَ عَلَى ٱلْأَعْمَىٰ حَرَجٌ وَلَا عَلَى ٱلْأَعْرَجِ حَرَجٌ وَلَا عَلَى ٱلْمَرِيضِ حَرَجٌ﴾ وأبوك وجدّك ما كانوا يفعلوا شيئاً إلّا بمشورتي وقالوا في المثل من لم يكن له كبير فليأخذ له مشير قال الشاعر [متقارب]

إذا ما عَزَمْتَ على حاجةٍ … فشاوِرْ كبيراً ولا تَعْصِهِ

وما تجد أحداً أدرى بالأمور منّي ومع ذلك إنّي واقف بين يديك على أقدامي أخدمك وما ضَجِرْتُ فتضجر أنت منّي

١٢،٣٩،١١ فقلت له يا هذا لقد أطلت عليّ الخطاب وأوجعت رأسي من كثرة الكلام فبالله عليك انصرف عنّي وأظهرت له الغَبَن وأردت أن أقوم وقد دنا منّي الوقت الّذي أنا منتظره والوعد الّذي أنا طالبه وأنا في كرب من ثقالة هذا النحس وكثرة كلامه فقال يا مولاي أنا ما أَعْتِبُ عليك وأنا متعجّب منك الّذي رأيتك بهذه اللحية وبالأمس

---

١ بي (في جميع النسخ): وَاسِي.

"After this the wretch kept up his talking and his raving till I said, 'May God divest my father of His mercy for having known one such as you!' but the wretch laughed at my words and said, 'There is no god but God! Glory be to Him who changes but is not changed! I can only suppose that your illness has affected you, for I see that your brain is deficient. Nevertheless, one grows wiser as one grows older. It must be the sickness that is making you talk nonsense. The Almighty has said, «Those who control their wrath and are forgiving of mankind,»[616] and the Almighty has said, «We have enjoined men to be kind to their parents,»[617] and it is reported on the authority of Anas ibn Mālik that the Prophet said, "Whoever pleases his parents pleases God and whoever displeases his parents displeases God," and the poet says: 11.39.11

Give to the poor when Fate treats you well,
And seize every chance to give alms.
Poverty's a hidden ill without cure,
Wealth an adornment that to ugly fronts adds charms.
Pass greetings around when you're out in society
And help your parents out of filial piety!

"'You are to be excused, however, my dear sir. The Almighty says, «There is no blame upon the blind or upon the lame or upon the sick.»[618] Your father and your grandfather would do nothing without consulting me, and, as the proverb has it, "He who has no older relative, let him take a counselor!" The poet[619] says:

If you resolve upon a thing
Consult one who is older, and do not disobey him!

"'You will find no one more experienced in affairs than me, and yet I stand before you ready to do you service and I have not lost my temper with you, even though you lost yours with me!'

"'Fellow!' I said to him, 'You have held me up and given me a headache with your endless talk. For God's sake, leave me!' and I made a show of ignoring him, and I wished to leave, for the moment I was waiting for and the hour that I sought had drawn close, while I was in a state of misery because of this wretch and his loquaciousness. Then he said, 'My dear sir, I don't blame you at all. I am delighted to see you today with this beard when just yesterday I used to carry you upon my shoulder and take you to the *kuttāb*!' 'By God's truth,' 11.39.12

كنت أحملك على كتفي وأمضي بك إلى الكتّاب فقلت له بحقّ الله احلق رأسي وقم عنّي (قال) فعند هذا كلّه لمّا رآني غضبت أخذ الموسى وسَنّه وتقدّم إلى رأسي وحلق منها بعض شعر ثمّ رفع يده وقال يا مولاي إنّ العجلة من الشيطان والتأنّي من الرحمن قال الشاعر [طويل]

تأنَّ ولا تَعْجَلْ لأمرٍ تريده　　وكن راحماً في الناس تُبْلَى براحمِ
فما من يد إلّا يد الله فوقها　　ولا ظالمٍ إلّا سيُبْلَى بظالمِ

وخير الأمور ما كان فيه التأنّي وأظنّك مستعجل وأنت قاصد حاجة وأنا أخشى أن يكون حاجة غير موافقة وأمر غير صالح فأخبرني فإن وقت الصلاة قد قرب ثمّ رمى الموسى من يده وأخذ الأصطرلابات[1] ومضى إلى الشمس وقال بقي لوقت الصلاة ثلاث ساعات لا تزيد ولا تنقص

فقلت له بالله عليك يا هذا اسكت عنّي فقد ضيّقت عليّ الدنيا وقد زهقت ١٣،٣٩،١١
روحي منك قال فتقدّم وأخذ الموسى وحلق شيئاً يسيراً ثمّ أرماه وصار يهدر عليّ في الكلام إلى أن مضى ساعتين وبقي ساعة واحدة وخشيت إن تأخّرت عن الموعد لا أدري كيف السبيل في الدخول إليها فقلت له احلق بسرعة ودع عنك كثرة الكلام فإنّي أريد أن أمضي إلى دعوة عند بعض أصحابي فلمّا سمع هذا النحس بذكر الدعوة قال إنّا لله وإنّا إليه راجعون والله يا سيّدي ذكّرتني جماعة عندي ضيوف ومرادي أصنع لهم طعاماً وما عندي شيء وأنت تحضر لي بجميع ما أطلبه ولا أروّح إلّا أنا وإيّاك وتشرّفني اليوم في محلّي ووليمتي أحسن من وليمة أصحابك فقلت خذ ما تريد واحلق بقيّة رأسي ودعني في حالي فإنّ الوقت ضاق ولا لي حاجة بالذهاب إلى منزلك وأحضرت له جميع ما طلب حتّى البخور العود ومرادي أنّ الله يصرفه عنّي حتّى أمضي إلى مطلوبي

---

١ بي: الأصطلابات.

I exclaimed, 'Just shave my head and leave me!' At this, seeing that I had lost my temper, he took the razor, stropped it, approached my head, and shaved off some hair. Then he lifted his hand and said, 'My dear sir, "Haste is the Devil's and patience the Merciful's." The poet says:

> Proceed with care, haste not in matters that concern you.
> Be merciful to men, and you will meet with mercy.
> There is no hand but God's is above it,
> No tyrant but shall meet with God's tyranny.

"'The best things are those that are undertaken with caution; yet I see that you are in a hurry and have something in mind, and I am afraid lest it be something unbefitting or improper, so tell me what it is, for the time of the prayer is close,' and he threw down his razor and took up the astrolabes and went into the sun and said, 'Three hours, no less and no more, remain until the prayer time.'

"I said, 'I beseech you by God, man, stop plaguing me with your words, for **11.39.13**
you have vexed me and depressed me!' So he approached and took the razor in his hand and shaved a little more. Then he threw it down again and went on blathering at me until two hours had passed and one hour was left and I was afraid that, were I late for the tryst, I would be unable to get in to see her, so I told him, 'Shave my head quickly and stop talking so much, for I want to be on my way to a party at a friend's house to which I am invited!' When the wretch heard mention of a party, he said, 'We are God's and to God we shall return! By God, Sir, you have reminded me that I have a company staying with me as guests. I want to make them food, but I have nothing. Just get me everything I ask for, and then you and I will go home, and you will honor me today with your presence at my place, and my banquet will be better than your friend's!' 'Take whatever you want, shave the rest of my head, and leave me be!' I said to him. 'Time is running out, and there is no need for me to go to your house,' and I had everything he asked for brought, even incense of aloes, all in the hope that God would rid me of him so that I could go to where I wanted to be.

١٤،٣٩،١١ فقال يا سيّدي وأنا الآخر عندي جماعة ملاح زيتون الحمّامي وضليع الفامي وسلوطح الفوّال وعكرشة البقّال وسعيد الحمّال وسُويد الفتّال وحميد الزبّال وأبو عكاشة البلاّن وقنبر الخرفان ولكلّ واحد منهم قصّة إن أردت أحكيها لك فأمّا حميد الزبّال فإنّه يرقص بالطار ويغنّي على المزمار وفي وصفه أقول [بسيط]

روحي الفداء لزبّال شُغِفْتُ به حلو الشمائل كالأغصان ميّالا
جاد الزمان به ليلاً فقلت له والشوق ينقص منّي كلمّا زالا
أضرمتَ نارك في قلبي فجاوبني لا غَرْوَ إن أصبح الوقّادُ زبّالا

(فامض يا سيّدي) معي إلى أصحابي واترك أصحابك فربّما إنّك تمضي إلى ناس يكونوا كثيرين الكلام فيشوّشوا عليك أو يكون فيهم واحد فضوليّ فيوجع رأسك وأنت قد صغرت روحك من هذا المرض

١٥،٣٩،١١ فقلت له غير اليوم فإنّ مرادي أمضي إلى أصحابي وامض أنت إلى أصحابك فقال هذا النحس معاذ الله يا مولاي أن أتخلّى عنك وأدعك تمضي وحدك فقلت له يا هذا إن الموضع الّذي أنا ماض إليه ما يتحمّل أحداً يدخله غيري فقال يا مولاي أظنّك اليوم في ميعاد واحدة وإلاّ كنت تأخذني معك وأنا أحقّ من جميع الناس وأساعدك على ما تريد وأنا خائف أن تكون امرأة أجنبيّة فتروح روحك فإنّ مدينة بغداد ما يقدر أحد يعمل فيها شيء ووالي بغداد جبّار وربّما يَصدِفك يرمي رقبتك فقلت له يا شيخ النحس أيش هذا الكلام الّذي تقابلني به وقد ملئت غيظاً وقد جاء وقت الصلاة وفرغ من حلق رأسي فقلت له الآن امض إلى أصحابك بهذا الطعام وأنا منتظرك إلى أن تعود وتمضي معي ولم أزل أداهنه وأخادعه وهو يقول لا أمضي إلّا معك ولا أدعك تروح وحدك حتّى حلفت له أنّي أنتظره لمّا يعود وأمضي أنا وإيّاه فأخذ جميع ما أعطيته له وخرج من عندي ثمّ إنّه أنفذه مع حمّال إلى منزله وأخفى نفسه في بعض الأزقّة

"Then he said, 'Sir, mine too is a charming company:[620] there's Zaytūn the Bathhouse Keeper, Big-Mouth, Salawṭaḥ the Bean Seller, 'Ikrishah the Grocer, Sa'īd the Porter, Suwayd the Ropemaker, Ḥāmid the Trashman, and Abū 'Ukāshah the Bath Attendant, plus Sheep-Larks, and each of them has a story that I, should you desire, will tell you. Now, Ḥāmid the Trashman dances to the tambourine and sings to the pipes, and I've composed to describe him: 11.39.14

My life I'd give for a trashman o'er whom I've gone crazy,
With the sweetest disposition, graceful as branches a-sway!
When Fate granted him to me one night I told him
(For I waste with longing whene'er he's away),
"You've fired up your love in my heart!" Said he,
"No wonder, when it's a trashman who's stoking the blaze!"

"'So, my dear sir, come with me to my friends and forget yours, for you may find yourself going to see people who talk too much and upset you, or one of them may be inquisitive and try your patience, given that your illness has made you so quick to fly off the handle.'

"'Some other day,' I said, 'for I intend to go to my friends and you must go to 11.39.15
yours.' 'God forbid, my lord,' this wretch then said, 'that I should abandon you and let you go on your own!' 'Fellow,' I replied, 'no one but me can get into the place I'm going to.' 'I think, my lord,' he said, 'that you have a tryst today with some girl, otherwise you would want to take me with you, but who is better suited than me to help you obtain what you desire? I fear, however, she may be some foreign woman who will get you into trouble, for no one can get away with anything in the city of Baghdad, and its governor is an ogre. He may catch you with her, in which case he will cut off your head.' I told him, 'You wretched old man, what nonsense is this you're throwing at me?' and I was filled with rage, and the prayer time had arrived, and he had finished shaving my head, so I told him, 'Take this food to your friends now, and I will wait for you to come back and then you can go with me,' and I kept on buttering him up and trying to fool him, while he kept saying, 'I won't go without you!' and 'I won't let you go on your own!' until I swore to him that I would wait until he came back and that then we would go together. At this he took everything I had given him and left, and then sent the stuff on with a porter to his house and hid himself in an alleyway.

١٦،٣٩،١١ ثمّ إنّي قمت من وقتي وساعتي وقد سلّم المؤذّن وضاق الوقت فلبست ثيابي وسرت مسرعًا وحدي إلى أن أتيت الزقاق ووقفت على الدار الّتي رأيت فيها الصبيّة وهذا التعيس المزيّن خلفي وأنا لا أشعر به فوجدت الباب مفتوح فدخلت فوجدت العجوز واقفة تنتظرني فطلعتني الطبقة الّتي للصبيّة فما أشعر إلّا وصاحب الدار قد عاد من الصلاة ودخل القاعة وأغلق الباب فأشرفت أنا من الطاق ورأيت هذا المزيّن قاتله الله قاعد على الباب فقلت إنّا لله وإنّا إليه راجعون من أين علم هذا النحس بي حتّى ساقه الله تعالى إليّ لهتك ستري ثمّ إنّ صاحب الدار ضرب جارية من جواره فأتى عبده ليخلّصها فضربه فصاح العبد فاعتقد هذا المزيّن الخبيث أنّه يضربني فصاح وخزق ثيابه ووضع التراب على رأسه وصار يقول قُتِلَ سيّدي في بيت القاضي واسيّداه واسيّداه فأقبلت إليه الناس وهو يصيح ثمّ مضى إلى داري والناس خلفه وأعلم أهلي وغلماني وقال لهم سيّدي قتل في بيت قاضي بغداد فجاءوني صارخين راخين الشعور وهو يصيح قدّامهم الله ينصر السلطان في القاضي قتل استادي

١٧،٣٩،١١ فسمع صاحب الدار ضجّة الخلق والصراخ والعياط والناس يقولون له تقتل في دارك أولاد الناس والمزيّن يقول واقتيلاه واسيداه فخرج وفتح الباب والناس يصيحون في وجهه وهذا النحس يقول الله ينصر فيك السلطان فقال يا قوم ما القصّة فقال له المزيّن تقتل سيّدنا في دارك فقال له وأين سيّدك حتّى أقتله فقال له هذا الخبيث المزيّن أنت ضربته بالمقارع وصار يصيح والآن ما بقي له حسّ وما هو إلّا أنّك قتلته فقال القاضي ومن أدخل سيّدك داري بغير أذني فقال له إنّه عاشق بنتك وقد دخل لها فلمّا جئت ورأيته ضربته وقتلته وما بقي يفرّق بيني وبينك إلّا السلطان أو

"I arose immediately. The call to prayer had been given and time was running out, so I dressed and rushed off, on my own, till I came to the alley and stopped at the house in which I had seen the girl, with this wretched barber, unbeknownst to me, following behind. I found the door open and I went in and found the old woman waiting for me behind the door, and she took me upstairs to the girl's quarters, but, before I knew it, the master of the house had returned from the prayer and entered the main hall and closed the door of the house behind him. I looked out of the window and saw this wretched barber, God strike him dead, sitting outside the door, and said to myself, 'To God we belong and to God we shall return! How did this wretch discover my whereabouts so that the Almighty could send him to expose me?' At this point, the master of the house struck one of his slave girls, and his slave came to intervene on her behalf, and he struck the slave too and the slave cried out, and this miserable barber thought the man was hitting me, and he shrieked and rent his clothes and threw dust on his head and started saying, 'My master has been murdered in the judge's house! Alas for my master, alas for my master!' so that people came from all sides in answer to his cries. Then he proceeded to my house, the people behind him, and informed my family and my servants, telling them, 'My master has been murdered in the house of the Judge of Baghdad!' and they came after me, screaming and with their hair untied, the barber in front of them yelling, 'God aid the sultan against the judge! He has murdered my master!' 11.39.16

"Hearing the noise of the crowd and the screaming and shouting and the people saying, 'Would you murder young gentlemen in your house?' and the barber saying, 'Alas for the slain! Alas for my master!' the master of the house came out and opened the door and the people yelled at him, while this wretch said, 'God aid the sultan against you!' 'What is the matter, good people?' he asked. The barber said to him, 'Would you murder our master in your house?' 'And where is your master,' said the judge, 'that I should murder him?' This miserable barber then said to him, 'You beat him with cudgels and he cried out, but now his voice has ceased, which means you murdered him!' 'And who put your master in my house without my permission?' asked the judge. He replied, 'He's your daughter's lover and he went to visit her, and when you came you found him and beat him and murdered him, and now either the sultan settles things between us, or you bring him out of the house right away!' The judge, who was covered with embarrassment and shame 11.39.17

تخرجه من بيتك في هذه الساعة فقال له القاضي وقد اعتراه الخجل والحياء من الناس إن كنت صادق ادخل أنت وأخرجه فنهض هذا الشقيّ ودخل الدار

١٨،٣٩،١١ فلمّا رأيته طلبت طريقاً أخرج منها أو موضعاً أهرب فيه فلم أجد غير صندوق كبير فدخلت فيه وردّيت عليّ الغطاء وقطعت الحسّ فالتفت هذا النحس الخبيث فلم ير غير الصندوق في المحلّ الّذي كنت فيه فأتى إليه وحمله على رأسه وقد غاب عقلي وخرج بي مسرعاً فلمّا علمت أنّه لا يتركني حملت نفسي ورميت روحي من الصندوق إلى الأرض فانكسرت رجلي وخرجت فرأيت خلقاً على الباب مثل التراب فصرت أنثر الدنانير على رؤوسهم فالتهوا عنّي وصرت أجري في أزقّة بغداد وهذا الخبيث النحس يجري خلفي ويقول احمد الله يا سيّدي الّذي خلّصك من القتل وأنا وراءك لا تخاف وما كان لك حاجة بعشقة بنت القاضي وعشق النساء صعب وصار يشنّع عليّ في الأسواق ويهتكني بالكلام إلى أن هربت منه في خان فقلت للبوّاب بالله عليك امنعه عنّي فقام عليه البوّاب ومنعه وقد زهقت روحي وأشرفت على الهلاك وأتيت إلى فقي وكتبت وصيّتي وأرسلتها لأهلي وأخذت معي جانب من الدراهم وسافرت وحلفت لا أسكن في بلد فيها هذا المزيّن التعيس

١٩،٣٩،١١ فلمّا جئت إلى بلدكم هذه دمشق ودعاني صاحب الوليمة ورأيت هذا الشقيّ جالس فما طاب لي الجلوس ولا الأكل وهذه يا جماعة قصّتي قال فالتفتوا إليه وقالوا له هذا الكلام صحيح فرفع رأسه وقال نعم وهو يحمد الله الّذي خلّصته وبكسر رجله ولا بضرب عنقه وانا عملت معه هذا الجميل فقالوا قاتل الله الأبعد هتكت الشابّ وغرّبته عن أهله وهتكت قاضي بغداد ثمّ إنّهم أخرجوه من عندهم وأكرموا الشابّ وتعجّبوا ممّا فعله معه وكلّ منهم مضى إلى حال سبيله وفي الغالب أنّ كثرة الكلام عند أرباب هذه الصناعة لكن هذا النحس زاد في الثقالة وعدم الذوق

٢٠،٣٩،١١ (ثمّ إنّ الناظم) بعد ذلك قال

before the people, said to him, 'If you are telling the truth, go in yourself and bring him out,' so this rascal went up and entered the house.

"When I saw him, I looked for a way of escape or a place in which I could take refuge, but all I could find was a large chest, so I got into that, pulled the lid down on top of me, and held my breath. This vile wretch looked around and seeing nothing but the chest in the room I was in, went to it and lifted it onto his head, while I was going crazy, and he exited with me in a hurry. When I realized that he was not going to let me go, I braced myself and threw myself from the chest onto the ground, breaking my leg in the escape. I saw that people were clustered around the door as thick as flies, so I started throwing gold coins over their heads, which distracted them, and I took off running through the alleys of Baghdad, this vile wretch running behind me saying, 'Praise God, my master, for saving you from being killed! I'm right behind you; don't be afraid! You had no call to make passes at the judge's daughter! Wooing women is a tricky business!' and he continued pursuing me with accusations of foul deeds through the markets and disgracing me with his words until I escaped from him into a caravansary, and I said to the doorkeeper, 'I beseech you in God's name, keep him away from me!' and the doorkeeper attacked him and stopped him from coming in. By this time, I was sick at heart and on the verge of expiring, and I summoned a jurist and wrote my will and sent it to my family. Then I took some money and traveled, and I swore that I would never live in the same town as this abominable barber. 11.39.18

"When I came to this city of yours, Damascus, the host of this banquet invited me and I saw this rascal seated here, so I could not bring myself to sit or to eat. Such, good people, is my story." Then they turned to the barber and said, "Is this true?" and he lifted his head and said, "Certainly! And he should praise God that I saved him, and that he only broke his leg and didn't get his head chopped off, and that I did him this favor!" "God strike you dead, you unspeakable wretch!" they said. "You disgraced this young man, exiled him from his family, and disgraced the Judge of Baghdad!" Then they expelled him from their company and did honor to the youth, marveling at what the barber had done to him, and each then went his way. Generally speaking, loquacity is a common trait among those who practice this profession, but this wretch went too far in his obnoxiousness and bad manners. 11.39.19

Next the poet says: 11.39.20

ص

٤٠،١١ وَيَجْلِسْ بِجَنْبِي إِبْنُ جَرْوٍ وَكُلْ خَرَهْ وَإِبْنُ كُلِ ٱلصَّكِّ ٱلنَّضِيفْ وَضِيفْ
وَإِبْنُ فِسَا ٱلتِّيرَانْ وَإِبْنُ خَرا ٱلحَسْ وَقَلُّوطْ وَٱلزِّبْلَهْ وَإِبْنُ كَنِيفْ

ش

١،٤٠،١١ هؤلاء مشايخ بلد الناظم افتخر بذكرهم وأجرى أسماءهم على لسانه والمعنى أنّه يقول إنّي إذا نزلت من المدينة وأنا مكسيّ لبدة وشدّ مشنير وأنا كما الكلب كما تقدّم ذكره وأتوا إليّ مشايخ البلد المذكورين وجلسوا بجانبي وهم ثمانية رجال

٢،٤٠،١١ (إِبْنُ جَرْوٍ و) الثاني ابن

٣،٤٠،١١ (كُلْ خَرَهْ و) الثالث

٤،٤٠،١١ (إِبْنُ كُلِ الصَّكِّ النَّضِيفْ) أي المتراسل بعضه إثْر بعض حتّى يخلّي القفا مثل عَلَم سيّدي أحمد البدويّ مثلاً وقيل إنّ الصكّ النضيف شرطه أن يكون من رجل شديد ويكون قفا الشخص مُصْلَح من غير شيء يمنع عنه الصكّ ويراسله بالصكّ بالسرعة والعجلة حتّى يحمرّ قفاه فعلامة نضافة الصكّ احمرار القفا وورمه

٥،٤٠،١١ (حُكِيَ) أنّ أبا نواس نادم أمير المؤمنين هارون الرشيد ليلة فأنعم عليه بجارية وأمر بحملها معه وقال لها إذا طلب منك الحاجة فصكّيه وكلّما أراد الطلب زيديه من

TEXT

wa-yajlis bi-janbī ʾIbnu Jarwin wa-Kul Kharah 11.40
wa-ʾIbnu Kuli l-Ṣakka l-Naḍīfa wa-ḍīf
wa-Ibnu Fisā l-Tīrān wa-Ibnu Kharā-Lḥas[621]
wa-Qallūṭu wa-l-Ziblah wa-Ibnu kanīf

And by me will sit Son-of-Puppy and Eat-Shit
and Son-of-Take-a-Good-Slapping-on-the-Back-of-the-Neck, and so on and so forth,
And Son-of-Ox-Fart and Son-of-Lick-Shit
and Big-Turd and Dropping and Son-of-Latrine

COMMENTARY

These are the shaykhs of the poet's village, whose names he takes pride in repeating and running off his tongue. The meaning is that he is saying: If I come back from the city wearing a felt cap and a turban with red fringes and I am like the aforementioned dog, the aforementioned shaykhs of the village will come to me and sit next to me, they being eight men altogether: 11.40.1

The first is *ʾIbnu Jarwin wa-* ("Son-of-Puppy and") the second is the son of... 11.40.2

Kul Kharah wa- ("Eat-Shit and") the third is... 11.40.3

ʾIbnu Kuli l-Ṣakka l-Naḍīfa ("Son-of-Take-a-Good-Slapping-on-the-Back-of-the-Neck"): that is, a slapping in which the blows follow one another in rapid succession, so that they leave the nape of the neck looking like the flag of Master Aḥmad al-Badawī, for example.[622] It is said that the requirements for a good slapping on the back of the neck are that it be administered by a strong man, that the recipient's neck be properly prepared, with nothing to impede the impact of the slaps, and that the slaps follow one another rapidly and with alacrity, so that they make the nape turn red, for the sign of a good slapping on the neck is the redness and swelling of the nape. 11.40.4

The tale is told that Abū Nuwās was keeping company one night with the Commander of the Faithful Hārūn al-Rashīd when the latter gave him a slave girl as a gift and told him to take her home with him. However, Hārūn al-Rashīd told her, "When he asks you to do it with him, give him a good slapping on the back of the neck, and the more he asks, the more you slap him." When Abū 11.40.5

الصكّ فلمّا وصل إلى منـزله وأراد منها الفعل نزلت في قفاه صكّاً وهكذا فلمّا أصبح أتى الخليفة وهو في غاية ما يكون من الألم لا يقدر يلتفت يميناً ولا شمالاً فقال له الخليفة كيف كانت ليلتك يا أبا نواس مع الجارية قال كانت طيّبة إلّا أنّ مولانا عوّدها عادة قبيحة فضحك منه وأنعم عليه بمال وغيره وقوله

١١،٤٠،٦ (وضيفْ) وأتى به لتمام البيت والرابع

١١،٤٠،٧ (إبْنُ فِسا التيرانْ) سمّي بذلك لأنّ أبوه كان انقطع مدّة في داره لمرض اعتراه وهو كثرة الفساء واتّخذ له محلّاً بين التيران يسمّى طوالة فصار يفسي فيها ليلاً ونهاراً فصار كلّ من شمّ رائحته يقول له ما هذا فيقول فسا التيران فسمّي بذلك والخامس

١١،٤٠،٨ (إبْنُ خَرا إلْحَسّ) سمّي أبوه بذلك لكثرة لحسه من الجلّة وهو صغير وقيل إنّه قلع عَرَقيّته ووضعها على الأرض وصار يخرى فيها حتّى ملأها وصار يلحس من حواليها فسمّي بذلك والسادس

١١،٤٠،٩ (قَلّوُطْ) مشتقّ من القَلْط على وزن الضَرْط والهَلْط يقال (فلان غلظ قلّوطه) بمعنى أنّه شبع من الرزق وبقي في الكفر أمر عظيم

١١،٤٠،١٠ والسابع من مشايخ البلد (الزِبْلَهْ) سمّي بذلك لأنّه كان في صغره مشغول بلمّ زبل الغنم وبيعه وكان هذا سبب سعادته وكان بينه وبين قلّوط صداقة في البلد فكان قلّوط دائماً فيها لا يفارقها والزبلة تارة يسافر وتارة يقعد فيها وكان قلوط هذا في وسطها سواء بسواء والزبلة في طرفها وكانوا أيضاً يهادوا بعضهم بعضاً وبينهم محبّة ومناسبة لأنّ الزبلة قريبة من القلّوط لكنّ ابن خرا الحس أعظم مَنْ في البلد وأكبر من الكلّ

Nuwās reached his house and wanted to do it with her, she rained slaps on the back of his neck, etc. The next day he went to the caliph in the greatest of pain, unable to turn his head to the right or the left. "What sort of a night did you have with the slave girl, Abū Nuwās?" asked the caliph. "She was great," the latter replied, "but you've taught her a very bad habit!" The caliph laughed and gave him gifts of money and other things.

wa-ḍīf ("and so on and so forth"): inserted in order to fill up the line. The fourth of those named is . . . **11.40.6**

ʾIbnu Fisā l-Tīrān ("and Son-of-Ox-Fart"): so called because his father was confined to his house for a period by a sickness that afflicted him, to wit, constant farting. He made a place for himself among the oxen in the thing that is called the *ṭuwālah* ("feeding trough") and farted there day and night, with the result that when anyone smelled the smell they would say to him, "What's that?" and he would reply, "ox farts," and that is how he got his name. And the fifth is . . . **11.40.7**

ʾIbnu Kharā-Lḥas ("Son-of-Lick-Shit"): his father was so called because he used to lick dung a lot when he was little. It is reported that he used to take off his skullcap and place it on the ground and shit in it till it was full, and then lick it out, and that is how he got his name. And the sixth is . . . **11.40.8**

Qallūṭu ("Big-Turd"): derived from *qalṭ* ("to produce a large, firm turd"), on the measure of *ḍarṭ* ("to fart audibly") and of *halṭ* ("to be flaccid and large (of the belly)"). One says, "So-and-so's turds have grown fat," meaning that he has become rich and acquired high status in the hamlet. And the seventh of the village shaykhs is . . . **11.40.9**

al-Ziblah ("Dropping"): so called because when he was young he used to busy himself picking up the droppings from the flocks and selling them, and this was the basis of his good fortune. A friendship existed in the village between him and Big-Turd. Big-Turd was always there and never left, but Dropping would sometimes leave and sometimes stay. This Big-Turd lived in the very heart of the village, while Dropping lived on the edge. They would send one another presents too, and there was both an affective and a familial relationship between them, for droppings are closely related to turds. Despite all this, Lick-Shit was the mightiest in the village, and the most senior of them all. **11.40.10**

(ومن النوادر) أنّ بعض الولاة من المغفّلين قال لكاتبه اكتب لفلان وأغلظ عليه وقل له يا خراء افعل كذا وكذا قال له الكاتب يا مولاي لا يصلح هذا فقال له حيث كان الأمر كذلك الحس موضع الخراء بلسانك والثامن ١١،٤٠،١١

(إبْنُ كَنيفَ) وكان فيها دائماً يتعاطى مصالح البلد وكان نديماً لقلّوط وابن خرا الحس إلّا أنّ ابن خرا الحس كان محبوب ابن كنيف في الصغر فلمّا كبر صار ابن كنيف نديماً له كما قال بعضهم مواليا [بسيط] ١٢،٤٠،١١

وِطْواطْ عشقْ خنفسا وصبحْ بها مجوبْ   وعملْ لها قصرَ جوّا بيت خلا من طوبْ
وحضّر النُقلَ والمأكولَ والمشروبْ   ما للنديم الخرا إلّا لِدي المحبوبْ

ثمّ إنّ الناظم قال ١٣،٤٠،١١

ص

وَأَفْـرَحُ بِٱللَّـهِ وَيَنْسَـرُّ خَاطِـرِي   وَهَـذَا مُـرَادِي يَا ٱبْنَ بِنْتِ عَـرِيفْ ٤١،١١

ش

هذا كلّه خطاباً لابن بنت عريف المتقدّم ذكره أي أنّه مترجّي من الله أن يبلغه مناه من سرقة الزرابين المتقدّمة ويمنّ عليه حتّى ينزل من المدينة بلبدة وكرّمشنير وله مقام ومقال ويجتمع عليه مشايخ البلد المتقدّم ذكرهم ولا يُحتاج لإعادتهم فإنّ الإعادة ما فيها إفادة وقد عرّفتُ أسماءهم باللفظ والذوق وملخّص القول أنّ الناظم يقول إن حصل لي هذا فهو غاية مرادي من الدنيا وتمام مطلوبي من اللذّات فإنّي كبرت ١،٤١،١١

An Amusing Story: a certain dull-witted governor told his secretary, "Write to so-and-so in harsh terms and say to him, 'You shit, do such and such!'" But the secretary said, "My Lord, that is not appropriate!" so the ruler told him, "In that case, lick the 'shit' off with your tongue!" And the eighth is . . . 11.40.11

ʾIbnu kanīf ("Son-of-Latrine"): he always took care of the needs of the village, and he was a crony of Big-Turd and Lick-Shit, though Lick-Shit had been Son-of-Latrine's bosom buddy when they were young. When he grew up, however, Son-of-Latrine became his crony. As a certain poet put it in a *mawāliyā*: 11.40.12

A bat fell in love with a beetle and woke the next day possessed,
And he built her then a palace inside a privy made of brick,
And he brought her nuts and food and drink—
What better boon companion could such a shitty friend possess?

Next the poet says: 11.40.13

TEXT

wa-ʾafraḥu bi-l-lammah wa-yansarru khāṭirī 11.41
wa-hādhā murādī ya-bna binti ʿarīf

And I'll rejoice in the throng and my heart will be happy
and this is my hope, O son of the daughter of ʿArīf!

COMMENTARY

All this is addressed to the aforementioned son of the daughter of ʿArīf. That is, he prays God to allow him to achieve his goal of stealing the aforementioned slippers and to grant him that he might leave the city with a felt cap and a turban with red fringes and have status and esteem, and that the shaykhs of the village listed above—and whose names there is no need to repeat, since repetition serves no function, and I have already given both the substance and the taste of their names—would meet with him. The poet says, in sum, "If I attain this, it will be all I could ask for or desire of this world, and the fulfillment of every pleasure I have longed for, for I have grown old and my wife has turned 11.41.1

والزوجة صارت عجوز عقيم وإذا منّ الله تعالى عليّ بما طلبته يبقى ررزق امراتي على الله لأنّه كريم وررزّاق العواجز وأنا على حدّ قول القائل [وزن غير معروف]

يا من طلب رِزْق ونالو   وقال بقى رزقُ امراتي
قم في الظلام سرّح دقنك   لا بدّ لك من خير ياتي

(أو أنّه) اختصّ بالطلب لنفسه وقال لعقله (المرا تاكل خرا) و(ألف دقن ولا دقني)

(ثمّ إنّه ختم) كلامه بالصلاة على النبيّ صلّى الله عليه وسلّم فقال ٢،٤١،١١

ص

وَأَخْتِمْ قَصِيدِي بِٱلصَّلَاةِ عَلَى ٱلنَّبِي   نَبِيّ عَرَبِيّ مَكِّيّ شَرِيفٍ عَفِيفْ ٤٢،١١

ش

١،٤٢،١١ وقد اقتدى الناظم بالحديث الشريف وهو قوله صلّى الله عليه وسلّم من صلّى عليّ في كتاب لم تزل الملائكة تستغفر له ما دام اسمي في ذلك الكتاب ومثل الكتاب النظم وغيره وفي الشفاء لابن سبع عن النبيّ صلّى الله عليه وسلّم قال أكثروا من الصلاة عليّ فإنّها تطفئ غضب الرحمن وتوهن كيد الشيطان والأحاديث الواردة في فضل الصلاة على النبيّ صلّى الله عليه وسلّم كثيرة

into a barren old woman, and if the Almighty grants me what I have asked for, provision for my wife will be up to Him, for He is Generous, the Provider for the Old, while I am as the one described by the poet who said:

> You who asked for bread, got it,
> Then said, 'Now what about my wife?'
> Get up early and primp your beard—
> Serendipity's a condition of life!"[623]

—or it may be that he intends his request to apply only to himself, thinking "a wife can eat shit" and "a thousand beards rather than my own."

Next he concludes his verses with blessings on the Prophet, God bless him and grant him peace, saying: 11.41.2

TEXT

wa-ʾakhtim qaṣīdī bi-l-ṣalāti ʿalā l-nabī 11.42
nabī ʿarabī makkī sharīfin ʿafīf

And I close my ode with blessings on the Prophet,
an Arab prophet, of Mecca, noble, sinless.

COMMENTARY

Here the poet is guided by the Noble Tradition in which the Prophet, God bless him and grant him peace, says, "The angels will never cease to ask for forgiveness for anyone who calls for blessings upon me in a book as long as my name shall remain in that book" (poetry, etc., counting as a book). In the *Cure* (*Shifāʾ*) of Ibn Sabuʿ[624] it says, on the authority of the Prophet, God bless him and grant him peace, "Call often for blessings upon me, for they quench the anger of the Merciful and undermine the wiles of Satan." The Traditions cited on the virtue of calling for blessings on the Prophet, God bless him and grant him peace, are numerous. 11.42.1

(ذكر بعض نوادر متفرّقة نختم بها الكتاب)

(قيل) تزوّج بعضهم بامرأة مات عنها خمسة أزواج فلمّا مرض هذا السادس صارت تبكي وتقول إلى مَن تَكِلُني بعدك فقال لها إلى السابع الشقيّ ١،١٢

(وحكي) أنّ بعض اللطفاء كان يكثر من الشراب سرًّا وكان عليه حَجْر من أبيه فبلغ والده ذلك فما زال يتتبّع أخباره إلى أن رآه ومعه قنينة الخمر فمسكها وقال له ما هذا فقال هذا لبن فقال ويحك اللبن أبيض وهذا أحمر قال صدقت ولكنّه كان أبيض فلمّا رآك خجل واستحى واحمرّ ولعن الله من لا يستحي فخجل أبوه وتركه وانصرف ٢،١٢

(وقيل) كان بعضهم إذا غضبت زوجته بادر إلى رفع رجليها واستعمال نكاحها فقالت له يوماً أنا كلّما اشتدّ غضبي عليك تأتيني بشفيع معك لا أستطيع ردّه ٣،١٢

(وقيل) دخل رجل مجنون على قاض وهو ماسك أيره وقال السلام عليكم فقام القاضي وكشف عن استه واندار به إلى المجنون وقال وعليكم السلام قال الله تعالى ﴿وَإِذَا حُيِّيتُمْ بِتَحِيَّةٍ فَحَيُّوا بِأَحْسَنَ مِنْهَا أَوْ رُدُّوهَا﴾ ٤،١٢

(وحكي) عن الأصمعيّ أنّه قال كنت عند الرشيد فقال من عندك يوانسك قلت ليس عندي أحد فلمّا ذهبت إلى منزلي أرسل لي جارية بديعة الحسن والجمال فوانستني بكلامها وخلعت ثيابي وثيابها وأكلنا وشربنا وأردت الفعل منها فلم ينتصب لي شيء واعتراني غاية الفتور فصارت تقلّب أيري بيدها وهو لا ينتصب وأنا منها في حياء وخجل فلمّا أيست منه قالت يا سيّدي دع أيرك فما منه حيلة ولا نفع ثمّ قامت ٥،١٢

Some Miscellaneous Anecdotes with Which We Conclude the Book[625]

It is said that a man married a woman who had been widowed five times before. When the sixth got sick, she started to weep and say, "To whom will you entrust me after you die?" The husband said, "To the wretched seventh!" 12.1

And the tale is told that a certain wit was a great drinker in secret, though he had been strictly enjoined by his father not to behave so. News reached his father of what was going on, and he followed reports of him until he came across him with a flagon of wine. When, however, he grabbed him and said to him, "What's this?" the son replied, "Milk!" "Give over!" said the father. "Milk is white, and this is red!" Said the boy, "I spoke the truth. It was white but when it saw you, it got embarrassed and felt bashful and blushed, and God curse those who have no modesty!" His father was abashed and left him and went his way. 12.2

And the tale is told that, whenever the wife of a certain man got angry with him, he would whip up her legs and set about pleasuring her. One day she said to him, "Whenever I lose my temper with you, you bring me an intercessor of yours to whom I cannot say no!" 12.3

And it is said that a madman went in to see a judge, holding on to his penis, and said to him, "Peace be upon you, and God's mercy!" The judge stood up, bared his backside, turned it towards the madman, and said, "And upon you be peace! The Almighty has said, «When greeted, return the greeting with one better or the same!»"[626] 12.4

And the tale is told that al-Aṣmaʿī[627] said, "I was with Hārūn al-Rashīd, and he said to me, 'Whom do you have at home to keep you company?' I replied, 'I have no one.' When I went back to my house, he sent me a slave girl of surpassing beauty and comeliness, who charmed me with her conversation and took off her clothes and mine. Then we ate and drank and made merry, and I wanted to do it with her, but I couldn't get it up and was completely overcome by lassitude. She tried moving my penis in her hand, but it still wouldn't go stiff, and my chagrin and embarrassment before her grew. When she despaired 12.5

وقالت لي نم على ظهرك حتّى أغسله وأكفّنه فخجلت منها ولم أقدر أخالفها فغسلته وكفّنته بمنديل ثمّ قالت قم صلّ عليه فقمت وأنا في غاية الخجل فتوضأت وصلّيت الصبح وسرت من وقتي إلى الرشيد فقال لي ما خبرك فقلت له يا أمير المؤمنين حكايتي غريبة وأخبرته بما جرى لي معها فضحك حتّى استلقى على ظهره وقال نحن أحوج إليها منك لصغرها وعوّضني جارية غيرها وعشرة آلاف درهم

٦،١٢ (ومات مجوسيّ) وعليه دين فقال بعض غرماءه لولده لِمَ لا تبيع دارك وتخفّف بها عن أبيك دينه فقال إذا بعت أنا داري وقضيت دينه هل يدخل الجنّة قالوا لا قال دعوه في النار وأنا في الدار

٧،١٢ (وقيل) كان رجل نحويّ اسمه زيد فرأى غلاماً يسمّى بكر فلمّا اختلى به قال له يا ولدي حرّك الأير حركة الإعراب * فإنّه فاعل بلا ارتياب * ومدّه إلى استك كالمدّ المتّصل * واجعل الهمز آلة له لئلّا ينفصل * وأطال الكلام فدخل رجل يسمّى عمرو فصكّ زيداً[1] وقال له أَعرِبْ ضرب عمرو زيداً فقام الولد وهو يجري ويقول وأَعرِبْ وخرج بكر هارباً

٨،١٢ (وقيل) مرض رجل نحويّ وكان بعيداً عن أهله فرأى غلاماً يعرفه من أولاد جيرانه فقال له امض إلى أهلي وقل لهم إنّ فلاناً قد أصابه داء أوجع رُكبَتَيْهِ * وآذى خُصيَتَيْهِ * وأسقم بَشَرَته * وزاد عِلّته * وأسهر مُقْلته * وأجرى عِبْرته * وصار يكثر على الغلام * من هذا الكلام * فقال له الغلام يا سيّدي اقْصِرْ أنا أقول لأهلك قد مات ولا يحتاج لهذا كلّه

٩،١٢ (وقيل) احتضر بعض البخلاء فقال له ولده أَوصِني فقال إذا جلست على مائدة الأكل وتكلّم معك إنسان فلا تزيد على قول نعم ولا تكرّرها فإنّك إذا كرّرتها ثانية فاتتك مضغة ثانية بتحريك فمك بها

---

١ بي: زيد.

of it, she said, 'Forget your penis, mister! It's a write-off!' Then she got up and said to me, 'Lie on your back so I can wash it and put it in its shroud!' I was too embarrassed to disobey her so she washed it and wrapped it in a handkerchief and said to me, 'Get up and pray for it!' So I got up, in an agony of embarrassment, and made my ablutions and prayed the morning prayer and went straight to see al-Rashīd. 'What's up?' he asked me, and I said to him, 'Commander of the Faithful, my case is bizarre!' and told him what had happened to me with her. He laughed until he fell flat on his back and said, 'We need her more than you, for her youth,' and he sent me another slave girl instead, plus ten thousand dinars".

And a Magian died with an outstanding debt. Some of the father's creditors said to his son, "Why don't you sell your house and pay off some of your father's debt?" The son said to them, "If I sell my house and pay off my father's debt, will he go to Heaven?" They said, "No." "Then leave him in Hell and me in the house!" said he. 12.6

And it is said that there was a grammarian whose name was Zayd,[628] and he saw a youth whose name was Bakr. When he found himself alone with him he said to him, "My boy, inflect my penis with the correct 'movements'[629] for it is an indubitably 'active' participle,[630] and extend it to your backside as one would a long open vowel between two words and glottalize it so that it does not break off in the middle,"[631] and went on at great length in this vein until a man called 'Amr came in and slapped Zayd on the back of the neck and said, "And put the correct inflections on "'Amr struck Zayd!'— at which the boy got up and ran off saying, 'And put the correct inflections on "And Bakr got out and ran away!"'" 12.7

And it is said that a grammarian got sick far from home, and he saw a youth whom he knew to be a son of the neighbors, so he told him, "Proceed to my family and tell them that So-and-so has been afflicted by a malady that has pained his knees and hurt his testes, ruined his complexion and aggravated his infection, denied sleep to his eye and made him cry," and went on at great length to the youth in the same vein. The youth said, "Sir, why don't I keep it short and tell your family, 'He's dead!'? Then we can drop the rest." 12.8

And it is said that a miser was on the point of death and his son said to him, "Give me your last will and testament!" The man said, "If you are at table and someone addresses you, just say, 'Yes,' and say it once only, for if you say it a second time, the moving of your jaws will make you miss a second chew!" 12.9

١٠،١٢ (وقال بعض الطُفَيْليّة) إذا طلعت الشمس على الفقير ولم يتغذّ نادى مناد من سماء سقف حلقه الصلاة على جنازة الغريب

١١،١٢ (وقيل) جاء رجل إلى امرأة بلحم فقال لها اسلقي بعضه فإنّه ينفع البطن واقلي بعضه فإنّه ينفع الظهر واشوي بعضه فإنّه ينفع الجماع فقالت له يا رجل ما عندنا لا قِدر ولا حطب والأولى أنّي أشوي الجميع

١٢،١٢ (ووقف بعض النحاة) على قصّاب وقال له هذا اللحم من الضأن الفَتِيّ أو من المَعْز الثَنِيّ قال هو من خِيار الضأن قال قد ذَبَحْتَهُ لِغَرَضٍ أم لِمَرَض فقال حتّى أتبلّغ به أنا وعيالي قال أَوَكان ذَكَرًا ذا خُصْيَتَيْنِ أَمْ أُنْثَىٰ ذات حَلَمَتَيْن قال كان ذكرًا ينطح الحائط يرميه قال أَفَكان يَمُجُّ الماءَ بِشِدْقَيْهِ أَمْ يَمُصُّهُ بِشَفَتَيْهِ قال كان يدلّي زلّومته في الماء ويشرب حتّى يشبع قال أَفَكان مَرْعاتُهُ الشِيحَ والبُعَيْثَرَان أَمْ العَصْفَ والرَيْحان قال كان يرعى من نبات الأرض أي شيء كان قال أَسَنَنْتَ شَفْرَتَكَ وحَدَّدْتَ مُدْيَتَك قال جعلتها لو وقعت على رقبة الأبعد قطعتها قال أَفَبَدَأْتَ بالبَسْمَلَةِ وأَظْهَرْتَ الحَيْعَلَةِ الّتي على وَزْنِ فَيْعَلَة وقيل فَعْلَلَة والصَحِيحُ الأَوّل فقال القصّاب لغلامه هات الجلد حتّى أقطعه على أكتاف هذا النحس الّذي أبطلنا وقطع رزقنا اليوم فلمّا سمع النحويّ ذلك شتم وهرب

١٣،١٢ (وحكي) أنّ بعض اللطفاء امتدح بعض الرؤساء بقصيدة فرسم له ببرذعة حمار وحزام فأخذهما على كتفه وخرج فمرّ به بعض أصحابه فقال له ما هذا فقال مولانا الأمير امتدحته بأحسن أشعاري فخلع عليّ خلعة من أحسن ملابسه فبلغ الأمير فضحك وأرسل خلفه وأجازه بجائزة حسنة

١٤،١٢ (وحكي عن الأصمعيّ) أنّه قال رأيت بالبادية جارية حسناء وعلى خدها خال أسود فقلت لها ما اسمك قالت مكّة فقلت ما هذه النقطة السوداء قالت الحجر الأسود

And a lazy freeloader once said, "If the sun rises on a poor man and he has not yet eaten, a voice will call the prayer for the funeral of a stranger out of the heaven of the roof of his mouth!"[632] 12.10

And it is said that a man brought his wife some meat and told her, "Boil some, for that is good for the belly, and fry some, for that is good for the back, and grill some, for that is good for intercourse." She said to him, "Husband, we have neither pots nor fuel. Let's just grill the lot!" 12.11

And a grammarian stood before a butcher's shop and said, "Is this the meat of the juvenile sheep or the mature goat?" The butcher replied, "It's the best mutton." The grammarian asked, "Did you slaughter it to be eaten or because it was ailing?"[633] "I slaughtered it," said the butcher, "so that I and my children might keep body and soul together." "Was it a male, possessed of testes twain, or a female, possessed of an equal complement of nipples?" asked the grammarian. "It was a male," said the butcher. "If it butted a wall, it knocked it down!" "Did it sip water through the sides of its mouth, or suck it up with its lips?" asked the grammarian. The butcher said, "It dangled its snout in the water and drank till it was full!" "Did it graze on wormwood and artemisia, or cornstalks and sweet basil?" asked the grammarian. "It grazed on any plants it could find!" said the butcher. "Did you whet your whittle and hone your hacker?" asked the grammarian. "I made it so sharp that, if it fell on your miserable neck, it'd cut it in two!" said the butcher. "Did you start with the *basmalah*[634] and pronounce the *ḥayʿalah*,[635] which some take to be of the measure *fayʿalah* while others take it to be of the measure *faʿlalah* (the former being correct)?" asked the grammarian. At this the butcher told his servant, "Get the skin so I can split it over the shoulders of this wretch who has wasted our time and brought my business today to a standstill!" On hearing this, the grammarian uttered an insult and ran off. 12.12

And the tale is told of a certain wit who eulogized a great man in an ode, for which the latter rewarded him with a donkey saddle and girth. The poet took these on his shoulder and left. One of his friends passed by him and said, "What are those?" The wit replied, "I praised our master the emir with my best verse, and he rewarded me with some of his best clothes!" Word of this reached the emir and he laughed and sent after him with a good reward. 12.13

And the tale is told of al-Aṣmaʿī that he said, "In the desert I saw a lovely slave girl with a black mole on her cheek. 'What's your name?' I asked her. 'Mecca,' she said. Then I said, 'What is this black spot?' 'The Black Stone,' she 12.14

فقلت لها إنّي أريد أن أطوف بالبيت وأقبّل الحجر الأسود فقالت هيهات ﴿لَمْ تَكُونُوا بَالِغِيهِ إِلَّا بِشِقِّ ٱلْأَنفُسِ﴾ فأخرجت لها صُرّة فيها بعض الدنانير وناولتها إيّاها فقالت ﴿ٱدْخُلُوهَا بِسَلَامٍ آمِنِينَ﴾ إن شئت فقبّل الحجر الأسود وإن شئت فادخل الحرم قال فأذهلني حسنها وجمالها

١٥،١٢ (قيل) سافر رجل مع جماعة وفيهم امرأة جميلة ومعها ولد جميل فزنا بالمرأة ولاط بالولد فقالت المرأة للولد أعرفه فلعلّنا إن رجعنا نظفر به ونعرض أمره على الحكّام فقال لها أمّا أنا فكان ظهري لوجهه وأمّا أنت فوجهك لوجهه فمعرفتك له أبلغ من معرفتي إيّاه

١٦،١٢ (وأرسل) بعض المغفّلين إلى صديق له يقوله [متقارب]

إذا ما ذكَرتُكِ يا مُنيتي يَسيلُ المخاطُ على لِحيتي
ولَيتَكِ عِندي إذا ما خَريتُ يكون لِسانُكِ في ثُقْبتي
نَسيمُكِ عَطّلَ ماءَ السّما وأَورثَني الخامَ في رُكبتي
إذا لم تَزُرني أنا مُذنِبُ فإنَّ الهوى سَهّلَ معدتي

١٧،١٢ (وقال المأمون) ليحيى بن أكثم وهو يعرّض له مَنِ الذي يقول [منسرح]

قاضٍ يرى الحدّ في الزناء ولا يَرى علَى مَن يَلوطُ من باسِ

قال أَوَما يعرف أمير المؤمنين من قاله قال لا قال يحيى يقوله الفاجر أحمد بن أبي نعيم الّذي يقول [منسرح]

أميرُنا يرتَشي وحاكِمُنا يَلوطُ والرّأسُ شَرُّ ما راسِ
لا أرى الجودَ ينقضي وعلى الـ ـأمّةِ والٍ من بني العبّاسِ

said. I said to her, 'I would like to circumambulate the House[636] and kiss the Black Stone.' 'Dream on!' said she. 'It is a land «ye could not reach save with great trouble to yourselves.»'[637] Then I pulled out a purse containing a few dinars and gave it to her and she said, '«Go into them in peace, secure!»[638] if you want, and kiss the Black Stone, and, if you wish, you may enter the Sanctuary.' I was amazed at her beauty and good looks."

And it is said that a man was traveling with a party that included a beautiful woman who was accompanied by a beautiful boy, and the man committed adultery with the woman and buggered the boy. Later the woman said to the boy, "I know him. Perhaps when we return we can get the better of him and expose him to the authorities." The boy said, "As far as I'm concerned, I had my back to his face but you had your face to his, so your evidence should be more telling than mine!" 12.15

And a simpleton once sent the following verses to a friend: 12.16

When I think of you whom I adore
The snot my beard flows o'er!
Would you were with me when I empty my gut—
You'd stick your tongue right up my butt!
Your breeze the rain in the skies does stem
And has filled my knees with a kind of phlegm!
If you don't visit me, I'm bound to die,
For love has set my stomach awry!

Al-Ma'mūn said to Yaḥyā ibn Aktham, as an indirect jibe, "Who was it that composed the verse that goes: 12.17

A judge who supports the severest punishment for adultery
But sees nothing wrong with those who commit sodomy?"

and Judge Yaḥyā answered, "Doesn't the Commander of the Faithful know the author?" "No, I don't," responded al-Ma'mūn. "It's by that profligate Aḥmad ibn Abī Nuʿaym," said Yaḥyā. "He's the one who also said:

Our Prince takes bribes, our Ruler
Stuffs boys, and the Boss is the worst kind of boss.
I don't see how such largesse can end
When the nation's ruled by the Banū l-ʿAbbās!"

فأفحم المأمون وسكت خجلاً

وممّا ينسب للحريريّ رحمه الله تعالى [طويل] ١٨،١٢

صَـديقُكَ في هذا الزَّمـانِ مُنـافِقٌ وخِـلُّكَ خَلٌّ دعْه واحذر بوائقَـهْ
ونَافِقْ فقـد آن النِّفـاقُ ولا تَخَـفْ كَسـادًا فـأحوالُ المُنـافِقِ نافقـهْ
وعرِّصْ وقُدْ واظلِمْ وبالفحش فافتخرْ فما رفـعتْ دنياك حُرًّا ولا ثقـهْ
وما فيك غيرِ الدِّينِ عيبٌ ولن ترى بـدهـرك إلّا مُـلْحِدًا وزنادقـهْ

ومثل ذلك قول الأبي صيريّ الأديب عفا الله عنه [وزن غير معروف] ١٩،١٢

ستّة في الهوى افعلهم بعـد الموت بهـم تُذكَر
اِتْمَخْوِلْ وعـرّص وافسق وغن وقـامـر واسكر

Al-Ma'mūn was too nonplussed and embarrassed to speak.[639]

And among the poetry attributed to al-Ḥarīrī,[640] may the Almighty rest his soul, we find: 12.18

In these times, your friend's a snake,
Your buddy tastes bitter—avoid him and his evil beware!
Play hypocrite, for hypocrisy's the rage
And hypocrites do well—your wares will find a buyer, never fear!
Pimp and pander, oppress and vaunt your vile doings,
For your world has produced no man noble or fair.
The only fault you can have is religion, for if you look round
Heretics and atheists are all you'll find here!

Similar are the words of that eminent man of letters al-Būṣīrī,[641] God excuse his sins: 12.19

Six things in love you ought to do
For which after death to be remembered:
Play faggot, pimp, and fornicate,
Sing, make bets, and be a drunkard!

(ونختم هذا الكتاب بأبيات من بحر الخرافات فنقول)

[رجز] ١،١٣

تمّ كتاب الهَلْس والتخريفِ   وما جرى في وصف أهل الريفِ
جعلته جزئين باختصارْ   فجاء كالزبلة في التيّارْ
لكنّه مع ثقل المعاني   وخبط عشوى يا ذوي العرفانِ
ولفظه الكثيف في المقالِ   وحَشْوِه مسائل الهبالِ
أبحاثه الّتي كما لحس الخرا   يا وجه الأصحاب حقيقًا لا مرا
فلَيسَ يخلو جَمعُه من فائدهْ   من نكتةٍ أو قصّةٍ مشاهدهْ ٢،١٣
وأصلُ ما ألجأني لفعلِهِ   وشرحِهِ ونسخِهِ ونقلِهِ
العارفُ الحَبْرُ وحيدُ الدّهرِ   وعالمُ الإسلامِ زاكي الفَخرِ
كانَ إمامَ مَصدَرِ الطّلابِ   وروضةَ العلومِ والآدابِ
ومعدنَ الجودِ معَ المطلوبِ   أعني الإمامَ أحمد السَندوبي
جزاه ربّ العرش جنّات النعيمْ   مع النظرْ لوجهِ مولانا الكريمْ
والله يرحمْ من قرا كتابي   هذا ويرشده إلى الصّوابِ ٣،١٣
ومن رأى فيه عيوبًا وخللْ   وسدّها فالشّخص يغروه الزَلَلْ
ولا تلمني فالسّماحُ أفضلُ   واعذرْ أخاك مُكرَهًا يا بطلُ

Let Us Conclude This Book with Verses from the Sea of Inanities

We declare: 13.1

Done is the book of bosh and drivel,
  With its description of the country people.
I made it, concisely, in two parts;
  It came out like a pipsqueak that from the beaten path departs.[642]
Yet, for all its obnoxious topics
  And blind stumblings, you gnostics,
Its language in expression unrefined,
  And all the silly arguments that therein you'll find,
And its inquiries that resemble the licking of shit,
  O best of friends, for sure and no doubt about it,
Taken as a whole it's not completely without merit 13.2
  By way of a joke or a story apposite.
And the prime mover that drove me to it,
  And to explain it, copy it, and duplicate it,
Was the Initiated Sage unique in his time,
  The Scholar of Islam of fame sublime,
He who was the leader to whom students would go,
  Of sciences and letters the very meadow,
Of excellence and fulfillment the source,
  Meaning the Imam Aḥmad al-Sandūbī, of course—
May the Lord of the Throne with gardens of ease reward him
  And with the sight of our Most Generous Lord award him!
And God have mercy on those who read 13.3
  This book of mine, and to the truth them lead,
And on him who finds therein some faults or flaws
  And mends them—for instinct to error all men draws;
And blame me not, but tolerance prefer,
  And excuse, good fellow, your brother, who could not demur,

والحمد لله على التَّمامِ ثُمَّ صلاة الله مع سلامِ
على النبيّ الهاشميّ أحمدا والآلِ والأصحابِ أَنْجُمِ الهُدى
ما غرّدتْ ساجعة الأطيارِ أو لاح بَرْقٌ في دُجى الأسحارِ

And praise be to God that it is ended.
    And may God's blessings and peace be extended
To the Prophet Aḥmad,[643] Hāshim's offspring,
    And to those stars of guidance, his Companions and kin,
As long as dove shall coo
    Or lightning in dawn's darkness glow.

Notes

1 Elsewhere (§11.33.10), al-Shirbīnī mentions that Falḥas is a dog's name, as does al-Jāḥiẓ (*Al-Ḥayawān*, 1:257); dogs are so called because Falḥas was the name of a proverbially greedy man (see, e.g., al-Maydānī, *Majmaʿ*: 1:234). The name may also be understood as Fa-lḥas ("Go lick!").

2 *Father* of ʿAmrah (Abū ʿAmrah) is "an idiom meaning pennilessness and hunger, and also a man who, every time he camped with a group, brought disaster with him, in the form of fighting and war" (al-Fīrūzābādhī, *Qāmūs*).

3 Neither place exists.

4 Literally "Hitch up your skirts for me and bend over."

5 According to a later reference (§11.4.5), Fasāqil was Abū Shādūf's paternal first cousin.

6 The words may be read two ways, depending on how they are divided: as above, in which case the literal meaning is "its length grew less," or as *qallaṭū lahā*, meaning "they excreted large, firm turds at it." Similarly, below, the words "(its width) rendered its length odious" translate *(ʿarḍuhā) ḍarra ṭūlahā*, which mean literally "(its width) harmed its length," may also be read *ḍarraṭū lahā* "they farted audibly at it."

7 See vol. 1, §5.2.7 on the proverbial stupidity of schoolmasters.

8 "O Umm ʿAmr . . . may be!": these lines are taken from a poem by Jarīr ibn ʿAṭiyyah (ca. 33–111/653–729) (*Dīwān*, 161); the remaining lines are anonymous.

9 Meaning, perhaps, the Bard of Shammirṭāṭī and Tall Fandarūk.

10 "This . . . ": the referent is unclear.

11 Umm Faswah: "She-of-the-Silent-Fart."

12 Dating to before the fifteenth century: cf. al-Ibshīhī, *Al-Mustaṭraf*, 1:43.

13 I.e., his wife.

14 Literally "Puppy, Son of Shit-Go-Lick."

15 "God . . . moisten his head-brick" (*Allāh . . . bashbish ṭūbatū*): a conventional expression, referring to the brick on which the head of a corpse rests in the grave.

16 The sense of *shirāʿah* is unclear.

17 "every Zayd and ʿAmr": i.e., "every Tom, Dick, and Harry."

18 Like a bard reciting the *Sīrat Banī Hilāl*, the poet opens with an address to the hero of the latter epic, Abū Zayd al-Hilālī Salāmah, though in al-Shirbīnī's version the poet's donkey and staff substitute for the steed and sword of the original.

19 Literally in the Arabic "and were not my father in his grave," which contradicts the context.

20 Literally "The one with the little spout."

21 Literally "The one with the turban."

22 I.e., Easter, when Copts traditionally color and eat eggs.

23 The poet, whom al-Shirbīnī quotes further below (§11.1.14), is unidentified; however, see also "al-Buhlūl" below (§11.10.6).

24 The attribution is dubious.

25 Ibn al-Rūmī (221–283/836–896) (*Dīwān*, 4:1592).

26 "patience fair" (*al-ṣabr al-jamīl*): reminscent of Q Yūsuf 12:18 and 83 «(My course is) a comely patience (*fa-ṣabrun jamīl*)» and Maʿārij 70:5.

27 The verses are unlikely to be by Ibn Muqlah. Ibn Ḥajar attributes them to Taqī al-Dīn ibn Razīn, i.e., Muḥammad ibn al-Ḥusayn ibn Razīn (d. 680/1281–82) (Ibn Ḥajar, *Al-Durar* 3/330).

28 The exemplars of awfulness named here are not to be found in the standard works on this topic and are probably invented for the occasion, mimicking, to some extent, the patterns of the names of the preceding four and having appropriately contrary meanings: Uṭrūsh, "Deaf"; Ibn Qaynah, "Son of a Slave Girl"; Qarnān, "Cuckold" (see al-Muḥibbī, *Qaṣd*, 2:160); Ibn Ayham, "Son of a Madman." The moral is that, in this hypocritical world, the worthy are neglected and the unworthy adulated.

29 Q Ṭāhā 20:106.

30 The lines "But when aroused . . . too far to keep" are attributed by Ibn Ḥamdūn to ʿAmr ibn Mālik al-Jaʿdī (Ibn Ḥamdūn, *Al-Tadhkirah*, 6:85).

31 Abū Shādūfi: i.e., Abū Shādūfin, with a meaningless short vowel supplied for the meter as throughout these texts (see further vol. 1, p. xlviii).

32 "These words are metered . . ." (*hādhā l-kalām lahu baḥr* . . .): al-Shirbīnī kicks off the commentary with a display of verbal virtuosity that evokes, through multiple puns and allusions, a range of literary and grammatical terms and conventions, along with comically irrelevant associations. One element is the pun on the dual meaning of *baḥr* (pl. *buḥūr*) as both "(poetic) meter" and "ocean, sea, large river," which is probably extended by reference to *madd* (see n. 34, at end), which in turn, and in another sense, may contrast with *qadd* (see n. 33).

33 "and tuned" (*wa-qadd*): in normal usage "shape." However, Dozy defines *qadd*, on the authority of a nineteenth-century source, as "*des paroles, qui ont les désinences grammaticales, adaptées à un air populaire*" (Dozy, *Supplément*). Similarly, Hava defines it as "musical tune" and, in Syrian colloquial Arabic, "popular tune, song."

34 "crooned" (*madd*): literally "stretching, protraction." Al-Shirbīnī may be using it here as a technical term under the rules governing Qurʾanic (but *not* poetic) recitation (*tajwīd*),

where it means "duration" in the sense of the number of beats assigned to each syllable (Nelson, *Art*, 24–27), or, more impressionistically, the "drawing out of the voice over long vowels (in Koran recitation)" (Wehr, *Dictionary*). Another interpretation would contrast *madd* with *qadd*, using the latter in its basic function as a verbal noun meaning "cutting (short)." This would imply that the words of the ode contain both pausal forms (*qadd*) and full forms (*madd*), which might in turn be interpreted to mean that they contain both colloquial forms (superficially similar to the pausal forms of formal Arabic in their lack of desinential endings) and formal forms, which is in fact the case. The association of *madd* in the sense of "tide" with *baḥr* "ocean/meter" is evoked, as is, further on in the same passage, yet another sense of *baḥr*, namely, "span (of a chain)."

35 In the following, al-Shirbīnī plays with the names of five of the sixteen normative poetic meters (see W. Stoetzer, "Prosody," in *EAL*, and van Gelder, *Sound*, 341–60): *al-ṭawīl* ("the Long"), *al-madīd* ("the Extended"), *al-kāmil* ("the Perfect"), *al-wāfir* ("the Exuberant"), and *al-basīṭ* ("the Extended," or "the Outspread," here translated "the Diffused"). The actual meter is *al-ṭawīl*, and there is no such meter as the "Long *and* Extended" (*al-ṭawīl al-madīd*).

36 *mutahābilun mutahābilun*: i.e., the meter *al-kāmil* (literally "the Perfect"), as stated, though the actual meter is *al-ṭawīl* (see preceding note). The Arabic spelling (متهابل) is unusual, in that prosodic mnemonics are normally written with the implicit nunation realized as a final letter *nūn* (i.e., متاهابلن) to allow complete representation of the syllable count; in the manuscripts of *Brains Confounded*, the nunation is suppressed throughout, as it is in the manuscript of *Risible Rhymes*, but has been realized in the translation. The mnemonic uses the root *h-b-l*, associated with "foolishness" and "doltishness" (see also vol. 1, p. xliii).

37 "the Meter of the Chain" (*baḥr al-silsilah*): in addition to the "meter/sea" ambiguity, al-Shirbīnī evokes both the nonstandard meter called *silsilah*, related to the Persian *dūbayt* meter (see van Gelder, *Sound*, 126–27) (even though the latter bears no relation to that of the verses quoted here) and the East Port of Alexandria, known as "the Sea of the Chain." Finally, the meaning of *baḥr* as "span (of a chain)" is part of the wordplay.

38 *halhalah halhalah*: i.e., LSL LSL, perhaps implying the rare meter *al-mutadārik*; the mnemonic is based on the root *h-l-h-l*, which includes the sense of "weaving (both cloth and verses) finely or flimsily."

39 Possibly a popular comic air or ditty, or a parody of some well-known song.

40 In works on prosody, verses representative of a particular meter may be presented in this "articulated" form, to demonstrate more clearly the division of the feet; cf. *Risible Rhymes*. The above division of the feet does not, however, conform to that

of *al-ṭawīl*, or any other, meter. The correct division is: *yaqūlu | Abū Shādū | fi min ʿuẓ | mi mā shakā*.

41 From the root *q-l-l* and unrelated to *qawl* (root *q-w-l*).

42 From the root *q-y-l* and unrelated to *qawl* (root *q-w-l*).

43 The last three forms all derive from the root in question, namely, *q-w-l*, and the last two are, indeed, forms of the verb itself; it is thus a specious and circular argument to speak of them as being etymons of *qāla* "to speak."

44 I.e., the Kaaba at Mecca.

45 The first day of Dhū l-Ḥijjah (the month of pilgrimage), 1074 fell on June 25, AD 1664.

46 That the author should apply such uncomplimentary terms to himself is, of course, surprising. One interpretation is that he held his listeners, as ignorant laymen, in such contempt that he regarded any attempt to bring true knowledge down to their level as no better than buffoonery, etc.

47 *The Thousand Lines on Grammar*: the *Alfiyyat al-naḥw* of Muḥammad ibn Mālik (ca. 600–72/1203–74), a very popular textbook of grammar in the form of a poem of about a thousand lines.

48 "Muḥammad, Malik's son, *has said*. . . ": the opening line of the *Alfiyyah*; in Arabic, the past tense may denote "an act which is just completed at the moment, and by the very act, of speaking" (Wright, *Grammar*, 2:1); thus, either the present ("he says") or the past ("he has said") is acceptable in such a context.

49 A piece of misdirection by al-Shirbīnī, for the poet seems to have been punning, and the first hemistich can also be read (with one metrically valid amendment) as meaning "Then he said, 'It is a keen sword (*māḍī*) in similar words (*bi-qawlin muḍāriʿin*)'/ Though that keen sword is in reality his" (without context, the exact sense of the second hemistich must remain obscure). This interpretation is supported by a verse by Yaḥyā ibn Aḥmad ibn Hudhayl al-Tujībī, where the same double entendre is found in a *nasīb*: the loved one's figure is described as . . . *sayfan ka-sayfi liḥāẓihī / fa-hādhā huwa l-māḍī wa-dhāka muḍāriʿuh* ("a sword like the sword of his glance/For the latter is a keen sword, the former its like" (al-Maqqarī, *Nafḥ al-ṭīb*, 5:489).

50 The following line is taken from one of the poet's famous panegyrics addressed to the Hamdanid ruler of Aleppo, Sayf al-Dawlah (al-Mutanabbī, *Dīwān*, 4:98).

51 "and silence the vowels of his verb": this may be understood both literally, i.e., "and silence (i.e., dissuade) him from moving to perform the action in question" and, taking the words in their specialized grammatical senses, "and put *sukūn*s (the signs written above consonants to show that they are not followed by a vowel) on the verb instead of vowels," referring to the use of jussive forms of the imperfect verb to form negative

imperatives; in other words, the hero of the panegyric completes his action before any can tell him "Don't!"

52 On such compound proper nouns, see vol. 1, n. 383.

53 Though *shādūf* is used today to describe the whole device (which works on the same principle as a well sweep), al-Shirbīnī's statement implies that it was, in his day, *abū shādūf* (literally "the thing with the cantilevered arm") that had that sense; thus the poet's *kunyah* would refer to the device itself, making the appellation more derogatory than if it were to mean simply "the person with the *shādūf*." The raising of water manually was among the most physically demanding, lowest paid, and least regarded of agricultural tasks in Egypt before mechanization. Pictures of the *shādūf* may be found in Lane (*Manners*, 327) and Hinds and Badawi (*Dictionary*, 975).

54 "scoop" (*qaṭwah*): "A vessel . . . with four cords attached to it . . . . Two men, each holding two of the cords, throw up the water by means of this vessel" (Lane, *Manners*, 328); the *qaṭwah* is made of leather.

55 I.e., they added the letters of prolongation ا (*alif*) and و (*waw*) to the original word شدف, making it شادوف; and, indeed, *fāʿūl* is an intensive pattern (cf., e.g., *jāsūs* "spy"), so that *shādūf* would be a logical formation from the root, in the sense of "that which constantly scoops."

56 This is misinformation, because the root of *ab* is *ʾ-b-w*, that of *āba* is *ʾ-w-b*.

57 I.e., Ibn Zurayq al-Baghdādī (d. ca. 420/1029) (*GAS*, 2:700–1); the line is from his famous *ʿayniyyah* called *Al-Qaṣīdah al-Andalusiyyah* (see, e.g., al-Ṣafadī, *Al-Wāfī*, 11:112).

58 *ābin*: sic, for *āʾib*.

59 See Vrolijk, *Bringing a Laugh*, 134 (Arabic).

60 "a perfect tense . . . verb" (*fiʿl māḍī*): in reality, the verb is imperfect. The word *māḍī* ("perfect") does not occur in Ibn Sūdūn's original.

61 *abū* . . .: an example of the rhetorical figure called "restraint," which will be referred to explicitly at §11.9.8 and §11.10.17.

62 See vol. 1, n. 430, on the use of letters to represent numbers.

63 Cf. Q Āl ʿImrān 3:12 *wa-yunshiʾu l-saḥāb*.

64 The verses are very similar to others written by Ibn Nubātah (686–768/1287–1366) about an Abyssinian youth, and the last hemistich is identical to Ibn Nubātah's (al-Ibshīhī, *Al-Mustaṭraf*, 2:230).

65 These verses occur in varying forms in disparate contexts; see, e.g., Ibn Khallikān, *Wafayāt*, 6:152ff., where they are described as having being addressed to a youthful Ḥasan ibn Wahb (later an important official in the Abbasid bureaucracy), after the latter objected to the judge's own advances.

66 These verses are quoted, with different frame stories and differences in wording, by, e.g., al-Masʿūdī (*Murūj*, 4:23) and Ibn Khallikān (*Wafayāt*, 6:152ff.), who attribute them to Rashīd ibn Isḥāq (b. 240/854, d. ?), and by al-Iṣfahānī (al-Iṣfahānī, *Al-Aghānī*, 18:91), who attributes them to Ibrāhīm ibn Abī Muḥammad al-Yazīdī.

67 Q Baqarah 2:155.

68 Q Sharḥ 94:5, 6.

69 See n. 304.

70 Q Sharḥ 94:1 «Have we not dilated thy bosom [with joy]?»

71 In Q Sharḥ 94:5 and 6, the word *ʿusr* ("hardship") occurs between two occurrences of the word *yusr* ("ease").

72 In fact, the meter requires an *i* after the *l*; by claiming that the word has no desinential inflection al-Shirbīnī may be pointing to the essentially colloquial character of the word when used in this sense, with *i*, versus literary *qull*.

73 Al-Shirbīnī later contradicts this by attributing the form without *ah* to the colloquial; both forms are, however, cited in the classical dictionaries (e.g., al-Fīrūzābādhī, *Qāmūs*, 3:40, s.vv. *qillah* and *qull*).

74 "the Red Death" (*al-mawt al-aḥmar*): i.e., "violent death" (Lane, *Lexicon*, 642).

75 This word occurs in the colloquial glossary of Yūsuf al-Maghribī (d. 1019/1610), who vocalizes it *ʿatr* and connects it to literary Arabic *ʿitrīf* (al-Maghribī: *ʿatrīf*), which he defines as "one who is base, licentious, daring, energetic, tyrannical, and overbearing" (al-Maghribī, *Dafʿ*, 30b). In modern Egyptian, *ʿitrah* means "strong, of outstanding personality" and is used, for example, of neighborhood heroes.

76 The poet is Ibn Sūdūn, to be found in Dār al-Kutub MS Adab 329 and related mansucripts of his *dīwān* (on which, see Vrolijk, *Bringing a Laugh*, 75, 104–5 English). I am indebted to Arnoud Vrolijk for this information.

77 Perhaps from Turkish *kulak* "ear, ear-shaped appendage, flap" and, in any case, without etymological connection to *qill*, etc.

78 The *qullah* is made of earthenware, the neck is narrower than the body, and it has an earthenware membrane pierced with holes that acts as a filter between the body and the neck (Hinds and Badawi, *Dictionary*, 971, illus.).

79 ʿAlī ibn al-Ḥasan, called Ṣurra Durr (d. 465/1073).

80 Al-Maydānī, *Majmaʿ*, 1:155.

81 These verses appear, with differences, in al-Shāfiʿī's collected works, where they are described as being of dubious attribution (al-Shāfiʿī, *Shiʿr*, 265).

82 "incarnation and corporealization" (*al-ḥulūl wa-l-tajsīm*): "After a long fight among the theological schools, the incorporeality of God was recognized by Islam . . . ." (Tj. de Boer, "Djism," in *EI2*). Al-Shirbīnī may be obfuscating here: al-Mujassimah is a word

used by their opponents to attack the Hanbalis and other theological conservatives, who, however, have no connection with the Ahl al-Ḥulūl, who were mystics whose belief in incarnation of the divine in the human was widely considered heretical; the celebrated mystic al-Ḥusayn ibn Manṣūr al-Ḥallāj (244–309/857–922) was executed in Baghdad for such beliefs.

83 See vol. 1, §4.2.2.

84 "Properly" in the sense that an *alif* would be attached to the word in the literary language as the sign of the accusative (making it نحيفا). The disappearance of most such inflections from colloquial Arabic is one of the features that most clearly separate it from the literary idiom.

85 Ibn al-Wardī (681–749/1292–1349) (al-Ghuzūlī, *Maṭāliʿ*, 1:81). For a discussion of the use made by fourteenth-century poets of the fact that *qamar* ("moon; beautiful person/face") and *qimār* ("gambling") share the same root in Arabic, see Rosenthal, *Gambling*, 143, where these verses are quoted in translation, with a difference in the two last words, al-Ghuzūlī reading *fa-hwa qamar* ("He is a moon") which, according to Rosenthal, may be taken as a pun meaning "He has won." Al-Shirbīnī reads *anti qamar* ("You (fem.) are the moon"), which should then mean "You have won!"

86 Q Ṣāfāt 87:88; the reference is to Ibrāhīm (Abraham) and his rejection of star worship.

87 *qaṭīm*: derived, according to Dozy, *Supplément*, from Latin *catamitus*.

88 Q Aʿrāf 7:133: "So we sent them the flood and the locusts and the *qummal* and the frogs and the blood"—al-Shirbīnī probably treats *qaml* and *qummal* as the same because of their identical consonantal skeletons; al-Bayḍāwī in his commentary glosses *qummal* as "full-grown ticks or, according to some, the young of the locust, before their wings sprout" (al-Bayḍāwī, *Anwār*, 1:356).

89 I.e., *Ḥayāt al-ḥayawān al-kubrā* by Kamāl al-Dīn Muḥammad ibn Mūsā al-Damīrī (742–808/1341–1405).

90 Al-Damīrī himself attributes this claim to "the Arabs" and dismisses it as "one of their lies" (al-Damīrī, *Ḥayawān*, 2:200).

91 Unit nouns typically are formed from collective nouns by the addition of the "feminine" ending *ah*; thus, *qamlah* really means simply "a louse," though al-Shirbīnī insists on creating a matching masculine form *qāmil* from the active participle.

92 Al-Shirbīnī's implication that *ʿuqrubān* and *thuʿlubān* are dual forms is spurious: even though they end in *ān*, formally identical to the nominative dual ending, they are singular nouns denoting the male of the species (though according to some authorities, *ʿuqrubān* may denote, rather than the male scorpion, the earwig or some other creature); nor could *ʿuqrubān* be dual in the verse—which is presumably of al-Shirbīnī's own composition—since its position in the sentence would require the genitive dual ending

ayn. Consequently, his contention on the basis of these forms that the dual may be used as a form of address to a single person, while not necessarily incorrect (see n. 93), is irrelevant.

93 Q Qāf 50:24 *alqiyā fī jahannama kulla kaffārin ʿanīd* "Throw into Hell every stubborn ingrate!" According to al-Bayḍāwī, the verb is either addressed by God to two persons (e.g., the two angels who guard Hell Fire) and is thus dual, or to one person but using the dual form for extra force (as al-Shirbīnī seems to imply here), or not dual at all but of the "energetic" form, i.e., *alqiyan*.

94 Al-Shirbīnī's quotation apparently conflates two sayings of al-Ḥajjāj's, namely, *yā Ḥarsiyyu-ḍrib ʿunuqahu* ("Strike his neck" (singular)) (al-Mubarrad, *Al-Kāmil*, 2:96)—a passage in which the words *yā ghulām* "Boy!" also occur—and *yā Ḥarsiyyu-ḍriban ʿunuqahu* ("O Ḥarsī, strike his neck") (al-Mubarrad, *Al-Kāmil*, 1:383), the latter using the energetic form (see n. 93); i.e., the quotation does not in fact support al-Shirbīnī's contention.

95 Neither word is etymologically related to *burghūth*, but the consonantal skeletons of the first two words, when joined, yield the consonantal skeleton of the latter (i.e., بر + غوث = برغوث).

96 These lines have not been located in al-Suyūṭī's works and are not quoted by al-Damīrī; they may be from the former's unpublished *Al-Ṭurthūth fī fawāʾid al-burghūth* (*The Ṭurthūth [a medicinal plant] on the Benefits of Fleas* (*GAL*, 2:154 and *Suppl.*, 2:192, no. 218); elsewhere, they are described as anonymous.

97 Al-Shirbīnī contends that all lice are female because the word for a single louse (*qamlah*) is grammatically feminine.

98 An introductory formula for riddles.

99 The diminutive is restricted in modern Egyptian to a closed list of words. However, the use of diminutives here and elsewhere by al-Shirbīnī imply that this class was productive in his day.

100 I.e., the words vary only in the absence or presence of a dot below the first letter, حمير (*ḥimmayr*) versus جمير (*jimmayr*).

101 *The Book of the Physick of the Poor* (*Kitāb ṭibb al-fuqarāʾ*): probably the *Kitāb al-fuqarāʾ wa-l-masākīn* (*The Book of the Poor and the Pitiful*) (*GAL*, 1:271) of Abū Bakr Muḥammad ibn Zakariyyā al-Rāzī ("Rhazes") (ca. 251–313/865–925).

102 Though metathesis may generate new forms in Arabic, al-Shirbīnī's proposed etymology is unlikely, because *ṣībān* derives from the root *ṣ-ʾ-b*, while *ṣubyān* is from *ṣ-b-y*.

103 The verb means "to soap"; the true verbal noun is *ṣabyanah*; *ṣībyān* ("boys") is for comic effect.

104 *Al-Qāmūs al-muḥīṭ* defines *nimnim/numnum* as "whiteness that appears in the fingernails of young people" (al-Fīrūzābādhī, *Qāmūs*, 4:183).

105 A variety of mint.

106 Cf. *nam*, sg. imperative verb: "Sleep!"

107 Al-Ḥarīrī: *Al-Maqāmah al-ḥalabiyyah* (no. 46) (*Maqāmāt*, 372).

108 Word puzzles are an ancient genre in Arabic literature (see further *EAL*, s.v. "lughz"); for other similar examples, see, e.g., al-Ibshīhī, *Al-Mustaṭraf*, 2:233–37.

109 Al-Shirbīnī explains later on (§11.18.5) that *ṭājin* ("casserole") may be deconstructed as *ṭa'* + *jinn*, i.e., "tread on (or screw) some jinn!" while *ṭāfiyah* (a metaphasis of *ṭā'ifah* ("company, group of people, etc.")) equals *ṭa'* + *fiyya*, i.e., "tread on (or screw) me!"; *yāsamīn* ("jasmine") is to be understood as equivalent to *ya's* ("despair") plus *mayn* ("lying").

110 "An old man and a maiden in the belly of a bird" (*shaykh wa-jāriyah fī baṭn ʿuṣfūr*): the sentence may also be read *shaykhun wajā ri'ah* ("an old man stabbed a lung" (while cutting up the bird)).

111 I.e., عُنّاب ("jujube fruit") since the first letter of the word is ع, called *ʿayn*, which also means "eye," leaving ناب "fang" as the rest of the word.

112 The word is unvoweled in al-Shirbīnī's text but is given here as in the autograph manuscript of Ibn Sūdūn's elegy on his mother's death quoted below (see Vrolijk, *Bringing a Laugh*, 57–58 Arabic).

113 Many of the children's words cited by al-Shirbīnī in the following passage are current in modern Egyptian Arabic. Those unattested today or used with a different meaning are: *namnam*—unattested (but cf. *namnim* "to nibble" and "to make tiny" (Hinds and Badawi, *Dictionary*, 887), in which latter sense the example given concerns food (al-Shirbīnī's sense is confirmed in the verses of Ibn Sūdūn's that follow); *buff*—used today to warn a child that food is hot (informants); *aḥḥ*—used today, inter alia, as "an exclamation expressing reaction to extreme heat or cold ~ ouch!" (Hinds and Badawi, *Dictionary*, 8); *wāwah*—today "a hurt place" (on a child's body) (Hinds and Badawi, *Dictionary*, 921), but see n. 117, below.

114 Compare the modern proverb *illi ʿāyiz id-daḥḥ ma-yqul-shi aḥḥ* "he who wants something nice shouldn't say 'Ouch!'" (where *daḥḥ* is understood by some to mean "eggs," so that the proverb implies that if you want eggs, you must put up with having your hand pecked by the hen).

115 Dozy, *Supplément*, 1:98 : "en parlant d'un chameau, rendre un son qui ressemble au glouglou de la bouteille."

116 I.e., the words are identical, except for the initial letter (أح, دح, ع).

117 In modern Egyptian, *wāwah* means "a hurt place, bruise, scratch," etc. on a child's body; this sense fits better in the verse that follows (see next note) and has been translated as such there.

118 "You who stole . . . 'Yumyum'": al-Shirbīnī fails to comment on the word *ninnā*, which is still current, as a "word used to lull a child to sleep" (Hinds and Badawi, *Dictionary*, 887).

119 The poem from which these lines are taken occurs in Vrolijk's edition (Vrolijk, *Bringing a Laugh*, 57–58 Arabic); see also ibid., 44–46 (English) for comments on this poem.

120 Literally "bend me, twist me."

121 I.e., the two words are identical in form (allowing for the conventional lengthening of the final vowel of *taḥnīnī* at the end of a verse) but different in meaning.

122 Al-Shirbīnī's formulation is unclear, but he probably means that there exists another type of body vermin in addition to those already named and it is called either *liḥḥays* or *liqqays* (probably diminutive forms, cf. *ḥimmayr*, etc., above). Neither word seems to be known today. Even al-Shirbīnī's equation of (the classical) forms *laḥisa* and *laqisa* is problematic, as the latter is not recorded in the lexica as meaning "lick," but rather, in the expression *laqisat nafsuhu*, "to be bad-tempered . . . to want to vomit" and in the expression *laqisat nafsuhu ilā* "to be greedy for a thing" (*WKAS*, 1084).

123 "according to the analogy of Fuṭays": see vol. 1, n. 366.

124 The word is no longer attested in these senses, but note modern Egyptian *malḥūs* "soft in the head, cuckoo" (Hinds and Badawi, *Dictionary*, 781).

125 Implying that the creature itself is rendered more harmful by virtue of the unpleasantness of its synonyms and associated words.

126 For no apparent reason, al-Shirbīnī here switches to Form II of the verb, which means "to give to lick."

127 Arab grammarians traditionally recognize three parts of speech, namely, the verb (*fiʿl*), the noun (*ism*), and the particle (*ḥarf* or *adāh*, which includes prepositions, adverbs, conjunctions, and interjections). Some grammarians, however, regard the interjections (*aṣwāṭ*) as "hav[ing], by either origin or use, a certain verbal force," because they are "either originally Imperatives . . . or equivalent to Imperatives." They therefore call them *asmāʾ al-afʿāl* ("verbal substantives") (Wright, *Grammar*, 1:296B), thus creating a "fourth part of speech," although the authority for al-Shirbīnī's naming this category "residual" (*khālifah*) is not clear.

128 Thus, in its more general sense, the word denotes "ring," though in relation to a garment it means the yoke or neck band.

129 Q Āl ʿImrān 3:180.

130 The verb means "to surround with a ring."

131 I.e., with the rearrangement of the dots, جبتك حمره becomes خنتك حمزه.

132 Though, in fact, *jāba* (root *j-w-b*) has no etymological relationship to *jabba* (root *j-b-b*).

133 The meaning of the verb is as given; *jubbatan* is for the argument.

134 At the beginning of the Ottoman period, Khāyir Bey, the Mamluk general turned Ottoman governor, "reportedly cut off half of every Mamluke's beard, handed it to him and said, 'You must abide by the Ottoman law, shave your beards, wear tight sleeves, and do everything like the Ottomans'" (Winter, *Egyptian Society*, 9).

135 Cf. al-Ibshīhī, *Al-Mustaṭraf*, 1:38.

136 I.e., tears and blushes.

137 *nakhīl*: "palms."

138 *minkhāl*: a variant of *munkhal* ("sieve").

139 The literary construction in which a verb is followed by a verbal noun of the same root (*maf'ūl muṭlaq*) gives an intensive sense; thus "which they shovel a shoveling" = "which they shovel intensively (or in great quantities)." In correct literary usage, the verbal noun would take the accusative ending *an*, but in the semi-colloquial, semi-literary poetic idiom employed here, this ending is dropped. The poet also plays with the internal form of the word (*jarf* is the standard verbal noun, *jarīf* an unattested form), a technique that is in fact typical of *sīrah* (epic) poetry, though in the latter such changes constitute a complex form of wordplay and provide much of the aesthetic pleasure, which does not seem to be the case here.

140 Because the pronominal suffix *hū* of *yajrufūhū* is masculine, while *nukhālah* is feminine; i.e., he should have said *yajrufūhā*.

141 Because the feminine pronominal suffix *hā* is a long syllable.

142 "truncation" (*tarkhīm*): "the rejection of one or more of [the] final letters [of a word]" (Wright, *Grammar*, 2:88A), though this applies primarily to vocatives, as in the example that follows.

143 The verse is by the pre-Islamic poet Imru' al-Qays; the translation is adapted from Arberry's *Seven Odes*, 62.

144 Fāṭim (in the Arabic Fāṭima or Fāṭimu) is the truncated form of Fāṭimatu.

145 I.e., one should understand the phrase as *shabīhu qishr al-nukālah yajrufūhu* "like *the husks* of bran that they shovel."

146 See al-Damīrī, *Ḥayawān*, 2:374.

147 Bashshār ibn Burd (ca. 98–167/714–84) (*Dīwān*, 2:189).

148 "They spared not one and let not one remain" (*mā khallā wa-lā baqqah*): al-Shirbīnī puns on two meanings of *wa-lā baqqah* in this colloquial verse: according to the first (as in the translation), *baqqah* is to be understood as a Form II verb, "it caused to remain"; according to the second, as a unit noun ("a bedbug"), thus "[and left] not one single bedbug."

149 See n. 6.

150 Q An'ām 6:74.

151 For an illustration of a present-day *maḥlabah*, see Hinds and Badawi, *Dictionary*, pl. A3.

152 For an illustration of a *qādūs*, see Hinds and Badawi, *Dictionary*, pl. E11.

153 The final *ih* is of special interest to the linguist, because it provides rare evidence for the behavior of a short vowel in a pre-modern colloquial dialect (the values of such vowels normally being hidden by the orthography). In this case, the ending *i(h)* of *qarrūfih* may be taken as evidence of an alternation between *i(h)* after consonants that are neither emphatic nor back, and *a(h)* in other environments in reflexes of the old Arabic "feminine" ending *a(h)* (see Blanc, *Perte*, and Davies, *Profile*, 81–85). Al-Shirbīnī provides another example below: *libbi(h)* for *libba(h)* (§11.23.9).

154 In fact, *kūz* is from the root *k-w-z*, *kazz* from the root *k-z-z*.

155 "the analogy of Fuṭays": see vol. 1, n. 366.

156 "Large handle-less earthenware jar used for storing and filtering water" (Hinds and Badawi, *Dictionary*, 389; pl. A7).

157 *qirr* (cited in the lexica as *qurr*): by stating that the word has "no vowel after the *r*," the author emphasizes that he is thinking of it in its colloquial form.

158 This fanciful etymology depends, for any semblance of plausibility, on the consonantal outline in Arabic script of the two putative etymons; thus, قِرّ (*qirr*) + وفِي (*wafiya*) = قروفي, which is equivalent in sound to *qarrūfi(h)*.

159 The letter *wāw* functions as both a consonant (*w*) and as the marker of the long vowel *ū*.

160 Using the *nisbah* ("relative") ending *ī* to form an adjective from the place name, as is conventional.

161 Q Naḥl 16:66.

162 I.e., she added *-ah*.

163 Literally "with nunation (*tanwīn*) and the vowel *i* after the *m*." Nunation is the addition of *n* to a short vowel at the end of a substantive and serves various grammatical functions in literary Arabic (see Wright, *Grammar*, 1:12) but is generally absent from the colloquial dialects. In this case, the form *yawmin* (which occurs twice more in the Ode) probably represents a conflation of *yawm* and conjunctionalizing *an* (*an al-maṣdariyyah*), meaning "on the day when."

164 Muslim fasts, such as that of the month of Ramadan, are restricted to the hours between sunrise and sunset.

165 The point echoes a wider position taken by the pious of the day, namely, that "the principle of *wara'* ('scrupulousness') . . . prohibits a man of religion from accepting favors from a ruler. Any material benefit which came from the rulers was *ḥarām* (morally tainted), because the rulers oppressed the people. Since the high officials could not maintain an

extravagant standard of living on their salaries, they must obviously have accepted presents from fellahs and other simple people" (Winter, *Society and Religion*, 263).

166 The ascription of partners to God (*shirk*), or polytheism, contradicts the fundamental tenet of the Muslim faith, that "There is no god but God."

167 See al-Ḥillī, *Al-Badīʿiyyah*, 262.

168 I.e., *fuq lī* and *fa-qlī* are identical in skeleton except that the second is augmented by the additional *alif* (which al-Shirbīnī counts as a consonant); on *al-jinās al-mazīd* see vol. 1, n. 242 and on *al-jinās al-muḥarraf* see Cachia, *Rhetorician*, 25.

169 I.e., the poet adds a dot above the letter ع so that عم ("paternal uncle") becomes غم ("grief") (paronomasia) and puns on the identicality of form of *khāl* ("maternal uncle"), which, in the inflected form in which it occurs in the verse, reads *khālī*, and of *khālī* ("devoid (of), empty (of)") in line-final "pausal" form.

170 I.e., ʿAlī ibn Abī Ṭālib.

171 I.e., Cain's murdering Abel; see Q Māʾidah 5:27–31.

172 "may the envious not prevail" (*al-ḥasūd lā yasūd*): a formula against envy and the evil eye.

173 The word is unattested but glossed below.

174 Al-Shirbīnī correctly identifies the colloquial form *aysham* (and the related *tayshimah* and *mayshūm* below) with the classical root *sh-ʾ-m*; however, this particular colloquial metathesis is no longer attested in Egyptian Arabic. On the other hand, *shūm* (brought in further on) is probably unrelated to this root.

175 As the story of Ṭuways (see Glossary) makes clear, the *mashʾūm* is not personally responsible for the dire events that become associated with his name; rather, he carries an aura of ill fortune.

176 Not the name of a tree but, apparently, of a quality of wood, cf. modern Egyptian *shūmah* "quarterstaff, cudgel."

177 Meaning, perhaps, that the poet would be happy to be in a situation in which condolences are required but would make even that gesture under protest.

178 The male sandgrouse flies long distances in the desert to fill its breast feathers with water, which its young then suck.

179 As usual, al-Shirbīnī disingenuously explains away a colloquial form (*minnū* versus literary *minhu*) as due to the constraints of meter (see vol. 1, p. xxxvii).

180 As above, *akhūhu* follows colloquial morphology (albeit with the addition of the pronominal suffix in literary form), while *akhīhi* conforms to literary grammar; the meter would not, however, be changed.

181 *khanfūr* is not considered an active participle form.

182 *Sic*, but should read "paternal uncle's"; see what follows.

183 I.e., Muḥaylibah.

184 I.e., Khanāfir son of Fasāqil.

185 Al-Shirbīnī insists on the literary voweling for these two forms (versus colloquial *yiqarraṭ/yiḍarraṭ*), thus turning them into pseudo-learned forms, presumably to emphasize their ludicrousness as objects of scholarly discussion.

186 The word has not, in fact, been mentioned before, unless al-Shirbīnī is referring to the immediately preceding sentence, in which case the "two forms" would be the formal and the colloquial vowelings.

187 The lines do not appear in Abū Nuwās's collected works, and the attribution is dubious.

188 "Earringed" (*muqarṭaq*): al-Shirbīnī's interpretation of the word in this sense is at odds with its generally accepted meaning, namely, "dressed in a close-fitting tunic," and also stretches the rules of the consonantal root system, by which *qurṭ* belongs to the root *q-r-ṭ*, while *muqarṭaq* belongs to *q-r-ṭ-q*.

189 Al-Shirbīnī plays on the double meaning of *bayḍ* as "eggs" and "testicles."

190 Perhaps the wolf spider, which carries its eggs conspicuously on its back.

191 The latter is a more formal term than *bayḍ*.

192 *Khiṣy* may also be read as *khaṣī* "eunuch," and, in the following, al-Shirbīnī appears to be making a joke along the lines of "it takes two eunuchs to make a whole man."

193 Al-Shirbīnī repeats the assertion regarding the related form *khiṣā* below, but there is no authority in the lexica for the use of either in this latter sense, and his following argument that the two words derive from one another is meaningless, in that they are (according to al-Shirbīnī) one and the same.

194 "and additionally they are in the position of annexation while it is in the position of the elevated and erected vowels": in grammar, *iḍāfah* ("annexation") is the genitive relationship between two nouns such as *ḥikmat allāh* "the wisdom of God" or *bayḍatu fiḍḍah* "an egg of silver," in which only the first noun may take the nominative (*rafʿ*, meaning, in nongrammatical usage, "elevatedness") or accusative (*naṣb*, meaning in nongrammatical usage "erection, construction") cases (see Wright, *Grammar*, 2:198–234). Al-Shirbīnī is saying that the testicles are equivalent to the second term in such a construction, while the penis, with its "elevatedness" and "erection," is equivalent to the first.

195 The lines have been attributed to Abū l-Ḥusayn al-Jazzār (601/1204–5 to 679/1280–81) (see Ibn Ḥijjah, *Thamarāt*, 48).

196 A further dig at the king, since the poet is saying that he is like both penis and testicles, while the king is like an anus that is large enough to accommodate both.

197 "No, may I be divorced—times three" (*lā ʿalayya al-ṭalāq thalāthah*): which may be read without a pause between *al-ṭalāq* and *thalāthah*, in which case it means "No, may I be triply divorced!" (the standard formula of irrevocable divorce, frequently used in oaths)

or with a pause in the same place, in which case it means "No, may I be divorced! Three [thousand]!"

198 *duldūl*: by analogy to modern Egyptian *daldil* "to dangle" but in the classical lexica "hedgehog."

199 *zubb*: in its reflex *zibb*, a standard, coarse, modern colloquial term.

200 *ayr*: a literary but still obscene term.

201 *ghurmūl*: "The penis . . . (in an absolute sense) . . . or a large and flaccid penis before its prepuce is cut off . . . or [the penis] of a solid-hoofed animal" (Lane, *Lexicon*, 2253).

202 *duldul*: presumably a by-form of *duldūl* above.

203 *dhakar*: another formal and not obscene term, occuring (as *zakar*) in modern colloquial Arabic.

204 *khuṣā* with *u*: albeit al-Shirbīnī does not, in fact, cite this form above.

205 I.e., *khiṣw* and, presumably, *khuṣw*.

206 I.e., *khuṣā* and *khiṣā*.

207 Ramzī mentions three villages of this name, of which the most important appears to be that on the northern edge of Cairo and which is also known as Khuṣūṣ ʿAyn Shams (Ramzī, *Qāmūs*, 2/1:33).

208 There is no such verb, though *khaṣā, yakhṣī* ("to geld") exists.

209 al-Ṭunayn: the reference is obscure; elsewhere (§11.29.9) *ṭunayn* is defined as "little sheaf of sugarcane."

210 In fact, the two words derive from separate roots, *līf* from *l-y-f* and *multaff* from *l-f-f*.

211 A favorite image of the classical poets, in the sense of a promise that is not kept or a person who fails to fulfil his promises.

212 The base form from which the "construct" form *nazlat* derives.

213 Ramzī lists four villages whose names appear in this form, with the definite article, and several dozen in which the word is the first part of a genitive construction (*nazlat* . . .; "the settlement of . . ."); the word appears to survive in modern Egyptian in this sense in place names only.

214 The verse that follows is taken from the *muʿallaqah* of Imruʾ al-Qays (*Dīwān*, 19), but the verse contains neither of the roots under discussion.

215 "As for those [peasants] who have plundered and burned villages and killed their inhabitants, they [the Inspectors] search for them and hunt them down using the best of means, wherever they may be on the face of the earth, be it even 'on the red bull's horn' [?], and apply against them the most severe and cruelest punishments slowly, so that they reveal the names of their partners, and then they seize these. [Having seized them] they flay them alive and break their hands and legs and recover from them the stolen

wealth. Thus they put an end to them all for the betterment of the world" (Shalabī, *Siyāḥatnāmah*, 434).

216 "However that may be" (*fa-ʿalā kull ḥāl*): this discreet disclaimer, and the framing of the whole passage in terms of "former times," appear to hint that the situation at the time of writing differed from that just described; the rest of the account focuses on injustices committed by Inspectors. In 1599, almost a century before al-Shirbīnī, the Turkish visitor ʿĀlī Muṣṭafā denigrated the Inspectors (*kushshāf*, sg. *kāshif*: "District Directors"), writing "Strange is also the despotry of the district directors (*kashif*) over the poor people, the tyranny and onslaught of a band of revenue farmers (*mültezim*) on the subjects (*raʿaya*) on the basis of the Circassian law. Some good-for-nothing, some roistering rough of the *jundis* of Egypt, who does not possess five aspers, pledges the revenues of a province and becomes a *kashif*" (Tietze, *Description*, 56).

217 "the suppression of the first term of a genitive annexation" (*ḥadhf muḍāf*): on "annexation" (*iḍāfah*), see n. 194.

218 "Ibrāhīm the Beloved" (Ibrāhīm al-Khalīl): i.e., "the Beloved of God," cf. Q Nisāʾ 4:125 «and God took Ibrahim as His beloved» (and similarly Isrāʾ 17:73); for the commentators' anecdotal explanation of the circumstances in which the epithet was first used, see Sale, *Koran*, 75 note f.

219 Ibn Nubātah (686–768/1287–1366) according to al-Ibshīhī (*Al-Mustaṭraf*, 2:34).

220 "juxtaposed contrasts in the wording" (*al-ṭibāq al-lafẓī*): i.e., "smile" and "tears," "weep" and "laugh."

221 The pre-Islamic poet ʿAlqamah (see *Al-Mufaḍḍaliyyāt*, nos. 119, 392).

222 These verses do not appear in al-Qāḍī l-Fāḍil's published works.

223 Al-Kumayt ibn Zayd (60/679–80 to 126/743–44) (*Dīwān*, 236).

224 Unlike other vultures, the Egyptian vulture (*rakhamah*; *Neophron percnopterus*) has largely white plumage.

225 "its two nests": perhaps meaning "on the head and in the beard."

226 A slightly different version of the above is to be found in his collected works (Ibn Durayd, 308).

227 Al-ʿAqīq and al-Liwā: literally, "the channel worn by a torrent" and "the winding sands," names inherited from and evocative of pre-Islamic poetry.

228 "they saw impurity," etc.: the point is unclear.

229 I.e., the poet says *shābat ʿawāriḍī*, with a nonanimate plural noun (*ʿawāriḍī*) following a feminine singular verb (*shābat*); this is, however, correct according to formal Arabic grammar, and al-Shirbīnī's insinuation that it represents a special rural usage is (presumably deliberately) misleading; moreover, the second of his two proposed alternatives

(*shābū ʿawāriḍī*) is itself incorrect in that the non-animate plural noun should not be preceded by a plural verb.

230 I.e., why does he use the form that is homophonic with the other sense mentioned rather than the less ambiguous verbal noun *nuzūl* ("descending")?

231 *Nazlah* is grammatically feminine, *nuzūl* masculine.

232 "the words of Abū Nuwās": not in his collected works.

233 See vol. 1, §5.3.14.

234 Cf. G. J. H. van Gelder, "Shiʿr," in *EI2*: "If traditions are to be believed, the great bards of the Dj̲āhiliyya considered that the poem was the speech of a god or of a dj̲innī (demon)."

235 Ibn al-Fāriḍ is buried in Cairo's Southern Cemetery, close to the Muqaṭṭam Hills, at the foot of al-ʿĀriḍ, the rocky outcrop on which stand the early Ottoman *khānaqāh* (lodge) and tomb of the Sufi Shāhīn al-Khalwatī.

236 Neither *ṣārī* (root *ṣ-r-y*) nor *ṣurr* (root *ṣ-r-r*) is related to *ṣāra* (root *ṣ-y-r*). The *ṣurr* (in other sources usually *ṣurrah*) was the annual cash allocation in support of the wages, pensions, and alms for various categories of servitors, guards, and beneficiaries attached to the Two Sanctuaries (al-Ḥaramayn) of Mecca and Medina, which had been administered from Egypt since the time of the Mamluks (see Shaw, *Financial*, 254ff.).

237 See n. 163.

238 "And ask the village" (*wa-s'al al-qaryah*): Q Yūsuf 12:82; the verse is used in textbooks on rhetoric as an example of "ellipsis" (*ījāz*) achieved through "curtailment" (*ḥadhf*).

239 The innuendo is either sexual or implies that he goes off with his crowbar to make holes in the mud walls of houses or animal pens and so enter and burgle them.

240 *shahlāṭ*: the word is unattested elsewhere.

241 The conquest of Egypt began in 18/639.

242 "The Muslim jurists disagree whether Egypt was taken by force . . . or by treaty . . . . Behind the theoretical dispute . . . lay the practical problem of how to legitimise any Muslim demands for increasing taxes without violating Islamic law" (J.-L. Arnaud and J. Jankowski, "Miṣr," in *EI2*).

243 See Ibn ʿAbd al-Ḥakam, *Futūḥ*, 87.

244 The two words are unrelated, *dīn* belonging to the root *d-y-n*, while *dīwān* is a Persian loanword, assimilable to the root *d-w-n*.

245 Meaning, perhaps, "different nations" (i.e., brings together Turks, Circassians, and others, with Egyptians).

246 The attribution is dubious; elsewhere, these verses are described as anonymous.

247 Al-Shirbīnī plays with the colloquial use of *rūḥ* as a reflexive pronoun ("I void my loose bowels all over *myself*") and its basic meaning of "spirit, breath of life," as though the poet had said, "I void my loose bowels on my Self."

248 Al-Shirbīnī's intent is not clear: it is a verb, *harra*, with which the commentary should be concerned, and not a noun; and the plural of *hirr* (if this is what is intended) is normally given as *hirarah*.

249 I.e., either "you will observe the kind of *hurār* just described" or, punningly, "you will observe that people have voided their loose bowels there."

250 The meaning of the verb is as given above.

251 I.e., *ḥidhā'*, its literary reflex.

252 *nisā'* . . . *niswah*: literary forms, in contrast to colloquial *niswān*.

253 Q Baqarah 2:195.

254 See §11.3.1.

255 I.e., Ḥassān ibn Thābit; on the accusations of cowardice against him, see Ḥassān ibn Thābit, *Dīwān*, 15.

256 River travel was faster and cheaper than travel by land. Gonzales, who traveled in Egypt in 1665–66, notes that the journey from Damietta to Cairo took five days and that there were daily sailings in both directions (Gonzales, *Voyage*, 71–72).

257 Presumably Masjid al-Khiḍr, a village on the west bank of the eastern branch of the Nile, near Quwisnā (Ramzī, *Qāmūs*, 2/2:202).

258 At this point, al-Shirbīnī substitutes the more colloquial form *ʿabā'ah* (equivalent to modern colloquial *ʿabāyah*) for the literary form *ʿabā(')* used in the verse.

259 Thus the *ʿabāyah* of Shirbīnī's day differed from that of today, which is usually plain black or brown (cf. Hinds and Badawi, *Dictionary*, 561, illus. 976; see also Lane, *Manners*, 30, 32).

260 Perhaps meaning the Prophet, his daughter Fāṭimah, his son-in-law ʿAlī, and their sons, al-Ḥasan and al-Ḥusayn.

261 In fact, the roots are unrelated: *ʿabā'*/*ʿabā'ah* are from *ʿ-b-'*, while *ʿabba*, etc., are from *ʿ-b-b*.

262 Several treatises dealing with the permissibility of listening to music (*samāʿ*) exist, the consensus of the polemicists being that "stringed instruments, the *kūbah* drum, and the *mizmār* [a reed instrument] are forbidden" because of their potential to distract the listener from his religious duties or because of their "salacious associations," the interdiction of the *kūbah* being attributed to its use by *mukhannathūn* ("effeminates") (Nelson, *Art*, 46). The exemption of the *nafīr*, though not mentioned in the best-known treatises, may be attributed to its use in war.

263 I.e., the adjective is being applied metonymically, and it is not the drum that is violent but the beating of it.

264 al-Ṣaghīrī: the name appears here and in the verses that follow in this form in all the witnesses, but no such person existed. Rather, the name is a misreading of the word *al-ṣafīrī*,

as found in verses that form part of an account of an apocryphal exchange between the Buyid chief minister and man of letters al-Ṣāḥib ibn ʿAbbād (326–85/938–95) and the celebrated author of *maqāmāt*, Badīʿ al-Zamān al-Hamadhānī (358–98/968–1008), as recounted by al-Ṣafadī (*Al-Ghayth*, 2:105). According to al-Ṣafadī (d. 764/1363), al-Hamadhānī farted in the presence of al-Ṣāḥib ibn ʿAbbād. Al-Hamadhānī explained the unfortunate noise as *ṣarīr al-takht* ("the creaking of the chair"), to which al-Ṣāḥib responded *bal ṣafīr al-taḥt* ("rather, the whistle of the fundament"). Thus the verses begin, according to al-Ṣafadī, *qul li-l-ṣafīriyyi*, meaning "Tell the ass-whistler . . . ." In addition to this, it should be noted that al-Ṣafadī was himself mistaken, for the verses first occur in the anthology *Yatīmat al-dahr* by al-Thaʿālibī (350–429/961–1038), where they refer not to Badīʿ al-Zamān al-Hamadhānī but to an otherwise unknown jurisprudent called al-Khuḍayrī who committed the same faux pas before al-Ṣāḥib ibn ʿAbbād, whose lines thus properly begin *yā-bna l-Khuḍayrīyyi* ("O Ibn al-Khuḍayrī . . .") (*Yatīmat al-dahr*, 3:198).

265 Cf., e.g., Q Anbiyāʾ 21:81 «And unto Solomon (We subdued) the wind and its raging.» *ʿūd*: "lute."

266 Abū ʿAbd al-Raḥmān Ḥātim ibn ʿUnwān (d. 237/851), known as "the Deaf" (al-Aṣamm), was an ascetic of Balkh, sometimes referred to, for his wise sayings, as "the Luqmān of this nation."

267 The following passage, in rhymed prose, is reminiscent in setting and tone of the *Agony of the Love-Sick Plaintiff and the Teardrop of the Weeper* (*Lawʿat al-shākī wa-damʿat al-bākī*) of Ṣalāḥ al-Dīn Khalīl ibn Aybak al-Ṣafadī (d. 764/1363) and may be intended as an *homage* to—or parody of—the latter.

268 Cf. Q Anʿām 6:95 «Lo! God (it is) who splitteth the grain of corn and the date pit (for sprouting)!»

269 I.e., "until he died."

270 Al-Ghawrī does have preserved works, mostly of poetry, but there is no record of treatises on fake farting.

271 Begins on D and has E flat, B half-flat, and F sharp.

272 "their transitions" (*nahazātuhum*): the meaning is unclear.

273 Al-Ḥillī, *Al-Badīʿiyyah*, 153.

274 The word occurs only in colloquial (modern Egyptian *yadōb*), and its etymology is not obvious; Fischer suggests that it comes from **yā duʾūb* "O cares! O pain!" with semantic and phonological contamination from *dōb/dhōb* "now, immediately," originating in **idhā huwa bi-* (Fischer, *Bildungen*, 156); al-Shirbīnī's connection of the word to *daʾb*, of which *duʾūb* must be a plural, is consistent with this, though the reference to the different root *d-b-b* (*dabb*, *dubb*, and *dabīb*, see below) is simply playful.

275 This practice, more often called *dabīb*, is referred to frequently in classical literature, as in the verses by Abū Nuwās cited earlier by al-Shirbīnī (vol. 1, §5.3.8); see further Bosworth, *Underworld*, 119–24 and, for its continuing prominence in the twentieth century, Dunne, "Sexuality," 187.

276 "calculating the money that I owe in tax and weighing out the tax in kind" (*ḥisāb al-māl wa-wazn al-kharāj*): here, and only here, al-Shirbīnī seems to make a distinction between *māl* and *kharāj* as taxes in specie and in kind; elsewhere (§11.8.3) he equates the two.

277 Bahāʾ al-Dīn Zuhayr (581-656/1186-1258) (*Poetical Works*, 92).

278 The terms that follow (*maẓālim, ziyādāt al-kharāj, ʿawāʾid, maghārim, kulaf, gharāmat al-baṭṭālīn*) refer mostly to illegal levies that grew up during the seventeenth century and lasted through the eighteenth (for further instances and a discussion, see ʿAbd al-Raḥīm, *Al-Rīf*, 135–38); see, further, Glossary, s.v. *maẓālim*.

279 Al-Maʾmūn visited Egypt in 214–15/829–30 to crush a series of Coptic revolts. The following paragraph is found, with differences of detail, in al-Maqrīzī (*Al-Khiṭaṭ*, 1:81).

280 Ramzī identifies the village with Tunnāmil al-Sharqī in the province of al-Sharqiyyah (Ramzī, *Qāmūs*, 2/1:174).

281 An error for Aḥmad ibn Abī Duʾād (see Ibn al-Zubayr, *Al-Dhakhāʾir*, 104), chief judge under the caliph al-Muʿtaṣim (r. 218–27/833–42).

282 I.e., by refusing the gift.

283 This paragraph is an abridged quotation from al-Maqrīzī, *Al-Khiṭaṭ*, 1:103 infra.

284 In his *al-Khiṭaṭ*, al-Maqrīzī explains that the term "land-based" (*kharājī*) applied to taxes on agricultural land, collected annually, and any "gifts" taken in kind from the peasants (al-Maqrīzī, *Al-Khiṭaṭ*, 1:103), while "lunar" (*hilālī*) applied to those that were levied on property and commercial enterprises and were collected monthly (ibid., 107). The fact that the latter fell on the urban classes may explain why they are condemned so vehemently in scholarly sources; the former affected only the peasants, and their legitimacy went unchallenged. Al-Maqrīzī goes on to mention that, after being abolished by Aḥmad ibn Ṭūlūn, the lunar taxes were reintroduced by the Fatimids, under the name of *mukūs* (ibid., 104).

285 "with or without the nunation in this verse" (*bi-l-tanwīn wa-ʿadamihi fī hādhā l-bayt*): any of the forms *wa-yawmin* (with nunation) or *wa-yawma* and *wa-yawmi* (without nunation) is metrically and syntactically defensible, the first possibility being the *wāw rubba* construction, the second and third being construable as the first terms of an *iḍāfah*; however, the first alternative, with nunation, has already occurred in the Ode (§11.6.1).

286 "The corvée" (*al-ʿawnah*): as al-Shirbīnī emphasizes in what follows, this form of compulsory labor was used exclusively on the tax farmer's private plot. Another term, *al-sukhrah*, was used of forced labor on public works, especially the maintenance of the irrigation system. The first sort of corvée was abolished in the early nineteenth century, the second in the period before and just after the British occupation in 1882, by which time year-round cotton cultivation had reduced the availability of labor during the summer.

287 Umm Waṭīf is a *kunyah* meaning literally "the mother of the man with the bushy eyebrows." Though the exact point of al-Shirbīnī's remark is obscure, there may be an allusion to the phrase *yā waṭfa* "You (feminine) with the bushy eyebrows" mentioned by al-Maghribī (*Dafʿ*, fol. 35a, 16; Zack, *Egyptian Arabic*, 314) as a term of abuse used by peasants.

288 These are beehive-like domes made by building up courses of dung cakes; a fire is then lit in the hollow interior to dry the dung to prepare it for use as fuel.

289 In traditional Egyptian society, women are rarely referred to by their given names.

290 "the big storage jar" (*al-zalʿah al-kabīrah*): the *zalʿah* is a "large storage jar with handles (usually for water)" (Hinds and Badawi, *Dictionary*, 377, pl. A10).

291 The meaning of both verbs is "to help," the form *ʿān* being a colloquialization of the literary Form IV *aʿāna*.

292 The roots *h-d-d* and *h-d-m* are not, in fact, related.

293 I.e., «Lo! Kings, when they enter a township, ruin it» (Q Naml 27:34).

294 I.e., the consonantal skeleton of the verb *hadd* (هد), repeated, is identical to that of the noun *hudhud* (هدهد).

295 Q Naml 27:20; see also vol. 1, n. 250.

296 In fact there is no relationship, *hudhud* belongs to the root *h-d-h-d* and *hadiyyah* to the root *h-d-y*.

297 "The gift of friends is on leaves of rue": see al-Ibshīhī, *Al-Mustaṭraf*, 1:37 (without explanation of the meaning).

298 Cf. Q Naml 27:17 «And there were gathered unto Solomon his armies of the jinn and humankind, and of the birds, and they were set in battle order.»

299 "nature's tongue": see vol. 1, n. 348.

300 An even less plausible etymology, as *hadhayān* belongs to the root *h-dh-y*, which shares only one consonant with *h-d-d*.

301 Al-Shirbīnī spells out the word in detail, perhaps because it constitutes an unusual colloquialized poetic, or pseudo-poetic, form of the literary Arabic *hādhā* ("this").

302 I.e., it is a (near) palindrome; though al-Shirbīnī uses the singular, the comment applies to both forms of the demonstrative (masculine, then feminine) used in the verse,

because *hādah* and *hādihī* have the same consonantal skeleton, the difference in the voweling being indicated by the meter.

303 I.e., the caliph ʿUmar ibn al-Khaṭṭāb (r. 13–23/634–44).

304 Perhaps Abū Wuhayb Buhlūl ibn ʿAmr, a "wise fool" who was a contemporary of Hārūn al-Rashīd (d. 193/809) (see al-Nīsābūrī, *ʿUqalāʾ*, 69–77, who does not, however, mention these lines) and who is "usually pictured as a cunning vagrant, wielding a staff or riding it as a hobby-horse" (Dols, *Majnūn*, 358)—to which "my reedling" (*quṣaybatī*) in the verse below refers. Or this "al-Buhlūl" may be identical with the Yaḥyā al-Buhlūl quoted by al-Shirbīnī earlier (§§10.14, 11.1.14). Verses attributed by al-Shaʿrānī to Buhlūl al-Majnūn ("Crazy Buhlul") (al-Shaʿrānī, *Lawāqiḥ*, 1:58) are closer in style and sentiment to those of al-Shirbīnī's "Yaḥyā al-Buhlūl" than they are to the verse quoted above.

305 Al-Shirbīnī takes terms such as "Coarse," "Moderate," "Hot," and "Moist" (see, e.g., §11.10.9 and passim) from Galenic medicine, which dominated the theory and practice of medicine in the pre-modern Arab world. The keystone of the Galenic system was the maintenance or restoration of *eukrasia* ("proper balance"), by practicing moderation in general and, especially, by maintaining a balance among foods consumed, according to their different humors; by including other qualities such as Coarse and Heavy, however, al-Shirbīnī's goes beyond the classical set of Hot, Cold, Dry, and Moist (see further Dols, *Majnūn*, especially 10–14).

306 Van Gelder (*Dishes*, 99 n. 123) notes that a similar statement, "Noble parents, low offspring," is attributed to Galen by ʿAlī ibn ʿAbd Allāh al-Ghuzūlī (d. 815/1412) in his *Maṭāliʿ al-Budūr* (2:55); this explains why al-Shirbīnī refers below to these words as a quotation.

307 On the evolution of this dish, which is found in Iran, Turkey, and parts of the Arab world in a wide variety of forms, see Aubaile-Sallenave (though the description there of Egyptian *kishk* as a "sweetmeat made from milk . . . flour and sugar" (Aubaile-Sallenave, "Al-Kishk", 127) appears to be based on Mehren's misreading of the above passage) and, for nineteenth-century Egypt, Lane's description (*Manners*, 488 n. 3).

308 *hirāsh* is usually defined as "quarreling, wrangling," but the author, seriously or not, asserts below (§11.10.13) that it is used here in the meaning given.

309 See vol. 1, §§2.5 and 2.26.

310 *Sic*: al-Shirbīnī seems to have forgotten that the second sort does not contain any beans and is presumably thinking of the first only.

311 Presumably al-Shirbīnī means "these three."

312 I.e., كعك (*kaʿk*), شاش (*shāsh*), and باب (*bāb*), and the longer examples that follow read the same forward and backward when only the consonantal skeleton is taken into

consideration and short and quiescent vowels (as in *kaʿk*) and inflectional endings (as in the Qurʾanic verses and the lines by al-Ḥarīrī below) are ignored.

313 Q Muddaththir 74:3.

314 Q Anbiyāʾ 21:33 and Ṣāffāt 37:40.

315 These verses are from *maqāmah* XVI ("al-Maghribiyyah") (al-Ḥarīrī, *Maqāmāt*, 113). The original contains a further three lines, each of them a palindrome.

316 I.e., they turned س into ش, etc., so that كس (*kuss*) became كش, implying that كشك (*kishk*) has some relation to كسك (*kussik* "your cunt").

317 The verbal patterns *mufāʿalah* (as in *muḥāraqah*) and *fiʿāl* (as in *niqār* and *hirāsh*) are often interchangeable.

318 *nayrūb . . . daylūb*: both words are unattested elsewhere.

319 Literally "a mischievous, or a slanderous, man" or "a strong man." The passage contains many confusing and seemingly circular statements, which may be deliberate, in view of the references to "confusion" and getting "mixed up."

320 Both *gharf* and *gharīf* are valid verbal-noun forms; al-Shirbīnī's comment complicates the issue for the sake, perhaps, of a dig at grammatical overanalysis.

321 I.e., "though I eat at night, I am hungry again the next morning," meaning that I cannot escape the belly's demands.

322 See §11.2.21.

323 Ibn al-Fāriḍ, *Dīwān*, 377.

324 Stewed fava (broad) beans, today called *fūl midammis*, remain perhaps the most important staple, after bread, of the Egyptian diet.

325 In reality, the last two forms belong to verbal Form I, whereas the first three belong to verbal Form II.

326 I.e., balances their humors, see n. 305.

327 "like a . . . ." (*mithl al-nuʿūt*): the word is unattested in the lexica in an appropriate meaning.

328 While *rīḥah* is indeed the colloquial word for "smell" and *rāʾiḥah* one of its literary equivalents, the former is, just as likely, a reflex of literary *rīḥah*, with the same meaning.

329 Here, *rāyiḥah* is the colloquial active participle from *rāḥ* "to go" and identical, except for the substitution of *y* for the glottal stop, with literary *rāʾiḥah* "smell."

330 "a cord" (*khayṭ*): i.e., the suspended rope using which small ferryboats are pulled from one side of a canal to the other.

331 I.e., the answer to the riddle that follows is "a ferryboat": the explanation may be that the ferryboat is "going and coming" across the canal; it comes from beneath the bank (the "wall"); it is "dead and living" because it is both inanimate and constantly moving;

it is flat on the "ground," i.e., the water, but could equally be described as sitting on it or standing in it; the sense of "atop a wall reclining" is unclear.

332 The formula *ʿalā (man)* is unattested elsewhere but is plausible as a genuine colloquial form, if *ʿalā* is taken as an optative verb (from *ʿalā* "to become high, elevated" etc.), in which case the use of the perfect tense rather than the more colloquial imperfect may be attributed to the specialized poetic diction of the epic style. Al-Shirbīnī describes this verb as a preposition simply because it is identical in pronunciation, and in his spelling, to the preposition *ʿalā* ("on"); the former, however, is more correctly spelled with *alif* (i.e., علا vs. على).

333 I.e., *nuṣṣ* is the colloquial (but not specifically rural) reflex of literary Arabic *niṣf* "half"; a *nuṣṣ/niṣf fiḍḍah* is a silver piece.

334 Al-Shirbīnī presumably means that the word *nuṣṣ* (نص) is orthographically a fragment of *niṣf* (نصف) and that it is up to the reader to supply the rest of the word.

335 Where "Fāṭim" is a conventionally shortened form of "Fāṭimu" or "Fātima"; the translation is Arberry's (*Seven Odes*, 62).

336 Q Sabaʾ 34:13 (of Sulaymān) "They made for him what he willed: synagogues and statues, and basins like reservoirs, and boilers built into the ground."

337 Kohl has been believed to strengthen the eyesight (see Lane, *Manners*, 36).

338 Shihāb al-Dīn Aḥmad ibn ʿUthmān al-Amshāṭī (d. 725/1325) (al-Ṣafadī *Aʿyān*, 1:288).

339 "wood" (*ḥaṭab rūmī*): literally "Anatolian fuel"—the standard Egyptian non-dung-based cooking fuel (*ḥaṭab*) of the time consisted of vegetable debris from the fields, such as sugarcane stalks; after the Ottoman conquest, however, real firewood was imported as a luxury item from the forests of Anatolia (*al-Rūm*) (Raymond, *Artisans*, 1:187).

340 Al-Shirbīnī paraphrases Ibn Sūdūn (Vrolijk, *Bringing a Laugh*, 136 Arabic, lines 11–12), who gives the name of the dish as "Gatherer of Loved Ones" (*mujammiʿat al-aḥbāb*); see further n. 344.

341 In present-day usage, "made of dry (as opposed to fresh or green) ingredients" (Hinds-Badawi, 111); see also Perry, "Būrān."

342 Accidentally or not, al-Shirbīnī here confuses *sāra* "to proceed" with *ṣāra* "to become," providing indirect evidence that the two had by his time come to be realized as homophones (*ṣāra*) as a result of regressive assimilation to emphatic *r*, as in modern Egyptian pronunciation.

343 This is the form in which the word occurs today.

344 Cf. Vrolijk, *Bringing a Laugh*, 134–36 Arabic. Ibn Sūdūn attributes these verses to "some person" and builds around them a commentary (a part of which al-Shirbīnī quotes below; see also vol. 1, p. xxii). They may have been a popular ditty: Ibn Sūdūn refers to

them as belonging to "what has become well known, spread far and near, and filled the ear" (ibid., 134 Arabic).

345 In modern Egyptian, "Abū Qirdān" is the name of the cattle egret, a common bird of the fields. Ibn Sūdūn specifies the voweling as given above (Vrolijk, *Bringing a Laugh*, 134 Arabic).

346 Eggplant.

347 I.e., the man said *mulūkhī yā* . . . ("My tearings! O . . .") and never completed the call.

348 I.e., ملوخي + يا = ملوخيّا.

349 Al-Ḥākim bi-Amri-llāh was famed for his eccentric ordinances, some of which—including perhaps that mentioned here—may be understood in the context of tensions between Shiites and Sunnis in Egypt at the time (see M. Canard, "Al-Ḥākim Bi-Amr Allāh," in *EI2*).

350 The lexica include neither term in an appropriate sense.

351 I.e., with suppression of the glottal stop of *jā'a*, formal reflex of colloquial *ja* ("he came"), plus substitution of enclitic *li* for *ilā*, also as in the colloquial.

352 The verbal noun.

353 The intransitive senses recorded for modern usage are "to force one's way; to step, stamp" (Hinds and Badawi, *Dictionary*, 290).

354 See n. 194; here however, al-Shirbīnī uses the term *muḍāf* loosely or by analogy, since what is omitted (in fact, replaced) is the logical subject of a verb.

355 "vapor" (*bukhār*): meaning perhaps the *pneuma* of Galenic medicine (see Dols, *Majnūn*, 2–22).

356 Al-Shirbīnī seems to imply that a peasant is unlikely to know so technical a term as *qulinj*, whose true etymon (as distinct from the facetious ones suggested by the author below) is the Greek *kolikos*, unless (as he points out below) he hears it from "a doctor or someone else."

357 These lines occur, with variations, as part of a longer piece attributed to him, uncertainly, in his collected works (al-Shāfiʿī, *Shiʿr*, 236).

358 *kānat*: the hemistich scans only if this word is read, as is possible in modern Egyptian, as *kāt*.

359 *qashaʿ* appears to have disappeared from modern Egyptian dialects except for those of the oases of the Western Desert (Behnstedt and Woidich, *Glossar*, 379).

360 This is the meaning in literary Arabic.

361 The first day of Dhū l-Ḥijjah, the pilgrimage month, of 1075 was AD 14 June 1665; al-Shirbīnī had also made the pilgrimage the previous year (see §11.1.3).

362 I.e., the thirty-second chapter of the Qur'an, called *The Prostration* (*al-Sajdah*) because believers prostrate themselves at the following verse: «Only those believe in Our

revelations who, when they are reminded of them, fall down prostate and hymn the praise of their Lord, and they are not scornful» (Q Sajdah 32:15).

363 Part of the call to the dawn prayer.

364 Q Isrā' 17:44.

365 See §11.11.11.

366 Cf. Q Kahf 18:19 «Now send one of you with this your silver coin unto the city, and see what food is purest there and bring you a supply thereof.»

367 Literally "of loosely hanging sleeves"; the translation is tentative.

368 The correct verbal nouns are *ball* and *billah.*

369 Since the sole realization of the root *q-l-q-s* attested in the lexica is the noun *qulqās*, *qalqasah* and its derivatives are probably nonce words. *Qulqās* derives from Greek *kolokasia*, whence the Latin.

370 I.e., *qulqās* is formed of *qul* ("speak!") plus *qāsā* ("it suffered"), the final *ā* of the second word being explicable as the pausal form of the accusative *qulqāsan*, explainable as the "accusative of admiration or blame" (*manṣūb ʿalā l-madḥ aw al-dhamm*).

371 Using the denominal verb.

372 See vol. 1, §3.43, where it occurs as the name of one of the village shaykhs.

373 A meaningless statement, as *dandūf* and *dandafah* (a verbal noun form) are of equal status in the same root.

374 From root *n-d-f* as against *dandūf*'s *d-n-d-f*, and hence, in reality, unrelated.

375 I.e., *jā'athu* is the literary reflex of colloquial *jatū*.

376 As in the case of "the *bīsār* came," see §11.12.7.

377 Cf. Hinds and Badawi, *Dictionary*, 704: *qaṣʿah* "bowl or basin without a base."

378 The word is attested in Egypt today only in the sense of "lid of a *mājūr*" ("earthenware kneading bowl") (Behnstedt and Woidich, *Glossar*, 469).

379 *qaṣʿah . . . quṣayʿah . . . faswah . . . fusaywah*: *quṣayʿah* and *fusawyah* are diminutives.

380 On such categories of figurative speech, see vol. 1, n. 236; here, however, al-Shirbīnī is clearly parodying this kind of terminology.

381 In modern Egyptian, *huwwa* is the standard third-person singular personal pronoun for both rural and urban dialects, versus literary *huwa*.

382 *Ḥanak* has the basic sense of "jaw" but is also used in derisive or vulgar speech to refer to the mouth itself.

383 A red herring, because it is not *fam* (and its irregular declension) that is at issue here.

384 See al-Ḥillī, *Al-Badīʿiyyah*, 82, where the verse is used to illustrate the device called *radd al-ʿajz ʿalā al-ṣadr*, i.e., using the same word at both the beginning and the end of a line of verse.

385 I.e., *tajrīf*, verbal noun of *yujarrifu*, is used here as an intensifier ("he shovels a shoveling" = "he shovels repeatedly or in great quantities, he shovels away") in the construction called *maf'ūl muṭlaq* ("objective complement," see Wright, *Grammar*, 2:54C ff.), which would require, under the rules of formal Arabic, an indefinite accusative, i.e., *tajrīfan*. One may also deduce from al-Shirbīnī's comment that the rhyme letter of the Ode is quiescent, even though many lines can be correctly construed, both metrically and syntactically, with final vowel.

386 See §11.12.12.

387 Jacques Berque, speaking of the first half of the twentieth century, remarks, "Les fromages, frais ou conservés ... ou même fermentés, *mešš*, constituaient ... le mets 'qui fait passer le pain'" (Berque, *Histoire*, 32).

388 Mentioned, if not defined, in the discussion of wheat groats (*kishk*) above, see §11.9.8.

389 Again, *wishsh* is the standard colloquial reflex of literary Arabic *wajh*, rather than a specifically rural form (see vol. 1, pp. xxxvi–xxxvii).

390 On this unusual curse form, see vol. 1, n. 29.

391 The table is that referred to in Q Mā'idah 5:114: «Jesus, son of Mary, said, "O God, Our Lord! Send down for us a table spread with food from heaven, that it may be a feast for us, for the first of us and the last of us, and a sign from Thee!"»

392 Q Baqarah 2:187.

393 Q Baqarah 2:249.

394 "Smoking" is expressed as "drinking smoke (or tobacco)" (*shurb al-dukhān*).

395 I.e., the letter *alif*, indicating the long *ā* in *māta* (مات), was omitted, so that مات + رد became مترد.

396 Presumably from *zunbūr* ("wasp; clitoris").

397 In the second of these forms, the spelling reflects the colloquial rather than the literary morphology (اطنبر versus تطنبر); thus, for consistency, one should read *miṭṭanbar* rather than *mutaṭanbir*, etc., in this sentence and the rest of the passage.

398 Of which the literal meaning may be "to play the tambourine" (*ṭunbūrah*) (see the author's reference to this instrument below).

399 "If you're ... hung" (*idhā kunta ālātī wa-ṭab'uka riqqī * ṭanbir bi-riqqah wa-'tabir bi-l-mashnūqī*): with puns on *ālātī* ("musician," from *ālah* "(musical) instrument"; also, "tool, penis"), *riqqī* ("gentle"; also interpretable as a relative adjective from *riqq* "tambourine"), and *ṭanbir* ("to play the tambourine"; also "to rub oneself against boys").

400 "All great Arab physicians whose works have been preserved warned against eating beef and recommended mutton. According to al-Rāzī, almost all meats, with the exception of mutton, cause illnesses" (Ashtor, "Diet," 130).

401 This sense of the word is discussed below, §11.20.5.

402 See §11.14.8.

403 *rafrāfah*: the word is not attested in the lexica, but, according to an informant, is used in the countryside today to refer to a feast held at the time specified, rather than a dish.

404 See the discussion of the implied logical subject at §§11.5.3 and 11.14.2.

405 Here al-Shirbīnī invokes the second meaning of the verb, "to resolve, determine."

406 The verb is employed with and without the following preposition *ʿalā*.

407 Al-Shirbīnī plays with the ambiguity of the conjunction *wa-* ("and"), which may denote synonymity (in which case *yaʿzim* and *yuḍif* would both be understood in the basic sense of "invite/play host to") or contrast (in which case *yaʿzim* should be understood in its other sense of "to determine (to do something)"); he also puns on the various senses of the root *ḍ-y-f* "to add, attach, join, annex" (hence *yanḍāfu* "to be added, be attached, be annexed (in the grammatical sense)") and *iḍāfah* "addition, annexation" on the one hand, and *ḍiyāfah* ("hospitality") and *ḍayf* ("guest") on the other. The grammatical usage of *iḍāfah* is further exploited below.

408 The second verbal noun, *ḍuyūf*, is a red herring, being merely the plural of *ḍayf* "guest."

409 On "annexation" (*iḍāfah*) in grammar, and the comic uses to which al-Shirbīnī puts it, see n. 194. In this passage, al-Shirbīnī focuses on another aspect of "annexation," namely, that the first noun, being definite by virtue of its position in the construction, may not end in *tanwīn* ("nunation," the endings *un*, *an*, *in*, from *nūn*, name of the letter *n*), the sign of the indefinite noun.

410 "puzzle word" (*muʿammā*): a form of riddle "solved . . . by combining the constituent letters of the word or the name to be found" (G. J. H. van Gelder, "Muʿammā," in *EAL*).

411 See above n. 108.

412 *Ṭāfiyah* is apparently a colloquial metathesis of literary *ṭāʾifah*; on al-Shirbīnī's deconstruction of the word, see n. 109.

413 I.e., take the word خذ ("take"), omit the dots above the letters so that it becomes حد and insert, in the empty (*fārigh*) space between the two letters, the word ما ("water" with omission of final *hamz*), and you get حماد (Ḥammād).

414 The name Shaḥātah (شحاته) (literally "begging") is explained as consisting of شُح ("avarice, miserliness"), followed by ا (the letter *alif*, the word *wālif* being interpretable as either equivalent to *wa-alif* ("and an *alif*") with elision of the glottal stop for the meter, or as an active participle meaning "friendly, familiar"), and finally by the letters ت and ه, together forming تِه, masculine singular imperative of the verb تاه "to lose one's way"; thus شحاته = ته + ا + شح.

415 Here it is the shapes and not the sounds of the letters that unlock the sense: thus, the name أحمد (Aḥmad) is envisioned as consisting of a ben tree (the أ), beneath which a worshipper bows down (the letter ح in its initial form حـ), while clasping a pearl (the

letter م in its medial form ـمـ), which is displayed (literally, suspended) in a bird's beak (the letter د).

416 I.e., instead of the formal reflex *hādhāka*; cf. n. 301.

417 See vol. 1, n. 258.

418 In fact, while all these "facetious plurals" share the root *kh-b-z*, the first two have no clear meaning, while the third means "bakers" and has no clear semantic connection to *khubbayz*; and, in fact, *khubbayz*, as a collective or mass noun, is unlikely to form a plural.

419 In other words, the word should be read in the verse as *khubbayza* (= *khubbayzah*, a feminine noun), which is in fact the standard colloquial form; however, in inscribing the verse, the author has disguised the colloquialism by pretending that the *a* represents the literary accusative ending.

420 Al-ʿAynī built the ʿAyniyyah *madrasah* in Cairo (still standing, opposite the house of Zaynab Khātūn, behind al-Azhar) but died before the Mamluk sultan Qāyitbāy came to power in 872/1468; there is no evidence that he ever lived in Dimyāṭ. A unique feature of the ʿAyniyyah was the Anatolian glazed-tile mosaic (destroyed during restoration in 1980) of the prayer niche, and this may explain al-Shirbīnī's characterization of the mosque; Ibrahim and O'Kane note that al-ʿAynī, who was originally from ʿAyntāb (modern Gaziantep) in southeastern Anatolia, "may have tried to underline his non-native origins by stylistic means, in order thus to stress his affinities with the ruling class" (Ibrahim and O'Kane, "Madrasa," 268).

421 The cotton teaser prepares cotton for stuffing mattresses, etc., or renews it after it has become compressed from use, by pulling a handful of cotton against the wire "string" of his bow and then releasing the string, thus fluffing the cotton. He usually works very fast, and it is the speed with which he grabs, processes, and crams the wool into the mattress that suggests the figurative use of the verb.

422 According to a *ṣaḥīḥ* ("sound," i.e., accurate and reliable) Tradition, these words were spoken by the Prophet to encourage his weary and hungry followers on a cold day as they dug the earthwork that allowed the Muslims to defend Medina and defeat the Meccans at the Battle of the Ditch (al-Bukhārī, *al-Ṣaḥīḥ*, *TIF*, 2871).

423 *Nadīf*, verbal noun of *anduf*, relates to the latter as *tajrīf* to *yujarrif* in the earlier use of the same construction; see n. 385.

424 See al-Shaʿrānī, *Laṭāʾif*, 668.

425 On the dropping of *-an*, see n. 385; al-Shirbīnī's assertion that the word نديف is to be read here as a diminutive, i.e., *nudayf*, "for the sake of the rhyme" is puzzling, since other line-final syllables *must* be realized as *-īf*; see, for example, *yaḥīf* in the third line (there being

no verbal form *yuḥayf*), and *līf* in the fourth line (there being no word **layf*). If it is contended that *īf* is an acceptable near-rhyme for *ayf* and that all rhyme words capable of taking a diminutive form should be treated as diminutives (e.g., one should read *nuḥayf* for *nuḥīf* in the opening line) and that, despite the difficulties (e.g., verbal nouns such as *nadīf* do not normally form diminutives), al-Shirbīnī's assertion that *ayf* is the default rhyme nevertheless remains entirely arbitrary, because these forms are identical metrically; thus the assertion has been ignored on the grounds that it probably represents no more than comic obfuscation.

426 The glottal stop with which first-person singular imperfect verbs begin is frequently elided when preceded by an open syllable in modern Egyptian (Mitchell, *Introduction*, 36); similar forms occur elsewhere in the Ode: *wa-hurru* (§11.6), *wa-baṭṭiṭu* (§11.21), *wa-bīʿū* (§11.37), and, again, *wa-luffū* (§11.38). As usual, al-Shirbīnī's presentation of the standard colloquial form as though it were a literary form adapted for the sake of the meter is unconvincing (see vol. 1, pp. xxxvi–xxxvii).

427 On such intensifiers, see n. 385.

428 *wa-baṭṭiṭu, wa-ḍarriṭu, wa-barbiṭu*: these three words are written in the manuscripts without initial *alif*, thus signaling the same elision described in the case of *w-aluffu* above (§11.20.5).

429 The basic sense of *ṭaḥīn* as a concrete noun is "flour," but the word is also used in the countryside to refer to harvested wheat as a foodstuff stored in the house to be ground as needed; the essence of al-Shirbīnī's question seems to be "What is the connection between a change in the nature of a thing and a change in its name?" Throughout the passage, al-Shirbīnī mimicks and perhaps mocks the concerns and language of scholastic theologians and philosophers.

430 The feast with which Ramadan ends.

431 *Maṭyab* and *maḥsan* (in the following line) are colloquialized forms *mā aṭyaba* and *mā aḥsana*, "verbs of surprise or wonder" (*afʿāl al-taʿajjub*), and the particle *a-yā* clearly is used here in an exclamatory sense to reinforce this usage; however, al-Shirbīnī insists on interpreting the particle as though it is being used in its more usual vocative sense, and so supplies a missing addressee, "people."

432 Perhaps *Zahr al-kimām fī qiṣṣat Yūsuf ʿalayhi l-salām* (*The Flowers in the Calyces on the Story of Yusuf, Peace Be upon Him*) by the mystic Ibrāhīm ibn Yaḥyā al-Awsī (687–751/1288–1350) (cf. *GAL*, 2:265, *Suppl.*, 2:377–78).

433 The celebrated treatise *Al-Qānūn fī al-ṭibb* (*The Canonical Work on Medicine*) by Ibn Sīnā (Avicenna). In his chapter on leprosy, Ibn Sīnā says, "If hot weather combines with bad food such as fish, jerked meat, coarse meats, donkey meat, or lentils, it is likely that leprosy will result, as happens frequently in Alexandria" (*Al-Qānūn*, 3:612).

434 I.e., without the inflectional endings of literary Arabic.

435 Al-Shirbīnī uses the term farcically here, as there is no real connection between the supposedly corresponding items.

436 See §11.10.11 for more on palindromes.

437 This definition is not, in fact, that given above.

438 *ʿalā l-nadā*; literally "at the dew."

439 I.e., "he is generous," "he has no generosity," and "generosity is the companion of excellence."

440 Cf. n. 153.

441 See vol. 1, n. 258.

442 *ʿalā rukbah wa-nuṣṣin*: literally "on a knee and a half."

443 Al-Shirbīnī is wrong: the poet in fact (see next note) meant "Prepare yourself for action!" (see Ibn Manẓūr, *Lisān*, s.v. *h-m-m*).

444 The pre-Islamic ʿAbd al-Masīḥ ibn ʿAmr al-Ghassānī (see, e.g., Ibn Ḥamdūn, *Al-Tadhkirah*, 8:11).

445 Of the *shimār*, Lane says, "The full sleeves . . . are sometimes drawn up, by means of a cord, which passes round each shoulder and crosses behind, where it is tied in a knot" (Lane, *Manners*, 32).

446 The form used in the verse is colloquial.

447 The literary reflex of the same word.

448 This parodies the *khuṭbat al-naʿt*, the second and more standardized of the two sermons delivered during the Friday prayer service, including all the main elements of the latter and much of its typical phrasing, and may be compared with Lane's translation of a sermon of this type from the second decade of the nineteenth century (Lane, *Manners*, 87–90). In both, the preacher begins with praise of God and His Prophet (Lane, 87: "Praise be to God, abundant praise, as He hath commanded . . ."; al-Shirbīnī: "Praise be to God, to whom for sure all praise is owed"), moves on to the exhortation and warning of the believers (Lane, 88: "O people, reverence God by doing what He hath commanded and abstain from that which He hath forbidden and prohibited"; al-Shirbīnī: "My people, why do I behold you of sweet rice with honey all unaware . . . . [H]ave nothing to do with foods that are coarse . . . ."), and moves via prayers for the victory of the ruler and the confusion of his enemies (Lane, 89: "Aid el-Islam . . . by the preservation of thy servant . . . our master the sultan . . . . O God, frustrate the infidels and polytheists . . . ."; al-Shirbīnī: "O God, bring us after dispersal all together, and grant victory, support, and safety to Sultan Sugar-Candy . . . And destroy, O God, the reprobates three . . .") to end with Q Anʿām 6:90 (Lane, 89: "Verily God commandeth justice . . . .

He admonisheth you that ye may reflect"; al-Shirbīnī: "He exhorteth you . . . that you may reflect").

449 I.e., the Kaaba, at Mecca.

450 The same words are attributed elsewhere to the pre-Islamic poet Taʾbbaṭa Sharrā and to Aḥmad ibn al-Ṭayyib al-Sarakhsī (d. 286/899) (van Gelder, *Dishes*, 109 and 151 n. 3).

451 On the topos of mutton as the lord of foods, see Finkel's discussion of a Mamluk *Rangstreit* pitting King Mutton against Sultan Sugar Cane; in the same article Finkel provides a translation of this passage from *Hazz al-quḥūf*. Goody, writing on Finkel's article, comments that "the conflict between meat and vegetables . . . is a class war" (Goody, *Cooking*, 133).

452 Q Hūd 11:61.

453 This parodies the "chain of authority" (*isnād*) that establishes the reliability of a Tradition; the names, some of which have occurred earlier, are either apparently meaningless (Sahlab, Mahlab, Zinṭāḥ) or comically absurd (Naṭṭāḥ "Head-Butter"; Qalīl al-Afrāḥ, "Having-Few-Joys").

454 Q Shuʿarāʾ 26:227; the same verse occurs in Lane's example (*Manners*, 88).

455 Compare Lane, *Manners*, 88: "O God, do thou also be pleased with the four Khaleefehs."

456 The fig and the olive are mentioned in Q Tīn 95:1 and the pomegranate in Anʿām 6:99 and elsewhere; the peach (*khawkh*) is not mentioned in the Qurʾan.

457 Compare Lane, *Manners*, 88: "And be Thou well pleased, O God, with the six who remain of the ten noble and just persons who swore allegiance to Thy Prophet Mohammad."

458 From *qirmiz* "cochineal," hence "the scarlet (dish)."

459 I.e., the Prophet Muḥammad.

460 Q Naḥl 16:90.

461 The poet was an unnamed cousin of Sharaf al-Dawlah, an ʿUqaylid ruler of Mosul (d. 453/1061) (see Ibn al-ʿAdīm, *Zubdat al-ḥalab*, 215).

462 I.e., Muḥammad ibn Saʿīd al-Būṣīrī (608/1213 to 694/1294–95) (see Glossary).

463 See al-Būṣīrī, *Dīwān*, 240.

464 The *ṭurṭūr* is a high, conical hat. A fatwa concerning the Muṭāwiʿah dervishes written in 1782 by Shaykh ʿAlī l-Ṣaʿīdī l-ʿAdawī refers to their wearing "palm leaf hats and *ṭarāṭīr* on which they put shells and feathers and bits of cloth, etc." (al-Ṭawīl, *Al-Taṣawwuf*, 1:85).

465 And thus resembles the end of a palm branch where it sprouts from the tree, another meaning of *qiḥf*. ʿĀlī Muṣṭafā, writing in 1599, describes the caps of the peasants as having "the shape of buckets emptied of their water" (Tietze, *Description*, 42).

466 "Un bonnet haut, couvert de drap et doublé de coton qu'on enveloppait d'un grand morceau de toile fine" (Raymond, *Artisans*, 1:325 n. 4).

467 From al-Shirbīnī's account, it seems that *libdah* (literally "(piece of) felt") was a generic term; that the *qaḥf*, the *ṭurṭūr*, and the "*libdah* that resembles a European hat" were specific styles thereof; and that all the latter were associated with Sufis and had strong negative associations at the time al-Shirbīnī wrote, being considered outmoded and uncouth. Despite al-Shirbīnī's emphasis on the outmodedness of the *libdah*, the term was in use in the early nineteenth century to denote "a white or brown felt cap" worn under the tarboosh or, among the very poor, on its own (Lane, *Manners*, 32). The *libdah* that is still in use in Lower Egypt has the form of a roughly conical cap of coarse brown wool, though it is apparently now worn only by peasants, among whom it is the "signe de majorité et de respectabilité" (Berque, *Histoire*, 30).

468 See vol. 1, §7.41.

469 Abū Nuwās: these verses do not occur in his collected works, and the attribution is dubious.

470 "furrow": i.e., "[are used to] plow," etc.

471 I.e., "and do not abuse him by reference to the latter and say to him 'you buffalo-cow' (*yā jāmūsah*)!"

472 Today an "earthenware tub for kneading dough, similar to a *maguur* . . . but smaller" (Hinds and Badawi, *Dictionary*, 796).

473 In fact, the literary rather than colloquial form of the same word, cf. *ṣalāt il-laqqān* "[Christian] ceremony of washing the feet" (Hinds and Badawi, *Dictionary*, 796).

474 In fact, the root of *yaluqqu* is *l-q-q*, while that of *laqqānah* is *l-q-n*.

475 I.e., he drops the glottal stop from the standard literary form *mal'ānah* (modern Egyptian *malyānah*).

476 A recipe is to be found in Khawam, *Cuisine*, 170. It resembles what today is called *mahallabiyyah* or *nisha*, i.e., blancmange.

477 The literary feminine singular relative pronoun.

478 The incident is recorded by both Yāqūt (*Udabā'*, 3:138) and Ibn al-Jawzī (*Al-Adhkiyā'*, 249). Yāqūt and Ibn al-Jawzī attribute the first fragment, attributed here to Abū l-ʿAtāhiyah, to ʿAlī ibn al-Jahm; that by al-Maʿarrī is from his *Saqṭ al-zand* (229).

479 The forenoon prayer is not compulsory and is performed from approximately half an hour after sunrise until midday.

480 Al-Shirbīnī implies that the name Waṭīf (root *w-ṭ-f*) derives from *ṭ-w-f* (root of *aṭwāf*, and also, below, *ṭawāf*) by metathesis.

481 See §11.9.6.

482 "Then enter the dome," etc: the comparison of the beloved's backside to a dome and the exploitation in the same context of the association of domes with buried holy men are commonplaces (see, e.g., vol. 1, §5.2.16).

483 A synonym of *laban*, in the latter's primary sense.

484 The substitution of *ghalw* for *ghaly* is also a solecism, in that the former belongs to the root *gh-l-w*, which denotes "exceeding normal limits, becoming expensive," etc., whereas it is the latter, which belongs to the root *gh-l-y*, that denotes "boiling."

485 See references to *khubz* above, §§11.19.3, 11.19.7.

486 I.e., because it is diminutive and hence hypercoristic.

487 Cf. Abū Nuwās, *Dīwān*, 3:126.

488 Ibn al-Fāriḍ, *Dīwān*, 343; the following line reads "That my hearing may witness the one I love, should he remain aloof, his phantom conjured by those words of blame, rather than by dreams."

489 From the description, *mafrūkat al-laban* resembled today's *Umm ʿAlī*, which is a "dessert of filo pastry, raisins and butter cooked in hot milk" (Hinds and Badawi, *Dictionary*, 37), but cf. *mafrūkah*, "type of fine maize couscous, usually eaten with milk and sugar" (ibid., 653, specified as rural).

490 See n. 385.

491 Though included in Ibn al-Fāriḍ's collected works (p. 380), these lines are attributed more authoritatively to Bahāʾ al-Dīn Zuhayr (581–656/1186–1258) (see Zuhayr, *Poetical Works*, 107 transl. 124, and al-Muḥibbī, *Nafḥat al-rayḥānah*, 4:368).

492 *fatt*; here and in the discussion that follows, Shirbīnī uses *fatt* and *taftīt* interchangeably to designate the dish that is today called *fattah* (cf. Hinds and Badawi, *Dictionary*, 638 "dish, consisting of hot broth or the like . . . poured over crumbled bread"; *fattit ʿads* "bread in lentil soup," etc.).

493 See §11.19.2.

494 See §11.27.2.

495 Q Muṭaffifīn 83:1; thus the verb *ṭaffafa*, of which *taṭfīf* and *muṭaffif* are, respectively, the verbal noun and active participle, has two contradictory senses (cf. Lane, *Lexicon*, 857).

496 What follows is a summary of the account of the martyrdom of al-Ḥusayn ibn ʿAlī Ṭālib (d. 61/680), grandson of the Prophet, as given in *Al-Kawākib al-durriyyah fī tarājim al-ṣūfiyyah* (1:100–104) by ʿAbd al-Raʾūf ibn Tāj al-ʿĀrifīn ibn ʿAlī ibn Zayn al-ʿĀbidīn ibn Yaḥyā ibn Muḥammad al-Munāwī (952–1031/1545–1621), a leading religious scholar and Sufi of the day. The work is also known as *Ṭabaqāt al-Munāwī* (*al-Munāwī's Biographical Dictionary*), and it is under this title that al-Shirbīnī introduces a direct quotation below. It is difficult to understand al-Shirbīnī's reasons for including this long, serious digression; conceivably the answer lies in the reference at the end of the passage (§11.31.14) to a difference of opinion concerning the resting place of al-Ḥusayn's head in Cairo, which implies that the issue was of concern to his contemporaries.

497 I.e., Sulaymān ibn Aḥmad al-Ṭabarānī (260–320/873–971), a leading compiler of collections of Traditions (al-Ziriklī, *Al-Aʿlām*, 3:121), though this excerpt was not found.

498 Al-Munāwī, *Al-Kawākib*, 1:102; see n. 496.

499 From al-Ṭabarānī, with minor differences (al-Ṭabarānī, *Al-Muʿjam*, no. 2814).

500 Ibn Saʿd, *Al-Ṭabaqāt*, 6:419, with differences.

501 Abū Yaʿlā, *Al-Musnad*, 2:176.

502 Abū Nuʿaym: probably Abū Nuʿaym al-Iṣfahānī (d. 430/1038), author of *Ḥilyat al-awliyāʾ*, is meant, but this story was not found there.

503 The tenth day of the month of Muharram, observed as a voluntary fast; hence the date of al-Ḥusayn's martyrdom was, according to the Gregorian calendar, October 10, 680.

504 I.e., the caliph Yazīd (r. 60–64/680–683).

505 Q Kahf 18:9.

506 Al-Shirbīnī refers presumably to al-Mashhad al-Ḥusaynī, or Jāmiʿ al-Ḥusayn, near al-Azhar mosque, which remains one of Cairo's most important shrines; however, al-Ṣāliḥ Ṭalāʾiʿ originally intended the mosque that bears his name and stands outside Bāb Zuwaylah to serve this purpose.

507 Apparently a noncanonical version of the "sound" Tradition that says, "No contagious disease, no evil omens, and the righteous augur—the fair word—pleases me." The sense would seem to be that all events, including illness, are to be attributed to God's direct intervention and not to other natural or supernatural forces.

508 Al-Shirbīnī repeats himself, seemingly having forgotten that he has already introduced the phrase.

509 Abū l-ʿAbbās Aḥmad ibn ʿAlī al-Būnī (d. 622/1225) was an influential writer on the esoteric sciences, with numerous works to his name, including many that are pseudonymous. The source of this quotation has not been identitifed.

510 "ewe": in the Arabic, *faṣīl* ("young camel"), a word also meaning "gap, divide"; for further similar anecdotes, see van Gelder, *Dishes*, 41.

511 I.e., *Mawāqiʿ al-nujūm wa-maṭāliʿ ahillat al-asrār wa-l-ʿulūm* (*GAL*, 1:443, *Suppl.*, 1:795 (19)).

512 On the depiction by Arab historians of the Umayyad caliphs as gluttons, see Van Gelder, *Dishes*, 26–27.

513 Al-Walīd was a famous bacchic poet; for these lines, see al-Walīd, *Shiʿr*, 45.

514 Q Ibrāhīm 14:15.

515 The name is given to several dishes (see van Gelder, *Dishes*, 70, and Rodinson, "*Maʾmūniyya* East and West").

516 *fisīkh*: use of the colloquial form here (versus *fasīkh*) seems justified in view of the etymology that al-Shirbīnī gives below.

517 Q Zukhruf 43:71, referring to Paradise.

518 See vol. 1, §5.2.2.

519 Q Dukhān 44:29.

520 Nuṣayb ibn Rabāḥ (d. ca. 108/726) (see, with differences, *Shiʿr Nuṣayb ibn Rabāḥ*, 130).

521 In fact the roots are unrelated: *b-k-y* "to weep," *b-k-k* "to ooze, exude."

522 See vol. 1, §5.2.2.

523 See §11.18.5.

524 I.e., drinks, as pigeons do, by sipping with their heads lowered, and not as do most other birds, which raise their heads and let the water run down their throats.

525 I.e., the Citadel of Cairo, on which work was initiated by Ṣalāḥ al-Dīn (Saladin) beginning in 1176. In al-Shirbīnī's day, the Citadel housed the Ottoman governor, various administrative offices and functional establishments, including the mint, and the barracks of two of the seven military corps stationed in Egypt (the Janissaries and the ʿAzab) (Raymond, *Artisans*, 1:1, 2, 10, 26).

526 These large structures, consisting of one or more conical towers several meters high, remain prominent features of the rural landscape.

527 "waterwheel jars" (*qawādīs*): Hinds and Badawi, *Dictionary*, 690, illus. 975.

528 Cf. Q Nūr 24:60.

529 "As for the number of visitors to a modestly sized bathing establishment, for the Ottoman period this has been estimated at between fifty and sixty people a day" (Warner, "Taking the Plunge," 51–52).

530 The employment of beardless boys in bathhouses was discouraged but widespread (Warner, "Taking the Plunge," 62).

531 In reality, the roots are *ḥ-w-m* and *ḥ-m-m*, respectively.

532 Q Ḥajj 22:19.

533 Q Ghāfir 40:18.

534 "he is diminished" (*inkhafaḍa*): meaning also "he is pronounced with an *i*."

535 I.e., invariable colloquial *Abū* has been used instead of literary *Abī*.

536 See §11.26.10.

537 I.e., they dropped *bi-* and the genitive marker *-i* that should be attached to the noun (according to literary rules). The author should perhaps also mention that they dropped the definite article (*-l-*) and explain the presence of the *Abū* of *Abū Shaʿnīf*.

538 *shaʿnafah*: meaning unknown.

539 In the literary language, a verb may be followed immediately by its verbal noun for emphasis (see n. 148); *faṭāyir*, however, is not a verbal noun but, as the author goes on to state, the plural of *faṭīr*, a concrete noun. Al-Shirbīnī appears to be assimilating to the literary construction a different, distinct colloquial construction, which allows, at least

in a few set phrases, the use of a concrete noun of the pattern CaCāyiC (such as *faṭāyir*) to similar effect, e.g., *ʿamal ʿamāyil* ("he did terrible things"). The expression *qashar qashāyir*, however, is his own, jocular, invention.

540 Properly speaking, *faṭāyir* is the plural of the unit noun *faṭīrah* and means "pieces (or cakes) of *faṭīr*," while *faṭīr* is a collective/mass noun and means "many-layered flaky pastry" in general. Similarly, *khamīr* is a mass noun and *ḥamīr* a simple plural.

541 Abū Qays ibn Rifāʿah (a contemporary of the Prophet Muḥammad; dates unknown).

542 A misquotation of a line usually attributed to the mystic poet al-Ḥusayn ibn Manṣūr al-Ḥallāj (244–309/857–922): "I am the one I love and the one I love is I / We are two souls incarnated in a single body" (see, e.g., Ibn Khallikān, *Wafayāt*, 2:141).

543 From his *Tarjumān al-ashwāq*, 42 (translation 139).

544 The poet compares himself and his beloved to a *ḥarf mushaddad*, a doubled consonant represented by a single letter distinguished by a special sign (*shaddah*).

545 Locusts and fish are eaten without being ritually slaughtered (G.-H. Bousquet, "Dhabīḥa," in *EI2*); the description "dead or alive" here apparently alludes to their non-slaughtered status rather than implying that fish and locusts may be eaten alive; thus the meaning is equivalent too "in any (edible) state."

546 Presumably referring to the Ḥaydariyyah, an originally Iranian antinomian Sufi movement founded by Quṭb al-Dīn Ḥaydar, who died ca. 618/1221–22 (Karamustafa, *Friends*, 3); on the Ḥaydarīs in Mamluk Egypt, see Sabra, *Poverty*, 28–31.

547 Islamic law requires that, in order to clarify the paternity of any children she may be carrying, a woman must wait for a specified period following divorce or death before remarrying.

548 Transmogrification into a living creature would imply the waiting period at the end of which return to the original marriage is possible, i.e., that for divorce (three menstrual cycles); that into an inanimate object, the waiting period at the end of which return is not possible, i.e., that for death (four months and ten days).

549 Ibn al-Rūmī, *Dīwān*, 809 (lines 1–3); sometimes also attributed to Abū l-Ḥasan ʿAlī ibn Faḍḍāl (d. 479/1086) (e.g., al-Zamakhsharī, *Rabīʿ al-abrār*, 1:446).

550 These and the following verses do not appear in al-Shāfiʿī's collected works. "Little Dog" and "Frayed" are puns on two famous names from pre-Islamic lore, Kulayb ("Little Dog") and his brother Muhalhil ("Ragged"), nickname of ʿAdī (or Imruʾ al-Qays) ibn Rabīʿah, so called because "he made poetry ragged, i.e., thin" (*halhala l-shiʿr, ay araqqahū*) (see Ibn Qutaybah, *Al-Shiʿr*, 297), which is taken by some to mean that he wove poetry finely (see Thomas Bauer, "al-Muhalhil ibn Rabīʿa", in *EAL*); he is said to have been the first to compose a *qaṣīdah* ("a polythematic poem with identical meter and rhyme," ibid.).

551 "he also said": in fact the verses are by ʿAbd Allāh al-Ḥumayḍī al-Andalusī (d. 488/1095) (see, e.g., Ibn Khallikān, *Wafayāt*, 4:283).

552 Attributed to Muslim ibn Ibrāhīm Abū l-Faḍl al-Sulamī al-Bazzāz (d. 455/1063), known as al-Shuwayṭir, in al-Ṣafadī, *Al-Wāfī*, 25:549.

553 Q Ḥujurāt 49:10.

554 All three of the slave girl's quotations are from Q Āl ʿImrān 3:134.

555 No such saying is to be found in the Christian scriptures; the words are attributed to Jesus by Ibn Qutaybah (*ʿUyūn*, 2:268) in some later sources and to al-Ḥasan al-Baṣrī (21–110/642–728) by al-Jāḥiẓ (*Al-Bayān*, 3:164).

556 Al-Ghazzī, *Al-Zubdah*, 57.

557 The story is told by the poet's grandson, ʿAlī Sibṭ Ibn al-Fāriḍ, in his biography of Ibn al-Fāriḍ (see Homerin, *Ibn al-Fāriḍ*, 47).

558 Al-Shaʿrānī reports that Yūsuf al-ʿAjamī al-Kūrānī (d. 768/1367) "was in the habit of educating his novices by a strange method: He did everything to thwart their natural inclinations in order to break down their willpower" (Winter, *Society and Religion*, 93).

559 "the Feast of the Slaughtering" (ʿĪd al-Naḥr): i.e., the Feast of the Sacrifice (ʿĪd al-Aḍḥā).

560 In modern Egypt, the word appears to apply specifically to a room built on top of a house, hence the figurative sense in which the plural *ʿalālī* is used by al-Shirbīnī and still today (cf. Hinds and Badawi, *Dictionary*, 598).

561 *Fī* can be used with a variety of locative and other functions in addition to its basic sense of "in, inside." Thus, in the two phrases *fī l-tall* and *fī l-jabal*, the preposition is used in a more generalized sense than in the phrase *fī l-dār*.

562 A crisis arose between the Mamluk and Safavid empires in the autumn of 913/1507, when the Safavids invaded a Mamluk vassal state in southeastern Anatolia. For the verses, see Ibn Ṭūlūn, *Mufākahat al-khillān*, 288, and al-Ghazzī, *Al-Kawākib*, I/297 (the reply is not found in these sources).

563 See al-Muḥibbī, *Khulāṣah*, 1:106, where these lines are said to have been written on Nebuchadnezzar's sword.

564 I.e., to slaughter for the feast.

565 *Dhibbān* is the literary reflex of colloquial *dibbān*.

566 The last form is unattested in modern Egyptian.

567 Q Ḥajj 22:73.

568 I.e., *Laṭāʾif al-minan* ("The Subtle Blessings"); see al-Shaʿrānī, *Laṭāʾif*, 295.

569 I.e., the imperfect preformative is *yi-*, as in modern Egyptian, rather than *ya-*, as in literary Arabic.

570 I.e., *yaʿuffu*; al-Shirbīni is, however, misinformed: the literary imperfect of the verb in this sense is *yaʿiffu*.

571 Al-Shirbīnī omits the second word of the phrase (*bi-ḥālu* "all") from the commentary.

572 *Akhadhtuhu* is the literary reflex of *khadtū*.

573 I.e., by the Prophet Muḥammad, who ascended into the heavens on his Night Journey (*al-Isrā'*); see Q 17, Sūrat al-Isrā'.

574 I.e., Paradise, Riḍwān being the guardian thereof. However, the reference is made even more apt by the fact that a park called the Garden of Riḍwān Bey existed and was "without peer in Cairo" according to Shalabī (*Siyāḥatnāmah*, 599).

575 I.e., the Prophet Muḥammad; see Q Qamar 54:1.

576 Shirbīn produced at least three distinguished scholars and Sufis before Yūsuf al-Shirbīnī's day, according to ʿAlī Mubārak (*Al-Khiṭaṭ*, 1:127–28): Muḥammad al-Shirbīnī, who lived on the eve of and predicted the Ottoman conquest (see al-Shaʿrānī, *Lawāqiḥ*, 2:118); Shams al-Dīn al-Khaṭīb al-Shirbīnī; and the latter's son ʿAbd al-Raḥmān ibn al-Khaṭīb al-Shirbīnī (al-Muḥibbī, *Khulāṣat al-athar*, 2:378).

577 "do not use it for its appointed purposes" (*wa-lam yaṣrifhā fī maṣārifihā*): the phrase evokes the *maṣārif al-zakāh*, i.e., the eight classes of alms recipient specified in Q Tawbah 9:60. Thus, the implication is that such nouveaux riches ignore their obligation to use their wealth to help those who are worse off.

578 "Divine Tradition": a communication to the Prophet by God that is not in God's precise words (and therefore not a part of the Qur'an).

579 These verses do not appear in his published works.

580 The relative merits of boys without and with beards are much debated in verse from Abbasid times, if not earlier; see, e.g. (for Abū Nuwās) Ibn Manẓūr, *Akhbār*, 9892.

581 The next three poems have already appeared (in different order) in al-Shirbīnī's earlier treatment of this theme, see vol. 1, §§7.39–40.

582 "another": the grammarian Muḥammad ibn Yūsuf ibn Ḥayyān al-Andalusī (d. 745/1344) (see al-Ṣafadī, *Al-Wāfī*, 5:273–74).

583 The first hemistich is by Abū Firās al-Ḥamdānī (320–57/932–68) (*Dīwān*, 34); see further vol. 1, n. 248.

584 Perhaps Fakhr al-Dīn Abū Bakr Muḥammad al-Ḥakkāk al-Ṣūfī (fl. 752/1351), a Syrian mystic (*GAL Suppl.*, 2:3).

585 On this rhetorical device, see vol. 1, n. 279; al-Shirbīnī means, jokingly, that "crone" and "virgin" occur in the opposite of chronological order.

586 Bashshār ibn Burd (ca. 95–167/714–784) (*Dīwān*, 4:117).

587 *The Westward Migration of the Banū Hilāl* (*Taghrībat Banī Hilāl*): one of the cycles of the *Sīrat Banī Hilāl* epic, which describes the movement of the originally Arabian Banū Hilāl tribe from Egypt to Tunis (see G. Canova, "Banū Hilāl, romance of," in *EAL*); parts of the epic are still recited in Egypt.

588 "Some say he used to teach . . . he knew . . . he possessed knowledge . . . he used to instruct . . .," etc: the basic sense of *ʿarīf* in common usage is "monitor in a school, who hears the students rehearse their lessons" (Lane, *Lexicon*, 2016). Al-Shirbīnī, however, exploits the tri-consonantal root *ʿ-r-f*, with its connotations of "knowledge" and "teaching" to string together a list of further, improbable, instructional roles for the *ʿarīf*, before getting around to this basic sense.

589 Q Māʾidah 5:38.

590 "if there is doubt (*shubhah*)": "In attempting to avoid as much as possible imposition of the severe *ḥadd* penalties . . . the jurists appealed to a prophetic Tradition instructing the believers to 'avert the *ḥadd* penalties by means of ambiguous cases'" (E. K. Rowson, "Shubha," in *EI2*).

591 The first line is by Abū l-ʿAlāʾ al-Maʿarrī (363–449/973–1058) (*Al-Luzūmiyyāt*, 1:391), the reply by ʿAlam al-Dīn al-Sakhāwī (d. 643/1245) (see al-Ṣafadī, *Al-Wāfī*, 7:110).

592 Amputation of the hand for theft is one of the *ḥadd* punishments, i.e., one of those specifically prescribed in the Qurʾan.

593 Al-Shirbīnī seems to imply that the two words are synonymous, though, in formal terms, *jāmiʿ* is more correctly applied to a large mosque used for collective prayer, while *masjid* is applied to a smaller mosque.

594 Typically, the worshipper removes his slippers on entering the mosque and places them near him while praying.

595 Major ritual impurity (*janābah*) is "caused by marital intercourse . . . [or] any *effusio seminis*" (Th. W. Juynboll, "Djanāba," in *EI2*), and one in this state cannot perform a valid prayer (*ṣalāt*), enter a mosque, or perform a number of rites.

596 Al-Būṣīrī was of rural origin and spent several years as a financial official in the Delta town of Bilbays.

597 A district called al-Rukn al-Mukhallaq ("The Perfumed Corner") lay south of Bāb al-Futūḥ (Raymond, *Marchés*, 86), and this street was probably located there.

598 "slippers as red as your face": apparently a popular joke, see vol. 1, §3.17.

599 Al-Būṣīrī plays with the colloquial expression *ʿala qafa min yishīl*, literally "on the necks of those who would carry them off," i.e., "there for the taking." On *qafā* ("back of the neck, nape") in insults, see vol. 1, n. 28.

600 Like other verses in mixed colloquial-classical style attributed to him by al-Shirbīnī, this is not included in al-Būṣīrī's works.

601 Al-Būṣīrī puns on *dukhūl*, literally "entering" but used here in the specialized sense of "fine singing, singing in tune," and its opposite, *khurūj* ("exiting; singing out of tune").

602 See Ibn Khallikān, *Wafayāt*, 2:98ff.

603 In Iḥsan ʿAbbās's edition of Ibn Khallikān, the name of this otherwise apparently unknown individual is given as Jamāl al-Dīn Maḥmūd ibn ʿAbd Allāh *al-Irbilī*. He may be Jamāl al-Dīn Muḥammad ibn ʿAbd Allāh al-Badīhī, man of letters, poet, and musician, who died in Cairo in 656/1258 and was therefore a contemporary of Ibn Khallikān (see al-Ṣafadī, *Al-Wāfī*, 26:275–76, where he is not called al-Irbilī but is said to have grown up in Mosul, which is not far from Irbil).

604 As al-Shirbīnī explains below, the verses exploit lines from a poem by Abū Nuwās that flatters the caliph by referring to the custom by which camels used to bring riders to a holy sanctuary, such as that at the Prophet's tomb in Medina, were released from further service. Thus the poet compares his visit to Ibn Khallikān's office to that of a poet to his master and a visitor to the Prophet's tomb in Medina, and he compares his stolen slippers to the now emancipated camel on which he made this pilgrimage. Abū Nuwās's verses are to be found, with some differences, in Abū Nuwās, *Dīwān*, 1:127.

605 I.e., if ʿIwaḍ is "recompense," as his name implies, for a pair of slippers, he can be no better than such himself.

606 *Muqaylī* is the diminutive of *maqlī* ("fried").

607 On this colloquial use of *laff* (literally "to wrap"), see §11.7.10.

608 See Marzolph and van Leuwen, *Arabian Nights Encyclopedia*, 1:405–6, where the story is described as belonging to "the core corpus" of the *Nights*.

609 I.e., with both Ibn ʿAbbās and his father, ʿAbbās.

610 The barber never does get around to saying how much of the day has elapsed, as his interminable sentence takes off in other directions.

611 The second month of the Hijri year.

612 Equivalent to AD 12 April 1352, though this was a Wednesday, not a Friday.

613 "the era of Our Lord Adam . . . of Alexander the Greek and . . . of the Persian reckoning": these three dating systems for the pre-Islamic period are described in some detail by al-ʿĀmirī (Rowson, "A Muslim Philosopher," 61–67). However, according to al-ʿĀmirī, the time elapsed between the creation of Adam and the first year of the Hijra (the era of Adam) amounts to either 6215 or around 4280 Persian years (depending on the method of calculation used) rather than the barber's 7000. The era of Alexander dates from the latter's arrival in Jerusalem (historically, 313), when he ordered the Jews to begin a new era, and thus the number of years elapsed before the Hijra should equal 935 years versus the barber's 320 years. The Persian era also dates from the creation of Adam.

614 Q Anbiyāʾ 21:7.

615 "the Aswan Mug" (*al-kūz al-aswānī*): Dozy (*Supplément* s.v. *kūz*) quotes Lane's comment in his translation: [the Aswan Mug] "seems to imply that the person thus named

was always like a mug, with open mouth, and insensible as flint to rebuke," referring to *aswānī,* meaning "flint."

616 Q Āl ʿImrān 3:134. The sense is completed in verse 136: "The reward of such will be forgiveness from their Lord," etc.; cf. the use of the same verse above (§11.35.13).

617 Q ʿAnkabūt 29:8.

618 Q Nūr 24:61.

619 A conflation of two lines by al-Zubayr ibn ʿAbd al-Muṭṭalib, uncle of the Prophet Muḥammad (see Ibn Sallām al-Jumaḥī, *Ṭabaqāt,* 205).

620 The names (which rhyme in the Arabic) are a mixture of the ordinary—though linked to low-status trades—such as ʿAkrashah, Saʿīd, Ḥāmid, ʿUkāshah, and the eccentric, such as Zaytūn ("Olives"), Big-Mouth (Dalīʿ al-Fāmī, presumably a distortion of *dalīʿ al-fam*), Salawṭaḥ (cf. *salṭaḥ* "to lie down flat, stretch out" (Hinds and Badawi, *Dictionary,* 509; cf. Lane, *Lexicon,* 1406 s.v. "islanṭaḥ")), Suwayd ("Little Black"), and Sheep-Larks (*Qunbur al-Khirfān*).

621 Kharā-Lḥas: i.e., Kharā Ilḥas (for the meter).

622 I.e., bright red.

623 Meaning, perhaps, that his wife is bound to get along somehow, and he need not worry about her himself.

624 Ibn Sabuʿ al-imām al-khaṭīb Abū l-Rabʿ Sulaymān al-Sabtī is mentioned by Ḥājjī Khalifah as the author of a work named *Shifāʾ al-ṣudūr* (Ḥājjī Khalīfah, *Kashf al-ẓunūn,* col. 1050); he is also quoted by al-Suyūṭī (*Al-Itqān,* 4:226) and mentioned several times by al-Damīrī (*Ḥayawān*).

625 The convention of ending a book with "miscellaneous anecdotes" is old, being present already in, e.g., al-Jāḥiẓ's *Mufākharat al-jawārī wa-l-ghilmān* (al-Jāḥiẓ, *Rasāʾil,* 4:125–38). Such anecdotes appear to have a structural purpose, touching on several of the themes of the book; in this case some are at the expense of grammarians, and the theme of disillusionment with the world, which recalls complaints of neglect with which the book opens, recurs.

626 Q Nisāʾ 4:86.

627 A less elaborate version of the same story appears in the *Kitāb al-Manẓūm wa-l-manthūr* of Aḥmad ibn Abī Ṭāhir Ṭayfūr (d. 280/893), where, however, the protagonist is a certain Salāmah ibn Fulayḥ and the caliph is al-Mahdī (Borg, "Lust," 158).

628 Zayd and ʿAmr (who makes an appearance below) are names used in examples of grammatical points memorized by schoolchildren, such as "ʿAmr struck Zayd," where ʿAmr stands for the subject of the verb and Zayd for the object; under this convention Bakr is usually the third actor, introduced when needed.

629 In Arabic, vowels are called *ḥarakāt* (literally "motions"); desinential inflection often consists of the addition of short vowels to the verb or noun.

630 "active participle" (*fāʿil*): meaning both "doer, actor" (in both the basic sense and that of "active partner in intercourse, fucker") and "active participle."

631 Al-Shirbīnī switches to the technical terminology of Qur'anic recitation, alluding to the *madd muttaṣil* (a long open vowel of two to six beats that links two words) and the *madd munfaṣil* (a long vowel occurring within a word and closed with a glottal stop) (see Nelson, *Art*, 25).

632 The "stranger" here is the food that has not been eaten, and the funeral is that held by his relatives for a man who has left his homeland and is presumed to have died (usually called "the prayer for the absent dead" (*al-ṣalāh ʿalā al-mayyit al-ghāʾib*)).

633 It is forbidden to sell meat from an animal that was not in healthy condition when slaughtered.

634 The utterance of the formula *bism illāh al-raḥmān al-raḥīm* ("In the name of God, the Merciful, the Compassionate").

635 The formula *ḥayya ʿalā l-ṣalāh ḥayya ʿalā l-falāḥ* ("Come to prayer! Come to prosperity!"), which occurs in the call to prayer; it is not, however, supposed to be used when slaughtering.

636 I.e., the Kaaba.

637 Q Naḥl 16:7.

638 Q Ḥijr 15:46; the reference in the original context is to the gardens of Paradise.

639 The incident is reported in various sources, with minor differences and with the verses from which these lines are extracted attributed to various poets (see, e.g., al-Khaṭīb al-Baghdādī, *Tārīkh*, 14:196; al-Masʿūdī, *Murūj*, 4:23).

640 al-Ḥarīrī: these lines are not found among al-Ḥarīrī's works, and the attribution is dubious.

641 al-Būṣīrī: these lines are not found among al-Būṣīrī's works, and the attribution is dubious.

642 "a pipsqueak that from the beaten path departs" (*ka-l-ziblati fī l-tayyār*): the line is reminiscent of the modern saying *ziblah wi-tqāwiḥ it-tayyār* (literally "a dung pellet, and it goes against the stream"), meaning "he's a nobody and he's out to change the world" (Hinds and Badawi, *Dictionary*, 365).

643 A variant of the name Muḥammad.

Glossary

ʿabāʾah "a long, wide garment made of wool with different-colored stripes, which the country people use as something to lie on in summer and as a cover in winter" (§11.7.10).

ʿAbd al-Malik (r. 65–86/685–705) fifth caliph of the Umayyad dynasty.

ʿAbd al-Wahhāb al-Shaʿrānī (897–973/1491–1565) a leading Egyptian Sufi of his time.

ʿAbd Qays an eastern Arabian tribe.

ʿAblah cousin and beloved of ʿAntarah (q.v.).

Abū l-ʿAtāhiyah Abū l-ʿAtāhiyah Ismāʿīl ibn al-Qāsim (131–211/748–826), a poet of Baghdad known for his pious and censorious verse.

Abū Ḥāmid al-Ghazālī (450–505/1056–1111), theologian, jurist, mystic, and religious reformer, author of *Iḥyāʾ ʿulūm al-dīn* (*The Revival of the Religious Sciences*).

Abū Ḥanīfah al-Nuʿmān (ca. 81–150/700–67), celebrated religious scholar of Iraq, after whom the Hanafi school of law is named.

Abū Nuʿaym Aḥmad ibn ʿAbd Allāh Abū Nuʿaym al-Iṣfahānī (336–430/948–1038), author of *Ḥilyat al-awliyāʾ wa-ṭabaqāt al-aṣfiyāʾ* (*The Adornment of the Saints and Classes of the Pure*), a biographical dictionary of early Islamic pious people, renunciants, and mystics.

Abū Nuwās Abū Nuwās al-Ḥasan ibn Hāniʾ al-Ḥakamī (ca. 130–98/ca. 747–813), one of the most famous poets of the Abbasid "Golden Age," especially in wine poetry and the love lyric. Though Abū Nuwās spent his most brilliant years in the service of the caliph al-Amīn, popular imagination has linked him with Hārūn al-Rashīd, al-Amīn's father. This popular Abū Nuwās is also the focus of numerous comic or instructive anecdotes.

Abū Ṣīr name of several villages, the one in the central Delta, on the eastern bank of the eastern branch of the Nile, probably being the one referred to in *Brains Confounded*.

Abū ʿUbaydah Abū ʿUbaydah Maʿmar ibn al-Muthannā (d. 209/824–25), philologist and historian of pre-Islamic and early Arabic history and culture.

Abū Yaʿlā Abū Yaʿlā Aḥmad ibn ʿAlī ibn al-Muthannā al-Mawṣilī al-Tamīmī (d. 307/919–20), an early and highly reputed transmitter of Traditions.

Ād and Thamūd ancient tribes of Arabia, both mentioned in the Qurʾan as having been wiped out by disasters in punishment for misdeeds (in ʿĀd's case, by a violent storm (Q Aʿrāf 7:65, Hūd 11:58, etc.) or a drought (Q Hūd 11:52), in Thamūd's by an earthquake (Q Aʿrāf 7:78) or a thunderbolt (Q Fuṣṣilat 41:13, 17)).

ʿAdnān according to traditional Arab genealogy ʿAdnān was the ancestor of the Northern Arabs, that is, those who inhabited the Hijaz and Najd and spoke Arabic proper, as distinct from the Arabs of the Yemen, who descended from Qaḥṭān and spoke a related language. Both ʿAdnān and Qaḥṭān descended from Sām ibn Nūḥ (Shem son of Noah).

Aḥmad al-Sandūbī Aḥmad ibn ʿAlī al-Sandūbī (d. 1097/1686), a scholar and teacher at al-Azhar (see vol. 1, p. xii).

ʿĀʾishah bint Abī Bakr (d. ca. 58/677–78) the favorite wife of the Prophet Muḥammad.

ʿAlī (ibn Abī Ṭālib), the Imam first cousin and son-in-law of the Prophet Muḥammad and fourth rightly guided caliph (d. 40/661). A highly venerated figure among Sunni as well as Shiʿi Muslims, he has become the attributive source of a vast number of maxims. None of the four sayings attributed to ʿAlī in this work is to be found in the standard collections.

Aʿmash, al- Abū Muḥammad Sulaymān ibn Mihrān al-Aʿmash (60–148/679–765), traditionist and transmitter of one of the fourteen canonical readings of the Qurʾan.

Amīn, al- al-Amīn Muḥammad (170–198/878–813), a son of Hārūn al-Rashīd; as a full-blooded Hashemite (descendant of the Prophet's ancestor Hāshim), he succeeded to the caliphate on the latter's death but was later overthrown by an older brother, al-Maʾmūn ʿAbd Allāh, the son of a slave.

Anṣinā Antinoe, in the district of Mallawī, near Asyūṭ, site of the tomb of Antinous, favorite of the Roman emperor Hadrian, who drowned nearby.

ʿAntar see *ʿAntarah.*

ʿAntarah (or ʿAntar) ʿAntarah ibn Shaddād al-ʿAbsī (fl. second half of the sixth century AD); pre-Islamic poet and hero of the folk epic *Sīrat ʿAntar*.

antithesis (muqābalah, ṭibāq) technically *muqābalah*, refers to a compound form of antithesis in which "there is more than one term on each side of the antithesis" (W. P. Heinrichs "Rhetorical Figures" in *EAL*, 2:659, s.v. *muṭābaqah*), whereas *ṭibāq* refers to "the inclusion of two contraries in one line or sentence" (ibid.); al-Shirbīnī, however, seems to use *ṭibāq* as a synonym of *muqābalah*.

ʿArab a woman's name, used conventionally for the Beloved.

ʿAshūrāʾ the tenth day of the month of Muḥarram, observed as an optional fast and celebration.

Aṣmaʿī, al- Abū Saʿīd ʿAbd al-Malik ibn Qurayb al-Bāhilī al-Aṣmaʿī (122–213/740–828?), the most celebrated of the early philologists and collectors of Bedouin poetry and language.

ʿAsqalān a city in southwestern Palestine, now called al-Majdal.

aṭwāf courses of dung cakes laid in a spiral; a fire is lit inside the resulting igloo-like structure to dry out the dung in preparation for its use as fuel.

ʿawāʾid ("customary dues") gratuities paid to officials in return for the performance of various services and counted among the *maẓālim* (q.v.) (see Raymond, *Artisans*, 1:124 and passim).

ʿawnah, al- see *corvée*.

ʿAynī, al- Abū Muḥammad Maḥmūd ibn Aḥmad ibn Mūsā Badr al-Dīn al-ʿAynī (762–855/1361–1451), Mamluk scholar and bureaucrat.

ʿayniyyah a poem with *ʿayn* as rhyme consonant.

Azhar, al- the mosque of al-Azhar: founded in 361/972, the mosque became Egypt's preeminent institution of learning (sometimes referred to as a mosque-university) during the Ottoman period (vol. 1, p. xxxix).

Bāb al-Naṣr "The Gate of Victory," a gate in Cairo's northeast city wall.

Bāb Zuwaylah Cairo's eastern gate, at the end of al-Ghūriyyah street, named after the Berber tribe al-Zawīlah, who were quartered nearby when the gate was built by the Fatimids in 485/1092.

Badawī, Aḥmad al- (596/1199–1200 to 675/1276), a widely venerated saint whose shrine is at Ṭanṭā, in the Delta, eponym of an antinomian, largely rural socio-mystical movement, the Aḥmadiyyah (unrelated to the modern Pakistan-based Ahmadiyya movement).

Baḥīrā a monk encountered by the Prophet Muḥammad when he accompanied a trade caravan from Mecca to Syria as a boy; according to Muslim tradition, Baḥīrā recognized the Prophet's status, while, according to the

Arab and Greek Christian traditions, he "became [Muḥammad's] inspirer and involuntary accomplice . . . in the composition of the Qur'an" (A. Abel, "Baḥīrā," in *EI2*).

bailiff (shādd and *mashadd)* a village official responsible for the maintenance of law and order and, in particular, for the payment by the peasants of their taxes.

Banū l-ʿAbbās the Abbasids, the descendants of the Prophet's uncle al-ʿAbbās ibn ʿAbd al-Muṭṭalib; they formed the third caliphal dynasty, taking power in 132/750.

Banū Umayyah the Umayyad dynasty, which ruled the Muslim world from 41/661 to 132/750.

Banū ʿUqbah a subtribe of Judhām/Judām (al-Maqrīzī, *Al-Bayān*, 18; Murray, *Sons*, 25).

Baqīʿ, al- the oldest Muslim cemetery in Medina.

Barmakī, Jaʿfar al- (150–87/767–803), member of the celebrated "Barmecide" family of leading officials at the court of Hārūn al-Rashīd.

basīsah a sweet pastry made with corn (maize) flour.

Basūs, War of al- the most famous of the *Ayyām al-ʿArab* ("Battle-days of the Arabs"), conflicts between tribes that provided the occasion for much of the heroic poetry of pre-Islamic Arabia.

bawshah according to al-Shirbīnī, the *bawshah* is a vessel used for cooking fava beans, wheat groats, and *bīsār* (q.v.); today, a rounded earthenware vessel for storing water, milk, clarified butter, etc. (Behnstedt and Woidich, *Glossar*, 40).

Bayn al-Qaṣrayn literally, Between the Two Palaces, a stretch of the street called al-Qaṣabah (today al-Muʿizz li-Dīn illāh Street); a main thoroughfare of medieval Cairo, originally a ceremonial ground between the Eastern and Western palaces of the Fatimids.

Birkat al-Fīl literally, the Pond of the Elephant, the second largest of the thirteen major ponds or lakes in Cairo in al-Shirbīnī's day (Shalabī, *Siyāḥatnāmah*, 374–75).

bīsār/bisārah fava beans mashed with *mulūkhiyyā* (Jew's mallow).

bisāriyah small fry of several species of Nile fish.

Blue Ocean and Piebald Canon, the (Al-Qāmūs al-azraq wa-l-nāmūs al-ablaq) a fictitious dictionary (see vol. 1, n. 127).

Brilliant Poem, the (Al-Badīʿiyyah) that is, *The Brilliant Sufficient Poem on the Sciences of Rhetoric and the Charms of the Badīʿ Style* (*Al-Kāfiyah al-Badīʿiyyah fī ʿulūm al-balāghah wa-maḥāsin al-badīʿ*), a poem in praise of the Prophet Muḥammad by al-Ṣafī al-Ḥillī (q.v.) that uses each of the major rhetorical tropes in turn.

Bukhārī, al- Abū ʿAbd Allāh Muḥammad ibn Ismāʿīl al-Bukhārī (194–256/810–870), renowned collector of Traditions, best known for his *Al-Jāmiʿ al-Ṣaḥīḥ* (*The Reliable Collection [of Traditions]*), a compilation of Traditions meeting the highest criteria of authenticity.

Būlāq the port on the Nile west of Cairo and separated from it, in al-Shirbīnī's day, by agricultural land.

Būlāq al-Takrūr a suburb of al-Jīzah (today called Būlāq al-Dakrūr).

Būnī, al- Abū l-ʿAbbās Aḥmad ibn ʿAlī ibn Yūsuf al-Būnī al-Qurashī al-Ṣūfī (d. 622/1225 in Cairo), a scholar of Maghribī origin and author of several books on the esoteric sciences.

Burdah, al- see *al-Būṣīrī.*

būrī a kind of gray mullet.

Būṣīrī, al- Muḥammad ibn Saʿīd al-Būṣīrī (608/1213 to 694/1294–95), a poet whose long panegyric of the Prophet entitled *The Mantle* (*Al-Burdah*) was immensely popular; few of the verses attributed to al-Būṣīrī by al-Shirbīnī are included in his published works.

carat (qirāṭ, pl. qarārīṭ) a twenty-fourth part; village lands were divided into lots, each equal to one twenty-fourth of the whole.

caudal paronomasia (jinās mudhayyal) repetition of homophonic elements (paronomasia) with the appendage of an additional dissimilar element, as in the saying *al-ʿār dhull al-ʿārif* ("Shame is the humiliation of the discerning") (al-Ḥillī, *Al-Badīʿiyyah*, 63).

Chosroes (Kisrā Anūshirwān; Persian Khusraw Anūshirwān*)* a Sassanid emperor (r. AD 521–79).

Christian of the village, the (naṣrānī l-balad) informal designation of the *ṣarrāf* (village tax collector), reflecting the dominance by Christians of the administrative and financial professions. ʿAbd al-Raḥīm states that the *ṣarrāf*'s functions included the assessment of the taxes (in terms of sown and fallow land, the latter being untaxed) and the assignment of the tax obligation on each parcel (ʿAbd al-Raḥīm, *Al-Rīf*, 43–46, 160); the *ṣarrāf* also maintained registers showing what each cultivator owed and how much each had paid.

Companions (of the Prophet) those Muslims who had contact with the Prophet Muḥammad during his lifetime. They are particularly honored as transmitters of Traditions.

copper piece (jadīd) see *silver piece (nuṣṣ).*

corvée, the (al-ʿawnah) compulsory labor on the tax farmer's demesne (*ūsyah/wisiyyah*); cf. *al-sukhrah.*

Damīrī, al- Kamāl al-Dīn Muḥammad ibn Mūsā l-Damīrī (745–808/1344–1405), author of several works on zoology, including a *Greater* and a *Lesser Life of Animals* (*Ḥayāt al-ḥayawān al-kubrā* and *al-ṣughrā*)—alphabetical encyclopedias listing etymologies of the names of animals, references to animals in the Qur'an, Traditions, and poetry, their uses in medicine, and so on.

Danaf, Aḥmad al- a popular archetype of robbers from early Islamic times who also appears as a leader of a band of forty rogues in *The Thousand and One Nights* (*Alf laylah wa-laylah*) and as the hero of a popular fifteenth-century romance, *Sīrat Aḥmad al-Danaf.* While his epithet is given by some scholars as *al-Danif,* meaning "the Sick," in Egypt today, where he remains a figure of the popular imagination, it is pronounced *al-Danaf,* possibly meaning "Sweetie-pie."

dārah a children's game of tag (see §§10.9, 11.19.5).

Day of Escape (yawm al-hurūbah) Lane, writing in the 1830s, says, in reference to urban weddings, "On the morning after the marriage . . . if the bridegroom is a young man, [a friend] generally takes him and several friends to an entertainment in the country, where they spend the whole day. This ceremony is called 'el-huroobeh' or the flight. Sometimes the bridegroom himself makes the arrangements for it; and pays part of the expenses, if they exceed the amount of the contributions of his friends; for they give nukoot [*nuqūṭ* 'gifts of money'] on this occasion. Musicians and dancing-girls are often hired to attend the entertainment" (Lane, *Manners,* 174).

Day of the Divine Decree (yawm al-qadr) more usually referred to as "the Night of the Divine Decree"; the night during Ramadan on which the Qur'an was first revealed to the Prophet; its precise date is not known, though it is generally taken to be that before the twenty-seventh day. Many believe that, on that night, those who are vigilant will be rewarded by having their prayers granted and their sins forgiven.

Dayr al-Ṭīn ("The Mud Monastery") perhaps the village of that name south of Old Cairo (Ramzī 1:77); see also *Ṣābūnī, Bridge of al-* below.

demesne (wisiyyah; also, in formal contexts, *ūsyah)* a private, tax-exempt grant of land sometimes made to a tax farmer in compensation for expenses occurred in the performance of his duties. The *wisiyyah* varied from one-quarter to one-half of the entire tax farm (ʿAbd al-Raḥīm, *Al-Rīf*, 96–100; Shaw, *Financial*, 22–23, 57–58).

dervish (faqīr, pl. fuqarāʾ) literally "poor man," that is, one who is "poor in God," a conventional term for a Sufi mystic; al-Shirbīnī uses the term mainly of mendicant rural dervishes.

dhikr literally "mentioning" or "naming" (of God), which, ritualized in various forms (with or without music, silently or audibly, accompanied, or not, by bodily movement), has become the central ceremony of most Sufi orders and groups.

Dimyāṭ Damietta, a town on the Mediterranean, at the mouth of the eastern branch of the Nile and, in al-Shirbīnī's day, Egypt's second city and its most important port for commerce with the eastern Mediterranean, handling the greater part of Egypt's rice exports (Raymond, *Artisans*, 1:166). Al-Shirbīnī's contemporary Wansleben says of it that, "Next to Cairo it is the greatest, most beautiful, the richest, the most populous, and the fullest of Merchants of all Egypt" (Wansleben, *Present State*, 67).

Dīrīnī, ʿAbd al-ʿAzīz al- (d. 697/1297–98), a Sufi reported to have been "possessed of magnificent states, noble conditions, famous miracles, and numerous written works, in the fields of commentary, jurisprudence, language, and Sufism, and much well-known verse . . . . His residence was in the countryside near Cairo" (al-Shaʿrānī, *Lawāqiḥ*, 1:172).

emir (amīr) "commander," a title given high-ranking military officers. By al-Shirbīnī's time, most tax farmers were emirs.

fālūdhaj a sweet dish made of wheat or starch with water and honey (Lane, *Lexicon*) or of almonds and sugar (Rodinson, *Recherches*, 149).

faqīh see *pastor*.

faqīr see *dervish*.

faqr see *poverty*.

Farazdaq, al- ("the Lump of Dough") nickname of the poet Hammām ibn Ghālib (d. 110/728 or 112/730).

farḍ ("duty") in Islam, "a religious duty or obligation, the omission of which will be punished and the performance of which will be rewarded" (Th. W. Juynboll, "Farḍ," in *EI2*).

Fātiḥah opening chapter of the Qur'an.

faṭīrah (pl. faṭīr, faṭāyir) a round or square of many-layered flaky pastry.

feddan (faddān, pl. fadādīn) a surface measure equal today to 4,200 square meters or 1.038 acres.

fiqī see *pastor*.

fisā l-kilāb a plant, "white pigweed"; literally "dog's fart."

foot soldiers (mushāh) the term *mushāh*, sometimes coupled with *jidʿān* ("brave lads"), appears to refer to the village's own armed forces, ready to take part in the raids and fighting for which the countryside was notorious.

Friend(s) of God see *God's Friends*.

ghafīr village guard or constable. "They prevented thefts and other crimes and gave warning of Bedouin attacks. They guarded the *multazim*'s [tax farmer's] house and the harvest and they watched the dykes to prevent their being tampered with out of season" (Rivlin, *Policy*, 29).

Ghawāzī, the a Gypsy group that traditionally makes its living from dancing and other entertainment.

Ghawrī, Qānṣawh al- (r. 906–22/1501–16), penultimate sultan of the Burjī Mamluk dynasty.

Ghuzz, the a term loosely applied, in al-Shirbīnī's time, to any troops of Turkic origin (from *Oğuz*, a group of Turkic tribes that moved west from Mongolia in the eighth century AD and were ultimately incorporated into the Muslim armies).

God's Friends, Friend(s) of God (wulāh, sg. walī) persons to whom God has vouchsafed esoteric knowledge "by transmission from Muḥammad, through a chain of elect masters, and also by direct inspiration" (Trimingham, *Sufi Orders*, 141, also 133–35).

ḥadd the *ḥadd* punishments are those specified in the Qur'an, including amputation of the hand for theft.

Ḥājj, al- title of a man who has made the pilgrimage to Mecca.

Ḥajjāj, al- al-Ḥajjāj ibn Yūsuf (41–95/661–714), Umayyad general and governor, famous for his harsh rule and chaste language.

Ḥākim bi-Amr Allāh, al- (r. 386–411/996–1021), sixth caliph of the Fatimid dynasty.

Ḥalabī, al- Nūr al-Dīn ibn Burhān al-Dīn ibn ʿAlī ibn Ibrāhīm ibn Aḥmad ibn ʿAlī ibn ʿUmar al-Qāhirī al-Shāfiʿī al-Ḥalabī (975/1567–68 to 1044/1635), author of a biography of the Prophet entitled *Insān al-ʿuyūn* (*The Pupil of the Eyes*), generally known as *Al-Sīrah al-ḥalabiyyah* (*Al-Ḥalabī's Biography*).

ḥālūm a kind of salted cheese.

hamziyyah a poem whose rhyme consonant is the letter *hamzah* (glottal stop, transliterated as ʾ).

ḥarām "forbidden by religion."

Ḥarām (tribe) see *Saʿd*.

Ḥarīrī, al- Abū Muḥammad al-Qāsim ibn ʿAlī l-Ḥarīrī (446–516/1054–1122), poet and man of letters, best known for his collection of fifty narrations in rhymed prose interspersed with verse (*maqāmāt*), in which he frequently uses puns and riddles.

harīsah "Any of a number of sweet confections made with flour, clarified butter and sugar" (Hinds and Badawi, *Dictionary*, 904).

Hārūn al-Rashīd (r. 170–93/786–809) fifth caliph of the Abbasid dynasty.

Ḥasan, al- (d. 49/669–70), older son of Fāṭimah, the Prophet Muḥammad's daughter and only surviving child, and of ʿAlī ibn Abī Ṭālib, the prophet's cousin; on his father's death, al-Ḥasan conceded the caliphate to Muʿāwiyah.

Ḥassān ibn Thābit Ḥassān Ibn Thābit ibn Mundhir al-Khazrajī al-Anṣārī (d. 54/674), a poet who supposedly lived sixty years before the coming of Islam and sixty years after the coming of Islam and was the Prophet's most prominent laureate.

Hijra the "migration" of the Prophet from Medina to Mecca; the Islamic (*hijrī*) calendar starts from the beginning of that year (18 July 622).

Hind a woman's name, used conventionally for the Beloved.

House of Binding, the (Dār al-Shadd) "a building which was maintained by the [bailiff] as a hotel for visitors in the village and as the headquarters of the *multazim* [tax farmer] and his agents. The *Fellahin* were provided with suitable quarters at the *Dar al-Shadd* until their accounts were settled, and the payments which they made in kind were stored there until they were disposed of" (Shaw, *Financial*, 55–56); the quarters would be for peasants from outlying villages under the authority of a single bailiff.

Ḥumaydī, al- ʿAbd al-Raḥmān ibn Muḥammad al-Ḥumaydī, a poet and physician and shaykh of the Cairo book trade. Although he does not give his dates, al-Khafājī (979–1069/1571–1659) includes him in his biographical dictionary of his contemporaries (al-Khafājī, *Rayḥānat al-alibbāʾ*, 2:114–16), and he would thus have been a (probably older) contemporary of al-Shirbīnī, who appears also to have been a bookseller (see vol. 1, p. xii).

Hurbayṭ a village, since disappeared, on the eastern branch of the Nile.

Ḥurr ibn Yazīd al-Tamīmī, al- a Muslim general sent by the caliph Yazīd to prevent the Prophet Muḥammad's grandson al-Ḥusayn from reaching al-Kūfah during the struggle over the succession to the caliphate following the death of Muʿāwiyah. Al-Ḥurr, however, joined al-Ḥusayn's forces and died with him on the battlefield.

Ḥusayn, al- (d. 61/680), younger son of Fāṭimah, daughter and only child of the Prophet Muḥmmad and wife of ʿAlī ibn Abī Ṭālib; following the death of the caliph Muʿāwiyah, al-Ḥusayn briefly contested the succession of the latter's son, Yazīd, and was killed in battle at Karbalāʾ, in Iraq.

Ḥusayniyyah, al- a residential neighborhood of Cairo, northeast of Bāb al-Futūḥ.

Iblīs Satan.

Ibn ʿAbbās ʿAbd Allāh ibn ʿAbbās (d. ca. 68/687–88), cousin of the Prophet, renowned as a recorder of Traditions, and a scholar of jurisprudence and Qurʾanic exegesis.

Ibn Abī Burdah, Bilāl (d. ca. 126/744), a judge and governor of Basra; of his approach to judging he said, "If two men come to me with a dispute, I decide in favor of the one I find the less tedious."

Ibn Adham Ibrāhīm Ibn Adham ibn Manṣūr (d. 161/778), seen by Sufis as a prototype and predecessor; Ibn Adham went bareheaded and barefoote gave his inheritance away, sought learning, fought the Greeks, and lived by the labor of his own hands.

Ibn Aktham, Yaḥyā (d. 242/857), chief justice of the Abbasid caliph al-Maʾmūn and representative in *adab* literature of the "supposed inclination of judges towards forbidden homosexuality" (Rosenthal, "Male and Female," 30).

Ibn al-ʿArabī Abū ʿAbd Allāh Muḥammad ibn ʿAlī ibn Muḥammad ibn al-ʿArabī al-Ḥātimī al-Ṭāʾī (560–638/1165–1240), one of the greatest exponents of metaphysical Sufism and author of several hundred works of prose and verse.

Ibn al-ʿĀṣ, ʿAmr (d. ca. 42/663), a Companion of the Prophet Muḥammad and one of his leading military commanders, who led the conquest of Egypt (19–21/640–42).

Ibn al-Fāriḍ ʿUmar ibn ʿAlī ibn al-Fāriḍ (576–632/1181–1235), a celebrated Sufi poet whose tomb "became a gathering place for all of Cairo's classes and, by the seventeenth century, a mosque for weekly worship unsurpassed in all of Egypt" (Homerin, *Ibn al-Fāriḍ*, 93). His verses remain popular today.

Ibn al-Khaṭṭāb, ʿUmar (r. 13–23/634–44), the second rightly guided caliph.

Ibn al-Mudabbir, Aḥmad (d. 270/884), director of finance (*ʿāmil al-kharāj*) in Egypt, under the Abbasid caliph al-Mutawakkil (r. 232–47/847–61); Ibn al-Mudabbir "introduced a number of new taxes . . . such as the one on cattle fodder . . . as well as the monopoly on caustic soda . . . . Hence he became the most hated director of finance for centuries" (Gottschalk, "Ibn al-Mudabbir," in *EI2*).

Ibn al-Rāwandī Abū Ḥusayn Aḥmad ibn Yaḥyā ibn Isḥāq ibn al-Rāwandī (fl. third/ninth century), a freethinker whose writings survive mainly as fragments in the works of his critics and are primarily concerned with the rejection of prophecy and of the intervention of the divine in the lives of men.

Ibn al-Zubayr ʿAbd Allāh ibn al-Zubayr (d. 73/692), prominent member of the ʿAbd Shams clan of the tribe of Quraysh and younger relative of the Prophet Muḥammad who, from Mecca, led an anti-Umayyad movement during the reigns of Yazīd and ʿAbd al-Malik.

Ibn ʿAmr al-Asadī, Minhāl a Kufan transmitter of Traditions.

Ibn ʿArūs a poet of quatrains with a moralizing tone and a distinctive, easily memorized rhyme scheme (ABAB) and rhythm, which still form part of the Egyptian folk-wisdom tradition and are sometimes sung to preface performances of the folk epic *Sīrat Banī Hilāl*. Sources differ as to the origins of Ibn ʿArūs (Qinā in Upper Egypt or Tunis; al-Shirbīnī refers to him as a "Pole of the Maghrib") and his dates.

Ibn Daqīq al-ʿĪd, Taqī al-Dīn probably intended is Taqī al-Dīn Muḥammad ibn ʿAlī ibn Wahb ibn Muṭīʿ (or Abī l-Ṭāʿah) al-Quṣayrī (or al-Qushayrī) al-Manfalūṭī (625–702/1228–1302), a scholar of Tradition, professor of jurisprudence, and, at one point, chief judge of Egypt, who was also a poet and the scion of a distinguished family of scholars with whom he bore the sobriquet Ibn Daqīq al-ʿĪd ("Son of Flour-of-the-Festival").

Ibn Durayd Abū Bakr Muḥammad ibn al-Ḥasan ibn Durayd al-Azdī (223–312/838–933), a central figure of the linguistic scholarship of his time and author of *Al-Qaṣīdah al-maqṣūrah*, a pedagogical poem on words ending in *-ā*.

Ibn Ḥajar Ahmad ibn ʿAlī ibn Ḥajar al-ʿAsqalānī (773–852/1372–1449), Egyptian Traditionist, scholar, biographer, and historian.

Ibn Khālawayh Abū ʿAbd Allāh al-Ḥusayn ibn Aḥmad ibn Khālawayh al-Hamadhānī (d. 370/980–81), eminent grammarian and litterateur.

Ibn Khallikān Aḥmad ibn Muḥammad Abū l-ʿAbbās ibn Khallikān (608–81/1211–82), celebrated biographer, author of the multivolume *Obituaries of Noted Men* (*Wafayāt al-aʿyān*).

Ibn Muqlah Muḥammad ibn ʿAlī Ibn Muqlah (272/856–57 to 328/904) systematized the six basic cursive scripts of classical Arabic calligraphy. He was three times vizier under the Abbasids and died in prison, having had one hand and his tongue cut off.

Ibn Saʿd ibn Abī Waqqāṣ, ʿUmar (d. 66/686), an Umayyad general and son of a well-known Companion of the Prophet.

Ibn Sūdūn ʿAlī ibn Sūdūn al-Bashbughāwī (810–68/1407–64), author of several verse and prose pieces, both serious and humorous, are collected in an anthology entitled *Nuzhat al-nufūs wa-muḍḥik al-ʿabūs*. Al-Shirbīnī quotes several of his verses and parodies, as well as a lengthy prose piece ("Funayn's Letter") from the anthology and refers to him as a source of his own inspiration (see vol. 1, p. xxii and §1.4).

Ibn ʿUmar ʿAbd Allāh ibn ʿUmar ibn al-Khaṭṭāb (10–73/613–692), son of the second caliph, noted for his piety and moral qualities.

Ibn Wāsiʿ, Muḥammad Muḥammad ibn Wāsiʿ ibn Jābir al-Azdī (d. 123/741), a traditionist of Basra.

Ibn Zāʾidah, Maʿn (d. 151/768), Umayyad and Abbasid governor, renowned for his generosity.

Ibn Ziyād, ʿUbayd Allāh (d. 67/686), Umayyad general, appointed governor of al-Kūfah by Yazīd in 60/679–80.

Imruʾ al-Qays Imruʾ al-Qays ibn Ḥujr, a poet of the sixth century AD, whose best known ode was one of those that, by tradition, are held to have been hung in the Kaaba at Mecca before the coming of Islam, and hence is known as his *muʿallaqah* ("suspended [ode]").

ʿInān (d. 226/841), a slave girl belonging to a Baṣran called al-Nāṭifī; she was renowned for the quickness of her repartee in verse, often displayed in joking contests with Abū Nuwās.

Inspector (kāshif, pl. kushshāf) official responsible for a minor province; the literal meaning of *kāshif* is "revealer, uncoverer." The duties of the Inspector in Ottoman Egypt consisted primarily of the maintenance of security and order, supervision of the exploitation of the land (including organization and monitoring of the irrigation system), and performance of imperial services (including payment of provincial garrisons and purchase of items required by the central authorities) (Shaw, *Financial*, 61). Wansleben comments that "a Cascief never ventures out in a Journy without a great train of Horse and Foot, and without expecting great matters" (*Present State*, 149), while Shalabī notes that the Nile flood cut them off from their districts during six months of the year, during which they appointed deputies, who traveled by boat to administer the areas (*Siyāhatnāmah*, 433) but that, "when the Nile recedes after three [*sic*] months leaving the land as mud, the peasants cast their seeds and put their feet on the land; then the hearts of the *kāshifs* and the officers and the tax-farmers are set at rest and they set off, with their troopers, to their provinces to sow their land" (idem, 434).

Inspector of Markets (muḥtasib) an official charged with the inspection of weights, measures, and prices and with maintaining public morality, who, as Lane noted in the Cairo of the 1830s, "occasionally [rode] about town, preceded by an officer who [carried] a large pair of scales, and followed by the executioners and numerous other servants" (Lane, *Manners*, 122).

inverted paronomasia (jinās maqlūb) that is, paronomasia in which the order of the homophonic elements is reversed, as in *āmālī* ("my hopes") versus *alāmī* ("my pains") (al-Ḥillī, *Al-Badīʿiyyah*, 67).

jawād a type of peasant shoe, synonymous, according to al-Shirbīnī, with *markūb* or *zarbūn* (kinds of slipper).

Jew's mallow see *mulūkhiyyā*.

Jibrīl the angel Gabriel.

Jisr, al- district on the western bank of the Tigris at Baghdad, opposite al-Ruṣāfah and originally connected to the latter by a bridge (*jisr*) of boats.

Jīzah, al- the settlement opposite Cairo on the west bank of the Nile (today usually spelled al-Guizah or Giza).

jubbah "long cloth coat of any color . . . , the sleeves of which reach not quite to the waist" (Lane, *Manners*, 30); it is open in front and usually worn over an under-robe.

Judām see *Judhām*.

Judhām (also Judām) a "Yemenite" (Qaḥṭānī) tribe that entered Egypt with the Muslim conquest and was present in the Delta (including the district of Hurbayṭ, close to Shirbīn) from at least the mid-eighteenth century. The name occurs three times in *Hazz al-quḥūf* to designate the opponents of the clan of Ḥarām and is thus apparently synonymous with Saʿd.

Juḥā protagonist of an enormous number of Egyptian (and other Middle Eastern) jokes and anecdotes, in which he often plays the role of the "wise fool."

Junayd, al- Abū l-Qāsim ibn Muḥammad al-Junayd (d. 298/910), a key figure in the development of the moderate Baghdad school of Sufism.

Kafr Dundayṭ a village in the district of Mīt Ghamr in the modern governorate of al-Daqahliyyah.

Kafr Hurbayṭ see *Hurbayṭ*.

Kalbī, Ḥakīm ibn ʿAyyāsh al- (fl. second/eighth century), Syrian poet, best known for his satirical verse.

Karbalāʾ a city about sixty miles south-southwest of Baghdad.

Khān of Abū Ṭaqiyyah, the complex of a depot, shops, and a hostelry built by the prominent merchant Ismāʿīl Abū Ṭaqiyyah (fl. 1580–1625), the remains of which can still be seen in Khān Abū Ṭaqiyyah Street, directly behind the Qalāwūn complex on Bayn al-Qaṣrayn (q.v.).

Khānkah, al- a town a few miles north of Cairo built around a Sufi hospice (*khānaqāh*) founded by the late seventh/thirteenth-century Mamluk sultan al-Malik al-Nāṣir Muḥammad ibn Qalāwūn.

kharāj land taxes; see also *māl (al-sulṭān)*.

Khawāmis, the name of the group that is the primary target of al-Shirbīnī's criticism of heterodox rural Sufi dervishes; vol. 1, p. xxx.

khayāl al-ẓill ("the shadow play") shadow plays, using leather cutouts on sticks held against a backlit screen, were popular entertainment, performed generally in colloquial Arabic with comic and often bawdy texts.

khushtanānak a sort of croissant made with butter and sugar and stuffed with almonds or pistachios.

kunāfah pastry made of vermicelli-like strands of dough, filled with pistachios or other nuts, and drenched in syrup.

kunyah a descriptive epithet consisting (for men) of the word *Abū* ("Father of") or (for women) of *Umm* ("Mother of"), followed by the name of the eldest son (in which case it is used as an honorific) or by a word denoting some characteristic of its bearer; thus, in the former case, a man with a son called Aḥmad may be known by the *kunyah* Abū Aḥmad (Father of Aḥmad), while, in the latter, the *kunyah* might also be translated as "He (or She) with . . . ," for instance, Abū Kirsh "The man with a (big) belly." Most of the *kunyah*s given by al-Shirbīnī are of the descriptive type, though not all of them yield a clear meaning.

kushshāf see *kāshif.*

kuttāb one-room school where children learn to recite the Qur'an, their ABCs, and arithmetic.

Lakhmī, Hishām ibn Ruqayyah al- Ibn ʿAbd al-Ḥakam (fl. third/ninth century), author of *Futūḥ Miṣr wa-akhbāruhā,* the earliest extant history of Islamic Egypt, drew on the reports of this person, who presumably accompanied ʿAmr ibn al-ʿĀṣ (q.v.) on the invasion of Egypt.

Laqqānah a village in the province of al-Buḥayrah, in the northwestern Delta.

lupine (turmus) the waxy yellow seeds of a leguminous plant of the genus *Lupinus*, still sold from street barrows as a snack.

Luqmān a legendary sage of pre-Islamic Arabia. Luqmān appears in the Qur'an (Q Yūsuf 12:31 and Q Raʿd 13:31) as a monotheist and a wise father giving advice to his sons and later became, in Islamic lore, the attributive author par excellence of wisdom literature.

Maʿarrī, Abū l-ʿAlāʾ al- Aḥmad ibn ʿAbd Allāh ibn Sulaymān Abū l-ʿAlāʾ al-Maʿarrī (363–449/973–1058), Syrian poet, prose writer, and skeptic.

Maḥallah (al-Kubrā), al- town in the central Delta and the center of Egypt's textile industry, in al-Shirbīnī's day as now.

Malik al-Ẓāhir Baybars, al- (r. ca. 658–76/1260–77), one of the greatest of the first (Baḥrī) dynasty of Mamluk sultans, Baybars conducted campaigns against several Christian states, including the Franks in Palestine and the Armenians.

Mālik, the Imam Mālik ibn Anas ibn Mālik ibn Abī ʿĀmir ibn ʿAmr al-Aṣbaḥī (d. 179/795), author of the earliest codification of Muslim law (the *Kitāb al-Muwaṭṭaʾ*) and founder of one of the four canonical schools of law.

Mallawī a town in Upper Egypt, south of al-Minyā.

mamluk a white male slave, generally from the Caucasus or neighboring regions. Most of these were destined to be trained as soldiers in the household of one of the major officers of the army or for the state.

Maʾmūn, al- (r. 198–218/813–33), seventh caliph of the Abbasid dynasty.

Manzalah, al- a town southeast of Dimyāṭ, on Lake Manzalah, on Egypt's northeastern coast.

maqāmah a composition belonging to a literary genre usually consisting of "collections of short independent narrations written in ornamental rhymed prose . . . with verse insertions, a common plot-scheme, and two constant protagonists: the narrator and the hero" (R. Drory, "Maqāma," in *EAL*).

maqṣūrah a poem rhyming in *-ā*.

marjūnah a storage basket.

Marqaṣ a village in the district of Shubrākhīt, al-Buḥayrah.

Marṣafah a village near Banhā, north of Cairo.

master (ustādh/ustād) title by which peasants address and refer to the tax farmer of their village.

matrad (pl. matārid) "a vessel of red pottery, smaller than the *shāliyah*" (§11.16.2); cf. modern Egyptian *matrid* "an earthenware vessel similar in shape to a *maguur* [kneading bowl]" (Hinds and Badawi, *Dictionary*, 810–11).

Māturīdī, Shaykh al- Abū Manṣūr Muḥammad ibn Muḥammad ibn Maḥmūd al-Māturīdī al-Samarqandī (before 260/873 to ca. 333/944), a Hanafi theologian, jurist, and Qurʾan commentator and founder of one of the main schools of Sunni systematic theology; his name refers to Māturīd, near Samarqand.

mawāliyā verse form characterized by colloquial features and consisting of four rhyming hemistiches in *basīṭ* meter.

maẓālim literally "injustices," unofficial levies that accompanied the creation of private, unofficial, tax farms on the backs of the official tax farms (Raymond, *Artisans*, 2/614–15) and that were "incessantly denounced, periodically abolished, but almost always re-instated" (ibid). Because most such levies were not catalogued or defined in the official tax registers (ibid, 135), the precise meaning of each is not always clear, and definitions in the secondary literature sometimes differ. Among the *maẓālim* were *ziyādāt al-kharāj* ("tax augmentations") (q.v.), *ʿawāʾid* ("customary dues") (q.v.), *maghārim* ("obligations"), and *kulaf* ("charges"). Ibrāhīm describes the resulting "tax accumulation" of these levies as absorbing much of the rural income and as one of the main causes of malnutrition among the rural population (Ibrāhīm, *Al-Azamāt*, 103, 126).

miḥrāb the recess in the wall of a mosque that indicates the *qiblah*, or direction of Mecca, which Muslims face when performing the five formal daily prayers.

minqalah "mancala," a game of the "sowing games" family.

mishammar a kind of *faṭīr*, or cake of flaky pastry, to be eaten with cream, honey, aged cheese, etc.

mishsh seasoned, milk-based liquid culture in which cheese is fermented.

muʿallaqah one of the seven odes that were, according to tradition, written on cloth in letters of gold and suspended in the sanctuary of the Kaaba in pre-Islamic Mecca and which, from early times, have been considered the best examples of pre-Islamic poetry.

Muʿāwiyah Muʿāwiyah ibn Abī Sufyān (r. 41–60/661–80), founder of the Umayyad caliphate.

mulūkhiyyā Jew's mallow (*Corchorus olitorius*), a leafy green vegetable.

Munāwī, ʿAbd al-Raʾūf al- ʿAbd al-Raʾūf ibn Tāj al-ʿĀrifīn ibn ʿAlī ibn Zayn al-ʿĀbidīn ibn Yaḥyā ibn Muḥammad al-Munāwī (952–1031/1545–1621), a leading religious scholar and Sufi of his time, author of the biographical dictionary of Sufis entitled *Al-Kawākib al-durriyyah fī tarājim al-sādah al-ṣūfiyyah*, also known as *Ṭabaqāt al-Munāwī*.

Muqawqis a title by which the Coptic patriarchs of Egypt were known to the Arabs and which, in Arab tradition, denotes "the individual who . . . plays the leading part on the side of the Copts and the Greeks at the conquest of Egypt" (K. Öhrnberg, "al-Muḳawḳis," in *EI2*).

muqaylī fried sprouted beans.

Mutanabbī, Abū l-Ṭayyib al- Aḥmad ibn al-Ḥusayn Abū l-Ṭayyib al-Mutanabbī (ca. 303–54/915–65), a renowned poet of the Abbasid age.

Muʿtaṣim, al- (r. 218–27/833–42), eighth caliph of the Abbasid dynasty.

Mutawakkil, al- (r. 232–47/847–61), tenth caliph of the Abbasid dynasty.

My Master (Sayyidī) title given eminent scholars and others, including those of earlier generations.

Nakhaʿī, Ibrāhīm al- Abū ʿImrān Ibrāhīm ibn Yazīd ibn Qays al-Nakhaʿī (50–96/670–715), a leading traditionist of his generation and authority for later jurists of various schools.

Nāṭifī, al- see *ʿInān.*

Nayrūz a major festival formerly celebrated on the first day of Tūt, the first month of the Coptic year, at about the height of the Nile flood; from Persian *nō rōz* ("new day").

Nifṭawayh literally "tar-complexioned," the nickname of Abū ʿAbd Allāh Ibrāhīm ibn ʿArafah ibn Sulaymān ibn al-Mughīrah ibn al-Muhallab ibn Abī Ṣufrah al-ʿAtakī al-Azdī (244–323/858–935), influential grammarian and philologist, whose works are mostly lost.

pastor (faqīh (colloquially fiqī), pl. fuqahāʾ) properly speaking, a *faqīh* is one learned in Islamic jurisprudence (*fiqh*). When speaking of the "ignorant *fuqahāʾ*" of the countryside, al-Shirbīnī seems to mean villagers who claim some learning (of dubious authority) and as such are the religious leaders of their villages. The anecdotes in the section "An Account of Their Pastors and of the Compounded Ignorance, Imbecility, and Injuries to Religion and the Like of Which They Are Guilty" (vol. 1, §4) imply that each village boasted one, who might also function as the village schoolteacher. Occasionally, *faqīh* is also used in its more formal sense.

Pillar of the Columns, the (in the text ʿĀmūd al-Ṣawārī, elsewhere usually spelled ʿAmūd al-Sawārī) a red granite column on what were, in the seventeenth century, the outskirts of Alexandria; it was popularly supposed to mark the tomb of Pompey the Great and was known to English travelers as "Pompey's Pillar."

poverty (faqr) lack of material wealth and, in Sufi terms, awareness of inadequacy in relation to God; by the second half of the thirteenth century, the term had become synonymous with Sufism itself.

Qāḍī l-Fāḍil, al- (529–96/1135–1200) ʿAbd al-Raḥīm ibn ʿAlī, known as al-Qāḍī l-Fāḍil ("the Virtuous Judge"), was a statesman, model of epistolary style, poet, and head of the chancery of Ṣalāḥ al-Dīn al-Ayyūbī (Saladin) from 566/1171.

Qādisiyyah, al- site of the battle (between 14/635 and 16/637) southwest of al-Kūfah at which the Muslims won a decisive victory over the Sassanid army, opening the way to their conquest of Iraq.

qafqūlah "earthenware cooking pot or milk pot" (Behnstedt and Woidich, *Glossar*, 389, s.v. *gafgūl*).

qaḥf (1) the broad, deeply indented, thorny end of the palm frond where it joins the tree; (2) a type of peasant hat; (3) a peasant (as a coarse, unpolished person).

Qalyūbī, Shihāb al-Dīn al- Aḥmad ibn Aḥmad ibn Salāmah Shihāb al-Dīn al-Qalyūbī (d. 1069/1659), a writer on jurisprudence, geography, medicine, and the occult sciences, and author of belles lettres; see vol. 1, p. xi.

Qarāfah, al- the great cemetery complex of Cairo.

qaṭāyif "small pancakes stuffed with nuts or other sweet filling fried and moistened with syrup or honey" (Hinds and Badawi, *Dictionary*, 709).

Qāyitbāy, Sulṭān (r. 872–901/1468–96), Mamluk ruler of the Burjī dynasty.

Qiblah the direction the worshipper faces when performing the ritual prayer (*ṣalāh*).

quotation (iqtibās) the use of a quotation from the Qur'an in poetry; this rhetorical device "consists of the poet introducing into his poetry deliberately a word or a verse from the Mighty Qur'an, and is of three types: praiseworthy and accepted, permitted but vulgar, and rejected and despicable" (al-Ḥillī, *Al-Badīʿiyyah*, 326–27).

Quḥāfah, al- a village in the province of al-Gharbiyyah.

qulqās a tuberous, starchy, taro-like root vegetable (*Colocasia antiquorum*).

Quraysh the tribe of the Prophet Muḥammad.

Quṣayr, al- a port on the Red Sea, about three hundred miles south of Suez and a major point of embarkation for pilgrims traveling to Mecca.

Rashīd Rosetta, on the mouth of the western branch of the Nile, a major entrepôt for trade between Cairo and Alexandria.

restraint (iktifāʾ) a rhetorical device by which "a poet produces a line of verse whose rhyme-word is dependent [for the completion of the sense] on a word that is omitted and that must be borne in mind if the meaning is to be understood but which the poet does not mention because the words of the verse themselves imply it; he thus relies on what the reader can be expected to know naturally for the completion of the sense" (al-Ḥillī, *Al-Badīʿiyyah*, 105).

rolling and unrolling (laff wa-nashr) in rhetoric, "an enumeration of terms followed by an enumeration of predicates or comments" (W. P. Heinrichs, "Rhetorical Figures," in *EAL*).

Rūm, al- Anatolia; literally "the Land of the [eastern] Romans," that is, the Byzantines.

Rumaylah, al- a large open space in front of Cairo's Citadel.

Ruṣāfah, al- a quarter of Baghdad on the eastern bank of the Euphrates.

Ṣābūnī, Bridge of al- (qanāṭir al-Ṣābūnī) a village called al-Ṣābūnī formerly existed south of Old Cairo between the districts of al-Maʿādī and Dayr al-Ṭīn and was associated with an island of the same name (now called Jazīrat al-Dahab) (Ramzī 1:77); this bridge may have linked the two.

Saʿd (or Judhām/Judām) with Ḥarām, one of two feuding armed factions into which the peasants were divided (see vol. 1, n. 13).

Ṣafī al-Ḥillī, al- ʿAbd al-ʿAzīz ibn Sarāyā Ṣafī al-Dīn al-Ḥillī (667/1278 to ca. 750/1349), a poet from Iraq who spent much time in Egypt at the courts of the last Ayyubids and first Mamluks.

Ṣaʿīd, the Upper Egypt, usually defined as Egypt south of Cairo.

saint's feast (mawlid, pl. mawālid) typically, the celebration of the birthday of a Muslim holy man, often associated with the Sufi group founded by that saint. The early Ottoman period in Egypt saw an efflorescence of *mawlid*s (Winter, *Society and Religion*, 178–80).

Ṣalībah, al- literally "The Cross-Shaped (Street)"; a major street running west from the north end of the square below the Citadel.

Ṣāliḥ al-Ṭalāʾiʿ, al- Abū l-Ghārāt Fāris al-Muslimīn al-Malik al-Ṣāliḥ Ṭalāʾiʿ b. Ruzzīk al-Ghassānī al-Armanī (495/1101–2 to 556/1161), a Fatimid general and governor of Egypt.

Samannūd a town in the central Delta, on the western bank of the eastern (Dimyāṭ) branch of the Nile, about twenty-five miles from Shirbīn.

sanjak (ṣanjaq) (originally a Turkish term, *sancak*, literally "flag") one of a group of military grandees, ranging at various times from sixteen to thirty-six or even more, who were promoted out of the officer corps of the Ottoman army in Egypt to act as counselors (and counterweights) to the viceroy and to occupy key positions in the Egyptian state apparatus.

sarkūj apparently an item of headwear or upper-body wear.

scholar (ʿālim, pl. ʿulamāʾ) a scholar learned in the religious sciences (such as Qurʾanic exegesis, jurisprudence, and prophetic traditions). Here, the term is used primarily of scholars associated with the mosque of al-Azhar, who often find themselves in conflict with the rural pastors known as *fuqahā'* (sg. *faqīh*, colloquially *fiqī*) (q.v.).

Shaʿbān the eighth month of the Islamic calendar, immediately preceding Ramadan.

Shāfiʿī, the Imam al- that is, Muḥammad ibn Idrīs al-Shāfiʿī (150/767–68 to 204/820), pupil of the Imam Mālik and founder of the school of law that, by the twelfth century AD, had become dominant in Lower Egypt and to which al-Shirbīnī belonged.

Shanashah a village, since disappeared, near Shirbīn.

Sharb, al- one of Cairo's principal cloth markets.

sharif a descendant of the Prophet Muḥammad.

Shīḥah sister of the hero Abū Zayd in the epic romance of the Banū Hilāl (*Al-Sīrah al-Hilāliyyah*).

Shirbīn Yūsuf al-Shirbīnī's birthplace, on the northern bank of the eastern branch of the Nile (see vol. 1, p. xi).

shovel-sledge (jarrāfah) a wooden, animal-drawn sledge used to clean and dredge canals and level fields. It is shaped like an equilateral triangle, with sides about three feet in length and a truncated front end from which descend two sides with raised edges.

Shubrā a village north of Cairo.

silver piece here translates *nuṣṣ* (pl. *anṣāṣ*), a silver coin minted in Egypt during the Ottoman period and the chief specie used for medium to large purchases; copper coins known as *jadīd*s were used for small local purchases, while gold coins were used for major purchases and transactions and foreign exchange (Pamuk, *Monetary History*, 66). The *nuṣṣ* remained the basic coin of Egypt until the coinage reform of Muḥammad ʿAlī, in 1834 (Pamuk, *Monetary History*, 95).

Sirw, al- village on the east bank of the eastern branch of the Nile, in the district of Fāriskūr, al-Daqahliyyah, near Shirbīn.

sow thistle (juʿḍayḍ) *Sonchus oleraceus*, a weed whose stalks may be peeled and eaten.

subūʿ the seventh day after the birth of a child, on which it is customary for the mother to be visited by her friends, who take part in various rituals to ensure the good health of herself and her child (cf. Lane, *Manners*, 504–5).

Suʿdā a woman's name, used conventionally for the Beloved.

sukhrah, al- compulsory labor on public works (especially the maintenance of the irrigation system); cf. *corvée* (*al-ʿawnah*).

Sulaymān Solomon.

Sulṭān Qizilbash ("Sultan Red-Hat") the Safavid ruler of Iran; from Turkish *kızılbaş*, in reference to the distinctive headgear of the followers of the Safavid shaykhs.

Sunnah ("custom") in Islam, an act approved because imitative of the practice of the Prophet.

surah chapter of the Qur'an.

surveyor (khawlī, pl. khawālī) "The [*khawlī*] . . . was responsible for determining exactly the limits of the village, the *Asar* [tax-paying] land of each cultivator, the nature and timing of the seeding and cultivation of each portion of the watered land, and the amount of tax owed by each cultivator. He was also charged with making sure that the waters in the irrigation canals were properly apportioned amongst the cultivated lands and that the irrigation canals and equipment of the village were kept in proper repair. The [*khawlī*] was elected by the cultivators and was their chief representative in the village administration" (Shaw, *Financial*, 54).

Suwayqat al-Sabbāʿīn a "little," that is, temporary, market west of Birkat al-Fīl (q.v.), southwest of Bāb Zuwaylah (q.v.).

Suyūṭī, al-Jalāl al- Jalāl al-Dīn Abū l-Faḍl ʿAbd al-Raḥmān ibn Abī Bakr al-Suyūṭī (848–911/1445–1505), one of the most prolific polymaths of medieval Arabic.

sycamore (jummayz) sycamore figs, the fruit of *Ficus sycamoris*, which resemble small pinkish figs with whitish pulpy flesh. A visitor to Egypt in the 1640s remarked that "it is the fruit of the poor, which costs them nothing except for the cooking" and notes that the fruit went untaxed, unlike that of other productive trees (Brémond, *Voyage*, 35).

Ṭalkhah chief town of the district of the same name in the province of al-Gharbiyyah, on the west bank of the eastern branch of the Nile.

tarjīl (pl. tarājīl) a type of peasant shoe, synonymous, according to al-Shirbīnī, with *markūb* or *zarbūn* (kinds of slipper) (q.v.).

tax collectors, tax-collection apparatus (dīwān) literally "council" or "bureau," the administration of Ottoman Egypt devolved through a series of *dīwān*s, with the High Dīwān (*al-dīwān al-ʿālī*) of the viceroy constituting the "principal executive and legislative council" (Shaw, *Financial*, 2).

Under this was the Registration Bureau of the Sultan (*al-dīwān al-daftarī al-sulṭānī*) and its subdepartment, the Bureau of the Daybook (*dīwān al-ruznāmah*), which was responsible for the "administering of the imposition, registration and collection of taxes and revenues . . . and their disposition" (ibid, 338). Reflecting the informal usage of the time, al-Shirbīnī applies the term *dīwān* to the local administrative apparatus of the tax farmer, which mirrored the national-level *dīwān*.

tax farm (iltizām) the right to collect the taxes of an area of land, a right that, at this period, was purchased at auction; as Shalabī put it, "The *multazim* [tax farmer] who buys the village . . . has to come up with the tax . . . . and whatever is left over is his" (Shalabī, *Siyāḥatnāmah*, 191). Tax farmers also acted as local administrators, overseeing the maintenance of the irrigation system at the local level, approving acquisition and transfer of land by villagers, and nurturing agricultural prosperity generally. In 1658–60, a quarter century before al-Shirbīnī wrote, there were 1,714 *multazims*, over 90 percent of whom were emirs (military officers). The *iltizām* system was abolished beginning in the winter of 1813–14 as part of Muḥammad ʿAlī's reforms in favor of a state monopoly of tax collection (Raymond, *Artisans*, 2:612–18; Cuno, *Peasants*, 2:25–27, 33–47; Winter, *Egyptian Society*, passim).

Thamūd see *ʿĀd*.

thawb a "large, loose gown" or a "shirt" worn by women (Lane, *Manners*, 45).

Thawrī, Sufyān al- Sufyān ibn Saʿīd ibn Marzūq al-Thawrī (97/715–16 to 161/778), a celebrated transmitter of Traditions.

Tradition (of the Prophet Muḥammad) (ḥadīth, pl. aḥādīth) an account of his words or deeds to which he gave his tacit approval. Traditions supplement the ordinances found in the Qurʾan and provide a model for the attitudes and comportment of the believer. They are categorized, based on the reliability of their chain of transmission, on a scale from *ṣaḥīḥ* ("sound") to *ḍaʿīf* ("weak"); an account that lacks all credibility is dismissed as *mawḍūʿ* ("concocted") or as *khabar kādhib* ("a mendacious report"). Of the twenty-three claimed Traditions occurring in the book, nine are fundamentally "sound" (albeit two of them occur with minor variations from the canonical wording), nine are "weak," "concocted," or "mendacious," and the rest fall in between.

ṭūbār a kind of gray mullet (*Mugil capito*).

Ṭūr, al- a town on the west coast of the Sinai Peninsula.

Ṭuways ("Little Peacock") nickname of Abū ʿAbd al-Munʿim ʿĪsā ibn ʿAbd Allāh (b. 10/632), a celebrated singer of Medina during the early days of Islam who was also known for the coincidence of events in his life with unhappy events, for "he was born on the day the Prophet (upon him peace and blessings) died, weaned on the day Abū Bakr [the first caliph] (may God be pleased with him) died, was circumcised on the day ʿUmar [ibn al-Khaṭṭāb, second caliph] (may God be pleased with him) was killed, and married on the day ʿUthmān [ibn ʿAffān, third caliph] (may God be pleased with him) was killed" (al-Iṣfahānī, *Al-Aghānī*, 4/39).

ʿūd the Arab lute.

urjūzah a poem in *rajaz* meter (LLSL | LLSL | LLSL, with a wide range of permissible variants), usually in rhymed couplets with different rhymes in each couplet, in which form it may be referred to as an *urjūzah muzdawijah*. "On account of [the *muzdawijah*'s] easy rhyming scheme, it proved particularly suitable for long narrative and didactic poems" (W. Stoetzer, "rajaz," in *EAL*) such as Ibn Mālik's versified grammar, *Al-Alfiyyah*. Al-Shirbīnī uses this meter for the two long poems with which he summarizes volumes one and two, respectively, of his book.

vizier (wazīr) "minister," a title borne by some Ottoman governors of Egypt (Davies, *Lexicon*, 130).

Wādī al-Tīh a valley in Sinai, at the head of the Gulf of ʿAqabah.

wajbah the duty, imposed on the villager, of providing the tax farmer (*multazim*) and other officials and their entourages and animals with food (§11.3.9–11).

Walīd ibn Yazīd, al- (r. 125–26/743–44) eleventh caliph of the Umayyad dynasty and a poet.

waqf an endowment, often made for charitable purposes such as the upkeep of a mosque.

Wāthiq, al- (r. 227–32/842–47) ninth caliph of the Abbasid dynasty.

wheat groats (kishk) hulled wheat cooked with sour milk, formed into balls, and dried.

Yāsīn the thirty-sixth Surah of the Qur'an.

Yazīd (r. 60–64/680–83) second caliph of the Umayyad dynasty.

Zāhidī, Imam al- Najm al-Dīn Abū l-Rajāʾ Mukhtār ibn Maḥmūd ibn Muḥammad al-Zāhidī l-Ghazmīnī l-ʿArramānī (362–428/972–1037), a Hanafi jurisprudent.

Zayd, Sultan Zayd ibn Muḥsin (b. 1015/1607), founder of the Dhawū Zayd dynasty of rulers of Mecca.

Zubaydah cousin and wife of the Abbasid caliph Hārūn al-Rashīd and mother of his successor, al-Amīn Muḥammad (q.v.).

Zukhruf, al- the forty-third Surah of the Qurʾan.

zummārah a cane or wood pipe with reed.

Bibliography

ʿAbd al-Raḥīm, ʿAbd al-Raḥīm ʿAbd al-Raḥmān. *Al-Rīf al-miṣrī fī l-qarn al-thāmin ʿashar.* Cairo: Maktabat Madbūlī, 1986.

Abū l-ʿAtāhiyah. *Ashʿāruhu wa-akhbāruhu.* Edited by Shukrī Fayṣal. Damascus: Maktabat Dār al-Mallāḥ, n.d. Photomechanical repr. of ed. Damascus: Maṭbaʿat Jāmiʿat Dimashq, 1965.

Abū Firās al-Ḥamdānī. *Dīwān.* Edited by ʿAlī al-ʿUsaylī. Beirut: Manshūrāt Muʾassasat al-Aʿlamī, 1998.

Abū Nuwās, al-Ḥasan ibn Hāniʾ. *Dīwān Abī Nuwās al-Ḥasan ibn Hāniʾ al-Ḥakamī.* Edited by Ewald Wagner and Gregor Schoeler. 7 vols. Cairo and Wiesbaden: Franz Steiner/Beirut and Berlin: Klaus Schwarz, 1958–2006 (vols. 6–7: indexes). The second edition of vol. 1 (2001) has been used.

Abū Yaʿlā, Aḥmad ibn ʿAlī ibn al-Muthannā al-Tamīmī. *Al-Musnad.* Edited by Ḥusayn Salīm Asad. 15 vols. Beirut: Dār al-Maʾmūn li-l-Turāth, 1410/1989.

Ahlwardt, Wilhelm. *The Divans of the Six Ancient Arabic Poets.* London: 1870, reprinted Osnabrück: Biblio, 1972.

Aḥnaf, ʿAbbās al-. *Dīwān.* Edited by ʿĀtikah al-Khazrajī. Cairo: Dār al-Kutub al-Miṣriyyah, 1954.

ʿAjlūnī, Ismāʿīl ibn Muḥammad. *Kashf al-khafāʾ wa-muzīl al-ilbās ʿammā shtahara mina l-aḥādīth ʿalā alsinat al-nās.* 2 vols. Beirut: Dār al-Kutub al-ʿIlmiyyah, 1988.

Ālātī, Ḥasan al-. *Tarwīḥ al-nufūs wa-muḍḥik al-ʿabūs.* Cairo: Jarīdat al-Maḥrūsah, 1889.

Alf laylah wa-laylah. Edited by al-Shaykh Qiṭṭah al-ʿAdawī. Cairo: Maṭbaʿat Bulaq, 1836. Offset, reprint edition, Beirut: Dār Ṣādir, n.d.

Alf laylah wa-laylah min al-Mubtadaʾ ilā l-Muntahā: ṭabʿah muṣawwarah min ṭabʿat Barislaw bi-taṣḥīḥ Maksīmīliyānūs ibn Hābikhṭ. 2nd ed. Cairo: Dār al-Kutub al-Miṣriyyah, 1998.

ʿĀlī, Muṣṭafā see Tietze, Andreas.

ʿĀmilī, Bahāʾ al-Dīn al-. *Al-Kashkūl.* Beirut: Dār al-Kitāb al-Lubnānī, 1983.

Amīn, Aḥmad. *Qāmūs al-ʿādāt wa-l-taqālīd wa-l-taʿābīr al-Miṣriyyah.* Cairo: Maṭbaʿat Lajnat al-Taʾlīf wa-l-Tarjamah wa-l-Nashr, 1953.

ʿAntarah ibn Shaddād. *Sharḥ Dīwān ʿAntarah ibn Shaddād.* Edited by ʿAbd al-Munʿim ʿAbd al-Raʾūf Shalabī. Cairo: al-Maṭbaʿah al-Tijāriyyah al-Kubrā, n.d.

Arberry, A. J. *The Seven Odes: The First Chapter in Arabic Letters.* London: George Allen and Unwin, 1957.

———. *The Koran Interpreted.* Oxford World's Classics. Oxford: Oxford University Press, 1982.

Armbrust, Walter. *Mass Culture and Modernism in Egypt.* Cambridge Studies in Social and Cultural Anthropology 102. Cambridge: Cambridge University Press, 1996.

Ashtor, Eliyahu. "An Essay on the Diet of the Various Classes in the Medieval Levant." In *Selections from the Annales, Sociétés, Économies, Civilisations*, edited by Robert Forster and Orest Ranum, 125–62. Baltimore and London: Johns Hopkins University Press, 1975.

Aubaile-Sallenave, Francoise. "Al-Kishk: The Past and Present of a Complex Culinary Practice." In *Culinary Cultures of the Middle East*, edited by Sami Zubaida and Richard Tapper, 105–39. London and New York: I. B. Tauris, 1994.

ʿAyyāshī, Abū Salim al-. *Al-Riḥlah al-ʿAyyāshiyyah (Māʾ al-mawāʾid)*, edited by M. Hajji. 2 vols. Rabat: n.p., 1977.

Baer, Gabriel. "Fellah and Townsman in Ottoman Egypt: A Study of Shirbini's Hazz al-Quḥūf." *Asian and African Studies* [Jerusalem], 8 (1972): 221–56.

———. *Fellah and Townsman in the Middle East: Studies in Social History.* London: Frank Cass, 1982.

———. "Shirbīnī's Hazz al-Quḥūf and its Significance." In Gabriel Baer, *Fellah and Townsman in the Middle East: Studies in Social History.* London: Frank Cass, 1982.

Baqlī, Muḥammad Qindīl al-, ed. *Qaryatunā l-Miṣriyyah qabla l-thawrah – 1.* Cairo: Dār al-Nahḍah al-ʿArabiyyah, n.d. [1963].

Bashshār ibn Burd, Abū Muʿādh. *Dīwān.* Edited by Muḥammad al-Ṭāhir Ibn ʿĀshūr. 4 vols. Algiers and Tunis: al-Sharikah al-Waṭaniyyah/al-Sharikah al-Tūnusiyyah, 1976.

Bayḍāwī, ʿAbd Allāh ibn ʿUmar ibn Muḥammad al-Shīrāzī al-. *Anwār al-tanzīl wa-asrār al-taʾwīl.* 2 vols. Beirut: Dār al-Kutub al-ʿIlmiyyah, 1999.

Bayhaqī, Aḥmad ibn al-Ḥusayn al-. *Kitāb al-zuhd al-kabīr.* Edited by ʿĀmir Aḥmad Ḥaydar. Beirut: Dār al-Janān wa-Muʾassasat al-Kutub al-Thaqāfiyyah, 1987.

Behnstedt, Peter, and Manfred Woidich. *Die ägyptisch-arabischen Dialekte* . Vol. 4, *Glossar Arabisch-Deutsch.* Wiesbaden: Dr. Ludwig Reichert Verlag, 1994.

Behrens-Abouseif, Doris. *Egypt's Adjustment to Ottoman Rule: Institutions, Waqf and Architecture in Cairo (16th and 17th Centuries).* Leiden: E. J. Brill, 1994.

Berque, Jacques. *Histoire sociale d'un village égyptien au XXème siècle.* Paris: Mouton, 1957.

Blanc, Haim. "La Perte d'une forme pausale dans le parler arabe du Caire." *Mélanges de l'Université Saint Joseph* 48 (1973–74): 376–90.

Borg, Gert. "Lust and Carnal Desire: Obscenities Attributed to Arab Women." *Arabic and Middle Eastern Literatures* 3, no. 2 (2000): 149–64.

Bosworth, Clifford Edmund. *The Mediaeval Islamic Underworld: The Banū Sāsān in Arabic Society and Literature*. 2 vols. Leiden: E. J. Brill, 1976.

Brémond, Gabriel. *Voyage en Égypte de Gabriel Brémond 1643–45*. Edited by Georges Sanguin. Collection des voyageurs occidentaux en Egypte 12. Cairo: Institut Français d'Archéologie Orientale, 1974.

Bukhārī, Muḥammad ibn Ismāʿīl ibn Ibrāhīm al-. *Al-Jāmiʿ al-musnad al-ṣaḥīḥ al-mukhtaṣar min umūr rasūl Allāh ṣallā Allāh ʿalayh wa-sallam wa-sunanih wa-ayyāmih*. 3 vols. Stuttgart: Islamic Thesaurus Society, 1421/2000–2001.

Burckhardt, John L. *Arabic Proverbs; or the Manners and Customs of the Modern Egyptians Illustrated by Their Proverbial Sayings Current in Cairo*. 3rd ed. London: Curzon Press, 1972.

Būṣīrī, Sharaf al-Dīn Abū ʿAbd Allāh Muḥammad ibn Saʿīd al-. *Dīwān*. Edited by Muḥammad Sayyid Kīlānī. Cairo: Muṣṭafā al-Bābī al-Ḥalabī, 1973.

Cachia, Pierre. *The Arch Rhetorician or the Schemer's Skimmer: A Handbook of Late Arabic badīʿ Drawn from ʿAbd al-Ghanī an-Nabulsī's Nafaḥāt al-Azhār ʿalā Nasamāt al-Asḥār, Summarized and Systematized by Pierre Cachia*. Wiesbaden: Harrassowitz, 1998.

———. *Popular Narrative Ballads of Modern Egypt*. Oxford: Clarendon Press, 1989.

Çelebi see Shalabī, Awliyā.

Coppin, Jean. *Voyages en Égypte de Jean Coppin, 1638–1646*. Edited by Serge Sauneron. Collection des voyageurs occidentaux en Egypte 4. Cairo: Institut Français d'Archéologie Orientale, 1971.

Crecelius, Daniel, and Abd al-Wahhab Bakr. *Al-Damurdāshī's Chronicle of Egypt 1688–1755: al-Durrah al-muṣānah fī akhbār al-Kinānah*. Leiden: E. J. Brill, 1991.

Cuno, Kenneth M. *The Pasha's Peasants: Land, Society and Economy in Lower Egypt, 1740–1858*. Cairo: American University in Cairo Press, 1994.

Damīrī, Kamāl al-Dīn Muḥammad ibn Mūsā al-. *Ḥayāt al-ḥayawān al-kubrā*. 2 vols. Cairo: Muṣṭafā al-Bābī al-Ḥalabī, 1978.

Davies, Humphrey. *A Lexicon of 17th-Century Egyptian Arabic*. Orientalia Lovaniensia Analecta 225. Leuven: Peeters, 2013.

———. *Seventeenth-Century Egyptian Arabic: A Profile of the Colloquial Material in Yusuf al-Shirbīnī's "Hazz al-quḥūf fī sharḥ qaṣīd Abī Shādūf."* PhD diss. University of California, Berkeley, 1981. Available from ProQuest Dissertations & Theses Global (order no. 8200073). http://search.proquest.com/docview/303007733.

———. *Yūsuf al-Shirbīnī's Kitāb Hazz al-Quḥūf bi-Sharḥ Abī Shādūf ("Brains Confounded by the Ode of Abū Shādūf Expounded")*, Volume 1: Arabic text. Orientalia Lovaniensia Analecta 141. Leuven: Peeters, 2005.

———. *Yūsuf al-Shirbīnī's Brains Confounded by the Ode of Abū Shādūf Expounded,* Volume 2: *English translation, Introduction, and Notes.* Orientalia Lovaniensia Analecta 166. Leuven: Peeters, 2007.

Dols, Michael W. *Majnūn: The Madman in Medieval Islamic Society.* Oxford: Clarendon Press, 1992.

Dozy, R. *Supplément aux Dictionnaires Arabes.* 2 vols. Leiden: E. J. Brill, 1881. Offset, Beirut: Librairie du Liban, 1968.

Dunne, Bruce W. "Sexuality and the 'Civilizing Process' in Modern Egypt." PhD diss., Georgetown University, 1996.

EAL = *Encyclopedia of Arabic Literature.* Edited by Julie Scott Meisami and Paul Starkey. 2 vols. London and New York: Routledge, 1998.

EI2 = *Encyclopaedia of Islam.* 2nd ed. Edited by P. Bearman, Th. Bianquis, C. E. Bosworth, E. von Donzol, and W. P. Heinrichs. Leiden: E. J. Brill, 1960–2009.

Finkel, Joshua. "King Mutton, a Curious Egyptian Tale of the Mamluk Period. Edited from a Unique Manuscript, with Translation, Notes, Glossary and Introduction." *Zeitschrift für Semitistik* 8 (1932): 122–48 and 9 (1933–34): 1–18.

Fīrūzābādhī, Muḥammad ibn Yaʿqūb al-. *Al-Qāmūs al-muḥīṭ wa-l-qābūs al-wasīṭ fī al-lughah.* 2nd ed. 4 vols. Cairo: al-Maktabah al-Ḥusayniyyah al-Miṣriyyah, 1344/1925–26.

Fischer, Wolfdietrich. *Die demonstrativen Bildungen der neuarabischen Dialekte.* The Hague: Mouton, 1959.

GAL = Brockelmann, Carl. *Geschichte der arabischen Litteratur, I–II.* Leiden: E. J. Brill, 1943, 1949; Suppl. I–III, Leiden: E. J. Brill, 1937–42.

GAS = Sezgin, Fuat. *Geschichte des arabischen Schrifttums, II.* Leiden: E. J. Brill, 1984.

Ghazzī, Badr al-Dīn Muḥammad al-. *Al-Zubdah fī sharḥ al-Burdah.* Edited by ʿUmar Mūsā Bashā. Algiers: al-Sharikah al-Waṭaniyyah li-l-Nashr wa-l-Tawzīʿ, 1972.

Ghazzī, Najm al-Dīn Muḥammad ibn Muḥammad al-. *Al-Kawākib al-sāʾirah bi-aʿyān al-miʾah al-ʿāshirah.* Edited by Khalīl al-Manṣūr. 2 vols. Beirut: Dār al-Kutub al-ʿIlmiyyah, 1997.

Ghuzūlī, ʿAlāʾ al-Dīn ʿAlī ibn ʿAbd Allāh al-Bahāʾī al-. *Maṭāliʿ al-budūr fī manāzil al-surūr.* 2 vols. Bulaq: 1299–1300/1882–83.

Gonzales, Antonius. *Voyage en Egypte du Père Antonius Gonzales 1665–1666.* Edited by Charles Libois. Collection des voyageurs occidentaux en Egypte 19. Cairo: Institut Français d'Archéologie Orientale, 1977.

Goody, Jack. *Cooking, Cuisine and Class: A Study in Comparative Sociology.* Cambridge: Cambridge University Press, 1982.

Greene, Daniel. "An Egyptian Rabbi Trickster." *Journal of American Folklore* 79 (1966): 608–30.

Guillaume, A. *The Life of Muhammad: A Translation of Isḥāq's Sīrat Rasūl Allāh*. Karachi: Oxford University Press, 1967.

Ḥājjī Khalīfah (Kātib Çelebi). *Kashf al-ẓunūn ʿan asāmī l-kutub wa-l-funūn*. Edited by Şerefettin Yaltkaya and Rifat Bilge. 2 vols. Istanbul: Maarif Matbaası, 1941–43.

Hanna, Nelly. "The Chronicles of Ottoman Egypt: History or Entertainment." In *The Historiography of Islamic Egypt (c. 950–1800)*, edited by Hugh Kennedy, 237–50. Leiden: Brill, 2001.

———. "Culture in Ottoman Egypt." In *The Cambridge History of Egypt*, edited by M. W. Daly, 2:87–112. Cambridge: Cambridge University Press, 1998.

Ḥarīrī, Abū Muḥammad al-Qāsim ibn ʿAlī ibn Muḥammad ibn ʿUthmān al-. *Maqāmāt al-Ḥarīrī*. 3rd ed. Bulaq: Dār al-Ṭibāʿah al-ʿĀmirah, 1288/1871.

Ḥasan, Muḥammad ʿAbd al-Ghanī. *Al-Fallāḥ fī l-adab al-ʿarabī*. Cairo: Dār al-Qalam, 1965.

Ḥassān ibn Thābit. *Dīwān*. Edited by Walīd ʿArafāt. Beirut: Dār Ṣādir, 1974.

Hilāl, ʿImād. *Al-Baghāyā fī Miṣr: Dirāsah tārikhiyyah ijtimāʿiyyah (min 1834–1949)*. Cairo: al-ʿArabī li-l-Nashr wa-l-Tawzāʿ, 2001.

Ḥillī, Ṣafī al-Dīn al-. *Sharḥ al-Kāfiyah al-Badīʿiyyah fī ʿulūm al-balāghah wa-maḥāsin al-badīʿ*. Edited by Nasīb Nashāwī. Damascus: Majmaʿ al-Lughah al-ʿArabiyyah bi-Dimashq, 1982.

Hinds, Martin, and El-Said Badawi. *A Dictionary of Egyptian Arabic: Arabic-English*. Beirut: Librairie du Liban, 1986.

Höglmeier, Manuela. *Al-Ǧawbarī und sein Kašf al-asrār: Ein Sittenbild des Gauners im Arabisch-islamischen Mittelalter (7./13. Jahrhundert): Einführüng, Edition und Kommentar*. Berlin: Klaus Schwarz, 2014.

Homerin, Th. Emil. *From Arab Poet to Muslim Saint: Ibn al-Fāriḍ, His Verse, and His Shrine*. Columbia: University of South Carolina Press, 1994.

Howarth, Herbert, and Ibrahim Shukrallah. *Images from the Arab World: Fragments of Arab Literature Translated and Paraphrased with Variations and Comments*. London: Pilot Press, 1944.

Ḥusayn, Ṭāhā. *Al-Ayyām*. 2 vols. Cairo: Dār al-Maʿārif, 1953.

Ibn ʿAbd al-Ḥakam, Abū l-Qasim ʿAbd al-Raḥmān. *The History of the Conquest of Egypt, North Africa and Spain = Futūḥ Miṣr wa-akhbāruhā*. Edited by Charles C. Torrey. New Haven: Yale University Press, 1922.

Ibn Abī l-Ḥadīd, ʿAbd al-Ḥamīd ibn Hibatallāh. *Sharḥ Nahj al-balāghah li-l-Sharīf al-Raḍī*. Edited by Muḥammad al-Faḍl Ibrāhīm. 20 vols. Cairo: Dār Iḥyāʾ al-Kutub al-ʿArabiyyah, 1963.

Ibn Abī ʿAwn. *Tashbīhāt*. Edited by M. ʿAbd al-Muʿīd. London: Luzac, 1950.

Ibn al-ʿAdīm, Kamāl al-Dīn Abū l-Qāsim ʿUmar ibn Aḥmad. *Zubdat al-ḥalab min tārīkh Ḥalab*. Edited by Khalīl al-Manṣūr. Beirut: Dār al-Kutub al-ʿIlmiyyah, 1996.

Ibn al-ʿArabī, Muḥyī l-Dīn Abū ʿAbd Allāh Muḥammad ibn ʿAlī. *Dīwān*. Beirut: Dār al-Kutub al-ʿIlmiyyah, 1996.

———. *Tarjumān al-ashwāq*. Edited by Reynold A. Nicholson. London: Royal Asiatic Society, 1911.

Ibn Dāniyāl, Shams al-Dīn Muḥammad. *Three Shadow Plays*. Edited by Paul Kahle with a critical apparatus by Derek Hopwood. Cambridge: Trustees of the E. J. W. Gibb Memorial, 1992.

Ibn Durayd, Abū Bakr Muḥammad ibn al-Ḥasan. *Dīwān*. Edited by ʿUmar Ibn Sālim. Tunis: al-Dār al-Tūnusiyyah li-l-Nashr, 1973.

Ibn al-Fāriḍ, Abū Ḥafṣ (Abū l-Qāsim) ʿUmar ibn Abī l-Ḥasan ʿAlī ibn al-Murshid ibn ʿAlī. *Dīwān Ibn al-Fāriḍ*. Edited by ʿAbd al-Khāliq Maḥmūd. Cairo: ʿAyn li-l-Dirāsāt wa-l-Buḥūth al-Insāniyyah wa-l-Ijtimāʿiyyah, [1995].

Ibn Ḥajar al-ʿAsqalānī, Aḥmad ibn ʿAlī. *Al-Durar al-kāminah*. Hyderabad: Dāʾirat al-Maʿārif al-ʿUthmāniyyah, 1929–31.

———. *Tahdhīb al-Tahdhīb*. Hyderabad: Maṭbaʿat Majlis Dāʾirat al-Maʿārif al-Niẓāmiyyah, 1907.

Ibn Ḥamdūn, Muḥammad ibn al-Ḥasan. *Al-Tadhkirah al-Ḥamdūniyyah*. Edited by Iḥsān ʿAbbās and Bakr ʿAbbās. 10 vols. Beirut: Dār Ṣādir, 1996.

Ibn Ḥanbal, Aḥmad. *Al-Musnad*. 6 vols. Cairo: Muʾassasat Qurṭubah, n.d.

Ibn Ḥijjah al-Ḥamawī, Abū Bakr Taqī al-Dīn. *Thamarāt al-awrāq*. Edited by Muḥammad Abū l-Faḍl Ibrāhīm. Cairo: Maktabat al-Khānjī, 1971.

Ibn Hishām, Muḥammad ibn ʿAbd Allāh. *Al-Sīrah al-nabawiyyah*. Edited by Ṭāhā ʿAbd al-Raʾūf Saʿd. Cairo: Maktabat al-Kulliyyāt al-Azhariyyah, 1974.

Ibn al-Jawzī, ʿAbd al-Raḥmān ibn ʿAlī. *Kitāb al-adhkiyāʾ*. Edited by Muḥammad ʿAbd al-Raḥmān ʿAwaḍ. Beirut: Dār al-Kitāb al-ʿArabī, 1986.

Ibn Khallikān, Aḥmad ibn Muḥammad Abū l-ʿAbbās Shams al-Dīn al-Barmakī al-Irbīlī. *Wafayāt al-aʿyān*. Edited by Iḥsān ʿAbbās. Beirut: Dār al-Thaqāfah, 1997.

Ibn Qayyim al-Jawziyyah, Muḥammad ibn Abī Bakr. *Al-Ṭibb al-nabawī*. Shubrā, Cairo: Dār al-Taqwā li-l-Nashr wa-l-Tawzīʿ, 2003.

Ibn Qutaybah, Abū Muḥammad ʿAbd Allāh ibn Muslim. *Al-Shiʿr wa-l-shuʿarāʾ*. Edited by Aḥmad Muḥammad Shākir. Cairo: Dār al-Maʿārif, 1966.

———. *ʿUyūn al-akhbār*. 4 vols. Cairo: Dār al-Kutub, 1925–30.

Ibn Manẓūr, Jamāl al-Dīn Muḥammad ibn Mukarram. *Akhbār Abī Nuwās*. Edited by Ibrāhīm al-Abyārī as an appendix to Abū al-Faraj al-Iṣfahānī's *Kitāb al-aghānī*, vols. 29–30. Cairo: Dār al-Shaʿb, 1979.

———. *Lisān al-ʿArab*. Accessed at http://www.baheth.info/.

Ibn al-Rūmī (Abū l-Ḥasan ʿAlī ibn ʿAbbās ibn Jurayj). *Dīwān*. Edited by Ḥusayn Naṣṣār. 6 vols. Cairo: al-Hayʾah al-Miṣriyyah al-ʿĀmmah li-l-Kitāb, 1973–81.

Ibn Saʿd (ibn Manīʿ al-Zahawī), Muḥammad. *Kitāb al-ṭabaqāt al-kabīr*. Edited by ʿAlī Muḥammad ʿUmar. 11 vols. Cairo: Maktabat al-Khānjī, 1421/2001.

Ibn Sallām al-Jumaḥī, Muḥammad. *Ṭabaqāt fuḥūl al-shuʿarāʾ*. Edited by Maḥmūd Muḥammad Shākir. Cairo: Dār al-Maʿārif, 1952.

Ibn Sīnā, al-Ḥusayn ibn ʿAlī. *Al-Qānūn fī l-ṭibb*. Edited by Saʿīd al-Laḥḥām. 4 vols. Beirut: Dār al-Fikr, 1994.

Ibn Sūdūn (al-Bashbughāwī), ʿAlī, see Vrolijk, Arnoud.

Ibn Ṭūlūn, Shams al-Dīn Muḥammad ibn ʿAlī. *Mufākahat al-khillān*. Beirut: Dār al-Kutub al-ʿIlmiyyah, 1998.

Ibn al-Zubayr (al-Qāḍī al-Rashīd), Aḥmad ibn al-Rashīd. *Kitāb al-dhakhāʾir wa-l-tuḥaf*. Edited by Muḥammad Ḥamīdallāh. Kuwait: Maṭbaʿat Ḥukūmat al-Kuwayt, 1959.

Ibrahim, Laila, and Bernard O'Kane. "The Madrasa of Badr al-Din al-ʿAyni and Its Tiled Mihrab." *Annales Islamologiques* 24 (1988): 253–68.

Ibrāhīm, Nāṣir Aḥmad. *Al-Azamāt al-ijtimāʿiyyah fī Miṣr fī l-qarn al-sābiʿ ʿashar*. Cairo: Dār al-Āfāq al-ʿArabiyyah, 1998.

Ibshīhī, Muḥammad ibn Aḥmad al-. *Al-Mustaṭraf fī kull fann mustaẓraf*. 2 vols. Cairo: Muṣṭafā al-Bābī l-Ḥalabī, 1371/1952.

Idrīs, Yūsuf. *Al-Farāfīr*. Cairo: Maktabat Ghurayyib, 1977.

Imruʾ al-Qays. *Dīwān*. Edited by Muḥammad Abū l-Faḍl Ibrāhīm. 4th ed. Cairo: Dār al-Maʿārif, 1984.

Irwin, Robert. *The Arabian Nights: A Companion*. London: Penguin Books, 1995.

———. "ʿAlī al-Baghdādī and the Joy of Mamluk Sex." In *The Historiography of Islamic Egypt (c. 950–1800)*, edited by Hugh Kennedy, 45–57. Leiden: Brill, 2001.

ʿĪsā, ʿAlī. *Al-Lughāt al-sirriyyah*. Alexandria: Maṭbaʿat al-Intiṣār, n.d.

Iṣfahānī, Abū l-Faraj al-. *Kitāb al-aghānī*. 24 vols. Cairo: Dār al-Kutub/al-Hayʾah al-Miṣriyyah al-ʿĀmmah li-l-Kitāb, 1927–74.

Jabartī, ʿAbd al-Raḥman al-. *ʿAjāʾib al-āthār fī l-tarājim wa-l-akhbār*. 4 vols. Bulaq: al-Maṭbaʿah al-Amīriyyah, 1880.

Jāḥiẓ, ʿAmr ibn Baḥr al-. *Al-Bayān wa-l-tabyīn*. Edited by ʿAbd al-Salām Muḥammad Hārūn. 4 vols. Cairo: Maktabat al-Khānjī, 1968.

———. *Al-Ḥayawān*. Edited by ʿAbd al-Salām Muḥammad Hārūn. 8 vols. Cairo: Muṣṭafā al-Bābī al-Ḥalabī, 1965–69.

———. *Rasā'il al-Jāḥiẓ*. Edited by ʿAbd al-Salām Muḥammad Hārūn. 4 vols. Cairo: Maktabat al-Khānjī, 1965/1348.

Jarīr ibn ʿAṭiyyah. *Dīwān bi-sharḥ Muḥammad ibn Ḥabīb*. Edited by Nuʿmān Muḥammad Amīn Ṭāhā. 3rd ed. 2 vols. Cairo: Dār al-Maʿārif, 1986.

Jurjānī, ʿAbd al-Qāhir. *Dalā'il al-iʿjāz*. Edited by Maḥmūd Muḥammad Shākir. Maktabat al-Khānjī: Cairo, 1984.

Karamustafa, Ahmet T. *God's Unruly Friends: Dervish Groups in the Islamic Later Middle Period 1200–1550*. Salt Lake City: University of Utah Press, 1994.

Kern, F. "Neuere ägyptische Humoristen und Satiriker." *Mitteilungen des Seminars fur Orientalische Sprache*, Section 2 (1906): 31–73.

Khafājī, Aḥmad ibn Muḥammad ibn ʿUmar al-. *Rayḥānat al-alibbā'*. Edited by ʿAbd al-Fattāḥ Muḥammad al-Ḥulw. 2 vols. [Cairo]: Maṭbaʿat ʿĪsā al-Bābī l-Ḥalabī, 1967.

Khaṭīb al-Baghdādī, Aḥmad ibn ʿAlī ibn Thābit al-. *Tārīkh Baghdād*. 14 vols. Cairo: Maktabat al-Khānjī, 1349/1931.

Khawam, René R. *La cuisine arabe*. Paris: Albin Michel, 1970.

Khayrī, Badīʿ, and Najīb al-Rayḥānī. "Kishkish Bak ʿUḍw fī l-Barlamān." *Majallat al-nāqid* (17 February 1929). Reprinted in Ḥasan Darwīsh, *Badīʿ Khayrī: al-azjāl al-badīʿiyyah wa-l-alḥān al-rayḥāniyyah*. Cairo: al-Majlis al-Aʿlā li-l-Thaqāfah, 2001.

Kumayt ibn Zayd, al-. *Dīwān*. Beirut: Dār Ṣādir, 2000.

Lane, Edward William. *Account of the Manners and Customs of the Modern Egyptians*. 5th ed. London: John Murray, 1860. Offset, Cairo: American University in Cairo Press: 2003.

———. *An Arabic-English Lexicon*. 8 vols. London: Williams and Norgate, 1865. Offset, Beirut: Maktabat Lubnān, 1968.

Le Cerf, Jean. "Littérature dialectale et renaissance arabe moderne." *Bulletin d'Études Orientales* 11, no. 11 (1932): 179–258.

Maʿarrī, Abū l-ʿAlā' al-. *Al-Luzūmiyyāt*. Edited by Amīn ʿAbd al-ʿAzīz al-Khānjī. Cairo: Maktabat al-Khānjī, n.d. [1924].

Maghribī, Yūsuf ibn Zakariyyā ibn Ḥarb al-. *Dafʿ al-iṣr ʿan kalām ahl Miṣr*. Introduction and notes by ʿAbd al-Salām Aḥmad ʿAwwād. Moscow: Dār Nashr al-ʿIlm, 1968.

Maqqarī, Aḥmad ibn Muḥammad al-. *Nafḥ al-ṭīb min ghuṣn al-Andalus al-raṭīb*. Edited by Iḥsān ʿAbbās. 8 vols. Beirut: Dār Ṣādir, 1968.

Maqrīzī, Taqī al-Dīn Aḥmad ibn ʿAlī ibn ʿAbd al-Qādir ibn Muḥammad al-. *Al-Bayān wa-l-iʿrāb ʿammā fī Miṣr min al-Aʿrāb*. Cairo: 1961.

———. *Kitāb al-khiṭaṭ al-maqriziyyah al-musammā bi-l-Mawāʿiẓ wa-l-iʿtibār bi-dhikr al-khiṭaṭ wa-l-āthār*. 2 vols. Cairo: al-Maṭbaʿah al-Amīriyyah, 1853. Offset, Beirut: Dār Ṣādir, n.d.

Marmon, Shaun. *Eunuchs and Sacred Boundaries in Islamic Society*. New York: Oxford University Press, 1995.

Marzolph, Ulrich. *Arabia Ridens*. 2 vols. Frankfurt: Vittorio Klostermann, 1992.

Marzolph, Ulrich, and Richard van Leuwen, eds. *The Arabian Nights Encyclopedia*. 2 vols. Santa Barbara: ABC Clio, 2004.

Masʿūdī, Abū l-Ḥasan ʿAlī ibn al-Ḥusayn al-. *Murūj al-dhahab wa-maʿādin al-jawhar*. Edited by Muḥammad Muḥyī l-Dīn ʿAbd al-Ḥamīd. 4 vols. Cairo: al-Maktabah al-Tijāriyyah al-Kubrā, 1958.

Maydānī, Abū l-Faḍl Aḥmad ibn Muḥammad al-Nīsābūrī al-. *Majmaʿ al-amthāl*. 2 vols. Cairo: al-Maṭbaʿah al-Khayriyyah, 1321/1892.

Mehren, A. F. *Et Par Bidrag til Bedømmelse af den nyere Folkelitteratur i Ægypten*. Copenhagen: Bianco Lunos, 1872 (summary in French, 23–24).

Michel, Nicolas. "Les Dafatir al-Gusur, source pour l'histoire du réseau hydraulique de l'Egypte Ottomane." *Annales Islamologiques* 19 (1995): 151–68.

Mitchell, T. F. *An Introduction to Egyptian Colloquial Arabic*. London: Oxford University Press, 1956.

Moreh, Shmuel. *Live Theatre and Dramatic Literature in the Medieval Arab World*. New York: New York University Press, 1992.

Mubārak, ʿAlī. *Al-Khiṭaṭ al-tawfiqiyyah al-jadīdah*. Cairo: al-Maṭbaʿah al-Amīriyyah, 1887–89.

Mubarrad, Abū l-ʿAbbās Muḥammad ibn al-Yazīd al-. *Al-Kāmil*. Edited by Muḥammad Abū l-Faḍl Ibrāhīm. 8 vols. Cairo: Dār Nahḍat Miṣr, 1981.

Mufaḍḍaliyyāt, Al-. Edited by Aḥmad Muḥammad Shākir and ʿAbd al-Salām Muḥammad Hārūn. Cairo: Dār al-Maʿārif, n.d.

Muḥibbī, Muḥammad Amīn ibn ʿAbd Allāh al-. *Khulāṣat al-athar fī aʿyān al-qarn al-ḥādī ʿashar*. 4 vols. Cairo: 1284/1867–68. Offset, Beirut: Dār Sadir, n.d.

. *Nafḥat al-rayḥānah wa-rashḥat ṭilāʾ al-ḥānah*. 5 vols. Cairo: ʿIsā l-Bābī l-Ḥalabī, 1967–69.

———. *Qaṣd al-sabīl fī mā fī l-lughah al-ʿarabiyyah min al-dakhīl*. Edited by ʿUthmān Maḥmūd al-Ṣīnī. 2 vols. Riyadh: Maktabat al-Tawbah, 1994.

Munāwī, ʿAbd al-Raʾūf al-. *Fayḍ al-Qadīr: sharḥ al-Jāmiʿ al-ṣaghīr min aḥādīth al-baṣīr al-nadīr*. 6 vols. N.p.: Dār al-Fikr, n.d.

———. *Al-Kawākib al-durriyyah fī tarājim al-sādah al-ṣūfiyyah aw Ṭabaqāt al-Munāwī al-kubrā*. Edited by ʿAbd al-Ḥamīd Ṣāliḥ Ḥamdān. 4 parts in 2 vols. Cairo: al-Maktabah al-Azhariyyah li-l-Turāth, 1994.

Murray, G. W. *Sons of Ishmael: A Study of the Egyptian Bedouin*. London: Routledge, 1935.

Mutanabbī, Abū l-Ṭayyib Aḥmad ibn al-Ḥusayn al-. *Sharh dīwān al-Mutanabbī*. Edited by ʿAbd al-Raḥmān al-Barqūqī. 4 vols. Cairo: al-Maktabah al-Tijāriyyah al-Kubrā, 1938.

Nadīm, ʿAbd Allāh al-, ed. *Al-Aʿdād al-kāmilah li-Majallat al-Ustādh*. 2 vols. Cairo: al-Hayʾah al-Miṣriyyah al-ʿĀmmah li-l-Kitāb, 1994.

———. "Al-Waṭan" in *Akhbār al-adab* 217 (September 2003, 13–16).

Nelson, Kristina. *The Art of Reciting the Qurʾan*. Austin: University of Texas Press, 1985. Reprinted Cairo: American University in Cairo Press, 2001.

Newmark, Peter. *About Translation*. Multilingual Matters 74. Clevedon, UK: Multilingual Matters, 1996.

Nicolle, David, and Angus McBride. *The Mamluks 1250–1517*. Men-At-Arms 259. Botley, UK: Osprey Publishing, 1993.

Nīsābūrī, al-Ḥasan ibn Muḥammad ibn Ḥabīb al-. *ʿUqalāʾ al-majānīn*. Edited by Fāris al-Kīlānī. Cairo: al-Maṭbaʿah al-ʿArabiyyah, 1924.

Nuṣayb ibn Rabāḥ. *Shiʿr Nuṣayb ibn Rabāḥ*. Edited by Dāwūd Sallūm. Baghdad: Maktabat Marwān al-ʿAṭiyyah, 1967.

OLA 141 = Shirbīnī, Yūsuf al-. *Yūsuf al-Shirbīnī's Kitāb Hazz al-quḥūf bi-sharḥ qaṣīd Abī Shādūf*. Vol. 1, *Arabic Text*. Edited by Humphrey Davies. Orientalia Lovaniensia Analecta 141. Leuven: Peeters, 2005.

Omri, Mohamed-Salah. "Adab in the Seventeenth Century: Narrative and Parody in al-Shirbini's Hazz al-Quhuf." *Edebiyat* 11, no. 2 (2000): 169–96.

Pamuk, Şevket. *A Monetary History of the Ottoman Empire*. Cambridge: Cambridge University Press, 2000.

Perry, Charles. "Būrān: Eleven Hundred Years in the History of a Dish." In *Medieval Arab Cookery, Essays and Translations*, edited by Charles Perry et al., 239–50. London: Prospect Books, 2006.

Pertsch, Wilhelm. *Katalog der Orientalischen Handschriften der Herzoglichen Bibliothek zu Gotha*. Leipzig: Landesbibliothek Gotha, 1859–93.

Raḍī, al-Sharīf al- see Ibn Abī l-Ḥadīd.

Rāghib al-Iṣfahānī, Abū l-Qāsim al-Ḥusayn ibn Muḥammad al-. *Muḥāḍarāt al-udabāʾ wa-muḥāwarāt al-shuʿarāʾ wa-l-bulaghāʾ*. Bulaq: Maṭbaʿat Ibrāhīm al-Muwayliḥī/Jamʿiyyat al-Maʿārif, 1287/1870–71.

Ramzī, Muḥammad. *Al-Qāmūs al-jughrāfī li-l-bilād al-Miṣriyyah min ʿahd qudamāʾ al-Miṣriyyīna ilā sanat 1945*. Cairo: Maṭbaʿat Dār al-Kutub al-Miṣriyyah, 1953–54.

Raymond, André. *Artisans et commercants au Caire au XVIIIème siècle*. 2 vols. Damascus: Institut Français d'Etudes Arabes, 1973–75. Reprinted Cairo: Institut Français d'Archéologie Orientale, 1999.

———. *Les marchés du Caire*. Cairo: Institut Français d'Archéologie Orientale, 1979.

Rivlin, Helen Anne B. *The Agricultural Policy of Muhammad Ali in Egypt*. Cambridge, MA: Harvard University Press, 1961.

Rodinson, M. "*Ma'mūniyya* East and West." In *Medieval Arab Cookery, Essays and Translations,* edited by Charles Perry et al., 183–97. London: Prospect Books, 2006.

———. *Recherches sur les documents arabes relatifs à la cuisine.* Paris: Librairie Orientaliste Paul Geuthner, 1950.

Rosenthal, Franz. *Gambling in Islam.* Leiden: E. J. Brill, 1975.

Rowson, Everett K. "Al-ʿĀmirī." In *History of Islamic Philosophy,* edited by Seyyed Hossein Nasr and Oliver Leaman. New York: Routledge, 1996, 1:216–21.

———. "Cant and Argot in Cairo Colloquial Arabic." *Newsletter of the American Research Center in Egypt* 122 (Summer 1983): 13–24.

———. "Male and Female: Described and Compared." In *Homoeroticism in Classical Arabic Literature,* edited by J. W. Wright and Everett K. Rowson. New York: Columbia University Press, 1997.

———. *A Muslim Philosopher on the Soul and Its Fate: Al-ʿĀmirī's Kitāb al-Amad ʿalā l-abad.* New Haven: American Oriental Society, 1988.

Ṣabbāgh, Mikhāʾīl ibn Nīqūlā ibn Ibrāhīm. *Al-Risālah al-tāmmah fī kalām al-ʿāmmah wa-l-manāhij fī aḥwāl al-kalām al-dārij.* Edited by H. Thorbecke. Strassburg: Karl J. Trübner, 1886.

Sabra, Adam. *Poverty and Charity in Medieval Islam: Mamluk Egypt 1250–1517.* Cambridge: Cambridge University Press, 2000.

Ṣabrī, ʿUthmān. *Riḥlah fī l-Nīl.* Alexandria: ʿUthmān Ṣabrī, 1965.

Ṣafadī, Ṣalāḥ al-Dīn Khalīl ibn Aybak al-. *Aʿyān al-ʿaṣr.* Edited by Nabīl ʿAmshah et al. Damascus: Dār al-Fikr, 1988.

———. *Al-Ghayth al-musajjam fī sharḥ Lāmiyyāt al-ʿajam.* 2 vols. Beirut: Dār al-Kutub al-ʿIlmiyyah, 1975.

———. *Ikhtirāʿ al-khurāʿ.* Edited by Fārūq Islīm. Damascus: Ittiḥād al-Kuttāb al-ʿArab, 2000.

———. *Kitāb nuṣrat al-thāʾir ʿalā l-mathal al-sāʾir.* Edited by Muḥammad ʿAlī Sulṭānī. Damascus: Maṭbūʿāt Majmaʿ al-Lughah al-ʿArabiyyah bi-Dimashq, 1972.

———. *Al-Wāfī bi-l-wafayāt.* 30 vols. Beirut, Wiesbaden, and Berlin: Franz Steiner and Klaus Schwarz, 1931–2005.

Sale, George. *The Koran: Commonly Called The Alcoran of Mohammed; Translated into English Immediately from the Original Arabic with Explanatory Notes, Taken from the Most Approved Commentators.* London: William Tegg, 1850.

Shāfiʿī, Muḥammad ibn Idrīs al-. *Shiʿr al-Shāfiʿī.* Edited by Mujāhid Muṣṭafā Bahjat. Mosul: University of Mosul, 1986.

Shalabī, Awliyā [= Çelebi, Evliya]. *Siyāhatnāmah Miṣr.* Translated by Muḥammad ʿAlī ʿAwnī. Cairo: Dār al-Kutub, 2003.

Shaʿrānī, ʿAbd al-Wahhāb al-. *Laṭāʾif al-minan wa-l-akhlāq fī wujūb al-taḥadduth bi-niʿmat Allāh ʿalā al-iṭlāq*. Cairo: ʿĀlam al-Fikr, 1976.

———. *Lawāqiḥ al-anwār fī ṭabaqāt al-akhyār (Al-Ṭabaqāt al-kubrā)*. Cairo: al-Maṭbaʿah al-ʿĀmirah al- Sharafiyyah, 1315/1897.

Sharīf al-Raḍī, al-. *Dīwān*. Edited by Maḥmūd Muṣṭafā Ḥalāwī. 2 vols. Beirut: Sharikat al-Arqam ibn al-Arqam, 1999.

Shaw, Stanford J. *The Financial and Administrative Organization and Development of Ottoman Egypt, 1517–1798*. Princeton, NJ: Princeton University Press, 1962.

Shoshan, Boaz. *Popular Culture in Medieval Cairo*. Cambridge: Cambridge University Press, 1993.

Spitta, Wilhelm. *Grammatik des arabischen Vulgärdialektes von Aegypten*. Leipzig: J. C. Hinrichs, 1880.

Suyūṭī, Jalāl al-Dīn ʿAbd al-Raḥman al-. *Al-Itqān fī ʿulūm al-Qurʾān*. Edited by Muḥammad Abū l-Faḍl Ibrāhīm. Cairo: al-Hayʾah al-Miṣriyyah al-ʿĀmmah li-l-Kitāb, 1975.

Ṭabarānī, Sulaymān ibn Aḥmad Abū al-Qāsim al-. *Al-Muʿjam al-kabīr*. Edited by Ḥamdī ʿAbd al-Majīd al-Salafī. 20 vols. Cairo: Dār al-Bayān al-ʿArabī, n.d.

Tanūkhī, Abū ʿAlī l-Muḥassin ibn ʿAlī al-. *Al-Faraj baʿd al-shiddah*. Cairo: Maktabat al-Khānjī, 1955.

Ṭawīl, Tawfiq al-. *Al-Taṣawwuf fī Miṣr ibbān al-ʿaṣr al-ʿUthmānī*. 2 vols. Cairo: al-Hayʾah al-Miṣriyyah al-ʿĀmmah li-l-Kitāb, 1988.

Taymūr, Aḥmad. *Al-Amthāl al-ʿāmmiyyah*. 4th ed. Cairo: Markaz al-Ahrām li-l-Tarjamah wa-l-Nashr, 1986.

———. *Muʿjam Taymūr al-kabīr li-l-alfāẓ al-ʿāmmiyyah*. Edited by Ḥusayn Naṣṣār. Vols. 1–3, 2nd ed. Cairo: Maṭbaʿat Dār al-Kutub wa-l-Wathāʾiq al-Qawmiyyah, 2002; vols. 4–6, 1st ed., Cairo: Maṭbaʿat Dār al-Kutub wa-l-Wathāʾiq al-Qawmiyyah, 2003.

Thaʿālibī, Manṣūr ʿAbd al-Malik ibn Muḥammad ibn Ismāʿīl al-. *Yatīmat al-dahr*. Edited by Muḥammad Muḥyī l-Dīn ʿAbd al-Ḥamīd. 4 vols. Cairo: Maktabat al-Ḥusayn al-Tijāriyyah, 1947.

Tietze, Andreas. *Mustafa ʿAali's Description of Cairo of 1599: Text, Translation, Notes*. Vienna: Verlag der Österreichen Akademie der Wissenschaften, 1975.

TIF = *Jamʿ jawāmiʿ al-aḥādīth wa-l-asānīd wa-makniz al-ṣiḥāḥ wa-l-sunan wa-l-masānid; al-kutub al-sabʿah al-matīnah fī aḥādīth al-sunnah al-sharīfah*. Vaduz: Thesaurus Islamicus Foundation, 2001.

Tifāshī, Aḥmad ibn Yūsuf al-. *Surūr al-nafs bi-madārik al-ḥawāss al-khams*. Edited by Iḥsān ʿAbbās. Beirut: al-Muʾassasah al-ʿArabiyyah li-l-Dirāsāt wa-l-Nashr, 1980.

Trimingham, J. S. *The Sufi Orders in Islam*. Oxford: Clarendon Press, 1971.

Ṭurṭūshī, Muḥammad ibn al-Walīd al-. *Sirāj al-mulūk*. Edited by Jaʿfar al-Bayātī. London: Riad El-Rayyes Books, 1990.

Van Gelder, Geert Jan, trans. *Classical Arabic Literature: A Library of Arabic Literature Anthology*. Library of Arabic Literature. New York: New York University Press, 2013.

———. *Of Dishes and Discourse: Classical Arabic Literary Representations of Food*. London: Routledge, 2000.

———. "The Nodding Noddles, or Jolting the Yokels: A Composition for Marginal Voices by al-Shirbīnī (fl. 1687)." In *Marginal Voices in Literature and Society*, edited by Robin Ostle, 49–67. Strasbourg: European Science Foundation/Maison Méditerranéenne des Sciences de l'Homme d'Aix-en-Provence, 2000.

———. *Sound and Sense in Classical Arabic Poetry*. Arabische Studien 10. Wiesbaden: Harrassowitz, 2012.

Vial, Charles. "Le Hazz al-Quhuf de al-Širbini est-il un échantillon d'adab populaire?" In *Rivages et déserts: hommage à Jacques Berque*, 170–81. Paris: Sindbad, ca. 1988.

Vollers, K. "Beiträge zur Kenntniss der lebenden arabischen Sprache in Aegypten." *Zeitschrift des Deutschen Morgenländischen Gesellschaft* 41 (1887): 365–402.

Vrolijk, Arnoud. *Bringing a Laugh to a Scowling Face: A Study and Critical Edition of "Nuzhat al-Nufūs wa-Muḍḥik al-ʿAbūs" by ʿAlī Ibn Sūdūn al-Bashbughāwī*. Leiden: Research School CNWS, 1998.

Walīd ibn Yazīd, al-. *Shiʿr al-Walīd ibn Yazīd*. Edited by Ḥusayn ʿAṭwān. Amman: Maktabat al-Aqṣā, 1979.

Wansleben, F. *The Present State of Egypt: Or, a New Relation of a Late Voyage into the Kingdom, Performed in the Years 1672 and 1673* by F. Vansleb [*sic*]. Translated by M. D., B. D. London: 1678. Reprinted Westmead, UK: Gregg International Publishers, 1972.

Warner, Nicholas. *Guide to the Gayer-Anderson Museum Cairo*. Cairo: Ministry of Culture/ Supreme Council of Antiquities, 2003.

———. "Taking the Plunge: the Development and Use of the Cairene Bathhouse" in *Historians in Cairo: Essays in Honor of George Scanlon*, edited by Jill Edwards, 49–79. Cairo: American University in Cairo Press, 2002.

Wehr, Hans. *A Dictionary of Modern Written Arabic*. Edited by Milton J. Cowan. 4th ed. Wiesbaden: Otto Harrassowitz, 1979.

Winter, Michael. *Egyptian Society under Ottoman Rule 1517–1798*. London and New York: Routledge, 1992.

———. *Society and Religion in Ottoman Egypt: Studies in the Writings of ʿAbd al-Wahhāb al-Shaʿrānī*. The Shiloah Center for Middle Eastern and African Studies: Studies in Islamic Culture and History. New Brunswick and London: Transaction Books, 1982.

WKAS = Ullmann, Manfred, with Anton Spitaler. *Wörterbuch des Klassischen Arabischen Sprache*. Wiesbaden: Otto Harrassowitz, 1970–.

Woidich, Manfred. "Materialen zur Kenntnis des Kairenisch-Arabischen." In *Leermiddelen voor de studie van de Arabische taal en cultuur* 2, 19ff. Amsterdam: Instituut voor het Moderne Nabije Oosten/Universiteit van Amsterdam, 1990.

———. "Zum Dialekt von il-ʿAwāmra in der östlichen Šarqiyya (Ägypten)." Part 1, "Einleitung: grammatische Skizze und Volkskundliches." *Zeitschrift für Arabischen Linguistik* 2 (1979): 76–99.

Wright, W. A. *Grammar of the Arabic Language*. 3rd ed. Revised by W. Robertson Smith and M. J. de Goeje. 2 vols. Cambridge: Cambridge University Press, 1951.

Yāqūt ibn ʿAbd Allāh al-Rūmī al-Ḥamawī. *Muʿjam al-udabāʾ*. Edited by Aḥmad Farīd Rifāʿī. 20 vols. Cairo, 1936–38. Reprinted Beirut: Iḥyāʾ al-Turāth al-ʿArabī, n.d.

———. *Muʿjam al-buldān*. Edited by Farīd ʿAbd al-ʿAzīz al-Jundī. 7 vols. Beirut: Dār al-Kutub al-ʿIlmiyyah, 1990.

Zack, Liesbeth. *Egyptian Arabic in the Seventeenth Century: A Study and Edition of Yūsuf al-Maghribī's Dafʿ al-iṣr ʿan kalām ahl Miṣr*. Utrech: LOT, 2009.

Zamakhsharī, Maḥmūd ibn ʿUmar al-. *Rabīʿ al-abrār wa-fuṣūṣ al-akhbār*. Edited by ʿAbd al-Majīd Diyāb. 2 vols. Cairo: al-Hayʾah al-Miṣriyyah al-ʿĀmmah li-l-Kitāb, 1991–92.

Ziriklī, Khayr al-Dīn al-. *Al-Aʿlām: qāmūs tarājim li-ashhar al-rijāl wa-l-nisāʾ min al-ʿArab wa-l-mustaʿribīna wa-l-mustashriqīn*. 8 vols. Beirut: Dār al-ʿIlm li-l-Malāyīn, 1990.

Zuhayr, Bahāʾ al-Dīn ibn Muḥammad. *The Poetical Works [by] Behà-ed-din Zoheir*. Arabic text edited by Edward Henry Palmer. 2nd ed. Amsterdam: Oriental Press, 1971.

Further Reading

Abū Fāshā, Ṭāhir. *Hazz al-quḥūf fī sharḥ qaṣīdat Abī Shādūf*. Cairo: al-Hay'ah al-ʿĀmmah li-l-Kitāb, 1987. [A study, not a text edition.]

Amīn, Aḥmad. *Fayḍ al-khāṭir*. Vol. 3. Cairo: n.p., 1965, 101–6. [Notice under the title *Dumyah fī dimnah*. All the information on the countryside contained in the same author's *Qāmūs al-ʿādāt wa-l-taqālīd wa-l-taʿābīr al-miṣriyyah* (Cairo: Maṭbaʿat Lajnat al-Ta'līf wa-l-Tarjamah wa-l-Nashr, 1953) is also taken, without attribution, from *Hazz al-Quḥūf*.]

Abd al Raheim, Abd al Raheim A. "*Hazz al-Quhuf*: A New Source for the Study of the *Fallahin* of Egypt in the XVIIth and XVIIIth Centuries." *Journal of the Economic and Social History of the Orient* 18/3 (October 1975), 245–70. [Translation of the next.]

ʿAbd al-Raḥīm, ʿAbd al-Raḥīm ʿAbd al-Raḥmān. "Dirāsah naṣṣiyyah li-Kitāb *Hazz al-Quḥūf*." *al-Majallah al-Miṣriyyah li-l-Dirāsāt al-Tārīkhiyyah* 20 (1973): 287–316.

———. *Al-Rīf al-miṣrī fī l-qarn al-thāmin ʿashar*. Cairo: Maktabat Madbūlī, 1986.

ʿAbd al-Raḥīm, ʿAbd al-Raḥīm ʿAbd al-Raḥmān, and Wāṭārū Mīkī. "Village in Ottoman Egypt and Tokugawa Japan: A Comparative Study." *Studia Culturae Islamicae* 7. Tokyo: Institute for the Study of Languages and Cultures of Asia and Africa, 1977.

Baer, Gabriel. "Fellah and Townsman in Ottoman Egypt: A Study of Shirbini's Hazz al-Quḥūf." *Asian and African Studies* [Jerusalem] 8 (1972): 221–56.

———. "Shirbīnī's Hazz al-Quḥūf and Its Significance." In Gabriel Baer, *Fellah and Townsman in the Middle East: Studies in Social History*. London: Frank Cass, 1982. [An expanded version of the preceding.]

———. *Studies in the Social History of Modern Egypt*. Chicago and London: University of Chicago Press, 1969.

Baqlī (al-), Muḥammad Qindīl. *Qaryatunā al-miṣriyyah qabla al-thawrah – 1*, with introduction by Muḥammad ʿĪsā Ṭalʿat. Cairo: Dār al-Nahḍah al-ʿArabiyyah, n.d. [1963]. [A shortened and expurgated version of *Hazz al-quḥūf*.]

Ben Cheneb, M. "Al-Shirbīnī." In *EI1*.

Davies, Humphrey. "The Use of Middle Arabic in Yūsuf al-Shirbīnī's *Hazz al-Quḥūf bi-Sharḥ Qaṣīd Abī Shādūf*" in *Proceedings of the First International Symposium (Louvain-la-Neuve, 11–14 May 2004) on Middle Arabic and Mixed Arabic Throughout History: The Current*

State of Knowledge, Problems of Definition, Perspectives of Research. Publications de l'Institut Orientaliste de Louvain. Louvain-la-Neuve; Institut Orientaliste de l'Université Catholique de Louvain, 2008.

———. "Yūsuf al-Shirbīnī." In *Essays in Arabic Literary Biography (1350–1850)*, edited by Joseph E. Lowry and Devin Stewart. Wiesbaden: Otto Harrassowitz, 2009.

———. "Yūsuf al-Shirbīnī's Hazz al-Quḥūf: Issues Relevant to Its Assessment as a Source for 17th-Century Egyptian Colloquial." *Al-Logha* 2 (November 2000): 57–78.

Dayfīz, Hamfirī (Humphrey Davies), and Madīḥah Dōs, eds. *Al-ʿĀmmiyyah al-miṣriyyah al-maktūbah: mukhtārāt min 1401 ilā 2009*. Cairo: al-Hay'ah al-Miṣriyyah al-ʿĀmmah li-l-Kitāb, 2013.

Ḍayf, Shawqī. *Al-Fukāhah fī Miṣr*. N.p.: n.d., 91–99.

Doss, Madiha. "The Position of the Demonstrative DA, DI in Egyptian Arabic: A Diachronic Inquiry." *Annales Islamologiques* 15 (1979): 349–57.

———. "Réflexions sur les débuts de l'écriture dialectale en Égypte." *Égypte/Monde arabe*, ser. 1, 27–28 (1996): 119–46.

El-Rouayheb, Khaled. *Before Homosexuality in the Arab-Islamic World, 1500–1800*. Chicago: University of Chicago Press: 2009.

Finkel, J. "King Mutton, a Curious Egyptian Tale of the Mamluk Period. Edited from a Unique Manuscript, with Translation, Notes, Glossary and Introduction." *Zeitschrift für Semitistik* 8 (1932): 122–48, and 9 (1933–34): 1–18. [Pages 132–36 contain a discussion and partial translation of *Hazz al-quḥūf*'s "sermon on different dishes" (§11.25.7–13).]

Goldziher, Ignaz. "Jugend- und Strassenpoesie in Kairo." *Zeitschrift des Deutschen Morgenländischen Gesellschaft* 33 (1874): 608–30.

Hamarneh, Walid. "Aḥmad Fāris al-Shidyāq." In *Essays in Arabic Literary Biography (1850–1950)*, edited by Roger M. A. Allen, Joseph Edmund Lowry, and Devin J. Stewart. Wiesbaden: Otto Harrassowitz, 2010. [Compares and contrasts al-Shidyāq, al-Shirbīnī, Ibn Sūdūn, and other humorous writers; see p. 323.]

Ḥamzah, ʿAbd al-Laṭīf. *Al-Adab al-Miṣrī min qiyām al-dawlah al-ayyūbiyyah ilā majī' al-ḥamlah al-firansiyyah*. Cairo: Maktabat al-Nahḍah al-Miṣriyyah, [1960?], 209ff. [Excerpts, with introduction.]

Hanna, Nelly. *Ottoman Egypt and the Emergence of the Modern World: 1500–1800*. Cairo: American University in Cairo Press, 2014.

Ḥasan, ʿAbd al-Jalīl. "Sawṭ al-ṣāmiṭīn yaʿlū." *Al-Kātib* (August 1994): 134–43. [Baer, *Significance*, 26: "One of the best articles on Hazz al-Quḥūf written in Egypt so far."]

Ḥasan, Muḥammad ʿAbd al-Ghanī. *Al-Fallāḥ fī l-adab al-ʿarabī*. Al-Maktabah al-Thaqāfiyyah 128. [Cairo]: Dār al-Qalam, [1965], 139–44.

Hathaway, Jane. *A Tale of Two Factions: Myth, Memory, and Identity in Ottoman Egypt and Yemen*. New York: State University of New York Press, 2003.

Howarth, Herbert, and Ibrahim Shukrallah. *Images from the Arab World: Fragments of Arab Literature Translated and Paraphrased with Variations and Comments*. London: The Pilot Press, 1944, 21–23. [Translation of the tale of the Persian *ʿālim* (see vol. 1, §§4.5–4.9)].

Kern, F. "Neuere ägyptische Humoristen und Satiriker." *Mitteilungen des Seminars fur Orientalische Sprache* (1906), Section 2, 37–42 and 64–65. [The first passage is a description of the work, the second a transcription and translation of an excerpt.]

Mehren, A. F. *Et par Bildrag til Bedømmelsa af den nyere Folkeliteratur I Aegypten*. Copenhagen, 1872, 37–71. [With résumé and glossary in French of words "peu usités dans la langue littéraire" (58–71).]

Mikhail, Alan. "A Dog-Eat-Dog Empire: Violence and Affection on the Streets of Ottoman Cairo." *Comparative Studies of South Asia, Africa and the Middle East* 35, no. 1 (2015): 76–95.

Muḥassib, Ḥasan. *Qaḍiyyat al-fallāḥ fī l-qiṣṣah al-miṣriyyah*. Maktabah al-thaqāfīyah 256. Cairo: al-Hay'ah al-Miṣriyyah al-ʿĀmmah li-l-Ta'līf wa-l-Nashr, 1971, 15–22.

Musawi, Muhsin J. al-. *The Medieval Islamic Republic of Letters: Arabic Knowledge Construction*. Notre Dame, IN: Notre Dame University Press, 2015.

Nallino, C. A. *L'Arabo parlato in Egitto. Grammatica, dialoghi i raccolta di vocabuli*. Milan: Editore-Libraio della Real Casa, 1900.

Omri, Mohamed-Salah. "Adab in the Seventeenth Century: Narrative and Parody in al-Shirbini's Hazz al-Quhuf." *Edebiyat* 11, no. 2 (2000): 169–96.

Peled, M. "Nodding the Necks: A Literary Study of Shirbini's *Hazz al-Quhuf*." *Die Welt des Islams* 26 (1986): 57–75.

Rowson, E. K. "Al-Shirbīnī." In *Encyclopedia of Arabic Literature*, edited by Julie Scott Meisami and Paul Starkey. 2 vols. London and New York: Routledge, 1998, 715.

Ṣāliḥ, Aḥmad Rushdī. *Funūn al-adab al-shaʿbī*. Cairo: n.p., 1956, 43.

Selim, Samah. *The Novel and the Rural Imaginary in Egypt, 1880–1985*. London: RoutledgeCurzon, 2004.

Spitta, Wilhelm. *Grammatik des arabischen Vulgärdialektes von Aegypten*. Leipzig: J. C. Hinrichs, 1880. [Texts VIII and X derive from *Hazz al-Quḥūf*; see Davies, 1981, *Profile*, 34–35.]

Van Gelder, Geert Jan. *Of Dishes and Discourse: Classical Arabic Literary Representations of Food*. London: Routledge, 2000 (a).

———. "The Nodding Noddles, or Jolting the Yokels: A Composition for Marginal Voices by al-Shirbīnī (fl. 1687)." In *Marginal Voices in Literature and Society*, edited by Robin Ostle. Strasbourg, 2000 (b), 49–67.

———. "Satire, Medieval." In *EAL*, 693–95.

Vial, Charles. "Le *Hazz Al-Quhuf* de Al-Širbini est-il un échantillon d'*adab* populaire?" In *Rivages et déserts: hommage à Jacques Berque*. Paris: Sindbad, ca. 1988, 170–81.

Vollers, Karl. "Beiträge zur Kenntniss der lebenden arabischen Sprache in Aegypten." *Zeitschrift des Deutschen Morgenländischen Gesellschaft* 41 (1887): 365–402.

Von Kremer, Alfred. "Aus einem Briefe von Prof. Dr. von Kremer an Prof. Fleischer." *Zeitschrift des Deutschen Morgenländischen Gesellschaft* 9 (1855): 847. [GAL II, p. 278, has "ZDMG 10" by mistake.]

Vrolijk, Arnoud. *Bringing a Laugh to a Scowling Face. A Study and Critical Edition of "Nuzhat al-Nufūs wa-Muḍḥik al-ʿAbūs" by ʿAlī Ibn Sūdūn al-Bashbughāwī*. Leiden: Research School CNWS, 1998, 138–40. [Reviews and critiques findings of Davies, *Seventeenth-Century*.]

Zakariyyā Saʿīd, Naffūsah. *Taʾrīkh al-daʿwah ilā al-ʿāmmiyyah wa-āthāruhā fī Miṣr*. Alexandria: Dār Nashr al-Thaqāfah, 1964, 240–49.

Zaydān, Jirjī. *Tārīkh adab al-lughah al-ʿarabiyyah*. Vol. 3. Cairo: Maṭbaʿat al-Hilāl, 1931, 276–77.

Zubaida, Sami. "Hazz al-Quhuf: An Urban Satire on Peasant Life and Food from Seventeenth-century Egypt." In *Food Between the Country and the City Ethnographies of a Changing Global Foodscape*, edited by Nuno Domingos, José Manuel Sobral, and Harry G. West. London: Bloomsbury Academic, 2014.

Index

About the NYU Abu Dhabi Institute

The Library of Arabic Literature is supported by a grant from the NYU Abu Dhabi Institute, a major hub of intellectual and creative activity and advanced research. The Institute hosts academic conferences, workshops, lectures, film series, performances, and other public programs directed both to audiences within the UAE and to the worldwide academic and research community. It is a center of the scholarly community for Abu Dhabi, bringing together faculty and researchers from institutions of higher learning throughout the region.

NYU Abu Dhabi, through the NYU Abu Dhabi Institute, is a world-class center of cutting-edge research, scholarship, and cultural activity. The Institute creates singular opportunities for leading researchers from across the arts, humanities, social sciences, sciences, engineering, and the professions to carry out creative scholarship and conduct research on issues of major disciplinary, multidisciplinary, and global significance.

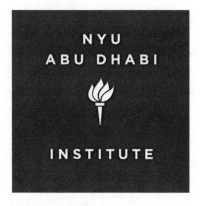

About the Typefaces

The Arabic body text is set in DecoType Naskh, designed by Thomas Milo and Mirjam Somers, based on an analysis of five centuries of Ottoman manuscript practice. The exceptionally legible result is the first and only typeface in a style that fully implements the principles of script grammar (*qawāʿid al-khaṭṭ*).

The Arabic footnote text is set in DecoType Emiri, drawn by Mirjam Somers, based on the metal typeface in the naskh style that was cut for the 1924 Cairo edition of the Qur'an.

Both Arabic typefaces in this series are controlled by a dedicated font layout engine. ACE, the Arabic Calligraphic Engine, invented by Peter Somers, Thomas Milo, and Mirjam Somers of DecoType, first operational in 1985, pioneered the principle followed by later smart font layout technologies such as OpenType, which is used for all other typefaces in this series.

The Arabic text was set with WinSoft Tasmeem, a sophisticated user interface for DecoType ACE inside Adobe InDesign. Tasmeem was conceived and created by Thomas Milo (DecoType) and Pascal Rubini (WinSoft) in 2005.

The English text is set in Adobe Text, a new and versatile text typeface family designed by Robert Slimbach for Western (Latin, Greek, Cyrillic) typesetting. Its workhorse qualities make it perfect for a wide variety of applications, especially for longer passages of text where legibility and economy are important. Adobe Text bridges the gap between calligraphic Renaissance types of the 15th and 16th centuries and high-contrast Modern styles of the 18th century, taking many of its design cues from early post-Renaissance Baroque transitional types cut by designers such as Christoffel van Dijck, Nicolaus Kis, and William Caslon. While grounded in classical form, Adobe Text is also a statement of contemporary utilitarian design, well suited to a wide variety of print and on-screen applications.

Titles Published by the Library of Arabic Literature

Classical Arabic Literature
Selected and translated by Geert Jan Van Gelder

A Treasury of Virtues, by al-Qāḍī al-Quḍāʿī
Edited and translated by Tahera Qutbuddin

The Epistle on Legal Theory, by al-Shāfiʿī
Edited and translated by Joseph E. Lowry

Leg Over Leg, by Aḥmad Fāris al-Shidyāq
Edited and translated by Humphrey Davies

Virtues of the Imām Aḥmad ibn Ḥanbal, by Ibn al-Jawzī
Edited and translated by Michael Cooperson

The Epistle of Forgiveness, by Abū l-ʿAlāʾ al-Maʿarrī
Edited and translated by Geert Jan Van Gelder and Gregor Schoeler

The Principles of Sufism, by ʿĀʾishah al-Bāʿūnīyah
Edited and translated by Th. Emil Homerin

The Expeditions, by Maʿmar ibn Rāshid
Edited and translated by Sean W. Anthony

Two Arabic Travel Books

> **Accounts of China and India**, by Abū Zayd al-Sīrāfī
> Edited and translated by Tim Mackintosh-Smith
> **Mission to the Volga**, by Ahmad Ibn Faḍlān
> Edited and translated by James Montgomery

Disagreements of the Jurists, by al-Qāḍī al-Nuʿmān
Edited and translated by Devin Stewart

Consorts of the Caliphs, by Ibn al-Sāʿī
Edited by Shawkat M. Toorawa and translated by the Editors of the Library of Arabic Literature

What ʿĪsā ibn Hishām Told Us, by Muḥammad al-Muwayliḥī
Edited and translated by Roger Allen

The Life and Times of Abū Tammām, by Abū Bakr Muḥammad ibn Yaḥyā al-Ṣūlī
Edited and translated by Beatrice Gruendler

The Sword of Ambition, by ʿUthmān ibn Ibrāhīm al-Nābulusī
Edited and translated by Luke Yarbrough

Brains Confounded by the Ode of Abū Shādūf Expounded, by Yūsuf al-Shirbīnī
Edited and translated by Humphrey Davies

About the Editor–Translator

Humphrey Davies is an award-winning translator of Arabic literature from the Ottoman period to the present. Writers he has translated include Aḥmad Fāris al-Shidyāq, for the Library of Arabic Literature, as well as Elias Khoury, Naguib Mahfouz, Alaa Al Aswany, Bahaa Taher, Mourid Barghouti, Muhammad Mustagab, Gamal al-Ghitani, Hamdy el-Gazzar, Khaled Al-Berry, and Ahmed Alaidy. He has also authored, with Madiha Doss, an anthology of writings in Egyptian colloquial Arabic. He lives in Cairo.